SUPER-SCENIC MOTORWAY

The University of North Carolina Press   Chapel Hill

Super-Scenic

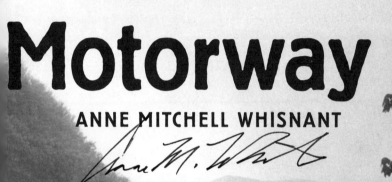

For Joe —
Who is working for the Parkway's
future! Enjoy this Parkway journey.

A BLUE RIDGE PARKWAY HISTORY

Motorway

ANNE MITCHELL WHISNANT

7 November 2006

SPEED
25
ZONE

© 2006

The University of North Carolina Press

All rights reserved

Designed by Richard Hendel

Set in Quadraat and Berliner types by Eric M. Brooks

Manufactured in the United States of America

This book was published with the assistance of the Fred W. Morrison
Fund for Southern Studies of the University of North Carolina Press.

The paper in this book meets the guidelines for permanence and
durability of the Committee on Production Guidelines for Book Longevity
of the Council on Library Resources.

Library of Congress Cataloging-in-Publication Data

Whisnant, Anne Mitchell.

Super-scenic motorway: a Blue Ridge Parkway history /
Anne Mitchell Whisnant.

   p. cm.

Includes bibliographical references and index.

ISBN-13: 978-0-8078-3037-6 (cloth: alk. paper)

ISBN-10: 0-8078-3037-2 (cloth: alk. paper)

1. Blue Ridge Parkway (N.C. and Va.) — History. I. Title.

F217.B6W47 2006   975.5 — dc22   2006011351

An earlier version of chapter 4 was published as "Public and Private Tourism
Development in 1930s Appalachia: The Blue Ridge Parkway Meets Little
Switzerland," in *Southern Journeys: Tourism, History, and Culture in the Modern
South*, ed. Richard D. Starnes (Tuscaloosa: University of Alabama Press, 2003),
88–113. Used with permission of the University of Alabama Press.

An earlier version of chapter 5 was published as "Culture, History, and
Development on the Qualla Boundary: The Eastern Cherokees and the Blue
Ridge Parkway, 1935–40," *Appalachian Journal* 24 (Winter 1997): 144–91.
Copyright *Appalachian Journal* and Appalachian State University. Used with
permission.

10 09 08 07 06   5 4 3 2 1

For David,

from the beginning of time, for all time

And for our boys, Evan and Derek

CONTENTS

ILLUSTRATIONS

ACKNOWLEDGMENTS

My six-year-old son, Derek, recently bounded into my study on a beautiful Saturday afternoon and begged me to play ball with him. "I can't," I said, "I have to keep writing." Writhing on the floor, he wailed, "You've been working on that book my whole life!"

He's right, but the truth is that I've been investigating the history of the Blue Ridge Parkway for nearly fifteen years, much longer than his whole life. Anything that consumes you for that long is bound to become part of your very self, but the Blue Ridge Parkway has shaped the contours of my life perhaps more profoundly than one might expect. While discovering the Parkway as a subject of study gave me a topic that I loved and thus rescued me from sinking into the quagmire that humanities research can become, seeing the work through to publication has intertwined with my entire professional and personal journey these past fifteen years. Despite the burdens this work has put on Derek and my other son, Evan, it is literally true that neither of them would even be here were it not for this project and that my life would not be configured as it is had I not started down this (actual and metaphorical) road. For the many good things that have come into my life along this Parkway trip, I am forever grateful.

My scholarly Parkway journey began serendipitously (as such projects often do) in August 1991 as I was thumbing through the (not yet computerized) card catalog in the University of North Carolina's North Carolina Collection. Hoping I might build on my earlier research on a woman doctor who had run a birth control clinic in Alabama in the 1930s, I pulled open the "B" drawer in search of references to birth control in North Carolina. However, the cards flipped instead to the entries for Blue Ridge Parkway—specifically, to references to Cherokee opposition to the road in the 1930s. Growing up, I had spent several summers in western North Carolina and had traveled the Parkway many times, so these cards caught my eye, and I began to investigate. Three months later, I had written a paper not on early birth control clinics in North Carolina but on the Cherokee resistance to land acquisition for the Parkway, now the subject of chapter 5 of this book.

As I developed the book, many faculty, friends, and colleagues at the University of North Carolina offered specific help and, just as important, general camaraderie and support. Within the congenial History Department community, several people especially stand out. Gretchen White was my first good friend in graduate school and made life bearable during the difficult first year. Lu Ann Jones and Laura Moore were unfailingly encouraging and interested in this project. Houston Roberson helped by faxing me needed grant application forms when I was living away from Chapel Hill and letting me camp in his apartment for a few weeks. Marla Miller has been my friend since we entered graduate school together in 1989, and her intelligence, warmth, and sense of humor made the experience much more pleasurable, especially that last year when we both raced to finish. I treasure our ongoing friendship, which has had the extra benefit of informing my developing identification as a "public historian" as this book has unfolded.

On the UNC faculty, William Leuchtenburg, a towering figure in writing the history of the New Deal, helped me launch this project and guided it in its earliest stages. Distinguished historian of the South Joel Williamson assisted me in creating a plan for a larger study built on the initial short paper on the Cherokees. Jim Leloudis helped me get a better grasp on North Carolina history. Altina Waller of the University of Connecticut generously shared her knowledge as an Appalachian studies specialist.

Special thanks go to Jacquelyn Hall, who read sections of my work carefully and quickly, offered thoughtful suggestions and support, and wrote numerous letters of recommendation for me with timeliness and a good spirit. I am grateful to her almost as much for the things she did not do: try to micromanage my work or impose her own agenda. By offering gentle guidance when I asked for it and by otherwise trusting me to find my way, she allowed me to move forward at my pace, follow my interests, and produce a work that reflected my process.

As I started in earnest on this project, a first task was to determine if sufficient archival sources existed to support a longer work. So I placed a call to the Blue Ridge Parkway headquarters in Asheville, North Carolina. From that moment forward, everyone on the park staff (and at the National Park Service more generally) has been unfailingly helpful, trusting, and generous in answering my numerous inquiries and in guiding me to helpful resources. Anyone who has ever criticized "government bureaucrats" has clearly not met these dedicated public servants.

Park curator Jackie Holt, for example, has patiently accommodated my repeated visits to the park archives and at a crucial point directed me to the park's important Lands Files, from which the Grandfather Mountain story took shape. Other members of the Parkway's Resource Planning and Professional Services Division (including David Anderson, Torin Dilley, Sheila Gasperson, Al Hess, and Gary Johnson) were hospitable to me on several Asheville research trips, giving me unlimited photocopying privileges, helping me sort through the park's large photograph collection and map files, clarifying Parkway landownership statistics, and volunteering information about materials that were critical to the development of the Peaks of Otter story in particular (chapter 6). In the Interpretive Division, Peter Givens and Patty Lockamy have given me several welcome opportunities to talk about my research with park staff. Former Parkway superintendent Dan Brown displayed a real interest in my project from the outset, giving me confidence that the park supported the work from the top down.

Special thanks go to Parkway management assistant Phil Noblitt, who as an interpretive specialist in the early 1990s had charge of the Parkway archives and who more recently has been the Parkway's public relations spokesperson. Phil has from the first gone far beyond what might be expected in offering practical help, a generosity that has flowed from his deeply informed, passionate enthusiasm for and understanding of the analysis I was developing. From opening the doors to the Parkway's well-organized and useful archives, which were in 1993 hidden in a third-floor room in an abandoned Veterans Administration hospital dormitory in Asheville (bring a battery-powered lamp, he advised!), to connecting me with all of the other park staff members I've mentioned, to helping me understand park operations, to touting my expertise to the regional media, Phil has been instrumental to the completion and success of this project.

From my first days reading materials by the sunlight through the windows of those Parkway archives through all of my work in many other repositories, I have found archivists to be one of the kindest, most knowledgeable, and most patient groups of people I have ever encountered. They are the backbone on which scholarship rests. At the National Archives in Washington, D.C., for example, I would have been lost without the aid of Richard Fusick, who guided me through the thicket of less-than-transparent finding aids to locate a treasure trove of boxes on the Parkway's development. The staffs at the Library of Virginia; the Memphis Public Library; the National Park Service's Harpers Ferry Center; the Franklin D. Roosevelt Library in Hyde Park, New York; the Library of Congress Manuscripts Division in Washington; the National Archives Southeast Regional Branch in Atlanta; the Asheville Citizen-Times; the Duke University library; the Southern Historical Collection and North Carolina Collection at UNC–Chapel Hill; the Pack Memorial Library in Asheville; the University of North Carolina at Asheville; and the North Carolina State Archives in Raleigh were similarly helpful in pointing me toward useful materials. I especially thank John White of the Southern Historical Collection for alerting me to a crucial group of Little Switzerland records that had not yet been listed in the finding aids. Nearer the end of the project, Lisa Coombes at the North Carolina State Archives enabled me to conduct a large-scale illustration search in a single day. Helen Wykle at the University of North Carolina at Asheville also gave generous aid in navigating that library's wonderful photographic collections.

Materials held in private hands have also been crucial. For me, one of the most exciting moments of the past fifteen years was the day my phone rang and I heard the lilting southern voice of Harriet Browning Davant on the other end of the line. The daughter of engineer R. Getty Browning, Harriet had called to talk with me about my (still unpublished) work on "Daddy," and she and her husband, Charlie, soon invited me to their Blowing Rock home to peruse her father's files there. She also arranged for me to meet her brother, Bob Browning, who later hosted me in another research foray into files in his Raleigh office. Tom and Jeannette Richardson of Bedford, Virginia (whom I have yet to meet in person), gave me unfettered access to their extensive personal collection of materials on the Peaks of Otter while those items were on loan to the Parkway in 2002. Without the insights emerging from these documents, I could not have developed chapter 6.

Several people on whom I called for personal recollections about the Parkway were also very generous. Interviews I conducted with former Parkway landscape architect Robert Hope and longtime environmental journalist Michael Frome helped clarify several points, while Hugh Morton took nearly three hours one afternoon in the midst of a torrential rainstorm to recount his story of the long battle over the Parkway route at Grandfather Mountain.

The connection with the Browning/Davant family would not have been made without the help of Blue Ridge Parkway Foundation founder and director Houck Medford. I have also been grateful to Houck for his invitation to serve on the foundation's Council of Advisers, affording me a vantage point from which to better understand and participate in debates about the Parkway's present and future challenges.

As I sought to shape all the information I had collected into a readable, publishable analysis, many other people have offered time and insights that have immeasurably improved the book. My acquisitions editor at the University of North Carolina Press, Sian Hunter, has professed confidence for nigh on nine years that this book would eventually see the light of day and has been cheerfully patient with my repeated extension of deadlines. Two anonymous readers provided encouragement and thoughtful suggestions for revision. I have also received support at the press at crucial moments from director Kate Torrey and designer and friend Rich Hendel as well as project editors Ron Maner and Pam Upton. Ellen D. Goldlust-Gingrich copyedited the manuscript with interest and care. John David Smith, then head of the North Carolina State University Public History Program, encouraged and facilitated my drafting of chapter 6 in his Introduction to Public History graduate course in the fall of 2002.

During the past three years, I have been fortunate to be a member of a remarkably intense and supportive women's writing group. Fellow "writing goddesses" Kirsten Delegard, Caroline Light, Ginny Noble, and Susan Thorne have given many of these chapters a high level of thoughtful attention and have suggested alterations that will save readers of this book from becoming confused or, worse, bored! From the first, the five of us clicked and became close friends, building a level of trust without which honest sharing and shaping of writing is impossible. If for no other reason, I now have to devise a new (if smaller-scale) writing project so that I can continue to spend time in the company of these smart, funny, politically engaged, warm, and generous women.

Funding and other tangible support from several sources has also facilitated my research and writing. The History Department at the University of North Carolina supported me throughout my graduate career with fellowships and teaching assistantships and awarded me a well-timed Mowry research grant that, in combination with the North Caroliniana Society's Archie Davis Grant, paid for a research trip to Asheville. A travel grant from the Franklin and Eleanor Roosevelt Institute in Hyde Park, New York, financed a delightful two weeks at the Roosevelt presidential library. The Graduate School at UNC paid for several weeks of research in Washington, D.C., with an Off-Campus Grant in the spring of 1994. The History Department, through the generosity of Doris G. Quinn, came through again with a grant that enabled me to devote my full attention to writing for seven months in 1996–97.

I have also benefited from financial support provided through the Phi Alpha Theta Manuscript Award (2000), which James Sweeney of Old Dominion University helped me secure. In addition, I am grateful to Richenel (Muz) Ansano, Cathy Davidson, and Rob Sikorski for giving me my first full-time job, at the John Hope Franklin Humanities Institute at Duke University, an offer of employment that brought my family financial stability at a crucial moment. At Duke, furthermore, institute director Srinivas Aravamudan and former executive director Cheri Ross were generous in numerous ways that helped ensure that my full-time employment did not derail this project.

Other colleagues at the John Hope Franklin Center—especially Kelli Anderson, Donna Boyd, Jason Doty, Sara Gronewold, Pamela Gutlon, Celeste Lee, Tori Lodewick, Mark Olson, Sharon Peters, Mindy Quigley, and Brett Walters—have offered direct help, friendship, and encouragement. Also at Duke, I have benefited greatly from the advice and friendship of Sally Hicks, senior writer at the

Office of News and Communications, who has helped me understand the complex workings of public media.

On a more personal level, other friends and family members have assisted me in countless direct and indirect ways. My parents, Norma Taylor Mitchell and Frank Joseph Mitchell, both historians by training, engendered in me an early enthusiasm for understanding the past. My mother accompanied me on an initial research trip to the isolated and lonely Blue Ridge Parkway archives. My father has enthusiastically read parts of my manuscript and asked probing questions. More than that, Mom and Dad have been constant cheerleaders for me all my life. All along, too, the financial support, cars, and, more recently, babysitting that they have provided have been critical to getting this book out the door. Their companionship since they relocated to North Carolina in 2001 has helped me to cope with new parenthood, working life, and the stresses of completing a project of this magnitude. I am so lucky to have such encouraging and unfailingly supportive parents.

My mother's tireless dedication to staying in touch with all of her relatives, far and near, paid off when she connected me with distant cousins Jack and Sheila Tiedemann, who hosted me at their home in Washington, D.C., for an astonishing several months while I worked at the National Archives and Library of Congress. The Tiedemanns' warmth helped compensate for the cold and snow that blanketed Washington during the early weeks of my research there. I still remember the warm bowls of oatmeal and the apricot nectar cakes that Jack and Sheila made and the weekly tennis matches in which they engaged me. I am sorry that Jack did not live to see this project appear in print.

Other relatives who also happened to live near archival repositories found themselves hosting a young researcher. I treasure the opportunities that trips to Asheville provided for me to spend extended time with my mother-in-law, Mary Neal Whisnant, and my wonderfully generous aunt, Faye Mitchell, with whom I made Christmas cookies during one visit. A native of Asheville and an inveterate reader, Mary Neal would have enjoyed this book; I so regret that she did not live to see it finished.

Other family members who did not specifically help with this project nevertheless reminded me of the loving support network in which I am privileged to live. Brothers- and sisters-in-law Richard and Elaine Whisnant and Norman and Kathy Whisnant have been hospitable on many occasions. I am glad to call them friends as well as relations. I feel the same way about my two smart and generous stepdaughters, Rebecca Whisnant and Beverly Shannon, who have brought laughter and fun into my world whenever they have visited.

Many of the people mentioned here have come into my life because of events cascading from a pivotal early suggestion I received from my fellow graduate student, Andy Kirkendall, who urged me to read David Whisnant's *All That Is Native and Fine: The Politics of Culture in an American Region* and to contact its author, who, I was surprised to learn, was on the UNC faculty in English. His book introduced me to the emerging literature of Appalachian studies, about which I was embarrassingly ignorant. Finding out about this field of inquiry enlarged and sharpened my understanding of the Blue Ridge Parkway's context and introduced me to a community of politically committed scholars and regional activists within the Appalachian Studies Association, at whose annual meetings I got my first opportunities to share my ideas before gentle and supportive audiences.

But my debt to David goes far beyond the connection to Appalachian studies and the insights provided in *All That Is Native and Fine*. When I finally called on him in the spring of 1993 to talk about my work, he was immediately enthusiastic, bolstering my early but still fragile sense that what I was doing had merit. But at length he became more than just an interested supporter: sharing what a mutual friend once called a "tribal" affinity, we fell in love and married (appropriately, in western North Carolina) in May 1995. David is my one and true soul mate: had this project never gone one bit further, I would at the moment I met him already have received its greatest reward.

But the project did go forward, and my relationship with David has shaped it in countless ways, not least through untold hours of conversations about the Parkway over the past twelve years. The analysis presented here has been greatly enriched by our ongoing dialogue. While David may have anticipated that marrying me would entail a good bit of thinking about the mountains and the Parkway, he surely did not envision the way the project would pervade our lives together. From our first camping adventure amid unrelenting rains near the Roosevelt Library at Hyde Park in the summer of 1994 through dozens of subsequent "vacations" that have incorporated Parkway research, we have taken hardly any trips that have not involved the Parkway.

David's level of personal investment in this project has grown consistently, too, especially since our sons were born in 1997 and 1999 and since I took a full-time job in 2002. This book would have taken even longer to complete than it has had David not collected archival materials, pored over the 1930 Census, made calls, gathered illustrations, entered notes into my database, and read and reread my chapters. The unflagging devotion to my success that all of this work represents has reinforced many times over David's tender and constant expressions of love and confidence. For all of this and for the companionship and happiness of countless sweet moments in our lives together, I love him more dearly than anything I write can possibly express.

Moreover, David has done all of this while being a splendid stay-at-home father to our two beautiful young sons, Evan David Whisnant and Derek Taylor Whisnant, whose whole lives have been shaped by their mom writing this book. While David's steady presence has eased my guilt about not having more time for them and while they have been as patient as young children can be with a project they only partly understand, I know that my preoccupation with this work has deprived them of my attention. The time has now come (and I'm glad that it has) for me to turn from the project that gave me my life to the life the project gave to me: to David and these little ones, whose days with me are passing far too quickly.

Parkway near Ice Rock and Alligator Back, milepost 242 in North Carolina, June 1946.
Photo by A. Rowe. Courtesy Blue Ridge Parkway.

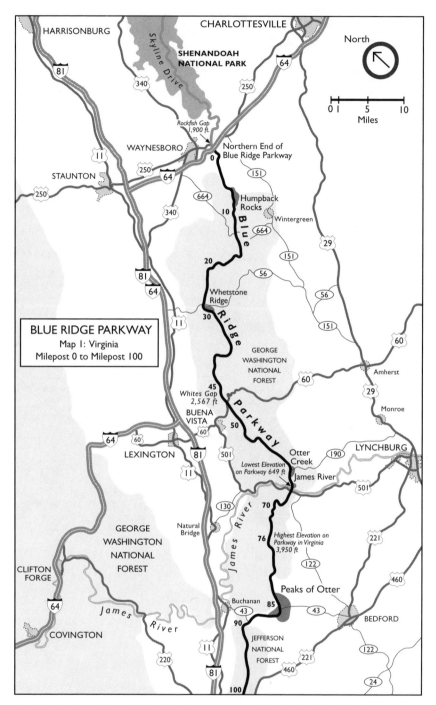

Blue Ridge Parkway. Map by Michael Southern, based on official National Park Service map.

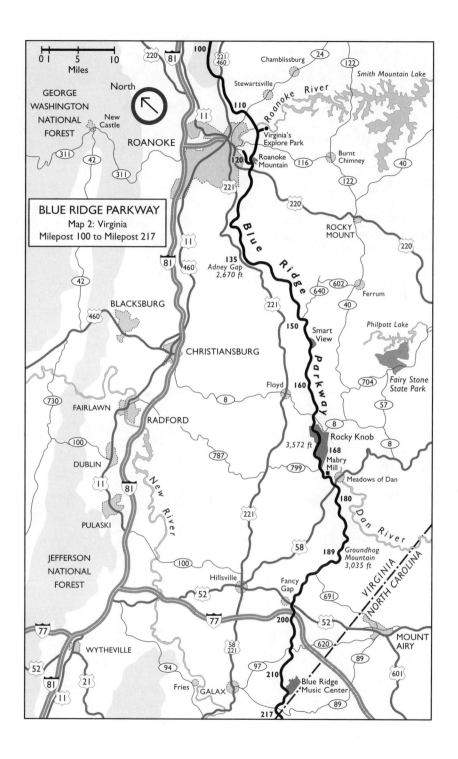

BLUE RIDGE PARKWAY
Map 2: Virginia
Milepost 100 to Milepost 217

GEORGE WASHINGTON NATIONAL FOREST

New Castle

ROANOKE

Chamblissburg

Stewartsville

Roanoke River

Smith Mountain Lake

Virginia's Explore Park

Roanoke Mountain

Burnt Chimney

ROCKY MOUNT

Ferrum

Philpott Lake

BLACKSBURG

CHRISTIANSBURG

135 Adney Gap 2,670 ft

150 Smart View

Fairy Stone State Park

Floyd

160

FAIRLAWN

RADFORD

3,572 ft

Rocky Knob

168 Mabry Mill

Meadows of Dan

DUBLIN

New River

180

Dan River

PULASKI

JEFFERSON NATIONAL FOREST

189 Groundhog Mountain 3,035 ft

VIRGINIA
NORTH CAROLINA

Hillsville

Fancy Gap

200

MOUNT AIRY

WYTHEVILLE

210

Blue Ridge Music Center

Fries

GALAX

217

North

0 1   5   10
Miles

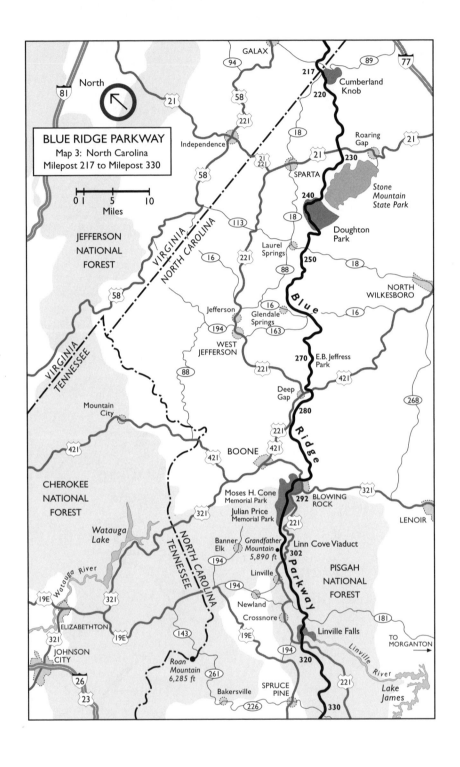

BLUE RIDGE PARKWAY
Map 3: North Carolina
Milepost 217 to Milepost 330

0 1   5   10
Miles

GALAX

94

81

21

58

221

Independence

217

220

Cumberland
Knob

89

77

18

Roaring
Gap

21

21
221

21

230

SPARTA

240

Stone
Mountain
State Park

JEFFERSON
NATIONAL
FOREST

58

113

18

Doughton
Park

16

221

Laurel
Springs

250

18

NORTH
WILKESBORO

58

Jefferson

88

Glendale
Springs

16

Blue

16

194

163

WEST
JEFFERSON

270

E.B. Jeffress
Park

221

421

VIRGINIA
NORTH CAROLINA

88

Deep
Gap

280

268

Ridge

VIRGINIA
TENNESSEE

Mountain
City

221

421

BOONE

421

321

421

CHEROKEE
NATIONAL
FOREST

541

Moses H. Cone
Memorial Park

292

BLOWING
ROCK

Watauga
Lake

NORTH CAROLINA
TENNESSEE

321

Julian Price
Memorial Park

221

LENOIR

Banner
Elk

Grandfather
Mountain
5,890 ft

302

Linn Cove Viaduct

PISGAH
NATIONAL
FOREST

Watauga River

194

Linville

Parkway

19E

321

194

181

ELIZABETHTON

19E

Newland

Crossnore

19E

Linville Falls

TO
MORGANTON

321

JOHNSON
CITY

143

320

Linville River

26

Roan
Mountain
6,285 ft

261

194

221

Lake
James

23

Bakersville

SPRUCE
PINE

226

330

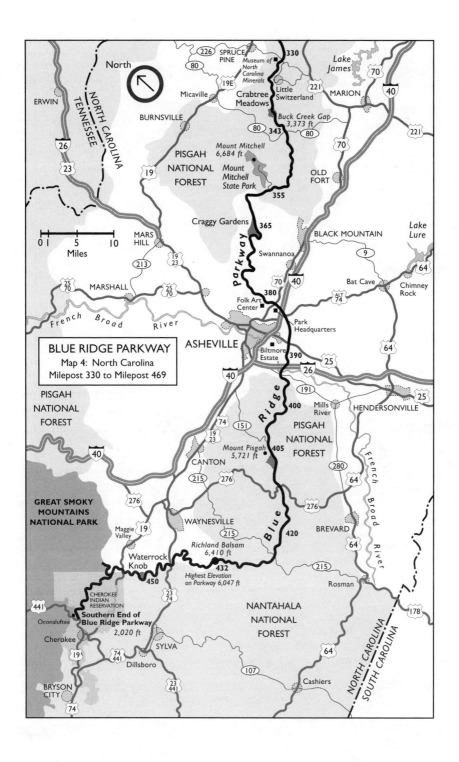

North

ERWIN

TENNESSEE
NORTH CAROLINA

226 · SPRUCE PINE
80
Museum of North Carolina Minerals
330
19E
Micaville
Little Switzerland
221
Lake James
70
MARION
40

BURNSVILLE
Crabtree Meadows
Buck Creek Gap 3,373 ft
80
221

26

23

PISGAH NATIONAL FOREST
80
343
80
70

19

Mount Mitchell 6,684 ft
Mount Mitchell State Park
355
OLD FORT

Craggy Gardens
365
BLACK MOUNTAIN
Lake Lure

0 1   5   10
Miles

MARS HILL
19 23
Swannanoa
9
64

213
70 40
Bat Cave
Chimney Rock

25 70
MARSHALL
25 70
380
ALT 74

French Broad River

Folk Art Center
Park Headquarters
64

BLUE RIDGE PARKWAY
Map 4: North Carolina
Milepost 330 to Milepost 469

ASHEVILLE
Biltmore Estate
390
25
26
191
25

PISGAH NATIONAL FOREST

40

400
Mills River
HENDERSONVILLE

74
151
19 23
Mount Pisgah 5,721 ft
405
PISGAH NATIONAL FOREST
280
64

French Broad River

CANTON
215 276
276

GREAT SMOKY MOUNTAINS NATIONAL PARK
40
276

WAYNESVILLE
215
420
BREVARD
64
215

Maggie Valley
19
Richland Balsam 6,410 ft
Blue Ridge

Waterrock Knob
450
432
Highest Elevation on Parkway 6,047 ft
Rosman
178

23 74

CHEROKEE INDIAN RESERVATION
Southern End of Blue Ridge Parkway 2,020 ft

441
Oconaluftee
NANTAHALA NATIONAL FOREST

NORTH CAROLINA
SOUTH CAROLINA

Cherokee
SYLVA
64

19
74 441
Dillsboro
107
Cashiers

BRYSON CITY
23 441

74

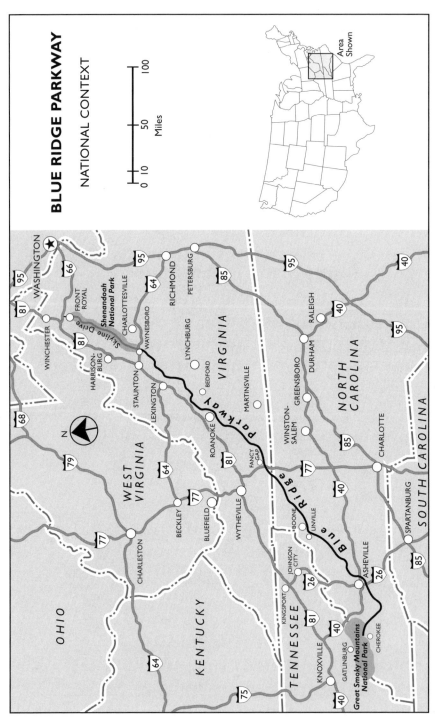

Blue Ridge Parkway: National Context. Map by Michael Southern.

SUPER-SCENIC MOTORWAY

INTRODUCTION
A NEW TRIP ALONG
A BELOVED ROAD

The first thing I remember is the silence. Late at night, sitting on the grass at the Waterrock Knob overlook near the southwestern end of the Blue Ridge Parkway, gazing into the darkness over Cherokee, North Carolina. Town lights and stars in the distance. A light breeze whistling, but at that hour, few visitors, few cars, and virtually no other sounds.

The year was 1986, and I was nineteen. It was my first summer away from home, and I was spending days waiting tables and scooping ice cream for Methodist ministers and the devoted faithful as part of the college student staff at Lake Junaluska United Methodist Assembly near Waynesville in the western North Carolina mountains. But evenings were free, and my friends and I would frequently go "up on the Parkway" to sit and talk.

At that time I did not realize that the Parkway itself had anything to say. Another five years would pass before I heard it speak. By then a history graduate student at the University of North Carolina at Chapel Hill, I was thumbing through the (not yet computerized) card catalog in the university's North Carolina Collection when I came upon a card that referred to a five-year campaign waged by the Eastern Band of Cherokees in the 1930s to prevent some of their lands from being seized for the Parkway. Land seizures? Opposition? How could something as peaceful and beautiful as the Parkway have stirred opposition? My curiosity aroused, I began to uncover the story this book tells.

The fifteen years that have passed between that moment and this one have been part of my nearly thirty-year journey up and down the Parkway. Before I was a summer waitress or a scholar studying the Parkway's history, I was simply one among millions of Parkway travelers. I first visited in the late 1970s, when my parents (like a long line of flatlanders before them) arranged for a summer escape from our home in beastly hot south Alabama to the coolness of the North Carolina mountains. In the decades since World War II, millions of travelers like my family have made this scenic highway through the Appalachian mountains of North Carolina and Virginia the most visited site in America's national park system.

It is easy to see why. In phrases used to describe the road since the 1930s, the Parkway is both a "park-to-park highway" joining Virginia's Shenandoah National Park with North Carolina and Tennessee's Great Smoky Mountains National Park and a wonderful "elongated park" in its own right. On a clear day, the views from the high southwestern end, where much of the road lies above five thousand feet, are breathtaking, the temperatures noticeably cooler than those down below. The rhododendrons at Craggy Gardens near Asheville burst into bloom in June; a few months later, the tree leaves swirl into fall with a rolling display of color. The gentle farmland of southwest Virginia is peaceful and green. Even on misty and foggy days (all too frequent at higher elevations), close-in views beckon: wildflowers, solitary log cabins in fields, split-rail chestnut fences, Ed Mabry's restored gristmill. All the sites are set in a tranquil and apparently undisturbed natural landscape and are complemented by rustic wooden park buildings and rough-hewn directional and informational signs (often embellished by an evocative Kentucky long-rifle logo). Whatever the weather or season, the trappings of modernity and commerce — power lines, billboards, snarled or speeding traffic, rumbling trucks, franchise restaurants, tract development — barely intrude. With the road stretching through 469 miles of mountains, traffic is dispersed and solitude easy to find even during the busiest "leaf looking" times of year.[1]

All along the road, the thoughtfulness of design and the love of the mountains and the outdoors that underpinned much of the Parkway's planning are palpably evident. Dramatically placed overlooks and frequent, varied trails for hikers of all abilities convey visitors to hundreds of picturesque spots. Numerous campgrounds and several rustic lodges provide places to eat and rest. Park staff are friendly and helpful, and visitor centers offer information on the road and the region. The whole experience is open to everyone at virtually no cost beyond what they pay in federal taxes.

There is little question that the Parkway serves a broad public good and does so beautifully on what has long been a modest budget. More than 20 million visitors drive parts of the road each year — people like Bob and Frances Allen, who have been coming to the Parkway since their honeymoon in 1955. "It's like being in another world," Bob Allen told the *Asheville Citizen-Times* in a 2002 interview for a feature story about "what makes this scenic highway so special." Paul Ingrassia of Waynesville was more specific: "People like to travel the parkway because they get glimpses of God. . . . They get glimpses of something outside of the realm of the world they are living in day to day. It's their little escape from the box of society."[2] For seventeen years (1972–89), the Peaks of Otter Lodge was "Our Thanksgiving Place" for the far-flung Mann-Middleton family of New Jersey, Georgia, Maryland, and North Carolina. Countless other families — like mine — have their treasured Parkway stories, which the nonprofit Blue Ridge Parkway Foundation has recently begun collecting in an online archive.[3]

To the degree that they think about it, most of these travelers probably see the Parkway as it is often profiled in popular and travel magazines — like the 1985 *Southern Living* cover story commemorating the fiftieth anniversary of "The Good Road of the Blue Ridge." The road, that article poetically noted, "celebrates every mile of the country through which it travels . . . without altering the countryside." Roadside exhibits, the author observed, "both honored and celebrated [the] unromantic life [of] mountain highlanders . . . stripped of clutter and pretense . . . full of independence [and] fueled by ingenuity and self-sufficiency." The piece concluded soothingly that "the parkway never seems an intruder among these mountains"; instead, it has become "evidence of how well, how honestly and how intelligently, we can treat the earth if we but try."[4]

That the road has this almost magical effect on those who drive it offers enduring testimony to the work of many whose voices are now silent. Some of the most important labor, obviously, was that of the landscape architects and designers, engineers, stonemasons, contractors, and workers who carved the Parkway into the Appalachian ridges and whose efforts have been explored and celebrated in many a publication and televised documentary and now on many a Web site. But obscured by the road's apparently seamless and effortless integration into the surrounding mountains is the fact that it is highly constructed (as opposed to natural), its shape as much a product of nearly seventy years of direct interventions and very worldly decisions as of the natural topography and scenery the Parkway showcases.[5]

While scores of popular books and articles have celebrated the Parkway's beauty and design, no scholar has ever inquired sufficiently into the road's history. Most discussions of Parkway history appear in travel guides or coffee table books.[6] The few available serious discussions have almost uniformly followed the by-now standard account offered in Harley Jolley's slender *The Blue Ridge Parkway* (1969).[7]

By these Jolley-derived accounts, the Parkway originated during the Great Depression primarily as a make-work project to provide jobs for an undifferentiated population of suffering mountaineers within an isolated and backward region; it was thus essentially a benign and broadly beneficial "road of peace" and a "godsend for the needy." Local citizens, who shared a common interest in building up the tourist industry, unanimously welcomed it. The several controversies that did erupt in the early years were relatively small speed bumps along the road to progress, neither reflecting significant costs associated with building the road nor revealing substantial social divisions. "From the beginning," Jolley concludes, "the Parkway . . . benefitted from the helping hands of countless people, each making a contribution toward the common goal of establishing a unique recreational highway." It was "a road for pleasure [that] emphasized the work of nature while de-emphasizing the work of man."[8]

While Jolley's book—sold through the years in all of the Parkway's visitor centers—is perhaps the main source of the myth for contemporary travelers, this version of Parkway history, like the road itself, had been under construction since the 1930s by Parkway partisans in Asheville, National Park Service officials, a few other scholars, and writers for the local and national press. The Parkway-boosting *Asheville Citizen* repeatedly characterized the road as the "salvation of tens of thousands of persons who lie along the route" and argued that it would be the "crowning achievement of its kind for making this mountain country the recreational center of Eastern America."[9] In the monthly *Blue Ridge Parkway News*, National Park Service officials added their own elements to the story, emphasizing that the road was "built FIRST for the pleasure and recreation of the people who use it."[10] Who could argue with that?

This Parkway "history" has achieved virtually canonical status. Newspaper articles by the dozens have sung these familiar refrains, as has the Park Service itself. A 1986 scholarly conference to examine the impact of "America's favorite road" opened with a slide show by Jolley and included presentations that called the Parkway "a Depression-era make-work project" to give "proud, but poor and isolated, mountain men jobs."[11]

Yet creating the Parkway scene and experience required more than the talents of landscape designers and engineers working unopposed in a stunning physical setting. Instead, "the Scenic," as local residents often called the road, was also political: its creation required the arbitration of many significant disputes over substantial issues across boundaries of power. Built beginning in 1935 through the cooperative efforts of North Carolina's and Virginia's state highway departments and federal agencies of President Franklin D. Roosevelt's New Deal and completed more than a half century later, in 1987, the Parkway has been as politically complicated and controversial as any other large public works development.

Travelers rarely see evidence of these aspects of Parkway history, however. Tourists seeking a glimpse of God might have been surprised to encounter instead Ashe County, North Carolina, resident S. A. Miller, who owned land along the Parkway route and complained to Roosevelt in 1937 that "the Park to Park highway isn't any benefit to us according to what they tell us. We aren't allowed to put any buildings near it and not even cross it to our land on the other side."[12] L. F. Caudill of Sparta, North Carolina, repeatedly ripped down the barricade on an illegal access road that connected his property to the Parkway. Connie Johnson of Alleghany County, North Carolina, for years resisted the Park Service's attempt to close off an old road that led from his land to the Parkway. D. S. Bare, another North Carolinian, wrote to his congressman that "it will ruin us people a long top of the mountin [sic] if they take all of the land for the road."[13]

Many Parkway visitors today would no doubt dismiss as a crank Fred Bauer of the Eastern Band of Cherokee Indians, who opposed the Parkway's intrusion into Cherokee lands and argued in 1939 that "a system of public roads, with freedom to stop at any farmhouse, and visit or trade as desired, would be enjoyed more than a restricted parkway with everything planned just so."[14] Yet rather than being enamored with thoughts of mountain scenery, Bauer and others in the Cherokee area—who had long anticipated construction of a much-needed state highway from the Cherokee reservation east to the nearest metropolitan area, Asheville—were dismayed to learn of plans to build a land-gobbling, limited-access scenic Parkway over the same route.

Perhaps more sympathetic would be the figure of Marie Dwight, the Charleston, South Carolina, woman who for twenty years had welcomed girls to Camp As-You-Like-It, near Little Switzerland, North Carolina. Learning that the Parkway was to be routed too near the camp that provided her only income, she protested that she "should not be interrupted and interfered with by the menace I feel a public highway to be, *immediately* adjacent to a resort where there are only women and young girls."[15]

At least two powerful North Carolina landowners and resort developers—Heriot Clarkson of Little Switzerland and Hugh Morton of Grandfather Mountain—shared similar concerns, but what traveler today would recognize in the beloved Parkway an undertaking that Clarkson and Morton characterized as a ruthless and destructive attempt to crush tourist enterprises in the mountains, build up the fortunes of greedy and self-important government bureaucrats, and wreck the scenery it purportedly sought to highlight?

In truth, people's views of the Parkway during its seventy-year history have varied greatly depending on their cultural frames of reference, their class position, their geographic location, and their particular needs. Yet these variations are nearly invisible to most present-day travelers because the Parkway landscape almost mysteriously conceals its history. The peaceful appearance molded by the landscape architects on the Parkway staff and federal and state engineers is infused with a romantic version of regional history presented in roadside historical exhibits. The history told at these Parkway stops, that is, has obscured the currents within Appalachian, southern, and indeed American history that produced the highway. Consequently, a tourist attraction that an early Parkway superintendent described as designed to open "great picture windows to expose a way of life hitherto heavily veiled from the eyes of the American tourist" in fact shows a highly idealized picture of that life into which the Parkway and the forces that produced it have not and almost could not be incorporated.[16]

Encountering the Parkway at first as a tourist, I know how beguiling and historically opaque the luminous (and apparently transparent) Parkway scene can be. And sometimes it is fine just to enjoy it for what it is, without looking deeper. Even after I started the research for this book, I traveled the Parkway many times just for fun. I have ridden with my husband and young sons on the little green school bus to the summit of Sharp Top mountain at the Peaks of Otter. We have had our picture taken in front of the Mabry Mill and listened to mountain music at the new Blue Ridge Music Center. We have hiked along the glorious ridge at Rocky Knob and perched the boys on rocks at the overlook across from crashing Linville Falls. We have set up a tent and cookstove at our favorite rhododendron-enshrouded campsite at Crabtree Meadows and have browsed the crafts at the Folk Art Center. We have snapped family photos at the Parkway's highest point, Richland Balsam (6,047 feet), and hiked with a three-year-old to the top of Waterrock Knob. I presently serve on the Council of Advisers for the Blue Ridge Parkway Foundation, whose goal is to raise funds to improve and enhance the Parkway. So it should be clear at the outset that I love the Parkway and relish the memories of the many experiences I have had there.

In this book, I want to take readers on a different journey—beyond the concrete and immediate experience of the Parkway traveler into the complicated and often contentious processes that brought the road into being. This book departs from a romantic view of the Parkway as a modern miracle and as pure gain for everyone involved and looks critically at the road's history as a project created by human minds and hands, paid for with public funds, in the service of some version of a public good. Approaching the Parkway in this way helps us to understand that the Parkway's appearance owes as much to essentially political decisions as it does to landscape design principles and engineering practices. The Parkway is a result of active decisions in which some people got what they wanted and others did not. Hence, understanding the Parkway's appearance at any given place requires knowing about local conditions and issues, the local pressures brought to bear on the project, and the interaction of both of these factors with the visions, policies, and plans of state and federal designers and policy makers.

In any such public works project (road, dam, school or library, urban renewal project, power line), some of the needs of some people obviously have to be sacrificed in the service of what one expects to be a broad and consensus-backed public purpose. Benefits rarely come without costs, and the two must be weighed against one another. When the government exercised its power of eminent domain to take land for the Parkway, people were displaced. Some lost homes and farms; others lost businesses.[17] Individuals and the public were asked to understand and accept that the public good served was great enough to justify the private sacrifices required.

But the key issues go beyond the question of whether some people suffered negative impacts. Some clearly did, and those impacts should be inventoried and understood just as clearly as the project's benefits (whether immediate or later as a result of multiplier effects).[18] The essential questions, however, are whether the benefits that accrued are in fact as broad and evenly distributed as the Parkway's supporters claim, whether the process by which the cost and benefits are distributed is fair, and whether those who bear the costs have a voice in the decision-making process or receive fair compensation for their losses.

The Parkway's final form was neither inevitable nor obvious to all. Nor was it foreordained by nature or completely preplanned by landscape architects who imposed (without significant conflict or opposition) their fully formed Parkway vision. At every point, the Parkway developed out of a dialogue (sometimes amicable, sometimes conflicted) among the parties planning for or affected by the project: National Park Service staff, state highway department officials, highway engineers, landscape architects, tourism entrepreneurs, regional and national political leaders, and adjoining landowners.

To foreground this process, this book's basic questions diverge from the topics that usually dominate discussions of the Parkway: large- and small-scale aesthetics (vista selection, landscaping, overlooks, built structures, signage, stonework, fences), engineering features (bridges, tunnels, cuts and fills, gentle spiral curves), and construction logistics (Civilian Conservation Corps and Public Works Administration workers, private contractors). Instead, I ask how and by whom the public good to be served by the Parkway was defined. What biases inhered in decisions about design and routing? Given that a scenic parkway undoubtedly (and perhaps rightly) privileges some needs over others, whose needs has it privileged? How rigid or flexible have Parkway standards been, and how fairly have they been applied? What problems were encountered in bringing the Parkway to particular localities with specific histories and needs, and how did government agencies and officials manage competing demands? Did some constituencies, by virtue of their position or relative power, exert more influence over Parkway development than might have been warranted while other affected individuals or groups had little voice in shaping the project? Was the public good co-opted in some instances in the service of private ends, and if so, how? Would different decisions at some points have more equitably distributed the costs and benefits?

These questions have already been asked about other public works projects, so why ask them about the Parkway, and why now? Part of the reason is that the Parkway has long been discussed (erroneously) as if it had appeared on the land fully realized, free of these constraints, controversies, and concerns. The other part of the answer is that the factors that have always shaped the Parkway both persist today and show no signs of disappearing. Inevitably, our (and our government's) decisions about how to manage these issues will determine the Parkway's future. Moreover, the ongoing erosion of public funds for public projects of whatever sort will undoubtedly intensify debates and require us all to think better about where the public good lies and what initiatives deserve public funding. In meeting these challenges, an uncritical vision of both the Parkway itself and the region through which it passes ultimately is not useful.

Furthermore, forgetting that the Parkway resulted from active choices among competing alternatives robs historical actors of their agency and suggests that we too are powerless in the face of impersonal historical forces. Yet we, like those who created the Parkway, can and must choose how we define and pursue the public good and how we go forward, both in relation to the Parkway itself and in regard to our constellation of publicly provided infrastructure and services. Seeing the contested nature of both the public good and "just compensation" to individuals and groups along the Parkway can help us think better about how to balance these competing needs.

So in the interest of helping us think both about these larger matters and about understanding and better managing this particular road, I want to take you on a Parkway journey different from the one you are perhaps used to. Like all Parkway journeys, this trip through history will take us past a succession of overlooks into the past: views sometimes panoramic and clear, other times partial and obscured by the fog of years and the overgrowth of layers of new vegetation. We will take the Parkway's trademark "ride a while, stop a while" approach, lingering at several favorite sites and passing by others for another time.

Our trip moves through time from the Parkway's beginnings in the 1930s through its completion in the 1980s. Using a series of case studies—our own set of scenic stops—we will examine many critical areas of Parkway development where the public good was debated, defined, and balanced against other considerations: Parkway design and routing, land acquisition and management, relations with landowners and regional business interests, inter-and intragovernmental dynamics, environmental impact, and interpretation of the history and culture of the Appalachian region to the public.

As we move along, it should become clear that rather than arising organically from the geography of the region itself and disturbing it little, the Parkway's physical form in fact inscribed on the landscape several critical political decisions made during its seventy-year history. Thus, the physical shape of the Parkway is as much a product of political processes as of the "natural" features of the mountain lands through which it winds. Rather than "de-emphasizing the work of man," as Jolley has argued, the Parkway quietly embodies parts of the very human story of the politics of public works and tourism development in the southern Appalachian mountains.[19]

To help us bear in mind that the Parkway emerged as part of larger regional and national processes, our trip begins with context. Chapter 1, "Roads, Parks, and Tourism: A Southern Scenic Parkway in a National Context," discusses how nineteenth- and early-twentieth-century efforts at building good roads, creating national and state parks, and promoting tourism generated the ideas, synergies, and conditions that eventually produced the Parkway when New Deal agencies made funding available for such projects in 1933. The chapter argues that the Parkway represented not a wholly new idea but rather the embodiment and fulfillment of long-term trends, ideas, models, and processes.

Chapter 2, "The Scenic Is Political: The Parkway and Asheville's Tourism Industry," examines the 1934 controversy between North Carolina and Tennessee over routing the southern end of the Parkway. It argues that Asheville's campaign for the Parkway revealed the close ties between Parkway supporters and tourism promoters in the North Carolina mountains. These close ties make clear that the Parkway's most fervent advocates originally conceived it primarily as a stimulus for Asheville's flagging tourism industry and an economy devastated by a decade of improvident boom development. The chapter further discusses the very different sort of Parkway that would have resulted had the Tennessee route been chosen.

Chapter 3, "We Ain't Picked None on the Scenic: Parkway Ideals and Local Realities," explores issues surrounding land acquisition, manipulation, management, and protection that have been and remain central to Parkway development. The chapter describes the evolution of Parkway regulations about access and use and the processes of land acquisition in Virginia and North Carolina. It assesses the effects of these policies on local residents and landowners, discusses their responses to the project, and analyzes their relative ability to force changes in the project. It concludes that the Parkway's appearance writes onto the landscape a number of decisions that either inhered in the scenic parkway design model or resulted from resolving specific problems with putting this kind of road in particular localities.

Chapter 4, "By the Grace of God and a Mitchell County Jury: Little Switzerland, Regional Tourism, and the Parkway," details the manipulation of the Parkway for private gain by North Carolina Supreme Court Justice and resort developer Heriot Clarkson in the late 1930s. Beginning in 1909, Clarkson developed Little Switzerland, the place on the North Carolina section of the Parkway where — as a consequence of Clarkson's battle with the North Carolina State Highway Commission — the Parkway right-of-way is at its narrowest and where commercial development is directly accessible from the road. To bend the Parkway (literally and figuratively) to his purpose, Clarkson skillfully manipulated political connections, the legal system, and public sentiment.

Chapter 5, "The Crowning Touch of Interest: Parkway Development, Cultural Landscaping, and the Eastern Band of Cherokees," looks at the Eastern Cherokees' opposition to routing the Parkway's southern end across their Qualla Boundary lands. The chapter details tribal negotiations with both the state and federal governments, explores intratribal disagreements over economic and cultural development, and discusses how Parkway development intertwined with New Deal policies toward Native Americans, especially with regard to Indian assimilation. It points out how an organized, culturally visible — though in many respects disempowered — group compelled changes in Parkway plans for their lands. Finally, the chapter engages the question of how local cultures and peoples would be presented to Parkway travelers.

Chapter 6, "Remembering the Peaks of Otter: Telling History on the Parkway Landscape," examines the history of the Peaks of Otter/Mons community in Virginia from the nineteenth century forward, with special attention to an entrepreneurial but nevertheless public-spirited group of local men who owned and developed the Hotel Mons and helped the National Park Service to acquire area land for the Parkway in the late 1930s. The chapter details how the Park Service reshaped the landscape at the Peaks from the 1940s onward and then looks at the service's attempts to tell an idealized version of Appalachian regional history at a site whose historic landscape had by then been largely obliterated.

Chapter 7, "From Stump Town to Carolina's Top Scenic Attraction: Private Interests and the Public Good at Grandfather Mountain," discusses the longest battle over Parkway lands, which stretched from 1955 to 1968 at Grandfather Mountain, North Carolina. The chapter explores Grandfather's history, including the logging threat in the 1930s and 1940s and owner Hugh Morton's development of a popular tourist attraction there in the 1950s, as well as Morton's claim that the National Park Service was willing to ruin the mountain by routing the Parkway higher on the mountainside than he preferred. Finally, the chapter suggests that Morton's environmentalism was closely intertwined with his desire to continue to develop a profitable tourist attraction at Grandfather and looks at how the conflict was emblematic of an emerging broader clash between privately developed tourism enterprises and federal officials managing the Blue Ridge Parkway. That clash, at its most intense in the early 1960s, represented the decline of the symbiotic relationship between private business owners and public officials that had brought the Parkway into being in the 1930s.

This journey will take us from a place many think they understand to one few would recognize, along a Blue Ridge Parkway almost no one knows. After traveling this road for fifteen years, however, I believe that we should (and can) know this path and that it will serve us—and the Parkway—better. In the process we will lose some naïveté and innocence, but at the same time we will move from myth to understanding, from unquestioning acceptance to critical analysis, from forgetting to remembering, from passivity to action.

In place of a Parkway miraculously laid on the land, we will find a road that sometimes hacked its way through the property of people who would have preferred that it go elsewhere. In place of a Parkway brought into being by generous citizens worried about the unemployed in mountain coves, we will see a project initially championed mainly by business officials who fretted about the future of the tourist industry they had built. Instead of a beloved byway that everyone agreed should come to the mountains, we will learn about a contentious project whose development was far more likely to be influenced by the wealthy, well-connected, or well-organized than by the average citizen or landowner. Instead of a project that nobly and consistently served the broad public interest, we will find a parkway sometimes co-opted by private concerns. Instead of a visionary and pioneering road that represented the embodiment of one brilliant landscape architect's planning genius, we will encounter a beautiful drive that was devised by the minds of many planners drawing on many past models, that emerged from many competing interests, and that was formed on the fly with nearly as many plans discarded as implemented.

None of these discoveries detracts from the Parkway's beauty or its perennial (and deserved) attractiveness to millions of travelers. But these phenomena remind us that such beauty and accessibility are not inevitable, self-sustaining, or without cost. As this "super-scenic motorway" emerged from human actions in specific historical contexts, so must it be preserved and protected in the present and future by those of us who love it—locating, defining, and defending in it a broad and equitable sense of the public good.[20]

ROADS, PARKS, AND TOURISM
A SOUTHERN SCENIC PARKWAY
IN A NATIONAL CONTEXT

In 1919, North Carolina attorney, resort developer, and Democratic Party activist Heriot Clarkson gave a speech, probably at a meeting of the newly organized Wilmington-Charlotte-Asheville Highway Association, which he served as a legal adviser.[1] "This is an age of progress," he exhorted. Quoting a South Carolina governor advocating the state's-rightist nullification law of the 1830s, Clarkson continued, "'He who dallies is a dastard and he who doubts is damned.'" What people want, he ventured "are results. Beneficial results, those that serve mankind, churches, schools, good roads—these are the great civilizers of the ages." The Wilmington-Charlotte-Asheville Road project, an effort to build "a hard-surface road from the mountains to the sea," he named "the greatest movement started in years." This road, he hoped, could be linked with roads to be built through federally owned lands in North Carolina's mountains. "The National Government," he reminded his listeners, "has spent millions of dollars on roads in Yellowstone Park, White Mountains and elsewhere." Given that fact, "What is the matter with our Congressmen, are they sleeping at the switch? We have the most beautiful scenic mountains in the world. Our government has acquired hundreds of thousands of acres—why not great hard-surface roads built approaching and through them?"[2]

With characteristic hyperbole, Clarkson previewed the boosterish spirit and identified several of the national and regional trends that fifteen years later would bring the Blue Ridge Parkway to the southern Appalachian mountains of North Carolina and Virginia. As a tourism developer (he had started his Little Switzerland resort getaway in the North Carolina mountains in 1909), a prominent state political figure, and a crusader for good roads, Clarkson was well placed to appreciate the possibilities offered by the emerging tourism–roads–national parks link that lay at the center of the accelerating development of the new national park system.

Nationwide, Good Roads advocacy, park building, and surging automotive tourism in the 1910s and 1920s heralded a new era of national park–oriented travel to which local boosters such as Clarkson hoped to hitch their economic wagons.[3] Throughout America, the phenomenal growth of the national park system between 1916 and World War II (greatly fostered by the New Deal) was inextricably tied to the spread of cars and the growth of tourism. Perhaps no project of this era exemplifies the national tourism–automobiles–national parks interconnection (and the many tensions within it) as fully as the New Deal's Blue Ridge Parkway—precisely the kind of "hard-surfaced road approaching and through" the scenic North Carolina mountains for which Clarkson had called. In North Carolina especially, the Blue Ridge Parkway appeared to offer tourism boosters, business promoters, road and park builders, and state government officials a not-to-be missed opportunity to realize long-term goals having as much to do with regional development as with national currents.

Both national trends and regional dynamics gave birth to the Parkway, and the roads-autos-tourism connection shaped the road in crucial ways. It was not (as it has generally been understood to be) a wholly new and imaginative idea for a road to be "laid gently on the land." How did this particular road come to lie on this particular land, and what can it can tell us about the cultural, social, economic, and political history and values of our or any other times?

EARLY PARK BUILDING IN THE UNITED STATES

The Blue Ridge Parkway emerged at the end of a century-long process of developing an American aesthetic and style for public parks, first in nineteenth-century cities and later in the huge expanses of national parklands. When they began to think about the Parkway in 1933, planners could draw on landscape architecture and park-planning experience that originated in Frederick Law Olmsted's nineteenth-century work on municipal and regional parks, more than thirty years of state park development, more than twenty years of parkway-building experience in other parts of the United States, more than a decade of road building in the national parks, and an evolving Park Service "rustic" design aesthetic. Thus, the Parkway—though longer and more ambitious in scope than any earlier parkway or park road—represented the fruition of long-term trends rather than a new model of park and road development.[4]

The ideas about scenery, parks, and presentation of landscapes that had been evolving in the United States since the early nineteenth century borrowed in turn from an earlier tradition of English landscape gardening. In nineteenth-century America, civic enthusiasm for carefully planned public parks designed by landscape architects, especially Olmsted and the many influenced or taught by him, produced numerous urban, suburban, and wilderness spaces with roads, paths, and plantings that harmonized with the surrounding natural landscape and highlighted its scenic qualities. From New York's Central Park (1858) to the many other municipal parks it inspired to the federal donation of Yosemite to the state of California in 1864 to the establishment of Yellowstone as a federal park in 1872, park development in the nineteenth century sprang from a growing sense of "seeing land as landscape." This aesthetic, according to historian Ethan Carr and others, celebrated scenic beauty as a core cultural value and landscape as an art form. Out of this sensibility grew what Carr calls the "landscape park concept" that would govern national park development from 1910 through the 1930s.[5]

Related to municipal park development were Olmsted's and others' plans in several cities beginning in the 1870s for integrated systems of controlled parkways to connect neighborhoods and parks. The system created by Olmsted's student, Charles Eliot, on the outskirts of Boston after 1893 exemplified the possibilities. Olmsted's sons' Denver Mountain Park system (initiated in 1912) also connected a series of outlying areas by scenic roadways, a plan that according to Carr became characteristic of park development in many western cities in the early twentieth century. Foreshadowing the later Blue Ridge Parkway, many early-twentieth-century park systems "featured curvilinear drives and paths that conformed to topography and offered constantly shifting views in a considered sequence."[6]

Eliot's park system around Boston also heralded a widening of the concept through the creation of municipal, county, and state park commissions that had the power to condemn and manage larger and larger areas of parklands (sometimes outside of municipal boundaries) for public health and aesthetic enjoyment. The movement for state parks in particular strengthened in the 1880s and 1890s, with New York's protection of Niagara Falls (1885), the creation of Minnesota's Itasca State Park (1891), and designation of the Palisades Interstate Park in New York and New Jersey (1895). Park commissions and systems soon emerged in Connecticut, Minnesota, Wisconsin, Ohio, Idaho, North Carolina, Indiana, and several other states. By 1920, the parks movement had spread nationwide and stood poised for exponential growth in the decade to follow.[7]

As the twentieth century proceeded, physical modifications of the landscape in the larger new state and regional parks were downplayed in favor of increasing emphasis on highlighting the scenery nature provided. Even the roads and paths needed for visitors, Eliot wrote in the 1890s, should be "mere slender threads of graded surface winding over and among the huge natural forms of the ground." Other physical improvements to these parks—such as Eliot's Boston system, Bear Mountain in Palisades Park, and Lake Itasca—were also designed seamlessly to foreground the natural scenery. Buildings and other facilities were carefully placed, and all construction was designed so that it blended into the landscape picture. Designers requested that grading follow the land's natural contours, gardeners emphasized woodlands management and planting of indigenous rather than exotic plants, and masons used native stone and wood to build visitor shelters, lodges, guardrails, and signs. The larger, more remote parks offered visitors a wider range of vigorous recreational options, including mountain climbing and hiking, fishing, camping, boating, and swimming. With these developments, Carr notes, the "American landscape park," born in the city, "moved to the country."[8]

In 1917, just in time for the advent of the national park system, Harvard landscape architect Henry Hubbard and librarian Theodora Kimball summarized much of what had been learned by two generations of landscape architects in their seminal textbook, *An Introduction to the Study of Landscape Design*. According to one historian of the Park Service, this book, which still dominated schools of landscape architecture as late as the 1950s, was likely "the single most influential source that inspired national and state park designers in the 1920s and 1930s." Hubbard and Kimball advocated an informal style they called "modern American landscape" that highlighted the use of indigenous plants, "natural" landscape scenes that were usually "partly the results of man's activity," and the development of "vistas" that included a "single central focal point . . . enframed by trees or other masses that screened all other objects" and created a "window that could be manipulated by the designer who could arrange one scene after another in a sequence." They pushed park builders to imitate natural forms in their buildings by using weathered local stone, rough posts, and thatched roofs to blend shelters and other structures into the landscape.[9]

Nearly as influential as Hubbard and Kimball was landscape gardening professor Frank Waugh of the Massachusetts Agricultural College, whose *The Natural Style in Landscape Gardening* (1917) was also widely read. Waugh promoted an approach to park planning that involved asymmetry, mass plantings, an emphasis on imitating natural forms, an attempt to create areas whose boundaries were nearly invisible, and the careful sequencing of scenes and views. All of these elements of design work, he claimed, concerned "intelligently letting alone a natural landscape."[10]

This expansion of the park concept received a major impetus from the growth of automobile-based tourism. As automobile ownership expanded and the national park system came into being, Carr argues, "automotive technology pervaded almost every aspect of how [national] parks were developed, managed, and used. Automobiles—and the crowds of tourists they conveyed—made the national park system as we know it possible."[11]

THE GOOD ROADS MOVEMENT IN
THE NATION AND THE SOUTH

Auto tourism depended on the development of good roads. When the Blue Ridge Parkway idea was first whispered in North Carolina in the summer of 1933, the state, like the nation, was only barely into its second decade of serious road construction. Late-nineteenth-century calls for better roads had finally begun to bring some change in first two decades of the twentieth century, as a network of improved roads spread across the northeast and as the federal government passed legislation in 1916 and 1921 providing funds to help states with road building. With the growing popularity and affordability of the automobile, a national (albeit disunified) Good Roads movement emerged, and by the 1920s highway construction across the country was booming.[12]

Within and beyond North Carolina, awful southern roads needed attention. In 1904, for example, only slightly over 4 percent of them qualified as "improved" in any way, and most of those were in urban areas. State and federal governments were slow to respond, and as of 1910 (when "improved" mileage had climbed to 7 percent), neither the federal government nor most southern state governments (Virginia's and Alabama's being the exceptions) allocated any money to help local governments with road construction.[13]

First to set about to change this situation were farmers' organizations, which advocated better roads to connect farms to nearby markets or to railroad hubs. The farmers' lobbies resisted levying additional taxes on their members to finance road building, however, and the early Good Roads organizations did not envision a state-controlled highway system. Domination of the Good Roads movement by farmers also limited broad public support by casting road improvement as primarily a farmers' problem. Not until business and industrial leaders joined the campaign did the Good Roads movement gain the momentum it needed to transform the southern landscape. Financially strapped local or county governments continued to manage road construction, which remained a decentralized and erratic process until the 1916 federal legislation.[14]

The automobile-induced transportation revolution arrived in earnest in 1910 (with more than thirty-two thousand Model Ts sold), and by the mid-1910s, momentum was building for road improvements. By 1912 North Carolina alone had at least sixty-five Good Roads associations. Car registrations soared to more than 25 million by the late 1920s as the American middle class took to the roads in droves. As people struggled to dig their new vehicles out of the muddy ruts of the old wagon roads, however, the clamor for better highways increased. Professional engineering training was becoming more widely available, and public relations campaigns for better roads galvanized citizens across the South.[15]

As the automobile-owning population and the automobile industry grew, the rationale for road improvements altered dramatically. Auto owners and industry leaders wanting to sell more cars began to see the auto as a replacement for the railroad, issuing calls for roads to serve interstate tourists and industries, not local farmers. Reform-oriented professionals who had always favored good roads as a means to southern progress and economic development had little difficulty switching to the new rationale, and they were soon joined by business leaders who previously had paid little attention to the Good Roads movement. One historian terms these people "highway progressives" who "paid only lip service to rural development issues and mentioned the concerns of farmers only as a means of getting them on the bandwagon to construct tourist highways. To highway progressives, good roads in the South clearly meant increased tourism, and that translated into economic well-being." The Good Roads movement thus turned in a new direction by 1915, and this change mirrored trends nationwide as interstate tourism and advocates of a federally funded, nationally connected system of roads came to dominate the enterprise.[16]

State leaders, however, had no clear idea of how to plan, build, or pay for the roads everyone now seemed to agree were needed. The old decentralized, county-controlled, locally financed, convict-labor road-building system seemed inadequate, but what could or should replace it? What role should federal and state governments play?[17]

As North Carolina's political leaders edged haltingly into the new age, Heriot Clarkson became central in spurring road building in the state. In his 1919 speech, he spoke for many prominent North Carolinians who had been trying to dig the "Rip Van Winkle state," left behind by progress, out of both the mud and legendary backwardness. Clarkson and other North Carolina 1920s highway progressives subscribed to a broader development creed that has been termed "business progressivism." This point of view translated into a willingness to throw the state's money and support behind social and infrastructure improvements that would make North Carolina more attractive to business and industry and, they hoped, help modernize the state.[18]

Deep-seated resistance to tax hikes to finance road building and a long-entrenched commitment to county control of highway construction restrained the state from creating a unified and professionally designed state road system until 1921. That year, after much publicity by the North Carolina Good Roads Association (by then the main state roads lobby) and with the somewhat lukewarm backing of new Governor Cameron Morrison, a bill written by a committee headed by Clarkson passed the state legislature, and the state highway system was born. A large bond issue and a gasoline tax, combined with federal monies allocated by the 1916 legislation, would pay for construction of a highway system (controlled by a newly strengthened State Highway Commission) that would link together all the county seats and other important destinations and join these roads to those of neighboring states. Throughout the rest of the decade, the state built highways at a frenetic pace, nearly tripling its mileage of improved roads. In the process, it become known as the Good Roads State.[19]

The 1910s and 1920s saw a flurry of driving contests and publicity to build public interest in the new possibilities for travel as well as numerous proposals for (and some actual construction of) ambitious cross-country interstate roads. Feeling ignored by the interstate trunk line schemes, farmers criticized the new highways, but their protests largely went unheeded as the profits to be made from new jobs, new industries, and new investments brought by long-distance highways were too great for middle-class southerners to ignore. By the end of the 1920s, the business community's vision of highway construction had handily won out.[20]

The Good Roads movement in North Carolina—and certainly in the mountains—seems always to have had a probusiness orientation, as tourism-related motives had long intertwined with the goals of helping farmers. Both the Buncombe Turnpike (completed in 1828 from Saluda Gap, South Carolina, near Greenville, north through Asheville and Warm Springs, North Carolina, to Greeneville, Tennessee) and the Yonahlossee Road (built before 1900 from Linville to Blowing Rock in North Carolina) had demonstrated roads' potential to attract tourists. One of the first Good Roads bodies in the South (and the first in North Carolina) was the Good Roads Association of Asheville and Buncombe County (1899). Although it catered to farmers' concerns, this association was characterized from the beginning by a more business-oriented outlook. Tourist promoters in Asheville saw better roads—often scenic drives through the sur-

Good Roads caravan, Hickory Nut Gap, near Asheville, North Carolina, ca. 1916.
Photo by W. Staley Wicker. North Carolina Collection, University of North Carolina at Chapel Hill.

rounding countryside—as a way to attract more tourists to the already-popular resort town. North Carolina Geological Survey head and Good Roads crusader Joseph Hyde Pratt pointed out as early as 1907 good roads' potential to attract auto-driving pleasure travelers. At a major road convention in Asheville in 1909, more than 360 delegates formed the Southern Appalachian Good Roads Association to promote an extensive system of long-distance tourist-oriented improved roads through the mountains, naming Pratt the new group's president.[21]

Pratt's organization proposed to begin with highways connecting Charlotte and Asheville, North Carolina; Knoxville, Tennessee; and Greenville and Spartanburg, South Carolina. Good Roads enthusiasts in North Carolina and elsewhere also proposed a series of "special highways" designed to spark interest in and generate local and private financing for roads in communities along the routes. Among six such highways planned for North Carolina was the Crest of the Blue

Arrival of stage, Warm Springs Hotel, Madison County, North Carolina, before 1886. The location of Warm Springs (later Hot Springs) along the Buncombe Turnpike made it attractive for tourists beginning in the 1830s. North Carolina Collection, University of North Carolina at Chapel Hill.

Ridge Highway (Pratt's idea), a direct precursor of the Blue Ridge Parkway. With this highway, tourism supporters in the mountains hoped to open the area's rich scenery to automobile drivers. Although Pratt raised some money for the road and his department completed surveys and even some construction on parts of the route, his idea would have to await the 1930s to become reality.[22]

In the other Blue Ridge Parkway state, Virginia, the entire road-building picture was different. Roads activism there, though strong early, became considerably more muted as the 1920s dawned. It petered out by the early 1920s when a fiscally conservative movement under State Senator Harry F. Byrd defeated an effort (similar to North Carolina's) to get a large road-building bond issue approved by voters. Relying on an increased gasoline tax to finance road building, Virginia lagged perhaps two decades behind North Carolina in improving the state's road system. With Byrd elevated in the 1920s to the governor's office and then in the 1930s to the U.S. Senate, and with his machine dominating Virginia politics into the 1960s, the defeat of the bond issue, according to one historian, "solidified a pay-as-you-go mentality . . . that would be the ideological basis for the state's fiscal policy for the next several decades."[23]

Road building and easy travel by automobile were crucial to the growth of a true national parks system and an ethic of national middle-class tourism. Although park development at the municipal, regional, and state levels had proceeded vigorously since the mid-nineteenth century, by the 1910s only seventeen national parks existed, and they were managed in a somewhat uncoordinated and often chaotic way. Lacking a distinct parks wing, the Interior Department had allowed railroads and other private commercial interests to build and manage hotels (such as the Northern Pacific's Old Faithful Inn at Yellowstone and the Atchison, Topeka, and Santa Fe's El Tovar at Grand Canyon) and other facilities for visitors in many of the parks.[24]

Vastly increased tourism in the 1910s brought dangers and opportunities for parks old and new. Uncontrolled visitors added new threats to the illegal grazing, poaching, logging, and plans for hydroelectric and irrigation projects (like the 1913 Hetch Hetchy Dam in Yosemite) that had already threatened to damage or destroy the parks' natural and scenic resources. The incursion of tourists generated a debate about how best to protect and manage the parks as well as a movement to create a separate federal parks agency.[25]

With the hiring of Stephen Mather to manage the national parks for the Interior Department in 1915, the movement for a separate parks agency gained momentum. Seizing on the opportunity presented by growing public interest in auto touring, Mather saw increasing the accessibility and public use of the national parks as the best way to build the constituency necessary to support creation of a federal parks agency. In short order, he and other advocates of a park service shepherded to passage the 1916 National Park Service Act (the Organic Act). It gave the National Park Service (NPS) a "dual mandate" to "conserve the scenery and the natural and historic objects and the wild life therein and to provide for the enjoyment of the same in such manner and by such means as will leave them unimpaired for the enjoyment of future generations."[26]

Discussions among pre-1916 advocates of the act clearly indicate that the meaning of "conservation" at this time included "efficient management" of the parks for public use. Indeed, many scenic preservationists who supported the Park Service believed that "tourism was the only 'dignified exploitation' of the national parks," a pursuit whose impacts were fairly benign and whose benefits in terms of justifying the exclusion of other, more destructive uses were evident. Even when they realized, as Mather did, that uncontrolled tourism might be damaging, early Park Service supporters—adherents to a long tradition of systematic park planning—saw controlled park development to serve tourists as the best route to scenic preservation. Science-based protection of natural resources played little role in the early management of the Park Service.[27]

As Mather sensed, park building, tourism, and road building generated a powerful synergy in 1916 and the years to follow. Mather believed that fostering travel to the parks was the surest way to build a national constituency for the new park system as well as for the new NPS. Indeed, the establishment of the independent federal Park Service occurred because of the prospect of mass visitation to the parks. As one historian has observed, by negotiating the shift to a rationalized park system through the encouragement of park visitation, "the state became actively involved in the promotion of national tourism."[28]

This promotion took several forms that had concrete results (both literally and figuratively) for the national park system's physical development. During the early years of the Park Service, Mather launched an aggressive publicity campaign to draw visitors to parks, changed policies to facilitate automotive travel, and encouraged road building to enable and control the influx. Publicity efforts, coordinated by journalist and publisher Robert Sterling Yard, included numerous articles in popular magazines and the distribution of 275,000 copies of the lushly illustrated *National Parks Portfolio*, millions of copies of a smaller *Glimpses of the National Parks* pamphlet, and countless other guides produced by local chambers of commerce and tourist bureaus.[29]

These promotional efforts combined with road building and the widening availability of cars to spur a great surge in park visitation by auto in the late 1910s and into the 1920s. This wave rolled in on the heels of decades of efforts by railroad companies and businessmen to entice travelers to the American West. As European travel had plummeted with the start of World War I, the See America First movement that had started among Western tourism boosters as early as 1906 caught hold. Promoters motivated by a mix of business acumen and patriotism exhorted Americans to tour their national natural treasures. These efforts built on—and their early reach was vastly expanded by—the longer-term project mounted by the transcontinental railroad corporations to construct tourist enterprises to attract visitors to western parks. When the parks became united under a single federal agency, they began to be transformed from a set of discrete attractions into a rationalized system of national riches symbolizing "the majesty and pride of the nation." Touring the parks became both an act of patriotism and a builder of a national consciousness.[30]

Mather and his staff believed that the parks could be "accessible and popular, but not vulgar" and that they could "bring in the crowds and yet . . . maintain an appearance of not being crowded." At the head of this effort within the Park Service was a cadre of landscape architects and engineers who dominated the early NPS leadership. Under their direction, the next two decades featured extensive tourism-serving construction of park facilities of all sorts (headquarters buildings, museums, roads, campgrounds, trails, hotels, shelters, and water and sewer lines), all built in a "rustic" architectural style developed to echo and blend with the natural scenery. While Mather's staff debated the types of tourism development that were "appropriate" for the parks, road construction in and between the parks clearly surpassed all other priorities during and after Mather's tenure.[31]

PARK ROADS AND THE WESTERN PARKS

National parks visitation soared from 335,000 in 1915 to more than 900,000 five years later and to more than 1.5 million by the mid-1920s. The new Park Service initially joined with private, municipal, and civic groups to designate, mark, and improve roads connecting the parks, and many of those groups, like Mather, envisioned park-to-park highways linking the parks. Good Roads advocates set up the National Parks Touring Association in 1919. One of the most important efforts was that of the National Park-to-Park Highway Association, formed (with Mather's active participation in 1916 as the Yellowstone Highway Association) to devise and promote a road linking the western parks. By 1920, the group's well-marked (though not fully hard-surfaced) route connecting all major western parks was complete.[32]

The rapid improvement of roads leading to the parks made it obvious to Mather that the roads within parks were in sad shape, and he pushed road building in the parks as one of the top priorities of his administration (1915–29). For Mather, providing for enjoyment while conserving park resources and leaving them unimpaired demanded the construction of well-planned facilities (including roads) to prevent visitors from destroying beauty through unbridled and random use.[33]

Wandering about on their own, independent of train lines, carriage routes, and established centralized hotels, auto travelers posed an acute threat. Mather's NPS hired numerous landscape architects and engineers over the next several years, secured funding in 1924 for the service's first large road-building program, and entered into a crucial interbureau agreement in 1926 with the Bureau of Public Roads (BPR) to manage and coordinate park road building under NPS direction. In 1927, at his urging, Congress authorized a ten-year, $51 million road-building program.[34]

The 1920s and 1930s soon became, in the words of a recent Park Service exhibit

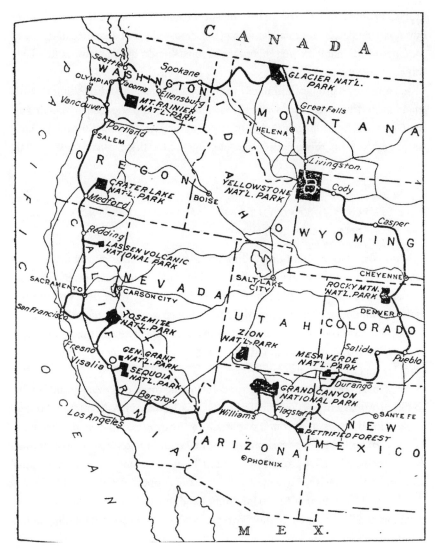

Map of the National Park-to-Park Highway, 1920. This loop connected western national parks. *Report of the Director of the National Park Service*, 1920; reproduced from Sutter, *Driven Wild*, 109.

on park roads, a "Golden Age of park road development." With landscape architects preeminent, road building in this period emphasized meticulous planning and careful placement of roads and other facilities to blend gracefully with their surroundings and to protect and showcase the park scenery. Many of the Park Service's most notable scenic road projects were completed in these years, including the Generals Highway in Sequoia (1926), the Zion–Mount Carmel Highway in

Zion Canyon National Park (1930), the spectacular fifty-two-mile Going-to-the-Sun Road in Glacier National Park (1933), the ten-mile Trail Ridge Road in Rocky Mountain National Park (1933), and the reconstruction of the Wawona Road entrance to Yosemite (1933).[35]

Each of these projects ultimately influenced the design and building of park roads in and between the two great eastern national parks (Shenandoah and the Great Smoky Mountains) that were central to the development of the Blue Ridge Parkway. But those parks came late, lagging the first western park by a half century.

PARKS FOR THE EAST: THE GREAT SMOKY MOUNTAINS
AND SHENANDOAH NATIONAL PARKS

With park development proceeding apace and a national consciousness developing about the potential economic, recreational, and patriotic benefits park tourism could bring, leaders in the eastern United States (where nearly two-thirds of the population remained in 1920) naturally hoped to get in on the park-building frenzy. For easterners, it was inconvenient that as of the early 1920s, only one national park (the small area in Maine that had become Acadia National Park in 1919) lay east of the Mississippi River.[36]

The tourist travel boom that occurred during the 1920s delighted groups in the southern Appalachians—particularly business leaders in Asheville—who had worked for decades to encourage tourism by creating regional park systems.[37] Their activism led to the development of the Great Smoky Mountains National Park in western North Carolina and eastern Tennessee. Simultaneously, Virginia tourism boosters, with Harry Byrd's enthusiastic support, set about establishing the Shenandoah National Park. Unfolding hand in hand with new highway construction, the development of these two parks set the stage for the building of the Blue Ridge Parkway, which would link them together.

In lobbying for eastern parks, North Carolina and Tennessee took leading roles. In 1899, about fifty leaders from several southern states gathered at Asheville's elegant Battery Park Hotel to consider establishing a national park in the Blue Ridge or Great Smoky Mountains.[38] They formed the Appalachian National Park Association (ANPA), and agitation for a southern mountain park, which had sputtered along sporadically since the 1880s, took its first organized shape.[39] Alarmed by the environmental destruction being wrought by the region's burgeoning timber industry, the ANPA hoped to protect some portions of the mountains.[40] But conservation was only one of the group's motives: the Asheville Board of Trade leaders who called the meeting doubtless knew that the continued success of their growing tourist industry (spurred to new vigor twenty years earlier by the railroad's arrival in the city) depended largely on preserving the surrounding scenery. Furthermore, the group acknowledged that anything that fouled the air or water endangered the city's and the region's reputation as a health resort.[41]

Whatever the ANPA's motives, however, its early efforts were unproductive. Powerful lumber interests in the region, dead set against removing good timberlands from logging, either resisted efforts at federal intervention in the region or pushed for a national forest—in which cutting would be permitted—instead of a park. Realizing the futility of trying to secure federal funding for a park at this juncture, the ANPA became the Appalachian National Forest Reserve Association and threw its weight behind the national forest movement. Thus thwarted, the early southern Appalachian park movement temporarily faded from view.[42]

The timber industry that squelched the park movement also brought massive changes to the southern Appalachians. The coming of railroads to western North Carolina spurred the industry's growth. By 1900, manufacturing of lumber and timber products had become the state's second-leading industry, and timber production continued to increase through the 1920s. Ohio-based Champion Fibre Company was the biggest industrial player, buying up land throughout the area and opening a massive mill at Canton, fifteen miles west of Asheville, in 1905. Champion employed thousands of people, and by 1930 its Canton plant had become the largest paper and pulp mill in the United States.[43]

As the leaders of the early Appalachian national park movement no doubt realized, unchecked growth in lumbering ultimately would prove incompatible with continued expansion of western North Carolina's tourism industry. Yet through the early years of the twentieth century, the two sectors grew hand in hand. Tourists and travelers who flooded Asheville and the surrounding countryside after the 1890s carried home news of the region's massive timber resources, fostering industrialists' and entrepreneurs' interest in the area, and the latter groups frequently involved themselves in the tourist industry.[44]

But the short-term and limited compatibility between tourism and logging could not last. By the 1920s, the timber industry had devastated western North Carolina's forests. Corporate loggers had clear-cut nearly 60 percent of the Smoky Mountains area, with particularly drastic effects on the North Carolina side. What loggers had not gotten, fires and floods had finished off, so that much of the landscape of western North Carolina had become decidedly unscenic.[45] The conservation movement, which had not completely died, finally brought about the creation of the Pisgah National Forest in western North Carolina in 1916. But Pisgah's goal of forest management for use did little to assure preservation of the scenery that was so important to the mountain tourism industry. The time was ripe for renewed agitation for more protective recreation-oriented national parks in the southern mountains.

The arrival of better roads and the automobile in the 1920s also made the need for protection and development of the southern mountains' scenic resources for tourists more urgent than it had been when park boosters held their 1899 meeting. Asheville and western North Carolina experienced a tourist and real estate boom in the 1920s unlike anything the area had previously seen.[46] With the tourist boom came a flood of requests from members of Congress to the fledgling Park Service for the creation of new national parks. Western parks' success in drawing tourists (and their money) spurred the demand, and Mather encouraged it, knowing that the establishment of more parks—especially closer to eastern population centers—would shore up support for the new federal agency among southern representatives.[47]

Asheville was joined by Knoxville, Tennessee, and at least thirty other mountain cities and towns in the renewed movement for a southern Appalachian national park in the 1920s. Tourism boosters in Knoxville's auto clubs, Chamber of Commerce, and business community founded the Great Smoky Mountains Conservation Association and hired a New York publicity company to promote ideas for a park and raise money to fund its development. The North Carolina legislature appointed a park commission to press the state's claims for part of the park. At the same time, tourism-boosting business leaders, entrepreneurs, and conservationists in Virginia organized the Northern Virginia National Park Association to lobby for a national park in the Virginia mountains. Interior Secretary Herbert Work, supportive of the general idea of a new national park in the East but inundated with requests and proposals, appointed the Southern Appalachian National Park Committee in 1924 to study the situation and select a site.[48]

Hearing of this development, Virginia boosters—with Byrd's enthusiastic support—organized quickly and lobbied for the Shenandoah. Supporters saw a Shenandoah park as a means of resource conservation, an engine of tourism development, and possibly even a magnet for industry. Like the supporters of the Great Smoky Mountains, the Shenandoah's leading boosters were largely private, business-oriented interests. In Knoxville, the main driver of the movement for the Smoky Mountains park was Chamber of Commerce President David Chapman. In Virginia, the main park supporters were George Freeman Pollack, outdoorsman and proprietor of the Skyland resort, in operation since the 1890s, and the business officials of Shenandoah Valley, Inc., which promoted the anticipated economic benefits of tourism for Virginia's mountains.[49]

The Southern Appalachian National Park Committee reconnoitered sites and weighed evidence presented by municipalities and pro-park groups and in late 1924 recommended two regions: the Virginia Blue Ridge and the North Carolina/ Tennessee Great Smoky Mountains. Park promoters in Virginia, western North Carolina, and Tennessee were overjoyed, but now they faced the more difficult task of raising money and political support for carving the parks out of long-settled regions wholly unlike the largely uninhabited areas that had been turned into national parks in the West. Congressional authorization for three eastern parks (Great Smoky Mountains in North Carolina and Tennessee, Shenandoah in Virginia, and Mammoth Cave in Kentucky) came quickly in 1925 and 1926, but at least another decade would pass before the states and the federal government acquired sufficient lands to open the parks: Shenandoah officially opened in 1936, with the Great Smoky Mountains National Park following four years later.[50]

As in other parts of the country, movements for national parks in the southern mountains and the agitation for better tourist roads into and through the region soon flowed together into a movement for roads to and into these new parks. In the states that were home to the three new eastern parks, this movement first took the form of agitation for what became known as the Eastern National Park-to-Park Highway, intended to join together Shenandoah, Great Smoky Mountains, and Mammoth Cave National Parks as well as some other scenic and historic sites. By the early 1930s, the scenic Skyline Drive within the Shenandoah National Park in Virginia was also under construction.

As the momentum for good roads increased, organizations popped up all over the United States to promote particular highways. Around 1928, the Eastern National Park-to-Park Highway Association, under the leadership of Representative Maurice H. Thatcher of Kentucky, began lobbying for a federally supported highway to join the three eastern national parks as well as Washington, D.C., and the historic sites being developed at Williamsburg, Jamestown, and Yorktown, Virginia.[51] The project, conceived as an eastern parallel to the West's decade-old National Park-to-Park Highway, had apparently caught the attention of official Washington by the spring of 1931, when Thatcher convened a meeting of road supporters and congressional delegations from the states involved as well as enthusiastic officials from NPS and the BPR. Conflict over the highway's route plagued the meeting, as North Carolina representatives battled successfully to have significant mileage built in their state, but the group finally agreed on an official map of the extensive project.[52] The Eastern National Park-to-Park Highway was to be a joint federal and state project and was to combine new construction with upgrading of existing highways.[53] It was to follow existing travel routes and would be a major trunk highway on which both recreational and commercial traffic would be permitted.[54]

Despite the grand plans, work on the highway moved agonizingly slowly, and North Carolina highway supporters fretted that their state was not doing enough to capitalize on the tourism potential of the developing Great Smoky Mountains National Park.[55] A year after official plans for the highway had been approved, early park-to-park highway enthusiast R. L. Gwyn of Lenoir pleaded with several North Carolina officials for more attention to (and funding for) the highway's construction.[56] To Governor J. C. B. Ehringhaus, Gwyn indicated that the depression-induced state budget cutting was especially harmful to the highway's progress and, in turn, to the western part of the state's long-term economic interests. But the penurious governor, his mind set on balancing the state budget, responded that although he supported the project, "all of our highway activities are seriously handicapped by lack of funds. The prospect for the next two years is not at all encouraging."[57] Indeed it was not. The highway department, like nearly every other state agency, suffered drastic cutbacks under Ehringhaus's austerity program, and most of the state funds remaining for roads were shifted from new construction to maintenance.[58]

As progress on the Eastern National Park-to-Park Highway remained slow and the depression closed in around North Carolina, the coalition that had supported the Eastern National Park-to-Park Highway fragmented. North Carolina tourism boosters, particularly in Asheville, worried that their city was being left out of the boom that was expected to come from travel to the Great Smoky Mountains Park. Park and tourism enthusiasts there and elsewhere in the state homed in on road improvements as key to the solution and began to focus on what the state and federal governments could do to help North Carolina provide better highway access from Asheville to the park.

The *Carolina Motor News* proposed that the N P S build parkways and roads within the park and even suggested a scenic parkway from Asheville to the park, a route underserved by paved roads. Leaders of the Asheville Chamber of Commerce, long involved in the movement for the Eastern National Park-to-Park Highway, called for federal relief funds to finance highway construction to and through the park. Charles A. Webb, editor of the park- and tourism-boosting *Asheville Citizen*, called attention to the "unnecessary delay" in completing paved roads from the North Carolina side of the park to Newfound Gap at the Tennessee–North Carolina state line and expressed hope that officials in his state had finally realized the "great

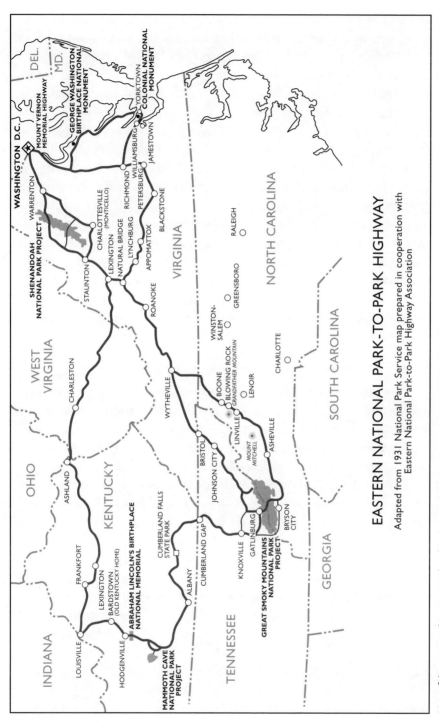

EASTERN NATIONAL PARK-TO-PARK HIGHWAY

Adapted from 1931 National Park Service map prepared in cooperation with
Eastern National Park-to-Park Highway Association

Map of the proposed Eastern National Park-to-Park Highway, 1931. Map by Michael Southern,

based on National Park Service map in John Garland Pollard Papers, Library of Virginia, Richmond.

advantage and tremendous value of this Park to all Western North Carolina." An Asheville attorney pleaded with Ehringhaus for construction of a parkway known as the Doggett Gap Road from Asheville to the park.[59]

As they began to contemplate ways to get their state into the thick of park-based tourism development, western North Carolina tourism leaders took a cue from Virginia, which in 1930 had secured a federal appropriation for construction of a scenic highway, the Skyline Drive, through the new Shenandoah National Park. The original Southern Appalachian Park Committee had tossed around the idea for a ridgetop highway through the park during the 1920s, but only the advent of the depression brought the concept to fruition. Virginia Conservation and Development Commission Chair William Carson, a Virginia businessman, revived the idea as a way to provide work for the unemployed. President Herbert Hoover had already been won over to the charms of the Virginia mountains, establishing his Rapidan Camp getaway there a few years earlier, so officials easily convinced him of the merits of a federally funded Skyline Drive through the park. He announced the appropriation in 1930, and construction began in 1931; by 1933, several hundred people were at work on the project, one of Hoover's little-acknowledged depression-relief measures. The advent of the New Deal boosted both the Skyline Drive's funding and its appeal as a relief project as the federal government sent Civilian Conservation Corps (CCC) recruits to continue the work. The first sections opened to travelers in mid-1934, and the highway became an immediate hit: nearly fifty thousand drivers flooded it during the first five weeks after its opening.[60]

Those best poised to benefit from the popularity of the Skyline Drive and the Shenandoah Park were the business leaders of Shenandoah Valley, Inc., who had guided the park's and the highway's early development. From the beginning they had touted the potential benefits growth in tourism would bring to the mountainous parts of Virginia, and Virginia state leaders joined in making such claims during the 1930s. And while the planners' motives were not entirely crass (many were also interested in protecting mountain scenery from logging and development), the dire transportation, employment, educational, and health care needs of suffering local mountain residents figured only tangentially in their thinking.

As the NPS and the state of Virginia became more involved in the park and Skyline Drive development, local citizens' needs faded even further from view. Severe controversy arose—as it did in the Great Smoky Mountains National Park—over the Park Service's policy of removing all residents from parklands to re-create the image of a pristine wilderness. Local residents also chafed at the Park Service's decision to charge a toll for use of the Skyline Drive and to close several other roads that crisscrossed the park, making travel in and around the park region very difficult, particularly given the poor condition of many local roads.[61] So while improvement of mountain residents' lives was often mentioned (particularly after the start of the depression) as a rationale for Skyline Drive construction, the forces driving the building of that highway were considerably more complex, and impoverished mountain residents' needs sometimes appeared to provide only a convenient argument for construction of a highway that had long interested business leaders for other reasons.[62]

A similar situation prevailed in western North Carolina, as business leaders watched the progress of the Skyline Drive and developed ideas for ways to improve roads through the local mountain scenery. Asheville Chamber of Commerce manager Fred L. Weede, a savvy veteran of Miami's 1920s tourist and real estate boom and one of Asheville's most vigorous boosters, was one of the first in North Carolina to see the potential of depression-relief measures to provide a means for accelerating stalled scenic highway construction in his state.[63] Writing in 1932 to North Carolina Senator Josiah W. Bailey, known to have been long interested in park-oriented road construction, Weede commented on Congress's appropriation of some relief funds and suggested that North Carolina might use its share for highway construction in and around the park. Virginia's success in securing money for the Skyline Drive particularly intrigued him. "In this connection," he wrote, "you may recall that . . . the Shenandoah National Park people got through a highway measure under the guise of relief for the unemployed and yet their park, as I understand it, is not nearly so far along in the matter of lands acquired as our Great Smoky Mountains Park."[64]

THE NEW DEAL AND THE BLUE RIDGE PARKWAY

In spite of Weede's prescient sense that depression-related relief money might be used for tourist road construction in the North Carolina mountains, the proposal for a scenic highway to connect the Shenandoah and Great Smoky Mountains National Parks seems to have originated in Virginia, among Skyline Drive and Shenandoah National Park proponents, although Weede undoubtedly played a pivotal role in Asheville leaders' lobbying to get the Parkway routed near their city (see chapter 2).[65] Ultimately, however, Virginia became the less enthusiastic of the two Parkway states in pursuing the project, which fit better with North Carolina's long-standing tourist-boosting ethos.

More important than with whom or where the idea originated is the general matrix from which the idea came—the growth and popularity of the national parks, the park-development initiatives that had been going forward in the southern mountains for several decades, the Good Roads and tourist highway movements, the old Crest of the Blue Ridge Highway plan, the massive growth in automobile tourism in the 1920s, the efforts in the early 1930s to build a highway connecting the eastern national parks, Asheville's long-standing desire for better roads from the city into the Great Smoky Mountains park, and the initial success of the scenic mountaintop Skyline Drive.

In this context, it is not difficult to understand how the idea of a scenic parkway to extend the Skyline Drive southwest to the Great Smoky Mountains National Park emerged. When President Franklin D. Roosevelt launched his massive New Deal, latent possibility, pent-up demand, and regional/local organizational readiness met opportune historical moment. Early in 1933, just as North Carolina's state funding for construction of the Eastern National Park-to-Park Highway was drying up, the Roosevelt administration began to contemplate public works projects to jump-start America's faltering economy.

The Parkway was authorized under the National Industrial Recovery Act, signed in June 1933, which created the Public Works Administration (PWA) to finance large-scale public works projects as a way of pumping money into the sagging economy and creating jobs in the construction of substantial structures that would be of long-term value to the nation. With many plans for such projects already well along but delayed for lack of funds, the NPS was a logical recipient for PWA monies. In the work program's first year, it funded more than 150 projects in national parks. While Park Service regular annual appropriations soared from about $10 million in 1933 to more than $25 million in 1939, the park system benefited hugely from the $218 million that flowed forth from the PWA, the Civil Works Administration, the Works Progress Administration, and the CCC.[66]

Creating a new agency to administer the $3.3 billion authorized for public works was an enormous task. Appointed to head the PWA was the meticulous and intense secretary of the interior, Harold L. Ickes. Mindful of the scandals that had rocked the Department of the Interior in the 1920s and the opportunities for corruption and graft in any public works program, Ickes set about assembling an administrative structure that would assure timely fulfillment of the PWA's goals without any impropriety. In July 1933, Ickes and his staff issued tough guidelines for PWA projects. Approved projects had to be integrated within a coordinated national plan and had to provide employment, stimulate industrial recovery, and produce something of long-term value. They also had to be technically and financially sound, and the agencies to whom money was given or loaned had to be capable of both finishing the projects and paying back any loans. Gradually—in the opinion of many critics, too gradually—an organization came together to find projects fitting these guidelines, and the public works monies began to flow. Throughout his tenure, "Honest Harold" Ickes kept the agency's hands clean.[67]

Some PWA money went outright to other federal agencies to pay for projects those agencies directed. Other funds went to states and municipalities as loans and grants for locally administered undertakings. The local and state-run projects took longer to implement as a result of a complicated approval procedure; the necessity of coordinating federal, state, and local agencies and laws; and the enormous number of project proposals that inundated PWA offices in the summer and fall of 1933.[68]

Despite the glitches and criticisms, over its six years' existence (1933–39), the PWA completed an extraordinary array of projects and contributed mightily to the development of the nation's infrastructure. By the beginning of 1935, the agency had initiated or completed more than nineteen thousand projects, with some work in nearly every U.S. county. PWA money built dams, hydroelectric projects, schools, courthouses, city halls, hospitals and clinics, railroad stations, municipal water and sewer systems, streets and highways, bridges, tunnels, and ports. In fact, the appropriation directly to highway construction was the largest such federal allotment ever made to that point. The PWA also funded the building of ships and airplanes for the military, slum clearance, and the construction of affordable housing. As of 1935, these projects had directly employed more than 2 million people while indirectly providing jobs for many others by stimulating demand for equipment and materials. Ickes estimated the total number of people benefiting from PWA expenditures by that time to have been nearly 10 million.[69]

The PWA sparked hope nationwide that some of the money could relieve the economic woes of particular regions. Thus, in the first hectic months of its existence, as Ickes described it, "a deluge of pleas for funds had already descended upon us. . . . The pressure from local communities was tremendous. Delegations of politicians, business men, contractors and 'leading citizens' laid siege to our offices in person, by mail, by telephone and by telegraph."[70]

The businessmen and "leading citizens" who converged on the PWA offices included a group from Virginia, North Carolina, and Tennessee lobbying in favor of a scenic parkway to connect the Shenandoah and Great Smoky Mountains National Parks. Proponents of the plan were fortunate to have powerful allies in federal agencies and a project that could plausibly be presented as having national rather than local significance. Consequently, the Blue Ridge Parkway proposal moved swiftly through the PWA review process.

The lobbying committee was formed in October 1933 under the leadership of

Senator Harry F. Byrd of Virginia with the help of Virginia Governor John Garland Pollard. But the idea of making this particular proposal had been born more than a month earlier, when Byrd visited CCC camps along the Skyline Drive with Roosevelt and Ickes. One early Parkway movement leader reported that as the president's entourage traveled along the beautiful new road, Roosevelt suggested the building of a scenic parkway from the Shenandoah to the Great Smoky Mountains, although Byrd later recalled that he had proposed the idea to Roosevelt. Whatever the case, the general concept was hardly original: a month after FDR's visit to the park, Gwyn was still lobbying for PWA funds to build the similarly conceived Eastern National Park-to-Park Highway.[71] The originating impulse came from regional boosters, not the Park Service. With so many urgings from so many sectors, some kind of scenic highway apparently was likely to be built: the question was simply what form the project would take.

With the influential Senator Byrd (at this point still a supporter of the New Deal) on the case and with $3.3 billion in PWA funds awaiting allotment, the park-to-park connector project gained a new momentum. By early October, Byrd was discussing the specifics of funding and construction with an enthusiastic President Roosevelt. Byrd and the governors of Virginia, North Carolina, and Tennessee also organized state parkway committees to drum up local support and look at specific routing issues. In North Carolina, former Eastern National Park-to-Park Highway boosters recognized their earlier ideas in this project and quickly lined up to support it. They unanimously recommended Gwyn for membership on the state's lobbying committee. Gwyn believed the new highway to be "a tremendous improvement on our original Park-to-Park Highway."[72]

In mid-October, Byrd called representatives from the three interested states to Washington for a strategy session. In attendance were high-level officials from all the agencies that would be involved in the eventual building of the Blue Ridge Parkway: NPS, the BPR, the PWA, and state highway departments. Also present were members of Congress from the three states as well as interested private citizens. Byrd told the group that he had spoken with Roosevelt and Ickes about the project and that although both had "expressed the deepest interest," they needed a concrete proposal before the idea could be put before the PWA for funding.[73]

Byrd's group appointed a small committee to prepare the proposal, which did not specify the Parkway's route except to imply that it would run through all three states. Each state's parkway committee was asked to come up with a particular routing suggestion for its section. The proposal written for Ickes's perusal suggested that the project be federally funded and involve no tolls or loans that states would have to repay, that $20 million immediately be allotted to the project, and that the Parkway be a newly constructed twenty-foot-wide roadway protected by a one-thousand-foot right-of-way to preserve roadside scenery. Even fiscally and socially conservative southern state leaders could support such a federally financed, business-enhancing, and gasoline-tax-boosting project.[74]

Ever worried that federal money might be spent for narrow purposes, Ickes initially greeted the group's proposal with skepticism, especially its suggestion that the project be funded entirely by the federal government. He wanted the states to pay at least part of the cost, noting that "while it is true that it would connect two national parks . . . its main service would be to the States and not to the parks." Thatcher, the president of the Eastern National Park-to-Park Highway Association, disappointed to see the disintegration of a project on which he had worked for years, urged Ickes to spend the PWA funds on the original park-to-park highway. That project, he argued, would serve a larger region and be more useful because of its design as a trunk highway permitting both tourist and commercial traffic.[75]

Ickes's approval of the scenic parkway project appeared unlikely. Ickes told Thatcher that "the final proposal as submitted called for the construction of this parkway . . . as a purely federal project. I do not believe that the Federal Government would be justified in entering into such a project at this time." Park Service director Arno B. Cammerer, one of the proposal's authors, informed a correspondent confidentially that "there seems to be little chance of having money allotted for the project."[76]

North Carolina partisans, undaunted by negative signals from Ickes and the Interior Department and energized by the thought of a federally funded boost to their struggling tourism industry, scurried around Washington lobbying for the new proposal. Powerful North Carolina Representative Robert L. Doughton, a native of the state's mountain region and a member of a family well known for its involvement in the state's Good Roads movement, arranged a private meeting with Ickes and found the secretary to be more receptive to the project than the press had reported. While Ickes still hoped that the states would help pay for the project, Doughton left the meeting hopeful that the parkway would be built.[77]

Other meetings and negotiations followed, including a critical conference between Ickes, North Carolina Congressmen Doughton and Robert Reynolds, Tennessee Senator Kenneth McKellar, BPR Chief Thomas MacDonald, and—signifying a direct link between the old Crest of the Blue Ridge Highway and the Blue Ridge Parkway—Joseph Hyde Pratt, now the head of North Carolina's Conservation and Development Commission. Somehow, by mid-November, after conferring with President Roosevelt, Ickes had become a supporter of the project as proposed. His acquiescence is somewhat surprising given his general opposition to road building in and around the national parks in defense of "wilderness" (a position articulated as early as 1933), but it was consistent with his use of his multiple official roles to expand the national park system. For the Parkway project, he insisted only that the states obtain the highway's right-of-way without cost to the federal treasury. Official approval of the Blue Ridge Parkway followed on 19 November 1933. Except for acquisition of the right-of-way, the PWA would pay the entire cost.[78]

Approval of the project was a triumph for pro-Parkway partisans from the three states. In the intense weeks between the October meeting in Byrd's office and the PWA's official approval of the project in November, supporters had convinced Ickes, Roosevelt, and others in Washington that a locally initiated and rather self-interested proposal had enough national significance to be taken on by the NPS, the BPR, and (crucially) the PWA as one of its few almost completely federally funded projects. In Weede's words, business-oriented state leaders had put their highway project through "under the guise of relief for the unemployed."[79] But in fact the unemployed figured but little in initial discussions of the highway, and who the major beneficiaries of the project would be nobody knew.

Early discussions between Parkway partisans and federal officials and nearly all early pronouncements emphasized the highway's likely benefits for the mountain tourist industry. Virtually none of the participants mentioned the destitute mountain citizens who would so dominate later accounts of the Parkway's early history. According to Byrd, for example, the Parkway would be "the greatest scenic road in the world and [would] attract millions of tourists." Hugh MacRae of Wilmington, North Carolina, a real estate developer who had built the upscale Linville resort community in the Grandfather Mountain region, saw the Parkway as a component in a recreational development plan for the area that would "assure its prosperity for all time." Reynolds told those convened in Byrd's office for the first official meeting that "the greatest industry in the world is not the building of automobiles, the steel, the mill or the tobacco industry, but . . . the tourist industry." The Asheville Chamber of Commerce leapt onto the Parkway bandwagon early and with gusto, worrying from the beginning that Tennessee might try to swipe valuable Parkway mileage from North Carolina. In the arguments of its strongest partisans, then, the Blue Ridge Parkway project was essentially congruent with North Carolina's "business progressive" outlook and with the overall tourism-promoting trajectory of parks and road development from the 1910s forward.[80]

Indeed, southern leaders who often resisted New Deal efforts to redistribute wealth or increase state spending on relief and social welfare welcomed park projects and the Parkway in particular. That Senator Bailey—not a supporter of the New Deal—could embrace the Parkway as a "very great benefit to the mountain section of North Carolina" clearly demonstrates the project's fundamentally conservative nature. In fact, from this perspective, the Parkway project was an ideal New Deal program for North Carolina politicians: it promised federal largesse for the ailing mountain tourist industry, required only small amounts of state funds for land acquisition, and posed little threat to the mountain region's basic social structure.[81]

In Virginia, where the effects of the depression were milder than in other states, Senators Harry Byrd and especially Carter Glass eventually became vocal opponents of much of the New Deal. Their long-entrenched pay-as-you-go mentality engendered a fiscally conservative response to the Great Depression that stymied state efforts at reform. Nevertheless, Virginia, like North Carolina, was willing to accept federal help that did not threaten to upend social structures. As the Richmond Times-Dispatch noted at the time, Virginia's political leaders were "great advocates for State rights when such advocacy meets their convenience, but when it doesn't, they believe in letting Uncle Sam hold the bag."[82]

National officials, however, focused on the rejuvenating possibilities of travel to the national parks rather than on local or state economic impacts. In the original Parkway meeting in Byrd's office, MacDonald, a major architect of the nation's federal highway system in its early years, cited the blistering summer heat in the South, which made it "very difficult for people to live . . . and go about their daily work," and argued that a mountaintop parkway would provide "an opportunity for a break in the monotony of hot days and hot nights in a cooler climate." MacDonald went on to say, correctly, that the time was ripe for park development in the East, closer to population centers, a view with which Cammerer concurred.[83]

Although several North Carolina partisans—Doughton, Reynolds, and Gwyn among them—reiterated these sentiments, their first interest was in particular segments of the economy of their home state.[84] The centrality of these more local concerns would become more evident as Parkway supporters in Asheville geared up their campaign to bring the new road near their city.

WHAT IS A PARKWAY?: A DESIGN AND CONSTRUCTION
PLAN FOR THE BLUE RIDGE PARKWAY

Like the Asheville partisans, many people were euphoric that a parkway was to be built, but as detailed planning proceeded, conflicts inevitably arose, many of the earliest as a consequence of the decision to build a scenic parkway instead of a regular highway. What, exactly, did that choice mean, and what were the interests and perspectives of those who would be involved in bringing the "elongated park" (as they called it) into being?

The design aesthetic and standards that governed the Blue Ridge Parkway grew out of the nearly century-old tradition of American park development, a decade of scenic road construction in the western national parks, and more than three decades of parkway building in other parts of the country. Some specific antecedents within the American parkway movement—the development of roads through parklike settings—were especially relevant.

The first real motor parkway in the nation was the Bronx River Parkway (1913). The idea originated with several members of the New York Zoological Society, who worried about increasing pollution in the Bronx River (which flowed through the Zoological Park and the city's Botanical Gardens) and who hoped that the construction of a parkway along the river would enable riverbank cleanup and discourage further dumping. Like most later parkways, it was an urban road, but it did include many of the features that came to distinguish a parkway from a regular roadway: it was protected by parklands on both sides; it did not allow invasive and dangerous access from adjoining properties; intersecting roads passed over it on bridges; it was carefully landscaped to ensure beauty and to eliminate unattractive roadside dumps and billboards; and, in keeping with its design as a leisurely recreational drive, it limited speeds, banned commercial vehicles, and featured recreational facilities alongside. Fifteen miles long and four lanes wide, the Bronx River Parkway was completed in 1925 at a cost of $15 million.[85]

Through the 1920s, New York continued to lead the nation in parkway construction (as it had in state park development), as Westchester County embarked on construction of a large park and parkway network. Long Island State Park Commission Chair Robert Moses directed development of another parkway system that included the Southern State Parkway, the Wantagh State Parkway, the Meadowbrook State Parkway, the Northern State Parkway, and several others. In the 1930s Moses built other parkways in hopes of relieving New York City's growing traffic problems, but these roads were designed mostly to provide uninterrupted, swift traffic flow, not recreation, leisure, and scenery. Thus, according to one observer, they "were not, for the most part, parkways at all" but instead represented early efforts at freeways.[86]

Other cities also built or planned parkways in the 1930s, and as in New York, usually constructed them alongside rivers, often with CCC aid. Riverside parkways that conformed more closely to the original idea of preserving greenery and

Along the Bronx River Parkway, 1922. Courtesy Westchester County Archives, Elmsford, New York.

providing recreation were built in Milwaukee (the Root River, Honey Creek, and Oak Creek) and Cleveland (the Strongsville-Brecksville River). Other early-1930s parkways included several built in the Washington, D.C., area, including the Mount Vernon Memorial Highway (later extended and called the George Washington Memorial Parkway) along the Potomac River.[87]

The parkways that preceded the Blue Ridge often tried—some more successfully than others—to combine visually attractive roadside landscapes with features that enabled easier and faster commuting. The road that succeeded best at doing both was Connecticut's Merritt Parkway (1930–40). This four-lane, 37.5-mile parkway—another in Moses's parkway system—sought to ease the increasingly congested commute from New York City to the Connecticut suburbs. According to its historian, the Merritt Parkway not only was "the most beautiful limited-access highway ever built" but also featured a design that "emphasized the pleasure of driving without sacrificing such mundane considerations as speed, efficiency, and safety." Protected by a three-hundred-foot-wide right-of-way, the Parkway had controlled access and use restrictions (buses and trucks were prohibited), and the route was decorated with extensive and thoughtful landscaping and creative, artistic bridges. Lacking the traffic lights present on the old road to New York, the Merritt did speed the commute time to the city, but as traffic increased, regulations had to be implemented to prevent some of the original rec- reational uses of the road, such as roadside picnicking, which had become dan- gerous and destructive. With time, the people who, according to historian Bruce Radde, "took too literally the *park* in *parkway*" were pushed out as the Merritt's objective of providing a faster commute overwhelmed the highway's recreational purposes. Nevertheless, when compared with later expressways, some of whose features it employed, the Merritt Parkway "was rooted in the picturesque, roman- tic landscape tradition of Frederick Law Olmsted. True to its name, it was de- signed as a way through a park."[88]

As the need for public works projects coincided with the New Deal's focus on conservation and recreation, federal agencies embraced the parkway-building trend with gusto. Along with the Blue Ridge Parkway, the NPS built two other similar parkways in the 1930s: the Colonial Parkway connecting historic sites in the Williamsburg, Virginia, area and the Natchez Trace Parkway following the old trading and Indian trail through Tennessee, Alabama, and Mississippi.[89]

Flushed with their initial success, New Deal road and park builders waxed elo- quent about the possibilities of parkway development. One Saturday afternoon in April 1935, BPR Chief MacDonald and NPS associate director A. E. Demaray went on nationwide NBC radio to tout the "Parkways of the Future." With the Marine Band mimicking the clatter of wagon wheels in the background, the narrator re- counted the steady progress of America's transportation revolution: from covered wagons to railroads ("telling the Indian that the White Man had come to stay!") to autos to airplanes and, now that "the past is gone but the future remains," to "parkways of the future." After musing on the recent rise in pleasure travel and park visitation, MacDonald and Demaray asserted, "We have found that the instinct of people to seek the open country or the gypsy trail is very strong." Park- ways, MacDonald suggested, would help people escape the "unsightly billboards . . . hot-dog stands and gas stations" that had sprung up along the nation's roads and would fulfill people's need for "natural scenic beauty." If the three parkways now under construction proved as popular as expected, "construction will be ex- panded. [It] may be that eventually a great parkway will lead from New England . . . south to connect with the Shenandoah–Great Smokies parkway, and on . . . into Georgia and perhaps to the Florida Everglades." His excitement building, Demaray linked the idea to a grand vision of America's westward progress: "I can, in imagination, see still other parkways stretching westward. . . . The pioneers opened that country for us . . . and we, in turn may open it up in an entirely differ- ent way to those who come after us."[90]

The ambitious scheme for a network of parkways crisscrossing the nation never materialized, however. Paradoxically, the vision was washed away in the next wave of automobile-inspired progress, the expressway. Indeed, according to one student of American tourism, the federal parkways were in no way typical of national approaches to road building but rather "stand in contrast to the nation's other highways built with federal funds."[91]

New Deal parkways, like roads built in the 1920s in the western national parks more generally, emphasized recreation and scenery and were only secondarily concerned with getting travelers quickly to a destination.[92] In many ways, then, these parkways, especially Blue Ridge and Natchez Trace, were less like the earlier (urban) parkways and more like national park roads traversing rural areas and serving a completely recreational purpose; however, the New Deal parkways were far longer than any of their precursors either inside or outside the national parks. In addition, unlike the roads through western parks (that is, through lands already in federal ownership), the new parkways thrust an entire "elongated park" through long-populated and developed areas. As a result, though in many respects they represented the culmination of long-developing trends, they required new thinking about regulations and design and generated substantial new challenges and conflicts.

The Natchez Trace Parkway was the most similar in design and conception to the Blue Ridge, and the two were usually paired in appropriations bills and NPS correspondence about New Deal parkway projects. Both were projected to be more than four hundred miles long, and they were subject to similar rules about financing, land acquisition, right-of-way protections, and other design standards. But unlike the Blue Ridge, whose great attraction was the surrounding natural beauty of the mountains, the Natchez Trace was to be a trip back hundreds of years in time along the path followed by countless Native Americans, explorers, traders, settlers, soldiers, and missionaries who had traveled from Natchez to Nashville. In particular, the Natchez Trace Parkway commemorated the route of the nation's second-oldest federal highway. Thus, while the Blue Ridge Parkway sought largely (although not exclusively) to showcase scenic grandeur and was thus routed across the ridgetops, the Natchez Trace was purposefully routed through an area of intense human activity. As the federal survey recommending the Natchez Trace Parkway's construction noted, "no outstanding scenery" lay along the proposed route. "The historic purpose," the document continued, "determines the value of the project rather than its natural scenic value."[93]

Both parkways, however, arose from local lobbying, and a comparison of their origins is revealing. The Blue Ridge Parkway emerged from activism of tourist-oriented businessmen (and nearly all the major actors in the movement to bring the Parkway to western North Carolina were male) in the mountains. In fact, early Blue Ridge Parkway enthusiasts, including the president of the Asheville Hotelmen's Association, had called explicitly for "big men familiar with mountains . . . to obtain for our state its proper recognition" in the attempt to get the Parkway. The president of the Asheville Chamber of Commerce concurred, begging Governor Ehringhaus to appoint "vigorous men well informed on mountain section" to his state parkway planning committee.[94]

The Natchez Trace Parkway, by contrast, sprang from the minds of historic-preservation-minded women: the Daughters of the American Revolution in Mississippi and the U.S. Daughters of the War of 1812 in Tennessee. As early as 1909, both organizations began marking the Trace with historic signposts. Accounts of the Trace's history published early in the century bolstered the women's activity and further stimulated interest in the Trace, as did the Natchez and Pilgrimage Garden Clubs' annual tours of Natchez-area antebellum homes. By 1933, the Natchez Trace Association, consisting of many "civic or patriotic groups," had formed and was lobbying for construction of a parkway along the Trace's route to memorialize the earlier road and to bring economic benefits to the region. Through this organization's efforts, in conjunction with the work of the Daughters of the American Revolution and of Mississippi's congressional representatives, construction of the Natchez Trace Parkway began in 1937.[95]

In both the short and long run, however, the men's scenic vistas proved more popular with the public (and with Congress) than did the women's historical commemorations. The Blue Ridge Parkway became the most visited NPS site in the nation (with 18 million annual travelers by the 1990s), with the Natchez Trace Parkway lagging behind in both visitation and appropriations. And while the Blue Ridge Parkway was finally pushed to completion in 1987, the Natchez Trace Parkway was not finished until 2005.[96]

The long construction timetables for both roads reflected the astounding bureaucratic and technical complexity of the undertakings. The Blue Ridge Parkway ultimately became a cooperative venture of the states of North Carolina and Virginia, the NPS, the BPR, and the PWA. The interrelationships among these agencies were complicated and tangled, but each had clear responsibilities. Locating engineers and other officials from the state highway departments made the initial decisions about routing through the mountains, which they passed on to federal officials for clarification and approval. In lieu of paying for any of the construction, the states acquired all the lands federal officials determined were needed and conveyed titles to the federal government at no cost.

Planning for, design of, and management of the Blue Ridge Parkway fell under the jurisdiction of the NPS, which officially took control of the project in 1936. But the engineering and construction of the highway were carried out by the BPR (under an interbureau agreement with the NPS, negotiated during the Mather years), with considerable assistance from the highway departments of the two states. On the ground, private contractors chosen through a competitive bidding process did the building, employing workers according to federal work relief rules. The CCC worked on several of the Parkway's recreation and camping areas, and the Works Progress Administration constructed some buildings along the road. Funding for most of the early road construction, however, came through the PWA and other depression-related emergency funding measures, at least until the early 1940s. Because the project's last link was not completed until 1987, subsequent funding had to come from other federal sources, especially the Mission 66 program of the 1950s and 1960s (see chapter 7).[97]

Construction on the initial twelve-mile section commenced just south of the North Carolina/Virginia border at Low Gap, North Carolina, in September 1935 under the direction of Durham contractor Nello Teer. On 11 September, a few men unloaded "several car loads" of heavy machinery (including a "huge dirt shovel") from a train at nearby Galax, Virginia, and work continued a few days later when more than a hundred men hired from the lists of the Alleghany County unemployed continued moving equipment and cleared brush and timber along the right-of-way. According to a North Carolina State Highway Commission official on the scene, the "first breaking of ground" took place on 19 September. "One thing noticeable about the work," a local paper observed, "is that all material and machinery with which to work have been purchased new." The huge diesel shovel, the paper continued, cost nearly twenty-five thousand dollars. Moreover, the newspaper reported, "Numerous caterpillar tractors are on hand and about a dozen large dump trucks will haul the dirt away from the shovel."[98]

As the agency ultimately in charge of the project, the NPS provided general guidance for construction according to standards developed specifically for New Deal–era parkway construction and issued in 1935 by Interior Secretary Ickes and the head of the NPS. Not incidentally, those standards became the source of much conflict (discussed in detail in chapter 3).

Controlling nearly all decisions about the Parkway's design was the basic premise that it was to be a scenic road. Scenery and recreation—the needs of tourists, rather than short-distance local travelers—were paramount, as they had been with all park development since the establishment of the NPS. The road was to be used only by passenger cars; commercial vehicles (buses and trucks) were prohibited. Roadside development was severely curtailed in hopes of preventing

Machinery and men from the Nello Teer Company at work on section 2-N2 of the Blue Ridge Parkway in North Carolina, 4 July 1941. Courtesy North Carolina State Archives, Raleigh.

the tacky, congested, and "unsightly" buildup that already marred the roadsides of many of America's regular highways (hotdog stands particularly worried the Park Service). To provide "an insulating strip of park land between the roadway and the abutting private property," the Parkway would have a wide right-of-way, and adjoining landowners were permitted no frontage rights or direct access from their property, in part because of threats to road safety posed by eateries, billboards, driveway entrances, and other distractions.[99]

The width of the right-of-way was intended to be about one thousand feet, although it varied along the route. In a few places, protective green space was preserved through a scenic easement, which left the land in the hands of the original landowner but imposed strict usage regulations on it; in most places, however, the land was bought outright (in fee simple). Whatever the means, the Parkway took much more land than an average highway required and more than many previous parkways had taken. The road therefore kept nearby landowners and residents at a much greater distance than had been the case with earlier roadways.[100]

Other design requirements intended to enhance the Parkway's safety and enjoyableness for travelers also hindered its use by local residents. Anticipating innovations that would later become standard on freeways and interstate highways, all intersections with other highways were to be handled via under- or overpasses to eliminate dangerous grade-level crossings. Furthermore, to reduce interruptions in Parkway traffic, access was to be tightly controlled via widely spaced entrances and exits. In some cases, the regulations specified, new regular highways would be built parallel to the Parkway to carry local traffic, and the states would be required to provide landowners whom the Parkway totally isolated with alternate access to local roads. In keeping with all of these requirements, the rights of adjoining property owners to connect driveways or other access roads to the Parkway would be tightly controlled, especially (as it turned out) on the North Carolina sections.[101]

PARKWAY CONTROVERSIES AND A COUNTERDISCOURSE

As officials and citizens in all three states initially involved in Parkway discussions realized the likely costs and benefits of building this project, conflict arose throughout the Parkway region. Most of the debate focused on how best to distribute the costs and benefits of a project most people assumed would (and should) go forward. Most conflicts therefore turned on questions of how various constituencies could channel to their advantage the benefits of road building, parks creation, and tourism.

These conflicts, which broke along many of the existing class and cultural fault lines that divided the southern mountain region, are the subject of much of the rest of this book. Putting 469 miles of scenic parkway through what was not an isolated region (in spite of pervasive and generally trusted accounts that held otherwise) could not help but reveal and exacerbate social and other divisions. Citizens along the Parkway corridor had mixed responses to the road. While the Parkway's potential as a boon to Asheville was evident, it was less clear what mountain residents not already involved in the tourist business would gain in the long term.

As these struggles unfolded, they revealed the Parkway's paradoxically (for a progressive New Deal project) conservative origins and its explicit class and cultural politics. As we have seen, the idea for the Parkway arose from the same tourism-boosting, business-progressive political matrix that had previously produced the Good Roads movement and at least a large measure of the agitation for national parks in the southern mountains. The project attracted the support of southern state politicians otherwise suspicious of and hostile to much of the New Deal. At length it would become clear that Parkway development—however beneficial to the broad public—was shaped by (and best served) citizens of power, wealth, and influence.

But even as the conflicts raged over particular aspects of the Parkway project, it became clear that most Parkway region citizens of all classes and social groups shared a fundamental faith in the synergy of roads, parks, and tourism to bring progress and economic development to the southern Appalachian region. Most participants in the debate simply sought to bend these trends to their benefit.

Hence it is important to ask whether anyone opposed the Parkway project and the development model it represented on more fundamental grounds. In fact, in the midst of the chorus of voices heralding the advent of the age of automobile tourism to and within the national parks, a few individuals sang a different tune. By the early 1930s, an Appalachian-based opposition to automobile-based tourism, especially the building of roads into wild and scenic areas and national parks, had begun to emerge. The enthusiasm for auto touring caused a cadre of conservationists to be, in historian Paul Sutter's words, "driven wild."[102] They framed a counterdiscourse to the development of the Blue Ridge Parkway that was far broader than critiques voiced by most of the opponents of any of its specific design elements.

The leading voices in this counterdiscourse included Aldo Leopold, Robert Sterling Yard, Benton MacKaye, Robert Marshall, Harvey Broome, and their allies who in 1935 founded the Wilderness Society. These men confronted head-on the impacts — social, moral, ethical, aesthetic, environmental — of what was by the 1930s two decades of road building and automotive tourism into America's wilderness and national park areas. Not coincidentally, furthermore, their plan to form an organization focused on roadlessness as the key to wilderness preservation emerged both at the time and in the place where the solidification of plans for the Blue Ridge Parkway was under way.

The organization began when Marshall, a forester with the Bureau of Indian Affairs, and MacKaye, the Knoxville-based founder of the Appalachian Trail who was at that time working for the Tennessee Valley Authority, got together in Knoxville at the October 1934 meeting of the American Forestry Association. The city was awaiting word on its fate in a pitched battle with Asheville for the southern end of the Parkway and consequent status as the gateway city to the Great Smoky Mountains National Park. Indeed, Marshall had visited Knoxville only two months earlier on a mission from Ickes to review the two proposed routes for the southern end of the road.[103]

On a day trip to Knoxville's outskirts, the two men drew up plans for the Wilderness Society, an organization defined by a "new preservationist ideal" seeking single-mindedly to keep large areas of wilderness free of cars and road building. The impulse for the new organization, Sutter notes, came as New Deal conservation and public works projects, "by emphasizing road building and recreational development, threatened wilderness." These projects, which included the Blue Ridge Parkway, capped off more than two decades of work to bring automobiles more easily into public park areas. Road building, society founders observed, represented the first step toward destruction of wild areas by other forms of development, commodification, mechanized incursion, rampant consumerism, and resource extraction. Trying to stop the destructive cascade at its origin, then, these men and their organization defined "wilderness" fundamentally as roadless areas.[104]

With the addition of Leopold, a noted preservationist writer; Yard, a former NPS publicist who had become a vocal critic of the service's prodevelopment policies and land management; and several other similarly committed men, the small group launched the society in early 1935, the same year that Parkway construction began. The group urged federal protection of large, roadless wilderness areas. It would be a long fight, as federal impulses and public sentiment were trending strongly in other directions.[105]

In the years to follow, wilderness advocates set their sights firmly on the interwar fascination with nature-oriented recreation and parks tourism, developments they pegged as direct expressions of twentieth-century consumerism. Through the roads-parks-tourism triangle in the national parks, the See America First campaign, the Good Roads movement, New Deal recreational projects, and rising auto tourism, nature—carefully packaged in units such as the "landscape parks" discussed earlier—had become something to be marketed, sold, and visited.[106]

Leopold had previewed his comrades' arguments as early as 1924. In contrast to developer Heriot Clarkson, who demanded to know why the government had not yet built "great hard-surface roads" all through federal lands in his state, Leopold asked, "Just what is it that is choking out our last vestiges of wilderness?" The answer, he said, "is not true economics at all, but rather that Frankenstein which our boosters have builded [sic], the 'Good Roads Movement.'" Although "entirely sound and beneficial in its inception," the movement had "been boosted until it resembles a gold-rush." Instead of gold, the "yellow lure" was "the Motor Tourist. . . . We offer up our groves and our greenswards for him to camp upon, and he litters them with cans and with rubbish. We hand him our wild life and our wild flowers, and humbly continue the gesture after there are none left to hand. But of all offerings, foolish roads are to him the most pleasing sacrifice."[107] Eleven years later, Marshall—the first to call for an organization to advocate for the protection of wilderness—wrote to Ickes that the Wilderness Society was needed "to counteract the propaganda spread by the Automobile Association of America, the various booster organizations, and the innumerable Chambers of

Commerce, which seem to find no peace as long as any primitive tract in America remains unopened to mechanization."[108]

Interwar wilderness advocates saw the trend of "knowing nature through leisure" as "not only a grave threat to wilderness but also a manifestation of a deeper pathology," the generator of an endless cycle of building and searching for an authentic hinterland that soon would exist only in memory. Or, as Broome, another Wilderness Society founder and a Knoxville attorney, wrote to Ickes in October 1933, just as the Parkway was being conceptualized, "a skyline link would split the whole mountain region wide open, and with the cleavage would vanish much of the spell of the primeval." Business would soon follow as "service stations of all kinds would necessarily have to be dragged up from the valleys to meet the needs of the motorists." The combination of the road, cars, and service stations, "all extraneous to the wilderness," would turn the road's surroundings into "but a mockery of the fresh, green, inviolate nature such a road is supposed to reveal."[109]

After the Parkway's construction had become assured, Broome's commentary became even more scathing. In a mid-1934 letter to the editor of *The Nation*, he inveighed against the selection of the ridgetop route favored by North Carolina Parkway boosters. "There is no accessible wilderness in Eastern America comparable in its extent, or in its primeval character, to this range," he asserted. "Those who would escape the din and rush of the machine age must plunge deeply into some natural environment. They know that they must place miles between themselves and the last house, railroad, and highway before the insulation becomes complete and the spell and peace of the wilderness can be felt." The wilderness viewed through a car window from the Parkway, he lamented, "is but the shell of the wilderness felt from the footpath."[110]

Despite these arguments, federal Parkway planners—egged on by those chambers of commerce Marshall so despised—elected to build the road across the North Carolina skyline. The process by which this outcome was assured is the subject of chapter 2. The results, as anyone who has traveled the road surely knows, were in many respects spectacular. No one can deny, as Sutter acknowledges, that the national craze of "getting back to nature" by car on the Parkway has provided millions of Americans with what many would call spiritual inspiration, opportunities to be outside in stunningly gorgeous spaces, havens from life's demands, and places for family togetherness or real solitude. Furthermore, these benefits have been made available nearly free of direct charge to anyone who wants to come.

But as the remainder of this book will also show, interwar wilderness advocates were right to call into question the close links between construction of the Parkway and the enterprise of consumerist tourism. The central tensions that lay within the Parkway project from its inception have issued from the internal contradictions created by the project's close alliance with those promoting tourism in the mountains. The struggle to maintain a semblance of wilderness—even of the "wilderness by design" favored by the Park Service—in the face of ongoing pressure from those seeking to profit has constituted a central strand of the Parkway story.[111]

More broadly, as numerous details of the following narrative will emphasize, just as the Parkway was to thread its way through nearly five hundred miles of rugged landscape, the policy challenge involved negotiating a complex array of dichotomies: long-term needs and large-scale enterprises versus short-term demands and local preferences, wilderness preservation versus wilderness access, providing needed services versus bald commercialization, the Wilderness Society's ultimately masculine ideal of the lone hiker in the solitary wilderness versus the needs and preferences of the broad public (male or female, old or young, hardy or weak, moneyed and leisured or less well-off, local or foreign), and—in some ways above all—the equitable distribution of costs and benefits. Along the way, many confrontations inevitably arose, many missteps inevitably were taken, and many compromises inevitably were made.

THE SCENIC IS POLITICAL

THE PARKWAY AND ASHEVILLE'S
TOURISM INDUSTRY

Sixty prominent North Carolinians fidgeted in their seats in the banquet hall of Asheville's imposing Grove Park Inn on a warm June night in 1934 as they listened to speeches from Asheville's city leadership and from National Park Service (NPS) director Arno B. Cammerer. The Asheville Chamber of Commerce had arranged the dinner in honor of Cammerer; North Carolinian (and now ambassador to Mexico) Josephus Daniels and his wife, Adelaide; and Anna Ickes, estranged wife of the interior secretary, all of them visiting the city as part of a tour through the Blue Ridge and Great Smoky Mountains that the Danielses had planned with the Ickeses more than a year earlier. When the time came for the trip, Harold Ickes, swamped with his duties in Washington and seriously distanced from his wife after years of intense marital conflict, elected to let her take the vacation without him.[1]

It should have been an exciting occasion for the Asheville citizens, but the inn instead bristled with tension and worry. Just as Cammerer, Anna Ickes, and the Danielses arrived in the city, the grapevine delivered awful news: a committee appointed by Harold Ickes to determine the exact route for the new scenic parkway had recommended the route advocated by Tennessee. Acceptance of the committee's recommendation would mean that the new road would completely bypass Asheville, the city with perhaps the most at stake. To make matters worse, Cammerer had served on the committee that submitted the dreaded recommendation.[2]

It was "the bluest crowd I have ever associated with," Josephus Daniels noted in his diary. He and many others in attendance had been involved in the original southern Appalachian national park movement, started in Asheville in 1899, and many more had worked throughout the 1920s to establish the Great Smoky Mountains National Park. Now, with the Great Depression casting its shadow over Asheville's tourism industry, business and civic leaders were hoping that the new Parkway would link the city tightly to the newly opened park, enabling Asheville to capitalize on the expected flood of travelers. But if the rumors about the committee's report were correct and the Parkway were diverted away from Asheville, one of the banquet attendees wrote a few days later, "our situation [will be] entirely and permanently hopeless."[3]

By the time of the Grove Park Inn gathering, Asheville's Parkway supporters had been fighting for more than six months to have the new road routed near their city. Although they had been delighted with Ickes's November 1933 decision to adopt the Parkway as a Public Works Administration (PWA) project, some among them had foreseen that gaining Ickes's general approval represented only the first step. Some of North Carolina's staunchest Parkway supporters—veterans of the often-contentious Eastern National Park-to-Park Highway movement—worried from the beginning that the cooperative spirit of the early meetings about the Parkway would eventually dissolve into a conflict between North Carolina and Tennessee over the route. "Tennessee should have never been mentioned in connection with" the Parkway, Lenoir businessman and longtime park-to-park highway promoter R. L. Gwyn fretted to Congressman Robert L. Doughton. Senator Josiah Bailey concurred, writing suspiciously, "I know just how the Tennessee people are. I had to deal with them on the Park-to-Park Highway. They want a road whether it is scenic or not."[4]

Gwyn, Bailey, and other North Carolina partisans had reason to worry about conflict, but the source of the problem ultimately lay within their state. The three states containing the Shenandoah and Great Smoky Mountains parks had put together the original proposal for the scenic highway, and proponents had assumed from the outset that it would touch all three. But the issue of specific routing had been left unresolved until after Ickes's approval of the project was secured. As early as October 1933, however, North Carolinians, urged on by Asheville Chamber of Commerce manager Fred L. Weede, among others, began to stir up support among western North Carolina civic organizations for what would become North Carolina's preferred route, following "the crest of the Blue Ridge from Blowing Rock by way of Linville, Linville Gorge, Altapass, Little Switzerland, Buck Creek Gap, Green Knob, Pinnacle, Mt. Mitchell, the Craggy Rhododendron Gardens, and on to the Great Smokies." This route would completely exclude Tennessee.[5]

When Ickes approved the Parkway, North Carolina and Tennessee—and more specifically the cities of Asheville and Knoxville—launched an intense yearlong battle over the routing. While the route within the state of Virginia was determined quickly, Tennessee and North Carolina developed incompatible proposals for the remaining mileage, and each lobbied federal officials for months in hopes of winning the "eastern gateway" to the Great Smoky Mountains National Park. Not until November 1934 was the issue resolved.

Tense and nerve-wracking as it was, the conflict gave Asheville-based North Carolina Parkway boosters (ultimately far more invested in the project than were Knoxville's citizens) ample opportunity to refine and articulate their vision for the new road. The controversy reveals much about the motivations of those who wanted the Parkway and about their reasons for embracing the project as an appropriate form of development for the region. As chapter 1 has made clear, the Parkway constituted both a locally generated idea that grew out of specific conditions in the southern mountains and the culmination of national trends in park, road, and tourism development. The New Deal offered an opportune moment for implementing Parkway supporters' long-cherished plans for boosting tourism. As the Asheville partisans, in particular, argued for their vision of the Parkway, they unwittingly revealed the class and cultural biases of a project many of them considered simply the "greatest thing that could ever happen for our section."[6] Many mountain citizens whose lives would be touched directly by the project remained nearly mute.

Thus, the process by which Asheville business leaders brought the road to western North Carolina highlights many of the social, economic, and cultural fault lines that crisscrossed the mountains in the 1930s. Attention to the details of that process calls into question the widely accepted but simplistic notions of a homogenous community of needy "mountain people," "outsider exploitation" of the mountains, and the Parkway as a benign project that helped everyone equally and harmed no one.

PARKWAY BOOSTERS: BUSINESS-MEDIA
COLLABORATION IN ASHEVILLE

Everyone from Secretary Ickes down realized that threading a new scenic highway through the southern Appalachian mountains would be a complicated task, both logistically and politically. Shortly after he approved the Parkway project, therefore, Ickes appointed a high-level committee to investigate the various routing proposals.

In Washington, Ickes handed off the routing problem to a three-member panel chaired by PWA regional adviser George L. Radcliffe of Maryland and filled out by Cammerer and Bureau of Public Roads (BPR) Chief Thomas H. MacDonald, the heads of the two federal agencies that had charge of the project.[7]

Meanwhile, in the fall of 1933, North Carolina Governor J. C. B. Ehringhaus appointed the nine-member North Carolina Committee on the Federal Parkway to devise a unified routing plan. The committee was chaired by J. Quince Gilkey of Marion, a member of "an old time family in Rutherford and McDowell counties."[8] Other influential members included real estate and insurance executive Rufus Lenoir Gwyn of Lenoir (longtime promoter of the Eastern National Park-to-Park Highway), U.S. Senators Robert R. Reynolds of Asheville and Josiah Bailey of Raleigh, Congressman Doughton, businessman Reuben B. Robertson (president of the huge Champion Fibre Company west of Asheville), and attorney Francis O. Clarkson of Charlotte (son of longtime roads booster and state Supreme Court Justice Heriot Clarkson, who had also developed a resort community at Little Switzerland). The committee was rounded out by two attorneys, Burnsville's Charles Hutchins, whose wife served in the General Assembly, and John P. Randolph, a Bryson City General Assembly representative. The committee was to work closely with the North Carolina State Highway Commission under the leadership of Chair E. B. Jeffress.[9]

Although the committee was filled with people experienced and well connected enough to be quite powerful and persuasive, in fact it proved weak and ineffective. Much of the initiative in devising North Carolina's route and plotting the state's tactics in the Parkway battle was seized by a small group of men associated with the Asheville Chamber of Commerce and the city's main newspaper, the *Citizen-Times*.[10] Given the role that chambers of commerce had long played nationally in park and road boosting, this was hardly surprising.

At the helm of the Asheville business community's efforts was Weede. Born in Iowa in 1873, Weede had come to Asheville in 1928, when he was hired to manage the Chamber. A former journalist, Weede had worked in the 1920s as publicity director and later manager of the Miami Chamber of Commerce. In 1925, he left the Miami Chamber for work in a real estate firm in the city. His years in Florida were marked by intense boosterism, efforts that had played a part in sparking a tremendous (and ultimately calamitous) tourism-inspired land and construction boom. A similar process was unfolding in Asheville, where Weede had vacationed for several summers before taking over at the Chamber, a position he held until he was pushed out in 1940.[11]

Energetic and driven, Weede applied his considerable promotional skills with gusto in Asheville, enlarging the city's fledgling annual Rhododendron Festival and encouraging the development of the Mountain Dance and Folk Festival, working for the construction of the city's first airport and its civic auditorium, playing a part in starting the city's burley tobacco market, and helping to convince the Dutch-owned American Enka Corporation to locate a huge new rayon plant outside Asheville in 1929. The Blue Ridge Parkway was Weede's kind of project: big, bold, and calculated to boost Asheville's tourism. Years later, Weede called bringing the Parkway to Asheville the "outstanding accomplishment" of his career and even claimed that he had conceived the idea. Although he exaggerated his role, he undoubtedly played a central part in the routing battle.[12]

Weede's first volley in the routing war was his late 1933 campaign to rally support for the Parkway among Asheville's civic organizations and within "every Chamber of Commerce in the central and western part of the state," which he called on to "use every means possible for getting support in all quarters for the North Carolina route." His efforts brought forth a deluge of enthusiastic letters to North Carolina's members of Congress and endorsements by the Asheville City Council and Chamber of Commerce as well as (according to Weede) "practically every luncheon and civic club in the city."[13]

In a media-business partnership mirroring the one that had prevailed during the real estate boom in Miami, Weede worked closely with the *Citizen-Times*, whose president and owner, New Deal enthusiast and Asheville attorney Charles A. Webb, pressed North Carolina's Parkway case particularly hard.[14] A three-term state senator and former chair of the state Democratic Executive Committee, Webb passionately pursued "the wholesome development of his beloved . . . region," whose mountains he called "our principal and compelling attraction." Webb's interest in the Parkway project in fact reached back to his turn-of-the-century work in the movement for a southern Appalachian national park; he was also involved in later efforts to establish the Great Smoky Mountains National Park. His commitment to the Parkway project ensured voluminous newspaper coverage of progress, editorials arguing North Carolina's position on routing, and full cooperation with Weede and others behind the scenes. The *Citizen* and the *Times* publicized the project intensely from the beginning, calling the Parkway's initial approval "Big News for Us" and labeling the scenic highway "far and away the most appealing project which has been suggested for this territory under the public works program."[15]

Closely allied with Webb and Weede in the Asheville business-media community and in the Parkway battle was George Stephens, a prominent developer and Webb's early partner at the *Citizen*. Their collaborative work on behalf of the Parkway helped to make clear that even such an innovative project would inevitably be embedded in long-standing political processes and networks within the state.

A native of Guilford County and a graduate of the University of North Carolina, Stephens was active in the Good Roads campaign. From the 1890s until the 1920s, he made his home in Charlotte, where he became one of that city's most active and important real estate developers. In this work, he imbibed the city and park planning ideas that were sweeping other parts of the country and formulated ideas that were to influence Asheville's campaign on behalf of the Parkway. Innovative and aggressive, Stephens partnered with older, more financially capable businessmen and burst onto the Charlotte business scene around the turn of the century with his work in the development of the Piedmont Park subdivision. There, Stephens and his partners pioneered the use in southern cities of restrictive covenants on the properties they sold, limiting Piedmont Park to fairly well-to-do whites who wanted to build homes away from the city's business districts.[16]

Also active in park development in Charlotte, Stephens became acquainted with nationally respected urban planner John Nolen, who converted Stephens to the gospel of city planning. In 1911, Stephens formed the Stephens Company to develop the prestigious new Myers Park suburb and hired Nolen to design it. The heart of the new neighborhood was a huge tract of rolling land that Stephens purchased from his father-in-law on favorable terms, an arrangement that left him free to invest most of his considerable wealth in improvements and amenities such as trolley service, gas lines, sewers, water lines, and (unusually for Charlotte at the time) paved streets. By some reports, Stephens poured a staggering six hundred thousand dollars of his own money into Myers Park in the suburb's first decade. He and a partner also purchased the *Charlotte Observer*, thereby ensuring favorable publicity for the development.[17]

Termed "one of the largest and most influential planned suburbs in the southeastern United States," Myers Park employed several innovations in residential neighborhood design: curving avenues following the contours of the land, considerable amounts of green space, and abundant trees and shrubs, "giving the suburb the look of a romantic semi-rural park." In Myers Park, most of the neighborhood streets were designed to discourage through traffic, and most of the nicest homes were tucked away from main thoroughfares. "Such design," historian Thomas Hanchett writes, "put Charlotte in the vanguard of suburban planning nationally." It also furthered the segregation of wealthy, white-collar suburbanites from the rest of the city's population. Myers Park shortly became Charlotte's preferred address, and wealthy citizens in suburbs throughout the South copied its design features.[18]

Myers Park attracted piedmont North Carolina's wealthiest and most powerful citizens. In addition to Stephens, the publisher of the *Southern Textile Bulletin* moved there, as did the head of Charlotte's First National Bank and many textile company executives, furniture manufacturers, hotel proprietors, and top managers from the Southern Power Company (later Duke Power). Thus, Myers Park came to be not only "a social hub of Charlotte's elite, but also a concentration of men who exercised tremendous power over the destiny of the Carolina piedmont."[19]

With Myers Park well under way, Stephens and Nolen set out in 1916 to convince Charlotte's city leaders to adopt a plan that would have linked disparate neighborhoods (wealthy and poor) together via public parks, boulevards, greenways, and parkways set around a planned city center. However, Charlotte's municipal leaders ignored the proposals, which were not picked up again for twenty years. Perhaps dejected about this turn of events, perhaps concerned (as he said) about his family's health, Stephens soon left Charlotte for Asheville, where he set up a new real estate holding company, the Appalachian Realty Company, which soon purchased the entire town of Biltmore Village from the Vanderbilt estate. Stephens continued his crusade for city planning—this time with greater success—as he convinced Asheville leaders to hire Nolen to devise a city plan.[20]

While city and suburban planning and development were his greatest passions, Stephens had his hands in other projects as well. With two partners, he formed the Southern States Trust Company in 1902 (predecessor to the North Carolina National Bank, later NationsBank and now Bank of America). While engaged on work on Myers Park, Stephens also developed the Kanuga Lake Club, a mountain resort community on fifteen hundred acres near Hendersonville and Flat Rock, North Carolina (where he had owned a summer home since 1898), to serve as a summer retreat for the homeowners moving into Myers Park. With a hundred-acre lake, tennis and golf facilities, horseback riding trails, and summer cottages, the Kanuga Lake Club was a successful enterprise for several years.[21]

When Stephens moved to town, Asheville thus gained an energetic, innovative, and well-connected new citizen. With broad experience in real estate, planned developments, and political maneuvering, a longtime interest in the mountain region, and an affinity for public parks, green spaces, parkways, and similar projects that fit humans into the environment, Stephens was a natural supporter for the Blue Ridge Parkway. According to some accounts, he and Weede were the first Asheville citizens to latch onto the Shenandoah–Great Smoky Mountains parkway idea in the fall of 1933, and by the winter of that year Weede had arranged for Stephens to head a Chamber of Commerce committee to coordinate plans for getting the Parkway routed near Asheville. According to Weede, however, the rest of the committee was never appointed, leaving Stephens and Weede free to orchestrate the Chamber of Commerce's activities. With his wide circle of acquaintances throughout the state and his close friendship with Governor Ehringhaus, Stephens became a valuable asset to North Carolina's Parkway campaign.[22]

ENGINEERING AND POLITICS:
NORTH CAROLINA'S R. GETTY BROWNING

Civic and business leaders in Asheville, however experienced and well connected, could not by themselves secure the Parkway for their section of the mountains, since the North Carolina State Highway Commission bore official responsibility for designating the route. Asheville's partisans would need the engineering expertise of Raleigh highway officials to make a convincing case. Furthermore, when Parkway construction began, getting it planned and built would entail the same cooperation of engineers and landscape architects that had characterized national-park development and road building since the N PS's creation in 1916.

At the head of the Highway Commission was native western North Carolinian and ardent Parkway backer Edwin B. Jeffress, who worked energetically on the routing issue during late 1933 and early 1934. But a paralyzing stroke the following August incapacitated Jeffress for months and ultimately ended his tenure on the commission.[23] Much of the commission's work on the route thus fell to senior locating and claim engineer R. Getty Browning.

Browning's critical role in bringing the Parkway to North Carolina and in determining the type of road that would be built has never been adequately explored. While Parkway policy officially emanated from elected or appointed officials in Washington and Raleigh, Browning (assisted by the similarly unelected Weede, Webb, and Stephens in Asheville) did much of the day-to-day work of designing, developing, and promoting the project. In addition, Browning's vision of what the parkway could be, derived from his notion of where the parkway should go, guided the initial design process. Press reports later called Browning the "architect of the Blue Ridge Parkway" and "the man who is responsible, more than any other man, for the location of the . . . Parkway in North Carolina rather than in Tennessee." Indeed, a 1950s-era document found in Browning's papers indicated that "the route which the Parkway follows in North Carolina was mapped for the Secretary of the Interior in 1934 by R. Getty Browning . . . and it is remarkable that although this map was made before any surveys were begun and was based upon information obtained by Mr. Browning by actually walking over the route, the finished Parkway follows it almost exactly." Although the document is unsigned, records dating from the 1930s support the contention that the North Carolina portion of the Parkway threads the mountains along Browning's route.[24]

Not only has Browning's role not been explored, it has been actively neglected in favor of attention to the activities of the Parkway's first employee, resident landscape architect Stanley W. Abbott. Especially within the NPS, which employed Abbott, historical accounts of the Parkway (often written by landscape architects) depict Abbott as the driving force behind the Parkway's early design and development. Thus, the longtime domination of the Park Service by landscape architects has extended not only to the degree of landscape architect control over project development but also to the telling of Parkway history.[25]

Abbott, who also served as the Parkway's acting superintendent before being called into World War II in 1943, was certainly important in designing the Parkway landscape after construction started in 1935. But his importance in conceptualizing the project was secondary to that of Browning, whose vision guided the initial placement of a large section of the Parkway in North Carolina and whose proposed route Abbott originally thought unworkable. Deciding where the Parkway would go guided the type of road that would be built and determined the array of views that visitors would see.[26]

Besides being a talented and technically capable locating engineer, Browning also proved an astute political mediator and negotiator with a remarkably broad sense of the myriad issues at stake in building the Parkway. Throughout his work on the project, Browning—a gregarious man who could "outwalk men half his age and . . . outtalk them too"—moved easily among high New Deal officials in Washington, state leaders in Raleigh, tourism and business boosters in Asheville, Cherokee Indians on the Qualla Boundary, wealthy and well-connected resort developers at Little Switzerland, and ordinary landowners through whose lands the Parkway would go.[27]

Born in the 1880s, the grandson of a famous hunter and storyteller whom he greatly admired, Getty Browning grew up camping, hiking, and hunting with his family in the Maryland woods. After studying in private schools and with private tutors, he learned civil engineering through correspondence courses during a period when university-based programs in civil engineering—particularly in the South—were few.[28] Browning thus became a pioneering figure in the developing field of highway engineering at the moment when large-scale road building was getting under way.

After working for several years on railroad, highway, and bridge location and construction in Maryland, Browning was lured to North Carolina in 1921 by the start of the state's massive new road-construction program. As head of the State

Highway Commission's Location and Right-of-Way Departments after 1925, he was responsible for highway location during the formative period of North Carolina's state-maintained highway system.[29]

A "stocky, muscular-looking man" with "the restless curiosity of a school kid and the stamina of a mountain climber," Browning energetically attacked highway locating problems, usually by walking possible routes before reaching a decision. By the 1950s, he proudly claimed to have hiked more than ten thousand miles in locating North Carolina highways. In 1952, the *Saturday Evening Post* called him the "last of the great on-the-spot highway locators" and the "unchallenged dean of location engineers."[30] During the battle over Parkway routing, Browning was one of the few participants who had seen firsthand the entire length of North Carolina's proposed route, and this direct knowledge served him well as he promoted the route in Washington.

As Parkway negotiations proceeded, Browning was frequently charged with entertaining federal officials who came to inspect the various routes. He reveled in his role as tour guide, leading a large delegation sent by Secretary Ickes's routing committee (the Radcliffe Committee) on a thrilling trek up and down through the North Carolina mountains—hiking up Mt. Pisgah, picnicking at Mt. Mitchell, driving to Grandfather Mountain and Blowing Rock, and ending at 4,055-foot Tompkins Knob before heading down the mountain to Winston-Salem. "I shall never be able to tell you," the committee chair wrote, "how greatly you assisted us in our efforts. . . . I do not see how any living being . . . could have been more resourceful . . . in showing us the points of interest."[31]

This apparently innocuous social note points up a key feature of Browning's negotiating strategy and style: he understood the importance of personal relationships in influencing political decisions, and he used his considerable personal charm to navigate the wrangling over the Parkway route. He mailed a small gift to Baltimore for the son of the routing committee chair and sent additional maps and a picture of Mt. Pisgah to another member, whom Browning also invited to go bear hunting.[32]

Gregarious and outgoing, Browning appears to have gotten along well with nearly everyone involved in the Parkway negotiations. After entertaining Josephus and Adelaide Daniels, NPS director Cammerer, and Anna Ickes as they toured western North Carolina at the time of the "blue" Grove Park Inn dinner, Browning especially hit it off with Ickes. When Cammerer arrived at the train station to accompany her back to Washington, he found her "happily ensconced with Mr. Browning entertaining her with some interesting tales."[33]

R. Getty Browning, chief locating engineer, North Carolina State Highway Commission, prided himself on walking every mile of proposed roads. Behind him is North Carolina's Pisgah range. Photo by Bill Shrout. Reprinted from the *Saturday Evening Post*. © 1952 Saturday Evening Post Society.

THE DEVELOPMENT OF NORTH CAROLINA'S
HIGH MOUNTAIN ROUTE

The Blue Ridge Parkway project—combining the quest to open areas of beautiful mountain scenery with difficult engineering challenges—captivated Browning from the moment he heard of it in late 1933, and it became his nearly all-consuming work from then until his retirement in 1962. Though he was a vigorous outdoorsman who conquered lengthy backcountry trails with ease, he always sought to enable "millions of our people . . . to enjoy the beauty of these heretofore inaccessible sections of our country," such as North Carolina's Craggy Mountains, where, he reported in 1934, "steep, rough hiking trails [were] the only means of access."[34] Taking a perspective counter to that of the Wilderness Society, he insisted that the high mountain route that he and the rest of the North Carolina partisans would adopt would serve a democratic end.

As soon as it looked as if Secretary Ickes would approve the project for funding in late 1933, Browning, his colleagues on the Highway Commission and the state Parkway committee, and the Asheville partisans set to work preparing North Carolina's routing proposal. As Weede recalled, he and Stephens scurried to Raleigh several times in late 1933 for meetings with the commission and Governor Ehringhaus. The Asheville contingent had from the first been set on a route that would take the Parkway past several of what they considered their region's finest scenic and tourist attractions: the early tourist center of Blowing Rock, lofty and storied Grandfather Mountain, dramatic Linville Falls, so-called "beauty spot of the Blue Ridge" Little Switzerland (developed, not coincidentally, by routing committee member F. O. Clarkson's father), Mt. Mitchell, the romantic and lovely Craggy Gardens, the city of Asheville, and then on to the newly created Great Smoky Mountains park via the Native American community at Cherokee. Just a month after Ickes approved the Parkway project, the Asheville group had convinced the state Parkway committee to endorse this route.[35]

By early 1934, the Highway Commission had tentatively investigated and approved the suggested route and, with considerable input from Browning, who knew the terrain intimately, had elaborated more specifically the route between Asheville and the park. Much of this part of the road, Browning wrote, would penetrate an "unbroken wilderness" near the Pisgah National Forest. He characterized this section as "the largest unbroken area . . . in this State which could be considered in connection with the Park [and which] by all means should be protected." It would, he asserted, be "a very great asset to the Parkway." Crossing Mt. Pisgah and the Balsam Mountains (at elevations above five thousand feet nearly all the way), the far southwestern part of the route would end on the reservation lands of the Eastern Band of Cherokee Indians. The state Parkway committee published the completed route proposal in booklet form in early 1934 for presentation to federal officials.[36]

Thus, a route initially promoted by the private business-media alliance in Asheville and a capable and persuasive but relatively low-level bureaucrat in Raleigh became the path officially advocated by the state. The Asheville Chamber of Commerce, with Weede at the helm, became the dominant voice concerning the state's internal routing process, making itself the arbiter of western North Carolina municipalities' requests for a piece of the expected parkway. As Weede later wrote, "As in all public works certain individuals thought they saw an opportunity to cash in, and get for their particular area the benefits that would accrue. . . . Some of these suggestions we accepted. . . . Some [groups] we informed [that] their plan could not possibly be considered because of geographic reasons.

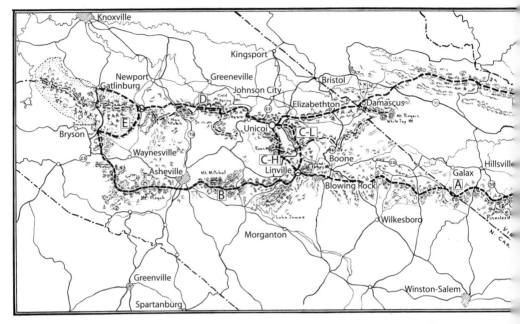

Proposed Shenandoah–Great Smoky Mountains National Parkway map, 1934, showing all
possible locations. Line A from the Shenandoah National Park to Linville, North Carolina, was
quickly agreed on. Controversy raged through the summer of 1934 over whether the Parkway

In most instances our disposition[s] of the proposals were accepted, possibly not
relished, but accepted. . . . We always found means to persuade or exert pressure
that solved the problems."[37]

In ensuring mountain counties' unified support and state officials' endorse-
ment of the route the Chamber favored, Weede observed drily, "iron hands [were]
sometimes necessary." By his account, even the State Highway Commission de-
ferred to the Asheville Chamber on some routing questions. Weede recalled that
after mapping out the route through the Balsams west of Asheville, Browning
and his crew requested Chamber approval before incorporating the map into the
state's official proposal. Although they enthusiastically endorsed the proposed
route, city and state elected officials from the governor to Asheville's mayor and
city council played only a small part in devising North Carolina's plan.[38]

THE TENNESSEE ROUTE

By adopting the Asheville-favored plan and thereby diverging from the original
1933 three-state conceptualization of the project, the state of North Carolina vir-

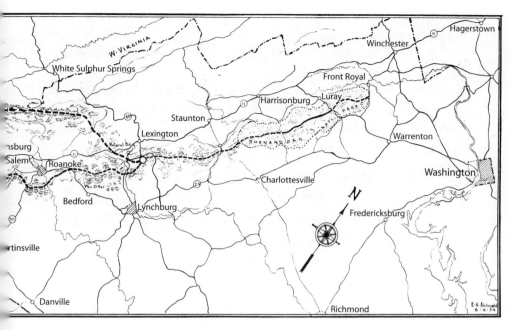

would follow line B (which North Carolina favored) or lines C-D-E (which Tennessee favored) from Linville to the Smokies. Final route follows line B. Drawing by E. H. Abbuehl, 4 June 1934. Courtesy Robert C. Browning.

tually ensured that an interstate routing battle would erupt. Tennessee's proposal for a Parkway that dipped into North Carolina before turning west at Linville to cross into Tennessee via Roan Mountain on its way to the Great Smoky Mountains park at Gatlinburg better fit federal officials' early idea for the Parkway. Tennessee's route, however, had a quite different character from North Carolina's and generally lay at lower altitudes.[39]

The Tennessee and North Carolina proposals shared the same routing from the North Carolina state line past Grandfather Mountain to Linville, North Carolina. At this point, however, instead of continuing toward the southwest, the Tennessee route would have turned west and crossed into Tennessee, passing the grand Roan Mountain (elevation 6,285 feet) on either a high route on Roan's slopes or a lower route through the adjoining valley on the way to Unicoi, Tennessee, just south of Johnson City. From there, the route would have turned southwest and crept near the North Carolina/Tennessee state line (within what is now the Cherokee National Forest) through the Nolichucky River Gorge, across Cold Springs Mountain, through the French Broad River Gorge to Delrio and Hartford, and then on to the Smokies, possibly via a fork around the park that would have taken visitors either to Gatlinburg or to Cherokee. The Tennessee route, Abbott wrote, offered "a variety of mountains, mountain stream valley, and broad river types of scenery," including some high rock cliffs, meadowlands, and woods—all in all, a "wide variety of interest." Its disadvantage, he observed, was its "relatively low elevation."[40] Though it did share Parkway mileage fairly equitably among the three states, this route bypassed Asheville, a significant drawback in the eyes of most North Carolina Parkway advocates.

THE FIRST HEARINGS AND ARGUMENTS: BALTIMORE, FEBRUARY 1934

With a flood of incoming letters and intense lobbying of federal officials by partisans from both Tennessee and North Carolina in late 1933 and early 1934, it soon became clear to federal committee chair George Radcliffe that hearings were needed to allow the committee to sort out the merits of each proposal. Radcliffe called representatives of each state to make their arguments in a three-day forum in Baltimore in early February.[41]

Joining Radcliffe at the hearing tables were several experts from both the NPS and the BPR. These professionals, the *Asheville Citizen* noted (somewhat ironically, in light of the intensity of the political debates and maneuvers that would surround the routing process), "were engaged . . . to select the location of the drive, so that political influences would be eliminated." Theodore Straus, a Baltimore engineer (sometimes associated with the origination of the Shenandoah–Great Smoky Mountains parkway idea) serving on the regional PWA advisory board, acted as Radcliffe's second in command. With him sat a team of engineers and landscape architects, most prominent among them consulting landscape architect Gilmore D. Clarke. Well-known, nationally respected, and highly experienced, Clarke was a pioneer in the nation's parkway-building efforts. He had supervised construction of the nation's first parkway, the Bronx River Parkway, and had subsequently served as landscape architect for the Westchester County Parkway Commission during its 1920s building campaign. Working with Clarke were NPS chief landscape architect Thomas C. Vint, BPR engineer H. J. Spelman, and newly hired Blue Ridge Parkway resident landscape architect Stanley W. Abbott.[42]

Abbott would become the Parkway's first superintendent and one of its principal early designers, but in December 1933, when he was hired to work on the project, he was an unknown and relatively inexperienced twenty-six-year-old only three years out of Cornell's landscape architecture program. He had worked with Clarke on the Westchester County Parks Commission, and this connection led to

Abbott's Blue Ridge Parkway position. For ten years, Abbott would head the Parkway project, designing the landscape for what would become the longest parkway yet built in the United States.[43]

At the Baltimore hearings, the outlines of the Parkway routing battle crystallized. Virginia's delegation presented its suggestions first. Although that state proposed two possible routes, representatives of the Highway Commission declared that they would support either, depending on what decisions were made in the Tennessee–North Carolina controversy. Virginia's day at the hearings was relatively uncontentious and consisted mainly of glowing if jumbled and rambling descriptions of the scenery and accommodations available along each of that state's possible routes.[44]

The hearings heated up the next morning, however, as North Carolina got its turn. Its twenty-six-person delegation included Governor Ehringhaus, most of the state's congressional delegation, most of the members of the state-appointed Parkway committee, Browning, Jeffress, other members of the State Highway Commission, and Stephens. For more than three hours, the North Carolinians presented their case for leaving Tennessee out of the Parkway picture and building all the non-Virginia mileage in their state.[45]

Ehringhaus managed North Carolina's carefully organized presentation. Following the state's official routing proposal as laid out by Weede and the North Carolina parkway committee but downplaying the more locally oriented motives that drove their fight for the Parkway, North Carolina's speakers took a national approach, foregrounding words Ickes had used in approving the project the previous November. "The President," Ickes had said, "has approved the proposed scenic Parkway connecting the Shenandoah and Great Smoky Mountains National Parks." Thus, "we are not quarreling with our sister states," Jeffress began; "we are simply contributing what we can today in an endeavor to make America's greatest scenic highway possible." The route they proposed, as state officials had argued in their January routing pamphlet, would connect "scenic vistas [that] will . . . measure up to and be worthy of the massed grandeur it links together."[46]

To demonstrate how the state's plan would achieve this — and doubtless hoping to appeal to the professional sensibilities of the landscape architects and engineers — North Carolina then pushed forward its chief technical expert and the person with the most firsthand knowledge of their route, Browning. Armed with several large maps, Browning patiently, professionally, and quickly took his listeners over highlights of the projected route, relating it to existing towns, roads, and rivers.[47]

He emphasized that the ridgetop route he envisioned not only would be less damaging to construct than other routes but also would be "the most direct, the most economical and the one which would provide . . . the greatest amount of scenery." Then Browning compared his route with that to be proposed the next day by Tennessee. While North Carolina's route would follow the mountaintops and thus feature "a high elevation all the way," Tennessee's would require heavy and destructive construction to negotiate the abrupt climbs and descents, resulting in an unappealing "zigzag" road. Pressing the advantages of his route, Browning noted that in building a scenic parkway, "it would be too bad to go in there and make deep cuts and fills and shoot these cliffs all to pieces and let the dirt run down over the mountain side," the likely (and unscenic) result if Tennessee's plan were adopted. But, he went on, "if you can follow the crest[,] where the cut and fill is diminished, we can lessen the cost of construction" as well as limit environmental damage. Furthermore, he stressed the spectacularly high elevations along the North Carolina–sponsored route, much of which would run above five thousand feet.[48] Before departing, Browning left each member of the committee with a small copy of the North Carolina route map.[49] His presentation had blended sophisticated technical knowledge, impeccable expertise, noninflammatory rhetoric, lucid articulation of a clear vision for a ridgetop Parkway, environmental concern, finely tuned aesthetics, astute politics, and a dramatic sense of the moment.

A stream of other speakers followed, most sticking closely to North Carolina's strategy of emphasizing how the state's route fulfilled the mandate for a scenic parkway. Where Browning had been cool, technical, and professional, however, these speakers delivered more fervently emotional testimonies about the wonders of North Carolina's natural treasures. As they told it, God had ordained the Parkway route by endowing western North Carolina with breathtaking mountains. Former Highway Commission chair Frank Page intoned that "you had just as well try to have a funeral without a corpse as to lay out a scenic highway . . . between these two locations" leaving out the North Carolina sections. "Now, we folks in North Carolina did not do that," he continued. "The Lord built these mountains." Senator Reynolds asserted that "in Western North Carolina God has presented to the world the most gorgeous section of America. . . . You can divert traffic, you can change your roads, but you cannot change those mountains that have been placed there." Representative Doughton claimed sweepingly that "nature has fixed where this road should be located. You must take the road to the scenery," he reminded the committee; "you cannot take the scenery to the road." This son of the mountains noted emotionally that "when you get out here to the Grandfather Mountain section, Blowing Rock, Grandfather Mount, Linville Gorge, and on to Mt. Mitchell . . . you will find that the Omnipotent Architect of the World has

carved and chiseled the most outstanding display of nature known to all creation."
North Carolinians would forsake heaven itself, Bailey told the committee, "for the
humble privilege of returning to the ridge along which the road is proposed to be
run." The overall message these officials preached to the Baltimore congregation
was that adoption of any route other than the one their state proposed would be
tantamount to spitting in the face of the Almighty.[50]

Truth be told, however, many of North Carolina's delegates had far more
worldly concerns on their minds, and they managed to get those concerns across
amid their soaring rhetoric about their mountains' splendor. Muted at this first
hearing, these arguments would grow louder over the ensuing months. If by giving their region its spectacular and superior scenery God had destined that the
Parkway be located in western North Carolina, it followed that God had given that
region its well-established tourist business, which would be irreparably harmed
by a mislocating the Parkway in Tennessee. For people in the mountains, Jeffress
asserted, tourism was the "natural business." The area's inherent attractiveness
to travelers, Stephens argued, had dictated the establishment of numerous resort
hotels costing millions of dollars in communities along the proposed route. "The
fact that those splendid hotels were erected along [the proposed line of the Park-
way], in spite of the non-accessibility of travel," Doughton continued, "is con-
clusive evidence that Nature there has ordained that this is a natural tourist line
of travel."[51] "If Gatlinburg were to become the official and only entrance to the
. . . Park," Jeffress pleaded, "certainly our folks in Western North Carolina would
feel that their birthright of sharing in the tourist business of America had been
largely diverted away from them." Furthermore, the committee had an obligation
to tourists to put the road where travelers already wanted to go, Bailey argued, "to
construct [it] where it is going to be of the greatest benefit to the tourists . . . who
spend billions of dollars in this country annually."[52]

The needy recipients of this endangered tourist-generated income, however,
remained vague in the North Carolina presentation. Most of the speeches that
discussed the issue referred simply to an undifferentiated tourist industry, while
others focused mainly on the idea that "this great development is for the people of
America." That phrase, however, came from Reynolds, who had just announced
that he was representing both the state of North Carolina and the American Automobile Association, of which he was a national vice president.[53]

The interests represented at this hearing thus were intertwined, and it was difficult to sort out what concerns were most driving the North Carolinians' pleas.
But as the months went on, it would become clearer that the benefits would not
flow as equitably as the high-sounding oratory implied. In particular, the central-

ity of the interests of Asheville's tourist entrepreneurs to North Carolinians' arguments would become increasingly evident. The Asheville partisans' fight exposed
the Parkway's origins at the center of the roads-parks-tourism triad that had by
then become such a powerful driver of American life.

Furthermore, the subsequent debate would also reveal that tourist development was much more a matter of human than divine agency—that is, tourism
occurred because certain people made certain decisions. As Dona Brown found
in her study of the development of tourism in nineteenth-century New England,

> To a modern eye, there may appear to be something inevitable about the
> growth of tourist industries. Wherever they have flourished, they seem to have
> emerged naturally out of the attractions of a particular place—its mountains,
> sea air, or quaintness. But nothing could be further from the truth. Just as riv-
> ers do not mandate textile mills, beaches alone do not make a resort. Nature
> alone does not make 'scenery,' and picturesque history alone does not make a
> quaint tourist destination. Tourism is not destiny, imposed on a community or
> a region by its geography or its history. Tourist industries were built by people.
> . . . [I]n every case, the industries were the product of human choices, made
> not only by visitors, but by natives as well.[54]

True though this was in North Carolina's case, the state's partisans most concerned with furthering tourist development in the mountains were content for the
time being to submerge their more local concerns and let their case rest mostly on
building the most scenic highway possible "to provide for the people of America,
and particularly for those in the eastern area, a chance for travel and recreation,
amid splendor and inspiration, that only mountains like these can provide."[55]

For the moment, this seemed like a good strategy. As Clarke noted at the close
of North Carolina's day at the hearings, "We want to find the most scenic route.
We will divorce it from politics."[56] But Tennessee's presentation the next day
proved that in fact that the scenic, like the personal, was indeed political.

North Carolinians attending the Tennessee presentation doubtless felt smug
as they watched the antics of Senator Kenneth McKellar, who argued his state's
case with accusations of bias and favoritism within the federal committee and
threats to use his influence in Congress to withhold funding for the road were
it not located to his liking. While the North Carolina delegates had begun their
testimony with Browning's calm and professional presentation of the advantages
of the route they favored, McKellar rambled, grumbled angrily about North Carolina's attempt to "grab" the highway, and repeated his call for the route to be
located "fairly" to all three states involved, meaning that half of the non-Virginia

mileage should go to North Carolina and half to Tennessee. Regarding North Carolina's proposal, he complained, "It is not right for one state or one community to seek an advantage over another."[57]

Radcliffe, denying that the committee he chaired was predisposed to favor North Carolina's proposals and perturbed by McKellar's contentious tone and his speech's paucity of concrete information, finally interrupted: "Senator, . . . I have not found out yet what you want, except in a general way. What I want to see is some concrete presentation." But such was not forthcoming until halfway through Tennessee's allotted time, when General Frank Maloney of the State Highway Department rose to speak, armed with detailed maps. Maloney gallantly tried to pick up the pieces after McKellar's disastrous speech, discussing the possible advantages of Tennessee's less-elevated route: relief from mountain driving, the beauty of the streamside sections, and the improved camping opportunities that a mix of high and low elevations might offer. Maloney tried to show that "the highway I have mentioned . . . would be of a scenic beauty that is unsurpassed" and that it would divide "the distance equally between the two states [and give] no one the advantage in any way." Other Tennessee speakers concurred, but, compared with the facts, fervor, and polish of North Carolina's presentation, the Tennesseans' case seemed vague, disorganized, whiny, and weak. Other than asking for equity in the treatment of the two states, they seemed unable to offer many compelling reasons why the Parkway ought to follow their route.[58]

The North Carolina delegates left the hearings encouraged and delighted with their performance, which seemed to have been well received by the committee. Clarke praised their efforts, stating publicly, "I never recall a presentation made in a more graphic or interesting manner," and Radcliffe seemed to open a door for North Carolina's case to be considered when he cautioned McKellar that achieving mileage balance between North Carolina and Tennessee should not be the "only controlling factor" in routing the Parkway.[59]

The North Carolinians knew, however, that a successful conclusion to the hearing was but a first step in what was likely to be a drawn-out battle. Thus, at Browning's urging and with assistance from Weede, Stephens, and the rest of the Asheville contingent, Doughton arranged a posthearing audience at which he, Stephens, and Ehringhaus presented President Roosevelt with an expensively produced red leather album full of "beautiful pictures in natural colors" of the scenic spots they hoped that the Parkway would include. It was a politically savvy personal touch thoroughly characteristic of Browning. The president was impressed, but months of investigation and negotiation still lay ahead before federal officials would settle the routing question.[60]

"STABILIZATION PROJECT":
ASHEVILLE'S CRISIS AND THE PARKWAY

In spite of lofty rhetoric about sublime scenery bestowed by an all-wise Creator on western North Carolina and the tourist industry that grew "naturally" out of such scenery, more basic economic concerns lurked beneath the surface throughout the first several months of the routing controversy. From the beginning, Asheville's business community argued that the new Parkway was the one hope for reviving the city's flagging tourist business. This argument was not without merit, for after a tremendous boom in the 1920s, Asheville had, by many measures, reached truly desperate straits by 1933. But, in truth, a drooping tourist industry was not the whole problem, and reviving it was not the only available solution.

Asheville as a Tourist Center

For many decades before the Western North Carolina Railroad arrived in 1880, Asheville had attracted visitors, but the new accessibility afforded by train service brought an unprecedented surge in tourism that lasted well into the 1920s. That period was something of a golden age for the city, with bold and grandiose construction projects, the building of luxurious hotels and city facilities, and the attraction of an impressive array of prominent and wealthy tourists and new residents.[61]

Late-nineteenth-century promotional and "local color" literature touted the city's healthful climate and portrayed the southern Appalachians in general as a mysteriously fascinating and isolated region where (either "backward" or "quaint," depending on one's point of view) remnants of American pioneer culture survived. Christian Reid's 1876 love story, *Land of the Sky*, historian Milton Ready writes, "painted an idyllic picture of Asheville and of Western North Carolina as a Garden of Eden whose inhabitants were caught in a curious time warp." Inspired by such accounts, travelers from throughout the nation flocked to Asheville and the surrounding hills. Many decided to stay, swelling the city's population from fifteen hundred in 1870 to more than ten thousand by 1890 and transforming it from a sleepy county seat into a bustling social center. Victorian-era city politicians and other prominent citizens encouraged the growth, publicizing the city as a health resort and pushing for reforms and enhancements to better accommodate the new guests. Starting with Mayor Edward J. Aston's 1877 revitalization and cleanup of the muddy and crowded town square and his construction of a new three-story brick courthouse, a long line of city-boosting officials fostered a building spree that transformed the skyline by the 1920s. Their promotional efforts and improvements soon made the city a health center and the home of several tuberculosis sanatoriums and other spas.[62]

As tourism flourished, wealthy, socially adept, self-confident, and ambitious entrepreneurs arrived in Asheville. Cleveland lumberman George Willis Pack fostered and financed a spree of new construction. Accompanying these Gilded Age and Progressive Era changes in the city's built environment was the installation of many other conveniences, including electricity, telephone service, street railways, and better water and sewer facilities. Tremendous sums of city money went for street paving and other improvements. Pack focused city leaders' attention on improvements to the city's still filthy and clogged Court Square, helped the city to open more parks and playgrounds, lobbied for the organization of a public school system in 1889, and provided funds for a downtown public library. Mayor Charles Blanton oversaw the outlawing of gambling and prostitution and urged creation of a city board of health. Pushing much of the development was the new Board of Trade (later the Chamber of Commerce), organized in 1898 under the motto "Transportation and Trade" to promote and publicize Asheville's progress and to advertise the city as a resort.[63]

To accommodate newly arriving tourists, Frank Coxe constructed the city's first high-class hotel, the Battery Park, in 1886. Perched atop an exquisitely landscaped high knoll, it sported in-room fireplaces, modern bathrooms, hot and cold water, elevators, steam heat, electric lights, dining rooms, ballrooms, a bowling alley, and billiard rooms. It became the city's social as well as visual center, catering to prominent families from Asheville and elsewhere.[64]

Visitor George Washington Vanderbilt, the grandson of railroad magnate Cornelius Vanderbilt, arrived in 1889 to build his mansion, the Biltmore House, on immense acreage he purchased on the outskirts of the city. Vanderbilt constructed an ostentatious 250-room French chateau with landscape design by Frederick Law Olmsted, completing the house in 1895.[65]

By 1900, nearly fifteen thousand people lived in Asheville, with almost fifty thousand more (plus the many tuberculosis patients in the sanitariums) visiting each year. The sojourners included successful Tennessee and St. Louis pharmacist Edwin Wiley Grove, who was so delighted with Asheville's salutary health effects that he soon moved there and quickly made his mark. Full of ideas and flush with the fortune he had made selling his popular quinine tonic, he bought land in 1905 in the Sunset Mountain section, developed an exclusive residential area, and opened the imposing and elegant all-stone Grove Park Inn in 1913. He also set in motion his plan for revitalizing downtown Asheville by demolishing

First Battery Park Hotel, Asheville, with trolley in foreground, before 1900. The hotel was built in 1886. North Carolina Collection, Pack Memorial Public Library, Asheville, North Carolina.

Coxe's Battery Park hotel, boldly razing the hill where it stood, and constructing a new hotel with the same name in 1924. He followed this with construction of the Grove Arcade (1929), with which he hoped to attract shoppers, businesses, and conventioneers as well as seasonal tourists to downtown Asheville.[66]

Thus, by the 1920s, development in Asheville was proceeding at a feverish pace, and the city appeared to be coming into its own as one of North Carolina's major urban centers. Yearly visitation topped 250,000, and the population continued to increase at a fantastic rate—79 percent between 1920 and 1928—to top 50,000 by the end of the decade. Only Charlotte and Winston-Salem grew faster, and it looked as if Asheville—already larger than Raleigh and Wilmington—would soon pass Durham and Greensboro to become the state's third-biggest city. According to one of the city's historians, many Asheville residents in the 1920s believed that within a decade, the city might even rival Richmond and Atlanta.[67]

Real estate values in the Asheville area shot up as developers (often fresh from the simultaneous Florida land boom) swarmed in; subdivided and sold lots; started large business, resort, and hotel developments throughout the city and the surrounding mountains; and speculated wildly. Construction of hotels (the new Battery Park, the Vanderbilt, and the Asheville-Biltmore) and expansion of city services and amenities (especially public parks, plazas, and extensive landscaping) proceeded apace, making the city more attractive to tourists. Yet another lavish new city hall was built, along with a fine new county courthouse. Down-

Grove Park Inn, Asheville, built in 1913. E. M. Ball Collection, D. H. Ramsey Library Special Collections, University of North Carolina at Asheville.

town's first skyscraper, the fifteen-story Jackson Building, went up in 1924. And after 1927, the Chamber of Commerce sponsored the Rhododendron Festival and the Mountain Dance and Folk Festival to draw even more visitors. The hiring of Fred Weede from formerly growth-happy Miami (where the land boom had gone bust in 1926) to head the Chamber in many ways symbolized the boosterism, optimism, and prosperity that ruled Asheville in the 1920s.[68]

While Asheville developed as the prime tourist center of western North Carolina, surrounding areas also capitalized on the growing tourist business. By the 1930s, roads (many paved) radiated out from Asheville to points of interest—the Craggy Gardens, Elk Mountain, Mt. Pisgah (topped by the Pisgah Inn, opened in 1920, and the Vanderbilt hunting lodge), the dizzying heights of the Balsam Mountains, the impressive Mt. Mitchell (at 6,684 feet the highest peak east of the Rocky Mountains), Lake Lure (with its resort and "commodious hotels"), and Chimney Rock (a privately owned mountain wonder, admission one dollar).[69] Just outside Asheville, the Biltmore Estate was also by this time open to the public.

Summer religious assembly grounds also dotted the region—Lake Junaluska (1913) for Methodists in Haywood County west of Asheville, Kanuga Lake (1909)

A 1908 Ford pulls away from Asheville's second Kenilworth Inn, completed in 1917.
The first Kenilworth Inn was destroyed by fire in 1908. E. M. Ball Collection, D. H. Ramsey
Library Special Collections, University of North Carolina at Asheville.

for Episcopalians to the south, and Ridgecrest (1907) for Baptists, Montreat (1897) for Presbyterians, and Blue Ridge (1906) for the Young Men's and Young Women's Christian Associations to the east. Perhaps a hundred youth camps (including Camp As-You-Like-It for girls) hid in many nearby mountain recesses. Exclusive privately developed summer home colonies also proliferated. One of the most successful was Little Switzerland, developed by Heriot Clarkson after 1909. Thomas Dixon, author of *The Clansman*, on which the film *Birth of a Nation* was based, tried during the 1920s to develop an artists' and writers' resort colony (a "refuge for creative thinkers," he termed it) at Wildacres, near Little Switzerland. Like this one, many similar developments flourished briefly and failed. Even the Eastern Cherokee Indians, whose reservation covered a large tract of land to Asheville's west, got in on the action from 1914 on, attracting tourists with an annual Cherokee Fair. Thus, the lure of a lucrative trade had drawn much of western North Carolina into the tourist business by the time the Blue Ridge Parkway proposal came along.[70]

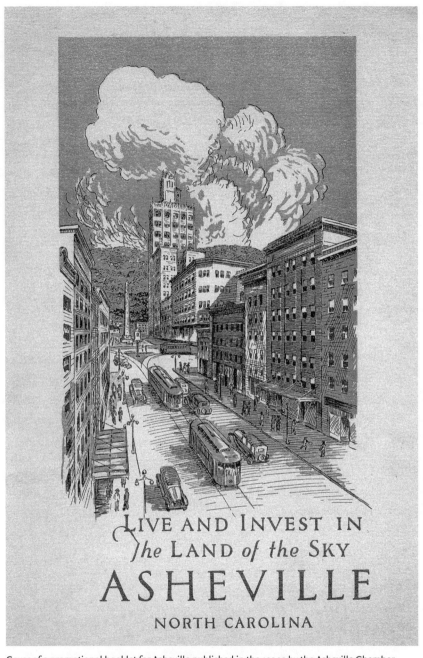

Cover of a promotional booklet for Asheville published in the 1920s by the Asheville Chamber of Commerce and Asheville Real Estate Board. Frank Coxe Collection, D. H. Ramsey Library Special Collections, University of North Carolina at Asheville.

The Depression and Asheville's Economic Crisis

As the Parkway routing question and the battle with Tennessee came to dominate the thinking of many business-oriented people in western North Carolina, however, the optimism and prosperity of the 1920s had turned into the despair and adversity of the 1930s. At the center of western North Carolina's woes was Asheville. As was the case throughout the nation, the boom there in the 1920s had been built on a shaky financial footing. Asheville paid for its 1920s building spree with more than $16 million in municipal bonds, many of which were issued to make up for falling tax revenues as the decade wore on. By 1930, Asheville's bonded indebtedness stood at nearly $24 million, the largest of any of the state's eight biggest cities and larger than the combined totals of Raleigh, Durham, Greensboro, and Winston-Salem. Furthermore, the collapse of the region's real estate market after 1926 left western North Carolina's largest bank, Central Bank and Trust, holding millions of dollars in loans on seriously depreciated lands and defunct developments. By 1928, the bank was declared nearly insolvent, but because of inaction by state banking commission officials, it remained open. Moreover, bank officers convinced Asheville city officials in 1928 and 1929 to leave in the bank's coffers large sums of Asheville's cash reserves to cover Central's daily operations and help conceal the severity of its troubles. This strategy staved off disaster for a couple of years, but by 1930, the game was over and the bank closed its doors, kicking the footings out from under financial institutions and municipalities throughout the western mountains.[71]

Asheville paid dearly for its irresponsible financial management and its trust in the big local bank, losing millions of dollars in city deposits in its collapse. Without money for operating expenses and unable to borrow more, the city defaulted on its massive boom-generated debts, which, with a proportionate share of county debt added in, amounted to more than $41 million by 1931. Although the officials who had dug the city into this financial hole were quickly tossed out and replaced with a more frugal and efficient new administration, Asheville would not fully recover from the disaster for decades. The debts were renegotiated, but stringent rules imposed to ensure their repayment limited Asheville's ability to borrow or spend money on further expansion of city services as late as the 1970s, when the debt was finally retired. In addition, tourist traffic dried up and population growth stalled, so that by the 1970s, Asheville still had a population of only about fifty-five thousand. Thus, the once-thriving metropolis stagnated, and the boundless optimism that had driven the tourist-oriented building boom turned by the early 1930s to a deep despair.[72]

The boosterish spirit of the 1920s nevertheless died hard. Many observers naively believed Asheville's woes to be temporary, and Weede, Webb, Stephens, and
other civic and business leaders continued to push projects such as the Rhododendron Festival, the Mountain Dance and Folk Festival, and especially the Blue
Ridge Parkway, all of which the men hoped would revive the sagging tourist industry. The *Asheville Times* encouraged citizens to "have faith in Asheville," and the
Citizen predicted a renewed surge in tourism with the impending opening of the
Great Smoky Mountains park.[73]

While many Ashevillians in fact had little faith in the city's government and
business community in the wake of the crash and doubtless remained skeptical of
new schemes for piling more of the city's eggs into the tourism basket, a tourist-
oriented, probusiness segment remained in control of the city's most powerful
organizations, especially the Chamber and the *Asheville Citizen-Times*. In the wake
of the burst 1920s bubble, these men bore most of the responsibility for bringing
another expensive tourist-serving development project (in the form of the Blue
Ridge Parkway) to Asheville in the 1930s. In many respects, it seemed that they
had learned little from the crash.

The Parkway as Panacea

By the time the Parkway routing issue came up for debate, however, Asheville
obviously could not finance continued infrastructure developments to attract
more tourists. Thus, by 1934 the truth was, as city leaders argued, that federal
assistance represented the city's only hope. Federal monies certainly provided the
bulk of the aid to Asheville's poor and suffering as the depression wore on; the
city's ability to pay for relief was limited, and the conservative state leadership
was disinclined to help.[74] In this context, the short- and long-term transformative
potential of an infusion of federal aid in the form of the construction of a splendid
new scenic highway looked like an answer to prayer.

The North Carolina delegates to the Baltimore hearing had a point, then, when
they argued that the committee ought to consider the fate of the area's established tourist industry. As the city's supporters increasingly emphasized, Asheville was at something of an economic crossroads: with federal help and the Blue
Ridge Parkway, it could recommit itself to tourism in anticipation of a new influx
of travelers to the Great Smoky Mountains National Park; conversely, without
the Parkway—and presumably therefore unable to fully capitalize on the new
park—it could look forward to eventual marginality as a tourist destination and
consequent economic collapse. Thus, the "naturalness" of tourism in the western

North Carolina mountains, which the state's delegation had stressed so forcefully at the Baltimore hearing, was called into question as Asheville leaders looked to a decidedly human solution to save the industry.

The situation ultimately proved considerably more complex than this stark choice indicated, but given the pro-tourism bent of Asheville's Parkway proponents, consideration of other alternatives became difficult. Both scenarios implicitly acknowledged that more than God-given scenery was needed to create tourism. Conscious policy decisions would ultimately determine the Asheville region's fate as a tourist destination.

When North Carolina proponents returned home from the Baltimore hearing, they had reason to believe in the effectiveness of their crucial, if muted, economic arguments wrapped in eloquent discussions of the scenic benefits their region offered. The official name given to the parkway endeavor in the wake of the hearings was the "Shenandoah–Smoky Mountain Parkway and Stabilization Project," and Radcliffe had reassured the delegation as the hearing concluded that the committee was aware that the Parkway "means a great deal in the way of economic rehabilitation, stabilization, development. . . . I want you to know that that phase of the matter is receiving very careful attention and consideration from us."[75]

But as winter passed into spring and the Radcliffe Committee continued its investigations, Asheville's pleas for help in rescuing its tourist business became more and more desperate as city leaders began to fear that arguments based solely on God-given scenery might not win the day. And the louder the economic arguments, the more evident the class and cultural lines that cut across western North Carolina society. Exploring the ways in which the Asheville business community lobbied federal officials in the months after the hearing gives the lie to the previously accepted idea, central to Harley Jolley's widely distributed book on the Parkway, that the project was primarily a "godsend for the needy."[76] The "needy" in question turned out to be the members of Asheville and western North Carolina's business community, whose voices dominated discussions of the Parkway, rather than poor, out-of-work rural mountaineers, whose interests were often invoked but who in fact had neither much say in determining the course of the project nor much to gain from it.

In the months after the Baltimore hearing, the Radcliffe Committee took at least two reconnaissance trips to inspect the Virginia, North Carolina, and Tennessee routes. Not surprisingly, Weede, Webb, Stephens, state Parkway committee members, and other prominent and well-connected western North Carolina citizens fluttered closely around the inspection parties on both of their visits to the Asheville region. Jeffress, who along with Browning hosted one of the visiting reconnaissance parties, encouraged these efforts. After a grueling day of travel in driving sleet along icy mountain roads, the group was welcomed to Asheville with a dinner at the Biltmore Forest Country Club, hosted by Champion Fibre's President Robertson and a group of civic leaders (including Weede and several officers of the *Citizen-Times*). Warmed and refreshed, the committee bedded down for the night at the posh Grove Park Inn.[77]

While Browning and Jeffress showed the committee the region's scenic glories on the ground, the Asheville newspapers and the "leading citizens" lobbying for the Parkway emphasized economic factors more strongly than ever while continuing to make the case for the North Carolina route. "The Scenic Parkway," the *Asheville Citizen* asserted, "would stabilize the tourist industry of this region as nothing else could do . . . and it would bring into being for the people of this region new and desperately needed opportunities. It is the bow of promise in their sky."[78]

And who were "the people of this region?" The *Citizen* wanted readers to understand that it was referring to the rural mountain poor. "The thousands of visitors who would travel [the Parkway] would bring to [locals'] doors a market for their labor, a market for the products of their little farms, a market for the various things which they would be able to make and sell. In no other known way can they hope to share in the benefits of the Recovery movement."[79]

The Tourist Industry and the Little Farms

As articulated by the *Citizen*, this argument—first made in a February editorial and repeated by Stephens at the Baltimore hearing—seamlessly conflated the interests of the "tourist industry" with that of the owners of "little farms" throughout the region. The way Stephens had introduced the topic exposed Asheville Parkway supporters' somewhat condescending view of their mountain neighbors. "It has been customary in almost all of our activities and interests of a public nature," Stephens contended, "for some one to find an under-dog that has to be taken care of." For Stephens, that "under-dog" was "our mountain people." Four hundred thousand of them, he went on, were "land-locked," for "the eddies of civilization somehow have shunted them up into these places." Calling on long-held stereotypes, Stephens elaborated: "Those people are almost a neglected race. Many of them speak the English of Chaucer." And perhaps more significantly, they are "the true type of pioneer American stock." Unfortunately, "the march of civilization has not brought them the things that it has brought to many other people." This fact Stephens attributed partly to the mountaineers' unwillingness to leave their mountain coves to sell farm products in urban areas where warehouses and other marketing conveniences were available.[80]

Glossing over the possibility that poor roads might have inhibited mountain farmers' mobility, Stephens blamed their inexplicable attachment to their land for their economic difficulties and noted that "the only way to give these people help is to take it to them." The Parkway, he concluded, would do just that. It would provide a livelihood for nearly half a million people as well as afford them the benefits of "contact with new ideas and new people." By providing employment in hotels and resorts as well as buyers for the "products of these little farms," the Parkway would "give them enthusiasm and hope, as nothing else . . . would do. And if it is not done, I can think of no other means and no other opportunity that these people will have for their future welfare." The *Citizen* remarked similarly that current New Deal programs such as the National Recovery Administration and the Agricultural Adjustment Administration offered little to people in the mountains, who were not workers in industry or growers of the crops targeted.[81]

Paradoxically, however, Stephens almost simultaneously lamented the fact that many mountain people had left their beloved coves when economic pressures became too great. "These people, many of them," he had told the Radcliffe Committee, "have had to leave the land that they were reared on, the land of their inheritance, and go down into the cotton mill regions to make a living." Increased tourist development along the lines he proposed, Stephens hoped, would keep the mountaineers in their homes by bringing tourists "right to [their] doors."[82]

In fact, neither economic circumstance nor highland topography but rather an entangling array of popular stereotypes about mountain people prevented Stephens from conceiving of other ways to help suffering mountain families or from considering that the tourism industry might be part of the problem. Tourism seemed to him a perfect development strategy for a "primitive" people who had—according to Stephens, the *Citizen*, and many others interested in the mountains in the 1930s—a "deftness at anything connected with handcraft." He insisted therefore that "the tourist is [the mountaineer's] market." And the sales possibilities were almost unlimited, he went on, for even Eleanor Roosevelt was ordering craft items from mountain workers.[83]

Ignoring the possibility that the construction of regular, paved highways might help those in the mountains who wanted to market their crafts, Stephens proposed the limited-access scenic highway as the ideal solution. "They have no means of getting these products out to the market," he insisted, "and in order to do that we must carry the market to them." As the Parkway would be designed, however, with its wide right-of-way, its limited private and public access, and its strict restrictions on roadside commercial development, it would offer average "isolated" mountain folk for whom Stephens professed such concern almost no opportunity for contact with the traveling public.[84]

Stephens's short speech invoked popular images of mountaineers that had long blinded people to the root causes of their difficulties and limited ideas about what might be done to help. Nevertheless, Stephens deployed the images in support of the Asheville partisans' case. By proposing handicrafts and tourism as remedies for mountain peoples' woes, he added his own confusing bit to a half-century-old conversation about the economic, social, and cultural features of southern mountain society. And as the history of the coming Parkway moved forward, he was by no means the last to do so.

From the latter half of the nineteenth century, when writers in search of local color joined timber, coal, and railroad entrepreneurs in search of abundant natural resources in "discovering" the southern Appalachians, various myths had spilled forth about the people who lived there. Appalachian people, the myths held, were an isolated, culturally unique Anglo-Saxon pioneer remnant, untouched by modernity and alternately backward (moonshiners or feudists) or quaint and noble (craftspeople and ballad singers). Such images proliferated via fiction and non-fiction writings for genteel popular audiences as well as in popular films and cartoons. From the 1850s onward, an unbroken stream of articles in the popular press, religious journals, and other publications supplied the stock phrases for the developing discourse about southern mountaineers: "a strange land and peculiar people" (1873), "our contemporary ancestors" (1899), "our kindred of the Boone and Lincoln type" (1900), "Anglo-Saxons" (1901), "simple, homeloving folk . . . heedless of the march of events" (1907), and the ubiquitous "hillbillies" (1915). Such characterizations even appeared in published collections of English ballads from the southern mountains and in widely read nonfiction studies of mountain life such as Samuel Tyndale Wilson's The Southern Mountaineers (which went through five editions between 1906 and 1915) and Horace Kephart's Our Southern Highlanders (1916). Concurrent with the Parkway routing battle, National Geographic promised that visitors driving through the new eastern national parks would encounter mountaineers in log cabins, "the friendly descendants of that sturdy stock which produced such men as Abraham Lincoln, Daniel Boone, Andrew Jackson, and Admiral Farragut." The New York Times informed readers that they would find along the new Blue Ridge Parkway "primitive mountain folk" whose speech was often laced with "a phrase or two of Anglo-Saxon origin almost without meaning to the modern grammarian."[85]

These ideas had certainly gained credibility within the leadership of the National Park Service, whose future director, Conrad L. Wirth (then with the NPS

Branch of Land Planning), visited Shenandoah National Park in 1933. In his memoir, Wirth recalled that the people in that area were "extremely poor and uneducated" and that they "spoke dialect that dated back to the late seventeenth-century English spoken by their forebears." Inbreeding was rampant, Wirth reported, leading to high rates of mental retardation. Nearly all families made moonshine, and their "one-room cabins" were filled with their numerous children. "It is hard to believe," Wirth marveled, that "that people could be so poor and isolated in the twentieth century within a hundred miles of the capital of the United States."[86]

In fact, as neither Wirth nor many other observers realized, the "mountain people" included many different social, economic, and cultural groups with vastly different historical experiences, as recent scholarship on the Appalachian region has demonstrated. The elite group of mountain people who had built Asheville into a decidedly modern tourist center and now lobbied for the Parkway should have recognized this fact. But the totalizing generalizations about mountain people and their lives popularized by nineteenth-century writers had become so widespread (even in Asheville) that they dominated many of the conversations about what should be done for the region.[87]

The writings about the region, for example, encouraged an influx of workers who hoped either to "uplift" the downtrodden mountaineers or to "preserve" or "revive" their disappearing but valuable culture. Thus, as booming coal, timber, and textile companies bought and transformed mountain land, drew former mountain farmers into wage work, and brought convulsive economic and social dislocation, church-affiliated home missionaries and other social and "culture" workers also came to the aid of mountain residents. While some such workers established health clinics and literacy and agricultural programs, most were partial to crafts and culture. The 1890s and subsequent decades saw the opening of numerous settlement schools and folk craft programs that shared those broad goals, and western North Carolina was a center of such efforts. Prominent handicrafts projects in the area included Asheville's Log Cabin Settlement, Allanstand Cottage Industries (1895), and Biltmore Industries (1901) and the John C. Campbell Folk School (1925) near Murphy. By the 1930s, the western North Carolina–based Southern Highland Handicraft Guild had become the principal arbiter of "mountain crafts."[88]

Even in the early twentieth century, however, some people did not believe that cultural erosion or "backwardness" lay at the root of Appalachian residents' problems or that cultural revitalization could provide an adequate solution to the region's poverty and suffering. Massive industrial development and associated structural changes had brought with them a host of problems — environmental damage, occupational injuries and diseases, disruption of communities and family life, economic instability—that many of the culture workers failed to address, and other voices called for a more substantive discussion of these difficulties and for a different set of remedies.[89]

Emma Bell Miles's 1905 *Spirit of the Mountains* criticized tourism as a mixed blessing at best. Others debated the benefits and drawbacks of textile work for mountaineers. Thomas R. Dawley argued in 1910 that removal of mountain residents to the mills represented a positive development, a position questioned by much research on the people themselves. Malcolm Ross's *Machine Age in the Hills* (1933) detailed the social costs of the coal mining industry, and in the mid-1930s radical Vanderbilt University theologian Alva Taylor spelled out a tough-minded perspective on "sub-marginal standards of living in the southern mountains" that emphasized how timber companies had "siphoned off [the region's wealth] into the cities and the centers of capital" while leaving in poverty the mountaineers who provided the labor needed for such enterprises.[90]

Only a year after Stephens invoked these popular myths to buttress the Asheville partisans' pro-Parkway arguments, writer and historian C. Hartley Grattan published in *Scribner's* magazine a remarkably clear-headed analysis of the structural ills facing the southern mountains. "The romantic Southern Appalachians," the epigraph proclaimed, "run into the cold facts of modern economics." Mountain subsistence farmers had never been as isolated as depictions had contended, and prior to the advent of industrialization, mountaineers had managed to eke out a decent living through a system of community interdependence. Industrialization, Grattan correctly noted, had created a demand for the region's rich natural resources, driving many farmers from their land, while the industries—usually owned by outsiders little concerned with local conditions—failed to provide adequate permanent employment to take the place of dwindling farm income.[91]

Grattan detailed how timber companies, aided by increasing railroad penetration of the mountains, denuded the landscape and sent profits out of the region. Coal resources had been similarly exploited and mishandled by outside operators—a "derelict industry," he called it, producing "outrageous conditions" in eastern Kentucky. Handled in these ways, he concluded, the region's rich natural resources had not provided an adequate standard of living for mountain people.[92]

Grattan held out little hope that manufacturing as currently conducted would improve living standards in the region because such industries generally depended on cheap, nonunionized labor. He dismissed the possibility that handicrafts or tourism could pull a majority of mountain residents out of their poverty, although he placed some hope in restructured, unionized manufacturing and perhaps cooperatively based craft making. The only long-term solution, he argued, was to reorganize the national economy to provide adequate jobs for all.[93]

The *Scribner's* article was just one of many studies that appeared prior to or during the 1930s that analyzed the economic changes that had rocked the southern mountains. Furthermore, tourism was by no means the only development option under discussion, and some observers were aware of the social costs that tourist-oriented development could entail. Although coal, timber, and textile companies had brought severe environmental, economic, social, and cultural costs, it was not clear, even during the tumultuous 1930s, that tourism was inherently better for local populations than more humane industrial or manufacturing development might be.

In any case, the rationales for the Parkway offered by George Stephens and the *Asheville Citizen* were not internally consistent, disregarding persuasive evidence that even if it did boost tourism in the region, the Parkway might not be a boon to the average mountain resident. Thus, at some level the decision to promote the road in this way seems to have resulted less from a wholehearted belief in the Appalachian myths than from a complicated conflation of those myths with a self-interested manipulation of the available competing arguments. A limited-access scenic ridgetop Parkway could neither bring the tourist market to the average western North Carolinian's door nor function as a much needed farm-to-market road. It would instead be most likely to increase tourist travel near established urban centers.

The *Citizen* nevertheless tried to make the case that the Parkway's effects would "diffuse themselves throughout the entire population of this entire region" as a consequence of improved business for existing tourist centers, resorts, and hotels, which in turn would create year-round employment and increased demand for local farm produce. The paper even proposed that the influx of new residents would help by raising mountaineers' property values. Stephens agreed with the *Citizen*'s contention that improvements in the tourist business would benefit everyone, for "the tourist is Western North Carolina's great cash crop."[94]

Yet only certain people in the mountains could profitably grow this crop. Throughout 1934, however, Asheville Parkway proponents continued to conflate the interests of a tourist-oriented business class with those of the masses of mountain residents and to use the plight of suffering mountaineers (portrayed in a way that was likely to resonate with widely held stereotypes) to justify reconstructing the region's Asheville-centered tourism industry. As North Carolina Parkway supporters became increasingly fearful that their route would not be selected, it became more and more clear that the fate of this industry was their central concern. In a June letter to Josephus Daniels, Little Switzerland resort owner Heriot Clarkson wrote with a note of urgency that "this road is either the life or death of Asheville. The tourist trade is the very hope of Asheville and if this road is routed elsewhere, it will hurt Asheville and western North Carolina beyond measure."[95]

THE RADCLIFFE COMMITTEE REPORT
AND ASHEVILLE'S "ACE IN THE HAND"

As Asheville's 1934 Rhododendron Festival opened, the Radcliffe Committee delivered the much-feared fatal blow, recommending the Tennessee-sponsored route.[96] The report was not made public until months later, but someone leaked the news to the Asheville supporters gathered to greet the Washington delegation at the Grove Park Inn on that June evening.

In light of the seriousness of Asheville's economic woes and civic boosters' certainty that the Parkway was crucial to the city's recovery, the North Carolina Parkway enthusiasts did not take this news calmly. Prominent Asheville lawyer Junius Adams, who attended the welcoming dinner, predicted that if the committee's report were accepted, Asheville would be "far worse off than if the Parkway were not built at all. . . . Something must be done, even if we have to go to the length of stopping the Parkway somewhere around the Virginia line. . . . If it is diverted into Tennessee . . . our situation is entirely and permanently hopeless."[97]

In subsequent editorials, the *Asheville Citizen* echoed his sentiments. "Our primary concern here," one piece said, "is not that there shall be a Scenic Parkway, [but] that IF there is a Scenic Parkway it shall be so located as to improve, and not to destroy, our natural advantages on this side of the mountains."[98] Faced with such a prospect, the North Carolina partisans swung into action to appeal their case to Ickes and Roosevelt.

But the North Carolinians had to tread carefully. Several signs indicated that Ickes in particular might not respond favorably to arguments that put too much stress on Asheville's economic situation and history of tourism dependency. While Asheville partisans had been pleased by the Radcliffe Committee's inclination to name the project the Shenandoah–Great Smoky Mountains Parkway and Stabilization Project, Ickes had firmly rejected the title. "I wish," he had written to Park Service officials in February, "that some shorter and characteristic name could be proposed. I especially object to the word 'stabilization.'"[99]

Doubtless mindful of the secretary's views, the North Carolina and Asheville boosters adopted a double-edged lobbying strategy. In the days and weeks after the report's submission, they relied heavily on what Weede later termed their "ace in the hand," the political skills of the influential Daniels.[100] And then, after a new hearing of their case had been assured, they sent in Browning, the most professionally credible spokesperson for their vision.

Daniels, the one Parkway booster with intimate connections in Asheville and Raleigh as well as major influence in Washington, had long pushed for the North Carolina route. Now serving as ambassador to Mexico, Daniels was the former secretary of the navy, the former editor (and still owner) of the *Raleigh News and Observer*, and a longtime supporter of the movement for the Great Smoky Mountains National Park. Daniels had been FDR's superior during World War I, when the future president started his national political career as assistant secretary of the navy, and the two men had subsequently stayed in close touch.

When Daniels arrived in Asheville in June 1934 with his wife and Anna Ickes and heard about the Radcliffe Committee's recommendation, he was furious. Remaining outwardly calm and cheerful, however, he and Browning accompanied Anna Ickes, Cammerer, and several others for two days of travel through the Great Smoky Mountains and back to the Danielses' summer cottage at Lake Junaluska Methodist Assembly. But the Parkway question weighed on his mind, and when Cammerer tried to arrange a fish fry for the group outside Gatlinburg, Daniels insisted that the party return immediately to North Carolina. "I had other fish to fry," he wrote in his diary. "I had promised to speak at Lake Junaluska Sunday morning, and besides I wanted us all, particularly Mrs. Ickes, to see what a parkway to the Park on that [committee-recommended] route would mean. It was so hot part of the way we almost wasted as we stopped to get a cool drink at Newport [Tennessee]." By contrast, he noted, the trip to Tennessee via the North Carolina–supported route had been "cool all the while."[101]

Back at Junaluska, Daniels huddled with Browning on the porch of his cottage as rain fell, plotting strategy. As soon as Anna Ickes left, Daniels scurried to Washington for a meeting with her husband; there, armed with Browning's maps and arguments, Daniels pleaded North Carolina's case directly to the secretary. On 18 June the ambassador had sent an urgent telegram requesting that Ickes postpone a decision on the Parkway route until the two could meet. Western North Carolina Congressmen Zebulon Weaver and Robert Doughton, along with Senator Josiah Bailey and several others, had also conveyed the state's objections. Ickes held a 21 June press conference at which he announced that he would hear from North Carolina partisans six days later. But Daniels's secret visit to Ickes on 25 June was sufficient to produce the sought-after delay in announcing a routing decision, and Ickes canceled the larger hearing in favor of speaking to Browning alone on 28 June. Key to Daniels's tactics was his portrayal of the North Carolina–supported route as the "scenic one" leading to the "natural eastern gateway" to the Smoky Mountains park at Cherokee. The Tennessee route he characterized as driven by "political" considerations. Daniels reported that Ickes agreed with this reasoning and "said he would not stand for any road based on political division." Having won over the secretary, Daniels arranged immediately to see President Roosevelt.[102]

The North Carolinians' connections with the president and the secretary proved decisive. It was not the first time Daniels had gone directly to his old protégé to discuss the Blue Ridge Parkway. The two had a long relationship of mutual trust and respect, and Daniels felt free enough with F D R to address the president in letters as "My Dear Franklin." Meeting with Roosevelt in a sweltering White House office on 26 June, Daniels presented North Carolina's case. "He grasped the whole situation," Daniels confided in his diary, "agreed that the route I urged was the best, and turned to his secretary and said: 'Make a note that I want to see Secy. Ickes about the Great Smoky Mountain National Park tomorrow.' He as much as said that the route I had outlined had his approval." Much relieved, Daniels left the White House and called Ickes: "He was grateful," Daniels reported, that "I had seen the President and that we all three had the same point of view."[103]

What appeared to have been most important to Roosevelt and Ickes was not so much the message but the messenger: someone whom they knew and respected and with whom they shared some history was delivering the by-now familiar arguments of Browning and the Asheville partisans. In the months after the secret conferences, they referred to "the route Ambassador Daniels advocates," as if that were the central fact about it. And the president and the secretary decided to oblige their friend and choose the North Carolina route even before Ickes held his final hearing on the issue in September, a hearing he admitted to F D R had been organized primarily to preempt charges of favoritism sure to erupt when Ickes overruled his own committee. Thus, within a few weeks of the Radcliffe Committee's unfavorable report, the tide again was turning in North Carolina's direction.[104]

The developments of late June, however, remained a closely guarded secret in North Carolina. To prevent an uproar among Tennesseans over North Carolina's backdoor maneuvers, news of Daniels's visit to Ickes and F D R was kept out of the newspapers and was conveyed only to a select few North Carolina insiders (including Weede, Webb, Stephens, Jeffress, and Browning). As Daniels left Washington, Bailey wrote reassuring letters "in strictest confidence" to Governor

Ehringhaus and members of the Asheville group, conveying at first only the cryptic message that "inside information is more favorable than you would imagine from what you have heard."[105]

As this back-channel maneuver unfolded, the pages of the *Citizen* continued to depict the routing battle as a fight for Asheville's life and the Parkway as bringing benefits to both the local tourist industry and the rural mountain poor. "These people," the paper asserted, deserved help because they were "pure American stock." Noting the lack of other large-scale industries or farms in the region, the paper argued that a scenic parkway would employ destitute mountain residents immediately in construction and later in tourist-related service industries while providing a steady market for their products. It would be "the biggest thing that has ever happened or that can be expected to happen for them."[106]

Why such benefits would not accrue to many of the mountain poor if the Parkway were located along the Tennessee-sponsored route was left unanswered. The paper's silence on this issue perhaps revealed Asheville supporters' ultimate concern for local business interests, a viewpoint confirmed in *Citizen* owner Charles Webb's private letters. Not mentioning Buncombe County's rural poor, Webb fumed that it was time "for us North Carolinians to begin to raise a little hell" to get the Parkway. East Tennessee, he noted bitterly, had never catered to tourists and had no "first-class tourist hotels" to compare with those of western North Carolina. "We have spent millions of dollars," he continued, "in building tourist hotels and in advertising Western North Carolina as a tourist center." At a Rotary Club meeting a few weeks later, Webb asked, "Are we going to sit quietly by and let what we have worked for all our lives be taken away from us?"[107]

North Carolina Parkway supporters thus waited nervously through the summer of 1934 for word from Washington and planned their next move. Daniels kept the pressure on with further letters from Mexico City to Washington, keeping Browning aware of his maneuvers.[108]

Ickes went ahead and designated the part of the route from the Shenandoah National Park to Blowing Rock, North Carolina, on which all parties agreed, and announced in late July that a decision on the controversial sections would await the outcome of further hearings in September. Browning dashed to Washington for more private discussions, offering to guide the secretary on a private tour of the North Carolina route. "I can assure you," Browning wrote, "that you need meet no other individual [or] group . . . as I can personally take you through the whole area." A bit disingenuously, he assured Ickes, "I am not acting as a partisan in this matter but simply as an interested citizen anxious to see this great question settled upon its merits." Although Browning was genuinely interested in building the most elegant Parkway possible, he also understood the importance of well-timed personal contacts in furthering what he knew was a political as well as engineering proposition.[109]

A "DREARY LITTLE MILL TOWN": KNOXVILLE AND THE PARKWAY

Partly because both the Radcliffe Committee report and the project's originating momentum favored their route, Tennessee Parkway partisans, though certainly vigorous in pursuit of their case, never worked themselves into a frenzy over the project as did their North Carolina counterparts. But the differences between the two states' levels of enthusiasm for the project also stemmed from differences in what was at stake for each.

Regional geography, the history of the Appalachian national park movement, and the three-state route suggested in early federal planning implied that the obvious city to take the lead in advocating and planning the Tennessee portion was Knoxville. Like Asheville, it was an old, established city (both had been founded in the 1790s) and the largest in the mountainous end of its state (Asheville's population was 51,000; Knoxville's 106,000). Knoxville had a substantial and diverse economic base and was situated about the same distance from the Tennessee entrance to the Great Smoky Mountains National Park at Gatlinburg as Asheville was from the North Carolina entrance at Cherokee. With proximity to the southern end of the Parkway, Knoxville stood to gain both economic advantage and an enhanced public image as the main gateway to the park. City boosters had been very active in lobbying for the Great Smoky Mountains National Park in the 1920s, partly because of the tourism it would channel into the city. City leaders and local businesspeople certainly would have been expected to try to galvanize the public on behalf of the Parkway.[110]

Although city leaders apparently initiated an early lobbying effort in Washington, they did not attempt as broad a public campaign as did Asheville.[111] One reason may have been that none of the proposed Parkway routes would have come closer than about forty miles from Knoxville. The North Carolina route, by contrast, would come right to Asheville's doorstep.

In addition, some Knoxvillians feared that the Parkway's projected ridgetop route would damage a park on which they had been working for a very long time. Support for Great Smoky Mountains park in Knoxville had come from a coalition of business and tourism boosters that included Chamber of Commerce President David C. Chapman as well as a cadre of conservationists whose interest stemmed from more personal, aesthetic, and psychic sources. While the boosters and preservationists had worked together on behalf of the park, their reasons for favoring the Parkway route into Knoxville differed completely. The preservationist group (centered around attorney Harvey Broome, planner Benton MacKaye, and the Smoky Mountains Hiking Club) favored the three-state Parkway route mainly because it did not involve building the road on the ridgetops they wanted to protect. By 1934, in fact, Broome and MacKaye had their sights set on preventing the incursion of more road-building projects into park and wilderness areas and had become focused on creating the Wilderness Society to pursue this agenda. Thus, one of the Knoxville groups most interested in the Parkway was engaged mostly from a defensive standpoint and was not likely to join a large-scale campaign in favor of bringing the road toward Knoxville.[112]

Other reasons for the two cities' disparate dynamics involved important differences between the cities themselves. Knoxville's relatively diversified economy was not tied strongly to tourism. Indeed, by the 1930s, Knoxville had a reputation as a "dreary little mill town" beset with racial and class tensions and other social ills born of years of first growth and then stagnation in the wholesaling, iron making, textile, apparel, furniture, and coal industries that dominated the city. A reader of the *Knoxville News-Sentinel* in the early 1930s would hardly have been aware that a local tourist industry even existed, although the Great Smoky Mountains National Park had been under development for nearly a decade. For Knoxville, the depression brought bank failures, factory closings, population loss, and (as in Asheville) staggering municipal bonded indebtedness. The *News-Sentinel* tried to buoy readers with hopeful tidings: in mid-August 1933, construction of five new business buildings downtown was announced as a "glowing indication to Knoxvillians" that the economic situation was improving. A few days later, news came that a factory to produce barnstorming airplanes was to be built.[113]

The greatest promise for the city's renewal, however, lay in the fact that Knoxville sat in the middle of the greatest New Deal project of them all, the multistate Tennessee Valley Authority (TVA), whose concrete (in both senses of the term) promise dwarfed any potential benefit from the contemplated park-to-park highway.

The TVA was created in May 1933 to bring multipurpose, integrated river basin development to the entire Tennessee Valley river system: agricultural reform, flood control, and public power development, together with the social, economic, and cultural development that would proceed from the synergistic linkages among these broad goals.[114] The project quickly drew fire from private power companies, but in its early days Knoxville leaders saw it as a godsend. Many of the TVA's offices were to be in Knoxville, and its first dam (named for Nebraska Senator George Norris, the TVA's most effective congressional champion) was to be built on the Clinch River only a few miles northwest of the city. Cities throughout the region were invited to build distribution systems for TVA power, cutting themselves loose from expensive private power monopolies.

Knoxville very much wanted in on the deal. "Let power development proceed, and with it the social betterment for the valley," urged a 1 August 1933 *News-Sentinel* editorial, and within days the TVA had leased four floors (more than one hundred offices) of the New Sprankle Building. A job office opened a few days later, and applications poured in at the rate of one thousand per day. Two dozen clerks were hired to handle the applications, and within weeks fifty thousand people had filed. Before the end of the month, engineering tests had begun at the Norris Dam site and the first blasts of dynamite echoed through the Clinch River Valley.[115]

Amid the roar, it would have been hard to discern the quiet movement simultaneously getting under way in the early fall of 1933 to plan a park-to-park highway. Though Tennessee representatives were involved in the October conversations in Virginia Senator Harry F. Byrd's office, whatever might happen on that front was much less compelling to Knoxvillians than the emerging TVA drama. The jobs would be welcome, and city businesses eagerly awaited orders for materials and services, but the overriding aim was to get Knoxville on the TVA power grid. "TVA Sets Low Municipal Power Rates," read a headline in mid-September, and the next day an editorial advised that "a great social test has started—a test to make cheap power lighten the burden of human labor. The TVA rates represent a 'New Deal' indeed for the Tennessee Valley—and the Valley should be quick to accept and to cooperate."[116] The TVA was, therefore, a very large bird in hand, while the park-to-park highway was at best a comparatively small one in the bush.

By November 1933, construction of the Norris Dam was well under way, the TVA's monthly payroll had reached $150,000, and city leaders were pouring all of their efforts into getting a bond issue passed to build a public power-distribution facility. The TVA was front-page news all through the fall. City electricity users, advised that they stood to save a million dollars a year, approved the bond issue by a ratio of two to one in late November, despite a heavy and deceitful campaign of opposition backed by the Tennessee Public Service Company, the local private power monopoly. The *News-Sentinel*'s first mention of what was to become the Blue Ridge Parkway did not appear until a few days later, and it was buried on page 10, much subordinate to an editorial announcing that TVA had rented an entire seven-story building and rejoicing that "Money [is] flowing into the city . . . in payrolls and orders for materials."[117]

Much of the city's attention during the early months of 1934 necessarily focused on efforts to buy out the private Tennessee Public Service Company's interest in city power-distribution facilities and on the infusion of huge sums of public funds to the TVA: $48 million in agency-development funds and perhaps $300 million for its first three dams. Secretary Ickes's late-1933 approval of the Parkway envisioned an initial projected federal expenditure of only $16 million. Indeed, the 1933 PWA allotment for the Parkway amounted to only $4 million.[118]

COMPETING VISIONS FOR THE PARKWAY:
GETTY BROWNING AND STANLEY ABBOTT

As Getty Browning labored through the summer of 1934 to rescue his ridgetop western North Carolina parkway, he confronted head-on the recommendations of Stanley Abbott, the twenty-six-year-old landscape architect the Park Service had hired a few months earlier to manage the project. In simultaneous June 1934 reports, the two men elaborated their quite different visions for the Parkway.

Five days before the Radcliffe Committee issued its recommendations, Abbott submitted to the National Park Service's chief landscape architect, Thomas Vint, (and through him to Cammerer) the conclusions from Abbott's five-month investigation of the competing routes. His report, undoubtedly the basis of the Radcliffe Committee's recommendations, came down in favor of the Tennessee route, with its varied valley and mountain scenery and elevations. In advocating this route, Abbott envisioned the Parkway primarily as a "Park to Park connection" that should thus be "as directional as possible consistent with its location in interesting territory." A Parkway traveler, that is, should "feel that by and large he is traveling on the shortest line between the two Parks." In addition, Abbott favored the varied scenery of the mountain-valley route proposed by Tennessee over the consistently high elevations of the North Carolina route. He also thought that the North Carolina route would be too expensive and damaging to construct.[119]

Abbott clearly assumed that most Parkway travelers would be driving all the way from one park to the other. Motorists, he felt, might "become tired with 500 miles of mountain scenery" offered by Browning's mountaintop North Carolina route, and Abbott argued that "the mountain parkway would not be used by a sufficient number of tourists nor have great enough recreation value to justify its construction." "It is believed," he continued impersonally, "that a mountain or skyline road is distinctly a type to be developed within a park such as Shenandoah National Park and that the idea is not adaptable in this region to a 500 mile Park to Park connection." In conclusion, he suggested that the Parkway might even be built (albeit with scenic features designed in) to accommodate regional passenger traffic, thus combining the paradigms of regular highway and scenic parkway to create a commuter parkway similar to those previously constructed elsewhere in the country. Abbott's rather conservative view thus adhered closely to previous models of scenic but utilitarian parkways.[120]

Browning's vision for the Parkway—more in keeping with dramatically scenic roads in western parks—was much closer to what the Parkway ultimately became than was Abbott's. Browning also had a better sense than did Abbott of the potential public response to such a project. At about the same time as Abbott was submitting his report, Browning mailed to the Radcliffe Committee a lengthy argument for his North Carolina route. In this document as well as in the two routing hearings held by federal officials, Browning articulated his vision for an all-mountaintop, truly scenic Parkway whose main aim was not merely to transport tourists from one place to another but also to present breathtaking scenery along the way.[121]

The fifty-one-year-old Browning, an avid outdoorsman and locating engineer with many years of experience considering alternative highway locations, called the Parkway "one of the most worthwhile engineering fetes [sic] of modern times." He described the spectacular sights to be seen at each juncture and the feasibility of construction along the route he proposed. Stunningly high peaks, distant views, dense woodlands, and stands of flora such as rhododendrons and laurels interested him most, and he argued that a ridgetop parkway would enable thousands of nonhikers to enjoy what he and other outdoor enthusiasts had seen. He argued passionately that "no where else in the United States, so far as I know, could such an excellent location for a parkway be found, if splendid scenery, high elevation, profusion of beautiful shrubbery, favorable climatic conditions, reasonable construction cost and accessibility from all sections of the country are to be considered." In contrast to Abbott, moreover, Browning thought that summer visitors seeking the coolness of high altitudes would be disappointed "to find [the Parkway] following the narrow, hot valleys at low elevations, when they might just as well have had the advantage of the cool, beautiful mountain route." "Shall the Parkway be just another highway," he asked the committee, "or shall it be a really outstanding, beautiful driveway through the most delightful and attractive country that the whole region affords?"[122]

As the summer of 1934 drew to a close, federal officials faced the fundamental challenge of choosing between Abbott's favored undulating, peaks-and-valleys Tennessee route and Browning's ridgetop North Carolina path. In determining

Photograph taken at Asheville-Hendersonville Airport, 19 June 1935, immediately preceding a flight over the route designated for the Parkway across western North Carolina. Many of the major early players in Parkway development are pictured: (*left to right*) Thomas Kesterson, Tennessee Valley Authority pilot; B. A. Batson, regional road engineer in the Tennessee Valley Authority's Land Planning Department; E. B. Abbuehl, landscape department of the National Park Service; William M. Austin, engineer from the Bureau of Public Roads; George Stephens, Asheville developer; R. Getty Browning, chief locating engineer, North Carolina State Highway Commission; and Stanley W. Abbott, resident landscape architect, National Park Service. Courtesy Robert C. Browning.

what travelers would see, the choice would be at least as important as the later (and much more often commented upon) landscape design.

THE FINAL HEARING: WASHINGTON, SEPTEMBER 1934

Ickes was tempted to take Browning up on his offer to guide him secretly through the North Carolina mountains, but the secretary of the interior was also mindful of Tennesseans' rising complaints of favoritism. Thus, he elected not to take a tour prior to his final hearings. Instead, he arranged for an August reconnaissance visit by a friend, forester Robert Marshall, who would soon become one of the founders of the Wilderness Society and who was not likely to be sympathetic to the North Carolina route as a consequence of his opposition to wilderness and ridgetop roads.[123]

In spite of cryptic private assurances emanating from Daniels's secret work, Asheville partisans spared no expense in preparing for the hearing. Newspapers throughout North Carolina reprinted pro-Parkway editorials supplied by the Citizen-Times, and the Chamber of Commerce drummed up support among civic clubs and citizens throughout the western part of the state. "The fever is hot," gushed Weede, who reported never before having seen residents of western North Carolina "so aroused and so united as they are on this matter." The Chamber chartered a train to ferry 240 "prominent citizens" (mostly business, civic, and political leaders) to the hearing and reserved ten rooms and a parlor in the Mayflower Hotel for the visitors' use. On hearing day, nearly four hundred cheering North Carolina supporters crowded the Interior Department auditorium. Tennessee likewise sent a trainload of partisans, making for a much more boisterous and public second hearing than the one in Baltimore seven months earlier. Despite Ickes's pleas that the standing-room-only crowd hold its applause, the rowdy groups cheered and clapped as their representatives rose to speak.[124]

North Carolina's top political leaders — Governor Ehringhaus and the state's senators and representatives — headed up the delegation. But the Asheville Chamber's Weede and Stephens prepared the state's ninety-minute presentation. And when the plan was announced, only ten minutes were allotted to Ehringhaus and only five to each congressional leader. North Carolina's hopes, and a full hour of the state's presentation — were entrusted to Browning. With newly drawn relief maps, charts, and a long pointer, Browning again put forward his vision for an all-mountaintop Parkway in place of the mountain-and-valley one proposed by Tennessee. Most presciently, unlike others who thought of the Parkway merely as an attractive means of connecting the two national parks, Browning argued that it was likely to become an attraction in itself. "This parkway is so long," he speculated, "that a great many people will probably not drive from one end to the other, so we thought that every mile of it ought to be located as carefully as possible."[125]

After Browning finished, four other speakers presented — more succinctly and more pointedly than they had in Baltimore — the remainder of Asheville's case. Citizen editor Robert Lathan, aided by Congressman Doughton, made the economic arguments, continuing to conflate the interests of the Asheville tourist industry with those of ordinary mountain citizens. He again insisted that subsistence farmers ("living back in the coves of those mountains" and "as patriotic a people as there are in the world") had the most at stake and would gain from jobs in craft making and sales of farm products. "These people live along that mountain, that is their home," he said, again deploying the stereotype. "[They] will never be at home elsewhere and you cannot take them to the industrial sections and keep them there. The only way to help them is to give them employment and the only way to do it is to bring the development to them. You cannot take them to the road, you must bring the road to them."[126]

But the North Carolina supporters could not afford to keep the focus on the cove residents for long, because even if the Parkway would help such people, the fact that they were spread throughout both western North Carolina and eastern Tennessee meant that their plight offered in itself no clear rationale for any particular route. Lathan therefore returned quickly to the Asheville boosters' central concern: "Our fear is that if this parkway leaves Asheville out of the picture, if we are 60, 70, or 40 miles away from it . . . we will be off the main stream, and instead of our condition being bettered, we feel it is going to be made infinitely worse."[127]

Then it was Tennessee's turn. Its delegates arrived far better prepared than they had been in Baltimore, with more concrete proposals, clearer justifications for their varied-topography route, and calmer rhetoric backed now by the investigations and recommendations of the Radcliffe Committee. That committee's report had never been made public, and the North Carolina partisans had yet to see it. To the North Carolinians' dismay, however, Tennessee's speakers had obtained a copy, and they used it to their advantage, arguing that the committee's investigations had been thorough and careful and that its suggestions ought to be followed. Bolstered by the report, Tennessee's representatives portrayed their position as fair and reasonable, emphasizing their state's willingness to share the Parkway while characterizing their sister state's efforts to monopolize the project as "selfish and greedy." Perceptively, one Tennessee congressman pointedly accused the North Carolinians of being concerned not with the national or even the broadly regional interests at stake in the project but only with the welfare of the city of Asheville.[128]

In a brief submitted along with their presentation, the Tennesseans bolstered their position further with a conciliatory proposal for a fork at the western end of the parkway to give entrances to the Great Smoky Mountains Park in both states. They argued with some merit that the North Carolina partisans had overstated the economic destruction that would befall Asheville were the Parkway to follow the Tennessee route. Responding to Asheville's argument that Knoxville and east Tennessee already had the TVA, the brief noted—just for good measure—that both Asheville and nearby Hendersonville had opposed building a contemplated Norris-like dam on the French Broad River.[129]

The brief also capitalized on the logical weakness of the North Carolinians' assertion that their proposed route would most help "cove dwellers." "The Tennessee route," the brief admitted, "does not traverse a region now provided with elaborate and costly tourist hotels and commercial highways." But, it continued, that route "does . . . provide innumerable desirable camp-sites and would be of inestimable value in providing the small mountain farmer with a new means of livelihood, and a new contact with people from other parts of the United States. We believe this latter feature would be of great benefit to both the traveler and the mountaineer. It is highly desirable that they know each other better."[130] Regional reconstruction through cultural exchange was not perhaps the strongest argument, but it was at least novel.

In spite of their outward confidence going into the hearing and the real strengths of their case, especially from engineering and scenery standpoints, the North Carolina delegation (with the exception of Browning) left the hearing shaken by Tennessee's presentations and particularly by that state's use of the Radcliffe Committee report. The North Carolina delegation subsequently backtracked, notifying N PS director Cammerer and others in Washington that North Carolina would be satisfied with a looped or forked Parkway that would serve both east Tennessee and western North Carolina (and include Asheville and most of North Carolina's desired route). Such an arrangement would, it was expected, be acceptable to the Tennesseans as well as to the Radcliffe Committee, which had mentioned that option in its report. In the days after the hearing, the North Carolina delegation also discussed other compromise routes in private meetings with Ickes, Cammerer, and other Park Service and Interior Department officials.[131]

This negotiating and backtracking again revealed the North Carolina partisans' central concern with the financial recovery of the city of Asheville and especially of its tourist sector. As the situation turned critical, their other arguments faded into the background. Above all, Asheville had to be on the route. Even Cammerer's suggestion to include Asheville but to exclude the rugged and breathtaking scenery of the Pisgahs and Balsams to the west in favor of a shorter and less scenic route into the park encountered a favorable response. "I told Cammerer," Charles Webb elaborated melodramatically to Josephus Daniels, "that if . . . the Parkway [is] located in Tennessee, as recommended (without a fork near Asheville), our tourist business would be destroyed." Lathan put it even more baldly to Ickes: "In pleading for a location of the Parkway which will serve this region, we are pleading for nothing less than the right to live."[132]

Browning seems to have been almost the only North Carolinian who did not panic in the wake of the hearing. He believed that the state's presentation had been effective, and he was confident that Ickes favored North Carolina's route. "I am not discouraged in the slightest," he told Daniels. "I believe that we are going to win."[133] Browning's confidence may have arisen from having been in particularly close touch with Ickes and Daniels in the wake of Daniels's June visit to Washington, perhaps giving him a firmer sense of the commitments that had been made by Ickes and Roosevelt. Browning empathized with Asheville business leaders' economic worries, but he had no personal stake in the Asheville tourism industry and more personal and professional interest in the proper location of the Parkway from an engineering and aesthetic perspective. He therefore approached the question with a broader view than that of the Asheville leaders, who by this time had succumbed to some of the "fairness" arguments they had earlier ridiculed among the Tennesseans.

Browning's vision for the Parkway prevailed in a follow-up brief submitted to Ickes under Governor Ehringhaus's signature a week after the hearing. According to the brief, the project

> belongs neither to Virginia, Tennessee, nor North Carolina. It is a national project and . . . must be in keeping with national, not local, desires and needs. . . . We cannot believe that the gentlemen who composed [the Radcliffe Committee], having once started along the crest of the great watershed and attained the high altitudes and the magnificent scenery that it presents, and the easy grade and alignment afforded by its gradually undulating surface, would have abruptly departed from this natural highway and laid out a route across the barriers of streams and gorges to seek the scenery of a few outstanding mountains, when scores of higher peaks lay along the course upon which they had started, unless they felt constrained by some sense of duty to place a part of the route on one side and a part on the other side of the State boundary line.

Although the brief went on to mention Asheville's economic situation and the possibility of a forked parkway, those concerns were buried at the end by Browning's confidence that his vision of a mountaintop parkway would prevail.[134]

That confidence proved well founded. Browning may have known the details of the assurances Ickes and Roosevelt had given Daniels or may have trusted in the ultimate irresistibility of North Carolina's scenery. Whatever the case, the other North Carolina supporters need not have worried as the fall of 1934 drew to a close. Ickes had long since decided what course he would choose. "As I think you know," Ickes assured the ever-vigilant Daniels after the hearing, "you and I see eye to eye with respect to this scenic parkway." In another letter, the secretary of the interior wrote, "I think I have succeeded in keeping every one quite in the dark as to what my own feelings are with respect to this parkway, and that I shall attempt to do until after the [November] election." Thus reassured, Daniels sent calming missives to his friends in Asheville, but with the election still several weeks away, the other North Carolinians were left to bite their nails while awaiting a final verdict.[135]

Asheville likely would get what it wanted, but whether that result would in fact be the best way to spread renewed prosperity to either Asheville proper or to the surrounding mountains was another question.

TOURISM VERSUS INDUSTRY AS A
DEVELOPMENT BASE IN THE LAND OF THE SKY

While the Asheville partisans had always portrayed the routing decision as a life-or-death matter, Asheville's situation was not in fact as dire as they suggested. The city certainly was in deep economic trouble, and the problems adversely affected the large hoteliers and resort operators as well as small farmers in the surrounding region who had found markets for their products in hotels and restaurants. But, contrary to the assertions of Weede, Webb, Stephens, and their colleagues, tourism was not the only game in town.[136]

In fact, the depression-induced decline in tourism in the region known since the late nineteenth century as the Land of the Sky marked the beginning of a transition to a more diversified and ultimately healthier and more resilient economy than the city had in its past and than many other counties of western Carolina would have in the years to come. According to Alex Tooman's economic study of tourist development in western North Carolina and eastern Tennessee, the lull of the 1930s, which ended the era of grand hotels and highly affluent tourists and delayed the growth of an automobile-driven, middle-class-based tourism economy, in effect opened a window for other industries to come into the region. Although many of these industrial jobs paid relatively low wages, they did provide an employment alternative to the tourism that so preoccupied Parkway partisans.[137]

The largest of the new plants was the Netherlands-based rayon producer American Enka, which opened in 1929 and by 1934 employed 2,500 people, almost all of them drawn from the surrounding rural areas. The same year, as the Parkway battle unfolded, about 1,300 people were making cotton blankets at Beacon Manufacturing in nearby Swannanoa. Sayles-Biltmore Bleacheries, established in 1927 to finish and dye cotton and rayon, employed another 475. Other large plants in the area by the early 1930s included the huge Champion paper mill in Canton, just a few minutes west of Asheville, which had begun operations in 1906 and employed more than 1,600 people by 1934.[138]

Moreover, even after the Parkway arrived, Asheville's tourist industry did not regain its pre-1930 proportions for decades, largely as a result of stringent restrictions imposed on the city's borrowing power in the wake of the disastrous 1920s boom. The region's other industries continued to grow, however, and by the late 1940s, according to Charles Webb, employed enough people (more than twelve thousand) to support nearly fifty thousand citizens, a figure close to the city's total population.[139]

Thus, from the 1930s collapse until at least the early 1970s, when tourist-oriented development began to accelerate again, tourism did not dominate Asheville's economy as it once had, providing no more than about 6 percent of total employment. While this figure was higher than the percentage supplied by tourism-related jobs in most surrounding counties or in the rest of the state, it also occurred, according to Tooman's analysis, in the largest and most diverse county economy in the North Carolina mountains, a situation that mitigated the tourist industry's ability to dominate the city's economic picture. In some sense, therefore, the crash of the 1930s ultimately facilitated growth of a healthier, more diversified local economy, while the Parkway's economic benefits turned out to be less dramatic than its partisans had predicted, partly because of the short duration of most travelers' visits.[140]

Slowly emerging data thus suggested that a continued slump in tourism might not mean prolonged economic depression. But many of Asheville's Parkway partisans were so heavily invested — both emotionally and no doubt financially — in the Asheville of the large hotels, rapid population growth, affluent tourists, and the fast-paced development of advanced city services tourists demanded that they could not interpret the data. In any case, the advent of the Great Depression brought that golden era of Asheville's history to an abrupt end. Nevertheless, the city's business leaders seemed unable to envision any future for Asheville other than one bound up in tourism.[141] Although Asheville had industries other than tourism, it neither had been dominated by industry nor thought of itself primarily as an industrial city. Moreover, for all its drawbacks, tourism spared the city the smoke and crowding that afflicted other industrial towns. Thus it seemed particularly galling to Asheville's boosters that an unattractive city such as Knoxville might steal Asheville's trademark business.

Finally, on 10 November 1934, the long-awaited word arrived: overruling the Radcliffe Committee, Ickes adopted North Carolina's route. Unexpectedly, there was no compromise, no sharing, no fork, and no loop, just a complete victory for the North Carolina cause. Tennessee would get no Parkway; North Carolina would get nearly 250 miles, with the remaining 220 going to Virginia.[142]

Employing arguments presented by the North Carolinians in their months of lobbying, Ickes cited several reasons for his decision: even without the Parkway, Tennessee already had the western entrance to the Great Smoky Mountains National Park at Gatlinburg; the North Carolina route was higher, cooler, and more scenic; and he was reluctant to "destroy a long-established business and lay waste economically a section that, by its initiative and energy, has built itself into a commanding position as a tourist area."[143]

Tennessee's Parkway supporters were, of course, incensed. The "Tennessee people are terribly mad and are threatening all sorts of opposition and obstruction," *Citizen-Times* company president Webb reported, adding that Senator McKellar and perhaps other members of Knoxville's pro-Parkway community might appeal directly to President Roosevelt. When they did so, however, Roosevelt told the Tennesseans firmly that he supported Ickes's decision and "that it was going to stand." A Knoxville *News-Sentinel* editorial a few days later called Ickes's decision "disappointing" but accepted it (somewhat naively) as "the result of a clash of honest opinions of disinterested parties." Ickes, the paper assured readers, was an "honest and fearless administrator." The paper enjoined Knoxvillians to "take this defeat gracefully" and expressed confidence that many of the benefits of the road would flow to Tennessee regardless of the route. Governor Hill McAlister admitted philosophically that probably nothing could be done about the decision.[144]

Asheville's Parkway supporters rejoiced. The "Dawn of [a] New Era for This Section," the *Citizen* called it, and city business leaders lined up to praise the ruling. Revealingly, the *Citizen*'s first articles in the wake of the announcement focused almost exclusively on the Parkway's promise of boosting the tourism business, making little mention of the road's potential to provide public works jobs for unemployed cove dwellers. In addition, most of the published postdecision commentary came from the city's business and political leaders, while little reaction was reported from either average Asheville residents or small farmers, many of whom would be dramatically affected by the arrival of the Parkway yet had been largely mute throughout the discussion of the new project. Their wishes and needs had played almost no part in the decision to encourage such development.[145]

As a consequence, the *Citizen*'s front-page headlines announcing that the Parkway decision was "Hailed as Great Victory by Entire State" and that "People Here Receive News with Delight" must be taken only to mean that certain sectors of the population in North Carolina and in Asheville welcomed the news in this way. Webb gushed that the decision "literally insures the growth and prosperity of this section," while Stephens promised that the Parkway "gives permanent and increased value to our tourist development." The "people" quoted as being delighted included a stream of business leaders: hardware merchant, former mayor, and Chamber of Commerce President Ottis Green; the president of the First National Bank and Trust; the vice president of Wachovia Bank and Trust; the president of the Asheville Real Estate Board; the managers of the Grove Park Inn and other large hotels; and the president of the Asheville Merchants Association.[146]

Subsequent *Citizen* editorials predicted that the Parkway would be an unalloyed blessing to western North Carolina; an editorial from the nearby *Hendersonville Times-News*, reprinted in the *Citizen*, made the central point: "The building of [the Parkway], like the development of Smoky Park, is a great tourist enterprise; and in the first place, Park and parkway are a commercial proposition."[147]

On the day after the announcement, the *Citizen* buried on an inside page a small article noting that the Parkway "Will Need Labor." Of the leading Parkway supporters quoted in the newspaper that day, only state Parkway committee chair J. Quince Gilkey mentioned the project's potential to provide work relief. Thus, if the Parkway represented a "godsend for the needy," it did so almost by accident. Although Asheville partisans had often cited the needs of the rural poor, it was clear by the end of the battle that the disadvantaged groups' plight had been mentioned mainly in the service of the urban elite group's cause.[148]

The celebrations that followed Ickes's decision masked critical political issues that would arise as Parkway construction got under way the following year. As the state initiated land acquisition and local landowners began to understand the large amounts of land that the scenic highway would require and the restrictions that would be placed on their use of the new road, it became evident that the project was not without significant costs to certain segments of the mountain populace. And if the Asheville-based partisans had overlooked those immediate costs, they had also failed to address the much more serious long-term question of whether encouragement of further tourist-oriented development in the North Carolina mountains would bring the benefits they predicted.

In her early and prescient book, *The Spirit of the Mountains* (1905), Emma Bell

Miles criticized the effects of tourist development in the southern mountains. She knew that the hospitality industry was already causing cultural and economic dislocation in east Tennessee and that the influx of tourists would bring mostly menial, low-paying jobs. She feared that mountain people would jump at these jobs as "an easy way of making money" and that cherished ways of life would erode. She did not chastise mountain people for being drawn to work in the tourism industry, but she warned that "too late the mountaineer realizes that he has sold his birthright for a mess of pottage. He has become a day laborer, with nothing better in store." Seasonal tourism employment provided only a "semblance of prosperity," she reminded her neighbors; it would disappear each winter, leaving "a broken people in poverty and despair."[149]

Studies undertaken in the 1930s and subsequently confirm Miles's concerns and raise serious questions about the economic, social, and cultural costs and benefits of tourism development. Several of these studies contested the possibility that tourist-related development alone could provide the uniform prosperity that the Asheville Parkway enthusiasts expected.[150]

Long-term trends confirmed these early analyses. In 1975, the North Carolina Public Interest Research Group released a study of the impact of recreational development in ten mountain counties (not including Asheville's Buncombe County). The report concluded that growing recreational development had served primarily to increase the proportion of lands in the hands of fewer and fewer absentee owners. Resort development offered "very little in the way of significant economic gains for the counties," with each major resort employing an average of only twenty-five people and with tourism-related employment comprising only a relatively small percentage of any county's total.[151]

Similarly, Tooman's 1995 study of the historical evolution of tourism and its effects on social welfare indicators (per capita income, median family income, seasonal unemployment rates, income distribution, measures of "social dependency," schooling changes, and infant mortality rates) in the North Carolina and Tennessee mountains emphasizes tourism's "significant limitations in bringing about improvement in well being for native residents." Tourism, Tooman argues, "does not constitute a viable stand-alone industry but rather offers beneficial supplemental income within a more diverse economy." Tourism alone, he concluded, "has serious limitations as a cure for underdevelopment especially if rapidity of economic improvement is desired. Ironically it is more effective in an environment where it is least necessary."[152]

Not the success of the tourism industry but rather its precipitous depression-induced decline and sluggish recovery ultimately created an opening in which

Asheville could develop a healthy, diversified economy in the years after the Parkway battle. In Buncombe County, such a diverse economy provided a base for a higher level of social welfare than that which prevailed in surrounding areas. The slow rebirth of tourism in this context permitted that industry to supplement rather than dominate the city's increasingly prosperous economy.[153] So while the 1930s did indeed begin a new era for Asheville, it was not the era the Asheville business community had anticipated, and it arose in spite of their efforts to reinvigorate the golden era of tourism.

Tooman's findings also call seriously into question the likelihood that a tourist-oriented development project such as the Parkway could significantly boost the economies of the more rural counties along its route. Although most of the counties he studied in far western North Carolina did not lie directly along the Parkway, his conclusion that tourism unaccompanied by high levels of development in other industries has been inadequate to raise mountain counties' living standards implies that the Parkway by itself was unlikely to dramatically alter the economic picture in areas outside of Asheville.

THE SCENIC IS POLITICAL

It is important, of course, not to overstate the power that Asheville's Parkway partisans ultimately wielded over the course of economic development in the western North Carolina mountains. It is also crucial to note that in spite of the highly political debates that surrounded Parkway routing, aesthetics ultimately played an important part in the location. As Ickes made clear, had the North Carolina route not also offered beautiful natural scenery, it would have been illogical to locate the Parkway in those areas. And even as they rushed to tout the new Parkway's hoped-for economic benefits for their city and region, the Asheville supporters acknowledged the assistance that the imaginative and visionary State Highway Commission engineering team (especially Browning) had provided to the cause by developing an all-mountaintop route that could have been supported on its aesthetic merits alone.[154]

Present at every stage of the negotiations, Browning remained confident throughout that his vision of the Parkway would eventually persuade Secretary Ickes. Time and again Browning had insisted that "good engineering is good politics" and that "a road properly located speaks for itself."[155] But in truth, even Browning did not wait for the Blue Ridge Parkway as he envisioned it to "speak for itself." Following the initial rejection of his route by the Radcliffe Committee (proving that scenery alone would not win the day), Browning realized that getting the Parkway built according to his vision would require him to promote it politically. So with patience and confidence, he planned, strategized, traveled, talked, drew maps, considered every angle of the highway's possible impact, lobbied influential people, sent pictures and other personal mementos to Interior Department and PWA representatives, appealed to the officials at two hearings with lucid and persuasive rhetoric based in his intimate knowledge of the project, and supported his arguments with dramatic graphic representations. In the end, his diligence paid off, his vision prevailed, and the resulting Parkway was stunningly beautiful.

Unlike many of his colleagues in the Parkway battle and unlike many more recent commentators on its history, Browning realized that the proposal for the Parkway was neither unproblematic nor uncontroversial. Many competing agendas and interests had to be balanced to pursue a project that he saw as a great democratic endeavor that would offer millions the chance to see natural wonders previously only accessible to those with his vigor. As the Parkway routing battle shows, "the Scenic" (as local residents came to call it) was political from the outset.

Nowhere would the political conflicts over distribution of the project's costs and benefits and the class and cultural fissures from which they sprang be more apparent than in the acquisition of land for the Parkway, handled in North Carolina by Browning's office. Only when this effort commenced in earnest in 1935 were views solicited and heard from most Asheville citizens and the surrounding mountain landowners. The land-buying process, like the routing battle, called on Browning to juggle—perhaps more sensitively than any of the other major Parkway players—the complex array of public and private political, ethical, cultural, environmental, economic, and aesthetic concerns. Browning faced the conundrum of always trying to choose a route that would, as he wrote, "be fair to all and at the same time insure the best location for the Parkway."[156] This task often was nearly impossible.

3

WE AIN'T PICKED NONE ON THE SCENIC
PARKWAY IDEALS AND LOCAL REALITIES

In January 1937, S. A. Miller, a farmer and small landowner in heavily rural Ashe County, North Carolina, took up his pen and in neat, flowing script, wrote a letter to Franklin Roosevelt asking the president to help with a problem with the "Park to Park high way." The right-of-way "goes through the middle of my farm [and] takes 20 acres" out of it, Miller explained, splitting his modest 70 acres into two parts. To make matters worse, "the state don't offer me the worth of my land, not counting the damages anything—They have ruined my spring and take all of my wood. They just offered me $5.50 dollars and said they would not give any more." This land, he continued, "is good land, and better than some, along the Blue Ridge Parkway, that they have payed big prices for. . . . Maybe some people would say," Miller went on, "that the land on the Blue Ridge isn't any good [but] we people have made our support on it and it is some good to us." The Parkway, by contrast, "isn't any benefit to us according to what they tell us. We aren't allowed to put any buildings near it and not even cross it to our land on the other side." Declaring his undying support for the Democratic Party, Miller concluded plaintively, "Will you please write me. And tell me if I am wrong. And what for me to do."[1]

On four pages of lined notepaper, Miller summed up some of the most important issues that arose in the process of land acquisition for the Parkway, which got under way in early 1935, immediately after Interior Secretary Harold L. Ickes resolved the routing controversy. The questions Miller raised about the distribution of Parkway costs and benefits—land requirements, impact on neighboring lands, settlement payments, and access and use—generated conflicts in place after place from the project's earliest days. Indeed, issues surrounding land—its acquisition, protection, manipulation, and management—have been and remain the central problems of Parkway development.

Given that a major purpose of the Parkway is to reveal beautiful scenery to the traveling public, it is not surprising that management of what came to be more than eighty thousand acres of land has generated such contention. What is surprising is that most discussions of the Parkway, its history, and its lands focus solely on the beauty of the surrounding topography and the ways that landscape architects created the stunning vistas—the landscapes, both distant and near, that attract Parkway visitors. As a result, the perdurable but only partly truthful story of the creation of the Parkway is primarily a tale of how landscape designers (preeminently Stanley Abbott) "painted with a comet's tail" on a large geophysical canvas, laying the Parkway "lightly on the land."[2] The stories of the many S. A. Millers who had to try to hang onto the comet's tail have had virtually no hearing.

The truth is that the Parkway's appearance today has as much to do with the resolution of essentially political conflicts with and among local citizens over Miller's issues as with landscape architects' work of placing the Parkway "lovingly . . . on the face of the earth." The Parkway's physical form ultimately inscribed on the land many elements of the region's complex political history and sociocultural system, reflecting the markedly unequal power of various individuals and groups of citizens to affect the project's development. Furthermore, its elongated design (with a nearly twelve-hundred-mile boundary and nearly five thousand adjacent landowners and neighbors) magnified its impact beyond what is suggested by the number of acres involved.[3] Because it is a narrow ribbon stretching 469 miles through twenty-nine Appalachian counties with differing social and economic conditions, its character necessarily changes along the way, quietly telling many stories of this region to those who know where to look.

On the ground, the politics of the Parkway's development have played out in two ways. First, some political choices were inherent in the Parkway's design. Adoption of a scenic parkway (rather than a conventional highway) model invoked certain class and cultural biases and influenced the distribution of costs and benefits. The resulting right-of-way requirements and access regulations carried the seeds for nearly all the battles that flared with affected landowners.

Second, the particular sociopolitical contexts into which the Parkway came shaped the implementation of the parkway model. Political conflicts over the impacts of Parkway design standards constrained planners' ability to implement the Parkway vision. As Parkway development played out in particular state and local contexts, as various individuals and groups worked to influence the project toward their ends, the resulting conflicts and compromises got written onto the Parkway landscape.

Miller understood how these interrelated processes affected him in the specific context that was Ashe County, North Carolina, about thirty miles south on the Parkway from the Virginia line. As the states bought land for the Parkway, he and other landowners along the route came to see that constructing a limited-access scenic road with a wide, protective right-of-way differed substantially from constructing a normal public highway. The benefits of such a road, landowners such as Miller came to realize, would be unevenly distributed. For their part, he and other small landowners would neither find the new road to be of much immediate practical use nor directly reap whatever long-term tourist-related economic benefits ensued. Instead, the rewards of increased tourist traffic would flow most directly to well-established, larger tourist operators and to towns and cities such as Asheville rather than to small farmers and other landowners trying to enter the tourism business.

It is no coincidence that Miller wrote from Ashe County, a place of about twenty-one thousand souls lying on the Blue Ridge's western slopes about 110 miles northeast of urbanized Asheville by way of the Parkway but a world away in terms of local needs, economic development, and sensibilities. Just as Buncombe County was a seat of Parkway boosterism, Ashe County—along with its neighbor to the east, Alleghany County—was a center of substantial small-scale opposition to the Parkway throughout the 1930s as well as of a piercing critique of the tourist industry during the 1960s.[4]

As the owner of seventy acres in a rural county where 95 percent of the land was in small farms (averaging just over sixty-three acres each), Miller typified landowners in the county, which borders Virginia on the north and Tennessee on the west. With land values averaging twenty-six dollars per acre in 1930, he had reason to complain about a five-dollar-per-acre offer. In addition, with only five hotels, restaurants, and boardinghouses listed in the 1930 census, the county did not have anything like the tourism infrastructure of other Parkway counties such as Buncombe or Ashe's nearer neighbors, Watauga, Wilkes, and Surry. Buncombe County, with only 60 percent of its land base in farms, reported nearly eighteen hundred such businesses, while Watauga had fifty and Wilkes and Surry more than one hundred each. Nearly 9 percent of Asheville's workers had jobs in tourism, while in Ashe County the figure was 0.1 percent. Miller's trenchant critique of the Parkway project arose from the involved county with the smallest percentage of tourist-related businesses.[5]

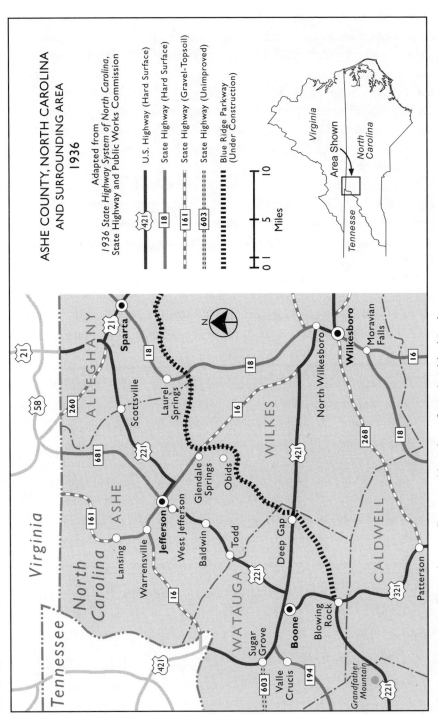

Ashe County, North Carolina, and surrounding area, with roads, 1936. Map by Michael Southern, based on official State Highway and Public Works Commission map.

Although he may not have realized the significance of the fact, Miller's residence in North Carolina rather than Virginia was also important. Landowners in North Carolina found the state asking for much more land and imposing more strictly the stringent Parkway standards than did landowners in Virginia. The different ways in which Parkway land was acquired in the early years in the two states illustrated the different outcomes possible on the landscape depending on whose needs were most obligingly accommodated. North Carolina's almost complete compliance with ideal (noncommercial, wide right-of-way, restricted access) Parkway standards produced a gorgeous and well-protected Parkway but was hard on landowners and led to many protracted conflicts. Virginia's resistance to consistently implementing the ideal represented in part a greater sensitivity to landowner concerns but resulted in a Parkway with a narrower protective right-of-way and many more interruptions — entrances and crossings created at the request of landowners.[6]

As the Parkway's costs and benefits sorted out during the land-acquisition and -management process, social fault lines that had begun to crack open during the Asheville boosters' battle to bring the Parkway to the Appalachian region yawned ever wider. Tremors small and large rumbled through the mountain region, and they — as much as topography or the work of landscape architects and engineers — molded the Parkway landscape.

THE LAND AND PEOPLE OF THE PARKWAY REGION

As much as ideas, ideals, visions, plans, and regulations had to do with how the Parkway came to be and look, they do not by themselves explain why conflicts large and small emerged. One also has to comprehend a myriad of local factors, circumstances, personalities, and details.

The 469-mile roadway threads through widely varying topography. The land at Humpback Rocks, the Peaks of Otter, Mabry Mill, or Volunteer Gap, Virginia, differs visibly from that at Doughton Park, Grandfather Mountain, Richland Balsam, or Cherokee, North Carolina. Beyond topography, however, the social and cultural geography (and related economies) of the Parkway's subregions shaped the road by determining the conflicts that emerged in building it. All of these factors affected how and to what degree the ever-shifting Parkway ideal could be implemented in specific places. Most importantly, these intraregional differences make clear that the Parkway came not into a region of generic "mountains" and undifferentiated "mountain people" but into a chain of subregions of widely differing character.

For 355 of its 469 miles, the Blue Ridge Parkway does indeed follow the Blue Ridge Mountains. It then turns in the vicinity of Mt. Mitchell, North Carolina, into the Black Mountains and across several other transverse ranges that protrude at right angles to the Appalachians' generally southwesterly course. In general topographical terms, the Parkway can be divided into three major sections: an undulating area north of Roanoke, Virginia; a rolling plateau from Roanoke south to about Blowing Rock, North Carolina; and a much higher, more visually dramatic, and rugged ridgetop stretch from near Grandfather Mountain south to the Great Smokies.

From the point where it connects to the Skyline Drive at Shenandoah National Park at Rockfish Gap, near Waynesboro, Virginia, at an elevation of about 1,900 feet, the road runs for its first hundred miles near the crest of the Blue Ridge Mountains that separate the eastern Piedmont from the Great Valley. Although elevations through this section average 2,500 feet, the altitude fluctuates as the road plunges near milepost 64 to its lowest point (649 feet) at the crossing of the James River before climbing thirteen miles later to its highest Virginia peak, Apple Orchard Mountain (3,950 feet). Near milepost 110, travelers pass Roanoke, where the Parkway lies about 1,500 feet above sea level as it follows the western slopes of the Blue Ridge across the Roanoke River Valley. Leaving Roanoke, it then traces the eastern rim of Blue Ridge plateau through the rolling farmlands of southwest Virginia. This section, too, averages 2,500 feet and offers visitors breathtaking distant views to the east from Smart View and Rocky Knob, but it lacks the dramatic heights that characterize the section north of Roanoke.

At milepost 216.9, the road enters North Carolina, still following the Blue Ridge south to Ridge Junction (milepost 355, near Mt. Mitchell), where it leaves the Blue Ridge for the spruce and balsam forests along the rugged and steep Black Mountains, Great Craggies, and, beyond Asheville, the Great Balsams. Elevations along this final section average 4,650 feet north of Asheville and 2,230 feet through the French Broad River Valley skirting Asheville's southeast side; higher elevations (some above 5,000 feet) prevail from Mt. Pisgah to Cherokee, where the road descends to enter the Great Smoky Mountains National Park. In this section west of Asheville, the Parkway reaches its highest point (6,047 feet) at Richland Balsam.[7]

Influenced by the topography, the Parkway's cultural landscape changes along the route as well, despite the popular image of a homogeneous rural and agricultural Appalachia. The 1930 Census illustrates vividly the differences Parkway builders encountered when they began moving dirt in the fall of 1935.[8]

Within each state, how did Parkway counties compare with non-Parkway ones in 1930? In Virginia, the counties through which the Parkway ran tended to be more white, less densely populated, and more rural and agricultural than the state as a whole. And despite the popular image of the Virginia mountains as a tourist destination, rates of employment in tourism reached only a little over half their statewide levels. Similar differences existed in North Carolina, although the gulf between the mountains and the rest of the state in several respects (except racial composition) was not as pronounced. North Carolina mountain counties as a whole were a bit more thinly populated (fifty-four persons per square mile compared to sixty-five statewide) and significantly more white dominated than was the state as a whole (94 percent white versus 70 percent statewide). The percentage of the land area devoted to agriculture (63 percent) in the mountains nearly matched that of the rest of the state (64 percent). Even so, the mountain counties were substantially more rural (91 percent versus 75 percent), and a higher percentage of workers (51 percent versus 44 percent) labored in farming. However, the percentage of workers in the Parkway counties who held jobs in tourist-related work (1.6 percent) was nearly as large as the percentage statewide (1.9 percent).

Aggregate figures for the Parkway counties mask internal differences, however. Both Buncombe County, North Carolina, and Roanoke County, Virginia, contained major urban centers (Asheville and Roanoke), and population densities in those counties were consequently much greater (144 persons per square mile in Buncombe and 120 in Roanoke) than they were elsewhere. In these urban counties, furthermore, the percentages of land devoted to agriculture were smaller (about 60 percent in both) and the percentage of citizens working in farming was drastically less (16 percent in Buncombe and 20 percent in Roanoke).

Comparing the seventeen North Carolina Parkway counties with Virginia's twelve also reveals several striking demographic and economic differences. Most obviously, North Carolina as a whole was growing much more rapidly than Virginia, with people pouring into its already more densely settled mountain region. In 1930, thirteen North Carolina Parkway counties had more than forty persons per square mile, compared to only four in Virginia. North Carolina Parkway counties, like the rest of the state, were growing, while Virginia's were losing population. Indeed, more than half of Virginia's Parkway counties had lost population in the 1920s, while only three of North Carolina's had done so. Virginia's mountain counties were, however, more racially diverse: five had black populations exceeding 10 percent, while only one North Carolina county (urbanized Buncombe) did so.

Despite North Carolina's greater population density, population in the Parkway region in both states remained heavily rural (over 90 percent). Land use differed, however. While just over 63 percent of the land in North Carolina's Parkway counties was in farms, 74 percent of that in Virginia was. More than half the land was in farms in eleven of Virginia's twelve Parkway counties but only in twelve of North Carolina's seventeen Parkway counties. Virginia farms also tended to be larger (averaging eighty-four acres to North Carolina's sixty) and more valuable (thirty-five dollars per acre to North Carolina's thirty-one dollars). A higher percentage of the populace worked in agricultural occupations in Virginia's Parkway counties (56 percent) than did so in North Carolina (51 percent).

Nevertheless, an agricultural economy remained much in evidence as the Parkway crossed from Virginia into northwestern North Carolina, where nearly 80 percent of the land in each of the first five counties (Alleghany, Surry, Ashe, Wilkes, and Watauga) was in farms and those farms employed nearly 70 percent of the workforce. By the time the Parkway reached its highest elevations (in its last four counties southwest of Asheville), however, less than 57 percent of the land was in farms. In two counties (Transylvania and Swain, where large parts of the Cherokees' lands were concentrated), farms covered less than 30 percent of the land. In the final two (ruggedly mountainous Jackson and Swain) more than 50 percent of the people worked in farming, but only because overall population density was so low. Swain County was suffering the greatest population outmigration of any North Carolina Parkway county: 12 percent of its citizens left during the 1920s. It also had the lowest per-acre land value (nineteen dollars).

Somewhat less tied to agriculture, North Carolina's mountain residents were more likely than Virginia's to work in either manufacturing or tourism (recreation, hotels, restaurants). In six of North Carolina's Parkway counties, manufacturing accounted for more than 15 percent of jobs, while this was the case in only three of Virginia's counties. Mountain Virginia's manufacturing was much more concentrated in the Roanoke metropolitan area, however, while North Carolina's was dispersed through many of its counties. In Roanoke, manufacturing far outranked tourism as an employer (23 percent versus 4 percent). In Asheville, by contrast, approximately 9 percent worked in each area. Though Roanoke's population of sixty-nine thousand was nineteen thousand larger than Asheville's, nearly twice as many Asheville's worked in hotels, restaurants, and boardinghouses and the percentage of the population engaged in such work was double that of Roanoke. Finally, tourism in western North Carolina was fairly dispersed throughout the region (as it had been since the nineteenth century) but was most heavily concentrated in three counties including and surrounding Asheville (Buncombe, Henderson, and Transylvania). A majority of Virginia's tourism industry was concentrated in counties from Roanoke north.

Within such an enormously varied context, state and federal officials began buying thousands of parcels of land, strung together in a nearly five-hundred-mile swath stretching through twenty-nine counties in two states, that would be required for the Parkway.

How Much Land?

Officials in charge of designing and building the Parkway through a populated landscape were venturing into uncharted waters. No previous parkway had approached the length or shared the exact goals of this one. No clear standards existed for how much land such a purely recreational parkway should take to protect what Stanley Abbott called the "unspoiled natural surroundings" and scenery from the "parasitic and unsightly border development of the hot-dog stand, the gasoline shack, and the billboard." A large roadside buffer clearly was in order. But in early discussions among state and federal officials and in the public press in 1933 and 1934, it was not clear how much land would be required. What was undeniable was the potential for significant direct impact on large numbers of landholders and businesses.[9]

Two features of the "elongated park" (a term used from the 1930s on) distinguished it from a regular highway and increased the amount of land required: its wide right-of-way and the even larger "recreation areas" that bulged out here and there along the route. These features increased land requirements far beyond those of typical 1930s highways, which usually had only a sixty-foot right-of-way. By 2004, the Parkway owned 80,214 acres outright (that is, in fee simple), 45,625 in North Carolina and 34,589 in Virginia.[10]

From whom and under what terms did the Parkway obtain this land? Well over half of it was purchased outright by either the state or federal government from private landowners. By the late 1970s, the state of North Carolina had provided nearly twenty-three thousand acres, while Virginia had purchased and donated nearly fifteen thousand. The rest has come from private donations or from the U.S. Forest Service (through whose lands more than 180 miles of the Parkway runs), which had as of 2004 deeded over fifteen thousand acres to the Parkway. Just over half of the land (forty thousand acres) was acquired prior to 1943. The state-run land-acquisition phase mostly concluded in the early 1960s, but federal legislation enacted in 1961 has allowed the National Park Service (NPS) to continue to purchase adjacent lands to protect views and natural and cultural resources, provide recreational opportunities, and improve safety by closing dangerous crossings and access roads.[11] In additional, conservation organizations also have recently bought lands to protect Parkway views.

Early in the Parkway's history, the states also purchased "scenic easements" on perhaps fourteen hundred acres in addition to lands bought outright. Scenic easement lands remained under private control while the Parkway bought the right to restrict the uses to which such lands could be put. Even before World War II, however, a Parkway staffer concluded that easement lands cost almost as much as fee-simple purchases and that enforcing easement restrictions was so difficult as to render the mechanism "most unsatisfactory." The scenic easement was, therefore, mostly abandoned by the 1940s.[12]

The use and later abandonment of scenic easements was emblematic of the fact that before World War II, Parkway development was dominated by a shifting series of policies through which planners worked out the parameters of an unprecedented project. By the end of the first decade of construction, however, the road's key design features were in place: a wide right-of-way, limited and controlled access, and exclusion of commercial vehicles.

In the early years of Parkway development, therefore, landowners along the Parkway found themselves entangled in a bewildering array of regulations emanating from several state and federal agencies. The states of North Carolina and Virginia were handling land acquisition along the right-of-way, while the N PS, aided by funds from the Resettlement Administration, was acquiring acreage for the five initial recreation areas. To further confuse matters, the Bureau of Public Roads (B P R) was in charge of construction and placed the work on the ground in the hands of private contractors. Such division of responsibility—combined with ever-shifting plans for the right-of-way, recreation areas, and access—created fertile ground for landowner frustration.[13]

Small Landowners and Small Parcels

Overall land-acquisition policies and figures alone do not capture either the magnitude or the exact nature of the Parkway's impact in specific places. The dispersal of its land takings in small parcels through twenty-nine counties, the road's tendency to divide and take only part of each owner's lands, and strict restrictions on use of the road by adjacent property owners magnified the project's impact.

The far larger Great Smoky Mountains National Park took most of its five hundred thousand acres from eighteen timber and mining companies and about eleven hundred small landowners. In contrast, the Parkway's roughly twelve-hundred-mile boundary came to adjoin lands owned by between four thousand

and five thousand different individuals. Data available from some sections suggest that the total number of landowners from whom land was taken may have exceeded the figure for the Smokies, even though nearly 40 percent of the Parkway's mileage passed through National Forest lands.

Along several of the Parkway's more populated segments, an average of five owners per mile saw their land taken. Seventy parcels had to be bought to build a single eight-mile section between Boone and Blowing Rock, North Carolina, during the 1940s. Along the thirteen-mile section (2-D) through Ashe and Wilkes Counties where S. A. Miller's property lay, the state of North Carolina obtained land from approximately eighty owners. Section 2-B (stretching only about eight miles through Alleghany and Wilkes Counties) was compiled from lands belonging to about thirty-five owners. Similarly, along the nine miles of Virginia section 1-S in Floyd and Patrick Counties south of Roanoke, about thirty-five owners were affected.[14]

Right-of-Way

Of the three key Parkway design features (right-of-way, limited access, and noncommercial use), planners had the most difficulty deciding on the width of the right-of-way. Early Parkway enthusiasts as well as all early press reports talked of a two-hundred-foot right-of-way. The initial proposal sent to Secretary Ickes from the committee of interested North Carolina, Tennessee, and Virginia citizens, however, called for a twenty-foot-wide road protected by a one-thousand-foot right-of-way. In approving the project, Ickes noted that the states had agreed to acquire "rights of way 200 feet in width where this Parkway crosses other than Federally owned lands." During the year following Ickes's authorizing memo, the press throughout the Parkway region cited this figure as definitive.[15]

Shortly after receiving the green light for the project, however, leading officials at the NPS began to think more ambitiously about the Parkway's land needs. In January 1934, an NPS regional engineer suggested to director Arno B. Cammerer that scenic easements should extend control beyond the two-hundred-foot right-of-way to limit "unsightly stands and buildings" and roadside signs. In July 1934 the NPS's right-of-way engineer made a detailed case to top officials for a one-thousand-foot right-of-way to be "adopted as a means of furnishing a satisfactory basis to begin the creation of that which may develop into a system of National Parkways."[16] Thus, as the North Carolina/Tennessee routing controversy raged throughout 1934, NPS planners were pushing for a right-of-way—or, at the least, for easement control—far wider than that being reported to the public.

By midsummer 1934, Ickes had agreed to require a minimum two-hundred-foot of right-of-way and as much as one thousand feet in cases where the extra expense would not be prohibitive. He directed that in cases where fee simple acquisition was not possible, scenic easement control be extended over the lands beyond the two-hundred-foot right-of-way. Both the N PS and the B P R adopted this policy as they issued their first official standards for right-of-way acquisition in August 1934.[17]

This policy underwent continual adjustment throughout the fall, changing in early 1935 from an absolute requirement to a more flexible one hundred acres per mile in fee simple, augmented by fifty acres per mile in scenic easements to allow for variations in topography and property lines. The new standard moved toward firmer federal control over a large expanse of Parkway lands, reducing the reliance on scenic easements. Applied uniformly, it would have translated into approximately 825 feet in fee simple and another four hundred feet in easement. At no point, however, was the right-of-way to fall below two hundred feet. By 1940, problems of enforcing development restrictions on lands that remained in private hands had generally induced the N PS to give up the idea of scenic easements. Through the first five years of Parkway development, one early N PS staffer recalled, "the right-of-way picture was one of constant jacking up of the standards."[18]

This "jacking up"—implemented without substantial public discussion, without publicity in the regional press (which was reporting very different information), and with little input from the states involved—complicated the land-acquisition process for state officials, who had originally agreed to the two-hundred-foot right-of-way. It also came as a shock to landowners who had read about the original standards in the press. These behind-the-scenes developments assured that the land-acquisition process would be far more controversial than some early Parkway supporters had expected. North Carolina Representative Robert L. Doughton, for example, had predicted confidently that land acquisition would be simple, with many property owners expected to donate the rights-of-way.[19] But those who had such expectations were in for a rude awakening.

The shock was greatest to landowners in North Carolina, where state leaders implemented the enlarged Parkway ideal more fully than did Virginia. Several factors, including different road-building histories and a generally lower level of enthusiasm for and engagement in the Parkway project among Virginia state officials, lay behind the divergent levels of commitment to the wide right-of-way. But as longtime Parkway superintendent Sam Weems later remembered, North Carolina's more enthusiastic embrace of the new standards ultimately derived from a single individual: "The difference between the broad right-of-way in North

Carolina and the stingy right-of-way in Virginia," Weems recalled, "is attributed to Getty Browning's interest in this Parkway." As Browning later remembered, "We realized very early that a greater width was necessary in order to properly insulate the parkway."[20]

Influential as he was, Browning could not have achieved such a result single-handedly. After ten years of aggressive bond- and tax-funded highway construction, North Carolina had a proud reputation as the Good Roads State, and many state leaders certainly recognized the Parkway's importance for enhancing tourism. Passage in 1931 of a law bringing an additional forty-five thousand miles of secondary roads into the state system gave North Carolina the largest state-maintained road system in the nation, a distinction it held into the 1990s. The consolidation, improvement, and expansion of the system proceeded despite the darkening depression as the State Highway Commission's available operating funds (now allocated more to maintenance than new construction) continued to increase, making it the state's wealthiest agency.[21]

With a decidedly pro-tourism bent, prohighway policies in place, and a still-increasing highway budget, North Carolina readily settled on acquiring 125 acres per mile in fee simple and little to no scenic easement acreage, thus adopting the concept of a wide right-of-way completely under federal ownership.[22] The good news was that North Carolina's enthusiastic embrace of the Parkway project produced a well-protected parkway in that state. But the bad news was that this policy also ensured that more conflict over land would take place in North Carolina than in Virginia.

While the matter of right-of-way width was quickly resolved in North Carolina, years of wrangling in Virginia meant that the early land-acquisition program there was, as a Parkway landscape architect later remembered, "really in a mess." From 1935 until at least 1939, construction languished as a consequence of the state's inability to furnish what federal officials considered a sufficient right-of-way. Five years into the project, the *Roanoke World-News* fretted that the state's failure to convey sufficient right-of-way lands might soon result in a diversion of Parkway appropriations to North Carolina. A year later, the *World-News* decried the "lack of cooperation between the State government and the Federal government" in building the Parkway in Virginia. The Park Service, the *World-News* asserted with some justification, "makes arbitrary and frequently changing demands," while the State Highway Department "regards these demands as unreasonable and extremely costly." As a result, "while both sit back and glare at each other, the public suffers, and a vast improvement promised as far back as 1933 remains at a standstill."[23]

The problems in Virginia developed in part because of latent conditions there. While "business progressivism" drove state-sponsored infrastructure and educational improvements in North Carolina beginning in the 1920s, Virginia was characterized by a more fiscally conservative "cautious progressivism." North Carolina approved and issued bonds to fund the 1920s expansion of its state road network, but Virginia citizens defeated a similar plan in 1923, opting instead for an increased gasoline tax.[24]

A leading opponent of bond financing for roads, Harry F. Byrd, was elected Virginia's governor in 1925. Byrd had long professed support for road building (especially in rural areas) as long as construction was funded through gas taxes and tolls. Under his leadership, Virginia, like North Carolina, took over maintenance of all state roads, created a highway trust fund, and built a state highway system. Without bond revenues, however, Virginia's road building fell far behind North Carolina's. As the depression descended, the "absence of a broader social conscience and an unwillingness to spend" limited Virginia's capacity to aid its citizens either through road building or by other means. Under Governor Byrd, his biographer concludes, "economy became another word for stinginess." As the New Deal opened, Byrd went to Washington as a senator and proved to be one of the Parkway's earliest proponents, but Virginia's policy makers retained the penurious Byrd's pay-as-you-go outlook for decades to come.[25]

The views and politics of other individuals also mattered. Not having had to fight for their Parkway miles, Virginia state leaders had not been whipped into the North Carolina–versus–Tennessee frenzy. Virginia officials only hesitantly embraced the Parkway, while Virginia State Highway Commission head Henry G. Shirley seemed hamstrung by restrictive state land-acquisition laws and was, according to at least one news report, overloaded with other duties. Stanley Abbott later recalled that Shirley posed the "greatest hurdle" the NPS faced as it approached right-of-way acquisition in Virginia.[26] Shirley's personal engagement in the Parkway project certainly did not match Getty Browning's. While Browning spared no effort to produce a spectacular Parkway, Shirley appeared most focused on the difficulty of wedging this unusual project into his existing road-building apparatus. And Shirley had no one on his staff who matched Browning's expertise, commitment, and passion.

In addition, however, Virginia officials rightly felt somewhat misled about Parkway requirements. Virginia had agreed, Shirley reminded BPR officials in 1935, to a two-hundred-foot fee simple right-of-way, but scenic easements were added, and "now they ask [for] 100 acres to the mile which will be something like 800 ft. . . . There is no possibility of getting any such width through Virginia."

Working through the first year to buy land on the basis of the original plan of two hundred feet (the maximum permitted by a 1934 Virginia law), Shirley felt certain that he had no legal basis for condemning more. Still, Shirley pledged cooperation with the effort to get an additional eight hundred feet in scenic easements and soon asserted that he had secured agreement from perhaps 70 percent of the first property owners through whose lands a two-hundred-foot strip had already been purchased. In early 1935, however, he informed Ickes that legal authorization did not permit a guarantee of the one-thousand-foot width through all the Parkway lands. Ickes responded that work in Virginia would not proceed without this guarantee.[27]

It was clear by the spring of 1935 that Virginia, like North Carolina, would need additional laws to permit acquisition of the widened swath of lands (whether in easements or fee simple) now required. Virginia's governor rightly worried, however, that blanket adoption of the wider standard would unduly burden valley farmers. Shirley, too, remained uncommitted to the wider right-of-way, particularly if it were taken in fee. In the fall of 1935, he said that the best he could do would be to buy the two-hundred-foot strip and try to obtain easements on either side. In the view of an NPS official, however, Virginia remained "unalterably opposed to a fee simple right-of-way in excess of 200 feet."[28]

By late 1935, a compromise began to emerge. A bill pending in the state legislature would allow condemnation of wider easements. Seeing that it was unlikely that Virginia would ever adopt unmodified the one hundred acres per mile in fee/ fifty acres scenic easement standard but trying to push Shirley's team away from relying on scenic easements, Park Service officials convinced him and his colleagues (who were finding easements unexpectedly expensive to buy) to rewrite the bill to allow the Highway Commission to condemn either eight hundred feet of additional scenic easement or (preferably) a smaller amount of additional land in fee simple as a protective buffer. The law passed in February 1936 despite what Shirley called a "storm of protest."[29]

Soon thereafter, Abbott and his staff began providing Virginia with land-acquisition plans that indicated the fee taking that NPS would accept in lieu of the eight hundred feet of easement. Abbott's office eventually wrote guidelines for the amounts of fee taking that could be substituted for the wider easements in woodlands, poor farmlands, and good farmlands, allowing for topographical and local variations.[30]

Still, Virginia seemed bogged in legal complications not present in North Carolina. Virginia's attorney general questioned in 1937 whether the Highway Commission or the Conservation and Development Commission had authority to acquire the land beyond two hundred feet. It took yet another state law in 1938 to vest this right clearly with the Highway Commission. In the midst of all of the negotiations and despite the progress that had been made, Abbott hesitated to convey "the impression that the Virginia right-of-way program is thoroughly satisfactory." In Virginia, he later recalled, "We settled for less."[31]

But as the Roanoke newspapers reported in 1937–38, even after the contorted right-of-way negotiations were settled, turnover of lands proceeded only sluggishly. Ickes threatened to suspend construction and reappropriate Parkway funds to North Carolina. Wrangling persisted into 1939, when Roanoke newspapers reported that federal officials shared blame for the delays. This assertion angered the Parkway staff, who advised top NPS officials that "this business of the State's using the public press to blame some one else for something that is largely their fault should be checked at once before this gets into a general cat and dog fight. It is so complicated that the public could never appreciate just what is involved."[32]

Two States and Two Ways of Buying the Land

After BPR and NPS engineers and surveyors flagged the exact route of the Parkway and informed the states of the lands desired, initiative shifted to the states for acquisition. However, the two states had starkly different highway-building cultures and enabling laws.[33]

Although legislation passed in the 1930s in both states allowed Parkway right-of-way lands to be seized through eminent domain, the situations were not functionally equivalent. North Carolina's swift transfer of title to the federal government offered many advantages (most importantly, certain protection of lands and a quick start to construction), while Virginia's slower process gave individual landowners greater consideration. But both systems contained the seeds of frustration and obstruction on the part of unhappy landowners in North Carolina and from unhappy NPS planners in Virginia.

In North Carolina, lands changed hands rapidly. To obtain a parcel, a State Highway and Public Works Commission official simply posted a map in the appropriate county courthouse informing landowners that the Highway Commission had "this day appropriated for use as a Federal Parkway the land described in this set of maps." Thus, at the moment the maps were posted, the lands became the property of the state and could be transferred quickly to the federal government. In practice, however, as Browning later related, "Almost invariably the people along the route were well informed that their land was being taken before the maps were posted."[34]

A rather cold statement that accompanied the maps informed landowners that they had the right to compensation. But trying to get this compensation mired owners in tedious negotiations that could drag on for years. If landowners filed claims, Highway Commission representatives would investigate and attempt to reach settlements. Landowners who disagreed with the judgments had until six months following the completion of construction on the land to petition the local superior court for an appraisal. That appraisal was performed by a board of three "disinterested" county landowners—a category that, given the complicated local politics of land acquisition, would necessarily have few members—who would determine the amount of damages the landowner should receive. If within twenty days either the state or a landowner objected, the case would go to a jury; otherwise, payment would be made. The process gave state officials power to take needed lands rapidly and decisively, but it also complicated the inauguration of construction while annoyed landowners awaited payment and final arrangements for their lands.[35]

In Virginia, however, title to a parcel could not be transferred until compensation had been agreed upon. Rather than simply posting maps in the courthouse, highway officials had to do field surveys, make arrangements for access, and appraise land before opening purchase negotiations. Landowners, for their part, could either accept a negotiated agreement with the state or force condemnation proceedings into the courts (a process undertaken by fewer than 15 percent of Virginia landowners).[36]

This system delayed construction and allowed some landowners to strip property of timber before the state could take control. In an urgent 1937 letter to Abbott, a Parkway landscape architect complained of an "epidemic of timber cutting" that had commenced along sections of the Parkway south of Roanoke: "It seems that as soon as a survey of a parcel of woods is completed, the owner decides that he had better get the timber off while he still is able to." Faced with NPS complaints, Virginia highway officials "have always contended there is nothing they can do as long as the land is still in possession of the owners."[37]

Recreation Areas

Further complicating land acquisition and compounding the possibility for conflicts and protest was the Park Service's plan for large recreation areas providing gas stations, gift shops, coffee shops, and camping, hiking, and picnicking at intervals along the highway.[38] Development of such areas impinged on many landowners who doubtless did not expect to be touched by the project and confused the land-acquisition process by bringing federal officials (in addition to the state right-of-way agents) onto the scene to negotiate for direct federal purchase of lands.

Lands for recreation areas came into federal hands through three main avenues: a depression-era arrangement that allowed direct federal purchase of lands with funds from a Resettlement Administration program for converting "submarginal" agricultural lands to other uses; transfer from the U.S. Forest Service; and donations by private individuals. Land for most of the major North Carolina recreation areas came either via private donations (the Moses H. Cone mansion and lands, the Julian Price Memorial Park, and the Linville Falls park) or by transfer to the NPS of National Forest lands already in federal hands (the Crabtree Meadows, Craggy Gardens, and Mt. Pisgah parks). The acreage for two North Carolina parks—Cumberland Knob on the Virginia–North Carolina line and Doughton Park (originally known as the Bluff) on the border of Wilkes and Alleghany Counties further south—was bought with Resettlement Administration funds. In Virginia, the NPS purchased lands for three large areas—Smart View, Rocky Knob, and Pine Spur—under the Resettlement Administration program. The Peaks of Otter area was assembled during the 1930s by direct (and fairly amicable) federal purchase of private lands and transfer of Forest Service lands.[39]

While the general notion that the Parkway should be widened at certain points to provide recreational opportunities had been discussed by FDR, Secretary Ickes, and NPS director Cammerer as early as late 1933, the first concrete plans did not emerge until a year later. Nineteen recreational parks (on lands to be purchased with federal funds) were soon approved as part of the first Parkway "master plan," although only four—two in each state—were well under way by the end of the decade.[40]

To justify recreational area development, Abbott argued that existing parks and National Forest areas would be unable to handle the volume of traffic expected along the Parkway. Furthermore, recreation area land purchases could be used to preserve "outstanding areas" that had been damaged by careless farming, deforestation, or commercialization. "Few of the show-places of the Parkway environs remain in an unspoiled natural state," Abbott observed, emphasizing "the need for public purchase and restoration if the area is to regain its one-time attractiveness." In addition, he noted, facilities for gasoline, food, and lodging could be provided in such areas.[41]

Over the years, as many as fifty-three recreational areas were proposed; of those, however, only thirty-one were developed, seventeen in North Carolina and fourteen in Virginia. They ranged in size from a few dozen acres to nearly fifty-five hundred acres at North Carolina's Doughton Park. Even at the sites that were developed, ambitious plans for inns, lakes, swimming areas, and other features devolved into considerably more modest facilities.[42]

At Virginia's Otter Creek recreation area, for example, a 1944 plan proposed an "elongated water feature park": a lake, swimming beach, and bathhouse, complemented by picnic grounds and a coffee shop. New plans in the 1950s called also for a gas station, camping areas, trails, and a lodge near the proposed lake. In the end, however, the park never materialized, leaving only a gas station (later removed), small restaurant, modest picnic area, creekside trails, and a mosquito-friendly campground.[43]

At other spots, such as North Carolina's Richland Balsam, Abbott's 1936 plan suggested that twenty-five hundred acres might be obtained on which to build a lodge, camping and picnic areas, and a service station. Though the area was, Abbott wrote, "in a sad state of repair" as a result of timbering, reforestation and cleanup could render the spot—with its splendid views of the Great Smoky Mountains—a "worthwhile" recreation stop. In the end, however, the area offered only a hiking trail and parking overlook.[44]

The gradual evolution of the plans for Parkway recreation areas indicated the experimental nature of the project and the planners' and supporters'—as well as the broader public's—incomplete vision of what the Parkway would entail. These changes also reflected the real challenges—such as the city of Danville's push for a hydroelectric dam that derailed plans for a recreation area at the Pinnacles of Dan on Virginia's stunning Dan River Gorge—of putting a comprehensive Parkway vision into place on the ground.[45] Some of the most perennially vexing challenges arose out of negotiations with the many hundreds of individual landowners from whom parcels (usually fairly small) were bought.

Landowners' Issues

In both states, landowners all along the road were frustrated by poor communication about land takings, low offering prices or delays in reaching settlements or sending payments, ever-changing demands and standards, and clumsy handling of forced relocations. Some of the problems undoubtedly are unavoidable in any large public works project, but some avoidable ones resulted from confusion about the parameters of this particular project and from state mishandling of parts of the process.

Troubles over land acquisition in North Carolina emerged early on out of the State Highway Commission's failure to communicate clearly, directly, and quickly with affected landowners. From 1935 to 1937, the commission apparently relied primarily on the posted maps to inform landowners of their rights and responsibilities as their land was being taken. As late as 1937, some landowners apparently still did not understand how much right-of-way the Parkway would require. Such official insensitivity raised landowner anxieties and opened a rift between the state and the NPS, which recommended more direct communication with landowners. Commenting on a complaint he had received from a property owner named Bare, an NPS engineer observed that until the service had stepped in to investigate, "there has been nobody in this region, or at least to see Mr. Bare, to explain the parkway project and negotiate for the purchase of the necessary parkway lands." He noted impatiently that "with regard to the Parkway, the policy of the State seems to be to keep the property owners uninformed." A lawyer working with Parkway residents similarly reported that although construction had begun, "people whose property and homes are involved tell me that no one has ever approached them or given them any information as to what they might expect."[46]

Realizing the critical role that state right-of-way agents played in keeping landowners' goodwill, NPS officials in the summer of 1936 admonished land representatives to explain to owners the details and purposes of land purchases. Agents "should never be curt and intolerant of simple questions asked by natives," taking care to act and behave in ways that would help create "a satisfied and sympathetic group of neighbors for the parkway project."[47]

Abbott concurred, suggesting that in addition to posting maps at the county courthouses, North Carolina officials should send letters about planned land acquisitions to all affected property owners. Browning agreed that "the owners are very hazy in regard to the method by which title has been taken to their property [and] they do not understand . . . why so much land is taken." He prodded his staff to speed up contacts with affected owners. But the magnitude of the undertaking was daunting. One of the Highway Commission's staff estimated in 1936 that along the fifty-seven miles of Parkway from the North Carolina/Virginia line south, at least two contacts with each owner would be needed—a total of nearly six hundred contacts. In 1937 the commission finally published an informational pamphlet for landowners that Browning hoped "would result in a better feeling on [the landowners'] part, and . . . make it easier for us to handle the claims with them."[48]

In Virginia, the initial problems had less to do with failing to notify people than with having to explain constantly changing standards to landowners. The state's reluctance to adopt the wider right-of-way standards entangled the land-acquisition department in two rounds of negotiations with many owners along several sections south of Roanoke. A few days before Miller had mailed his letter of complaint to the president, Frazier E. Kelley, a farmer whose family had been in

Floyd County, Virginia, since 1840 and who stood to lose about sixteen acres to the Parkway, wrote to FDR that "as a tax payer and a small land owner, I am writing you for advice and protection of my small home." Already, he explained, "I sold the government a strip 200 feet wide throgh [sic] my land for to build a Road on." Now, "they want 800 feet more and they don't want to pay me but $15.00 per acre."[49]

Floyd County, not surprisingly, had in 1930 the smallest number of hotels, restaurants, and boardinghouses (ten) of any of Virginia's Parkway counties and was in the section of the Parkway in Virginia with the lowest percentages of employment in tourism-related industries (0.5 percent for Floyd, Patrick, Carroll, and Grayson Counties, the four Virginia Parkway counties nearest the North Carolina line). Like North Carolina's Ashe County, Floyd County was completely rural, with most of its land in farms and most of its people working in agriculture. While average farm sizes there were somewhat larger than in Ashe County (ninety-five acres versus sixty-three), average per-acre valuations, according to the 1930 Census, were slightly lower (twenty-two dollars compared to Ashe's twenty-six).[50]

As Miller's and Kelley's letters suggest, landowners in both states resisted the low valuations put on their lands and the limited compensation offered for the inconveniences the Parkway caused. The lands in question on his farm, Kelley noted, had cost him one hundred dollars per acre. Worse, the latest taking "cuts of[f] what I have left from water." Forty-eight years old and "very near disabled to work," Kelley asked for help in getting "what I paid per acre and a reasonable damage on what is left so I can buy me land some where els[e] to live on and support my family." "Please," he implored the president, "answer this at once and let me know what you can do for me."[51]

The states had considerable interest in paying as little as possible for Parkway lands. With the state under the control of fiscally conservative governors throughout the 1930s, North Carolina officials pressured the Highway Commission to hold down payments for Parkway lands. During the first year of Parkway land acquisition, tightfisted Governor J. C. B. Ehringhaus had worried about the problem of high settlement claims. "I hope you will not think it improper for me to suggest," he wrote to North Carolina Senator Josiah Bailey, "that there should be as little publicity about this question of acquiring the rights-of-way as possible, in view of the fact that such publicity invariably excites the cupidity of those who have lands to sell." Ehringhaus consequently argued that "the less publicity we have about rigid Federal right-of-way lines the better for us on our end of the matter."[52]

For its part, the commission hid details of financial settlements for fear of driving up prices. One commission claims adjuster wrote to Browning in 1937 that "the information in regard to the cost and estimated cost of Parkway lands is confidential and should not be made public. . . . It will greatly hinder the settlement of claims for property owners to be able to compare the settlements and proposed settlements on each project. [This] information [should] be withheld until all claims have been settled." The adjuster explained candidly three years later that "our policy has been to adjust the claims for the lowest priced land first and then to reach the larger claims in order that the higher prices will not effect [sic] the first adjustments."[53]

Prices paid for lands varied greatly over time and space as land-acquisition officials dealt with the demands of small farmers, timber companies, tourist operators, and a Native American tribe. Prices reflected topographical considerations and usage-related market value as well as intangible factors such as the relative power and influence of landowners. Recognizing variations in the current uses of future Parkway lands, in 1935 the NPS staff issued guidelines for paying landowners. "Cultivable land" would bring between eight and forty dollars an acre, depending on its quality, while "grazing land" should command between six and twenty-five dollars an acre. "Cutover land and timber land" would bring between one and five dollars an acre, exclusive of any merchantable timber on the property, which would be appraised separately. Within each range, the land's hilliness, soil type, drainage, and accessibility would help determine the exact price. Browning reported in 1938 that land-acquisition costs to his state had ranged from five dollars per acre for cutover timberland to more than two hundred dollars an acre for "highly developed meadow land." By late 1939, North Carolina's average payment per acre for the approximately fourteen thousand acres acquired was about thirty-seven dollars, including payment for improvements (homes, barns, and other buildings).[54]

The per-acre average crept up as a result of North Carolina's settlements with two influential and powerful landowners along the middle section of the state's part of the Parkway, the Linville Company (owners of the Linville resort and Grandfather Mountain) and the Switzerland Company. By 1941, North Carolina had paid an average of forty-five dollars per acre for land itself (fifty-eight dollars if improvements were included), and three years later, North Carolina had spent about $1.28 million (including land costs, planning, and legal fees) for just over fifteen thousand acres. Land costs including improvements comprised about $1 million of this figure, resulting in a per-acre average of about sixty-seven dollars.[55]

Average land costs in Virginia appear to have been similar, but, as in North Carolina, huge variations occurred among owners. On Parkway section 1-s through Floyd and Patrick Counties, for example, tax valuations of land bought for the

Parkway ranged from about $2.50 to $5.25 per acre. But purchase prices for land along this section between 1936 and 1938 ranged from $11 to $200 per acre, with a majority of owners getting $40 or less. Further south, in Carroll County, Parkway lands had cost the state an average of more than $90 per acre by 1940. The slightly more than ten thousand acres Virginia had purchased by 1943 had cost just over $818,000 (including court costs, survey and planning costs, and payments for lands), of which land purchase costs (including improvements and damages paid to owners) amounted to about $560,000, or about $56 per acre.[56]

Because of the large variations, however, averages fail to tell the whole story. Ashe County Superior Court records for 1938–40 document many settlements that approached one hundred dollars per acre. Here, North Carolina highway officials' fears of a snowball effect caused by informed and somewhat more organized cooperation among landowners — apparently orchestrated by a local attorney — produced an avalanche of perhaps forty suits in which landowners rejected the sums initially offered after courthouse maps were posted in late 1935.[57]

By 1937, the claims adjuster handling land settlements in what he termed this "built up area" that seemed to be moving toward more intense tourism and second-home development worried about the large awards the local appraisers were making to owners who had filed these suits. "The Commissioner," he wrote to Browning, "appears intent on allowing the Plaintiffs in each case practically as much as [they] had asked for, paying no attention to values or to testimony or to statements made by representatives of the . . . Highway Commission." The attorney handling the cases, the adjuster continued, repeatedly alleged that "practically the entire farm or tract of land was destroyed because of its being cut off from access to the road." In one dispute involving three acres of easement lands and a relocated local road, the commissioners awarded ten thousand dollars. At this rate, he concluded, "it would not take these Commissioners long to pay off the entire bonded indebtedness of Ashe County."[58]

When these cases reached Superior Court, however, the Highway Commission and most landowners had settled by consent for approximately one hundred dollars per acre. Still, landowners' frustration spilled forth. In 1938, several plaintiffs claimed that the Parkway's taking of three of their one hundred acres had resulted in the "complete isolation of the remainder of the premises." The damages, they alleged, totaled five thousand dollars. In final settlement, however, they received $276. Despite these sorts of conflicts and the displeasure expressed by landowners, most Parkway land purchases in both states, like this dispute, were eventually settled by negotiation.[59] Nevertheless, orchestrated opposition had an effect in Ashe County.

While many landowners worried about how much they would be paid, others, particularly in North Carolina, wondered if they would ever be paid. Landowners could see their lands taken over, made subject to strict NPS usage regulations, and trampled or torn up for Parkway construction while they continued to live there, awaiting a claims adjuster and negotiation of an acceptable settlement. The attorney for four landowners along one of the North Carolina sections, for example, complained in 1937 that "the State Highway and Public Works commission entered all of this property without any notice to us, tearing down our fences, cutting down our timber, digging roads through our property, turning out water in volume on our valuable land, polluting our springs and otherwise depredating."[60]

The fact that money had not yet changed hands and that the state temporarily allowed them to remain in their former homes confused many landowners regarding the issue of who controlled the lands. While these four landowners, for example, complained about Highway Commission damage to "their" lands, the commission's general counsel retorted to their lawyer, "The point you are allowing to confuse you is that you talk about our acts of trespass upon your client's land. . . . This land has not belonged to your client since the day the map was filed in the courthouse. All they have had since that time was a claim against the State of North Carolina to pay for the land, and they themselves have been either trespassers or tenants at will since that time."[61]

Other former landowners faced an even more basic dilemma: unable to use the seized lands in their accustomed ways but still awaiting the arrival of the compensation check, they had no money either to invest in other lands or to relocate.

Park Service personnel, frustrated by confrontational encounters with former landowners still living on seized lands and eager to see the residents removed as NPS policy directed, agreed that the state's policy was unworkable. Writing to North Carolina State Highway Commission staff, NPS officials noted that "most of our serious trespass trouble on the Blue Ridge Parkway has been due to such continued occupances by persons who have not been paid for their lands."[62]

The NPS therefore recommended in 1937 that no more deeds be accepted from the state until former owners had been evicted from the premises. The North Carolina State Highway Commission hurried to comply, sending notices later that year informing 225 landowners on the first five sections of the Parkway that they had to vacate the seized lands before the end of the year. On this same stretch of road, removal also meant that nearly 140 houses, barns, stores, and sheds had to be torn down or hauled away. The process of depopulation was, in places, quite daunting, but the NPS continued through 1938 to push the state to speed the settlement of claims and to force former landowners to vacate the lands — giving the federal government actual as well as legal control — whether or not payment had been made. Abbott wrote to Browning that these landowners "are causing us a great deal of concern, due to the improper use of the land which is entirely contrary to the landscape program."[63]

Abbott's attitude was emblematic of a Park Service that in the 1930s generally viewed residents on lands newly incorporated into parks as problems to be removed. Working to open the new national parks in the East, NPS officials often spoke of "preserving" spectacular wilderness lands for tourist use, but as several recent studies have pointed out, considerable NPS development was required to (re)-create attractive "wilderness" areas there. Unlike the process involved in creating the great western parks, the development of the new eastern parks involved removing most traces of years of human habitation and use (farming, logging, even tourism) in new park areas, which were not the isolated and pristine sanctuaries they were touted to be. As the Blue Ridge Parkway project got under way, thousands of longtime residents were being moved out of the Great Smoky Mountains and Shenandoah National Parks. This policy generated several lengthy but ultimately unsuccessful court battles initiated by angry former residents of what was now parkland.[64] The criticism apparently did not faze NPS officials, who vigorously pressed the removal policy.

Landowners' frustration also mounted when they came to understand how the Parkway differed from regular highways in terms of access to, crossing of, and use of the road. The flood of requests for Parkway access or crossing rights that poured into both state and NPS offices and the large amount of time spent discussing how the Parkway would relate to the surrounding highway network highlighted the road's significance to adjoining landowners. Perhaps no issue surpassed the matter of access and crossing in demonstrating the inherent conflict between accommodating nearby landowners' needs and building a spectacular Parkway that would provide tourists uninterrupted views of mountain scenery.[65]

In their attempts to mollify small landowners and buy needed lands, NPS and highway officials (especially in North Carolina) repeatedly touted the project's benefits, claiming that loss of lands would be offset by closeness to the new road. But, in reality, neither NPS nor state officials were quite so naive. A Park Service official candidly admitted in 1936 that "it is more desirable to terminate [Parkway land suits] as soon as possible, because it is very doubtful if the Parkway with its wide boundary of land and restricted access will, in a direct way, create any benefits for the owner of the adjoining land."[66]

Landowners soon learned how the access restrictions considered crucial to creating a safe and beautiful Parkway also greatly reduced the likelihood that the road would become a useful travel route for most locals. But state laws also dictated different outcomes in Virginia and North Carolina. Federal policies provided that Parkway neighbors would not be stranded without outside access and required the states to rebuild or reroute disrupted local or state roads. As a senior NPS official noted approvingly in 1935, however, North Carolina acquired lands based on the assumption that the abutting owner had no inherent right of access to the Parkway. In Virginia, however, "the complete exercise of the restricted frontage policy is impossible" because of existing state laws granting each adjoining owner access at one or more points as long as the highway commissioner did not find that the accesses created traffic safety hazards. Virginia law therefore presumed an owner's right to access unless it was expressly forbidden in the deed. During the first few years of Parkway construction, Park Service officials consequently felt that they had to permit the states to allow a few landowners direct connections to the Parkway for private residential and farm-related travel or for access to other parts of bisected lands. Nevertheless, the NPS official continued, "every effort should be made to reduce access points to the minimum."[67]

Many Parkway neighbors found the division of their lands especially inconvenient and clamored for permission to cross the road. Several Ashe County landowners supported their 1938 Superior Court claim for five thousand dollars in compensation for three acres of seized property with a petition that described the problem. Although the taking was small, the owners claimed that their lands had been "completely cut off from any state or public road [and that] the former approach by which [they] went to and from their lands [had been] severed by a deep and precipitous cut, a part of the Parkway road." The Park Service, the owners reported, had refused to allow them access, and they consequently believed that "the Parkway road is not and will not be of any service, commercial or economic value to the lands through which it passes, or is adjacent thereto."[68]

Recognizing the severity of the problem, state and federal officials issued access and crossing permits relatively freely during the first two years of Parkway construction. By the late 1930s, however, the number of such private accesses and crossings permitted, especially in Virginia, had begun both to compromise the Parkway's restricted-access character and to endanger travelers' safety. NPS associate director A. E. Demaray reported in 1937 that one twelve-mile section was crisscrossed by 26 public and private roads and that another fifty-mile section had 150 such accesses. "I consider this entirely too many," Demaray wrote to officials in both states, enjoining them to make other arrangements for divided properties.[69]

Parkway in North Carolina at milepost 237, section 2-C, just north of Doughton Park, with Parkway crossing, n.d. Courtesy Blue Ridge Parkway.

One solution NPS officials suggested in late 1937 was that the state purchase a number of "residues"—small areas cut off from larger blocks of land on the other side of the Parkway—so that the need for crossings would diminish. For Parkway officials, decreasing the number of access and crossing roads went hand in hand with adopting a widened right-of-way. "I hope," Demaray wrote to Virginia highway commissioner Shirley in 1937, "we may lift the standards still higher in future work."[70]

Exhausted and exasperated by the ongoing lifting of standards, however, Shirley resisted changes in access rules as he had the increased right-of-way requirements. Responding to Demaray's repeated complaints about the large number of connecting roads in Virginia, Shirley accused the N PS official of being "so far removed from the constant touch of the general public that your Department, I do not think, clearly understands their attitude." According to Shirley, closing Parkway entrances (most of which he asserted would never be used) antagonized property owners, who had "no conception of what you are attempting to do." An owner so treated, he continued, "gets in his mind that N PS people are making the parks for the ultra-rich and idle class; that he is paying for most of it and you are taking right-of-way from him that he is entitled to."[71] The class politics of the Parkway, evident since the early days of Asheville's 1934 routing campaign, were thus not lost on Virginia's citizens or its highway commissioner.

North Carolina highway officials, by contrast, shared the Park Service's concern and from the outset resisted many nearby residents' requests to access the new road. After meeting with Browning about the access issue, the assistant Parkway superintendent wrote that the state and N PS agreed about the importance of not leaving any family "cut off from the outside world." Nevertheless, he reported that "Mr. Browning stated that he had no sympathy with the small saw mill man who wanted to use the parkway as an access to getting out a little timber that was now made accessible by the parkway. . . . The parkway is a park and as such [is] not a means of getting into places that [have] formerly been inaccessible."[72]

It is clear that neither state was operating in a class-neutral manner. However lacking in sympathy for the "small saw mill man," Browning had gone on to request that "in the event that some development such as a hotel or some other 'desirable' development be proposed which would only be possible by access to the parkway," the N PS should "consider such a request on its merits."[73]

The bias was especially evident in state officials' dealings with North Carolina companies that wanted to use the natural resources on their property. Champion Paper and Fibre Company, for example, owned significant timber acreage along the route, and the Linville Company planned to harvest timber and shrubbery and to mine building stone from its five thousand acres in the Grandfather Mountain area as well as to develop recreational and home sites along the mountain ridge to complement the company's established resort. The presence of such large players, concentrated in the section of the Parkway south of Ashe County between Blowing Rock and Mt. Mitchell, complicated land acquisition and pulled North Carolina state officials between their genuine desire to preserve the scenery along the Parkway corridor, their hope of encouraging "desirable" tourist development, and their need to avoid draining state coffers with astronomical acquisition payments.[74]

With less than wholehearted cooperation by Virginia and enthusiastic but somewhat contingent cooperation by North Carolina, the NPS moved in the late 1930s toward a harsher stance on private access roads. By mid-1938, the problem of the abundance of private access permits had become so severe (especially in Virginia) that Secretary Ickes informed the states that no additional permits would be granted and instructed officials to attempt to acquire residual tracts of land to eliminate the problem. Although this policy was not rigidly and consistently enforced until it was written into official 1941 NPS guidelines, it did signal growing sentiment within the Park Service for tighter control of the new Parkway.[75]

The enforcement of this policy also widened and focused differences between state and Park Service responses to pressure from business leaders. Whereas state officials continued frequently to request that NPS bend access rules to assist powerful local owners, the Park Service, more removed from the local political scene, became more uniformly insistent on enforcing the rules. As the North Carolina State Highway Commission chair informed a Salisbury attorney for Blue Ridge Oil Company, which owned land along the Parkway on which it wanted to install a gasoline station, "It is . . . very hard to obtain from the Park Service even so much as a public access[,] and private accesses are on the black list."[76]

Related to access was the use of the Parkway by vehicles deemed commercial. By the late 1930s, NPS policy firmly prohibited commercial traffic, but the categories of "commercial" and "pleasure" did not well contain all the regional traffic. Parkway assistant superintendent Sam Weems reported in 1940 that the NPS had for several years been inundated with requests in both states to allow school buses and rural mail carriers — neither of which fit neatly into Parkway rules — to use the road. "In most instances these requests have not been granted," Weems wrote, explaining that "by permitting school buses and similar traffic use of the Parkway we remove one of the strongest reasons for maintenance of the secondary State roads in the Parkway vicinity, [which] are, under the very best conditions . . . not comparable to the . . . Parkway." The states did in fact show some tendency to let maintenance of their highway systems slide in areas where the Parkway was built. Writing in 1942, as demand to open the Parkway to commercial traffic was growing, Abbott reported that "the States have not touched many of the secondary roads since the Parkway was built because of the general feeling that the Parkway could be used when the state roads got too bad."[77]

By the late 1930s, Parkway officials had realized that to contain commercial development through the corridor, limits on access had to be combined with appropriate state decision making regarding the maintenance of nearby public roads. To this end, in 1939 Abbott urged North Carolina highway officials not to take

Parkway through Virginia along section 1-P south of Roanoke, 1939. A grade crossing connects the Parkway to adjoining property. The Virginia Parkway sections south of Roanoke were riddled by private access and crossing roads. Photograph by J. K. Hillers. National Archives and Records Administration, College Park, Maryland.

into the state highway system every "joint-use" or "semi-public" road that gave several landowners access to the Parkway. "This . . . is one of the best controls we have over the commercial development of lands contiguous to the Parkway, and [it] would be entirely lost should the road which gives entrance to these properties become *legally a public* road."[78] Parkway development, access control, and state road policy thus also shaped private and commercial activity throughout the region.

Just as these policies were beginning to be solidified, the World War II emergency pushed a temporary relaxation of Parkway usage restrictions, and commercial haulers and school districts received permits to use the road. When the war ended, school boards in Virginia requested short-term continuation of the policy. Parkway authorities initially denied permission on the grounds that states were responsible for furnishing adequate school bus roads, and a "storm of protest descended through the mails and visitation to the [Parkway] office." The Floyd County School Board and representatives of the Virginia Highway Department "converged on [the Parkway] Superintendent" to explain the impossibility of bringing county roads up to par in the current school year. Considering that some children might be unable to attend school, Parkway officials relented.[79]

Taken together, the access and use issues brought to the fore the critical inter-relation of the Parkway with the surrounding communities. While Parkway development shaped private land use and local commerce, local needs, land use, and road development were also likely to impinge on the Parkway. Parkway managers, lacking the ability to control all lands within the road's "viewshed," saw that maintaining the Parkway scene in the face of these other pressures would be an enduring challenge.

Unequal Benefits: Concessions and Tourist Entrepreneurs

Also close to the heart of much of the conflict over the Parkway was the question of how its promised commercial benefits would be distributed. Scattered evidence suggests that many Parkway neighbors had taken Asheville and other supporters seriously when they touted those benefits for small farmers out in the mountain coves. Some adjoining landowners clearly hoped to establish tourist businesses. But once again, landowners' expectations ran head-on into the restrictions that would make a scenic Parkway different from a regular highway. Moreover, small entrepreneurs generally lacked the support of state officials (especially in North Carolina) in their efforts to develop commercial ventures near the Parkway. The plans of many entrepreneurs—fledgling and small, large and established—also ran afoul of the NPS, which was determined to keep tight control over the types of commercial enterprises permitted.

Demaray articulated both of these hindrances to local entrepreneurial aspirations when he informed landowner and businessman L. F. Caudill of Sparta, North Carolina, of the NPS's "intention . . . to establish and control by proper leases of parkway land service and supply stations necessary to serve the volume of traffic on the parkway. Persons owning land adjoining the parkway land should not plan to begin any business venture as it will be impossible to build any access drives to the parkway and without such a drive a business could not succeed."[80]

Weems reported a few months later that, like Caudill, "numerous owners of land adjacent to the Parkway are planning to establish typical highway soft drink and confectionary stands." This problem was especially serious in Virginia, where construction had progressed far enough to allow adventuresome travelers to attempt to drive the new road, and on other sections where land acquisition was stalled. Weems and the Parkway staff wished to "remove from the land owners' mind the idea that they will be able to commercialize on the early visitors of the Parkway." An NPS press release reiterated the point, instructing that "owners of land lying within the wide right-of-way which is to be acquired . . . will gain nothing by attempting to commercialize on prospective parkway traffic."[81]

Although many of these squabbles with local landowners occurred while land acquisition was incomplete and owners were unclear about the status of their property, the landowners' hopes and NPS's response highlighted the two sides' differing expectations. Access restrictions and the wide right-of-way would minimize opportunities for adjoining landowners to capitalize on Parkway traffic. And that was not the end of the bad news for landowners who thought that they would reap commercial benefits from the new road. As Demaray's letter to Caudill indicated, the NPS's plans to operate its own concessions at several points along the highway would further undercut local entrepreneurs' chances of attracting business.

Stanley Abbott and other NPS staff members had argued from the beginning that some accommodations, food, and gasoline would need to be provided along the route to supplement facilities available in nearby towns. In late 1934, in his first major brief on the "type and scope of development proposed" along the Parkway, Abbott anticipated that direct government operation of such facilities would provoke cries of government interference with private enterprise and suggested leasing the rights to operate Parkway concessions to local businesspeople.[82] The concessions issue did not surface again for almost three years, however, after land-acquisition controversies had settled somewhat.

By 1937, letters from local citizens and out-of-town developers alike began streaming into Parkway and NPS offices, inquiring about possibilities for entrepreneurship. Two self-described "middle-aged women" with "graduate degrees in home economics and . . . experience in teaching," for example, proposed to develop "attractive, comfortable, well-kept cabins—a high class place . . . for tourists able to pay more than the minimum rates." Having "some money to put into the business" ready at hand, the women were doubtless disappointed to receive the Park Service's standard response: no concrete plans for accommodations along the Parkway had yet been made. Deterring the women even further, the response noted blandly that when Parkway concessions were developed, they would go "to well-financed individuals or concerns to operate all the facilities within certain designated areas, rather than have many small independent operations."[83]

With the restrictions on access and development, such a policy severely limited the possibility that local citizens—whether small farmers or private tourist operators—would benefit directly from the expected influx of travelers. The president of the Blowing Rock Chamber of Commerce doubtless spoke for many when he asked the NPS director if gas stations, restaurants, and inns would be run by the government or leased; he also wanted to know what steps the NPS would take to advertise off-Parkway businesses to travelers. Established entrepreneurs in the area also fretted that government-controlled concessions might pose a threat to business. The Park Service's acting director pledged the agency's "hearty cooperation" in promoting local businesses, even though no advertising signs or billboards would be permitted. And lest there be any misunderstanding, he outlined again the NPS's plans for strategically located accommodations leased to private concerns. But because development of such facilities still lay in the future, the issue was, for the moment, moot.[84]

Nevertheless, discussions at all levels again revealed the divide between North Carolina officials and the NPS about the Parkway's usefulness to North Carolinians and about the Parkway's role in promoting tourist development. Mindful of the assurances that in-state Parkway supporters had given about likely economic benefits to the tourist industry, the commission's lead attorney insisted that "we shall strenuously oppose the utilization of the lands conveyed to the Federal Government for the purpose of granting exclusive concessions to be operated for private profit."[85]

As was slowly dawning on North Carolina officials, though, the initiative and power to direct Parkway development had by 1940 passed from state into federal hands, and the NPS held sway over most decisions about the new road. Although Park Service officials provided reassurances that plans for concessions called only for modest day-use gas stations, souvenir shops, and coffee shops at widely spaced intervals in areas where local businesses were few, North Carolina officials still worried that an NPS-sanctioned "government controlled monopoly" was poised to siphon off the new tourist business.[86]

The potential for such criticism, combined with the slow progress of Parkway construction, caused the NPS only gradually to push its plans for concessions. While Abbott was impatient for some tourist facilities to be opened along completed sections, other NPS officials advocated a measured approach. Washington's view prevailed, and on the eve of the call for concessionaire bids in 1940, Abbott reassured anxious North Carolina business leaders that the Park Service "is not at all inclined to favor a wholesale development of public operator units on the Parkway lands proper. Neither is it the intention that such public operator units . . . should be so placed as to be in competition with existing facilities."[87]

When the Park Service finally called for bids for contracts on filling stations and coffee/souvenir shops in 1940, the agency in some respects seemed sincerely inclined to try to attract bids from smaller-scale businesspeople and local entrepreneurs. Bid announcements went to all who had inquired about concessions possibilities, and the call for bids was advertised widely throughout the region. At the same time, however, the NPS structured bid regulations to exclude all but well-financed, experienced operators prepared to run all the concessions on open sections of the Parkway in one of the two states. At this point, that would have meant two facilities in each state: in North Carolina, a picnic-supply shop at Cumberland Knob Park and a coffee shop at Bluff Park (later Doughton Park); in Virginia, similar installations at Smart View and Rocky Knob. The bidder also needed to commit to a ten-year lease and to agree to strict NPS oversight of business design and management. An initial investment of thirty thousand dollars was required to undertake the North Carolina concessions, with forty thousand dollars required in Virginia. And a bid bond of five thousand dollars had to accompany the proposal.[88]

With even midlevel management salaries running between two thousand and three thousand dollars a year and the annual income of most Parkway neighbors doubtless much less than that, average mountain citizens were unlikely to have such sums. In addition, these sums had to be raised quickly, since construction on concessions buildings was to begin within sixty days of the contract being awarded. These financial barriers, combined with the NPS requirement that any concessionaire have "personal experience" with managing such operations, virtually insured that locals would never have direct access to Parkway travelers via roadside shops.[89]

Furthermore, bid regulations clearly indicated that the NPS intended to maintain stringent standards in the types and quality of accommodations. Parkway coffee shop and gas station owners would, for example, be permitted to sell only approved products (that is, souvenirs "comprising only native handicraft articles of the Blue Ridge Region") at Interior Department–fixed prices. Shop and station buildings would have to be built according to NPS-approved plans.[90]

By several accounts, too, many areas near the Parkway lacked adequate overnight facilities, and as the 1940s progressed, Parkway officials increasingly felt that the NPS had a responsibility to provide at least some accommodations until private development could catch up with anticipated demand. One Parkway official also argued that "the Parkway needs an adequate demonstration of tourist facilities . . . something between the swank Roaring Gap and Linville developments for the rich, and the roadside honky-tonk development now existing everywhere."[91]

Perhaps partly as a result of the strict financial requirements and partly because of factors beyond NPS control, by the initial deadline, the service received no complete bids for the first sets of concessions and had to reopen the bidding process a few months later. The NPS again invited "private business men or corporations familiar with the gasoline and food business" to "interest themselves in the possibilities." But the operator requirements remained the same, and despite many inquiries from interested North Carolina and Virginia businesspeople, no "definite proposals from responsible parties experienced in carrying on operations of this type" were forthcoming. "No aspect of Parkway work during the year," Abbott wrote, "has been as disappointing as the perfunctory response to the advertisement for a Parkway operator." The large numbers of visitors already traveling the 140 miles of open Parkway had begun to complain about the lack of facilities, and many more, he argued, were being kept away completely by the absence of convenient food and gasoline. Thus, in the wake of the unsuccessful bid solicitations in 1940, the Park Service began private negotiations with several of the "interested companies" in hopes of getting some facilities open by 1942.[92]

These negotiations proved more fruitful, and by early 1942 the Interior Department had granted the initial concessions contracts to National Park Concessions, a "non-profit distributing corporation" that had already been operating the concessions at Kentucky's Mammoth Cave National Park. The company had been set up as part of the Park Service's move to nationalize what had since the nineteenth century been a chaotic concessions system involving dozens of private operators. National Park Concessions had a "semiofficial connection" to the federal government, with two NPS staff members serving on the five-person board of directors along with three "private citizens" who were "old hands in the operation of national park facilities." Board members received salaries, and profits were to be plowed back into development of further tourist facilities in the national parks. The company moved quickly to establish a facility on the new Parkway and by spring had opened a sandwich shop at the Cumberland Knob recreation area just south of the North Carolina/Virginia line. Managing the shop were a husband and wife brought in from Mammoth Cave.[93]

The arrangement with National Park Concessions was concluded just as tourist travel declined at the onset of World War II, and the full range of concessions development did not take place until after the conflict ended. Nevertheless, the early debates surrounding the establishment of NPS-administered concessions and the process of awarding the early contracts to National Park Concessions set basic standards that would guide NPS thinking about the commercial establishments to be allowed along the new road. By awarding the first contract to a large outside firm, the NPS signaled decisively that North Carolina and Virginia entrepreneurs—especially small-scale businesspersons—would not be favored.[94]

This decision, combined with the frontage and access restrictions, meant that area residents hoping to capitalize on the Parkway tourist flood had to set their sights on building off-Parkway businesses to attract travelers willing to explore nearby towns—probably not what many locals envisioned when they heard boosters' arguments about the benefits the new scenic highway would bestow. In the years to follow, local businesspeople and Parkway leaders would tussle repeatedly about how best to alert travelers to shops, restaurants, motels, and other off-Parkway landmarks without turning the Parkway primarily into a regional advertising operation.

WEAPONS OF THE STRONG AND WEAK: MAKING LOCAL VOICES HEARD

As Parkway policies jelled, widely varied responses to the road reflected the great diversity of class, cultural, and personal interests and concerns within the population of the mountain region. Because mountain residents' reactions to the Parkway ran the gamut from enthusiastic cooperation to fierce opposition, it is difficult to generalize about "mountain people" and the Parkway. But a few observations are possible.

First, different landowners had markedly different success in shaping the implementation of Parkway standards on their properties. Some owners of adjoining lands changed the outcome favorably for themselves—by forcing a different routing through their lands, by eliciting large payment settlements in return for their losses, by pressuring the states to reduce land requirements, or by gaining direct Parkway access. More dispersed, unorganized, less powerful, or less well-connected landowners whose opposition to the project was just as urgent, however, failed (especially in North Carolina) to alter the course of Parkway development. Decisions all up and down the Parkway determined who would benefit and who would not. As a result, the Parkway's appearance at any given spot owes as much to the adjudication of these conflicts as to the implementation of an overall Parkway "vision" by landscape architects.

Moreover, although the Parkway clearly began as a pet project of the Asheville area's tourist-oriented businessmen and although Parkway policies frequently favored larger business and tourist interests, the new road did not uniformly and consistently benefit the relatively wealthy existing tourist sector. Largely as a consequence of the fact that the Parkway fell under the control of the N PS, whose officials were removed from the pressures of in-state politics, Parkway policy and restrictions frequently upset mountain tourist operators as much as smaller farmers and adjoining landowners, who could neither capitalize on the new road commercially nor use it freely for their personal transportation needs. The periodic disagreements over the N PS's concessions policy provide perhaps the clearest example of the conflicts between federally directed tourist development and private, local tourist operations.

In the Park Service's hands, the Parkway was not to be simply a means by which members of western North Carolina's wealthy business community could expand tourism as they wished. In fact, two of the Parkway's most vocal opponents were wealthy, influential North Carolina tourist operators: Judge Heriot Clarkson of Little Switzerland (chapter 4) and Grandfather Mountain owner Hugh Morton (chapter 7).

And even wealthier landowners not in the tourist business sometimes found themselves in conflict with the N PS and the state of North Carolina as Parkway development proceeded. Bertha Cone, the widow of textile magnate Moses Cone, owned an extensive summer estate, Flat Top Manor, near Blowing Rock. She was alarmed to learn that the Parkway would cut across the entrance to her property and possibly destroy a beautiful hemlock hedge she and her husband had nurtured for fifty years. In hopes of getting the Parkway route adjusted, she wrote letters throughout the 1930s to everyone she could think of, starting with her friend Josephus Daniels, whom she begged to intercede with Secretary Ickes. Daniels obliged, but she eventually wrote directly to Ickes and even implored Representative Robert Doughton to take her case to F D R. "I have wondered," she wrote, "what our President would say if the State wanted to make a road through the Hyde Park place!" Growing ever more bold, she finally wrote to Roosevelt herself.[95]

Although N PS officials initially insisted that the Parkway route could not be altered, Cone refused to budge, finally asking that her estate be left intact at least until her death. Compromise-oriented Highway Commission officials, fearful of having to pay another huge cash settlement, pushed the N PS to study other routes, and the agency obliged. Officials studied routing alterations and informally agreed that land acquisition in the Flat Top area could be postponed until after Cone's death. Cammerer also assured Cone that the Parkway could be built without destroying her hedge and that plans for the Blowing Rock region remained under discussion and construction through her lands lay years in the future. In the end, their gentle treatment paid off: Cone left her property to the state, which deeded it to the Park Service. The lands were eventually developed into the Moses Cone Memorial Park.[96]

The Cone case and simultaneous controversies unfolding at Little Switzerland and Linville demonstrated that socially prominent citizens along the Parkway corridor could wrest far more attention, concessions, and (sometimes) large cash settlements from the N PS and the Highway Commission than could poorer and less organized smaller landowners. Only in Ashe County, where one or two activist lawyers seem to have taken the lead, did numerous small landowners even contest land payments in court.[97] Their sole other option — unified, collective political opposition — remained largely untapped during the 1930s.

Except for the Eastern Band of Cherokees, a politically organized and savvy group of otherwise disempowered landowners (see chapter 5), small landowners and Parkway neighbors in North Carolina who expressed opinions about the Parkway usually did so individually (and sometimes covertly) by contesting their land values and forcing court hearings; by conducting isolated acts of vandalism, insurgency, and defiance; or by penning courageous but sporadic and ultimately ineffective correspondence — that is, through what James C. Scott has called "weapons of the weak." The frequency of these occurrences, combined with the numerous reports by N PS and state officials about troubles with landowners, betrays a significant degree of unrest among those most directly affected by the land-hungry and restrictive new Parkway. A good bit of that unrest, it is clear, stirred in Ashe and Alleghany Counties.[98]

Many marginalized southerners protested by correspondence in the 1930s. Jacquelyn Hall and her coauthors have described the impassioned letters southern textile workers wrote to President Roosevelt and other government officials as "extraordinary correspondence between ordinary people and their government" whose significance "can scarcely be exaggerated." Otherwise largely politically powerless southern millhands "inhabited a world in which letter writing was a political act of enormous courage."[99]

The letters written by Blue Ridge Parkway neighbors also reflected a courageous attempt at political expression by a largely powerless constituency. These letters, however, were neither as numerous nor as focused as the letters from textile workers, possibly because Parkway neighbors did not know where to direct their complaints. Furthermore, the level of risk involved in writing a letter against land seizure for the Parkway did not equal the level of risk braved by textile workers, who faced the possibility of losing their jobs and homes.

D. S. Bare of the Ashe County town of Obids hoped a letter to Doughton, an Alleghany County native, would bring changes in the Parkway route. "You know," Bare wrote, "that it will ruin us people a long top of the mountin if they take all of the land for the road & write of way." Bare complained specifically that the wide right-of-way would gobble up his yard, gardens, and cherry trees as well as a neighbor's house. A further annoyance was the way the surveyors "came throgh my corn & tramped and brocke & pulled my corn up the other day when they could have avoid it."[100]

Doughton's reply addressed few of Bare's specific concerns. Reminding Bare that no land would be seized without just compensation, the congressman advised, "Do not let the matter worry you, for I am satisfied that in a few years, after the Parkway is completed . . . and the people see the great benefits to our Country, everyone will be thankful to our Government and to the Democratic Party for giving such generous consideration to the Mountain people of Western North Carolina." Realizing that at least part of the problem was Bare's poor understanding of the regulations, N P S and state officials sent investigators to survey the situation and explain the right-of-way and the compensation process. Bare subsequently "took a more reasonable attitude toward the whole matter," Browning reported. But the end result for Bare was the same: unable to force even the temporary changes in N P S plans that Bertha Cone had won, he saw his land appropriated for the Parkway.[101]

While Bare's situation was resolved fairly quickly, the volume of landowner complaints made it clear that many area residents had yet to be convinced that the Parkway would be, in Doughton's words, "the greatest thing that has ever come to Western North Carolina." Like landowners waiting for the Highway Commission to pay them, citizens awaiting federal settlements for lands to be taken for recreation areas also felt repeatedly misled. The treatment of poor farmers whose lands were to be incorporated into the Bluff (Doughton Park) recreation area (in Alleghany County) seemed especially cruel. Having agreed in 1935 or 1936 to sell their lands, Bluff area landowners remained unpaid in 1937, although they had been forbidden to till the lands since agreeing to sell. "It is a real hardship that is being imposed upon them by their Government," R. C. Jennings told Senator Robert Reynolds. Perhaps in response to such complaints, the N P S hurried to mail checks to Bluff landowners. By mid-1938, the paperwork for most of the original thirty-nine parcels was nearly complete, and most of the landowners had moved out of the area.[102]

The N P S nevertheless continued to treat roughly the landowners in the Bluff area. For their part, small landowners there and elsewhere seemed unable to develop a coordinated strategy that would provide them with leverage with either the state or the NPS. The troubles experienced by World War I veteran Eli Richardson and his neighbors, Amanda Osborne and George Cleary, appear fairly typical, as do their individualistic responses to perceived mistreatment, which reveal their naïveté, lack of organization, and powerlessness. The NPS condemned the Richardson, Osborne, and Cleary tracts after most of the land for the Bluffs had already been acquired. Richardson had offered to sell his property in the early round of acquisition, but the NPS was uninterested, leading him to believe that he would be left untouched, and he built what NPS officials described condescendingly as a "cheap frame three or four room house" on his land. However, NPS plans still placed his tract in the middle of the Bluffs' projected picnic area, and in late 1938 he and the other two landowners were shocked when the Park Service moved to acquire their three small tracts. Moreover, Parkway construction was proceeding, and Richardson complained (as an NPS official reported) that "dynamiting through the cut near his house made it so dangerous that he has been forced to move out." Richardson demanded that NPS pay his rent while he had to live elsewhere.[103]

The NPS, however, focused on getting title to the Richardson, Osborne, and Cleary lands at the lowest possible cost. Officials rejected the landowners' claims that the value of their lands had increased as a result of the presence of the Parkway and balked at a judge's recommendation of one thousand dollars for the Richardson tract and fifteen hundred dollars for the Osborne parcel, hoping instead to negotiate lower settlements directly with landowners and threatening that if they refused to compromise, no deal would be made.[104]

Osborne and Cleary held out to get the prices set by the hearing judge, but Richardson, unable to live in his house and unable to afford rent elsewhere, had little option but to sell at whatever price the Park Service would give. Understandably bitter about the way he had been treated, he wrote to Secretary of the Interior Ickes that the NPS "had the offer of this property in 1935 and said thay did not want it so just as soon as I built my house Sam P. Weeams sneaks around and trys to take it for nothing so I have bin out of the place 14 months through cort cost and the use of my place I am out $700.00." Soon after writing to Ickes, however, Richardson agreed to a compromise of five hundred dollars. When Osborne and Clearly continued to hold out for more money, the NPS dropped its claim to their lands.[105]

Even after settling with Richardson, the NPS continued to treat him callously. Not yet having received his payment but unable to live in his small house, Richardson asked that the NPS allow him to salvage the windows to use in building another home. The Park Service refused, noting that the settlement had been reached on the basis on the property remaining as it was. When her mother's illness and her husband's role in the war effort left her family in need of money, Osborne wrote to Eleanor Roosevelt to say that she had reconsidered her decision. But the change of heart came too late: federal officials replied that no money was available for further land acquisition in the Bluffs area.[106] As Richardson, Osborne, and Cleary found, the complaints and resistance of smallholders proved no match for the NPS's delay and divide-and-conquer tactics. Richardson, Osborne, and other small landowners who could not afford to hire lawyers could do little but write plaintive (and seldom productive) letters.

A few owners went beyond letters, however. Because the states and the Park Service early on had difficulty policing Parkway lands, some residents displeased with the coming of the new road or with their treatment by federal and state officials took matters into their own hands: trespassing; carving illegal access roads; venturing onto the noncommercial road with trucks; plowing, seeding, and fencing in Parkway lands; and cutting timber on what was to be the right-of-way. In 1939, Weems, the assistant Parkway superintendent, sought authorization to hire additional rangers because "we are losing some timber at points along the route, and damage from grazing, illegal trespass, etc., are constantly being reported." The problem of commercial vehicles on the Parkway became most acute during World War II, when rubber and gasoline rationing increased the appeal of traveling on the Parkway when doing so saved driving time. Park Service officials eventually relaxed the regulations and permitted commercial haulers to use the Parkway for the duration of the war.[107]

In the mid-1930s, Sparta, North Carolina, landowner L. F. Caudill gave the NPS fits with his repeated illegal attempts to access the Parkway from his lands. Caudill had owned an Alleghany County general store for twenty years when the state appropriated just over seventeen acres of his land in 1935, blocking travelers' ready access to his establishment. Caudill was eager to move his business to the Parkway, but in 1937, after learning that he would not be permitted to do so, he forged an unauthorized Parkway access from his property. In the fall of that year, NPS officials barricaded the entrance, only to find it reopened the next day. They rebuilt the barricade, and a Parkway patrolman waited in nearby bushes to see what would happen. Caudill soon appeared and ripped down the second barricade, at which point he was arrested. The NPS launched only a tentative prosecution of Caudill, however, because as late as 1938 he had not been paid by the state of North Carolina for the lands appropriated three years earlier. When negotiations regarding his payment began, the Park Service dropped the charges against him.[108]

Obids, North Carolina, landowner Hamp Ashley frustrated the Park Service even more when he refused to stop using an illegal access road from his lands. Between 1938 and 1942, Parkway rangers blocked the illegal road at least five times and warned Ashley not to use it, but every time, an angry Ashley, who had understood that this sole access road to his lands would remain available after Parkway construction, removed the barricades.[109]

Such small but attention-getting acts of defiance irritated the N P S, but timber cutting posed the most serious challenge, and state and federal officials' varied efforts to stop the cutting generally had little effect. To preserve the natural scene, federal regulations barred landowners from cutting trees or shrubbery during the land-acquisition process. But many landowners saw logging as the only way to squeeze a little profit from their lands prior to state or federal takeover. Some landowners cut the timber because they misunderstood the status of their lands, but others did it—the N P S suspected—deliberately to protest either the state's sluggishness in paying for the seized lands or the fact that the lands were being taken.[110]

In one instance, according to Abbott, the owner of a "large black walnut" along the Parkway right-of-way was warned not to cut the tree but replied that he "hadn't been paid for the land and expected to use it as he saw fit until he was paid." In another case, federal officials sent the sheriff to the home of an Alleghany County man who said that he "cut the trees out of resentment because, as he says, a sufficient consideration had not been offered them for the land." Abbott complained that "cutting and sale of the timber cannot be controlled in the face of this attitude."[111]

In the fall of 1936, land seizures and North Carolina's slowness in mailing out payment checks disrupted and angered the entire Ashe County community of Glendale Springs. On Halloween night, apparently as a gesture of protest, someone felled twenty-three trees across the Parkway and piled other logs and rubbish on the roadway. While investigators initially fingered a group of fourteen youths who had been on the Parkway that night, they also suspected that the young men and women could not have wreaked such destruction unaided. The Interior Department's special investigator noted darkly that "circumstances point to several disgruntled property owners along the parkway. These men have reputations as particularly mean characters." The investigator explained that finding and punishing the perpetrators would be difficult because "the natural extreme reticence of all these mountaineers [has] made it impossible to find anyone who would say that they knew who cut the trees." Invoking timeworn stereotypes, the investigator added that the incident had occurred in a "remote mountain section of North

Carolina [that] was practically isolated until the building of the Blue Ridge Parkway." In this area, he reported, "considerable resentment" was evident among many of the mountain people, much of it "due to the fact that the parkway is being built through land [they] formerly owned, . . . for which many of them have not yet been paid." And, whether the resistance resulted from "natural reticence" or from legitimate anger at the callous treatment by the Highway Commission and the NPS, it was clear to investigators that the Glendale Springs community solidly supported the vandals. "Without exception" and despite several attempts to pressure or cajole witnesses to talk, "every mountaineer interviewed declared he or she knew absolutely nothing about it except that some trees had been cut." The case remained unsolved and was closed without any prosecutions.[112]

The Glendale Springs incident came when NPS officials were beginning to realize the severity of timber cutting and other forms of trespass. In hopes of curtailing such practices, Parkway officials in the fall of 1936 hired their first ranger, an Alleghany County native. But the ranger proved ineffective because the same community solidarity that had characterized the Glendale Springs case made government officials reluctant to prosecute in local courts. In another Alleghany County timber-cutting case, NPS employees feared that the outraged owner might turn a court case against the service by claiming that the amount of land taken from him exceeded the Parkway's real needs. The NPS investigator reported "some local resentment by the mountain people against the parkway project. . . . [T]hat feeling of resentment may be reflected by a biased jury."[113]

State officials also hesitated to prosecute such cases. The Highway Commission's head attorney feared that "the sympathy of local officials toward dispossessed land owners would be sufficient to cause magistrates to dismiss the trespass cases." Thus, even if such actions did not ultimately change the course of Parkway development, timber cutting and other forms of trespass or vandalism represented effective ways that landowners could annoy and frustrate their antagonists. Just a few months after the man's hiring, Parkway officials realized that the unavoidably ineffectual Parkway ranger had become the "laughing stock of the community."[114]

"CHILDREN PLEASURE-BOUND": PUBLIC RELATIONS
RESPONSE IN THE BLUE RIDGE PARKWAY NEWS

Class-related discontent continued to simmer throughout the corridor as land acquisition and construction advanced in the late 1930s. By 1938, Browning, the state's locating and claim engineer, reported to NPS officials that such unhappiness was hampering land buying, and he asked the Park Service to do a better job of explaining the Parkway to local residents. "We have recently heard a great many rumors and different stories of what regulations will apply to the Parkway," Browning observed, with "these statements coming from individuals living in that locality. Some contend that it is a 'rich man's road,' and that the local people will not be permitted to use it."[115]

To address what the NPS somewhat disingenuously termed this "misunderstanding on the part of the local people" and to remedy widely acknowledged deficiencies in communication, the Park Service in late 1937 began publishing a public relations newspaper. Five hundred copies of the first issue of the Blue Ridge Parkway News went out to individuals, schools, churches, and stores in the Parkway's path as well as to interested citizens who were not technically Parkway neighbors, such as Asheville's Fred Weede and officials at chambers of commerce throughout Virginia and North Carolina. As construction affected increasing numbers of people, circulation grew rapidly, reaching nearly three thousand by June 1938 and cresting at four thousand in early 1941 before publication ceased during World War II.[116]

The three- or four-page mimeographed News, written by Abbott and his staff, represented an experiment both in providing information and in constructing a discourse that would justify the Parkway's existence to sometimes angry and frustrated local people. The publication explained plans for the road, addressed problems that had plagued its relationship with landowners, and tried to encourage in its neighbors a sense of responsibility for maintaining its beauty. In launching the Blue Ridge Parkway News, Park Service officials revealed that they had realized that the success of their new creation depended greatly on the cooperation of local residents.

An early item on the agenda of generating local goodwill was a campaign to clear up confusion about the purpose of the Parkway ("a special kind of road built FIRST for the pleasure and recreation of the people who use it, rather than for the business of life") and to differentiate the new road from regular highways. In a friendly and informal tone, the News stressed that "the parkway is not a 'local' road; it is a 'national' road," but assured landowners that state highway systems would adequately provide for local commercial travel and daily activities. In this context, the paper chattily discussed the rules governing Parkway access and use (primarily "a matter of safety") and enjoined local residents to help preserve scenery by refraining from cutting timber on Parkway lands and by helping to prevent forest fires. The News constantly emphasized the reasonableness of Parkway regulations, soft-pedaled local opposition to and conflict surrounding the road, and invited "all concerned" along the route to "continue to work together" to keep the scenic Parkway scenic. Abbott also explained to 150 mountain schoolteachers to whom he sent copies of the News that the NPS hoped to use the paper to make mountain residents see that their children would be "the principal beneficiar[ies], economically, educationally and culturally from this rather vast undertaking."[117]

After sections of the Parkway formally opened in 1939, the Blue Ridge Parkway News urged "that all of us who are 'at home' in the Blue Ridge should be helpful and hospitable" to the "out-of-state tourists" expected to visit the region. Tourists "from the 'low' country and the big towns," the News explained, "are not used to the mountains," and "the Blue Ridge will seem a strange land to them indeed."[118] No Parkway official or supporter had ever suggested that the land itself was "strange" or that visitors would have trouble relating to it, and this odd warning seems to have been directed at the perceived strangeness of mountain people. Parkway officials apparently were cautioning mountaineers to avoid validating common stereotypes of themselves.

The publishers of the Blue Ridge Parkway News at Parkway headquarters in Roanoke evidently took the rather sanguine position that patient, friendly explanation and education would calm most citizen unrest and bring mountain people of all classes into harmonious agreement about the benefits of the new road. Indeed, by the early 1940s, Stanley Abbott believed that the educational campaign was paying off. Reporting to NPS superiors about his recent Parkway inspection trip with a congressman named Carter, Abbott recounted an incident that had reinforced his confidence. Before turning off the Parkway at Linville, Abbott recalled, he and the congressman had encountered "three very colorful mountain women [who] emerged from the woods on the roadside, each with a gunny sack filled with galax leaves." "I stopped the car," Abbott continued, "and inquired as to where they had been picked. The slatternly leader of the group pushed her snuff stick to one side and parried, 'We ain't picked none on the Scenic. We knowed you can't pick them near the road.'" "This impressed Mr. Carter as an evidence that the rangers had done some educating," Abbott concluded.[119]

But the incident also revealed a deep-seated acceptance within the NPS of stereotypes about mountain people. Those attitudes would become increasingly apparent after the war as the service began to interpret for travelers the Parkway corridor's natural and human history.[120] Indeed, as early as 1940, Abbott and the Parkway staff had begun work on an interpretive plan that hinged at least in part on the use of local people to add color to interpretive displays. In the early years of Parkway development, adherence to these stereotypes also hindered government officials' ability to understand the strength, depth, complexity, and legitimacy of local complaints about the project. While some resistance certainly stemmed from misunderstanding and poor communication (problems potentially fixed by the *Blue Ridge Parkway News*), much of the opposition festered because local citizens understood all too well that they could neither pick galax leaves nor make much other practical use of "the Scenic."

Not local residents but Park Service officials were the principal victims of misunderstanding. As publication of the *News* commenced, N PS associate director A. E. Demaray revealed in a letter to Browning this fundamental misreading of local citizens. Demaray attributed complaints about Parkway policy prohibiting trucks and other commercial vehicles to what he imagined to be citizens' worry that they would be unable to drive their multiuse family farm trucks to picnics on the Parkway. "Local citizens," he wrote, should be assured that they had "just as much right to use the parkway . . . with their pleasure vehicles as any other citizen" and that their trucks would be allowed on the Parkway "when the cargo is one of children pleasure-bound." Following this line of thought, the *News* reassured citizens in a 1940 article on "Trucks and Outings" that, as long as the Parkway was used for pleasure rather than for commercial hauling, it was open equally to everyone.[121]

POWER AND THE PARKWAY

As the contentious land-acquisition and early construction processes had made clear, local residents, some of whom had been struggling with the state highway commissions and the Park Service for five years, well knew that the most burdensome question did not involve the use of farm trucks for Parkway picnics. For mountain residents of all classes along the road's route, the construction of a wide, protected, restricted-access scenic parkway designed for leisure and recreational travel had serious implications in terms of land seizures, access and usage rights and restrictions, and short- and long-term economic possibilities.

But while the construction of the new Parkway disrupted the lives and work of mountain area residents — from farmer S. A. Miller to wealthy widow Bertha Cone to the owners of Little Switzerland and Grandfather Mountain — the initial costs of the project fell most heavily on smaller, poorer, and less-well-connected mountain residents, while its benefits and usefulness more often accrued to wealthier citizens. Although these landowners did not organize an opposition movement, the letters and individual acts of resistance and protest that emanated from places such as Ashe County provide evidence that many local people understood exactly what was at stake. Small landowners and Parkway neighbors, especially in places where tourism had not yet caught on, recognized the class biases that had inhered in the project from its inception, and they naturally asked what was in it for them.

The *Blue Ridge Parkway News* also made clear, however, that isolated and individualized grumbling, letter writing, and defiance could not command significant attention or wrest substantial policy changes from either the state governments (especially North Carolina's) or the Park Service. While NPS and state officials realized that, left unaddressed, widespread landowner discontent could damage the Parkway and delay the project, they also knew that such small-scale resistance ultimately posed at best a moderate threat, and they consequently did not take small landowners' complaints very seriously. Instead, they believed that a newsletter that calmly presented the project as benign and democratic would be enough to pacify most landowners and allow the government to push the project forward. Government officials judged that no large-scale changes to land and access policies were required in response to disorganized resistance from small landowners, and no such changes were implemented. On the contrary, as the 1930s progressed, the NPS reinforced precisely those requirements and restrictions (large-acreage fee simple acquisition and severely limited access rights) about which such landowners had complained most vociferously.

Larger, wealthier, better-connected, and/or better-organized landowners proved to have more power to thwart the project's development through entire sections of the mountains. They thus forced the government to go beyond publication of a chatty newsletter and to respond to grievances with policy changes or large settlement payments. Ashe County citizens forced larger-than-normal land payments. Bertha Cone's beloved hedge was left undisturbed during her lifetime. And the Switzerland Company's Heriot Clarkson and Grandfather Mountain's Hugh Morton (both large-scale tourism developers) turned the ostensibly noncommercial Parkway toward their emphatically commercial ends.

If other disgruntled Parkway landowners had pursued different tactics, could they have forced policy changes? Two 1936 examples suggest an affirmative answer to that question, but both incidents occurred under circumstances quite different from those in which most North Carolina landowners found themselves. A statewide referendum in Vermont turned down a similar parkway proposal for some of the same reasons North Carolina landowners were upset about the Blue Ridge Parkway: opposition to large-scale land acquisition by the government, fear of interference with locally owned commerce and tourist facilities, and a feeling that the highway was not needed.[122] Closer to home, tribal organization enabled members of the Eastern Band of Cherokee Indians, individually largely disempowered and poor, to force state and federal officials to debate more seriously and respond more substantially to many of the same arguments small landowners had raised. The Cherokees' vociferous protests necessitated more than a bland monthly newsletter. But the rest of the Parkway corridor's small landowners were not similarly organized, and, unlike their Vermont counterparts, the Parkway landowners were not offered a referendum on the issue. Their protests, therefore, were largely ineffectual in their time and have been mostly forgotten by ours.

BY THE GRACE OF GOD AND A MITCHELL COUNTY JURY

LITTLE SWITZERLAND, REGIONAL TOURISM, AND THE PARKWAY

Found among North Carolina Supreme Court Justice (and long-time Good Roads crusader) Heriot Clarkson's family papers was a story told in biblical cadence titled "Thunder and Lightning over Little Switzerland":

> Many years ago there came into these mountains a lawyer who was fascinated by their loveliness. . . . He found an irregular mountain-side over looking a valley so breath-taking in its entrancing charm that he decided to settle there [and] he called it 'Little Switzerland.' . . . Hence . . . he set for himself a task of transforming a rugged and isolated mountain view into a resort to which the tired materialists of a nation might come, look, and be renewed by the sight of an ethereal grandeur rarely known to man. . . . Suddenly, there swept upon this mountain paradise, the arm of the State Highway and Public Works Commission. . . . Here came the booted figures of 'engineers,' measuring and condemning and taking. . . . A commission which might well have named a great scenic highway for Heriot Clarkson, as the discoverer and popularizer of the beauty of our western highlands, instead, elected to condemn the heart of his mountain retreat.[1]

With dramatic flourish, this document captured the flavor and intensity of the conflict brewing at Little Switzerland, North Carolina, in the late 1930s as the State Highway Commission seized part of Clarkson's resort community for the Blue Ridge Parkway right-of-way. Although the document is vague as to authorship—Clarkson reported that it was sent to him by "a friend"—the manuscript bore Clarkson's editing marks and reflected both his interpretation of the Highway Commission's actions and his tendency toward colorful overstatement.[2] Hyperbole aside, however, the document raised a central question about Parkway development: what implications would the government-sponsored tourism project have for the long-established, privately developed tourist industry in the mountains? Wherein lay the "public good" that this public works project was supposed to serve, and how could it be found in the midst of competing public and private needs and demands?

Clarkson mailed "Thunder and Lightning" to a colleague while waging a furious battle with Highway Commission officials in the state's major newspapers, complementing his ongoing court case. Clarkson's boldness in conducting his war on both fronts reflected his significant power in state politics. The outcome — a large cash settlement for the Switzerland Company and drastic changes in Parkway regulations through Clarkson's resort lands — made it clear that, for someone rightly situated, Parkway development was subject to alteration and manipulation, despite the Blue Ridge Parkway News's assertions to the contrary.

Although Clarkson's complaints about Parkway land acquisition were the same as those expressed by many landowners in the Parkway's path, as a state supreme court judge, wealthy resort owner, and longtime Democratic Party power broker he was uniquely positioned to take his fight into North Carolina's newspapers and courtrooms. At Little Switzerland, the Park Service and the North Carolina State Highway Commission learned the hard way that a few conciliatory issues of the Blue Ridge Parkway News were not enough to quiet a determined and powerful opponent.

The battle at Little Switzerland represented a pivotal moment in early Parkway development, with the careful balance between propping up the southern Appalachian tourism industry and serving a broader public good threatening to come undone. If Parkway travelers are often amazed and thankful that the Parkway is not a tacky commercial corridor resembling Gatlinburg, Tennessee, or Maggie Valley, North Carolina, they likely do not realize how easily it might have become one. In fact, the Parkway's early development was much more closely intertwined with the broader history of tourism (and especially private tourism development) in the mountains than has generally been understood.

When Asheville and North Carolina battled Tennessee for Parkway mileage, officials within North Carolina's state government bureaucracy held the twin goals of promoting state tourism and building a beautiful public parkway in careful alignment. The Parkway, in their view, seamlessly served the ongoing project of tourism development in the state.

Yet as the 1930s and 1940s wore on, state officials found themselves having to choose sides between powerful private tourism promoters and the federal Park Service, which pursued tourist-oriented policies in a more public-spirited way. As the Blue Ridge Parkway came into being, the shape, scope, and impact of "tourism development" were often contested by people (in both the public and private sectors) who often shared little beyond a general interest in promoting it.[3]

No early struggle over developing the Parkway illustrates the growing conflicts between public and private tourism models better than does the episode at Little Switzerland, an exclusive resort for well-to-do white lowlanders developed in the 1910s by Clarkson.[4] There, on the rather precipitous side of a mountain, dramatic tensions emerged between local and state-level Parkway boosters, who tended to promote the Parkway largely for the economic benefits it could bring to established tourist centers such as Asheville (and Little Switzerland), and Park Service officials, who focused on the larger good of opening up areas of exceptional scenery to public enjoyment. For state officials charged with obtaining a right-of-way through Clarkson's land, the dilemma over how both to promote tourism in the state and to preserve the integrity of the tourist-drawing attraction they were creating proved difficult to negotiate. The encounter presaged a longer and fiercer conflict in the 1950s and 1960s with another private developer, Grandfather Mountain's Hugh Morton (see chapter 7).

RACE, RUM, AND ROADS: HERIOT CLARKSON AND NORTH CAROLINA POLITICS

By the time of his three-year late-1930s battle with the State Highway Commission, Clarkson was already well known throughout North Carolina. Now seventy-five years old, he had emerged first in local and then in statewide Democratic politics at the end of the nineteenth century.[5]

The child of a South Carolina planter family that had moved to Charlotte after losing its property during the Civil War, Clarkson graduated at the top of his class from the University of North Carolina in 1884 and began practicing law in his adopted hometown. By 1887, he held his first political offices (alderman and vice mayor), from which he entered the turbulent state politics of the 1890s. In those years, white Populist farmers and black Republicans—crushed by the crop lien system, sharecropping, increasing concentration of wealth in the hands of merchants and businessmen, and economic depression—joined together to form the Fusion coalition, which stormed the halls of the state General Assembly in 1894 and took the governor's mansion from the long-ruling Democrats in 1896. Piloting the ship of state for the first time since Reconstruction, this interracial, class-based political union eased the tax burden on farmers and workers, raised taxes on railroads and businesses, limited interest rates, appropriated more money for public schools, reinstated an elective rather than an appointive system for selecting local government officials, and made the voting process in state elections more democratic and more open to blacks and lower-class whites.[6]

The brief period of Fusion government posed a thoroughgoing threat to the undemocratic, racially exclusive, hierarchical, and probusiness Democratic Party that had dominated the state since the end of Reconstruction. Enraged Democrats scrambled to recover their power, restore what they considered to be the proper hierarchy (in which only upper-crust whites influenced state politics), and thwart Fusionist reforms. Democrats leapt on race as the issue with which to split the Fusion coalition and launched what one historian has termed "the most massive white supremacy campaign the state had ever seen." Through fraudulent elections, a well-financed public relations campaign touting the dangers of "negro rule," and episodes of outright violence, Democratic leaders intimidated black and poor voters and stirred up the racial animosity that always lay just below the surface. Editor and future Parkway supporter Josephus Daniels used the *Raleigh News and Observer* to denounce Fusion rule and portray the state's African American population in a degrading and terrifying light. Democratic leaders throughout the state organized "red shirt" clubs that staged threatening public parades against Fusion rule, broke up Populist and Republican meetings, and, in Wilmington, sparked a violent mob riot in which whites chased locally elected black officials and a prominent black newspaper editor out of town and killed as many as thirty black citizens. By 1898, the Democrats' campaign had broken the Fusion coalition and restored the party to firm control of the state legislature.[7]

Clarkson emerged into state politics during this nasty campaign, and his early political career almost exactly tracked the events in the Democrat-Fusionist fight. He first ran for the state General Assembly in 1896, but, like many other Democratic candidates that year who were crushed in the Fusion landslide, he was disappointed to go down in a narrow defeat to a candidate he later claimed had been supported mostly by black voters. That same year, he organized in Charlotte one of the state's first local red shirt clubs.[8]

When the Democrats retook the state legislature in 1898, Clarkson was one of the elected candidates. He rose as a leader over the next two years as the Democrats solidified their control of state politics by passing a disfranchisement amendment to the state constitution in 1900. While details of Clarkson's part in the disfranchisement campaign are hazy, he clearly played important legislative leadership and extralegal roles. Years after the Democratic triumphs, Clarkson's former law partner boasted that the judge "led the fight for White Supremacy through adoption of the Grandfather Clause in the State Constitution and did yeoman service in the ensuing 'red shirt' campaign." Clarkson led a parade of about six hundred white supremacists on horseback through downtown Charlotte, where they rallied at a city park in support of disfranchisement.[9]

Clarkson explained his support for disfranchisement in a 1900 speech in Gaston County before an "appreciative and enthusiastic audience" of "several hundred people" by saying that he "felt kindly towards the negro, and did not like to deprive him of his ballot, but that it was necessary to do so to maintain good government." Taking away the ballot from black citizens, he continued, "was like correcting a child." The "illiterate negro had abused his power and had to be punished by being deprived of his vote. . . . God had drawn the color line and trouble would come unless we followed the laws and kept the two races separate and distinct."[10]

Clarkson also fervently advocated the prohibition of the manufacture and sale of alcoholic beverages, organizing liquor opponents first in Charlotte (where sales were ended in 1904) and then statewide, winning election as president of the state Anti-Saloon League in 1907. His work helped bring voter approval in 1908 of statewide Prohibition, and he continued to support the antiliquor movement locally and nationally throughout the rest of his life.[11]

Thus, his many political activities placed Clarkson squarely within the group of new probusiness, pro–New South Democratic leaders that came to dominate North Carolina in the late nineteenth century. But like other prominent Democrats in his circle of friends, most notably Daniels, Clarkson advocated some semiprogressive reforms aimed at working- and lower-class citizens. In some of the opinions he wrote while serving on the state supreme court, he supported workers' right to organize unions and to receive compensation from their employers for job-related injuries. He also worked to establish and maintain homes and reformatories for prostitutes, unwed mothers, and other "wayward women"; for black juvenile delinquents; and for the mentally ill. Conversely, he consistently upheld through court decisions the racist "separate but equal" doctrine.[12]

More directly relevant to his later stand against the State Highway Commission in the Parkway battle was his work in the state Good Roads movement of the 1910s. Although he was not a leader throughout the entire campaign, he played a critical part in its last stages when he chaired a committee formed by members of the major state Good Roads associations that authored the bill that became the basis for the State Highway Act of 1921. This law set up the state-built and -maintained highway system and established the State Highway Commission, which later became Clarkson's nemesis. Clarkson also managed the 1920 gubernatorial campaign of North Carolina's Good Roads governor, Cameron Morrison, and Morrison rewarded Clarkson with a post on the North Carolina Supreme Court in 1923, where he sat when the Parkway battle commenced.[13]

LITTLE SWITZERLAND: "PROMINENT AND NOTED PEOPLE"
IN THE "BEAUTY SPOT OF THE BLUE RIDGE"

During his years as a powerful Democratic Party stalwart, Clarkson also established his summer resort colony in the North Carolina mountains. He found the perfect spot in the summer of 1909 as he rode a mule to an isolated mountaintop offering sweeping panoramic views and an ample supply of fresh springwater. Rushing home to Charlotte, he rounded up nine other men — drawn from among his associates in the city's professional, business, and real estate community — to invest in his venture. Within two months, the investors had signed a contract to buy as much of the Grassy Mountain and Chestnut Ridge property as they could from the local families who owned it. By early fall, the investors had incorporated the Switzerland Company to run the development, which soon came to comprise more than eleven hundred acres straddling Mitchell and McDowell Counties.[14]

Planning for Little Switzerland, as the investors named the resort, began in earnest in early 1910. One hundred acres of the land (purchased for about $11 per acre) would initially be offered in one-acre parcels for $150 (soon $300) for home sites. To ready the lots for cottages, the company installed a water and sewer system (planned to empty into a stream six hundred feet down the mountain) and set to work improving railroad and wagon access. Clarkson used his influence to have a Carolina, Clinchfield, and Ohio Railroad station moved to within two miles of the resort, and by 1910, a company-financed toll road connected the station to Little Switzerland. That summer, Clarkson's widowed sister, Ida Clarkson Jones, opened the Switzerland Inn, which quickly became the center of the new community. In the ensuing months, Jones advertised the new resort by entertaining both prospective homeowners from the Charlotte area and local residents from the surrounding mountains at a series of parties, picnics, and celebrations.[15]

Cottage construction proceeded slowly at first, with only Clarkson and his Charlotte law partner building homes by 1911. But before long, about twenty people — like the initial investors, mostly Charlotte-area attorneys and businessmen — had bought lots, and four of them immediately built summer homes. Road development on the lands continued apace, and Clarkson built a general store and post office in 1911. In 1912 he had a telephone line installed, virtually

Switzerland Inn, Little Switzerland, North Carolina, probably soon after it was built in the 1910s. North Carolina Collection, University of North Carolina at Chapel Hill.

the only modern convenience available at the resort until electricity arrived in the 1930s. With ten more cottages built between 1913 and 1916, the colony began to take shape.[16]

The ardently Episcopalian Clarksons helped organize the Church of the Resurrection in 1913, and a South Carolina woman opened Camp As-You-Like-It for girls the following year. A boardinghouse, Echo Cottage, opened several years later, and about the same time, the Raleigh Business and Professional Women's Club built the Swiss Chalet for members' use. A community center, Geneva Hall, was built in 1929, and enlargement of the water system followed, making the resort a relatively self-sufficient community by the early 1930s.[17]

At the same time as the resort was growing, several original Switzerland Company investors died or sold out to Clarkson or other members of his family, who gradually consolidated their hold over the resort. When he ascended to the state's supreme court in 1923, Clarkson handed over day-to-day management of the company to his son, Charlotte attorney Francis O. Clarkson. Until his death in 1942, however, the elder Clarkson remained the central power within the company.[18]

LITTLE SWITZERLAND AND STATE ROADS POLICY

The years during which he launched Little Switzerland were the same years in which Heriot Clarkson found himself in the midst of North Carolina's Good

Roads campaign. In fact, concern with improving access to Little Switzerland may partly account for Clarkson's involvement in the campaign, since it quickly became clear that the roads built to bring wagonloads of tourists from the train station were inadequate for automobiles.

In 1917, four years before passage of the statewide Highway Act, the Switzerland Company sponsored a large bond issue to enable McDowell County to build an automobile road into the development from the towns below. And when the Clarkson-written highway act passed the legislature, one of the first results in the Little Switzerland area—certainly not coincidentally—was approval of a state-maintained road (initially designated as Route 19) between Marion (seat of McDowell County), and Bakersville (seat of Mitchell County), via Little Switzerland, using some of the roads already built or sponsored by the Switzerland Company.[19]

In some respects, a controversy that arose over Route 19 presaged the battle over the Parkway right-of-way. Route 19 did not follow the shortest path between the two county seats, and by the late 1920s, some Spruce Pine residents (also served by the road between Bakersville and Marion) called for abandoning it in favor of a shorter route that would bypass Little Switzerland. Clarkson launched a campaign to keep the state-maintained route open through the resort. A crucial tactic in his effort was to organize a "Citizens' Committee" comprised of real estate agent Reid Queen (now running the store and post office at Little Switzerland), Ida Clarkson Jones, and several local men whom the Clarksons considered friendly to the development. As a similar group subsequently would do during the Parkway conflict, the Citizens' Committee waged its battle for Route 19 via a pamphlet melodramatically titled *A Plea for Honor and Justice* that argued in favor of retaining the longer route. The state's decision to continue to maintain the road from Marion into Little Switzerland was critical for the resort's prosperity. At least twelve more cottages were built in the years that followed, bringing the total number by the early 1930s to roughly twenty-five, and by the end of the decade, that number had grown to about sixty.[20]

Thus, during the more than twenty-five years between the founding of Little Switzerland and his fight with the State Highway Commission over the Parkway right-of-way, Clarkson had gained valuable experience and skill in manipulating state policy for his personal benefit and for that of the other notables who made up the colony.

From the beginning, Little Switzerland cottage owners and summer visitors were an exclusive group. To insure that the development attracted only the "right" people, deeds carried restrictive covenants, increasingly common tools to separate wealthy from poor, black from white, and businesses from residences. Little Switzerland's covenants stipulated that the one-acre lots could not be subdivided or contain more than one home and that they were to be used only for residences or farming. No business development other than that authorized by the company (the post office and general store in the early years) was permitted. And, in keeping with Clarkson's long-held segregationist views, Switzerland Company deeds specified that the land "shall never be owned or occupied by persons of the colored race." Thus, the deeds—and, no doubt, the high prices of lots (by the 1930s, up to six hundred dollars per acre)—tended to keep the poor and black out of Little Switzerland, and the restrictions ensured that the community would remain exclusively a leisure colony and would not attract the sort of business development that would provide year-round jobs for local residents.[21]

Not surprisingly, then, most of the cottage owners and tourists at Little Switzerland by the 1930s were, as one ad proclaimed, "prominent and noted people." Several North Carolina lawyers, a state senator, the presidents of several Charlotte-area companies, a supreme court judge from Louisiana, and doctors, musicians, and other professionals from North and South Carolina, Georgia, and Florida built homes at the resort, as did ardent Good Roads activist Harriet Morehead Berry.[22]

Nevertheless, on the eve of the Parkway battle, Little Switzerland was not a totally homogenous community. A 1936 advertisement for the resort noted, for example, that "the most modest" home at Little Switzerland cost three hundred dollars and the most expensive fifteen thousand dollars. The cheaper homes likely belonged to one of the fifteen "more enterprising" local families who had built "substantial and attractive" homes on farmlands at the development. Indeed, during the first decades of the resort's existence, Little Switzerland newcomers developed relationships of friendship and mutual interdependency with several native Mitchell and McDowell County families, most notably the Buchanans, the Hollifields, and the McKinneys.[23]

These relationships rested largely on the summer employment Little Switzerland homeowners and the company offered local citizens. Local carpenter and contractor Alphonzo "Fons" McKinney, for example, built a home for his family on Switzerland Company lands shortly after the community opened and, accord-

ing to one of the Charlotte-based homeowners, "was of great service to the growing community." In the years before automobile travel to the resort was possible,
members of the Hollifield and Buchanan families drove hacks loaded with visitors up the company's toll road from the train station. Company records show
that McKinneys and Hollifields built the Kilmichael Tower observation platform
in 1935, constructed roads, and performed other labor throughout the late 1930s
and early 1940s. Another member of the large McKinney family lived on company
lands as a caretaker for the members of Charlotte's Cansler family, who built an
expensive two-story "cottage" equipped with a Delco electrical system on their
large acreage. According to one longtime Little Switzerland homeowner, the
Canslers situated the caretaker's small home close enough to the main residence
that requests for assistance could easily be shouted down the mountain to the
McKinneys.[24]

As the development's historian later remembered, summer cottagers came
to depend heavily on local women and men for help in managing household
chores and caretaking at private homes, the Switzerland Inn, the camps, and the
Echo Cottage as well as for the carpentry, plumbing, and masonry work needed
in building new structures for the village. Little Switzerland visitors also bought
handmade products from several local craftspeople, including chairs from the
Woody family of Spruce Pine and gemstones from Roby Buchanan of Hawk.[25]

Notwithstanding elite residents' dependence on local people's energy and
skills, the resort's historian portrayed the "mountain friends and their ways" in
condescending and stereotypical terms: as "clans" of noble, "proud and independent" mountain people who spoke "picturesque mountain speech," made quilts,
displayed a "natural fatalism" in the face of tragic events, and raised their enormous families in log cabins. The patriarch of the McKinney family, she wrote, had
four wives and fathered forty-two children.[26]

News reports in the 1930s characterized Heriot Clarkson as a great friend of
the seventy-five or so local families living at or near his resort. "We's just one big
family up here," he told a reporter in 1937.[27] Yet the relationship between Little
Switzerland homeowners and visitors and local residents clearly was always lop-
sided, with locals dependent on tourists and cottagers and with homeowners and
visitors displaying a combination of paternalistic concern for and outright conde-
scension toward local residents.

While mountaineers were said to refer to Clarkson as "the judge," for example, Clarkson "call[ed] every mountaineer by name" as he drove to Little Switzerland in his Model T. Another report noted disingenuously that local people were
"never conscious of Justice Clarkson's official position." A journalist with whom

Clarkson drove down the mountain in 1937 recalled that "we encountered seven or eight ruddy-cheeked mountain children. 'Hello, Judge Clarkson!' they all bubbled, affectionately. His face flushed with a warmth of pleasure, he . . . plied them with questions, then gave them all the pennies he could produce from his pockets." The reporter concluded that "that incident reflects . . . the bond of affection existing between him and these mountain children." Another article explained that Clarkson had "consistently strengthened [his mountain neighbors'] faith in his leadership; and he has firmly rooted himself in their esteem. His tutelage of Little Switzerland . . . and his championing of the rights and best interests of its people have been inspiring, to say the least."[28]

Looking after the mountain residents, prohibiting alcohol at Little Switzerland, eliminating the possibility of blacks owning homes there, and interesting himself fervently in road development in and around the community, Clarkson created for himself at Little Switzerland a small utopia where he could pursue the elitist, racist, and paternalistic social vision he worked for in the disfranchisement, Prohibition, and Good Roads campaigns.

Members of the Clarkson family, for their part, portrayed themselves as the saviors and protectors of such mountain people, even when opportunistically conflating the interests of the Switzerland Company with those of local residents and disguising political maneuvers designed to manipulate public policy in the company's favor as activism on behalf of locals. Descriptions written on the eve of the Parkway fight recounting Clarkson's successful effort a decade earlier to keep open Route 19 provide a glaring example.

While it was clear in 1929 that retaining the state-maintained road was critical for the continued progress of Little Switzerland as a tourist colony, newspaper articles as late as 1937, written with the Clarksons' cooperation, described the battle as having been waged by the Clarkson family mainly on behalf of the mountain residents. This portrayal flew in the face of evidence that inhabitants of Spruce Pine had called for closure of the road in favor of a more direct route. An article in the *Charlotte Observer* cast Ida Clarkson Jones as a "modern Pauline Revere," reporting that when news of the possible closure of Route 19 came, the sixty-six mountain families who lived along the road and depended on income from tourist traffic "swarmed down from their hillside homes and confronted Mrs. Ida Clarkson Jones . . . who, they knew, had their commonwealth at heart." When word came that a hearing would be held in Raleigh about the highway's fate, Jones "bounced into her station wagon and dashed off into the night, rousing her neighbors at every cabin. During her ride a terrific storm released its pent-up fury. Thunder boomed. Flashes of lightning streaked the sky. . . . But . . . she rode onward, un-

daunted, her purpose clear. Presently she had aroused all the sleepers and therefore a fair-sized motorcade swept down the highway. . . . They rolled into the
capital city before ten o'clock next day, weary, haggard, their clothes soaked; yet
still alive to the responsibility of their task."[29] As at the famous Battle of Kings
Mountain a century and a half earlier, stalwart mountaineers rallied and fought
bravely, and to the Clarksons' great benefit, both Route 19 and Little Switzerland
were saved.

Thus, by the late 1930s, Heriot Clarkson had fifty years of experience in local
and state politics, more than twenty years of practice in getting what he wanted
for Little Switzerland, and a lifetime of portraying himself as a fearless crusader
for high principle. As the State Highway Commission set out to take some of
Clarkson's lands for the new federal Parkway in 1937, officials were dealing with
a formidable and experienced foe.

WRECKAGE AND RUIN AT LITTLE SWITZERLAND?:
THE BLUE RIDGE PARKWAY, THE STATE HIGHWAY COMMISSION,
AND HERIOT CLARKSON

Despite that history, it must have come as a shock to North Carolina Highway
Commission officials to find themselves in conflict with Heriot Clarkson over the
Parkway, for Clarkson and his son, Francis, had from the first been involved in
North Carolina's massive lobbying effort to bring the Parkway along a route that
(not coincidentally) would take it near Little Switzerland. Even as relations be-
tween the Highway Commission and the Clarksons began to sour in 1937, Francis
Clarkson wrote that the Parkway "will be in my opinion the greatest single asset
of its kind in the State of North Carolina."[30]

Heriot Clarkson at first seemed to see the Parkway as a potential asset to his
always somewhat isolated development. In a cordial 1935 note to state engineer
R. Getty Browning, Clarkson suggested a possible route through the development
that would bring travelers within a short distance of his newly built Kilmichael
Tower observation deck (to which he charged admission). His positive tone continued through midsummer 1937, when glowing Clarkson-approved newspaper
articles about the resort advertised the fact that the Parkway would pierce the development and opined that the new road "doubtless . . . will prove a boost . . . and
will serve to bring [the resort] added patronage."[31]

Although many reports depicted Little Switzerland (now with twelve hundred
acres and about sixty homes) as thriving, some evidence indicated that the community needed just such a boost. Although a long article/advertisement in the

Kilmichael Tower observation platform at Little Switzerland, North Carolina, 4 July 1935.
The Parkway settlement Heriot Clarkson received for the development included an access road
from the Parkway to the tower, where visitors were charged admission to take in a mountain view.
North Carolina Collection, University of North Carolina at Chapel Hill.

Asheville Citizen boasted that "there is no indebtedness on the Little Switzerland
property," many similar resorts had failed as the Great Depression descended.
Clarkson rightly worried that a depression-induced drop in tourist travel might
bring to his development a similar fate. And, indeed, Switzerland Company financial records for 1937 indicate that even if it was not seriously in debt, the company was losing money. Later records suggest that the Clarksons may have been
using their personal funds to keep the development afloat. By Clarkson's account,
his family had by the late 1930s poured at least $150,000 (and perhaps as much
as $200,000) into the resort, which, the family later claimed, had never made a
profit. Company records from 1944, two years after Clarkson's death, indicate
that the company still owed his estate more than $10,000.[32]

Thus, Heriot Clarkson, always eager to advertise and promote his development, must have viewed the coming of the Parkway to Little Switzerland as a great
opportunity. Even as his conflicts with the North Carolina Highway Commission
escalated in the summer of 1938, the *Asheville Citizen* quoted him as saying that

routing the Parkway through Little Switzerland "was the natural action to take. My place enjoys wide recognition as the beauty spot of the Blue Ridge. . . . Now the federal government, by routing its driveway through Little Switzerland, shows its determination that motorists from distant states and places shall have the opportunity to drink in the marvelous sweeping views and natural beauty of this wonderland."[33]

As negotiations over the Parkway's acquisition of a route through his lands progressed, however, Clarkson also became intrigued by the possibility of making the land-condemnation procedure work to the Switzerland Company's advantage. The original Parkway partnership between private promoters such as Clarkson and the state and federal governments slowly disintegrated into a conflict that illustrated fundamental differences between public and private approaches to tourism development.

Like many other area landowners, Clarkson was initially and perhaps legitimately alarmed by the Parkway's thousand-foot right-of-way. He was also annoyed by the state's sluggishness in letting him know what parts of the Switzerland Company's property would be affected and was frustrated by the state's delay in working out payment for the lands to be taken. By mid-1936, a worried Clarkson was pushing state officials to lobby the National Park Service (NPS) for a reduced right-of-way through Little Switzerland. With relations still cordial between Highway Commission staff and the Clarksons, the state obliged, in keeping with its desire to foster the local tourist industry as well to save money on land acquisition. The Highway Commission's chair advised the Park Service director that narrowing the right-of-way at Little Switzerland "would not reduce the beauty of the Parkway but might enhance it through the furnishment of better opportunity for the right kind of local development. Furthermore, [it] would save this State a very considerable cost."[34]

Park Service officials seemed convinced that trying to acquire a wide fee-simple right-of-way through a developed area such as Little Switzerland would be prohibitively expensive, so superintendent Stanley Abbott replied that NPS would accept a reduced right-of-way through the development. By December 1936, the state (with federal approval) presented new plans to take a strip averaging slightly more than the minimum two hundred feet wide (accompanied by a small scenic easement) through three miles of Clarkson's resort.[35]

Thus, when the official land-acquisition process for the Little Switzerland section finally commenced in the spring of 1937, state and federal officials had already gone a long way to reduce potential damage to the development. Clarkson, for his part, initially attempted to reach an out-of-court settlement with the state for three hundred dollars per acre while threatening that the Switzerland Company would demand five hundred dollars per acre if the case went to court. The road, he was now claiming (despite the right-of-way concessions already made), "has wrecked the Western part of the Switzerland Company property for any further development for summer visitors."[36]

Having paid an average of just over thirty dollars per acre for all the land so far acquired for the Parkway and simultaneously embroiled in delicate negotiations with the Eastern Band of Cherokee Indians and the nearby Linville Improvement Company for much larger tracts, the Highway Commission was not disposed to pay Clarkson three hundred dollars an acre, especially when Browning and the rest of the staff believed that damage to the development would be far outweighed by future benefits.[37]

Unpersuaded, Heriot and Francis Clarkson became more adamant that the new road would irreparably harm the development. Their arguments increasingly turned on the still unresolved issue of accesses to and crossings over the Parkway from the community. The state, for its part, acquired title to the Switzerland Company property in 1937 and then transferred control of the eighty-eight acres to the federal government in the spring of 1938. With this transaction completed and with their offer of a negotiated settlement rejected, the Clarksons hired a team of prominent lawyers and filed suit in the Mitchell County Superior Court in hopes of getting $50,000 (approximately $575 per acre) in "just compensation."[38]

Following normal procedures for condemnation cases, the Mitchell County courts appointed three local appraisers to assess the damages. The appraisers awarded the Switzerland Company $27,000 (slightly more than $300 per acre) plus some interest, more than the Company's original compromise offer of $22,500. Worried that such a large settlement would push up land prices for other lands it needed in the area, the Highway Commission appealed to the county superior court, where the case went before a judge and jury in March 1939. The Switzerland Company received an award of $25,000 with the stipulation that several access roads (under discussion with the Park Service since 1937 but not approved until the trial was well under way) from company property to the Parkway be provided. Although this was only half of what it was demanding, the company agreed. Still believing this sum to be excessive, however, the Highway Commission appealed to the state supreme court, on which Clarkson sat.[39]

As the case wound its way through the courts, the Clarksons consistently argued that without guarantees of access from the development, the Parkway would hinder Little Switzerland's future growth. "The road," they maintained, "is like a Chinese wall or canal. . . . You could not get on or off it, and it has bottled up and destroyed the western section of our development . . . making useless . . . hundreds of acres of land." And indeed, when they initially filed suit in the spring of 1938, the Clarksons had few assurances that Little Switzerland would retain adequate access to and crossings of the Parkway even though it would divide the resort. The state had requested the access points in 1937, but a reluctant Park Service withheld approval until at least 1939. Without such access, the integrity of the resort was indeed threatened. Furthermore, the Clarksons — now owners of 80 percent of the Switzerland Company stock — had poured considerable funds into having building lots surveyed, roads constructed, sewer and water lines laid, the observation tower built, and other improvements made. The loss of either the lands and lots themselves or of access to them involved costs and considerations that did not pertain in areas where the lands the Parkway required were largely undeveloped. Thus, the Clarksons argued, the costs of routing the Parkway through Little Switzerland went far beyond the value of the eighty-eight acres taken. The Clarksons also asserted that the long delay in reaching a settlement had crippled the resort's growth.[40]

For these reasons, therefore, Heriot Clarkson asked for the largest settlement yet demanded for Parkway right-of-way in North Carolina. Indeed, he estimated that the fifty thousand dollars asked for in the lawsuit was less than the real damages to the development, which his more generous accounting set closer to seventy thousand dollars.[41] Officials at the State Highway Commission thought even the lower sum too high. Their assessment of the Parkway's effects on Little Switzerland differed dramatically from Clarkson's, and they fought the influential judge with their own set of compelling arguments.

The commission contended that Clarkson had wildly overstated both the value of the lands and the detrimental impact of the Parkway. To bolster their claim, they cited tax valuations of Switzerland Company lands, which were much lower than the amount the Clarksons demanded. Commission officials further argued that far from being prime development lots, as much as two-thirds of the lands taken for the Parkway could not be developed because they were rugged and steep tracts that, Highway Commission attorneys noted, had "heretofore been inaccessible and not marketable at any price" and that "in nearly 30 years [had] brought no income and offered no opportunity of development."[42]

Acknowledging that the Parkway posed difficulties not encountered with a regular highway, however, commission officials reiterated the numerous special accommodations already arranged to minimize negative Parkway impact on the resort. Most important was the 1937 decision to reduce the right-of-way to two hundred feet, a concession made for no other individual or company, leaving the right-of-way on the Switzerland Company's lands narrower than at any other point in North Carolina. Furthermore, contradicting the Clarksons' claims that they had no assurances of access to or crossing of the Parkway, Highway Commission officials countered truthfully that they had worked for months to convince a grudging N PS to permit several accesses and crossings at Little Switzerland. One of the access roads, they noted, would allow drivers to visit Kilmichael Tower and would thus "bring hundreds of sight-seers within reach of this tower [for] every one that came before." The commission thus argued that the Parkway would help rather than harm the resort and that as a result the Clarksons' proposed settlement sum was excessive.[43]

Nevertheless, when the state supreme court (with Clarkson recusing himself) split three to three on the Switzerland Company case in the fall of 1939, effectively upholding the Mitchell County Superior Court's verdict, Heriot Clarkson felt vindicated. By December of that year, the Switzerland Company had its twenty-five-thousand-dollar check.[44]

Although defeated in court, Highway Commission officials were right in predicting that the Parkway would benefit Little Switzerland. Rather than suffering "wreckage and ruin," Little Switzerland thrived. In late 1939, the company promptly paid its attorneys and most of its outstanding debts with the receipts from the Parkway settlement. Heriot Clarkson gleefully told relatives and Little Switzerland property owners that "now we will have the Switzerland Company free from debt, except what they owe me" and that "the Company will not have to go into bankruptcy and will remain [a] going concern." "I have been able to beat up the State Highway and Public Works Commission, in seven trials," he gloated, and "we now own this beautiful mountain development."[45]

More than simply rescuing the company from financial difficulty, however, the settlement package markedly enhanced the development's accessibility and potential profitability. And shrewd as he was, Clarkson knew it. "I have never known such a vindication and victory in the history of the State," he bragged, "$25,000 . . . and then to reduce the damages[,] they give special and general benefits by plastering our section with entrances and underpasses. It shows the wisdom of suing them. We now have everything we should have." Energized by his victory, Clarkson set out immediately to capitalize on the new opportunities. There were new lots to be sold and hundreds of acres still to be developed, and electric lights soon would arrive. Direct access to the Parkway, which opened to traffic through Little Switzerland in 1939, was plentiful. Company advertising in the wake of the lawsuit touted the fact that Little Switzerland was the "Only Resort Directly on the Blue Ridge Parkway."[46]

Little Switzerland's rapid development in the decades after the building of the Parkway bore out the founder's optimism. The resort's historian wrote in 1982 that the Parkway had brought the "expansion of Little Switzerland's horizon" by attracting more travelers and making interesting destinations near the resort more accessible to Little Switzerland visitors. The community spilled over onto neighboring ridges, and new developments sprouted on its fringes. Roads were paved, and a new lodge (visible from the Parkway) and general store were constructed.[47]

Heriot Clarkson died suddenly in 1942 and did not see his colony expand in the aftermath of the Parkway settlement. But his vigorous fight unquestionably set the resort up for its later vitality. Indeed, Clarkson turned the coming of the purportedly noncommercial new road directly to his private company's commercial advantage. Instead of fighting what he had frequently portrayed as a defensive battle to save his development from disaster, Clarkson in fact waged his anti-Parkway campaign primarily with the hope of maximizing his company's return in the short run by getting a high payment for his seized acreage and in the long run by assuring that Parkway tourists could not miss Little Switzerland. His complex but brilliant array of strategies and his ultimate victory underscored the ambiguous and multidimensional nature of the Parkway project and exposed the multiple agendas that shaped its early development.

LAWYERS, LOCALS, AND LANGUAGE:
HERIOT CLARKSON'S WINNING STRATEGY

How did a private developer manipulate the Parkway project so completely to his advantage when so many other Parkway landowners — often making identical complaints and harboring similar hopes — failed to force significant changes in project plans? The answer lay in Clarkson's personal power, his wealth, his high position and longtime influence in state politics and government, and his significant potential to disrupt the progress of land acquisition by forcing a pricey settlement that would set a precedent that the Highway Commission feared would raise land-acquisition prices along a long section of the road. He also employed a shrewd political and cultural strategy through which he co-opted small landowners' complaints, manufactured a "grassroots" movement in support of the Switzerland Company, used the state's newspapers to publicize his version of events, and skillfully mobilized existing discourses to depict his crusade as a contest of good and evil and to generate the maximum possible public and private sympathy. Finally, he exploited a fundamental tension at the heart of the Parkway project

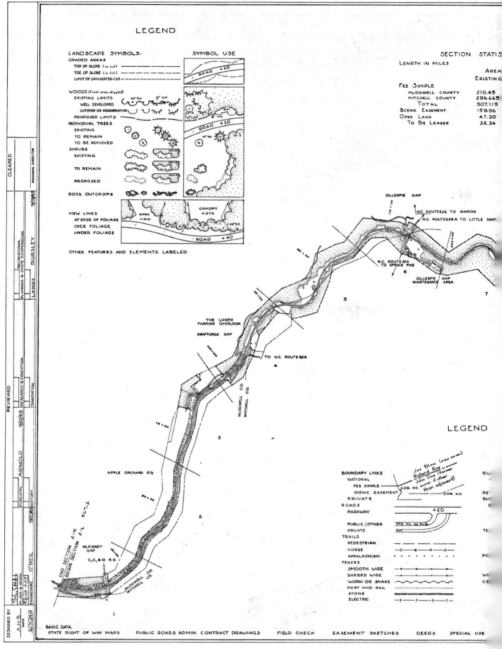

Parkway Land Use Map, Section 2-L, including Little Switzerland, 1949. This map shows the Parkway as it was built, including the roadway and right-of-way lands. The narrowing

MAP LAYOUT

RECOMMENDED ~~Geo. F. Deeming~~ DATE 8/29/49
Superintendent

RECOMMENDED S. W. ABBOTT DATE 9/21/49
Regional Landscape Arch

APPROVED T. J. ALLEN DATE 9/22/49
Regional Director

U. S. DEPARTMENT OF THE INTERIOR   NATIONAL PARK SERVICE

PARKWAY LAND USE MAPS
SECTION 2-L   McKINNEY GAP TO GOOCH GAP
BLUE RIDGE PARKWAY

SCALE ~ 1" = 1000'

PLANS AND DESIGN DIVISION
ROANOKE , VA. OFFICE

DELIN. BY: A.H.B.   DATE 6/30/49   CHECKED BY: W.A.J.   DATE 7/1/49

DATA AS OF JUNE 30, 1949 | DWG. No. | PKY-BR 2L-2062 | COVER SHEET OF 15 SHEETS

of the Parkway corridor through Little Switzerland (upper right-hand end) is evident.

Courtesy Blue Ridge Parkway.

itself: between its goals of aiding the ailing tourism industry in western North Carolina and of providing an uncluttered, scenic drive through the mountains.

Not surprisingly for a well-connected and wealthy judge and politician, Clarkson's first move in early 1938 was to hire a top-flight team of eight lawyers—including his son, Francis, as well as Guy T. Carswell, M. L. Edwards, Fred Hamrick, John C. McBee, W. T. Berry, and J. W. Ragland. Leading them was former North Carolina governor J. C. B. Ehringhaus, who had been in charge of state government during the North Carolina–Tennessee routing controversy. As it turned out, this legal team cost the Clarksons more than six thousand dollars—nearly a quarter of their settlement—but afforded them maximum flexibility in arguing the case. Ehringhaus's well-known political face gave the case credibility, while Francis Clarkson's involvement allowed Judge Clarkson to direct the day-to-day legal maneuvers from behind the scenes. Mitchell County attorneys acted as local front men for court actions: for example, McBee accompanied Heriot Clarkson to file the suit "so that we can keep it quiet except in the mountain country."[48]

Clarkson knew, however, that a team of sophisticated lawyers alone would not win his case, particularly when longtime Highway Commission general counsel Charles Ross, an old nemesis, was shrewdly arguing the Highway Commission's case in the pages of the *Raleigh News and Observer*. The verbal contest in the press started almost as soon as Clarkson's suit was filed, when the newspaper ran a blistering initial story—based largely on a "confidential tip" and a lengthy interview with Ross—reporting that the Switzerland Company was seeking a "large sum" in damages. The article stressed the accommodations that Parkway officials had previously made to reduce damage to Little Switzerland and reminded readers that the resort already had easy highway access. The article doubtless left readers wondering why Clarkson was so angry.[49]

Incensed, Clarkson retaliated with an article that cited his claims in the case. But simultaneous reports undermined his efforts by disclosing the low tax valuations for Switzerland Company lands. An editorial compared those tax values (less than sixteen thousand dollars for the company's several hundred acres in Mitchell and McDowell Counties) with the fifty thousand dollars demanded in the Clarksons' suit. The pro–Highway Commission *News and Observer* articles continued into the summer of 1938, one of them repeating almost verbatim the text of the Highway Commission's legal briefs arguing that the Parkway would help Little Switzerland.[50]

By July, a furious Clarkson decided that the Switzerland Company needed to mount a more coordinated response to the unfavorable publicity. A first step was to arrange for the publication of the company's legal arguments. The *News and*

Observer obliged, but it recapitulated the company's brief in a mocking tone that would have made it difficult for the public to take seriously the claims.[51]

The Clarksons also set to work organizing residents of the Little Switzerland area to support their cause. "I am going to get five or six mountaineers here who are willing," Heriot Clarkson wrote to Francis, "to issue an article, carefully prepared, . . . to the people of the State, especially officials around Raleigh." Instructing his son to have maps printed showing the Parkway route through Little Switzerland, the judge added that Ida Clarkson Jones "will head the list of mountaineers." Clarkson had used this strategy before, not only in the Route 19 fight but also in mid-1937, when, in an attempt to convince the Highway Commission to settle out of court, he had organized nineteen supposedly disinterested locals to testify to the high value of the Switzerland Company's property. The group's statement, apparently dictated by Clarkson, was again signed by members of local families that performed much of the manual labor at Little Switzerland — eight McKinneys, two Buchanans, and three Hollifields — as well as Reid Queen, the Switzerland Company's real estate agent and postmaster as well as a resident, and the manager of the resort's store, E. B. Osborne, who was also Clarkson's brother-in-law.[52]

Later in the summer of 1938, the Clarksons organized a "mass meeting" at the resort's Geneva Hall community center, which, the minutes reported, "was attended by a crowd of mountain people from this section." The group's leaders, however, were pillars of the Little Switzerland Community: Queen became the group's chair, and its secretary was Ray Deal, a consultant for the Southern Mining and Development Company who had built at Little Switzerland in 1933. In language that could only have come directly from the Clarksons, the "mass meeting" responded to the pro–Highway Commission articles in the *News and Observer*. Resolutions spelled out the alleged damage the Parkway had wrought at Little Switzerland, denounced Highway Commission attorney Ross for his attempt to "muck-rake the Switzerland Company," and asserted that "the amount of damages claimed by the Switzerland Company, on account of the wreckage of its property, is reasonable and just and should be paid." Whereas the newspaper had implicitly portrayed Heriot Clarkson as a high-handed and greedy businessman, the meeting asserted that "Justice Clarkson has been with us on the mountains for nearly thirty years and he has done more for this section of Western North Carolina than any man that has ever been on it and has built up a development on a plan unequaled in the Nation." The meeting concluded by appointing a committee to "keep up with . . . this case and see that it is not tried in the newspapers of this State." That committee, like others the Clarksons had organized in the past, included locals who worked for the resort. Touting Little Switzerland's contribution to the local economy, the Clarksons thus portrayed what was in fact the loyalty of a small and select group of area residents who were beholden personally to the Clarksons as well as to the Switzerland Company as the broad consensus of a representative group of mountain people.[53]

"It was a fine meeting of sturdy mountain men," a pleased Heriot Clarkson wrote in the days after the gathering, forwarding to Francis Clarkson a copy of the group's resolutions with instructions to have them printed in the *Charlotte Observer*. Not relying on the newspapers alone to present their case, however, the Clarksons also published and had mailed to hundreds of North Carolinians a pamphlet, *What Citizens Think about Attorney Chas. Ross' Attack on the Switzerland Co. and Its Stockholders*, containing the mass meeting's resolutions, the company's legal brief, and other pro–Switzerland Company documents. "People are now getting the true facts," a satisfied Heriot Clarkson wrote to his son; "we have [the Highway Commission] on the run." Containing his optimism, however, he cautioned Francis to "be patient—work & win."[54]

The *News and Observer* ridiculed the pamphlet and attempted to expose the mass meeting as the Clarkson-orchestrated exercise that it was. "Get the pamphlet folks," it advised readers, "it is truly spicy reading. . . . Anyone who has read an opinion written by Associate Justice Clarkson will harbor little doubt as to [its] authorship." Countering the Clarksons' attempts to distinguish between their personal interests and those of the Switzerland Company, the paper highlighted Clarkson's role in the lawsuit: "Little Switzerland is as much Mr. Associate Justice Heriot Clarkson of the State Supreme Court as Mr. Justice Clarkson is Little Switzerland. One is almost of the other."[55]

The newspaper battle stretched throughout the rest of 1938 and into 1939, as the *News and Observer* defended its coverage and resisted the Clarksons' intensifying efforts to tell their side of the story. The Clarksons persistently threatened legal action to pressure the Raleigh paper toward more balanced reporting, forcing the newspaper to print a detailed letter to the editor from Francis Clarkson spelling out the Switzerland Company's version of events. The Clarksons also planned and paid for a large advertisement bearing the headline "A Plea for Simple Truth and Justice" that put forth their case again in advance of the initial hearing of their case before the appraisers.[56]

Although the Clarksons' efforts to correct further "errors" in the Raleigh paper continued into 1939, Heriot Clarkson seemed to feel that the fall 1938 publicity campaign had gone far toward rehabilitating his name and the image of Little Switzerland. Ross, Clarkson wrote to a colleague, "behind closed doors with the

'News and Disturber' tried the meanest piece of assassination that has ever been attempted in the State." Brightening, he added, however, that the company's public revisions to the newspaper's reports had made the state's "just thinking people sensitive to the fact that our Company is honest and right."[57] These statements exaggerated both Ross's and the *News and Observer*'s transgressions and the ultimate significance of the Switzerland Company's battle, but the hyperbole was typical of Clarkson. Indeed, the language and imagery he employed in presenting the company's case were as important to his strategy as were his tactical decisions to employ eight lawyers, orchestrate the "mass meeting," and argue his case in the state's major newspaper.

Just as he was a master of political maneuvering, Heriot Clarkson also had an uncanny instinct for cultural manipulation, and he skillfully drew on several powerful discourses in shaping a narrative of his effort to wring "just compensation" from the Highway Commission: the language of war (particularly of rising world tensions in advance of World War II); familiar language, symbols, and narratives of the Bible; and the American popular creed of freedom, capitalism, and private property. Deploying these discourses, he presented himself both as one among many aggrieved property owners and entrepreneurs along the Parkway and as a lone and noble freedom fighter in a grand cosmic cause.

Comparing himself and his company to Japanese-occupied China, Italian-occupied Ethiopia, and German-occupied Austria, Clarkson described Ross as a "pygmy Hitler." "Now is the time to collar him," Clarkson wrote, observing that "the trouble in Europe is due to the fact that they did not collar a mad-dog before." Basking in the glow of victory in 1940, Clarkson bragged, "I did not do like [British Prime Minister Neville] Chamberlain—go around with an umbrella in my hand—I took a big stick when I thought we were in danger and they were trying to destroy me."[58] Combined with his demonstrated political savvy, Clarkson's winning rhetorical strategy resulted in a force that no other Parkway opponents had previously matched.

Clarkson seemed instinctively to understand that to mute criticism and increase his chances of prevailing, he must at every turn tell his story in resonant language. He seized the opportunity to mobilize the rhetoric and fears of national financial calamity. "Almost every development in Western North Carolina has broken," he observed in the company's mid-1938 complaint, "and if I can help it, by the grace of God and a Mitchell County jury, this development shall not be 'Gone With the Wind.'"[59]

A fellow attorney with experience in Parkway land-acquisition cases encouraged Heriot and Francis Clarkson to manipulate public understanding of the case, observing that "the psychology of these cases is as important as any civil case that I have ever appeared in. . . . There is something inherent, deep-rooted, in most Tar Heels that every man should have and enjoy the fruit of his own labor and when his property is taken for the public . . . he should be fully compensated."[60]

The Clarksons took this advice to heart. Francis Clarkson wrote to a Greensboro newspaper editor that the reason that Little Switzerland had avoided falling "into the hands of the Receivers" was that his father had "put everything he has ever made into the place and the proceeds of every piece of land sold has gone back into the investment." Writing to Raleigh editors, Francis Clarkson aligned the Switzerland Company with "the people of North Carolina[,] who believe in law and order and justice" and who "will never submit to having their property confiscated and destroyed for public use without 'just compensation.'" Heriot Clarkson's correspondence to state officials took on a more menacing tone: writing to Browning in early 1939, the judge warned that "'Truth is great and will prevail.' You just cannot destroy and bankrupt the Company and get away with it. A jury of this country will never permit it." An ominous final note added a religious gloss to the arguments about free enterprise and private property: "You know you cannot get away from the great stories in the Bible. One is that of Ahab taking Naboth's vineyard. . . . The tragedy came: turned out of office, then death came and his two sons gone. You watch your step." Closing, he quoted Galatians 6:7: "Whatsoever a man soweth that shall he also reap."[61]

When the jury awarded the Switzerland Company twenty-five thousand dollars, Heriot Clarkson worked diligently to be sure the verdict was not viewed as a vindication of one man's or even one social group's interests. Instead, he broadly labeled the court's decision "a victory not only for our Company but for the people in general." The verdict proved, Clarkson declared, "that men cannot sit back in offices in Raleigh and Washington, like King John of old, and force a free people to accept the injustice . . . and not allow a jury to say what was just compensation. It was a victory for the courts and the jury system." Furthermore, in a posttrial letter, he assured the "People of Mitchell County" that the award "maintains the fundamental principle that no man's land can be taken for public purposes without 'just compensation.'" Finally, in a statement that served to conflate Clarkson's personal and business interests with those of average landowners and hence perhaps obliquely to dissuade local citizens from protesting future second-home development in which he might have an interest, Clarkson said that because of the case's outcome, "when people . . . wish to locate in Mitchell county and purchase homes there, they may do so with the assurance that no crown of thorns will be pressed on their brows and that their property and personal rights will be safe."[62]

Clarkson thus transformed what was mainly a personal quest to wring from the state a generous payment for his resort property into a holy battle on behalf of American liberty, private property, and economic progress and stability. His statements attempted to preempt any criticism of the Switzerland Company's actions as an abuse of Clarkson's personal political power, an effort to co-opt smaller landowners' legitimate complaints about the Parkway, or a crass attempt to shape the project (and taxpayer dollars) to serve the interests of a wealthy developer.

Clarkson's strategy had its limits, however, especially after Parkway lands passed into federal hands. When he tried the same tactics in a 1940 dispute with the Park Service over road signs advertising Little Switzerland that Clarkson had placed on Parkway property, N PS officials dug in their heels. The Parkway superintendent wrote to his supervisors that "in view of the many troubles that have developed through the Little Switzerland area we believe it is time for the government to take a firm stand on the question of ownership of this tract." Top N PS officials agreed, noting that to be fair and to preserve Parkway scenery, they could not afford to set an "undesirable precedent" by making an exception to the no-advertising rules. Despite Francis Clarkson's plea to the N PS director that "the Government ought to rejoice in helping to build up the property along the new Parkway. [We] hope that you will see to it that these matters are adjusted" and his threats either to sue the Park Service or to take the matter to Secretary of the Interior Harold L. Ickes, the Park Service refused to make any further accommodations for the Little Switzerland resort. The matter eventually faded away.[63]

The episode—taken together with the two-year land battle that preceded it—illustrated many of the conflicted class and intra- and intergovernmental dynamics that shaped the early Parkway development. The Parkway as it originated in the minds of most of its North Carolina supporters was intended primarily to be an engine for tourist-oriented economic growth. If that had been its only goal, Clarkson's demands might have caused little stir. The Little Switzerland conflict, however, brought into the open an unresolved issue at the project's core: how to reconcile the Parkway's goals of boosting regional (mostly privately run) tourism and of serving a broader public good by building a spectacular, protected, scenic road. As R. Getty Browning and other state and federal officials walked this tightrope, they usually found it fairly easy—in the name of maintaining Park Service standards—to reject small mountain landowners' pleas for access or frontage rights. But state officials' divided loyalties and the project's inherent internal ambiguity meant that when the complaining party was a well-connected and well-financed operator such as Heriot Clarkson with the "right kind" of tourist business, requests could not be dismissed so effortlessly.[64] When Clarkson complained, state officials had to listen, as did N PS bureaucrats, especially as long as they depended on state cooperation to obtain Parkway lands. In the long run, however, Park Service officials were most concerned with fitting the Parkway into the national park system, with providing new recreational opportunities for eastern travelers, and with preserving or creating beautiful natural scenes. Once in control of the Parkway, they had less patience than did state employees with the demands of a persistent and powerful local landowner and entrepreneur who threatened to undermine what they believed were the project's guiding principles.[65]

These guiding principles included a vision for the cultural scenery to be displayed along the road, to be provided primarily by small farmers and the Eastern Band of Cherokee Indians, not by larger tourist developers. As chapter 3 demonstrated, despite their centrality to Parkway plans, these small landowners had little power to influence Parkway development. The Cherokees, however, were able both to wield power and to question the Parkway's presentation of regional culture, and they did so at the same time that the conflict at Little Switzerland was unfolding.

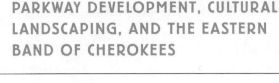

THE CROWNING TOUCH OF INTEREST
PARKWAY DEVELOPMENT, CULTURAL LANDSCAPING, AND THE EASTERN BAND OF CHEROKEES

5

The Switzerland Company's case irritated R. Getty Browning and the Highway Commission; consumed considerable time, money, and energy; and bared fundamental conflicts between government agendas and those of powerful private entrepreneurs and landowners. But as a tangled web of political and cultural issues and a direct early threat to the Parkway's completion, Heriot Clarkson's battle could not compare with officials' five-year struggle with the Eastern Band of Cherokee Indians over a right-of-way for the Parkway's final fifteen miles across their reservation in western North Carolina. Interior Department officials found themselves in a quandary that pitted the supposedly enlightened New Deal policies of the Bureau of Indian Affairs (BIA) against both the Park Service's park-development initiatives and the Interior Department's continued tendency to take a paternalistic stance toward Native Americans.[1]

For Browning and his staff, securing the Cherokee right-of-way brought an unanticipated lesson in the complexities of Indian identity and an unwanted foray into the confusing arena of federal Indian policy. For the Eastern Band, the fight over the Parkway provoked an intense internal battle over the best route to Indian economic and cultural survival in twentieth-century America. The intermingling of these agendas illustrated, perhaps better than any other episode in the Parkway's early history, that its meaning and impact, the politics of its advent, and the sources of its support and opposition depended greatly on local context.

By 1940, when the Cherokees finally consented, under intense pressure from both state and federal planners and from elements within the tribe itself, to grant the right-of-way, they had extracted from the government a much more favorable settlement than was originally offered and had forced officials to listen to local concerns about the Parkway and to consider the possibility that the project did not have North Carolinians' unanimous support. Similar episodes in the gnarled politics of development would be played out again and again on the lands of indigenous and marginalized people in Appalachia, throughout the United States, and worldwide as the century progressed.

For several reasons, the Cherokees succeeded where other disempowered constituencies failed, mounting an organized critique of the Parkway. Most importantly, despite their internal divisions, the Cherokees—unlike mountain white families north of Asheville—were organized as a political unit long before the Parkway came along. Living within the clear geographic confines of their Qualla Boundary lands, they had a discrete ethnic and cultural identity, and their tribal government gave them the political and legal means with which to combat the Parkway. Moreover, at a time when the federal government was newly attentive to Indians' concerns, their protest fell on potentially sympathetic ears.

The Eastern Band of Cherokees stood alone among western North Carolina's less prominent citizens in sustaining opposition to the Blue Ridge Parkway's massive land requirements and its limited accessibility. The Cherokees focused for state highway department and federal officials the questions that many people outside the Asheville area expressed individually: Whose interests did the Parkway serve? Whose highway was it? Was a scenic parkway the highway that most western North Carolinians needed? As these questions were raised on the Cherokee reservation, they revealed that the class and cultural politics of the early development of the Parkway were more complicated than many Parkway enthusiasts and federal and state policy makers either anticipated or liked to admit.

FOUNDATION FOR OPPOSITION: THE LEGAL AND
ECONOMIC STATUS OF THE NORTH CAROLINA CHEROKEES

In the 1930s, when the Great Smoky Mountains National Park opened at their doorstep and the Blue Ridge Parkway plans were announced, the Eastern Band of Cherokees controlled nearly sixty thousand acres of mountain land, located mostly in Swain and Jackson Counties in western North Carolina. Some twenty-two hundred Indians called the reservation (the main part of which is named the Qualla Boundary) home. The depression hammered the Cherokees, whose economy was already foundering following the collapse of the lumbering industry. Many bereft former lumber workers now eked out a meager living through subsistence farming, with the assistance of Tribal Council policies focused on improving Cherokee agriculture. But the tribe's limited base of arable land (estimated at less than 15 percent of the reservation's acreage in 1900 and possibly as little as 5 percent by the 1930s) prevented farming from providing a sufficient livelihood for most members. Sale of timber cut on the reservation generated some funds, and the Tribal Council provided relief money to the worst-off, but a new source of tribal income was clearly necessary.[2]

Many of the Cherokees saw tourism as a plausible solution, especially with the recent opening of the new national park (with which the reservation shared a boundary), but not all members of the Eastern Band agreed about how to build such an industry. The federal government, with its Parkway proposal, presented one set of options. Initially, however, many Cherokees from both acculturated and traditional factions resisted the Parkway and federally sponsored tourism. They judged the plan to be another federal government attempt to take Indian lands and exploit Indian culture for the benefit of whites. Other Cherokees advocated a more conciliatory approach and hoped that the Parkway would boost the band's fledgling tourism industry, which revolved mainly around the successful Cherokee Fair, held every October since 1914. Behind this disagreement lay an ongoing struggle within the band and even within some individual Cherokees regarding how Indians should relate to the federal government and the degree to which Cherokees should assimilate both economically and culturally into mainstream America.[3]

The tribe's complicated legal history exacerbated these essentially political disagreements. Those who lived on the reservation in the 1930s were descended from a small band of Cherokees who had avoided the great removal and Trail of Tears of the 1830s. This group had subsequently purchased several tracts of land in western North Carolina, which the state had helped them to retain after the Civil War. The Indians' legal standing solidified in 1889, when Chief Nimrod Jarrett Smith obtained a state charter organizing the Eastern Band of Cherokee Indians as a corporation. This status allowed the band to conduct business, take cases to court, and act as a political unit. The charter provided for tribal self-government via a Tribal Council (fifteen members elected every two years) and a principal chief and vice chief (elected every four years). Simultaneously, the band received federal recognition as a tribe, which meant that the BIA stationed an agent in Cherokee and that the agent exercised some control over tribal affairs.[4]

This dual recognition (by the state as a corporation and by the federal government as a tribe) produced a confused legal situation for the band. Were they citizens of North Carolina or of the United States, or were they "wards" under direct control of the federal government? Both the state and the national governments exercised authority in certain areas, and jurisdictional lines sometimes blurred. The fact that the Indians owned their land as a corporation and conducted their business through an elected Tribal Council also complicated questions of governmental power over their property. Because no one seemed to understand fully who had legal control, federal agents allowed the Tribal Council considerable latitude in running the Cherokees' affairs.[5] This autonomy set the stage for the band's resistance to the Blue Ridge Parkway. Resistance was not monolithic, however, and disparate interpretations of this legal history among the Cherokees served as sites around which differing temperaments and values coalesced into diverse strategies of resistance.

THE INDIAN NEW DEAL

Complicating matters was the fact that the conflict over Parkway routing through Cherokee lands erupted in the midst of an intense debate among Native Americans over the Indian New Deal. This set of policies, initiated by new Indian Commissioner John Collier and anchored by the 1934 Indian Reorganization Act (IRA, also known as the Wheeler-Howard Act), revolutionized federal management of Native American affairs.[6]

By the time he became commissioner in 1933, Collier had for more than a decade led a chorus of critiques of the assimilationist policies of the BIA from his post as founder and executive secretary of the American Indian Defense Association. The former New York City social worker's involvement with Pueblo Indians and white "regionalist" reformers in New Mexico in the 1920s convinced him that "Pueblo culture, and tribal life in general, must survive, not only in justice to the Indian but in service to the white."[7]

Collier and the regionalists were part of a larger community of 1920s thinkers seeking salvation for modern America in romantically conceived Native American cultures. As Robert Dorman describes in *Revolt of the Provinces*, many American artists and intellectuals of the era were "stricken by a growing sense of cultural disintegration." From this disquieted group, the regionalist movement arose, Dorman continues, to undertake "the task of cultural rejuvenation, seeking inspiration from the fresh materials of indigenous America." These regionalists sought in Native American cultures "an integrating aesthetic . . . to heal the breaches of modernity." Regionalists assumed that in spite of pervasive threats to Indians' cultural survival, Native American culture held the seeds of ancient communally based societies from which could be squeezed an antidote to the "tragedy of modernization." Regionalists and their allies believed that they bore responsibility for preserving and protecting this source of healing cultural salve. Regionalist interest, predictive of Collier's Indian reforms in the 1930s, became particularly focused on the community-reviving potential of Indian arts and crafts.[8]

Like the regionalists, Collier believed that Indians could show a fragmented and individualistic, "shattered" and "directionless" white America how to live more cooperatively and how to value the aesthetic more and the material less. To do so, however, Indian groups on the brink of extinction would have to reclaim their artistic and cultural traditions, gain a measure of political autonomy, and revert to a system of communal landownership instead of assimilating and owning property privately, as policies based on the Dawes Act of 1887 had recommended. Throughout the 1920s, Collier urged overhaul of the BIA along these lines, insisting that assimilation "must be replaced by [policies] that [respect] Indians as human beings with a dignity and culture of their own."[9] As Indian commissioner, Collier got the chance to implement his vision.

Departing from the old emphasis on assimilation, the federal government under Collier's programs invited Indians to retain their traditional ways of life. Viewed by many Americans as an enlightened program, the IRA and associated directives from Collier's office ended the allotment system, which, unsound in design and riddled with abuses, had eroded Native Americans' land base from 138 million acres in 1887 to about 52 million acres in 1934. Collier's reorganization plan allowed tribes to regain control of their not-yet-allotted lands and provided money for purchasing new acreage. The act (on which tribes could vote) also encouraged Indians to organize communally to govern themselves and manage their property via tribal councils and dispensed funds for tribal economic-development ventures. Furthermore, in direct opposition to the long-established push to make Indians more like whites, Collier's BIA promoted the production and sale of traditional Native American crafts and the preservation of Indian languages and culture through its Indian Arts and Crafts Board and its Anthropology Unit. In sum, according to one scholar of federal Indian policy, the Collier administration followed new principles in federal-Indian relations: "appreciation for Indian culture, concern for Indian self-determination and self-government, and a movement toward tribal economic activity."[10]

The foundation for much of Collier's thinking about the bankruptcy of modern society and the possibility for rejuvenation from Indian sources had been laid during his frequent camping trips in the mountains of north Georgia and western North Carolina. There, in his early twenties, Collier witnessed the timber industry's rape of southern mountain forests and the scattering of mountain families into piedmont textile mills. "This experience," he wrote later, "of men in groups, men in a noble folk-life, interrelated with a nature they were helpless to save; this was my gateway into our very wide world of the wastage of nature joined with the wastage of human cultures." Furthermore, as he hiked and camped, Collier became acquainted with a Cherokee boy who served as his guide. The boy was to be the first link in a long chain of contacts between Collier and the Eastern Band, with whom he "found [his] own thoughts and emotions bound in" and to whose history he devoted a chapter of his memoirs.[11]

When Collier's Indian reforms commenced in 1934, therefore, he likely anticipated few problems in dealing with the Eastern Cherokees, with whom he felt such a kinship. Already working under a system set in place by a North Carolina charter similar to that proposed by the IRA, the Eastern Band initially seemed disposed to adopt the new program, and members voted their general approval of the IRA in mid-1934. Increasingly, however, a more acculturated faction within the band objected that by encouraging "tribalism," the act discouraged Indians' individualism and undermined their ability to assimilate and survive in a white-dominated world. Nationally, significant Indian opposition to the Indian New Deal coalesced in the American Indian Federation (AIF). Formed in 1934 and eventually attracting about four thousand members, this organization was pan-Indian, assimilationist, often right wing, anticommunist, and anti-BIA. Group members' central tenet was summed up in the motto of their (failed) candidate for commissioner of Indian Affairs: "The Only Good Bureau Is a Dead Bureau."[12]

Among the Eastern Cherokees, the leading spokespersons against both the Indian New Deal and the Blue Ridge Parkway were AIF members (and husband and wife) Fred and Catherine Bauer. Throughout the 1930s, the Bauers campaigned against the IRA, effectively preventing the band from adopting a new constitution as required to fully implement the act. When the Parkway proposal came along, the Bauers viewed it through the lens of their opposition to the IRA and their suspicion of the overall New Deal agenda.[13]

THE ADVENT OF THE PARKWAY AT CHEROKEE

When first proposed, the Blue Ridge Parkway appealed to the Cherokees because it appeared to address pressing problems of travel on the reservation. Existing highways led out only to the north (to Gatlinburg) and west (to Bryson City). Hoping to get a paved road to the urbanizing and industrializing counties to the east (to Waynesville and especially to Asheville), the Tribal Council agreed in January 1935 to grant a two-hundred-foot right-of-way for the Parkway through the relatively heavily populated Soco Valley section, one of the mountainous reservation's two or three major flat tracts suitable for farming and development.[14]

Some Cherokees saw such a highway as a crucial part of their plans for future tourism development. Soco Valley residents, who had been expecting the state to build a highway through their valley for two or three years, also hoped to use the paved Parkway for access into the town of Cherokee. Earlier in the 1930s, the council had given a right-of-way sixty feet wide to the state for a highway through the reservation on a route close to that proposed for the Parkway. When plans for the Parkway came along, the state had directed the money set aside for that highway elsewhere, assuming, as did Cherokee officials, that the Parkway would replace the other road. With this history in mind, North Carolina Highway Commission officials anticipated few problems with routing the scenic highway through Indian lands.[15]

The Cherokees quickly became concerned, however, about rumors that the Parkway would take much more than two hundred feet of right-of-way and that it would not be the usable, accessible highway they wanted. Their worries soon reached Collier, who wrote to National Park Service (NPS) director Arno B. Cammerer outlining the Indians' questions. In late February 1935, Fred Bauer, who lived in the Soco Valley, rushed to Washington for a meeting with Collier and NPS associate director A. E. Demaray. Bauer interrogated them about the right-of-way, access to the Parkway, the payment the Indians might expect to receive for their lands, and NPS plans for operating concessions along the highway.[16]

Preparing for the trip to Washington, Fred and Catherine Bauer had trouped through the reservation's coves circulating an anti-Parkway petition. "Nearly all who saw the petition signed it, and most willingly," Catherine Bauer reported; "they were so glad that someone was trying to do something to help them." The Bauers had been quick to see the potential problems the Parkway presented to the Cherokees, and the 271 members of the band who signed the petition agreed. "The park highway," they asserted, "will not benefit us, and will take out of cultivation much land needed by the Indians." While her husband delivered the petition to Washington, Catherine Bauer wrote to Eleanor Roosevelt detailing concerns about the highway. Roosevelt forwarded the letter to Collier.[17]

Collier quickly realized that the Bauer opposition could split the Eastern Band and thwart all federal initiatives under way on the reservation. In an effort to head off divisive quarreling, he urged officials at the NPS and the State Highway Commission to move cautiously in negotiating for the right-of-way. In addition, Collier believed that Indians should decide for themselves what course they should take. Thus, in mid-March he instructed Cammerer that no construction or other work on the Cherokee Parkway sections should begin until the matter was resolved to the satisfaction of the Eastern Band. By mid-April, the NPS had halted its surveying work in the Qualla section and the work of the North Carolina Highway Commission also had wound down.[18]

Throughout the spring, Interior Department officials agonized over how to handle the unanticipated problems. BIA and NPS leaders planned a carefully worded message from Secretary of the Interior Harold L. Ickes to inform tribe members fully about the Parkway plans and to reassure them that the government would not coerce them to accept a highway they did not want. Writing to Cherokee Agency superintendent Harold Foght in late April, Collier discussed the forthcoming secretarial message, adding that "the tribe must not consider themselves under pressure to agree to anything."[19]

Ickes's letter arrived in Cherokee in May, possibly via Fred Bauer, who had traveled to Washington again that month. "I have been told," Ickes wrote, "that the Cherokee Tribe is not in favor of the proposed location. If you do not want the road to be built where the National Park Service desires it to go, it will not be built." Nevertheless, he continued, the Cherokees should understand the NPS's plans before making a final decision. Ickes then confirmed the fears of the Bauers and their supporters: the Parkway's right-of-way and easements would take or control an area nearly one thousand feet wide in many spots, consuming much more valuable Soco Valley farmland than originally expected. Restrictions would prohibit commercial development alongside the road, and adjoining residents would not have direct access to the new highway. Nevertheless, Ickes projected that granting the right-of-way would ensure increased tourist traffic to Cherokee trading posts and their planned hotel and rising sales of Indian-made products, and he explained the payment that landowners would receive for lost homes and property. He then reiterated that "this entire matter will be decided by the Cherokee Tribe." He had no desire, he assured, "to urge the Tribe against its wishes to accept this program."[20]

Tribal leaders took seriously Ickes's statement, but his discussion of the Parkway's likely benefits was not enough to placate the Soco Valley residents who were about to lose their land. As their February petition had noted, this was not the highway they needed or expected. Foght agreed with them and wrote to Ickes that "the land to be purchased and the easements required cover virtually every acre of tillable land in the Soco Valley."[21]

Foght was correct. While about half the proposed route from Soco Gap to Cherokee village snaked through difficult, hilly terrain, the last five or six miles pierced the rich bottomlands along Soco Creek. The level portion of the valley

Parkway section 2-z, milepost 461.6–469.1, 1935. The original location proposed for the Parkway through the flat and heavily agricultural Soco Valley section of the Eastern Band of Cherokees' lands was on the right at the edge of the woods. Courtesy Blue Ridge Parkway.

was no more than three-tenths of a mile wide in most spots, bounded on either side by sharply rising slopes. Thus, a thousand-foot taking for the Parkway would have swallowed the valley whole. People already short of farmland in a time of economic hardship viewed this sacrifice as too great. In light of these consider-ations, the Tribal Council met in emergency session in June 1935 and rescinded its approval of the right-of-way. Fred and Catherine Bauer were relieved, feeling that they had saved the Cherokees from a major blunder.[22]

THE BAUERS AND THE CHEROKEE OPPOSITION

At the time the council changed its mind, neither Fred nor Catherine Bauer held a position of political power within the Eastern Band. In fact, they had moved back to North Carolina from Michigan only two years earlier, after many years' absence. But Fred had grown up on the reservation in the home of his great-uncle and great-aunt, James and Josephine Blythe, and his mother was part Cherokee. His father, a prominent white Raleigh architect, had overseen the construction of the North Carolina governor's mansion in the late nineteenth century and had designed many other structures in the capital city. Shortly after Fred's birth in late 1896, his mother had died, and his father had sent him to live with his mother's relatives on the reservation. Fred's father committed suicide about eighteen months later.[23]

Bauer attended the Indian schools on the reservation before leaving for Pennsylvania's Carlisle Indian School. By that time, Carlisle, founded in 1879 as the prototype of off-reservation boarding school education directed toward Indian assimilation, was in serious decline. Bauer, however, seems to have almost completely adopted the basic philosophy that underpinned the Indian educational system: "The solution to the Indian problem lay in the rapid assimilation of the race into American life." After serving in the military in World War I, he returned to Indian boarding schools as a physical education teacher and coach. By this point, however, the heyday of such schools had passed. Opponents of the rapid-assimilation philosophy charged that such institutions were both ineffective and cruel. Under such pressure, many of them, including the one that employed Fred and Catherine Bauer, finally closed in the early 1930s. Out of a job, Bauer returned to the Cherokee reservation in 1933 to farm and work on several relief projects, including highway construction.[24]

Articulate and passionately interested in Indian issues, Catherine Bauer, a white Cornell graduate who also worked as a teacher in Indian schools in Michigan and on the Qualla Boundary, was a full partner with her husband in their crusade against the Parkway and the Indian New Deal. Collier's programs, the couple charged, would "impoverish the Indians" and "set up models of Communism for the American public to gaze upon, in the hope they will desire the same for themselves."[25]

During the spring of 1935, the Bauers battled the Indian New Deal on several fronts. As teachers, they focused particularly on changes coming to the Cherokee schools as a result of Collier's policies. In line with the new encouragement of Indian crafts, ceremonies, history, and language, Indian schools in Cherokee, under the direction of resident BIA agents, had begun once again to include such subjects in their curricula. Furthermore, the agents had slanted the offerings toward vocational education and away from the more academic subjects that other North Carolina children were required to study. The idea was to give Cherokee children the skills they would need to live within a Cherokee society, which officials assumed would (and should) remain separate and marginal.[26]

This emphasis rankled the Bauers and others on the reservation who thought that the route to Indian success in white America was through greater assimilation and individualism rather than through a reintroduction of traditionalism and communalism. the Bauers trusted little in the federal government and wanted to end what they perceived as government interference in Indian affairs and paternalistic treatment of Native Americans, whether under the guise of the Dawes Act or under the auspices of the subsequent IRA.

Shortly after the Bauers returned to North Carolina in 1933, Catherine began substitute teaching in the reservation schools and then took a permanent job in a new Cherokee school near the couple's home in the Soco Valley. Fred Bauer expected to be named a coach in the reservation schools. By the spring of 1935, alarmed by the use of a book on the Russian economy in one advanced class, Catherine became convinced that the schools were teaching communism. With the support of one or two other teachers, she lambasted the educational reforms. She and her husband even organized a strike or lockout against the schools in which some families briefly withheld their children from classes to protest BIA-initiated changes.[27]

In an attempt to quiet the hubbub, Foght fired Bauer from her job at the Soco school. He also posted signs around the reservation threatening the government-funded relief jobs of Cherokees who opposed the Indian New Deal, although he quickly realized that the signs were a poor tactic and had them removed. At the same time, according to Foght, Fred Bauer and some other "white" Indians who backed him held "weird night meetings" and plotted a takeover of parts of the tribal government. In the midst of this flurry of activity, the indefatigable Bauer traveled to Washington to confer with Commissioner Collier about these concerns and those related to the Parkway.[28]

These brewing tensions, combined with the Bauers' likely resentment of Catherine Bauer's firing, erupted in violence at least twice: once when bureau opponents allegedly drew knives and threatened the agent and his deputies, and once when Catherine Bauer and a supporter visited the Soco Day School and "after a brief altercation . . . seized [a] chair and rushing forward threatened to beat [one of the teachers] over the head with it."[29]

Whipped into a frenzy by the activist Bauers, confused and understandably suspicious about the changes in federal policy, concerned about erosion of tribal farmlands, and caught in a depression-induced spiral of fear and despair, enough Cherokees came to the Bauers' side by the fall of 1935 to elect Fred Bauer as the tribe's vice chief. Bolstering him on the Tribal Council was Pearson McCoy, another critic of the BIA and federal policy. Although this turn of events afforded Bauer more power than ever to frustrate federal and state plans, Qualla Boundary Cherokees in fact voted inconsistently. While selecting Bauer, they chose as principal chief a supporter of the IRA and the BIA, Jarrett Blythe. This divided strategy set the stage for escalating conflict over the Parkway.[30]

Blythe was descended from a line of Cherokee leaders, most prominently his great-grandfather, Nimrod Jarrett Smith, who had obtained the Cherokees' corporate charter in 1889. Born in 1886 on the Cherokee reservation, Blythe, like Bauer, attended the Cherokee Elementary School and then left for the Indian boarding schools. Blythe attended an interracial program for blacks and Indians at Hampton Institute in Virginia as well as the Haskell school in Kansas. He worked in Montana and Detroit before moving back to Cherokee in 1927 to take jobs in the Agricultural Extension Service and in forestry for the Cherokee Indian Agency. During the depression, Blythe supervised road-building crews of the Indian Emergency Conservation Work Program (the Indian wing of the Civilian Conservation Corps). To complicate matters, Blythe was Fred Bauer's cousin, the son of James and Josephine Blythe, who had raised Bauer. Jarrett Blythe and Fred Bauer had grown up as brothers, although Blythe was ten years older. In the years to come, the two would find themselves increasingly at odds. Neither ever acknowledged the family relationship during their public confrontations about the Parkway.[31]

BLYTHE, THE BAUERS, AND THE PARKWAY CONFLICT

The 1935 tribal election that brought both Blythe and Bauer to power set the stage for several more years of negotiations, accusations, stalemates, and setbacks before a compromise Parkway route emerged. On many occasions, agreements appeared on the verge of adoption, only to break down under continued scrutiny from the Bauers. Not until Fred Bauer was forced from office in 1939, leaving Blythe as the unchallenged spokesperson for the tribe, was the route from Soco Gap to the Great Smoky Mountains park firmly established.

Mixed Messages

Early on, Blythe and Bauer agreed that the Parkway should not pass through the Soco Valley. From the beginning, however, Blythe looked for a compromise and, according to Catherine Bauer, initially "stated that it would be useless to protest." Even after the Tribal Council denounced the plan in the summer of 1935, he continued to negotiate, causing the Cherokee leadership to send a series of mixed messages to Washington. Because of the wording of Ickes's May 1935 letter, Bauer and the council members expected that the June 1935 vote would be the last word on the Parkway project. But according to Bauer, Interior Department officials and Highway Commission representatives failed to get the message that the Indians had completely rejected the Parkway.[32]

Soon after the vote, BIA agent Foght and Blythe wrote to Ickes expressing a much more conciliatory position than the council had intended. Their letter outlined the many Cherokee objections to the Soco Valley route but instead of flatly rejecting the whole plan suggested that the tribe would be open to the highway if it followed a slightly different path. "The Cherokee Indians desire to go on record," the letter continued, "assuring the Secretary of the Interior and the Commissioner of Indian Affairs that [we] as a tribe are eager to cooperate . . . and are anxious to have the highway pass through the reservation, if this can be done without too great a loss." The letter went on to report that the Cherokees had finished plans for their craft shop, trading post, and hotel "to be managed as cooperatives" under the IRA. Seeming to confirm the Bauers' fears, the writers noted that the implementation of these plans "awaits only the final location of the Parkway."[33]

Coinciding as it did with continuing reports in the *Asheville Citizen* that Blythe and Foght supported the New Deal and welcomed plans to run the Parkway across the reservation, this letter alarmed Parkway opponents within the council. Several members countered the newspaper articles and the letter with a telegram and letter in which they reiterated concerns about the farmland the Parkway would take and repeated the council's resolution that "we do not wish to have the road built through our Reservation." An oblique reference to Foght's letter made their point: "Council is of the opinion that you desire an immediate answer of 'yes,' or 'no' without argument or excuse. If other reaches your office, we ask that you please disregard the same, for it will not be the sentiment of the Indians."[34]

News of this letter infuriated Foght, who suspected that the Bauers were behind it. According to Catherine Bauer, Foght unfairly accused his secretary of leaking word of his and Blythe's letter and tried to blackball the Bauers. "I state it to be a fact," she wrote, "that [the secretary], and all other friends we have at the Agency, dare not be friendly to us any longer, for fear of a transfer, or a discharge from" Indian Service jobs. In Bauer's account, the federal agent was coercing Cherokees to be "100% FOR the NEW DEAL" or risk losing their jobs, a scary prospect in a time of privation.[35] Thus, tensions ran high and divisions ran deep on the Qualla Boundary in the summer of 1935.

With such confusing signals from Cherokee, Interior Department and state officials waffled throughout the summer about what to do in regard to the southernmost Parkway sections. North Carolina Parkway supporters in particular pushed for further negotiations with the Cherokees, and in a statement prominently publicized in the *Asheville Citizen*, North Carolina Representative Zebulon Weaver opined, "I feel that when I explain the situation to Secretary Ickes he will have the Indian Bureau to make an investigation and take steps to revoke an action by the tribe which in my opinion is not to their best interest."[36]

The contradictory results of the August tribal elections doubtless caused even more uncertainty about whether the earlier council vote was final. By the end of September, Ickes had decided to continue negotiating with the Cherokees for a slightly altered Soco Valley route. Throughout the fall, State Highway Commission officials and Interior Department representatives plotted new tactics. Even Collier seemed optimistic about the possibility of getting the Cherokees to cooperate if they were offered other farmlands in exchange for the right-of-way, as Browning had suggested. "I believe," Collier wrote, "we should send somebody down to the Cherokee Reservation who has not yet tried to induce the Indians to accept the parkway, and see on this new basis whether he cannot convince the Indians of the desirability of the Parkway project. I believe it can be done."[37]

Such confidence proved misplaced. As planned, Browning and another State Highway Commission representative appeared before the Tribal Council in December 1935 to ask for the right-of-way. Again, however, the council scotched the request.[38]

Although twice rebuffed, state and federal officials clung to the hope of running the Parkway through the reservation. Almost before the ink was dry on the council minutes, Ickes called Browning to Washington for another strategy session with NPS and BIA officials. The press mentioned the possibility of simply condemning Indian lands but noted that "Secretary Ickes, it is believed, would never consent to this." Ickes did, however, pressure the Cherokees in the newspapers, releasing a statement shortly after the council meeting in which he accused the Indians of "standing in their own light" by resisting a highway that would bring them so much beneficial tourist traffic. Participants in the December meetings floated more ideas for further concessions to the Indians, including the possibility of opening the Parkway to commercial traffic on the reservation — a tacit acknowledgment of the Cherokees' need for a full-use public highway — but Park Service officials rejected this lowering of Parkway standards. Finally, Ickes announced that the Interior Department had compromised as far as it could and that the next move would be left up to the Cherokees.[39]

The Cherokees kept sending confusing signals, however. Always vigilant, Fred Bauer asked Ickes why, after the council had conclusively voted down the Parkway right-of-way, state and federal officials kept pestering the Cherokees with more proposals. "It seems," Bauer wrote, "that you have been grossly misinformed as to the wishes of the Indians." Foght, the source of some of that "misinformation," wrote to Browning three days later that "the fact remains that this particular council action was not an honest expression of the wishes of the people." Foght assured state Parkway officials that patience and persistence might eventually be rewarded: "I am convinced that at least 85% of the property holders along the highway, even now, are willing to sign a petition for the road."[40]

Such a petition, sent by Foght, arrived in Ickes's mail in early January 1936. It claimed disingenuously that "no Government employee has had anything to do with inspiring or circulating the petition." The signers, Foght continued, "represent approximately two-thirds of the land owners adjacent to the proposed highway." Even though they "did not state in so many words that they are anxious to have the Government condemn the necessary right-of-way," he reported, they wanted the Parkway to come to the reservation. The petitioners emphasized that "an unthinking group, a group which is in, we hope, temporary control of the policies of our Tribal Council, are doing us tremendous harm in blocking the inter-park highway from coming through our reservation."[41]

Clearly referring to the Bauers, the signers insisted that Parkway opponents had little personally at stake in the debate and were simply using the issue to thwart the New Deal. The group asked Ickes to "please defer action in taking the highway away until we see if we cannot break the influence of those who are misleading us." About thirty people signed the document. Foght kept the pressure on with a follow-up letter to Collier later that month, naming the stumbling blocks to Parkway approval as Pearson McCoy (a "contested Indian and a constant trouble maker") and Fred Bauer. The two, he reported, "have, up to this time, blocked every attempt in the Tribal Council to pass a favorable resolution—by means of intimidation and threats of bodily harm."[42]

A Land-Exchange Strategy

Encouraged by Foght's missives and apparently by favorable signals from Chief Blythe, federal and state officials continued throughout 1936 to draft new proposals to entice the Cherokees to grant the right-of-way. Most promising was Browning's idea of finding some fertile land in the Great Smoky Mountains National Park to give the Cherokees to compensate for the farmland that the Parkway would take. By May, Ickes was ready with a concrete plan, which Asheville observers and Superintendent Foght predicted the Cherokees would find acceptable.[43]

But once again, optimism proved premature: the Cherokees confounded expectations and frustrated Parkway supporters by narrowly voting against the land-exchange package at their March 1937 meeting.[44] Foght fumed. The meeting, he reported, had lasted several days, and an early poll had indicated that a majority of the members of the Tribal Council favored accepting the package. So excruciatingly complicated were local politics, he lamented, that quick and decisive action had been thwarted. Indeed, he complained,

> It is impossible to get the Cherokee Indians to vote on a problem until they have all had repeated opportunity to make their speeches. So they adjourned over Sunday, which I knew would be disastrous as it would give certain individuals the opportunity they were seeking. . . . [W]hen we met Monday morning three of our staunchest supporters had gone over to the opposition, making inspired talks against the parkway, with the result that when the vote came we lost six to five. . . .
>
> Threats of personal violence were made against the persons who changed their vote. This kind of thing we are up against constantly. . . . A majority of the property owners along the proposed right-of-way are in favor of granting the right-of-way and easements, and [are ready] to accept the exchange of lands.

Foght asked the if the BIA would countenance an attempt to remove Bauer from his position, since he did not meet the requirement that the vice chief be at least 50 percent Cherokee. If Bauer were not ousted, Foght warned, "the majority [will] continue to suffer these unwarranted proceedings directed by him and two others. There is a growing feeling here that this thing should stop. . . . Were it not for this little clique," he sighed, "all would be well."[45]

Panic in Western North Carolina

Few though they may have been, the "little clique" had by this time worked Parkway supporters from Asheville to Raleigh to Washington into a frenzy of activity and worry. State officials and Parkway boosters in Asheville grew fearful that continued Indian resistance might cause the hard-won southern end of the Parkway to be rerouted or not built at all. Evidence in the summer that Ickes had directed the surveying of alternative routes from Asheville to the Great Smoky Mountains National Park via Gatlinburg fueled the panic. One of Asheville's major Parkway boosters, George Stephens, described the alarm raging among Parkway enthusiasts, who had recently met with their old ally, Josephus Daniels: "It was further brought out that the Park Service was using this Indian situation to leave the route from Asheville to the Smoky Mountains undetermined. [Some] vigorous action in this matter needs to be taken."[46]

Officials at all levels of government as well as Parkway proponents in North Carolina's business community increasingly dismissed the Bauers' concerns as the rantings of extremists, but the Bauers' arguments resonated with enough Cherokees to ensure continued resistance to government plans. In particular, the Bauers' appeals struck a chord with Cherokees mindful of a history of federal abuses and suspicious of the increased federal control that the Indian New Deal seemed to propose. Catherine Bauer explicitly invoked past wrongs to question current policies: "Does the Parkway," she demanded in a 1935 letter, "contemplate celebrating the 100th anniversary of the GREAT REMOVAL by another GREAT REMOVAL?" Even Chief Blythe admitted that those who joined with the Bauers in fearing that turnover of the Parkway right-of-way was a first step toward federal confiscation of the entire Qualla Boundary for the Great Smoky Mountains park had a point. "They have still not forgotten" the removals of 1838, he told a congressional committee during the controversy.[47]

Cherokee misgivings were well founded in light of current events as well. Observant Cherokees could not have helped noticing that the NPS was at that time removing white Appalachian residents from their homes as it took over their lands for incorporation into the Great Smoky Mountains National Park. Furthermore, early plans for that park had indeed proposed incorporation of some Cherokee lands, and although that threat appeared to have subsided, many Cherokees doubtless suspected that federal officials had not completely abandoned the idea.[48]

For their part, the Bauers also saw the Parkway plans as interwoven with the agenda of the dreaded Indian New Deal. In their view, the federal government (working through the IRA) would first convince Indians to revive their crafts and traditional ceremonies and then would bring a scenic highway through the reservation and make the Cherokees a BIA-controlled park exhibit. The BIA and Foght, Fred Bauer remembered years after the controversy, stood "ready to remold the Cherokees into the Bureau notion of real Indians, with culture and traditions and glamour." In an article published in North Carolina newspapers during the struggle, he explained that "we welcome the touring public to enjoy the beauty and recreation we have. . . . In opposing the Parkway, we are not depriving anyone of the opportunity to travel through our lands. Rather we are offering a much more free opportunity for the public to come in contact with the real life of the Indians as it is lived today."[49]

Moreover, the Bauers thought that the Parkway's limited number of access points and insulated character would cause problems because, by necessity, the picture of Indian life presented along the highway would be controlled by the Interior Department. "Most 'trading post Indians,'" so created, Fred Bauer wrote, "do not give a true picture of the Indian of today. A system of public roads, with freedom to stop at any farmhouse, and visit or trade as desired, would be enjoyed more than a restricted parkway with everything planned just so." Elaborating, he pressed his point: "We do not want you to pass through without seeing more than a feathered 'trading post Indian,' and go back to New York or Boston believing that we Cherokees are living that old life. We live much the same as our white neighbors, and this you will never see from the Blue Ridge Parkway."[50]

Paranoid as some of Bauer's ideas may have been, his distrust of the Interior Department and fear of cultural exploitation were not entirely unwarranted. Parkway developers, supporters, and press reports about the highway did in fact frequently employ stereotypes about Indian life and clearly envisioned the highway as an avenue not only into a natural wonderland but also into the primitive white and Indian cultures thought to exist in the Appalachian region. Such a paradigm guided the Parkway's historical interpretation program, inaugurated in the late 1930s, and became especially salient (as chapter 6 will discuss) at Virginia's Peaks of Otter recreation area.[51]

In any event, even before the Parkway project was devised, the Park Service clearly had seen the Cherokees as an asset to park development plans in the southern mountains. Nearly two years before the Parkway came on the scene, the *Asheville Citizen* shared with readers the NPS's intention to market the Cherokees as one of the Great Smoky Mountains National Park's key attractions. "The education program for the national park," the paper reported, "is expected to utilize to the fullest the folk-lore of the Cherokee Indians and the native white inhabitants of the region. The presence of the Cherokee Indians on a reservation adjoining the national park on the North Carolina side offers many opportunities for dramatic preservations and other features, such as games of Indian ball, old-time Indian dances, archery and blow-gun contests." The paper reported that the Smoky Mountains park superintendent was hoping "that the Cherokees will keep up their work in arts and crafts and their ceremonial dances and athletic contests. These things . . . are tremendously interesting to the average tourist, and the Indians should find fine markets for their arts and crafts among the hundreds of thousands of tourists who are expected to visit the park in the future."[52]

North Carolina officials echoed the superintendent in their 1934 arguments in favor of their suggested Parkway route: "This route also ends at the Cherokee Indian reservation. . . . These Indians lead an agricultural life but their cabins, their council house, the baskets, pottery, bows and arrows they make, their dances and games have changed but little from what it was when the white man first came into their mountain fastness. These people form a picturesque and interesting feature for visitors to the Smoky Park."[53]

Secretary Ickes expressed similar sentiments a few months later when he wrote, "It is frankly admitted that the greatest value of this road will be to the white people living all over the country, who will be made happy by seeing the beauty of the Cherokee Reservation." Throughout the Cherokee battle, the press continued to run articles similar to one in the *Charlotte Observer* that tantalized potential Parkway visitors with images of "closemouthed Cherokee Indians of brownish, reddish, and coppery hues [who] will furnish the crowning touch of interest to everyone who motors over the Blue Ridge parkway."[54]

Thus, while the Bauers embraced the general Cherokee enthusiasm for tourism-oriented development, they were troubled by the thought of government-directed tourist programs capitalizing on Cherokee traditions, however understood. The Bauers especially criticized the BIA-sponsored cultural revivals and the crafts cooperatives planned under the Indian Arts and Crafts Act for the Eastern Band and other tribes. In a blazing statement before Congress, Fred Bauer contended that "the Cherokee Indians, who . . . have adopted most of the white man's civilization, are being re-educated to be Indians. Tribal regalia of feathered headdresses, beaded costumes, moccasins, tom-toms, forgotten ceremonial dances, Indian arts and crafts, and even the Cherokee language is being taught to the children and revived among the adults." The BIA, he added, "whose ideas of rehabilitating the Indians extend no further than to turn him back into a primitive state, hopes to exploit the Indian further by commercializing him. . . . All of these elaborate plans hinge upon the Parkway."[55]

The plan for crafts marketing seemed particularly sinister to the Bauers. The Arts and Crafts Act, they argued, had put the manufacture, marketing, and selling of Indian crafts solely under federal control, and they reported that an investigation conducted by the Cherokee Council, bolstered by other studies, had found that craftspeople working under such auspices were earning very little. "Not only for the Indians," Bauer observed, "but for all craft workers in the Great Smokies, this idea of making a living in weaving and pottery is a failure and a farce." Bauer reported that Cherokee weavers, basket makers, and potters were earning fifty to sixty dollars a year from their labors, adding that "not only has the Federal Government embarked in the Indian arts and crafts business, but it is using sweatshop methods to produce the articles."[56]

The Bauers' criticisms were borne out by an extensive 1933–34 study of the conditions under which craftspeople (mostly women) in the southern Appalachians worked. Conducted by the Women's Bureau of the Labor Department, the study found that crafts producers labored under a wide variety of conditions in small and large enterprises organized in a variety of ways (some did piecework at home, for example, while others worked in commercial enterprises and still others labored in craft shops or schools backed by benevolent agencies). No matter where they worked, however, craftspeople endured long hours under difficult conditions, often with little control over either the design or marketing of their products. The 1933 median income from crafts was fifty-two dollars a year, a wage that compared poorly with that earned in southern factories (usually about six hundred dollars a year).[57]

The Bauers believed that without Parkway and BIA control, the Cherokees could develop and run a tourist industry along state highways while gaining other income from the leasing of reservation land to tourist operators who had the capital to open stores and accommodations. Several years later, Catherine Bauer compared development strategies and outcomes in Gatlinburg, on the western side of the Great Smoky Mountains park, with those at Cherokee, on the eastern side. While Gatlinburg beckoned visitors with interesting shops, good roads, and plenty of places to stay, tourists entering Cherokee were disappointed by the "scarcity of overnight accommodations, the limited parking space, [and] the lack of sidewalks." Cherokee's buildings, she commented, "are taking on a run-down appearance."[58]

In the interest of what she termed "a greater western North Carolina," Bauer went on to examine the reasons for the differences. The crux of the problem, she insisted, was that tourist development at Cherokee had been seriously "retarded" by NPS and BIA efforts to establish federally supervised cooperative tribal tourist enterprises on the reservation in conjunction with the coming of the Parkway. BIA restrictions on Indian use of tribal lands, she contended, choked off proposals to lease Cherokee lands to private outside tourist operators, strangled private initiative in determining the kinds of facilities to be built, and limited individual profits by requiring tourist dollars to be funneled into tribal coffers. Gatlinburg, in contrast, prospered as a consequence of "the investment of private capital and the initiative of people who believed in private enterprise and were willing to proceed in the traditional American manner of doing business." The same capitalist magic could work at Cherokee, she concluded: "If Indians are ever permitted to live like men instead of children, they will readily take their places in the American scheme of things, and will have no need of [the BIA] to wet nurse them along."[59]

Bauer's arguments closely followed her husband's interpretation of Eastern Cherokee history, and the Bauers were in complete agreement about the bureau's and Parkway planners' notions regarding Indian culture and acculturation. In these crucial respects, the tribe's internal disputes about Cherokee history, Cherokee culture, and development policy intersected with planning for the Blue Ridge Parkway.

In Fred Bauer's view, the Eastern Band's unique legal standing—their ownership of their lands, their corporate charter, and other factors deriving from arrangements made when they avoided removal in the nineteenth century—differentiated them from western Native American groups, which had always been recognized as tribes and lived on true federal reservations. Bauer read the history of federal dealings with the Eastern Cherokees as a story of gradually increasing federal control (via the BIA) that was not warranted given the Cherokees' original independence. In short, Bauer thought that since the 1860s, the federal government had tried to squeeze the Eastern Cherokees into an ill-fitting legal model drawn from western Indians' experiences. "The terms 'reservation' and 'tribe' and 'tribal' have seemed appropriate to Congress and the public, because we are Indians," he wrote. "However, these terms suggest a primitive existence upon lands *reserved* for Indians from the public domain. These terms detract from the dignity of citizens who bought their lands individually and became subject to the laws of this State."[60]

To Bauer, the root cause of the growing BIA control over the Eastern Band was the displacement of the facts of Eastern Cherokee history by what he termed the "Mooney myth," drawn from the writings of ethnologist James Mooney, who studied the Cherokees in the 1880s and published his findings in 1900. The Mooney myth centered on the supposed sacrifice made by the Cherokee hero Tsali that enabled the Cherokee remnant to come down from their mountain hiding places and remain in North Carolina while thousands of other Cherokees were marched to Oklahoma. Mooney's account also distorted the complicated history of Eastern Cherokee land acquisition, according to Bauer, glossing over the important points that the nineteenth-century Cherokees had purchased their land individually (rather than communally as a tribe) and had received U.S. citizenship. Bauer asserted correctly that the band had acquiesced to federal control of its lands during the 1920s only in anticipation of the eventual allotment of lands to individual Cherokees. John Collier's administration, however, had halted the allotment process before Cherokee lands could be divided, leaving the Eastern Band stuck with more federal control than many among them had foreseen.[61] Much of the difficulty with the Park Service and the BIA in the 1930s, then, stemmed from competing accounts of this complicated and unique history that left unresolved many questions of the basis for and nature of Cherokee tribal identity.

CIRCUMVENTING BAUER AND THE COUNCIL

Whatever the merits, North Carolina state highway officials and Parkway supporters had long since grown weary of hearing the Bauers' objections. In mid-1937, these North Carolinians and their allies in Washington began to search for ways to circumvent the uncooperative Tribal Council. Some, including Josephus Daniels, favored state condemnation of the land under the power of eminent domain. But the Interior Department devised another strategy: it persuaded Congress to pass legislation to allow a land exchange (contingent on turnover of the Soco Valley right-of-way) if the Cherokees voted for the swap in a general referendum to be held within sixty days. Fred Bauer's belief that the land exchange was "bait to trick Indians into voting for the Soco route" still influenced many Cherokee voters, however, and Chief Blythe, fearing that the compromise would be defeated, never called for the vote.[62]

Stymied by that inaction, Ickes, Browning, and other Parkway planners tossed around ideas for routing alternatives throughout the fall of 1937 and into the following spring. Ickes frightened North Carolina Parkway supporters by seeming at times to favor several routes that entirely circumvented the Cherokee reservation—routes that Browning and his colleagues feared would bring the Parkway to a "shocking anti-climax" near the Great Smoky Mountains National Park.[63]

Aware that Ickes was considering this course, Browning scurried about western North Carolina in the fall of 1937 looking into other possibilities to solve the Cherokee problem. In December, the engineer discussed the matter with Ickes. The following March, Browning, NPS associate director Demaray, Ickes, and Collier again huddled, pondering the question of how to neutralize Fred Bauer. Browning proposed that the Indian Service offer Bauer a job on another reservation, in which case "opposition to the parkway would subside very quickly," but Collier demurred.[64]

THE RIDGE ROUTE PROPOSAL

Thwarted in his strategy for removing Bauer from the scene, Browning returned to North Carolina and worked out yet another proposal, which he and Highway Commission Chair Frank Dunlap presented to the Cherokee Council in May 1938. Forced to take seriously the Bauer objections, Parkway planners finally abandoned the Soco Valley route and suggested a new "ridge route" across the reservation. To sweeten the pot, they offered to pay the Cherokees at least forty thousand dollars for the land, a sum that all parties agreed to be more than adequate. This higher route would afford travelers gorgeous scenery from elevations as high as those along the rest of Parkway and would allow the Park Service to open an end-of-the-road tourist area at Flat Creek (elevation five thousand feet). That site, Browning noted, offered an "unsurpassed panorama of the Great Smoky Mountains" and a view at sunset that "is one of the loveliest I have ever seen." Furthermore, the new route would take land "along the top of a high, rocky ridge which is quite unsuitable for cultivation, orchards or pasture and where there is but little merchantable timber." Even more enticing for the Indians was the promise that if they accepted the ridge route, North Carolina would build a state highway, which the Indians had always preferred to the Parkway, through the Soco Valley. Easily accessible and lacking the Parkway's restrictions, such a highway would facilitate the tribe's turn toward tourism, something both Bauer and Blythe wanted.[65]

In retrospect, the ridge route compromise seems such an obvious solution that it seems odd that policy makers took so long to see it. Placing the final miles of the highway down in the Soco Valley would have represented an anticlimactic departure from the ridgetop location followed by the rest of the Parkway, especially in North Carolina. Furthermore, locating the highway through agriculturally marginal, uninhabited lands was clearly preferable to relocating most of the valley's residents. The plan was simple, appealing all around, and logically compelling, but state highway officials had been planning a highway through the Soco Valley for so long that they seem to have had difficulty prying themselves away from using that route for the Parkway.

Chances for Tribal Council approval of the ridge route compromise looked good. The new BIA agent, C. M. Blair, reported that on the eve of the meeting, "in talking to the council members, including the Assistant Chief, Fred Bauer, . . . we were of the opinion that the resolution would pass unanimously." To their great consternation, however, the council rejected the new agreement, perhaps because of misinformation spread by Fred Bauer.[66]

By now, Browning had become "desperately afraid" that the Indians (and Bauer in particular) would derail his dream project. Still, Browning and Dunlap persisted, hoping that Ickes might now intervene directly. At a July meeting in Washington, however, Ickes rejected this suggestion and only grudgingly gave an exhausted and frazzled Browning and Dunlap thirty days (later extended to sixty) to continue to work for Cherokee approval of the ridge route compromise. Browning and Dunlap dejectedly made their way back to North Carolina. Dunlap

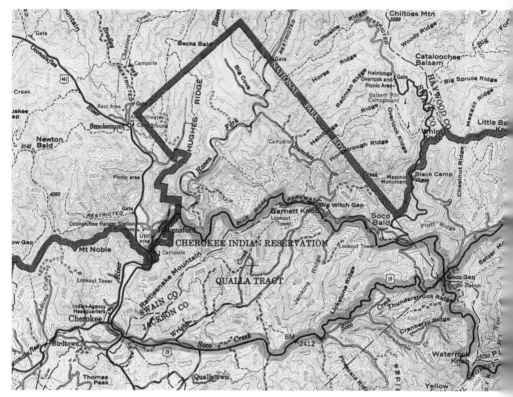

Map showing U.S. 19, the original route proposed for the Parkway through the Soco Valley, and the final Parkway route across the Qualla Boundary's higher ridge to the north of the original route.

was pessimistic: "All this would appear to be good but I honestly believe that Mr. Ickes must himself say something to the Indians and anything short of this is not going to produce much results."[67]

Dunlap's prediction proved correct, but not for lack of trying by Browning, Blair, and Blythe. In August, Bauer uncovered a deceptive plan by the agent (in collaboration with Blythe and with the knowledge of Browning and Dunlap) to "secretly" secure council members' approval of the ridge route without a formal council meeting, thus neutralizing Bauer's influence. The agent had taken a typed copy of a resolution similar to the one rejected by the council in June to council members' homes, where he had tried to convince them to sign it. At least three council members endorsed the resolution, while several others indicated their general support but declined to sign before speaking with Bauer. Later, according to Bauer, the agent had again attempted an informal canvass of the council members. Apparently based on this action, North Carolina newspapers reported (incorrectly and to Bauer's horror) that the Tribal Council had approved the Parkway route. In letters to the governor and the secretary of the interior, Bauer labeled the sneaky tactics a "conspiracy to defraud the Cherokees of lands for [the] Parkway."[68]

Now, however, more than three years after the state had first approached the Cherokees, the tide was turning against Bauer as officials and even some journalist supporters of the Parkway movement increasingly chafed at his obstructionism. A former owner of the *Asheville Citizen*, long a staunch Parkway partisan, asked the publisher of the *Charlotte Observer* to suppress the anti-Parkway, anti-BIA articles the Bauers were sending to North Carolina newspapers until negotiators resolved the issue.[69]

Under pressure from Browning, Daniels, and others and convinced that the Bauers' beloved AIF had ties to the Nazis, Ickes finally softened his resistance to more forceful intervention. Daniels again came to the aid of his friends in North Carolina, encouraging Ickes to overrule the obstructionists at Cherokee. As Daniels confided to Browning, "I . . . have told [Ickes] that, as the Great Father of the Indians, he should be able to use parental authority." When the sixty-day deadline passed without favorable action, Ickes was ready to do just that. After another meeting with North Carolina officials, Ickes directed Interior Department legal advisers to investigate the prospects for a federal or state seizure of the Cherokee right-of-way. By spring, officials had determined that congressional action would be needed to authorize such a confiscation, and Browning, Daniels, Ickes, and Cammerer set to work writing the necessary bill.[70]

As another winter passed without agreement and the Bauers persisted in their press attacks on the New Deal and the Parkway, Chief Blythe worried about possible public antipathy toward the Cherokees for their continued resistance. While explaining to Bauer that "the whole state of North Carolina has a strong feeling of resentment against his attitude," Blythe also worked with Blair to convince the editor of the *Raleigh News and Observer* not to print any more of the Bauers' articles. Dunlap wrote to Blythe that while his conciliatory attitude had been a "bright spot in the clouds," North Carolinians would begin to think that they "would be definitely better off if the Indians were somewhere else" should a solution not materialize soon.[71]

THE END OF NEGOTIATION: LEGISLATIVE WAR

In the spring of 1939, North Carolina politicians, with the acquiescence of Interior Department officials, finally declared legislative war on the Indians. Congressman Weaver introduced the bill to give the secretary of the interior the authority to seize the right-of-way; in return, the Indians would receive generous payment for their land and be permitted to purchase additional land in the nearby national park.[72]

While the bill was in preparation, rumors flew that Bauer would stand fast in his opposition. This time, however, federal and state officials had hardened considerably toward Bauer and dispatched a Federal Bureau of Investigation agent to Cherokee to determine the sources of opposition to the Parkway there. According to a Parkway supporter, the agent reportedly had been "sent directly from Washington, but we do not know by whom. (Don't much care.)"[73]

In July, the House Committee on Public Lands convened hearings on the Weaver bill. A confused Cherokee Council sent both Blythe and Bauer to testify as official representatives and defenders of the band. There, Blythe spoke sympathetically of those among his constituency who did not want the Parkway and noted that all band members objected to the Soco Valley route. He went on say, however, that the compromise ridge route was fair to the Indians and should be adopted.[74]

As expected, Bauer persisted in his objections. Playing on Indians' historically grounded fears of government mistreatment, he mixed specific complaints about the Parkway (its huge land requirements and its easement and use restrictions) with his general distaste for the federal government's new Indian policy. He also expressed dismay at the actions of Secretary Ickes, who, Bauer correctly recalled, had initially told the Indians that the Parkway would not come through if they did not want it. Bauer warned that the "cleverly drawn" confiscation bill would be "just one more stain upon the honor of the United States of America" and argued again, however implausibly, that the implementation of the Indian New Deal on the Qualla Boundary in fact hinged on the building of the Parkway through the reservation.[75]

Bauer asserted that dividing the reservation with the Parkway would be a first step toward incorporating half the Indians' lands into the Great Smoky Mountains National Park. He observed that the bill gave little guarantee that the Indians would receive the promised payment. He complained that because the bill did not specify the route for the Parkway, there was danger of a revival of the hated Soco Valley route. He claimed that any mention of consulting Indian leaders about the eventual route represented mere "camouflage," "just so many meaningless words."[76]

Bauer then laid out his view of how the Parkway project fit into the BIA's larger plans to revitalize Indian traditional culture for commercial exploitation. Echoing the A I F's anticommunist position, he attacked the Indian Bureau for scheming to set up "a model soviet community with so-called cooperatives on this parkway" and to "landscape the Indians into the park entrance . . . for the entertainment of rubbernecked tourists."[77]

Asked by a committee member why he had reached an entirely different conclusion on the Parkway issue than had Chief Blythe, Bauer responded that Blythe had acceded to government plans because as tribal chief and holder of a B I A job, "his bread and butter comes from the Government pay check."[78] If Bauer and Blythe had ever been close as kinfolks, they were now bitterly at odds as tribal leaders.

Bauer Ousted

In the fall 1939 tribal elections, held four years after the controversy had emerged, Cherokee voters finally had the opportunity to choose between Blythe and Bauer in the race for tribal chief. The Parkway issue was central to the campaign, with Blythe promising to implement the ridge route compromise on the condition that North Carolina agree to build the promised state highway through the Soco Valley. Perhaps tired of the turmoil on the reservation and possibly convinced that the more accommodating Blythe was now likelier to assure negotiation of a more favorable agreement in light of the impending passage of the Weaver bill, Cherokee voters reelected Blythe their chief by an overwhelming margin (788 votes to Bauer's 161). They also threw out two of Bauer's staunchest backers on the council. Hearing this news, Blair, the B I A agent, rejoiced that at last the Cherokees had "really cleaned house."[79]

Ridge Route Compromise Approved

The election results improved the mood of North Carolina highway officials, and Highway Commission Chair Dunlap predicted hopefully that the result "will enable us to carry forward our work on the Parkway without any further trouble." Indeed it did. Under Blythe's leadership, the Tribal Council in February 1940 approved the ridge route right-of-way, provided that the pending bill specified the Parkway route, assured the forty-thousand-dollar payment for the tribe's land, and required the state to build the regular highway through the Soco Valley. By the summer of 1940, Congress agreed to the compromise package, and after five years of haggling, the right-of-way matter was finally solved. Despite Dunlap's view that "this is a most absurd sum of money to give for this right of way," state payment of the forty thousand dollars and turnover of the deeds to the right-of-way followed in January 1941. North Carolina moved quickly to construct the promised state highway (now U.S. 19), which was completed during World War II.

The Cherokee sections of the Parkway opened in the 1950s, with Cherokee leaders participating in the dedications.[80]

THE POLITICS OF HISTORY AND
CHEROKEE TOURISM DEVELOPMENT

After his triumph over Bauer, Blythe served as the Eastern Band's principal chief for twenty-four years. Ironically and to the Bauers' acute disappointment, Blythe's ascendancy insured the implementation of tourist-oriented development plans based on the Mooney myth. The victory of this interpretation assured a growing emphasis on the Cherokees' primary identity as Indians in both cultural and political senses as well as a muting of those aspects of Eastern Cherokee history that foregrounded individualism, assimilation, and distance from the BIA.[81]

Under Blythe's leadership, the Eastern Band followed a development strategy that combined private investment with government- and tribally financed enterprises. The tourism industry that this mixed strategy produced during the next several decades has been anchored by the joint tribally and privately sponsored *Unto These Hills* outdoor drama, which since 1950 has repeated for visitors the inaccurate account of Eastern Cherokee history centering on the apocryphal but romantic story of Tsali, which Fred Bauer deplored. Whether tribal, state, private, or mixed, however, almost all tourist operations at Cherokee have traded on identification of the Cherokees as Indians — either as generalized Hollywood Indians in brightly colored, Plains-style "chiefing" outfits or more specifically as Cherokee Indians depicting eighteenth-century Cherokee life at the Oconaluftee Indian Village. Neither version of Indianness embraced the complex economic, political, social, and cultural realities of the Cherokees' lives in the mid-twentieth century.[82]

In spite of his supporters' success in forcing relocation of the Parkway, Bauer seemed later in his life to think that his group had in many ways won the proverbial battle but lost the war. In his view, despite the change in the Parkway routing, the Eastern Cherokees had still been landscaped into the western North Carolina national parks. Much of the town of Cherokee's tourist industry was, however, developed with private funds, and Bauer apparently did not anticipate the possibility that his faith in private enterprise was at odds with his fears of Cherokee cultural exploitation. With the cooperation of many Cherokee citizens and the tribal government, private entrepreneurs at Cherokee ultimately played a large role in this cultural landscaping project, often trading on the very misrepresentations of Indian culture the Bauers had feared from BIA-sponsored programs.[83]

When they united behind Jarrett Blythe, compromised on the Parkway route, and tossed out Fred Bauer, members of the Eastern Band opted for a particular blend of tradition and modernization. Completely distrusting the federal government's ability to treat Indians fairly and suspicious of federal control of the marketing of Cherokee culture, Fred and Catherine Bauer thought that the best protection for Cherokee interests was a Cherokee-built and -controlled tourist industry based on a free-enterprise model and on full assimilation into mainstream white American values and lifestyles. Blythe, conversely, cooperated with federal officials but opposed complete assimilation and emphasized Cherokee cultural and political distinctiveness in the tourist facilities he helped the tribe to build.

The ironies and paradoxes of this outcome are striking. Fred Bauer joined an all-Indian organization and opposed the federal government not because he favored retaining Indian cultural traditions but because he wanted Indians to assimilate. Most important to his thinking was his contention that the Eastern Cherokees' distinctive legal and political arrangements dating from the nineteenth century had put the band on a road to individualism and assimilation and had afforded them a freedom from the strict federal oversight given to western tribes. Blythe, however, compromised with government strategies, supported the Indian New Deal, and worked for continuation of BIA involvement on the Qualla Boundary not because he was insensitive to Indianness but because he judged that government-sponsored, tribally organized tourism might serve both to garner income and to maintain and reinvigorate Cherokee cultural traditions. Despite their radically different strategies, then, both men identified strongly with aspects of their Cherokee heritage, and both were firmly situated within a protracted and conflicted discourse among the Eastern Cherokees about their legal, political, and cultural status. Although they differed in their proposed mechanisms for moving the band forward economically, neither fundamentally questioned tourism as a development strategy.[84]

More broadly, the five-year struggle at Cherokee illustrates the multifarious and knotty issues raised by both the Indian New Deal and the Blue Ridge Parkway. Although they were roundly dismissed as cranks and eventually repudiated by their community, the Bauers—smart, feisty, and alert to some of the larger implications of the changes coming to their region during the New Deal—provided some of the most sophisticated and consistent critiques of both projects voiced from North Carolina in the 1930s. Recent scholarship on the Indian New Deal has supported the Bauers' sense that despite its laudable intentions, Collier's BIA continued traditional federal paternalism toward Indians and sometimes pushed its agenda with a heavy hand. As one student of the period has written, Collier "was so firm in his convictions of what was right for the Indians that he sometimes imposed conformity or manipulated the Indians to behave in ways that he thought best." At times, this tendency engendered an attitude of intolerance within the bureau toward those who opposed the Collier program. Other scholars have agreed that Collier's BIA was caught in a conflict between its goal of increasing Indian autonomy and its assumption that Indians were unable to manage their own resources without federal oversight. Furthermore, in spite of his stated support for Indian cultural diversity, Collier tended to impose a single plan for the ordering of Indian society on tribes of various histories and viewpoints. Thus, the Bauers' sense of the internal contradictions within the Indian New Deal—particularly their charges of harassment and pressure from the BIA agents at Cherokee and their fears of increased Bureau control—have been corroborated by later analyses.[85]

The advent of the Parkway project added an additional layer of complexity to debates under way on the Cherokee reservation; conversely, discussion of the Parkway in the Cherokee context raised some issues that were never as clearly articulated by other affected mountain residents. In relation to the Indian New Deal, Parkway planners' attempt to take Cherokee lands must have seemed an alarming contradiction to the IRA's stated intent of helping Indians restore their land base. The juxtaposition of these two projects no doubt heightened the fears of Cherokees already disposed to distrust the BIA. In addition, the Cherokees' awareness of federal efforts to revitalize and market their culture made them acutely sensitive to the potential for Park Service manipulation and distortion of that culture in Parkway exhibits, something 1930s Appalachian whites—themselves the objects of some analogous NPS cultural marketing—never collectively called into question.

Furthermore, the Cherokees' unique legal relationship to their land forced them to confront the proposed Parkway land turnover as a community rather than as individual landowners, and their complicated political situation bought them time to consider all of the project's implications. Emboldened by their political autonomy, the Cherokees publicly voiced many of the same objections to the Parkway's land requirements and restricted access that led many other landowners to grumble privately. In bringing these questions into the public spotlight, the Eastern Band put together the most coherent counterargument offered in the 1930s to the assurances of Asheville's business-oriented Parkway boosters that the road would be the panacea for western North Carolina's ills.

With a long-vested interest in a severely sagging tourism economy, the Asheville partisans most responsible for the Parkway's construction in western North Carolina could not objectively ponder the fact that the Parkway served their needs better than it did those on the Cherokee reservation, where land was scarcer and the regular state highway system was less well developed. In Cherokee as in no other place in the North Carolina mountains, however, Asheville-based Parkway boosters as well as Highway Commission staffers and federal officials had to face the possibility that the Parkway did not answer all mountain constituencies' needs. The intensely political five-year process Parkway planners endured to alter plans for the highway on the Cherokee lands taught some hard lessons indeed.

The routing modifications made in response to Cherokee opposition, however, were relatively small ripples on the seas of change coming to western North Carolina. By the end of the 1930s, the Great Smoky Mountains National Park had opened and Parkway construction was well under way. As the years passed, the Great Smokies and the Parkway would become the most popular attractions within the national park system. Large-scale tourism development had arrived, and with its advent, the Cherokees—and Appalachian whites as well, for that matter—encountered dilemmas that have faced marginalized peoples the world over as private and public commercial and industrial development has increasingly encroached. Mining operations, forest cutting, dam and highway construction, and other harbingers of the progress of modern civilization have thrown indigenous peoples worldwide into turmoil. In the United States in particular, federal use of eminent domain to seize Native American lands for public works projects grew more common as the twentieth century passed. As at Cherokee, the BIA has often facilitated such efforts with the assistance of tribal councils manipulated and co-opted by outside interests. By the 1960s, such tactics had helped spawn the growth of the vocal American Indian Movement to oppose the destruction of Native American communities and lands.[86]

Although quite different in some important respects from that later movement, the Eastern Cherokee opposition to the Parkway—and the internal tribal debates about tradition, modernization, culture, and history that the process triggered—constituted an early episode in the struggle of native and marginalized American peoples to deal with the demands of twentieth-century industrialization and development. Years would pass before many other western North Carolinians would follow the Cherokees' example and band together to fight development efforts they judged to be harmful to their communities.[87]

REMEMBERING THE PEAKS OF OTTER

TELLING HISTORY ON THE PARKWAY LANDSCAPE

Born in the Peaks of Otter community in Bedford County, Virginia, in the 1870s, Dr. E. L. Johnson practiced medicine for more than fifty years, reportedly delivering more than six thousand babies and serving as the Bedford County medical examiner. In Johnson's youth, the Peaks community had bustled with the activity produced by the twenty-odd families who lived within in a two-mile radius: a church, a school, a lodge, a hotel, two mills, traffic along the local turnpike, and a thriving tourist trade. Into the 1920s, that tourist trade, centered around the cozy Hotel Mons and the breathtaking views from Sharp Top mountain, flourished as more than four thousand visitors came to the area each summer.[1]

In 1960, National Park Service (NPS) staff interviewed Johnson about life in the area (by then under NPS jurisdiction as one of its Parkway recreation areas) in his childhood. The Peaks of Otter, he told them, "is a ghost-town today compared with what it was 75 years ago, when I was a child." Assessing the site a decade later, the Parkway's first staff historian, F. A. "Andy" Ketterson Jr., agreed. "The Peaks of Otter community area has been so altered," he lamented, "that, except for the mountains themselves, the area bears no physical resemblance to the man-made area that existed there at the turn of the century."[2]

By the early 1970s, when Ketterson arrived, it did indeed appear that the Parkway at the Peaks of Otter must have been built through a nearly uninhabited landscape. Most of the buildings that constituted the old community were gone; not even the footings of the Hotel Mons remained. The Park Service had converted the few structures it had kept to a decidedly rustic appearance, projecting an image of the area as a pioneer outpost. The farmhouse (known as the Johnson Farm) owned by one of the last families to sell to the federal government had been stripped of its weatherboard siding and added porch, so that it now stood as a lonely log cabin in a grassy field. Visitors could reach it only after a long walk that gave the impression of great distance from any other habitation, community center, or travel route.

The isolated picture did not result from organic forces of social evolution, even though by the 1930s, when the Park Service entered the picture, the once-vibrant community had already begun to decline. Instead, during the thirty years after it took possession of the lands for the recreation area, the N P S intentionally obliterated most of the evidence of the community that had once hummed there, creating instead a beautifully designed but historically empty ghost town. Park Service efforts literally re-membered—reassembled—what the N P S's guidelines term a "historic vernacular landscape" (one that evolved out of people's use of the area) into a "historic designed landscape" (one explicitly planned by a landscape architect or other professional). The process starkly illustrates both the dynamic quality of so-called cultural landscapes (landscapes intentionally created as such by human activity) and the layering of multiple uses over time and space that has created most of the landscapes in which we live daily.[3]

In 1972, Ketterson embarked on a thoroughgoing reexamination of the version of history told at the Peaks of Otter site. But remembering the Peaks of Otter—that is, reconstructing and presenting the documentable history of that particular place—proved challenging on a landscape so radically altered.[4] Despite Ketterson's efforts and at least two intensive research initiatives that followed over the next twenty years, as late as 2002 the landscape still presented an idealized and misleading picture more in keeping with the Parkway's imperatives of landscape design than with any responsibility to inform the public about the area's true history.

Visitors leaving the Peaks of Otter Lodge to walk to the Johnson Farm in 2002, for example, crossed under the Parkway to the open field where the Hotel Mons once stood. There, they faced a fork in the hiking trail. Park Service maps indicated that hikers could reach the farm by way of either of the two diverging paths, but signs at the spot directed walkers to take the much longer of the two routes. Meanwhile, signage for the shorter walk, passing through the field by the Hotel Mons site, was so minimal that few first-time visitors could be expected to be able to follow it. By its markings on the landscape in 2002, then, the Park Service still left the distinct impression that the farm was isolated and remote. The story of the area's historical connectedness and dynamism remained as hidden as was the shorter, more direct path to the Johnson Farm site.

The Peaks of Otter clearly illustrates the internal contradictions of the NPS's goals on the Parkway. Creating an aesthetically beautiful, idealized recreational landscape in keeping with the overall Parkway vision has not been very compatible with conveying regional history—complicated and multilayered as it is—to the traveling public. The Park Service's handling of this task—complicated still further over time by the agency's institutional evolution—has impeded public understanding of the constructed nature of the Parkway and of the choices that have given shape to it.

Thus, understanding both the NPS's almost total transformation of the landscape at the Peaks of Otter and the difficulty of telling history there requires the untangling of at least three stories that unfolded simultaneously. To do so is to understand how re-membering has hindered remembering.

Story 1: Tourism at the Peaks

The process by which the Park Service took ownership of the Peaks of Otter site, designed and built its Parkway and associated structures, and created the picturesque scene that greets visitors today is a part of the logical and linear continuation of the ongoing use of the site as a tourist destination since the early nineteenth century. The NPS has been merely the latest in a series of actors—beginning with nineteenth-century turnpike builders and innkeepers and continuing through local businessmen and hoteliers in the early twentieth century—who generated tourist traffic at the site.

Story 2: A New Layer on the Landscape

The story at the Peaks—and, indeed, that of the Parkway more broadly—is also more than just an account of another phase in tourism development. The NPS's work at the site constitutes an abrupt break with the past in which a new, designed landscape overwrote most evidence of an older, vernacular, organically produced one. Differently from earlier individuals or groups that had tried to develop the site primarily by capitalizing on the inherent beauty of the surrounding mountains, the NPS set about to create a central attraction—the Parkway—set in carefully controlled, designed surroundings. Paradoxically, this latest landscape of tourism at the Peaks drew self-consciously on idealized elements of nineteenth-century regional history and culture to round out its picturesque scene.

Story 3: "Great Picture Windows":
Telling History on a Compromised Landscape

The first two stories are not, in themselves, especially problematic. As in most places and times, the new replaces the old. Some processes continue; others end. But the first two stories are also linked by the related yet separate transformation of the NPS itself from an agency that focused primarily on natural resources to one that gradually became the arbiter of much of America's historical and cultural preservation and interpretation.

After the mid-1930s, at the outset of the Parkway's design and development, the NPS received the additional legal mandate to interpret the history and culture of sites under its management. At the outset, this agenda appeared to intertwine compatibly with the Parkway landscape architects' plans to open "great picture windows" on Appalachian life and culture. Paradoxically, however, in opening those windows, the NPS found itself drawing the curtains on much of the past it was — to a greater and greater degree as the twentieth century wore on — charged with exhibiting and interpreting.[5]

Thus, the NPS not only created a new landscape of tourism at the Peaks but also took on the charge — using the new landscape as a text — of telling a story of the old community, the major evidence of which the Park Service had obliterated. The NPS version of history that ultimately emerged at the Peaks better fit a pictur-esque vision of nineteenth-century rural life (created mostly as a part of landscape architects' attempts to design a beautiful setting) than it did the facts of life at the Peaks of Otter. Thus, two of the Parkway's goals within the general NPS frame-work — to present an idealized and aesthetically appealing picture of rural Appala-chian life within a carefully designed scenic landscape and to help tourists under-stand something about regional history — coexisted increasingly uncomfortably, creating what remains one of the Parkway's central management conundrums.

Viewed from a national perspective, the Peaks of Otter story thus contains many features familiar to students of historic preservation: an overweening focus on pioneer, agricultural landscapes; sparse attention to the twentieth century; a tendency to fix inherently fluid landscapes at a particular point in time (prefer-ably the distant past); the gulf between documentable history of a site and the presentation offered; and the profound impact of preoccupations at the time of a site's creation on the history presented there. Documenting these often humor-ous mutilations of "history," indeed, has become something of a cottage industry in historical scholarship. All of these impulses, at play at countless sites across America, proved an exceptionally good fit as they were brought to bear on the Appalachian region, which has for more than a century been (mis)understood by Americans as a rural backwater (or back region, in Dean MacCannell's terms) unchanged by historical process.[6]

The evolution of the Peaks of Otter site from the 1930s to the present and the Park Service's management during that time also illuminate many features of the NPS's emergence as the major arbiter of historic preservation in the United States. As the Parkway was developed, the NPS gradually appropriated the discourse and methods of the budding, professionalizing historic preservation movement.

Yet the adoption of rigorous preservation and interpretation standards has proceeded somewhat erratically, subject always to conflicting institutional impulses and shifting funding priorities. If, in the 1930s, when plans for the Peaks of Otter were first drawn up, no comprehensive preservation policies guided NPS planners managing the site's remaining structures, the site's condition by the 1990s revealed that NPS preservation policy development since the 1930s had far outpaced the service's ability to bring many of its properties into line with its stated policies. The agency also had not learned how to include itself within the array of actors acknowledged to have added layers to a site's present configuration.[7] As it tried to rationalize recreational and aesthetic concerns within its mandate to interpret history, presentations at many of its vernacular landscapes, like that of the Johnson Farm, exhibited dramatic shifts as agency policies evolved. Within this framework, we turn to the Peaks of Otter's three stories.

STORY I: THE "MONS HABIT"
PRIVATE TOURISM DEVELOPMENT AT THE PEAKS

Before the Parkway

The Peaks of Otter is a triangular area consisting of several thousand acres lying among three peaks in Bedford County along Virginia's Blue Ridge, about thirty-five miles north of Roanoke. The three Peaks—pointed and rocky Sharp Top (3,875 feet), smoother and more wooded Flat Top (4,001 feet), and smaller Harkening Hill (3,350 feet)—surround a beautiful rolling valley where today lie the Park Service's Peaks of Otter Lodge, the artificial Abbott Lake (named for Stanley Abbott), a visitor center, a 144-site campground and camp store, and a small gas station. Because of the relative flatness of surrounding lands, the Peaks stand out, and the summit of Sharp Top affords a dramatic view. As a venerable tourist respite, the Peaks was one of the sites Abbott identified in his first plan, drawn up in late 1934, for a string of recreational "bulges" along the Parkway—areas of outstanding scenery where larger amounts of land would be acquired to offer Parkway travelers a wider array of facilities.[8]

At least since the arrival of European settlers in the Bedford County area in the mid-eighteenth century, Virginians had known of the beauty of the Peaks of Otter. The area's fortunes had subsequently risen and fallen with the progress of road development. Beginning with the construction of a turnpike running from Liberty (now Bedford) to Buchanan across the Blue Ridge by way of the Peaks of Otter in the late eighteenth or early nineteenth century and continuing through the arrival of the Parkway in the 1930s, the level of accessibility by road was always key to the unfolding of life at the Peaks.[9]

Throughout the nineteenth century, the Peaks area was one of a number of relatively accessible scenic spots in Virginia. The Liberty-Buchanan Turnpike provided the crucial east-west connection to towns on either side of the Blue Ridge, and the situation improved considerably after 1851, when citizens of Bedford and Botetourt Counties organized the Buchanan and Bedford Turnpike Company to upgrade the rocky road. Supporters of turnpike improvement included members of the sheep-farming Benjamin Wilkes family, which by then owned the Peaks and hoped to expand the family's nascent hotel business there.

The business of catering to travelers along the road, begun with the opening of a small "ordinary" in the 1830s, soon expanded with the establishment of the Otter Peaks Hotel in the 1850s. Providing accommodations for at least thirty, offering stage service to Liberty (Bedford) timed to correspond with local train schedules, and beginning to charge tolls to visitors ascending Sharp Top and Flat Top, the entrepreneurial owner of the hotel, Leyburn Wilkes, took tourism at the Peaks to a new level as he sought to draw visitors rather than simply to serve those who happened by on their way somewhere else. The publication in that same decade of drawings and travel stories of the Peaks area by popular artists and writers in national magazines such as *Harper's Monthly* widened the region's fame and doubtless boosted the hotel's business. Nearly seven hundred people struggled their way to the Sharp Top summit in the summer of 1858, by which time the complex included an eight-room hotel, two distilleries, a stable, and a rock shelter at the top of the peak. Several slaves (of which Bedford County had many) helped the owners to run the operation in the pre–Civil War years.[10]

As this tourist enterprise grew in the 1850s, the family whose farmstead would later become the focus of NPS interpretive efforts bought land and settled in the Peaks area. John T. Johnson, whose father had been born in 1790 and had farmed in next-door Botetourt County, purchased 102 acres (to which he later added) straddling the Botetourt-Bedford County line and adjoining the Wilkes lands on the side of Harkening Hill. There, in the years surrounding the Civil War,

Nineteenth-century graphic artist David H. Strother (known as Porte Crayon) published several drawings of the Peaks of Otter in *Harper's* magazine in the 1850s. These two views show Sharp Top from the hotel and a distant view of Sharp Top and Flat Top. North Carolina Collection, University of North Carolina at Chapel Hill.

Johnson's farm prospered with its sheep herd, distillery, and potato crop. In 1884 Johnson sold the farm to his son, Jason.[11]

After the Civil War, the Johnson Farm and the Wilkes family's nearby tourist enterprises developed in tandem, with the tourist operation expanding through clearing of lands and the addition of an apple orchard, two distilleries, henhouses, stables, many other outbuildings, and miles of new fencing. Despite the destruction of the original hotel by fire in the 1870s and subsequent Wilkes family squabbles and legal battles that eventually led to the division and sale of the twenty-eight-hundred-acre property at auction in the 1880s, the area continued to thrive.[12]

Indeed, a late-nineteenth-century boom in nearby Roanoke, induced by its selection as a hub for the Norfolk and Western Railroad, reverberated north into Bedford County in the 1880s and 1890s, setting off a smaller development frenzy in which local citizens and outside developers organized land development companies and changed the name of the county seat from Liberty to Bedford City. At the Peaks, the boom inspired the owners of the old Peaks hotel site (a couple originally from New York) to build a new hotel they named the Mons (Latin for mountain) in 1897. A businessman from Baltimore purchased the Peaks in the 1890s and continued to charge tolls for treks to Sharp Top, where a rock shelter provided crude overnight lodging.[13]

As the twentieth century opened, the Peaks area was alive with the activities of tourists and the twenty or so families of both races that called it home, created community institutions and traditions, and made their livings by farming, raising livestock, tending fruit orchards, distilling, and catering to turnpike traffic and tourists.[14]

With the construction of the Hotel Mons, the community took on a more defined shape. A one-room school opened near the hotel, and the hotel's owner donated land to build a church/meeting hall for local residents. The area continued to attract the attention of developers from inside and outside of Virginia, as the Hotel Mons then went through several owners in the first two decades of the new century. Guests visited from nearby Bedford, Lynchburg, Roanoke, and Richmond as well as from Boston, Kansas City, Pittsburgh, Cincinnati, Buffalo, New Orleans, El Paso, Philadelphia, Detroit, Toledo, Los Angeles, and New York.[15]

Jason Johnson; his wife, Jennie; and their seven children ran the farm in the shadow of Harkening Hill, with Jason using his carpentry skills to update and expand the house. The family attended Baptist churches in both Botetourt and Bedford Counties, and the couple sent one son, E. L., to the Medical College of Virginia, where he learned the skills he would later need to serve the Bedford population for more than half a century.[16]

The changes that eventually led to the Peaks becoming a Parkway recreation area began before 1920, when a group of Bedford men took control of the county's scenic jewels—Sharp Top and Flat Top—as well as the Hotel Mons from their Maryland and Minnesota owners.[17] Soon thereafter, the federal government purchased nearly twenty-five thousand acres of mountain land near the Peaks in Bedford, Rockbridge, and Botetourt Counties for incorporation into the newly developing National Forest system.

To accomplish the first purchase, five well-connected Bedford men organized the Peaks of Otter Corporation in 1914 with an eye toward purchasing and developing the Peaks and the hotel site. In 1916, they reached a complex four-way agreement with the federal government, the owners of the hotel, and the owners of the Peaks that gave the corporation ownership of more than 580 acres at the Peaks, with the federal government purchasing for the National Forest most of the remaining 1,527 acres. Peaks Corporation–owned property now included the Mons and ninety-five acres, twenty-nine acres at the summit of Flat Top, seventy-two acres on the peak of Sharp Top (with its buildings, access to the summit, and the right to charge tolls), and various other lands.[18]

The new owners aimed to bring tourism-based prosperity to the Bedford area. Local druggist Walter L. Lyle, the entrepreneurial owner of an elegant home on the city's East Main Street, headed the corporation. Dr. B. A. Rice and former Bedford city manager William C. "Buddy" Ballard were also partners. In addition to Lyle, the most active members of the group were Thurston W. Richardson (publisher of the *Bedford Bulletin*) and attorney and former circuit judge Hunter Miller.

Suffused with boosterish optimism about Bedford, Richardson embarked on the Peaks project after having promoted a number of other improvements to the Bedford area, including bringing in telephone service and building a town-owned hydroelectric plant on the James River. Miller, who later served in the Virginia legislature, shared Richardson's enthusiasm for the project as well as a real sense of public-spiritedness in planning for its development.[19]

The new Peaks of Otter Corporation immediately set to work upgrading the resort and improving travelers' access. The area's tourism and road supporters tended to be the same people, as was the case in Asheville and indeed nationwide. Not surprisingly, the corporation's leaders saw improved roads as key to success in promoting the Peaks. Perhaps coincidentally, the year after the corporation purchased the lands there, Richardson, who already served as head of the Bedford Board of Trade's Road Committee, was elected president of the Roanoke-Lynchburg Highway Association, which lobbied for improvements to the Lynchburg-Bedford-Roanoke road. But beyond this project, which might not have directly helped the Peaks of Otter, Richardson also sought to have the state build a road through National Forest Service lands to the Peaks from Natural Bridge, a long-popular scenic site about fifteen miles to the northwest on the other side of the Blue Ridge. Hoping to capitalize on travelers' interest in other Virginia sites, Richardson argued that such a road would "give tourists the most magnificent trip that can be found in the Eastern United States, taking in . . . Luray Cave, Grottoes, Natural Bridge, the mountains and the Peaks of Otter."[20]

To attract more tourists, Richardson knew, the company would have to overhaul the Hotel Mons. Relatively small and dilapidated after years of neglect, the hotel had still "done a good business" in recent years, but the new owners immediately began to plan a new building. Completed by 1920, the new hotel more than doubled the available rooms. The new structure became the Hotel Mons, while the older building was dubbed the Annex. Three small guest cottages (including Peaks View and Road View, each with its own bath) rounded out the little cluster of white frame lodging facilities, all trimmed in green, connected by wooden boardwalks, and surrounded by a white fence. The corporation leased the complex to two couples who had longtime ties to the area and who managed the operation during the summers.[21]

The Peaks was not a luxury retreat, yet throughout the 1920s and early 1930s it attracted a steady stream of week-at-a-time return visitors with the "Mons habit." Accommodations were comfortable but by some accounts rather "homely." The main building boasted a large front porch lined with rockers, and guests could gather in the large living room with a huge stone fireplace where, the final proprietor recalled, "a cheery fire burned on cool days and rainy evenings." Including the Annex and the cottages, a total of about forty-four guest rooms housed one hundred people. Visitors in all the buildings shared baths and washed their faces using a pitcher of water and a bowl on a washstand in each room. The "somewhat uncertain" electrical generator, kept in a shed behind the hotel, "cast a flickering incandescence over the evening activities of the guests." When it failed, oil lamps lighted the guests' games of bridge or charades.[22]

In the attractive Mons dining room, waitresses in "smartly pleated aprons" fluttered around twelve large square tables, serving three home-cooked meals a day of country ham, fried chicken, lamb and veal roasts, vegetables, biscuits, and fresh fruit, eggs, and milk and butter. While one 1920s-era brochure noted that the resort's recreational facilities consisted mainly of "nature," the hotel also offered hiking, horseshoes, dancing, tennis, and croquet. Other visitors amused themselves with storytelling, singing, reading, and indoor games, and children played in a playhouse. By the late 1920s and early 1930s, guests could also take horseback

Hotel Mons complex, Peaks of Otter, 1920s. Courtesy Blue Ridge Parkway.

expeditions to Sharp Top (a twelve-hundred-foot climb), swim in a swimming pool, play miniature golf, and listen to entertainment by "musical artists, public speakers, readers and clog-dancers" brought in by Eugene and Fredonia Putnam, professionally trained musicians who had become the hotel operators. Guests in those years danced to the music of a "bouncy jazz pianist" (possibly an African American man from Bedford named Tiny Johnson) who frequently entertained at the hotel. From time to time, a band from Bedford would come for a "gala evening." For all of this, guests paid between $3.00 and $4.00 per person per day or $17.50 to $20.00 per week.[23]

But neither the facility itself nor the activities it offered served as primary draws for guests. Years after she checked out the final visitor in the fall of 1936, Myriam Putnam Moore, the Putnams' daughter, recalled that "the whole actuality of Hotel Mons" was both "a location and a state of mind." People came for food and relaxation in a gorgeous natural setting in (as one brochure described it) the "social atmosphere . . . of an old Virginia country home" where the managing couple aimed to be "the host and hostess . . . and guests are made members of one large family."[24]

The source of some of the family feeling at the Hotel Mons was the presence of a real family not far away. While the Peaks of Otter Corporation had been at

Members of the Bryant family lean on the fence at their farm at the Peaks of Otter, ca. 1925. The farm complex included numerous outbuildings, a large garden, and extensive farmed fields. A road passed directly through the property. Courtesy Blue Ridge Parkway.

work improving its property at the Peaks, the third generation of the Johnson family to live and farm at the Peaks of Otter had come into ownership of the family's property just around the mountain. In 1921, Jason Johnson sold 134 acres of his land to his son-in-law, Mack Bryant, who already owned another 106 acres nearby. Mack moved his wife, Callie, and their seven children into the farmhouse. The Bryant family would own the place until the arrival of the Park Service, and throughout the 1920s and 1930s, the Bryants maintained a close relationship with the hotel.[25]

Like the two generations before them, the Bryants (with all family members working) ran an extensive farm, producing nearly all they needed and selling a considerable surplus for cash. With almost 240 acres under cultivation, the farm blossomed with large field crops (hay, oats, corn), and produced prodigious quantities of vegetables. Apple, peach, pear, and plum trees flourished, as did chickens, dairy and beef cattle, and hogs and a prized stock of horses for farm work and transportation.[26]

The Bryants lived as part of an interdependent community in the Bedford-Botetourt area. They ground their corn at a nearby mill and bought coffee, sugar, and flour in local stores while selling their surplus produce to stores, individuals,

Bryant/Johnson Farm at the Peaks of Otter, ca. 1920. Courtesy Blue Ridge Parkway.

and a local cannery. With neighbors from other farms, they cooperated on larger tasks such as quilting, butchering cattle and hogs, and sawing wood for the winter. Their children attended the Mons community school and later the Botetourt County schools. Mack Bryant and one of his sons joined the local men's lodge. The family went to church regularly, and Callie Bryant routinely entertained between twenty-five and fifty guests at Sunday dinner.[27]

The Mons Hotel, less than a fifteen-minute walk away, provided both cash income and social contact. The Bryant children earned money by working for the hotel or its guests, and hotel regulars frequently walked up to visit the family, bringing trinkets for the children and admiring Callie's flower gardens surrounding the house (from which she sold bunches of flowers for the hotel dining tables). By one account, the Bryants even cooperated with one of the couples managing the Mons to build a swimming pool for the community and the tourists, served by water from the Bryants' spring in return for an annual payment of twenty-five dollars. The Bryant family and its farm thus became essential parts of what made the Mons experience so attractive to visitors, and the hotel constituted a key element in the family economy.[28]

More than either the hotel or the Bryant family, however, the real attraction for tourists at the Peaks of Otter was the mountains. From the nineteenth century on, Sharp Top had drawn intrepid hikers and horseback riders to its rocky top, where the little "rock house" shelter had perched since the days of the Wilkes family. One of the Peaks Corporation owners estimated that his company's efforts to improve roads to the Peaks area starting in 1917 and its later efforts (with Forest Service aid) to upgrade the trail up the mountain had dramatically increased visitation from its pre-1916 average of about one thousand people a year to nearly five times as many in 1925. Corporation owners were certain—perhaps with some justification—that this part of their property was the greatest potential moneymaker.[29]

In the 1920s and 1930s, fifty cents would admit one adult to the summit (half the price charged at Mt. Mitchell and Chimney Rock, North Carolina, and Natural Bridge, Virginia). The proprietors the corporation engaged to manage the Sharp Top portion of the operation collected the tolls at the bottom of the mountain and offered food in a pavilion at the summit as well as overnight accommodations for perhaps thirty people in one of several small cabins. Whether or not they came to the Hotel Mons, tourists loved Sharp Top, where Mons advertising claimed they had "an unobstructed view in every direction for nearly a hundred miles." Filtered through the "peculiar blue haze" that often settled over the mountains, sunrises on Sharp Top were especially dramatic. The last hotel proprietor remembered how groups of young people came to the Peaks from Roanoke or Lynchburg on Saturday evenings to climb Sharp Top, lugging picnic breakfasts to eat on the summit the next morning. "Many a Sunday School class," she recalled, "thus greeted the Sabbath morn, read their Scripture lessons by the gleam of sunrise on the heights, sang hymns, and felt happy and uplifted." One of the Sharp Top managers estimated that on one Sunday morning in 1929, more than four hundred people crowded onto the mountaintop for a dawn prayer service.[30]

But as the 1920s wound down and the Great Depression dawned, corporation owners were disappointed by their resort's performance, which seemed to lag further and further behind comparable sites. Instead of steadily increasing, visitation at both the hotel and Sharp Top peaked in the mid-1920s and then slid downward. At the Mons, which in the early 1920s was filled to capacity by 1 July and remained busy through August, the crowds thinned as 1926 and 1927 wore on. By the time the final proprietors were in place after 1928, their daughter later recalled, the hotel was "doin' alright" to have eighty of its possible one hundred beds full most of the time. At Sharp Top, too, 1927 visitation was off by nearly a thousand from its 1924 numbers, and the owners despaired of ever seeing it sur-

The Peaks of Otter in the distance (Sharp Top on the left and Flat Top on the right) with the city of Bedford in the foreground, 1938. Norfolk and Western Historical Photograph Collection, Digital Library and Archives, University Libraries, Virginia Polytechnic Institute and State University, Blacksburg.

pass five thousand in a season. Gross receipts from Sharp Top tolls and summit lodging barely broke two thousand dollars in 1926, while profits came to about half that.[31]

The Bedford owners frequently complained that other scenic attractions in the southern Appalachians were booming and pointed out that tourism was growing as a consequence of expanded automobile ownership. Thurston Richardson tallied up the figures in an article in his *Bedford Bulletin*: in 1930, Virginia's Luray Cave took in more than $80,000, while revenues at nearby Endless Caverns soared over $150,000. At the nearest competing attraction, Natural Bridge, more than one hundred thousand visitors paid a dollar apiece in 1930. In North Carolina during the same year, more than seventy-five thousand people passed through the gates at Chimney Rock, only a sleepy backwater fifteen years earlier.[32]

The Peaks Corporation's owners knew that just as the key to the Peaks' rise as a tourist destination in the nineteenth century was the relatively good state of transportation into the area (improvement of the cross-mountain turnpike, combined with railway service to Bedford), the explanation for the area's sluggish growth in the 1920s and 1930s was the lack of good access. Although the area had been relatively easy to reach prior to the advent of the automobile, auto-friendly road improvements nearer other resorts had begun to shunt tourists along smoother routes. Thus, with the spread of automobile transportation, an area that had never before been particularly isolated became much more so by the dawn of the Great Depression.[33]

At the heart of the problem lay the breakdown of the formerly busy cross-mountain turnpike route from Bedford west through the Peaks to Buchanan. At its own expense and with the help of convict labor, the company had made some improvements to the road to the Peaks from Bedford (then Highway 10, present Highway 43), and company advertising attempted to put a good face on the situation around 1930 by reassuring the public that the twelve-mile trip from the train at Bedford was easy, following a "good, safe dirt and macadam road all the way." In fact, the road's quality varied along its length, going from clay to lime dust to crushed rock. The grim reality of travel to the Mons, however, was that guests arrived over "the mean and narrow dirt road, Rt. #43 from Bedford City, in motor cars panting and steaming with engines overheated from the climb. Many came by train to Bedford, and by hired car to the Peaks; but more in their own autos." Even Peaks Corporation leaders privately agreed that getting to the Peaks by auto was exceptionally difficult and that the "rough, steep, and narrow" road from Bedford discouraged automobile traffic. By 1930, coming to the Peaks by automobile from Buchanan to the west had become impossible: the road had "practically been abandoned."[34]

By the late 1920s, the lack of attention to the Buchanan-Peaks half of the route particularly troubled the Peaks owners. The development of the Lee Highway, running northeast to southwest through Virginia's Great Valley on the west side of the Blue Ridge and connecting tiny Buchanan to Roanoke to the south and Lexington to the north, promised to bring a new stream of travelers to within twelve miles of the Peaks. Yet without improvement of the road between the Peaks and Buchanan, travelers along this important trunk route would not be able easily to reach the Peaks of Otter.[35]

Richardson realized, however, that with the needed road improvements, the area could become a tourist destination on par with Natural Bridge, which lay right on the Lee Highway. Indeed, with the road open, the bridge's annual "great crowd" of one hundred thousand visitors might simply be invited "to come on over to the Peaks," as upgrading of the Buchanan-to-Peaks route would shorten the driving distance by nearly fifty miles. Richardson even confidently predicted that the Peaks would draw more repeat business than Natural Bridge: wrote Richardson of that attraction, "Once seen, the novelty wears off"; however, "the thrill of the top of the Peaks is a never ending delight that is just as intense on the hundredth visit as it was at the first."[36]

Starting in 1927, when visitation began to decline, Richardson and his colleagues set out to arrange for improvements to the road between the Peaks and Buchanan. They lobbied the Virginia Highway Commission to undertake construction in the area while working for locally financed upgrading of the route. The company sought partnership agreements with Bedford and Botetourt Counties and the U.S. Forest Service (which owned much of the surrounding land). Peaks of Otter, Inc., Richardson suggested, might contribute nearly half of the project's costs, which were estimated to run more than one hundred thousand dollars. With strong citizen support, especially in Bedford, the counties also appeared disposed to contribute. When the state approved the takeover of the Peaks-Buchanan project into its system with the passage of the Secondary Roads Act of 1932, improvements seemed at last to be forthcoming. But construction work remained excruciatingly slow to get under way.[37]

As they watched this drama drag on with no change in the travel situation and as income at the hotel and Sharp Top continued to dwindle, Richardson and his colleagues realized that the original company investors could not, by themselves, provide the funds needed to develop the Peaks of Otter into a profitable venture on par with Natural Bridge. As early as 1927, Richardson had undertaken what became an increasingly desperate attempt to raise cash for improvements to the site, including plans for construction of an automobile road to Sharp Top and possibly a new hotel, a lake, and even a golf course. In 1931, the corporation tried to raise funds by selling additional stock to the public. And from 1927 to 1932, Richardson and Hunter Miller tried to interest owners of other Virginia resorts and other wealthy individuals around the country either in investing in an expanded version of the existing corporation or in buying the property outright. Although losing control of the land was not the outcome Richardson and his colleagues preferred, the Peaks and the Hotel Mons were indeed unofficially up for sale for between $150,000 and $200,000. Unfortunately, in the depths of the depression, there were no buyers despite Richardson's confident predictions of the enterprise's future profitability.[38]

As the depression worsened, the corporation floundered. Simultaneously, the Bryant family at the Johnson Farm saw their fortunes sour. With multiple sources of cash income, they had prospered in the 1920s, improving the farmhouse by weatherboarding the entire exterior, replacing the wood shake roof with tin, enlarging windows, adding screens, and upgrading the kitchen. Even in the early 1930s, when depression, drought, and Mack Bryant's stroke and subsequent death battered the family, they bought two automobiles, further enlarged the house, and added an outhouse to the property in compliance with a new state law. Always, as they were able, the family improved its condition.

But the Peaks community on which the family relied was scattering—selling out to the Forest Service in some cases or moving to other places to get jobs. Faced, too, with declining fertility of their lands, the Bryant children gradually married and left the home place. As the community dried up, the school and church closed. And with the Hotel Mons mired in a downward skid, the Peaks of Otter community's days appeared to be numbered.[39]

The Peaks and the Parkway

At this moment of crisis, word arrived in the fall of 1933 that the federal government—encouraged by Virginia Senator Harry F. Byrd—was considering building a scenic highway from the Shenandoah National Park to the Great Smoky Mountains National Park via the Peaks of Otter.[40]

Always alert for propositions that might finally bring needed road connections and hoped-for prosperity, Hunter Miller leapt on the Parkway project. Virginia Governor John Garland Pollard appointed Miller (by now a state senator) to the Virginia committee charged with developing a route for the Parkway, guaranteeing that Miller would be present at all early planning meetings to lobby for routing through the Peaks of Otter.

This time, road-routing politics turned favorable for the Peaks: Virginians planning their part of the route in 1934 were united around the proposition that it go from the southern end of the Skyline Drive in the Shenandoah park to the Peaks of Otter. From that point southward, Virginia delegates to the national hearings on routing were divided, but no matter. Given that the state had also finally begun work on the Mons-Buchanan link, the Peaks at last would get its roads.[41]

Richardson was no doubt pleased to hear that his beloved Peaks of Otter would get its deserved traffic, although he died in early 1934, before plans became final.[42] With political maneuvering shifting to Washington, however, it was perhaps just as well that Miller, who was better positioned to make the Peaks Corporation's views known, stepped up as the company's major spokesperson, a role he would continue to play until his death in the early 1960s.

Miller and Bedford's booster community agreed that encouraging routing of the Parkway through the Peaks of Otter represented their best hope to put their mountains on the map as a major tourist destination. They soon began lobbying, however, for more than just routing. Knowing that federal officials were planning to develop wider recreation areas along the Parkway, Miller and the Bedford Chamber of Commerce initiated a spring 1934 campaign in which former governor Pollard, the chair of the Virginia Commission on Conservation and Development, and officers of chambers of commerce throughout the area flooded Park Service officials with letters and petitions suggesting that the government buy the Peaks of Otter in its entirety for a Parkway recreational area. By December 1934, it looked like this wish too might come true: Stanley Abbott wrote a two-thousand-acre acquisition at the Peaks of Otter into his initial plan for the "type and scope of development proposed" along the Parkway.[43]

What remained was to negotiate purchase terms for the recreation area lands, which extended beyond the central seven hundred acres or so that the Peaks of Otter, Inc., owned to include other tracts also in private hands. This process was not completed until the early 1940s, as several thorny issues had to be resolved.

The first question was how to arrive at a fair valuation for the Peaks Corporation's highly desirable lands, and on this issue, Peaks owners and federal officials started their negotiations oceans apart. The owners initially set their price for 673 acres, including the Hotel Mons and the summits of both Sharp Top and Flat Top, at $300,000, which they quickly lowered to $250,000. Miller claimed, however, that even at this price, the transaction would represent a sacrifice by the corporation, whose independent appraiser valued the lands at $750,000 (more than $1,100 per acre) and advised sale at no less than $400,000 (about $600 per acre). The federal appraisal of the lands, based primarily on the existing use of and improvements to the property and not on speculative projections of the lands' potential for generating income, suggested a price of about $42,000. Trying to offer something the company might conceivably accept, the government proposed in 1936 to buy the corporation's lands for $60,000 (almost $90 per acre).[44]

With this gulf, several corporation owners apparently became eager to hold onto the property and continue to seek means for developing it privately, especially given that the state road improvements to Buchanan and Bedford were at long last under way. At times during the negotiations, other private purchasers may have tempted Peaks Corporation officers to look elsewhere for a buyer. But largely as a result of the steadfastness of Miller, who negotiated throughout on a friendly basis with Abbott and other Park Service officials, the corporation refrained from undertaking private development and held out for a settlement with the federal government. Miller seemed genuinely to believe that the federal government could do a better job of developing the Peaks area for public use than the company could. "I do not hesitate to say," he wrote to an NPS official in Washington, "that personally I have great ambition to see this particular piece of scenery developed under the supervision of Mr. Abbott." The Peaks could be, he believed, "outstanding among the National Parks of this country."[45]

Negotiations with high-level Washington officials continued for many months, and corporation officials were divided about what to do. Although their company had virtually no liquid assets, Miller and his partners sought to wring some profits out of their investment while selling to the government. Finally in 1936, the two sides reached an agreement by which the government would buy the lands for sixty thousand dollars and the Peaks of Otter, Inc., would receive a ten-year concession permit to charge tolls for trips to the Sharp Top summit (via a new road that had been brought up to automobile standards by Civilian Conservation Corps workers from the nearby camp at Kelso) and to provide meals and lodging to visitors there. This way, Peaks owners expected, they would finally see the fruits of their long investment.

In accepting the offer, Miller noted, "We are so strongly impressed with the fact that the development of this property will be so closely connected with the development of the National Parkway, and feeling that it all should be done under the supervision and direction of the National Park Service, that we have decided to make the sacrifice and accept this proposition." Whether the corporation's owners were truly as public-spirited as this letter indicated or whether they had finally given up (under the pressure of company debts) and taken the best offer they had gotten in a decade of trying to sell is not clear. But by 1937 they had signed the agreement and the federal government had control of the core of the Peaks lands. The Mons Hotel closed its doors for good.[46]

Federal officials still had to obtain the rest of the acreage needed for the recreation area—some to be transferred from the Forest Service, some still under private ownership. Partly because he knew that full development of the area (which would not occur until the Park Service had sufficient lands to implement its plans) would provide the only basis on which the corporation could reap profits from the Sharp Top concession, Miller worked doggedly with NPS to arrange the purchase of these remaining lands. A lack of federal funds for this purchase, which unlike land purchases at several other Parkway recreation areas could not legitimately be made under federal submarginal lands laws, complicated the process.[47] And lacking the power of condemnation, the Park Service had to secure the voluntary agreement of landowners (including the Bryant family at the Johnson Farm) to sell.

In this process, which unfolded for five years after Peaks of Otter, Inc., had sold its lands, the corporation worked in an unusual public-private partnership in which Miller and the corporation's president, W. L. Lyle, acted almost as agents of the federal government. The Park Service, for its part, modified and expanded its concessions agreement with the corporation. Concerned about the environmental and visual impacts of significant building (parking, lodging, and restaurant facilities) atop Sharp Top's rocky peak, Abbott agreed to a plan under which the corporation would open facilities at the base of the mountains (near the former Hotel Mons site) and operate a bus service to Sharp Top instead of charging tolls for individual automobiles.

For their part, Miller and his associates agreed to buy the remaining lands and donate them to the government. Callie Bryant's family sold its farm (now ninety-nine acres) to Peaks, Inc., for thirty-five hundred dollars in 1941, and the corporation soon deeded the site to the Park Service. The plan for the rest of the lands unraveled, however, because some landowners held out for what the corporation and the NPS felt were "exorbitant" prices. The NPS finally bought the remaining lands in 1942. By the early 1940s, then, land problems at the Peaks of Otter were mostly resolved, and construction had begun on the roadway through the area. It opened to traffic with a crushed stone surface before construction stopped for World War II.[48]

Throughout the land-acquisition process, Hunter Miller and his associates cooperated willingly with the Park Service to pursue both the public-spirited goal of providing a well-developed park at one of Virginia's most beautiful places and the corporation's interest in positioning itself favorably to profit from what its leaders continued to predict would be a bonanza when the recreation area finally opened. The harmonious confluence of private and public interests at this site contrasted markedly with the contentious public-private conflagration that simultaneously unfolded at Little Switzerland, North Carolina (see chapter 4) and later dogged the Park Service at Grandfather Mountain (see chapter 7). It remained to be seen, however, how well Miller's and his colleagues' cooperative spirit would ultimately serve them.

In superimposing a new layer of tourism over the landscape at the Peaks of Otter, the N PS pressed forward the forces of modernization (federalization of lands, road building, and greater and more profitable development of the area's long-recognized tourism potential), generating new conflicts with local residents. The Park Service, like the Wilkes family in the nineteenth century, the Yankee investors at the turn of the twentieth, and the Bedford businessmen of Peaks of Otter, Inc., confronted perennial questions about the site. On what basis could and should they make it attractive to travelers? How could the imaginative, mythical, intangible, but restorative qualities of the place best be maximized and made available to the public?

Park Service plans included elements that had served well in the past (good food, comfortable lodging, and friendly service) as well as some new features, especially a landscape architect's sense of the picturesque and a feeling for history. Paradoxically, however, the N PS proceeded to erase most evidence of the area's local history and ultimately wrote out of the story even the local businessmen of the Peaks Corporation who had so helped to bring the project to fruition.

By the mid-1940s, the Park Service had nearly four thousand acres with which to work at the Peaks of Otter. Laborers quickly cleared away much of the physical evidence of the community that had once thrived there. The Mons school, the local lodge, and the entire Hotel Mons complex, now quite dilapidated, were razed in 1939–40 as Thurston Richardson's daughter sadly looked on. The Park Service decided to retain many of the buildings at the Bryant/Johnson Farm, however, and in the late 1940s and early 1950s documented and photographed them in preparation for eventual interpretive presentation. Until the 1960s, however, the farm site lay virtually neglected.[49]

Park Service personnel focused instead on developing the other tourist facilities at the recreation area while the Peaks of Otter Corporation (still strapped for cash) awaited long-expected profits. When Parkway construction stopped with the outbreak of World War II, however, the Parkway remained incomplete through the Peaks, further improvements were still needed to the road to Sharp Top, and promised bus service to the peak was delayed. More than ten years after the corporation had sold its lands, its first paying passengers finally ascended the mountain on the Sharp Top bus during the summer of 1948. The corporation also

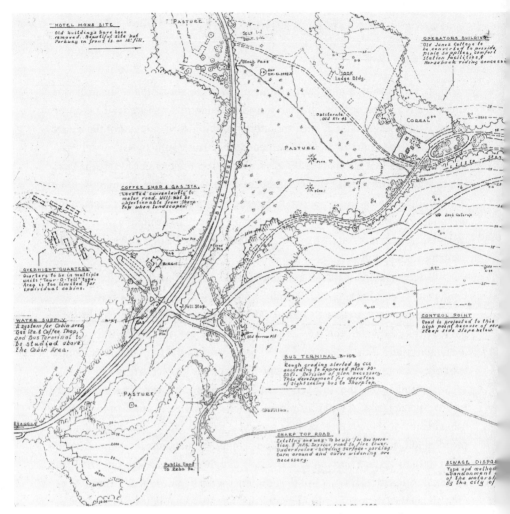

Preliminary National Park Service development plan for the Peaks of Otter, 1944. Shows roads to be obliterated or relocated, demolition of Hotel Mons buildings, and suggested reuse of community buildings. As finally developed, Abbott Lake took the place of the central pasture, with the Peaks of Otter Lodge built next to the lake. Courtesy Blue Ridge Parkway.

at this time opened a tearoom and small gift shop in the bus station the NPS built at the bottom of the mountain.[50]

This situation was not what Hunter Miller and the other Peaks corporation members had envisioned when they sold their lands in 1937. Assuming that the Park Service would complete the Parkway through the Peaks within two years, Miller and his associates had reserved the right to operate the concession for ten years, a period they thought ample to recoup their losses and gain some of the long-hoped-for profits. With the bus service finally under way, in 1950 Miller and his colleagues arranged a five-year extension of their contract, thinking that they now surely would begin to realize their long-held dreams.[51]

But it was not to be. Several problems conspired to deny them any such windfall. First, the company started its operations in 1948 in sad financial shape. Debts incurred during the 1930s, when the company had sold its lands at what it deemed an artificially low price and had extended company funds to help the NPS buy other lands, continued to accrue interest. Investments necessary to start up the concession operation after World War II, including buying the Sharp Top bus, added to the deficit, which by the early 1950s approached twenty thousand dollars. Since the 1930s, company officials and their family members had logged many hours of work without compensation, and the company's perennial inability to raise substantial cash for a major advertising campaign or to upgrade facilities hindered growth.[52]

Even if it had been able to generate the money, the Peaks might not have had enough travelers to make the concession pay during this period. Despite the fact that the Park Service graded and surfaced the road with stone before World War II, Parkway construction in that area proceeded at a far slower pace than anticipated. Not until 1952 did hard-surfacing appear. And despite this milestone, the slow pace of construction on other critical Virginia sections a short distance north and south of the Peaks may have hindered the growth of visitation there. In particular, neither the James River crossing to the north nor the section around Roanoke to the south was finished until the 1960s, no doubt causing some travelers to bypass altogether the seventy-mile section of the Parkway containing the Peaks of Otter.[53]

By the end of the 1950s, the original Peaks of Otter group found itself completely squeezed out of the concessions operation. Parkway and NPS officials had consistently treated the corporation members poorly. When the delays caused by World War II and slow Parkway development had necessitated the extension of the original ten-year concession contract, the NPS doled out extensions only in increments of two to five years. By the mid-1950s, corporation leaders realized that they needed a twenty-year contract to give them both the incentive to undertake major infrastructure improvements and the ability to raise the funds to pay for those improvements. The Parkway's largest concessionaire, National Park Concessions, had received such long-term contracts, but the NPS was unwilling to do so for the Peaks Corporation, rendering its standing at the park tenuous throughout the 1950s.[54]

Changes in the NPS policy on concessions at the end of the 1950s worsened an already bleak situation. With the advent of the national Mission 66 plan to upgrade National Parks facilities (discussed in chapter 7), Parkway construction and facilities development also accelerated. Parkway officials announced in November 1956 that they would divide the Parkway into large sections and seek a single concessionaire to operate all the facilities in each section. At the Peaks, the new concessionaire would have to build—at its own expense—a planned lodge and restaurant along with other facilities at nearby Otter Creek and Whetstone Ridge, improvements that would cost an estimated half a million dollars.

While Parkway officials assured representative Webster Richardson that the Peaks company could bid on the contract, Richardson knew that unless he and his associates could secure substantial loans, which he thought unlikely, they would not be able to embark on such a venture. With some justification, he accused Parkway officials of bias against small operators, charging that the service's true goal was to give National Park Concessions, a quasi-private nonprofit company largely under the control of the Park Service that had operated a large number of Parkway concessions since the 1940s, a complete chokehold on contracts.[55]

By the late 1950s, the remaining Peaks corporation leaders felt jilted, especially given the diligent work that Hunter Miller and W. L. Lyle had put into making the Peaks recreational area and the Parkway a reality. Company officials complained to Parkway superintendent Sam Weems, whom they did not find as cooperative as Stanley Abbott had been. They wrote and visited their representatives, including Senator Byrd, and appealed directly to the NPS director. And in a last-ditch December 1957 effort, hoping to secure funding partly through the Small Business Administration, they perhaps foolishly submitted a bid for the twenty-year contract for the new, enlarged concessions region.[56]

But it was to no avail. A fall 1958 letter brought news that "your company's operations at this location . . . will be concluded at the end of this current season." A larger company with a similar name, the Virginia Peaks of Otter Company, would take over the Peaks concessions as well as the rest of the Parkway facilities north of Roanoke, with a twenty-year contract. The new company was based in Charlottesville and was controlled by different investors, some with experience running food service operations in bus terminals around the South. This development, an embittered Webster Richardson wrote to the NPS director, came about despite the fact that "these concessions [were] the chief remuneration we were to receive for our property when it was transferred to the government." "It is tragic, indeed," Richardson continued, "that those who worked so hard and sacrificed so much, not only financially but of their time and effort, during the lean years, should be forced out when the time looks bright to make a profit, at long last."[57]

As a sad epilogue to the Bedford men's long history at the Peaks, Hunter Miller, writing in a trembling hand two years before his death in 1961, resigned himself to the situation, maintaining as always that the operation could have been a big moneymaker if not for unfortunate circumstances and never blaming the Park Service, in whom he had perhaps an unjustified trust: "If world war 2 had not delayed us so long and the bridge over the James River had been completed while we were in business," he said, "I believe we could have realized some substantial profit on our stock, but the luck seemed to be against us."[58]

If so, then luck was also against the new concessionaires, who in 1965 were still waiting for the operation to turn a profit. Despite rapid development of several new facilities (including by 1963 the Peaks of Otter Lodge) and investment of perhaps $800,000 in the Peaks of Otter, Otter Creek, and Whetstone Ridge sites, the new company found itself with a nearly $250,000 deficit at the end of the 1964 season. Ongoing construction at the site (including the building of Abbott Lake) and continued problems with the completion of the rest of the Virginia Parkway links depressed traffic at the Peaks well into the 1960s.[59]

With the departure of the original Peaks of Otter company, the locally initiated quest to turn the area into a profitable tourist enterprise came to a close. In marked contrast to the episodes at both Little Switzerland and Grandfather Mountain, the more public-spirited men of the Peaks of Otter Corporation had tried to make their money by working in tandem with the Park Service, an approach that did not serve them well.

In a different way, their situation made clear again some of the critical lessons of Parkway development: those who wielded wealth, political connection, and a confrontational style tended to have much greater success molding that development to their agendas than did either those who lacked access to the levers of power or, in this case, those who tried more congenially to go along. Bedford was no Asheville, and the men of the corporation, though not poor or unsophisticated, were not the shrewd and well-connected political operators that Little Switzerland owner Heriot Clarkson and Grandfather Mountain owner Hugh Morton were.

Thus, the Parkway development bias in favor of the organized and powerful rolled on. The answer to the question of how beneficial the road might be to small local entrepreneurs yet again was "not very." And the evolving story of tourist development at the Peaks of Otter turned to a new page with new characters, the Park Service and its larger-scale concessionaire partners.

At the same moment and at one of the same places Parkway tourist operations were moving from small and local to extensive and consolidated, the history the Park Service was beginning to present there emphasized a stereotypical
rural isolation that gave no hint either of the area's actual history or of the dramas
brewing in Parkway policy discussions. The emerging presentation came out of
a cultural interpretation program, under development since the late 1930s, that
merged with Parkway landscape architects' romantic landscape-design paradigm
to produce a radical reconstruction (literally a re-membering) of the landscape at
the Peaks. Therefore, while in many senses the Park Service's history at the Peaks
continued the long story of the site as a tourist center, Park Service treatment of
the site overwrote the landscape and its history in a dramatic and misleading
way.

The idealized portrait of pioneer Appalachia installed at the Peaks was perhaps
unproblematic as long as it remained primarily a part of a pretty landscape there.
Tourist developers are not obligated to retain all features of the previous owner's
operations when they redevelop a site. Over the years of the Peaks of Otter's development, however, the Park Service evolved institutionally into a major authority
on the preservation and presentation of America's historical past and sought self-
consciously to recount Appalachian history to Parkway travelers. Consequently,
the pretty landscape of the Peaks of Otter presented a conundrum for park historians and the public. Left with a landscape stripped of almost all evidence of its
history, the NPS would find it nearly impossible to instruct the public about the
historical forces that had shaped the site, including those that had brought the
area into Park Service hands.

Issues of historic preservation and representation along the Parkway thrust
themselves forward as the project's state-directed land-acquisition phase wound
down after 1943 and initiative for development shifted to the NPS. As the depression waned, Stanley Abbott and his staff at Parkway headquarters in Roanoke
turned their attention from basic routing, design, and land acquisition to landscape development and cultural interpretation, raising many questions that had
lain quietly in the background during the early years.

During the Parkway's first decade, only the Cherokee fight had demanded significant discussion (needed everywhere) of the cultural implications of bringing a
tourist parkway through a region in which human history was as interesting (and
important to travelers' understanding) as were natural surroundings. But since at

least 1939, the NPS had planned to showcase both the natural and the cultural/ historical landscapes along the Parkway. Early planners hoped that the Parkway would open "great picture windows to expose a way of life hitherto heavily veiled from the eyes of the American tourist."[60] At the Peaks, that hope translated into a romantic and misleading development plan.

Initial plans for historical interpretation emerged from major New Deal–era federal policy changes that had for the first time brought the NPS (and the federal government more generally) into the business of managing the nation's historic sites. Pushed by NPS director Horace Albright, President Franklin D. Roosevelt signed two 1933 executive orders transferring control over many federally owned historic sites from other agencies to the NPS. Two years later, with Park Service support, Congress passed the Historic Sites Act, boosting the NPS's role in historic preservation by authorizing Park Service cooperation with state and local governments in preserving historic sites. The act also officially launched the NPS into interpretation of the nation's history to the public at its parks through museums, exhibits, and educational programs. Throughout the 1930s, the NPS historical staff grew and became professionalized.[61]

These policy changes came about at least partly in response to the success of Colonial Williamsburg, developed with private funds during the 1920s. According to one historian, the work at Williamsburg invited Americans to believe that "given enough time, money, and expertise, a reasonable facsimile of the past could be recreated almost anywhere." The Historic Sites Act authorized the NPS to rebuild historic structures, but early efforts did not bode well for accuracy grounded in research. One of the first Park Service reconstructions, the George Washington birthplace (1932), turned out to be "the wrong size, . . . the wrong shape, and [facing] the wrong direction on the wrong site." Generally, according to one NPS historian, the agency's historical parks from the outset "often bore little resemblance to the way they had appeared during their historic periods. Features once present had vanished or changed; new features intruded." Debates raged for years about the appropriateness of reconstructing absent structures, and individual parks pursued a wide variety of strategies.[62]

Inexperienced as the NPS was at the task, drafting a cultural landscaping and interpretation plan for an area as burdened with cultural stereotyping as the southern Appalachian region was risky at best. Indeed, early interpretive plans for both the new Great Smoky Mountains National Park and the Blue Ridge Parkway hardly offered a closely researched and documented perspective. A 1939 Park Service press release describing plans for the Smokies noted that "many pioneer structures are to be found in the Park. . . . Here, where so-called progress failed to penetrate, is preserved a pioneer culture which dates back over a century and a half. Industries, domestic arts, ballads and many forms of speech remain unchanged. Spinning, weaving, milling, tanning, cobbling and various other activities, — some of which have become major industries in the world beyond the mountains, — have been retained in the original primitive forms and are of considerable historical value."[63] A more concise statement of conventional (and historically groundless) "wisdom" about the southern mountains could hardly be found.

Thus it is not surprising that the Park Service's first major reports on the historical and cultural resources of the Parkway region, completed after a 1940 inspection of the corridor by Parkway rangers, an NPS historical technician, and the NPS regional supervisor of historic sites, repeated these timeworn stereotypes. Indeed, the images in the heads of Park Service personnel seemed to have more to do with what cultural artifacts they were prepared to identify than did the actual sites along the roadway. Part of the 1940 report noted, for example, that the inspection team did not visit the part of the Parkway in North Carolina from U.S. 421 south to beyond Linville because the ranger informed the other team members that "there was nothing of particular interest for our purpose along this portion of the road."[64] Although this nearly forty-mile section contained the huge estate of textile magnate Moses Cone and the fashionable resorts at Linville and Little Switzerland, the story of the development of mountain tourist retreats for the wealthy (a story that in fact stretched well back into the early nineteenth century) was not a part of the tale the Park Service was prepared to tell.

Instead, the service wanted to present "some insight into the problems of the pioneers with their 'long rifles' who first penetrated the area, as well as the problems and life of their descendants." As events unfolded, however, the long rifles stayed and the descendants nearly disappeared from the picture as the early interpretive impulses (from the central NPS bureaucracy down to the local park level) focused on pioneer buildings and mountain handicrafts.[65]

Park Service personnel sent out to identify historical resources focused almost exclusively on "the early settlers of the mountains." Some of the first recommendations for the interpretive program reflected much of this preoccupation with the pioneer history of the Parkway corridor, even in the face of countervailing evidence. Despite the fact that the large and relatively heavily populated and farmed portion of the parkway visited by the inspectors included "only three log cabins" among countless houses of later design and materials, these structures received top priority in the 1940 recommendations. Characteristically, one inspector was disappointed to learn that the "old Mabry Mill" was "not very old, dating perhaps between 1900–1920." But from a distance, he pointed out, "the building is well weathered and appears much older than it is" and thus might work in a display. Based on the early historians' inspection report, the chief of the NPS's Museum Division argued that "the surprisingly small number of cabins along the Parkway emphasizes the need for their stabilization." Accordingly, the first four buildings to be preserved along the Parkway would be the three log cabins and the Mabry Mill—all selected, Abbott explained, "for their picturesque architecture and the interest of the legends which surround them."[66]

To his credit, one NPS historian noticed in 1941, when the preservation program was being inaugurated, that Ed Mabry's "modern constructed farm house," just behind the gristmill, was "a product of the miller's own effort" and well represented "an effort of the older mountain settlers to improve their standards of living." He recommended that the house be preserved to show that "no matter how isolated some of the mountain homes may be there was always a tendency to improve their living condition." While Abbott expressed sympathy with this sentiment, he decided that the house had to come down to make way for parking at the site. He outlined a plan to dismantle it in a way that would permit later reconstruction, but Mabry's home was razed by the summer of 1942 and has never returned.[67]

Abbott and the early Park Service historians, like so many who had worked in the southern mountains before them, were especially committed to preserving and reviving mountain handicrafts. Mountain residents' "struggle for existence, and their ingenious efforts to create small comforts of life have left a trail of handicraft which in simplicity and often crudity have proven to be both artistic and useful," noted one of the 1940 inspectors. The other inspector suggested that the cabins he had found could be restored and staffed with an "inhabitant of pure mountain stock" who would "treat his field as he would ordinarily" and make only "genuine" craft articles for display and sale. The two inspectors recommended that the Park Service foster a revival of traditional handicraft production by inviting the "more skilled producers of authentic handicraft" to "install their shops along the parkway right-of-way." In the face of the observation that even the Southern Highland Handicraft Guild's outlets were selling many machine-made items, however, the historians recommended that the Parkway shops "should be subject to careful supervision by the National Park Service." The report concluded by lamenting the damaging effects of industrialization and urbanization on people's minds and spirits, suggesting that a Parkway display of mountain life and handicraft would be a refreshing antidote.[68]

With these markedly ill-informed recommendations in hand, Parkway staff

Blue Ridge Parkway passing Mabry Mill, Floyd County, Virginia, 1937, before mill restoration. Ed and Lizzie Mabry's white frame house (built in 1914) is visible behind the mill. Their house was later taken down and replaced by the Matthews Cabin, brought in from another county. Courtesy Blue Ridge Parkway.

(with the assistance of laborers from the Civilian Conservation Corps) soon set to work planning for the restoration of the three cabins and the mill. By late 1942, work on the Brinegar cabin in North Carolina and the Mabry Mill in Virginia was nearly complete and Abbott was drafting the first master interpretive plan for the entire Parkway. Abbott's draft hinted at the breadth of the Park Service's thinking about the Parkway's role in interpreting Appalachian life. Despite the clear right-of-way lines, it noted, the Parkway's "true boundary is fixed only at the horizon." The Park Service ownership lines, it continued, afforded control over the "immediate foreground of a far flung picture." Design policies, Abbott's draft concluded, had made the roadway "the narrator of the whole story of the mountains," which should include representations of the "lived-in mountains" as well as both managed and wild natural scenes.[69]

Abbott argued that because "a Parkway can deliberately set out to interpret the whole story of a vast countryside," this park was different from more self-contained national parks. To his credit, Abbott acknowledged that the story to be told included elements of modernization and change. But believing as he did that "the old pioneer ways lasted longer here in these cool vales of life than anywhere else in America," his recommendations followed those of the earlier historians, focusing primarily on the Parkway's role in preserving the "pioneer cabins . . . , the grist mills, and the traces of old fence" that were parts of mountain life "swiftly passing, and, but for the Parkway, . . . passed in many parts."[70]

Ironically, however, while Park Service staff expressed such enthusiasm for the material signs of mountain people's lives, they also worked hard to keep most actual mountain residents off "the Scenic." Officials worried, in fact, that, left to mountain people, the picture of mountain life presented on lands adjacent to the Parkway would "result in a scene of poverty rather than one of rural pioneer life." Partly to prevent this possibility, the Park Service hired an agronomist to coordinate a program of soil conservation and leasing Parkway lands back to mountain farmers, whom they instructed in better — and more picturesque — farming methods.[71]

A belief that the Appalachian mountains had "supported a living civilization isolated from the outside world and little affected by it" continued to drive the interpretive program well into the 1960s. A 1994 study of agricultural landscapes along the Parkway noted that Stanley Abbott's "concept of the 'Museum of the Managed American Countryside' implied an aesthetic based not on the stark poverty of farm families, the eroded fields, and the cut-over woodland, but on idyllic pastoralism."[72] Nowhere was this more evident than in the NPS's long-delayed work at the Johnson Farm.

Re-Redoing the Johnson Farm

The Park Service began to erase the history of the Peaks of Otter by demolishing the Hotel Mons complex in 1939–40, leaving only an empty grassy field where summer crowds had once played lawn games and rocked on the porch. The clapboard Johnson farmhouse, however, had been left intact but was ignored after some stabilization work in the late 1940s.[73] But with the mid-1950s infusion of Mission 66 funds, park staff began to develop an interpretive strategy for the farm site.

In 1964, the Parkway's landscape architect and naturalist recommended revamping the site — now consisting of only four of the perhaps nine buildings that had been there when NPS received the lands — to appear as it might have looked around the turn of the twentieth century. The superintendent approved the plan. The fact that, as the report noted, the Park Service had "no documented information on the history of these buildings" did not deter the Parkway staffers (which did not include a trained historian) in their quest to "perpetuate the rapidly disappearing story of the pioneer mountain farm in the Southern Appalachians." To

Mabry Mill site as developed with reflecting pool and working waterwheel, 1952. Parkway paved at left. The mill has long been one of the Parkway's most photographed sites. Photograph by L. S. Tuttle. National Archives and Records Administration, College Park, Maryland.

create this picture, the report recommended removing the siding to expose the log understructures of the house and another building. It also directed that the tin roofs on three of the structures be taken off and replaced with wooden shakes.[74]

To its credit, in 1966 the Parkway initially engaged historical architect Charles Grossman to direct the restoration. Had the Park Service been willing to hear his suggestions, prepared after a lengthy and careful tour of the property, interpretation at the site might have come much closer to revealing its actual history.[75]

Grossman suggested that the house could be used as it was, without major structural changes, to show the evolution of life in the Blue Ridge. Instead of removing the weatherboarding, as the earlier NPS internal report had proposed, Grossman advocated leaving it in place to show "that people even here in these mountains when they had the opportunity to get new materials and better materials they were just as anxious to improve their homes as you and I are today." He went on to observe that the home had been near a transmountain road and that "these people out here lived just as well as they possibly could. You think of a mountaineer as Snuffy Smith. They weren't like that at all. They were hard working people and they liked nice things just the same as anybody else."[76]

Rather than conjuring up an idealized image into which to recast the house, Grossman suggested that NPS let "the building itself [be] your specifications" for restoration. "In other words," he clarified, "we don't improve it and we don't take anything from it." This house as it was, he concluded, "would be a very good interpretation of the mountain people who lived as graciously as they could under the circumstances."[77]

But for some reason not evident in the record, Grossman soon resigned from the project, and the park staff, under the leadership of its landscape architects (to whom pretty scenes were more appealing than historical accuracy), went on to implement the recommendations of the idealizing 1964 report. Workers removed the tin roof, reduced the size of a window that had been enlarged in the 1920s, pried off the clapboard siding, tore off the porch and rear addition, and exposed the considerably smaller log cabin that was indeed underneath the Johnson/Bryant house. For four years, the lonely cabin stood in an apparently isolated field. Neither the Bryants nor the swarms of visitors to the Hotel Mons would have recognized the family's former home.[78]

Grossman's unheeded recommendations came at a moment when the NPS mandate as an agency in charge of preserving historic properties and telling American history was again being dramatically enhanced, as it had been in the 1930s. Urban redevelopment ("renewal") projects of the 1960s had encouraged rampant destruction of historic structures nationwide. In response to an outcry from preservationists at Colonial Williamsburg and elsewhere, Congress passed and Lyndon Johnson signed the National Historic Preservation Act in 1966. The legislation established a national historic preservation policy and authorized a National Register of Historic Places (to be administered by the NPS) to give protected status to locally, regionally, and nationally important historic sites and structures under both private and state ownership. Enhanced by Executive Order 11593 in 1971 and subsequent amendments, the Historic Preservation Act required federal agencies to locate and nominate properties they owned for the National Register and to "exercise caution" while surveys were under way to see to it that possibly eligible structures were not "inadvertently transferred, sold, demolished, or substantially altered." With the creation of the National Register and the unification of several of the NPS's historical divisions, its status as the nation's history agency rose once again to new heights.[79]

Johnson farmhouse as cabin, 1971. Courtesy Blue Ridge Parkway.

Yet these new policy mandates seem to have had little effect on the telling of history at NPS sites. Simultaneous changes within the agency during the 1960s and early 1970s diminished the importance and status of professionally trained historians and cultural resource interpreters. These changes took place despite the release of a 1962 report by a high-level NPS committee that roundly criticized the service's interpretive program. Lack of centralized control, the report found, had resulted in widely varying standards for park historical programs. Like several that followed in the coming decade, this report also found that education and training of the interpretive staff were generally dismal. By the late 1960s and early 1970s, the staff had become deprofessionalized by changes in the NPS job-classification system, and the service subsequently became dominated by low-level technicians.[80]

Given the Park Service's developing role as the nation's major protector of history and its ongoing difficulty in telling the history of sites under its management, it is not surprising that developing a program of historic and cultural education along the Blue Ridge Parkway was a mixed and disjointed process. The confused state of the Johnson Farm site when historian Andy Ketterson arrived in 1972 was emblematic of problems throughout the national parks.

Whatever the poor state of training for park historical staff nationwide, Ketterson was an educated professional with ten years' experience as a historian and interpreter at several other N P S sites. He quickly realized that the lack of documentary evidence would make it impossible to present the Johnson farm as it had been in the late 1890s. "I think the period selected for restoration and the reason for selecting that period were unsound," he said bluntly in a 1972 report. But Ketterson still thought the project had value. Like Grossman, Ketterson recommended using the house itself as a historical source and pointed out that "by restoring the Johnson Farm House to the 1920s–30s period, we have an excellent opportunity to show the full evolutionary cycle that more than one mountain home underwent." Ample photographic and oral history documentation was available to guide planners in returning the house to that era's appearance, whereas leaving it in its present turn-of-the-century state required "a whole lot of guessing." Drawing on insights offered by one of the Bryant sons, Ketterson went on, "Mountain people didn't live in log cabins and cook in fireplaces because they thought it was fun, or cute, or quaint. The lived in this fashion for very basic economic reasons. When they had a chance to upgrade their property, they did."[81]

The desolation of the landscape surrounding the farm still presented an interpretive challenge. Noting that "there is nothing else at the Peaks of Otter to indicate that there was ever a community center or . . . community activity there," Ketterson recommended the creation of a historical "base map" to indicate the 1920s and 1930s locations of long-eliminated structures, paths, roads, fields, and gardens. The lack of such an understanding of the historical landscape, he theorized, was probably why "we bring our visitors in by means of a footpath that I do not believe existed in historic times, instead of bringing them in over the historic access road to the Johnson Farm[, thereby creating] a false impression of the isolation in which the dwellers at the Johnson Farm lived." In reality, Ketterson observed, "they were relatively unisolated. They lived near a small community and their access by road appears to have been the road through the present [ranger housing] area."[82]

Reflecting the growing body of professional standards being developed for historic preservation work, Ketterson lamented the lack of care taken during the 1968 "restoration" of the farmhouse. No one had written a detailed plan for treatment of the site, no one had made measured drawings of the house as it was before the work began, no one had taken adequate photographs of the house inside and out, no one had documented the work that was done, and no one had salvaged or kept any of the original materials (such as the roof tin and siding) that were removed.[83]

With Ketterson's report, some changes occurred in the Parkway's interpretive plan. The NPS soon approved an "interpretive prospectus" from Ketterson's office that incorporated his recommendations that the farm be returned as closely as possible to its 1930s appearance. Construction teams again swarmed the house, rebuilding the porches and extra rooms that had been demolished and reinstalling the white siding and tin roof.[84]

Joining a trend that had swept the Park Service after the mid-1960s, the interpretive prospectus also recommended developing a "living history" component with costumed interpreters. In the summer of 1974, the NPS hired Mel and Karen Lee to live in the house and demonstrate life on a 1930s farm. The Lees were returned Peace Corps volunteers who had become deeply interested in certain popular(ized) aspects of Appalachian regional culture and history. Self-described "*Foxfire* book addicts," the Lees had delved into local history, read widely on Appalachian ballads, and become self-taught crafts makers. Karen Lee had taken up spinning and weaving; Mel Lee had begun building lap dulcimers. In hopes of connecting more fully with the romantic pioneer Appalachia that fascinated them, they had moved for a winter into a one-room log cabin with no electricity or telephone, cooking on a wood stove and reading by candlelight. At the same time, however, Karen Lee had worked as a computer programmer, and Mel Lee had entered graduate school in pursuit of a counseling degree. Looking to turn their passion for Appalachian lifeways into income, they had approached the Shenandoah National Park about working as craft demonstrators and were referred to the Parkway. The Lees' proposal arrived at the Parkway offices just as the Parkway staff was contemplating the addition of living history to the Peaks of Otter site.[85]

In their time at the Johnson Farm (the summers of 1974–76), the Lees tried to follow the park interpretive specialist's daunting mandate that "the entire situation . . . be indistinguishable from the 1930's in the farm's appearance, in our appearance and activities, manner of speaking, and gestures." During their first two seasons in residence, the Lees lived full time in the farmhouse and used no "hidden conveniences" (one of which would have been an indoor bathroom) except the showers at the nearby ranger housing. Assisted by park staffers, they procured furnishings for the house that approximated those remembered by living members of the Bryant family. The Lees demonstrated or involved farm visitors in a wide variety of activities, including playing the dulcimer, spinning, cooking, and gardening, greeting visitors so convincingly that some unsuspecting tourists apologized for intruding on a privately owned farm. The Lees' compelling initia-

Johnson farmhouse being reconstructed to 1920s appearance, 1973.
Porch that had been removed is being put back on. Courtesy Blue Ridge Parkway.

tive drew media attention in Virginia and attracted a dramatically increased number of visitors to the farm in 1974. Many of these visitors, Mel Lee reported, appre-
ciated the efforts being made to live in what they perceived to be authentic 1930s
fashion. One woman, for example, "contrasted the 'purity' of her experience at
the farm with a trip to Williamsburg, which was spoiled when she discovered the
Raleigh Tavern's cookies were baked in electric ovens in the basement."[86]

In their first season, the Lees were aware that the minimal guidance from
park staff and a dearth of historical information hampered their ability to present an accurate picture. "There always seemed to be rumors of a treasure trove
of information on the farm which lay somewhere in Asheville," Mel Lee wrote in
his 1974 end-of-summer evaluation, "but these goodies of information seldom
trickled down to us." With little information and overly enamored (like generations before and after them) with a popular but romantic vision of pioneer Appalachia that focused on handicrafts, music, and "folkways" of dubious historical
authenticity, the Lees' early interpretive efforts, Mel Lee later admitted, presented
a picture that had little to do with the specific history of the Johnson Farm. The

Johnson farmhouse after restoration, 1973. Courtesy Blue Ridge Parkway.

Lees' initial approach to their work at the farm—typical for the times—reflected both the still-undeveloped state of critical historical scholarship on Appalachia, the influence of books like the recently launched *Foxfire* series (first mass-market volume issued in 1972) and the legacy of the 1950s and 1960s folk revival. While working at the farm, for example, Mel Lee made, marketed, and demonstrated the so-called Appalachian dulcimer, newly (though not deservedly) brought to popular attention by folk revival musicians as an indigenous, pan-Appalachian traditional instrument. At the end of their first summer, the couple recommended that the Peaks of Otter visitor center stock British collector Cecil Sharp's 1918 collection of ballads, Kentucky mountain singer Jean Ritchie's autobiographical but nonetheless romantic *Dulcimer Book*, Richard Chase's rather fabricated versions of Appalachian folk tales, and John Jacob Niles's idiosyncratic *John Jacob Niles Song Book*. In keeping with current thinking about the region, they also recommended installation of a shop selling "authentic mountain crafts."[87]

More years would pass before the first major revisionist studies of Appalachian culture and cultural work (Henry D. Shapiro's *Appalachia on Our Mind* [1978] and David E. Whisnant's *All That Is Native and Fine* [1983]) emerged to provide a critical perspective on the longtime fascination with these elements of the region's history. But even without these resources, the Lees were born learners, and they soon became dissatisfied with what they gradually realized was a stereotyped presentation. As Mel Lee later told it, the epiphany came about a month after they had started their first summer's work, when the Park Service held an open house at the farm site to publicize the living history project. "I was playing dulcimer and Karen was spinning in front of a glowing fire in the fireplace in the living room, the very picture of domestic bliss," Mel Lee remembered. "In the course of the day some members of the Bryant family came by . . . and started telling us how things were different when they lived there. . . . We were quickly informed that they certainly didn't spin and their mother would have been outraged at the thought of them going barefoot, and what's that funny looking instrument you're playing?" The revelations were sobering. "Our approach to interpreting the farm began to change," Lee recalled. "We both felt that having met these people we owed it to them to tell their story accurately."[88]

Determined to get the information they needed, the Lees partnered with a local couple who were dedicated amateur historians and launched a research project that included dozens of oral history interviews. By 1975, they had produced a remarkable five-volume compilation of information on the site's history. With funding from the NPS, the research initiative allowed the Lees to shape their presentations in a way more "specific to this particular farm and community." In their second season, they emphasized (sometimes using a participatory approach that visitors loved) the farm's close relationship with the Hotel Mons, the area's historic connection to tourism and travel routes, and the farm's relative wealth. In the 1920s, the study noted, the area was "latticed with roads," the location of many of which could still be seen. The present landscape, the Lees became increasingly aware, fell far short of displaying the documentable 1920s and 1930s scene. Though pleased (as were members of the Bryant family) that the house was again clapboarded, the Lees lamented the mowed lawn that had replaced the fence around the house, the lack of a root cellar to store potatoes and apples, and the absence of farm animals.[89]

Despite the Lees' efforts to move beyond a romantic and generic presentation of "Appalachia," the power of the notion of an isolated people clinging to old ways remained strong. A farm visitor who photographed a barefoot Karen Lee sitting in a rocker stringing beans from the garden later won a prize for her photo, described in the contest literature as a picture snapped when the photographer stumbled on what Mel Lee later described as "this woman from yesteryear, still living the traditional lifestyle in her ramshackle old house." Never mind, Lee chuckled, "that the woman in question had . . . a degree in mathematics and worked the rest of the year as a computer programmer."[90] With the historic landscape compromised as it was, one couple could go only so far in reshaping visitors' ideas.

The expanded interpretation effort ended after 1984, when budget cuts and changing priorities curtailed the Parkway's interpretive program. With the end of living history at the Johnson Farm, interest in the site diminished. The farm lay mostly dormant until 1990, when, in the midst of the flowering of scholarship on the Appalachian region that followed the Lees' tenure, the Park Service commissioned a professional historian to write a historic resources study and historic structures report on the site. Again, mountains of data were assembled into a readable form, complete with detailed recommendations for changes that would help the site more accurately recount the now amply documented history of tourism, farming, and community at the Peaks of Otter. "The continuous human occupation of the area for thousands of years, the community matrix of agriculture, tourism, and commercial trade, the well-documented evolution of a mountain farm and farm family through three generations, and the interdependence of white and black families in a small, mountain community," the authors urged, "present opportunities for cultural preservation and cultural interpretation that will make Parkway visitors appreciate the complex history of mountain life and enhance their Parkway experience." The study observed that the Johnson Farm was "one of the richest sites for cultural interpretation along the entire Blue Ridge Parkway" but that none of its history was available to visitors. "Making one's way up the path and finally reaching the farm," the authors wrote, "it is easy for the visitor to feel that this surely was an isolated mountain farm, idyllic and out of the ebb and flow of the changing currents of history." Echoing Ketterson's report written nearly twenty years earlier, the study concluded that "the potential for interpretation barely has been tapped."[91]

The 1990 study recommended reconstruction of several additional farm structures, rebuilding of the footings of the Hotel Mons, clear marking of the roads that linked the farm to the hotel and the towns beyond, development of maps showing the whole Peaks community and its infrastructure, and design of an interpretive program that emphasized the continuity of tourism at the Peaks of Otter. The authors called for closer cooperation between the present Peaks of Otter Lodge and the park interpretive staff in making information on the Hotel Mons and Johnson

Farm available to visitors and perhaps for redesigning the hotel dining area to recall elements of the Mons.[92]

Most of the recommendations went unheeded, however, and by the dawn of the twenty-first century the Peaks of Otter site remained much as it was in 1990. Despite the prodigious work that made it one of the best-documented sites on the Parkway and burgeoning scholarship on the wider Appalachian region, the NPS seemed unable to shake its commitment to the comfortable old myths. The Parkway's competing commitments to picturesque landscape and accurate history continued to clash. The repeated recommendation that the rest of the site be upgraded to reflect how unisolated the farmstead really was—by better marking of the Hotel Mons site and identifying the farm's access road—still failed to materialize.[93] As late as 2002, signs at the site still directed visitors up a long and circuitous (literally mis-leading) path to reach the farm rather than pointing out the relatively quick route available through the former Mons site. No effort had been made to provide access to the farm along the former roadway through the ranger housing area. The meandering path to the farm site remained as testimony, inscribed on the landscape, to the divergence between the Parkway's vision of Appalachia and the real history of the places through which the Parkway runs.

RE-MEMBERING AND REMEMBERING:
CONSTRAINTS AND CONTRADICTIONS

Such contradictions have characterized much of the Blue Ridge Parkway project over its history. At other Parkway sites, pioneer themes have been central to the park's interpretation of mountain life, to the exclusion of most other elements of the region's complex history. A 1950 master plan articulated the driving idea of the Parkway's interpretive efforts: the Parkway's mission was to "make accessible . . . representative sections of the Appalachians, assuring the visitor the opportunity to appreciate scenes of great natural beauty and traces of the homespun culture of the mountain people without threat of despoliation by commercial development." Native mountain people, the plan observed, would be "living exhibits" of a region "touched only by the backwash of history."[94]

In many other places, as at the Peaks, the Park Service deliberately removed or camouflaged inconvenient conflicting evidence that history had indeed touched people's lives in the mountains. At the Mabry Mill, for example, in the 1950s, when park officials tore down the owner's 1914 frame house (a structure quite typical of mountain farmsteads by that time), they replaced it with a log cabin trucked in from another county. They erected displays on blacksmithing and whiskey making while neglecting to mention the timber industry that had been so dominant and devastating in many parts of the region until the eve of Parkway construction. Elsewhere, displays on "typical mountain farms" emphasized isolation and primitiveness and ignored both the diversity of mountain life and mountain farmers' longtime involvement in community networks and in the larger market economy.[95]

A striking example of the NPS's inability to deal with the multidimensional history of the southern Appalachians was its quandary about how to handle the Moses Cone estate, over which the service finally gained control in 1949, several years after owner Bertha Cone died. Lavish and extensive, the estate was built in 1900 near the long-established wealthy resort community of Blowing Rock, North Carolina, by textile baron Moses Cone. The property was older than the Mabry Mill but did not fit as easily into the pioneer scene the NPS was striving to re-create. Park officials deliberated for years about how to use the estate, tearing down many of its outbuildings and even considering razing the manor house itself, which they initially concluded was not historically or architecturally important. Finally, in 1951–52 the Park Service established there a museum of pioneer life and a crafts sales center run by the Southern Highland Handicraft Guild, which was dominated by studio-trained crafts makers. During the 1960s and 1970s, agency officials contemplated building an entire "early Americana" village to display farm life, crafts and, more generally, the "centuries-old culture" of mountain people, which had supposedly persisted into the twentieth century in spite of the penetration of railroads, mining, and timber companies. But the project failed to materialize, and the NPS never really contemplated allowing the Cone estate's history to dictate interpretive efforts at the site.[96]

The Park Service's choices at the Cone estate showed how determined it was to make the Parkway, in Stanley Abbott's words, "an elongated museum of folklore." And those choices prevented other voices, perspectives, and meanings from being heard as development proceeded after World War II. No matter how obviously misshapen, pieces that did not fit into the developing Parkway scene were shoehorned into Abbott's model, and few participants in the project were either inclined or able to challenge the picture.[97]

And, some might say, why should they? Many constituencies have considerable investment in the Parkway as it is, and numerous impediments stand in the way of a thoroughgoing reconceptualization of the picture of Appalachian history exhibited. An obvious one is the Parkway itself, as built. Even some historic preservationists now view the road in its entirety as a unique and historic designed landscape deserving preservation as it is (stereotypes, confusions, and all). Turning the Parkway wholesale into a museum of documentable history would thus violate other long-standing principles of the road's design and purpose.

In addition, historic sites such as those on the Parkway are to a degree trapped by the "heritage of incomplete landscapes" at living history museums and the preferences of "escapist audiences" by now inured to the charming fictions of Colonial Williamsburg.[98] Moreover, the Parkway landscape as it has been designed represents an enormous public investment and has so overwritten the vernacular landscape that reconstructing the past even at a single location such as the Peaks of Otter would now be practically impossible. Perennially strapped for cash for even routine maintenance and staffing, the Park Service would face monumental expense in modifying the large and widely dispersed array of buildings and sites expressive of its dominant mythology.

Probably more importantly, from the standpoint both of the large-scale corporate tourism industry in the southern Appalachian mountains and of many an individual traveler, the Parkway as it is has been a resounding success — especially, perhaps, for "escapist audiences." Why alter elements that bring 20 million visitors to the region each year, many of whom come for the natural scenery and outdoor recreation and are little concerned with regional history? It is also far from clear that those who are drawn to the Parkway by its "historical" scenes would be pleased with any revised rendering that professional historians might offer. Thus, to tamper with the pervasive and persistent public affection for the "good road of the Blue Ridge" would be a political move fraught with some peril.[99]

Scholars who have analyzed Americans' fascination with the past and with visiting historic sites have outlined the complicated agendas (individual, economic, and political) that historic site "time travel" serves. What travelers often seek, David Glassberg suggests, is a very personal "sense of history," a way to locate themselves both in particular places and in a long-term historical continuum. Often, however, David Lowenthal argues, this interest in the past stems from and feeds a warm nostalgic feeling for everything vaguely old. "If the past is a foreign country," he notes, "nostalgia has made it 'the foreign country with the healthiest tourist trade of all.'" Tourists to the past, he further observes, "flock to historic sites to share recall of the familiar, communal recollection enhancing personal reminiscence. What pleases the nostalgist is not just the relic but his own recognition of it, not so much the past itself as its supposed aspirations, less the memory of what actually was than of what was once thought possible."[100]

The Parkway certainly has catered to such travelers. As Stanley Abbott insisted in a 1958 interview, the Parkway's Mabry Mill, Brinegar Cabin, and split-rail fences (and Johnson Farm, no doubt) offered evidence "of a simple homestead culture and a people whose way of life grew out of the land around them. . . . The mountaineer buildings we acquired to preserve within the holdings of the Parkway . . . have resisted the whitewash brush, the Sears Roebuck catalog, and the tar paper of Johns Manville. They are as interesting a part of the Blue Ridge as the natural scene around them."[101]

Tourists drawn to a prettified "colonial" Williamsburg or to a version of the southern Appalachian highlands reflecting Abbott's nostalgic sensibility would, several historians have pointed out, likely be bitterly disappointed by the actual past, complete with its dirt, disease, poverty, peeling paint, and garbage and horse manure in the streets—or, in the case of the Parkway, by denuded timbered landscapes, eroded soil, poor housing, and dilapidated hotels. As Anders Greenspan observes in his recent history of Colonial Williamsburg, historic sites tied to the tourism industry must in some way "present a version of the past that is more geared to attracting visitors than repelling them." Many visitors, another commentator on Williamsburg notes, "neither want nor expect to learn disturbing information about the past." Exploring the past, Lowenthal further notes, allows people to find "what we miss today. And yesterday is a time for which we have no responsibility and when no one can answer back."[102] A degree of irresolvable incompatibility thus exists between profitable tourism and complicated history telling.

Even if there were no conflict of motive, it is far from evident that the way would be clear for real truth telling. As scholars have recently pointed out, our understanding of the past is so profoundly shaped by present needs, abilities, and preoccupations that the dream of uncovering and representing the "true" past is inherently flawed. As the Peaks of Otter's three stories make clear, many factors and agendas are at work at any so-called historic site. There are layers upon layers of stories. Many scholars, therefore, have abandoned the search for historical "reality" in favor of investigating the constructed nature of every site and the constantly shifting content of our individual and collective historical memory. They recognize that "history" (how we tell about or understand the past) and "the past" (how the past was really lived) do not—and probably cannot—match.

Historic sites, James W. Loewen has written in his often-humorous *Lies across America*, "are always a tale of two eras": the time they are depicting and the time of the designation of the historic site (that is, the time of the remembering). Further complicating matters, the creators of many sites are motivated not by the desire to tell history but by the impulse to display celebratory and inspiring heritage, something American travelers throughout the twentieth century were conditioned to seek.[103]

With this tangle of agendas working at any historic site, what some historians—notably Michael Kammen in *Mystic Chords of Memory*—find most interesting about the story of historic sites, museums, and the project of historical remembrance in American history is the process through which these enterprises reflected and contributed to the construction (and reconstruction) of a personal and collective historical memory. From this perspective, analysis of the "second era" of any historical representation (that is, the moment of the telling) and a related "third era" (that is, the moment of the seeing) are more crucial than getting at "objective" truth about the period being remembered.[104]

If tourist audiences are generally escapist and really do not care to understand exactly what they are seeing, then perhaps none of this matters to anyone except scholars. But some recent evidence suggests that we may have underestimated the public's intelligence, ability, and desire to engage with complex histories. Roy Rozenzweig and David Thelen's survey of the historical sensibilities of fifteen hundred Americans during the 1990s found that people were intensely engaged with history, though generally not with the history of professional historians, schools, and textbooks. In fact, the authors asserted that the study's "most significant news" was that "we have interested, active, and thoughtful audiences for what we want to talk about." The public's problem with history, Rosenzweig and Thelen concluded, was not that they were overly patriotic or escapist and could not tolerate hearing about difficult, unsettling, gloomy, or uninspiring historical realities (the horse manure in the streets). The problem was rather that they found the history as presented in schools and textbooks boring and disconnected from their lives. History as seen at historic sites and museums, however, was active and alive. These participatory sites were energizing and relevant. Feeling connected to the past, visitors could direct their encounters with history and take away the resonant meanings. Mel Lee's account of a "magic Saturday evening" when visitors assumed the roles of Mons Hotel guests visiting the Bryant family at home certainly supports this contention.[105]

This is encouraging news, but given the manifest deficiencies of many historic sites and museums, Rosenzweig and Thelen also made a disturbing discovery: their respondents believed historic sites and museums to be some of the most accurate sources for learning history. Indeed, survey participants "trusted [museums] as much as they did their grandmothers."[106] The gulf between the constructed nature of sites and what the public thinks they are seeing is clearly wide.

Given the multiple layers embedded into any historic site and the public's expectation that sites will be trustworthy and true, and given that scholars realize that there is no monolithic or easily identifiable "truth," could or should anything be done to rectify the presentation of history at the Peaks of Otter (or on the Parkway more generally)? The answer is a (conditional) yes. Although it is impossible to tell the full truth, there are nevertheless both truer stories to be told and compelling reasons to try to do so. Indeed, it is at this junction between public interest in history and public trust of historic sites that the Parkway falls short. And it is at this point that the possibility for telling a truer story lies.

Historic sites are not the only venues in which the reality-versus-representation challenge must be faced and the public kept clear about what it is and is not seeing and being told. Documentary films are an instructive analogue. However transparently "truthful" they may be taken to be by the viewing public, they inevitably present—from particular perspectives and for varying purposes—intricately constructed versions of carefully selected aspects of past and present realities. The classic (and still influential) documentaries of the 1930s (Pere Lorentz's *The River*, for example) pretended to an omniscience and a transparency that the best recent documentarians have come to understand is neither desirable nor achievable. On the contrary, recent filmmakers' "self-reflexive" films endeavor to keep viewers aware—as an organic part of the exposition—of the filmmaker's general agency and particular point of view and choices.[107] Viewers may agree or disagree with the arguments of *Fahrenheit 9/11* (2004) but can hardly be unaware that it is Michael Moore's film.

The great failing of the Blue Ridge Parkway in the telling of history is, therefore, its lack of self-reflexivity—its disinclination to acknowledge itself and its designers and creators (especially but not only the National Park Service) as actors, both in producing the scene being offered and in narrating the road's history and the history of the region of which it is a part. Instead, at the Peaks of Otter and elsewhere, the NPS has preferred that the Parkway itself appear to be a transparent reporter of an essentially static historical picture.

But at the Peaks of Otter, a truer understanding might emerge by allowing the telling of the three stories untangled in this chapter: the long-running story of tourism and community along a historic travel route, the story of the Park Service's arrival and its work with local tourism boosters to create the Peaks of Otter recreation area, and the story of the Park Service's struggles to make the compromised landscape tell a tale that only barely approximates what happened at the site. Intelligent visitors deserve to see all the processes that have created the place where they are.

Including the Parkway itself (and all of the changes it brought) in the history the NPS tells is important for reasons beyond a historian's interest in simply getting the facts straight. History itself has a politics: different stories serve different interests and have different potential to support or challenge the status quo.[108] For the Peaks of Otter, we must ask who is doing the constructing, what (intentional or unintentional) political ends that construction may serve, and what contrary lines of analysis it may hinder.

The presentation of an idealized and romantic picture of the Appalachian region impairs the public's ability to think about the Parkway and about tourism more broadly as agents of change in the southern Appalachian region. Most fundamentally, as the story at the Peaks of Otter vividly illustrates, a region "touched only by the backwash of history" and populated by an agricultural pioneer remnant would never have produced the urban tourism boosters who most fervently promoted the Blue Ridge Parkway. The entire project—like the Peaks of Otter recreation area itself—clearly emerged organically as part of the more than hundred-year tale of tourism and development in the southern Appalachians. When the time came to build the Blue Ridge Parkway, local constituencies and issues molded its shape on the landscape at every turn, from its routing to the extent, type, and condition of the lands through which it winds to the views both distant and near that it offers.

But when the Parkway is set in the romantic and mostly ahistorical scene presented at the Peaks of Otter, Mabry Mill, or the Moses Cone estate, both the political forces molding its landscape and their differential effects across class and cultural lines are masked from public view. The history of the Parkway's development at this one place, then, illustrates how the Park Service participated actively in the long cycle of change in a region and at the same time sought to erase both itself and the forces that brought it there from the motionless historical scene it presented.

Shrouding the agency of tourism boosters, state officials, and the National Park Service masks the fact that the Parkway resulted from adopting certain possibilities and rejecting others. It allows people to believe that the Parkway they see was simply a miraculous and foreordained outcome. Without a means of understanding the Parkway as a product of a particular historical process involving regional conflict, political negotiation, and compromise, the public can hardly grasp the practical, often political pressures and cost-benefit calculations that have always shaped the Parkway's development.

Nowhere is the gulf between public understanding and the facts of a very political battle greater than in the retelling of the story of the Parkway's final "missing link": the Parkway segment around North Carolina's Grandfather Mountain. There, in a thirteen-year battle, owner and developer Hugh Morton turned the Parkway's history of collaboration with the tourism industry against it and manipulated the project's internal political contradictions to great personal advantage. With astonishing ease and effectiveness, Morton cloaked his highly political battle in its own myth, characterizing his private goals as broadly public-spirited. Caught unarmed, NPS staff failed to effectively articulate the public interest at stake, to alert the public to the power politics of the conflict, and hence to fend off Morton's manipulation. At Grandfather, the price of buying into a simplistic and romantic historical picture built on myth became abundantly clear.

FROM STUMP TOWN TO CAROLINA'S TOP SCENIC ATTRACTION PRIVATE INTERESTS AND THE PUBLIC GOOD AT GRANDFATHER MOUNTAIN

In late May 1955, as they had many times before, members of R. Getty Browning's staff in the Locating Department of the North Carolina Highway Commission posted maps at the Watauga County courthouse in Boone, seizing lands for the Blue Ridge Parkway by invoking the state's powers of eminent domain. The tract taken this time included 779 acres on the side of Grandfather Mountain, one of the most beautiful and unusual landmarks in North Carolina. Like many others before him, Hugh M. Morton of Wilmington, North Carolina, suddenly became the lands' former owner for whom the next step would be to try to negotiate just compensation.[1]

An entrepreneurial and ambitious thirty-four-year-old from a prominent and well-connected Wilmington family, Morton was in the process of transforming the mountain—which he had inherited only three years earlier—into what he was already billing as "Carolina's Top Scenic Attraction." He was also transforming himself into a major player in state politics, largely through a number of highly visible fights with the National Park Service (NPS) over Parkway policies.

Morton was determined to resist the taking. At the end of June, finding Bureau of Public Roads (BPR) contractors making test borings for a proposed tunnel, the "former owner," double-barreled shotgun in hand, ordered the men off the mountain. In the next few months, Morton managed to turn the state bureaucracy—until then highly cooperative with the Parkway project—against the federal park officials from whom the instructions to take his lands had come. Using language that would have wide and long-lasting appeal, Morton argued that Grandfather Mountain's "wild, rugged, unconquered terrain is the basis of

[its] beauty" and that "a super highway through the middle of it will destroy that charm." A scant two years later, the North Carolina State Highway Commission, in an unprecedented move apparently orchestrated directly by Morton, deeded the lands back to him.[2]

This two-year take-and-give-back episode was the opening battle in the most protracted and public struggle in the Parkway's history. The subsequent thirteen-year conflict over the routing of the Grandfather Mountain segment constituted just one part of Morton's multipronged twenty-year attack on the Park Service's management policies as they affected the Parkway's relationship to privately owned tourism businesses. The land battle alone indirectly postponed into the 1980s the completion of the Grandfather section, which became the Parkway's final link. There, at the dramatic and technologically sophisticated Linn Cove Viaduct, which floated the roadway on piers above Grandfather's rocky shoulders, dignitaries officially dedicated the completed Parkway in 1987, fifty-two years after the first shovelful of dirt was turned.[3]

How did Morton manage—as despairing Parkway Superintendent Sam Weems asked in 1965—to "bring to a screaming halt a $100 million plus Federal project jointly designed and agreed upon in good faith?"[4] A large part of the answer lies in Morton's crafting of an appealing story to describe his reasons for opposing the Parkway plans for Grandfather. Mobilizing the mountain itself as a resonant symbol both of individual property rights and private enterprise and of public spirited environmental protection, Morton has for fifty years obscured the real complexity of the conflict and created a cause almost no one could counter.

This story of the Parkway's "missing link" has by now become a cherished part of North Carolina's folklore.[5] The account (repeated in recent years on North Carolina public television and in a number of major daily newspapers) usually goes something like this: Morton's problems began because the NPS "wanted a route over the top of Grandfather." North Carolina highway engineers obligingly but illegally condemned the land along this line, and Morton fought back heroically. To build along this ill-conceived route on a "rugged mountain that didn't deserve to be conquered," as he phrased it, "would have been like taking a switch-blade to the Mona Lisa." The Park Service's route, the tale asserts, would have "require[d] too much land," would have come "within a football field of the [mile-high] swinging bridge" (Morton's major attraction), and "would have seriously damage[d] the natural beauty of the terrain." Morton—characterized as a "pretty humble fellow" and an "arch conservationist" who over the years has "done what he can to protect and preserve the beauty and natural wonder of the mountain he so clearly loves"—thus told the Park Service "to find another way." And since the NPS in fact already had an adequate route for the Parkway in lands lower on the mountain that Morton's family had, depending on the account, either given or "sold for a song" to the state in 1939, Morton justifiably held out for a "middle route" that "would do minimum damage and be less costly." Despite the years of wrangling and some criticism of him for "holding up the Parkway," Morton fought the NPS until it adopted his compromise middle route. Morton generously "donated all of the right-of-way needed" for it, and the NPS built the technologically ingenious Linn Cove Viaduct to protect the ecologically sensitive zone through which the Parkway wound.[6]

Like most myths, this account tells a victor's version of events, compresses time sequences, attributes causal relationships where none existed, and oversimplifies and distorts what really took place. The story's villain, the Park Service, undoubtedly botched its handling of the Grandfather case and mismanaged its relationships with local private entrepreneurs from the 1950s onward. But its favored route at Grandfather was neither as illogical nor as potentially damaging as Morton claimed. Morton, for his part, has developed some genuine environmentalist credentials but has done so mostly in the period after the Parkway battle was resolved. And his interests at Grandfather were considerably more complicated than suggested by the popular yarn about how "in the best traditions of the frontiersman, one North Carolinian battle[d] the National Park Service for the preservation of a mountain."[7]

Deeper investigation reveals, too, that the stakes in the conflict were far greater than just the question of where the Parkway would cross Grandfather. The equilibrium of public needs and private interests, local exigencies and broad policy concerns that the often-competing constituencies involved in the project had sought to achieve in the Parkway's first twenty years was knocked askew. Multiple interest groups that had claims on the Parkway project were rebalanced. Coalitions that had supported the project since the 1930s split apart as the Parkway—by now the most popular site in the national park system—came into its own as an actor in regional politics and as the NPS tried (with mixed success) to wrest more complete control of the project from local and state constituencies. The difficulty of bridging internal tensions between the Parkway's goals of providing recreational enjoyment and beautiful natural scenery for the traveling public and bolstering the private regional tourism industry became ever more apparent.[8]

In addition, the timelessness of the mythological narrative ignores the fact that the Parkway's battle over the "missing link" unfolded on an ever-changing historical landscape as well as an evolving physical one. In truth, as Morton grew older, his arguments changed in response to alterations in the national context, public discourse, and the challenges of managing his increasingly lucrative property. In the Cold War era, his anti-Parkway arguments traded largely on the conservative rhetoric (similar to that of Heriot Clarkson) of protecting private enterprise and property rights from government infringement. But as a tide of conservationist-based criticism rose against the Park Service in the late 1950s and 1960s, Morton adopted the more progressive (and public-spirited) language of natural resources protection. By the 1970s and 1980s, when the matter was concluded, a national environmental movement and Morton's evolving sensibilities retroactively vindicated his earlier emphasis on protecting the mountain.[9]

Because the perdurable and appealing Grandfather Mountain story itself helped to determine the outcome of the longtime conflict there, understanding why the Parkway lies where it does in that section and why it took so long to finish must begin with dismantling this tale and examining in turn each of its elements and claims.

THE LAST MILES AND THE MISSING LINK:
FINISHING THE PARKWAY IN A MISSION 66 FRAMEWORK

During the Parkway's first decade (1933–43), most of the route had been fixed, right-of-way and access regulations had been formulated, and much of the land had been acquired. Ownership of state-acquired land passed to the federal government and legislation officially named the road the Blue Ridge Parkway (1936). Construction had gotten under way on nearly 330 miles of the road's projected 469-mile length, and 170 miles were paved and fully opened to travelers. Another 123 miles were graded and surfaced with crushed stone. Except for the section around Roanoke, most of the rest of the Virginia portions had been started. West of Asheville, where little work had begun, construction was imminent on the sections crossing the Qualla Boundary lands of the Eastern Cherokees and connecting the Parkway to the Great Smoky Mountains National Park. Civilian Conservation Corps, Works Progress Administration, and Civilian Public Service workers had followed in the path of the private road contractors, rehabilitating jagged construction scars with grass, native plants, and miles of picturesque split-rail fences. They had also installed picnic tables, restrooms, and shelters; carved out camping areas and trails; and built roads and water and sewage systems at the five open recreational areas. The historical interpretation program had been launched with the restoration of "four more or less old structures" to form, in Stanley Abbott's words, the first in a series of "wayside exhibits planned to illustrate the provincial life of the backwoods country." Federal appropriations for the project had topped $20 million, while the states of North Carolina and Virginia had together spent nearly $2 million on land acquisition.[10]

During World War II and the following decade, by contrast, Parkway development stalled as N P S funding levels dropped precipitously and failed to rebound. A Park Service budget that had stood at $33.5 million in 1940 plummeted to $4.7 million in 1945 and still stood at only $32.5 million in 1955. At the same time, the national park system expanded rapidly from 161 park areas covering 21.5 million acres to 181 areas encompassing 24 million acres. Visitation increased from 17 million in 1940 to more than 50 million in 1955, and Parkway visitation changed similarly. Although wartime travel restrictions, rationing, and shortages caused a dramatic drop from the 900,000 who had traveled the Parkway in 1941, by 1946 visitation surged above 1.2 million, catapulting the Parkway to the top of the list of all National Park areas. In 1955, the number of Parkway visitors reached 4.5 million.[11]

Parks everywhere strained under the weight of the huge visitor influx—the public "loving the parks to death," as someone put it at the time. From Parkway planners' point of view, however, things were looking up. Weems noted optimistically in 1954 that new Federal Aid Highway Act funds and expected inclusion of the Parkway in future federal highway appropriations would spur the Parkway to completion.[12]

Thus, by the time Browning's staffers posted the state's maps in Watauga County in the spring of 1955, the Parkway had passed through its difficult postwar decade. Although planning, land acquisition, concessions, and recreation area development had moved steadily ahead, construction progress had been languid. Only three new sections totaling about thirty-two miles had opened to travelers in the decade since the end of the war.[13]

The real revolution in national parks funding came in 1956—just as the Grandfather Mountain conflict heated up—with the advent of the Mission 66 program, a ten-year plan of vastly increased funding and development aimed at resurrecting and dramatically expanding the nation's deteriorating park infrastructure in time for the N P S's fiftieth anniversary in 1966. Costing close to $1 billion by its conclusion, Mission 66 set about to upgrade parks' physical facilities to provide "enjoyment without impairment" for the huge influx of visitors: new roads, trails, parking areas, campgrounds, and water, sewer, and power systems; rehabilitated historic structures; and new park buildings including many visitor centers.

Supporters of the Park Service's traditional emphasis on bolstering recreational tourism viewed the unprecedented Mission 66 program as a "renaissance" for the national parks. But partisans of the growing environmental movement objected to what they saw as the "urbanization" and destruction of the wilderness character of the parks by such intense development and to the program's modernist architecture, which clashed with the more rustic styles of earlier Park Service buildings. Some environmentalists believed, historian Richard Sellars says, "that the bulldozer was the appropriate symbol for Mission 66" and suggested later that the Park Service needed "a Mission 76 to undo the harm done in Mission 66." Mission 66 nevertheless contributed mightily to making outdoor recreational spaces accessible and usable for millions of Americans.[14]

For most supporters of the Parkway, the Mission 66 funds and bulldozers were a welcome sight. With the Parkway named a priority project and allocated $32 million, it looked as if the ambitious undertaking would at last be finished. Focused mostly on construction of the road itself, plans for the Parkway—announced in July 1956—also envisioned the appropriation of approximately $4 million to develop more lodging, restaurant, and other visitor accommodation facilities at several recreation areas. In the end, Mission 66 provided perhaps 75 percent of the funds invested in the Parkway's construction, bringing the road within 5.5 miles of completion by the program's end. Those 5.5 miles lay in Section 2-H, the Grandfather Mountain section for which the State Highway Commission had appropriated lands in 1955, angering Hugh Morton.[15]

The Parkway's exact route at Grandfather Mountain had been left unresolved since the late 1930s. Soon after Mission 66 was announced, the NPS's acting director wrote to North Carolina Governor Luther Hodges to explain the program's potential benefits and impressing on him the "need for early action" by the State Highway Commission in turning over the deeds for the remaining rights-of-way. Probably because of the sudden importance of pushing forward Parkway land acquisition, Browning retired as chief locating engineer to devote his full attention to the Parkway as the Highway Commission's "federal parkway engineer."[16]

"WE GAVE THEM EVERYTHING THEY ASKED FOR":
THE 1939 RIGHT-OF-WAY AGREEMENT

Finalizing the Parkway route at Grandfather during the 1950s was complicated by a disagreement over whether the route there had in fact already been decided and the lands already bought in the 1930s. Throughout his conflict with the Park Service, Morton maintained that the 1955 effort to get new lands at Grandfather was one of a "string of attempted broken promises and agreements." Specifically, he asserted, "in the late thirties [my family] provided at modest cost a total of seven and one-half miles of Parkway right of way" at the maximum width allowed under state law.[17]

While the state indeed had purchased some lands at Grandfather in the 1930s, federal officials' commitment to use one section of those particular lands for the Parkway was always quite soft. The 7.5 miles of right-of-way at Grandfather had been bought in two segments, the first purchased in 1938. In 1939, fearing that development and timbering by the financially pressured company that owned the mountain might damage the scenery planned for the Parkway, state officials had paid Morton's uncle, Nelson MacRae, and his Linville Improvement Company twenty-five thousand dollars for 488 acres of right-of-way along an additional four-mile section (a fairly generous fifty-one dollars per acre) even though the NPS still had not officially designated the exact route it planned to use there.[18]

Although the fact that the route at Grandfather had not been firmly set was clear to all parties, the seeds of the subsequent conflict with Morton lay in this confused episode: When Browning's office posted maps for the 1955 acquisition, Morton (who had not been involved in the 1939 transfer, which involved lands for the same Parkway segment but different from those specified on the 1955 maps) immediately claimed that the state already had all the land it needed or was entitled to get. His legal argument initially rested on the 1930s state authorizing legislation, which, in compliance with federal standards, stated that a "reasonable right of way" for the Parkway would consist of 125 acres per mile in fee simple. Morton judged that the 1955 acquisition, when added to the 1939 purchase, gave the state between three and four hundred acres per mile along the disputed segment.[19]

While this argument persuaded State Highway Commission officials to return the 1955 lands to Morton in 1957, the legal argument lost force the next year when Browning and the Park Service came up with a revised plan that met the standard of 125 acres per mile. Furthermore, the state attorney general ruled in 1962 that the state had authority to acquire the additional lands.[20] Nevertheless, the existence of the 1939 transaction confused and complicated from the outset a controversy that ultimately turned on other arguments and was driven by other concerns. How had this baffling state of affairs developed?

A "RUGGED, UNCONQUERED WILDERNESS"?:
ENTREPRENEURS, TIMBERING, AND TOURISM
DEVELOPMENT IN A NEAR–NATIONAL PARK

Throughout his fight, Morton claimed that construction along the Park Service's desired Parkway route would destroy Grandfather's "rugged, unconquered wilderness qualities." But the reason state officials rushed ahead with the 1939 purchase of a right-of-way was that precisely those qualities were at risk of being damaged by the mountain's owners—Morton's development-minded maternal relatives, the MacRae family, who seemed likely to exploit a mountain that virtually everyone considered an incomparable prize. The ensuing conflict provides a textbook example of the malleability of notions of "nature," "wilderness," "conservation," "preservation," and "protection" and their sometimes only tangential relationship to verifiable changes on particular ground.[21]

Long before the Parkway was envisioned, park proponents had hoped to create a national park at the Blue Ridge's highest peak (5,964 feet), whose rocky ridge (ancient quartzite thrust up from the Piedmont 1.1 billion years ago) resembles the face of an old man looking skyward in "calm and passionless repose," according to an 1870 description. A 1907 account rhapsodized over the "Great Stone Face of the Grandfather . . . carved in rock and plumed with ferns . . . the furrows of his face . . . worn by the lapse of time." In the early years of Parkway routing, everyone agreed that the Parkway should come to Grandfather Mountain: both the North Carolina- and Tennessee-supported routes had included it.[22]

Since the 1880s, the mountain had been owned by the MacRae family of Wilmington, prolific industrial, agricultural, and tourism developers whose business enterprises eventually spread throughout the state. Virtually all biographical accounts venerate the family patriarch, Hugh MacRae, an MIT-educated industrialist, as a public-spirited citizen, but he was not always above using force to get his way. In 1898 he helped lead a vigilante mob of Wilmington's white citizens in a rampage in which the offices of a black-owned newspaper were torched and many black citizens were murdered as part of what historian Timothy Tyson calls the turn of the century's "bloody counterrevolution" that crushed growing black political power in the South.[23]

In first decade of the twentieth century, MacRae developed several Wilmington-area suburbs and the popular Lumina pavilion at Wrightsville Beach and went on to head the Wilmington Cotton Mills Company and the Wilmington Gas Light Company as well as several of its successors. He was also intensely interested in agricultural innovation, working out ways to support year-round grazing by his dairy herd on his Pender County farm. He sponsored a number of planned farming communities in southeastern North Carolina, enticing European settlers to take advantage of the long growing season. His successful efforts there inspired development of the New Deal rural resettlement community of Penderlea.[24]

Before launching his Wilmington-area enterprises, MacRae had worked for several years as a mining engineer in mica, feldspar, and kaolin mines in the

Spruce Pine and Burnsville areas of the North Carolina mountains. While there in 1887, he and other members of his family joined with other investors (described in an early company brochure as "capitalists from Boston, New York, Philadelphia, North and South Carolina, Missouri and Kansas") to form the Linville Land, Manufacturing, and Mining Company (later renamed the Linville Improvement Company). The company, one of many large timber and mining concerns to buy up Appalachian mountain lands in the late nineteenth century, purchased sixteen thousand acres including Grandfather Mountain in what are now Watauga, Avery, and Caldwell Counties. The company was not the first to be interested in the area's timber resources. Some of the lands purchased near the Linville River had already been so completely timbered that local residents nicknamed the area Stump Town. Indeed, a 1932 account of the origins of Linville noted that "in 1891 the ground now occupied by Linville had been cleared and stumped so clean that it looked like a desert bordered with trees."[25]

MacRae and his collaborators were in fact part of a group of capitalists who followed the railroads into the southern Appalachian region after the 1870s in search of lumber to take the place of exhausted northern and midwestern resources. These entrepreneurs launched a thirty-five-year timber boom that brought greater (and faster) ecological and sociocultural change to the Appalachian region than had any other previous form of human activity.[26]

The devastation already evident near Linville apparently did not deter Linville Improvement Company investors, who expected to use the land for both timber and tourism, a pattern already familiar in the southern Appalachians. After 1875, MacRae's major partner, Samuel Kelsey, had built the mountain getaway of Highlands on a similar platform of mining, timbering, and tourism. In the 1890s, the Linville Company began to develop part of its mountain lands along the Linville River into the town of Linville, envisioned as a planned community with private homes, industries, and full town services. Somewhat ironically, the cover of the first advertising brochure for this "resort for health and pleasure" featured an image of a tree stump.[27]

Initially ten miles from the nearest railroad stop at the iron mining town of Cranberry and beset by early financial difficulties and conflicts among the founders, Linville was slow to take off. To improve access, the company in 1891 built the Yonahlossee Road around Grandfather Mountain to connect the new development to Blowing Rock, eighteen miles to the east. A scenic but twisting route that an early traveler said "hug[ged] the mountainside closely" and "came like a belt of sunshine falling through shade," the Yonahlossee improved substantially on the rough wagon roads that were the norm for the area. "With every turn" along

Cover of 1880s promotional booklet for the village of Linville, North Carolina.
North Carolina Collection, University of North Carolina at Chapel Hill.

the Yonahlossee, an early brochure promised, "there opens before the vision an entrancing panorama of graceful forest-clad summits above and lovely valleys below."[28]

Drawn by "four splendid horses prancing between ornamental mazes of laurel and pine, passing mirthful falls and crossing streams like 'liquid silver,'" the stagecoach that carried tourists from Blowing Rock to Linville brought them to the "cheerful accommodations" provided by Linville's major attraction: the large and well-appointed Eseeola Inn, built by the company the year after the Yonahlossee Road was finished. Despite ongoing problems with debt, the Linville Company and the MacRae family continued to develop the community, building roads, streets, and a lake and attracting visitors and new summer homeowners with good fishing, a golf course, and riding stables. By the early 1900s, Linville nevertheless "still resembled a mountain outpost rather than a town."[29]

Whatever the attractions of Linville itself, timbering kept the resort afloat from the beginning. Company owners had promoted the timber resources of the area to potential home buyers and had operated a profitable sawmill on West Fork

Eseeola Inn at Linville, 1908. North Carolina Collection, University of North Carolina at Chapel Hill.

Creek that employed as many as thirty local men. They shipped lumber to Piedmont furniture factories and to the company's own furniture shop and provided the chestnut bark that covered Linville village summer homes. The World War I–era timber and iron ore boom brought the extension in 1917 of the East Tennessee and Western North Carolina's "Tweetsie" narrow-gauge railroad near the village, with service to Boone and points west. As historian Timothy Silver has observed of logging in the nearby Black Mountains, "thanks to the trees . . . local people got to sample the good life in modern America."[30]

Under the leadership of Hugh Morton's uncle, Nelson MacRae, the Linville resort flourished in the 1920s and early 1930s, with a new eighteen-hole golf course designed by premier Pinehurst, North Carolina, planner Donald Ross; several more summer homes; expansion of the Eseeola Inn; a new stable and riding ring; and plans for a larger, two-hundred-room hotel. By the 1930s, access was further improved by the paving of the Yonahlossee Road as it was leased to the state as part of U.S. 221.[31]

From its beginnings, Linville, like Little Switzerland, attracted an upscale clientele. A 1932 account of the Eseeola Inn's 1892 opening recalled that it had drawn "the finest gathering of high class people that has ever greeted the opening

Sawmill on the Linville River in Burke County, North Carolina, n.d.
North Carolina Collection, University of North Carolina at Chapel Hill.

season of a new mountain place in North Carolina." Later descriptions by Parkway officials characterized the community as "one of the finest resort developments [along] the entire Parkway" and as a "swank . . . development for the rich."
Stuart Cramer Jr., a Charlotte-area textile manufacturer, for example, built a large
new custom home at Linville in 1935, to which he annually moved his household,
"including domestic help." William McWane, head of Birmingham's McWane
Cast Iron and Pipe Company, was another Linville regular. Greensboro's Spencer
Love (founder of Burlington Industries) owned a home, as did Gastonia textile
maker A. G. Myers. Future Duke Power president Norman A. Cocke also owned a
Linville home.[32]

As at Little Switzerland, Linville's summer residents developed what the
community's historian rather generously called a "symbiotic relationship [with]
mountain people." In reality, the locals constituted a servant class, with women
working in the hotel, other small lodges, and private homes as housekeepers and
maids and men gardening, working as carpenters or plumbers, maintaining bri-
dle trails, or serving as caddies on the golf courses. With the company's blessing,
local residents also built some homes for themselves, planted gardens, and har-
vested firewood on company lands. Tensions occasionally emerged between local

white employees and the professional African American hotel workers brought in to cook, wait tables, and serve as bellmen, but black workers by and large lived separately from Linville's whites.[33]

During the 1920s and 1930s, golf and the Eseeola were the main attractions of Linville, but Grandfather Mountain itself had always been central to planning for the development. The company's first brochure asserted that the mountain "has been reserved as an extensive park, where the natural features of mountain and forest will be protected," and another early brochure termed Grandfather "the greatest attraction in this region, in fact in North Carolina." The company arranged to deed the top of Grandfather to a trust, whose managers were to protect it "for public use," but by 1916 MacRae judged this arrangement unsatisfactory. At that point—just a few months before the NPS was established but after many years in which park boosters in the southern mountains had been agitating for an eastern national park—he inquired with officials in Washington about giving fourteen hundred acres at the top of Grandfather to the Interior Department or the Forest Service (which had recently bought some other lands in the area for the just-designated Pisgah National Forest) "as a national park." A year later, as a result of these discussions, Congress authorized the interior secretary and the new Park Service to "accept for park purposes any lands and rights of way, including the Grandfather Mountain, near or adjacent to the Government forest reserve in Western North Carolina." Park Service head Stephen Mather rejected the donation, however, when it became clear that the Linville Company intended to retain ownership of (and perhaps profit from) all the lands around the donated summit, which at the time was, according to historian Michael Frome, "barren of trees."[34]

As the movement for eastern national parks gained strength with the 1924 establishment of a federal Southern Appalachian National Park Committee to choose a site, the idea of a national park at Grandfather Mountain revived. Park boosters in North Carolina lobbied the committee to select lands encompassing Grandfather Mountain and the nearby Linville Gorge. Rallied by Hugh MacRae, Grandfather-area supporters included officials of the Asheville and Charlotte Chambers of Commerce; Joseph Hyde Pratt's Western North Carolina, Inc.; the *Asheville Citizen-Times*; the towns of Linville, Blowing Rock, and Boone; the state-appointed North Carolina Park Commission (also established in 1924); and timber companies that owned land in the Great Smokies (and thus opposed locating a park there). The federal committee (and Congress) ultimately rejected the Grandfather site, however, in favor of the Great Smokies and Shenandoah areas. But North Carolinians' support of the Grandfather-Linville region—though eventually redirected to the campaign to raise funds for the Great Smoky Mountains National Park—died hard.[35]

In 1921, shortly before this flurry of park-boosting activity, Hugh MacRae's daughter, Agnes, and her husband, Julian Morton, had a son, whom they named Hugh MacRae Morton. Young Hugh grew up in Wilmington but spent his boyhood summers in Linville. While there, as a teenage camper at Camp Yonahnoka, he took up photography, a skill he went on to employ as a student at the University of North Carolina, as an army photographer in the South Pacific during World War II, as a freelance press photographer in North Carolina, and ultimately as the promoter of Grandfather Mountain.[36]

During Morton's boyhood, Linville thrived, but by the mid-1930s, both the community and the Linville Company had again fallen on hard times despite an ongoing combination of tourist-oriented development at Grandfather and further exploitation of the mountain's timber resources. In the early 1930s, the company generated a small profit by widening an existing horseback trail into an unpaved one-lane toll road to lead visitors from Highway 221 up to a wooden viewing platform at the Cliffside overlook on Grandfather. But the company's efforts to build up its tourism income suffered a blow in 1936 when fire destroyed the main Eseeola lodge building.[37]

In desperate straits, the company returned to its old mainstay, timbering. In the early 1930s, the company sold timber rights on parts of the mountain to Champion Paper and Fibre Company, which had operated an enormous pulp and paper mill at Canton, North Carolina, since 1908, for a reported seventy thousand dollars. The *Asheville Times* in 1933 described a deforested north slope now "covered with a deep layer of trash" and being overtaken with "thick growths of chokeberry and blackberry bushes, which render any early reseeding very unlikely." Forest fires followed the timbering and had, the *Times* noted, "burned over much of the east end" of the mountain. As hard times deepened, the company saw possible financial salvation in further sale of timber, building stone, and shrubbery (laurel and rhododendron) from the mountain's slopes, even though (according to another federal investigation done in 1935) "almost all the timber . . . has been cut, [and] a great deal of interest has been destroyed." Company representatives also mulled over the potential of some of Grandfather's ridges for real estate and recreational development.[38]

The accelerated timbering at Grandfather alarmed some North Carolinians, who by now could see the widespread devastation decades of timbering had wrought throughout the region. In 1933, representatives of several regional women's clubs, mostly in the Lenoir area, petitioned Congressman Robert Doughton

Lumbering operations at Grandfather Mountain, Section 2-H, February 1934. In the 1930s, timber companies, including Champion Paper and Fibre, removed spruce, balsam, fir, and hemlock trees from Grandfather over plank roads such as the one shown here. Courtesy Blue Ridge Parkway.

for federal protection of the mountain to stop the "vandalism" of Grandfather's spruce and fir forests by timber interests (including Champion). Nearby landowner and early Parkway promoter R. L. Gwyn, a supporter of the purchase of Grandfather by the Forest Service, reported in 1935 that substantial portions of the spruce and balsam on Grandfather that he and the women's clubs had lobbied the government to protect "has been sold and much of it removed, and the removal of the remainder is now going on at a rapid rate." By 1936, even the highest officials at the Park Service in Washington were reporting with dismay that "for the past several years now the paper company has been rapidly denuding the entire area of the timber stand and barren areas and fire hazards are evident in all directions."[39]

Such reports about Grandfather also unnerved Highway Commission officials such as Getty Browning, who wrote in April 1936 that the cutting was "a very serious matter insofar as it affects the Parkway." "I can think of no way to prevent further destruction of the timber," he continued, "unless the route of the Parkway can be definitely fixed and the right of way taken over by the State." In May, Browning alerted Stanley Abbott that the Linville Improvement Company had offered for sale another stand of virgin timber alongside the Yonahlossee

Road (U.S. 221). Noting plans to put twenty miles of the Parkway through this area of "outstanding beauty," Abbott urged speedy movement on route flagging in the area and assured Washington officials that Browning would "do everything in his power" to convince the Linville Company not to sell the timber until the Parkway land acquisition could be started. The chair of the Highway Commission pleaded with the N P S's associate director to "to decide promptly how the Park- way is to run across Grandfather and flag the route so that we can take possession of the property that we need and prevent further deforestation." The B P R engi- neer responsible for mapping the route in this area forwarded preliminary maps to the state a few days later but noted that they were based on existing surveys of the Yonahlossee Road and that "we have not flagged a Parkway line through this area."[40]

The problems Parkway planners faced at Grandfather epitomized the generally compromised natural environment out of which the eastern national parks were created. A half century of industrial-scale timbering and related fires, flooding, soil erosion, and the disastrous chestnut blight had left much of the area taken in by both the Parkway and the Great Smoky Mountains National Park a treeless wasteland. In many places, Parkway landscape architects thus found their job to be one of rehabilitation rather than preservation. As Abbott had lamented in a 1934 report on planned recreation area development on the Parkway, "Few of the show-places of the Parkway environs remain in an unspoiled natural state. The predominance of cut over forest, cultivated farm land and the commercialization of the few protected scenic types has greatly reduced the recreation values. There is a total absence of natural lakes and the muddy condition of the streams and rivers in all seasons due to erosion has nullified the outstanding beauty of these water features." This situation, Abbott concluded, created the "need for public purchase and restoration if the area is to regain its one-time attractiveness."[41]

By the 1930s, then, Grandfather Mountain, like much of the rest of the southern Appalachians, was far from an "unconquered wilderness." Indeed, the conquest was proceeding at such a pace that North Carolina Highway Commission officials felt an urgent need to take hold of the lands the Parkway would require at Grandfa- ther. Thus although the official route at Grandfather had not been flagged, during the summer of 1936 state officials posted the first of two sets of land-acquisition maps in Avery and Caldwell Counties for land owned by the Linville Company. The second set described 488 acres of Linville Company land straddling the exist- ing Yonahlossee Road/U.S. 221. In 1939, the state finally received explicit approval from top-level N P S officials in Washington to acquire these lands for the Parkway (in effect, taking over part of the Yonahlossee Road). Shortly thereafter, a legal agreement (though not a deed) filed in Avery and Caldwell Counties consummated the sale of the property to the state for twenty-five thousand dollars. Wording in the agreement plainly connected this purchase with "Land Acquisition, Blue Ridge Parkway, Project SPP-18, Section 2-H." Despite the heavy timbering, the lands' scenic values had not yet been entirely lost. A Highway Commission press release noted that the "Parkway right of way . . . embraces a considerable quantity of original growth timber, some especially beautiful balsam, hemlock, and spruce."[42]

In negotiating this settlement, the Highway Commission paid the Linville Company only half what the company asked, still a generous $51 per acre. Taking place a few months before the resolution of the Little Switzerland case for more than $280 per acre and a year before the finalizing of the Cherokee settlement at $30 an acre, the Linville payment was at that time "the most expensive single claim" for right-of-way in North Carolina. Although this was nearly $40 per acre more than the Highway Commission's claims adjuster had originally recommended for lands he said were "mostly unsuitable for any development[,] being steep and rocky," the Highway Commission's chief attorney justified the higher price by noting that these lands were the only large tract with valuable frontage on an existing paved highway, the taking of which would isolate and render much of the rest of the property undevelopable. Thus, far from selling its lands "for a song," as several 1962 newspaper accounts later told it, the Linville Company had in 1939 arranged a highly favorable and expensive settlement.[43]

Other parts of the generous arrangement made with the Linville Company revealed the State Highway Commission's ongoing alliance with prominent business developers. State negotiators, in clear contradiction to stated Park Service policy, permitted the Linville Company to retain access to the Yonahlossee section of the Parkway at four points until the state could construct a new public highway to serve the remainder of the company's property in that area. After the execution of the basic agreement with the company, the commission's claims adjuster unsuccessfully pressed the Park Service to approve further accesses from company lands to the Parkway, noting that President Nelson MacRae "has one of the finest resort developments in the entire Parkway which will be quite in harmony with the nature and use of the project."[44]

Company representatives, including Nelson MacRae, who handled the negotiations on the company's behalf, had supported the Parkway since the beginning, hoping that it—or at least the payment for the lands—would help revive their resort. Some evidence also suggests that the impetus for the slightly unusual settlement stemmed at least partly from Highway Commission attorney Charles

Ross's desire to help his "very good friend," Hugh MacRae. As Weems, the Parkway superintendent, later remembered, Ross said "that he would like to settle with the Linville Improvement Company as they needed the money."[45]

The Parkway settlement did not bring an immediate end to the company's difficulties, however. Timber orders declined and the sawmill closed in the late 1930s. Sales of summer homes languished. Heavy rains from a 1940 hurricane produced a devastating flood — possibly exacerbated by timbering on the mountain — that swamped Linville and washed out (permanently, it turned out) parts of the railroad connection to Boone. Visitation slumped, company debt mounted, and Wilmington banks pressured Hugh MacRae to dump the resort from his portfolio. In the early 1940s it appeared that the community might collapse. Troubles mounted in 1942 when company president Nelson MacRae, crushed by stress, committed suicide. Linville clearly was "at its lowest ebb."[46]

"SAFE FROM RUINATION": HARLAN KELSEY'S ATTEMPT TO PURCHASE GRANDFATHER

The flooding was perhaps emblematic of long-term trends of environmental exploitation at Grandfather. Paradoxically, by plunging the Linville Company further into the doldrums, it compounded the likelihood of continued damage to the mountain and intensified many people's feeling that only federal or state protection could stave off complete deforestation. With the reservation of access for the Linville Company to lands above the Parkway section of the Yonahlossee Road, the 1939 Parkway right-of-way arrangement clearly did not greatly reduce the risk of the destruction of the mountain's long-admired scenic values through continued logging or resort development.[47]

Despite their disagreement with the state about the arrangements to be made with the Linville Company, Blue Ridge Parkway and Park Service staff may have allowed state officials to proceed because they had an altogether different plan for Grandfather in mind, one that would trump the limited solution the state had arranged and eliminate the problem of the access roads and encroaching development.

On the eve of the announcement of the Linville Company settlement, Abbott wrote to the director of the Park Service to say that "the only logical plan for development of this resort region would provide for conservation of Grandfather Mountain in a wild state — this from the point of view of both the Parkway and the resort towns themselves." "Ideally," he continued, "Grandfather Mountain should be Federally owned or controlled through State or Federal purchase with a minimum of private reservations remaining on the land." As the Linville settlement was being announced, in fact, Abbott had launched his staff on a small research effort to determine costs of buying the needed lands. This study indicated that a purchase of between thirty-five hundred and forty-five hundred acres for perhaps thirty-five dollars per acre "would save this outstanding mountain." On the basis of these findings, the Park Service inquired whether the State Highway Commission could assist in the purchase. The commission's chair, however, rejected the idea of paying more than the five dollars an acre that federal agencies were customarily paying for similarly cutover "ordinary forest land."[48]

Still, the idea did not die. In 1940, the MacRae family seems to have initiated yet another effort to get Grandfather into federal hands, this time through a search for private funding coordinated by well-connected longtime family friend Harlan Page Kelsey, a landscape architect and horticulturalist formerly of Linville but now living in Massachusetts. Long associated with the national parks movement (he had been one of the five members of the Southern Appalachian National Park Committee and had pushed hard to have the committee choose the Great Smokies as one of its designated park areas), Kelsey had also been president of the Appalachian Mountain Club and a key adviser for early NPS directors Stephen Mather and Horace M. Albright. Kelsey's connection to the MacRaes and Linville also stretched far back: his father, Samuel T. Kelsey, had been an original Linville Improvement Company investor and had, according to company advertising, "selected the town site" for Linville during the 1880s.[49]

Sometime in 1940, the MacRaes asked Kelsey to help them sell Grandfather to the NPS as a Parkway recreation area, but Park Service director Arno B. Cammerer declared that his agency had "absolutely no funds" for the acquisition. However, one of Cammerer's successors, Newton Drury, confirmed that the service would welcome the donation of Grandfather and surrounding lands as a Parkway recreation area. Abbott's 1941 Blue Ridge Parkway "master plan" included an eight-thousand-acre recreation area at Grandfather Mountain. The plan acknowledged that "there have been extensive timbering operations in this area for several years" and that, as a result, "there is a great amount of slash that has been left, constituting a very serious fire hazard." But a large percentage of lands remained wooded, and the plan contemplated leaving them as undeveloped "wilderness" with trails and picnic areas.[50]

Intermittent discussions continued, and in 1942, Hugh MacRae, now in his late seventies and recovering from the death of his son, Nelson, approached the North Carolina Department of Conservation and Development about buying the mountain. The department, like the NPS, was interested but lacked funds. Later that year, MacRae enlisted Kelsey (on commission) to find "some wealthy person or persons who would be willing to purchase these mountains and donate them to the Park Service." Thus, Kelsey persisted. "Linville is my old home," he reasoned. "I have a particular affection for Grandfather and Grandmother mountains, and I want to see them in the perpetual care of the National Park Service." Despite his friendship with the MacRaes, however, he confided to Cammerer that Grandfather "has been badly mauled and manhandled by the Linville Company, through necessity I suppose, but that doesn't help the mountain any." Trying to enlist former NPS director Horace Albright's support, Kelsey wrote urgently, "This area must be under the permanent protection of the National Park Service and safe from ruination by the Linville Company or any one else."[51]

Arriving at an acceptable price for the desired lands was a challenge, given the MacRae family's and NPS appraisers' wildly different valuations for the property. Shortly after Nelson MacRae's death, Hugh MacRae noted the Linville Company's precarious financial state and wrote to Kelsey that the company would not be able to disregard "the intrinsic value of the mountain and [make] the equivalent of a large donation toward the success of the [park] plan." "Fair consideration" for the value of the lands, he argued "cannot be approached successfully on an acreage basis" (which would take account of timbering damage and produce a low valuation). He reminded Kelsey that a price of $1 million had previously been mentioned but said that the company would accept less. Hugh MacRae's son-in-law, Julian Morton, by 1943 presiding over the Linville Company, proposed what Kelsey considered a fair price of two hundred thousand dollars for twelve thousand acres (nearly seventeen dollars per acre) but estimated the true worth of the mountain at fifty dollars per acre. Given the previous logging, however, Drury judged even the two-hundred-thousand-dollar price too high. Still Kelsey pushed the idea, proposing in 1944 a campaign to raise a half million dollars to buy nearly fifty thousand acres—much of the area between Blowing Rock and Linville—which he described as "virgin or semi-virgin," to "do the job right." Such a large park, he argued, would "successfully foster the return of a wild-life fauna."[52]

Both Kelsey and Drury viewed the situation as urgent, not least because of statements made by Linville Company representatives about their plans for the mountain. In 1942, Hugh MacRae had proposed a system of roads on both sides of Grandfather in conjunction with an expanded Parkway there. Kelsey, who thought that the company's toll road and observation platform had already "done very much to spoil the beauty of the mountain as a natural park," told MacRae that he was alarmed by this idea: "If you carried out your idea of extending the road system on top of the mountain, making of it another Blowing Rock or even a Chimney Rock, then its value as a National Park . . . is ruined forever." Kelsey acknowledged that both his father and MacRae had dreamed of making Grandfather into a "great playground center" but surmised that "both you and he had in mind more the exploiting of the mountain for the purposes of making money for the Linville Company rather than dedicating the mountain itself as a beautiful natural object . . . unspoiled." Kelsey's words again foregrounded the competing discourses about natural resources use, conservation, and protection that had been circulating since the days of John Muir, Gifford Pinchot, and Theodore Roosevelt.[53]

As the 1940s wore on, Grandfather teetered on the brink of intense exploitation likely to be worsened when demand for timber products spiked at the end of the war. "I have not exaggerated the danger of destruction," Kelsey wrote to Albright, "for the Linville Company apparently must either sell or undertake lumbering operations which would of course render the area unfit for park purposes." Indeed, Julian Morton warned Kelsey directly a few days later that war conditions and a lack of income had forced the company to cut timber on its lands, although "not on the Grandfather Mountain proper." The company's need to raise cash was acute, and Morton warned that if the Linville Company property was not sold within a year, "we will most probably start timbering much closer and on other parts of the property. . . . We are going to continue to cut timber," he threatened, and "are going to sell either the timber or the land as a whole to the first purchaser that will pay us a satisfactory price." While he agreed that "we would rather see the property made a park," he emphasized that "we are not going to hold it indefinitely, hoping it will eventually become a park."[54]

While discussions dragged on for nearly a year, the Linville Company sold the Linville resort development and approximately 3,000 acres to another private concern for $160,000. Finally, in early 1945, Morton, MacRae, and the Linville Company gave Kelsey an option to purchase 5,555 acres of land including Grandfather and Grandmother Mountains for what Kelsey thought was a fair price — $165,000, or about $30 per acre — expressly for donation to the Park Service. Wide differences persisted over the cost, however. Weems, an experienced land appraiser who had managed land acquisition in the 1930s for the Parkway recreation areas at Cumberland Knob, the Bluff (Doughton Park), Rocky Knob, and the Peaks of Otter, judged this sum "excessive for the type [of] land involved."[55]

Despite these reservations, Weems and Stanley Abbott, now back from the war to his position as the Parkway's resident landscape architect, worked closely with Kelsey throughout 1945 and into 1946 to identify the boundaries of lands the

Park Service would eventually want to include in a Grandfather Mountain recreation area. The lands on which Kelsey held the option were considered the minimum the Park Service needed. Officials had set their sights on a much larger park area — at least twenty-six thousand acres, part of which was already in Forest Service hands. Kelsey, who had long hoped for an even larger acquisition, worked as an intermediary between the NPS and the Linville Company.[56]

From late 1944 through 1947, Kelsey orchestrated a public relations campaign to convince North Carolinians of the need to rescue Grandfather and worked to develop a Grandfather Mountain Park Association to round up private and state funds to buy the core Linville Company–owned lands. It was an "urgent challenge," he repeatedly emphasized; Grandfather was "threatened with immediate calamitous destruction of its virgin glories by lumbering operations and other commercial exploitation." "Shall Grandfather Mountain Be Saved?," he cried in the statewide press, in national parks and planning journals, and even in the U.S. House of Representatives.[57]

As the campaign proceeded, relations between the MacRae/Morton family and Kelsey deteriorated. Although Kelsey's ties to Linville and the MacRaes went back years and although the family had enlisted his help in the 1940 efforts to sell Grandfather to the government for a park, Kelsey came to doubt the family's and the company's ability and inclination to preserve Grandfather. Julian Morton's bald warnings that the company would continue timbering if the mountain were not sold certainly heightened Kelsey's fears. And after Morton died suddenly of a heart attack at age forty-nine in 1945, Kelsey worried about dealing with Hugh MacRae, whom he now distrusted.[58]

Despite Kelsey's apparent success in enlisting at least the verbal support of two governors, the State Conservation and Development Commission, former NPS director Albright, other important figures in the development of national parks, and longtime Parkway supporters at the *Asheville Citizen-Times* and Chamber of Commerce as well as prominent North Carolinians statewide, he failed to raise any substantial pledges beyond a single commitment of ninety thousand dollars (apparently from John D. Rockefeller Jr.) before his option to purchase Grandfather expired in the spring of 1947. Surprised by this outcome, given the energetic support of prominent North Carolinians for a park at Grandfather in the 1920s, Kelsey bitterly observed that "North Carolina has many multimillionaires and it is a sad commentary that they hemmed and hawed till my option ran out." For another year, he hoped that the purchase option might be renewed, but when Linville Company representatives declined to do so, Kelsey pulled himself out of an eight-year entanglement that had become too financially and emotionally draining.[59]

By this point, the situation at Grandfather Mountain had changed dramatically from the early 1940s. At that juncture, the company was in a weak position and was reeling from fire, floods, Nelson MacRae's suicide, debt, and the wartime decline in travel. By 1948, improved economic conditions, brightening finances, and the emergence of new leadership within the Linville Company had made selling Grandfather to the Park Service far less likely.

Post–World War II changes in company leadership played perhaps the largest role in altering the prospects for a Grandfather Mountain recreation area on the Parkway. Kelsey had worried that Hugh MacRae, whom Kelsey claimed in 1948 had "declared he would not give a dime towards acquiring any park or public area!" presented the greatest obstacle to his plans. But the rising influence in the still financially strapped company of a small group of wealthy Charlotte-area businessmen led by Duke Power executive Norman A. Cocke also posed challenges.[60]

The greatest risk to Grandfather in the late 1940s, Kelsey judged, "lies in the strong possibility of the Linville Company selling out to a group of wealthy Linville summer residents, including Norman A. Cocke . . . for *real* exploitation." The fact that Hugh Morton's sister had recently married Cocke's son gave Kelsey additional pause, as he felt that Cocke was "a bitter foe of National Parks and National Forests" who "hoped both would be given back to private citizens to be utilized (exploited) by them." Kelsey confided to Weems that on a recent trip to Wilmington, Kelsey had gotten "direct evidence that [Cocke] and the Linville Company were in collusion to block any and all National Park and National Forest extensions if not 'get rid' entirely of existing Reservations!" Kelsey felt certain that Cocke had discouraged the rest of the company leadership from renewing Kelsey's Grandfather purchase option.[61]

"RICH CROPS OF TOURISTS": HUGH MORTON AND
THE DEVELOPMENT OF GRANDFATHER MOUNTAIN

Cocke indeed played a major behind-the-scenes role in preventing the Park Service from getting what it wanted at Grandfather, working quietly as legal adviser to Hugh MacRae's grandson, Hugh Morton, who returned to North Carolina after World War II service in the South Pacific to take the helm of the Linville Company. The mostly cooperative relations among Kelsey, the Linville Company, and state and federal officials became markedly more contentious as the entrepreneurial young Morton took a more combative stance toward the Park Service than anyone in the Linville Company previously had. The change had much to do with the new plans for the Linville Company and Grandfather Mountain that Morton sketched soon after his arrival.

Those plans hinged on developing and marketing the mountain itself as a tourist attraction and on doing so more aggressively than anyone had envisioned. After Morton took the reins, he effectively mobilized the rhetoric of "protection," "wilderness," and "nature" — previously invoked mainly by the advocates of public purchase of the mountain — in favor of his private development agenda. The compatibility of that agenda with the imperatives of environmental preservation, however, would remain an arena of substantial disagreement.[62]

Unlike other family members who had run the Linville Company and had focused their tourism development efforts on golf, the Eseeola Inn, and summer home construction in the Linville community while seeing Grandfather mainly as a striking associated natural feature whose financial potential lay mainly in its natural resources, Morton viewed the mountain itself as the company's greatest tourist attraction.

This difference in perspective became clear during Kelsey's campaign, when Morton took exception to Kelsey's repeated public assertions that unless the mountain came under federal protection, it would suffer "immediate calamitous destruction" by "the exploiter armed with axe and saw, to devastate and despoil." "There is one aspect of your campaign that does not appeal to us," Morton wrote to Kelsey in late 1946. "Portrayal of the Linville Company as the villianous [sic] woodman, axe held high, preparing to devastate Grandfather down to the last sprig of chlorophyll," Morton explained, "is contrary to our opinion of ourselves, and we had just as soon not be looked upon in such a light." Not acknowledging the company's history of threatening, encouraging, and facilitating logging on its lands, Morton further asserted that the company had no plans for further lumbering and that instead it hoped to develop the mountain with improved tourist facilities should the sale not go through. Grandfather's beauty, he wrote to Kelsey, "would be the commodity which we would sell." In a 1947 *Raleigh News and Observer* article, Morton further noted that "all the timber on the 5,500-acre tract will not yield as much income as will several rich crops of tourists."[63]

Morton's plans brought him into almost immediate conflict with those still interested in making Grandfather a publicly owned park. Although Kelsey had withdrawn, efforts to see his plan through continued into 1948. North Carolina's National Park, Parkway, and Forest Development Commission, established by the state legislature in 1947, formed a Grandfather Mountain Committee that recommended that the commission sponsor purchase of the fifty-five-hundred-acre Grandfather "core" that Kelsey had tried to buy and donate to the Park Service. Noting that the area was "steep and rocky" and undevelopable and had been thoroughly timbered in the 1930s, the committee concluded that protection from further timbering and commercial development would allow the red spruce to return and render the mountain a site that "rivals in natural beauty any mountain peak in the Great Smoky Mountains National Park" (a "wilderness" recovering at the time from being heavily clear-cut during the first three decades of the twentieth century). The committee advocated accepting the ninety-thousand-dollar pledge Kelsey had raised and asking the Linville Company to donate the other ninety thousand dollars of the cost of acquisition.[64]

The commission unanimously accepted its committee's recommendations, and Superintendent Weems was optimistic as the commission prepared to approach Morton and the Linville Company. A dubious Kelsey, however, was not surprised to hear from Weems in early fall the "sad news" that in a "show down" meeting in which they had also roundly criticized the Park Service and declared the Parkway a failure, Hugh Morton and two other Linville Company stockholders had told the commission that Grandfather Mountain was not for sale "at any price." The nearly decade-long attempt to acquire Grandfather as a Parkway recreation area crashed to an abrupt halt.[65]

With the prospect of public purchase dead, Morton drew up plans for development of the mountain: straightening and paving the toll road up the mountain, improving the observation platform, and promoting the mountain through more extensive advertising. Such advertising for the 1947 summer season more than doubled the company's 1946 income from the toll road, leading Morton to conclude that "Grandfather Mountain shows promise of being an excellent long-term investment for the Linville Company."[66]

Grandfather Mountain ultimately became an excellent long-term investment primarily for Hugh Morton. After years of financial struggle, the company, now mostly divested of its holdings in the Linville development itself, dissolved in the summer of 1952, less than a year after patriarch Hugh MacRae died at age eighty-six. The company's assets were quickly distributed to its shareholders. Taking title to the more than four thousand acres that constituted his share, Morton became sole owner of the entire mountain.[67]

Morton immediately began to implement his long-held plans. Within three months of the Linville Company's dissolution, he borrowed money, widened the original toll road to two lanes, and bulldozed and blasted it up nearly to the mountain's summit. There, at the end of the road, he built a "mile-high swing-

Postcard advertising Grandfather Mountain as "just off the Blue Ridge Parkway," n.d.
Reprinted with permission from *Postcards of Historic Blowing Rock* (Blowing Rock, N.C.:
Blowing Rock Historical Society, 2002).

ing bridge" (dedicated in September 1952) to convey walkers over an eighty-foot
chasm (a mile above sea level) to the mountain's Linville Peak, where they could
take in exhilarating panoramic views. The suspension bridge, a narrow walkway
strung on steel cables between two large platforms, cost Morton fifteen thousand
dollars. To regain the cost of these improvements, which one mid-1950s report
estimated at one hundred thousand dollars, Morton increased the price of admission to the mountain from fifty cents for car and driver (twenty-five cents for
additional passengers) to ninety cents per person. He also immediately ordered
letterhead proclaiming Grandfather "Carolina's Top Scenic Attraction."[68]

Building on the success of the annual Singing on the Mountain gospel music
and preaching event started by one of the Linville Company's local employees in
1924, Morton added new activities through the mid- and late 1950s: kite-flying
contests, sports car events, photography clinics, and a Scottish music, dance, and
athletic festival, the Highland Games, inaugurated in 1956, that drew throngs of
visitors. To be sure people knew about what Grandfather now offered, Morton
marketed his expanding array of attractions and events through newspapers,
magazines, radio, roadside billboards, and even a "non-commercial movie" about
Grandfather that he made available to schools and organizations throughout the
state. His efforts met with dramatic success: by 1956, roughly two hundred thou-

sand people visited, up from only twelve thousand a decade earlier. By 1958, gross annual receipts had grown from ten thousand dollars to one hundred thousand dollars. It was this only recently developed but already highly lucrative and promising asset that Hugh Morton had in his portfolio when he entered renewed negotiations regarding Parkway routing across his mountain in the mid-1950s.[69]

In 1961, in the midst of those negotiations, Morton launched an additional wave of development near the mountaintop, adding a large new visitor center with a two-hundred-seat assembly hall, snack bar, gift shop, and observation deck. By the time the Parkway routing question was finally resolved in 1968, the mountain that Morton ever afterward insisted "didn't deserve to be conquered" by the NPS had been partially timbered and paved, crowned with a swinging bridge and several other decidedly nonnatural structures, and swarmed with visitors. Twinned with the ubiquitous swinging bridge icon was the mountain's new mascot, a black bear named Mildred, who arrived from Zoo Atlanta in 1966, at once evoking the (now safely captured) wildness of the "unconquered" mountain and the warm fuzziness of sentimentalized, marketable nature.[70]

"SOLD DOWN THE RIVER": THE FRACTURING OF THE ROADS-PARKS-TOURISM ALLIANCE IN NORTH CAROLINA

At the same time he was building Grandfather Mountain into what he was determined to make North Carolina's top tourist attraction, Morton traveled the state promoting tourism-oriented initiatives and became one of the state's most prominent and widely recognized business and political figures. In the late 1940s and early 1950s, Morton presided over his hometown of Wilmington's first Azalea Festival (1948), was anointed Man of the Year by the North Carolina Junior Chamber of Commerce (1948), became vice president of the Wilmington Chamber of Commerce, was elected president of the North Carolina Press Photographers Association (1949), and was named to the North Carolina Board of Conservation and Development (1951). In a four-page 1950 spread, The State magazine profiled the "versatile and energetic" twenty-nine-year-old Morton as a "fireball" and a "dynamo." In 1956, he threw himself into state politics as publicity director for Luther Hodges's successful gubernatorial campaign, starting a long (and useful) line of close associations with North Carolina's Democratic governors.[71]

Through a series of battles with the Park Service in this period, Morton became a major spokesperson for North Carolina's commercial tourist operators, especially in the mountains. The conflicts centered not on environmental concerns but on the Parkway's policies and practices regarding the promotion of local tourism facilities and attractions, N PS plans to build and operate visitor accommodations (coffee shops, gift shops, gas stations, lodging), and repeated proposals to impose entrance fees or tolls. This climate of suspicion and mistrust complicated efforts to decide on the Parkway route at Grandfather Mountain.

Within a wider framework, the conflicts between Morton and the N PS shifted coalitions, loyalties, and alliances that had remained fairly stable since the Parkway's inception. From the mid-1940s to the mid-1960s, the Park Service found itself increasingly at odds with both the state of North Carolina and local tourism boosters, two constituencies whose support had been critical at the Parkway's birth. In this period, the symbiotic alignment of roads, parks, and tourism backers that had given rise to the Parkway broke apart. Morton was the central figure in this shift.

The first conflict flared only months after Morton took over the Linville Company, but the issues resurfaced again and again during the 1950s. Throughout, Morton insisted first that the Parkway's overarching purpose should be to serve and promote North Carolina's tourism industry and second that N PS had thus far failed to do so, instead putting itself in competition with that regional industry. In making these critiques, he laid bare a central tension within the Parkway project: how could the road promote and serve the region's tourist industry without becoming its captive? And where, in this mix, was a sense of the public good inherent in this publicly funded public works project?

Morton, for his part, mobilized his understanding of the Parkway's history to the benefit of both Grandfather Mountain and the tourist business community more broadly: "Loyal North Carolinians, particularly resort operators and persons benefitting directly from their enterprises," he observed quite accurately in 1946, "brought the Blue Ridge Parkway to North Carolina." But problems had developed, he judged, because the Parkway administration failed to understand the project's responsibility to the state's tourist industry. Consequently, he wrote, "the original enthusiasm for the Parkway is now conspicuously absent along the completed sections," where "resort operators, large and small, have to the man already bitterly tasted the existing Parkway disregard of their endeavors to eke out a living." "Right or wrong," he concluded early on, "there are many who stoutly contend that the Parkway has done their business more harm than good." North Carolinians enamored in the 1930s with the prospect of tourist-induced prosperity brought by the Parkway, he charged, had been grossly misled.[72]

Signs on the Parkway

Morton's hostility to the Park Service seems first to have been sparked by a conflict early in 1946 when, in the midst of his initial efforts to increase tourist traffic at Grandfather, he requested that the Park Service erect "one small directional sign reading 'Grandfather Mountain 1'" at the intersection of the Parkway and U.S. 221. Predictably, given the earlier response to a similar effort by Little Switzerland's Clarkson, the Park Service refused, a response Morton claimed cost him five thousand dollars in lost business that season. What he portrayed as a minor request, he reported, had ballooned into a "tedious hair-splitting wrangle about Grandfather Mountain being 'commercial.'" Working the next year through a tourist-promotion organization called the North Carolina Travel Council, Morton convinced Park Service officials to put up small signs at Parkway intersections with major roads, indicating distances to nearby lodging, gas, or attractions. In 1947, Morton finally got the small sign he had wanted. But the signage issue festered into the 1950s, when, in the midst of the battle over the Parkway route across Grandfather, Parkway staff removed the Grandfather sign.[73]

Visitor Accommodations

The issue of the Parkway's role in advertising nearby attractions and accommodations mushroomed beyond a dispute over a few signs as Parkway visitation rocketed upward after the war. Morton and other businesspeople hoped to profit from the surging traffic. Parkway staff worried, however, that travelers would be dismayed to be unable to find adequate overnight lodging and food near the Parkway. "Tourist accommodations," Weems concluded in late 1945, "are sorely needed along the Parkway." Whether as a result of his limited understanding of the long history of tourism development in the region (scores of inns, lodges, and resorts had in fact dotted the western North Carolina and Virginia mountains since the early nineteenth century) or as a consequence of existing conditions, Weems doubted that nearby communities could spawn sufficient facilities. Resurrecting the venerable myth of isolated Appalachia, he lamented, "We spend millions of dollars building an outstanding Parkway for the tourist, only to turn him loose in a region which, until very recently, has known very little of the outside world."[74]

Seeking to document the scarcity of accommodations Weems lamented, a staff member from the NPS concessions office visited the mountains in 1946 and reported that snacks, groceries, and gasoline were plentiful near the Parkway but that nice overnight lodging and places to eat larger meals were harder to come by.

Later surveys similarly revealed that in the northwestern North Carolina section near the Bluff (Doughton Park), where an estimated fifty thousand people per month traveled the Parkway in 1948, convenient lodging and food were scarce. Sparta, the nearest town, was eighteen miles away and had neither a hotel nor a "sizeable restaurant." Travelers would have had to go twenty-five miles to North Wilkesboro to find that town's single hotel. Boone, forty miles distant, also had one hotel. Browning concurred with the NPS assessment of the situation. With hotels and motels in the region already overcrowded and Parkway travel growing, Browning urged Parkway officials to "think . . . of the necessities and comfort of these Parkway travelers . . . and do we have adequate facilities to care for them."[75]

While private development had stagnated during the war years, it was probably reasonable to think it would rebound after the conflict ended. The Park Service, it appears, may have underestimated the ability of regional business interests (neither isolated nor unsophisticated) to meet visitors' needs. In the years after the war, tourism operators in the mountains joined together for several promotional campaigns. In 1946, a group of western North Carolina business leaders, government officials, and educators formed the Western North Carolina Associated Communities to press tourism development in the counties west of Asheville. In 1949, the group spawned a subsidiary, the Western North Carolina Tourist Association, which served hotel, tourist court, gift shop, and service station owners from eleven mountain counties. The group hoped eventually to set regulations for tourist facilities and to devise a rating system to help increase consumer confidence. Though some of its efforts foundered, the Western North Carolina Associated Communities and the mountain tourism promoters thrived, and between 1950 and 1970, the number of motels in western North Carolina increased threefold. Most were owned by western North Carolina citizens.[76]

Despite all of this activity, the NPS seemed determined to shut out local entrepreneurs from the Parkway accommodations business, perhaps because of at least two contradictory strains within Park Service history. First, Weems's view that the Parkway had penetrated a previously isolated region, while consistent with long-cherished myths of Appalachia, may have owed more than he realized to long-standing NPS policy about visitor accommodations, originally developed to serve the needs of western rather than eastern parks. The first Park Service director, Stephen Mather, and his successor, Horace Albright, had believed, according to one historian, "that the existing parks were all so remote and of such limited access that only large-scale concession monopolies stood a chance of financially surviving and developing them." Consequently, concessions policy drawn up in

1928 provided that the interior secretary could grant concessions contracts without even securing competitive bids. This monopoly concessions policy remained in place even through reforms in the 1960s.[77]

Park policy, in turn, was built on a de facto system dating from the 1870s in which a few large private companies (often associated with the railroads) had been allowed to completely dominate park concessions and visitor services in the vast western parks. During Harold Ickes's tenure at the Department of the Interior in the 1930s and 1940s, the Park Service moved to begin nationalizing park concessions, as the establishment of National Park Concessions (NPC) indicated. But the rather confused public-private concessions system persisted through the 1950s despite growing concessionaire unrest, charges of poor service to visitors, and numerous federal studies, rulings, and policy changes. Further reform came in the 1960s in the form of new federal legislation that minimally restricted the rights of monopoly concessionaires while preserving their preferential right to contract renewal.[78]

Thus, in their conflict with Morton, Park Service officials were operating on the basis of longtime assumptions about how accommodations in the parks were to be provided while trying, in response to growing criticism, to appear less beholden to private business than had traditionally been the case. This combination of impulses, it seems, caused them to anger Morton and other mountain business leaders by ensconcing monopoly concessions on the Parkway and by taking a surprisingly strict stance against "commercialization" in the form of promoting local businesses from the Parkway.

Parkway concessions policy, as evidenced at the Peaks of Otter and elsewhere, favored large operators and the quasi-public NPC over local businesspeople. Indeed, NPC's formation in 1942 and its immediate certification as the major Parkway concessionaire had long been a key factor restricting local operators' access to Parkway travelers. Though NPC was said to be a "nonstock, nonprofit organization" whose income would be plowed back into "developments in the public interest," it was in fact a Park Service–spawned entity run by a number of former NPS employees.[79]

Having NPC in place solved the immediate problem of getting an operator for early facilities, but it also later created an awkward situation for Parkway staff trying to defend the Park Service from accusations of government takeover of all concessions. At best, NPC created the impression of tied-in individuals getting preferred access to choice spots. But more substantively, its virtual monopoly over Parkway concessions outlets (in this period it operated all of them except the bus service to Sharp Top at the Peaks of Otter) truly did exclude local businesses in a region that was — unlike the western parks — neither isolated nor sparsely populated.[80]

Morton and his allies in the travel industry felt that the answer to the tourist accommodation problem was not increased development of government-sponsored facilities on the Parkway proper but a redoubled effort to advertise and direct travelers to locally owned hotels, restaurants, and other businesses, which, as traffic increased, would expand their offerings. Morton's group thus bristled at two major proposed expansions of visitor facilities on the Parkway in the 1940s and 1950s.

The first came in 1948, when the Parkway constructed a long-planned visitor complex (coffee shop, gas station, and twenty-four-room lodge) at the Bluff (Doughton Park), twenty-five miles south of the North Carolina line. This development sparked a showdown with Morton at the August 1948 meeting of the North Carolina Park, Parkway, and Forest Development Commission, held, perhaps coincidentally, at Linville. In view of the "lack of consideration given to private enterprise, facilities and attractions along the Parkway in publicity and signs," Morton argued, the Parkway would "do more harm than good" for the tourist industry. He characterized the Bluff development as "just the beginning" of a "trend toward government operation of the tourist business." A year later, Morton again lambasted the N P S in a talk to the Asheville Board of Realtors, describing a conspiracy by the Park Service to replace the privately owned tourism industry in North Carolina with a "socialized" one. Morton's criticisms — bolstered by calls from other unnamed "citizens in the Linville, Boone, Blowing Rock section" for better cooperation with local entrepreneurs — spilled into various state newspapers, where, according to another Parkway staffer, "considerable hue and cry was raised."[81]

Countering Morton, Weems tried repeatedly to explain that the N P S sought to provide accommodations only in areas where private enterprise had not offered them. Citing the service's unsuccessful attempt at the outset of World War II to solicit bids from local businesses to run the first few Parkway concessions (including facilities at the Bluff), Weems painted the turn to the then newly formed N P C as a move of last resort. He furthermore proclaimed agreement with Morton's pro–private enterprise stance, asserting that "if I believed" that the government was trying to monopolize visitor accommodations, "I would be ashamed to be connected with the Blue Ridge Parkway."[82]

In September 1949, just after Morton's Board of Realtors appearance, Weems's staff refuted Morton's charges in a long memo to the director of the N P S. Locating parkways away from "built-up communities," Weems noted, was a "first principle," especially in light of a large-scale postwar review of NPS concessions policy and consultation with industry representatives that had concluded that "where adequate accommodations exist or can be developed by private enterprise outside, accommodations shall not be permitted." He reminded the director that "no community has been left without ample access to the Parkway" and that Parkway signs in North Carolina now included information about hotels, gas stations, and restaurants in nearby towns. Finally, a free Parkway information pamphlet gave more information about those facilities, and an expanded regional guide was under development in conjunction with the states' tourist bureaus. "Any observant traveler on the Parkway," Weems asserted, "should have no difficulty finding his way around the Parkway vicinity or in locating the accommodations of his choice."[83]

In early 1950, a high-level conference with NPS director Newton Drury framed new agreements that quieted the controversy for a few years. The Park Service scaled back some of its facilities plans and agreed to enhance (mostly at public expense) Parkway signs about what was available in local communities. Travel interests in the Parkway region agreed to create a regional promotional organization, and the Parkway consented to distribute pamphlets about regional attractions. Regional interests formed the Blue Ridge Parkway Association later that year, and by 1956 Parkway rangers handed out fifty thousand copies of the association's advertising booklet listing nearby amenities and attractions. Nevertheless, having acquiesced to most of Morton's demands, the Park Service still asserted that it would develop further facilities that might be needed "in the interest of the public."[84]

Weems remained wary, however, of making the Parkway a "publicity agent for private interests." And Morton remained unconvinced that the Park Service was not trying to undermine those interests. Weems at first suspected that Morton's anti–Park Service campaign represented merely a ploy for attention, since at the time (1949), the only tourist attraction Morton even partly owned was the (still modest) Grandfather Mountain toll road. Naively (in view of later developments), Weems initially dismissed Morton: "I do not consider him of sufficient importance to warrant the service's entering into a newspaper debate over his short-sighted campaign in behalf of the 'little man' for unrestricted concession privileges along the Parkway motor road. I think he would like nothing better than just that."[85]

Even though the matter stayed quiet for a while (partly because in the early 1950s the Park Service lacked funds to build new facilities), developments at the Peaks of Otter (see chapter 6) proved that Morton's complaint about the relative chances for the "little man" to get contracts to operate facilities along the Parkway had merit, and the issue continued to fester.

It erupted again in 1956, just one year after Morton's lands were appropriated, when Mission 66 funding provided $4 million for new Parkway visitor accommodations: seven gas stations, five cafés, seven gift shops, two coffee shops, and two lodges. Morton and his allies in the Blowing Rock and Boone Chambers of Commerce pounced on the proposals, hiring an attorney to press their case with the Interior Department and Congress, issuing a flyer proclaiming "We Are Not Going to Sit Still while the Tourist Business Is Sold down the River," and asking for help in resisting the "sinister" plans to commercialize the Parkway with "an empire of Government sponsored tourist facilities."[86]

By this point, Morton's connections around the state allowed him easily to generate a broad campaign against NPS plans. Thus, he quickly arranged a meeting with the chair of the North Carolina National Park, Parkway, and Forest Development Commission; began conversations with members of the state Department of Conservation and Development (of which he was a member); spoke to the Asheville Tourist Association; discussed the issue with leaders of the Asheville business community and at the Asheville Chamber of Commerce and Citizen-Times; and dashed off a letter to Governor Hodges, for whose reelection campaign Morton had just directed publicity. With the governor's knowledge, Morton also quietly circulated a report articulating his arguments (especially against NPC) to the Conservation and Development Board and state parks officials in the weeks before they were to meet with Parkway officers to hear more about the plans. Within a very short time, the board requested that the NPS delay building the new facilities until public hearings could be held.[87]

Weems labored to counter Morton's campaign. In meetings with state agencies and in several public hearings, the Parkway superintendent explained that facilities would not be built where accommodations "exist or can be developed by private enterprise outside" and that, when approved for the Parkway, they would be bid upon, built, paid for, and operated by "private enterprise." But NPC's continued involvement of as the major "private" entity on the scene doomed the Park Service's attempt to combat Morton's arguments. In internal correspondence if not publicly, Weems acknowledged that having NPC in the picture handicapped him. In 1956, he suggested that the Park Service regional director should make a "clear statement as to our future relationship with NPC, which seems to me ought to be phhht!"[88]

Meanwhile, reviving images of revolutionary-era mountain men, the *Charlotte Observer* wrote of "hotel, motel, restaurant or scenic attraction operators" in the region between Asheville and Roanoke "march[ing] forth from the valleys beneath the scenic . . . Parkway to shake angry fingers at the Park Service from every available forum." Indeed, as the controversy dragged on, Morton's opposition found adherents among a variety of civic and tourism-promotion groups.[89]

In the face of this tide and hobbled by the NPC link, Weems and other Park Service officials allowed Morton and his allies to set the terms of the debate primarily around the fairness (or unfairness) of the concessions bidding process. They seemed unable to highlight the broadly appealing goal of serving the public and upholding the Parkway's statutory requirement to connect the Shenandoah and Great Smoky Mountains parks with a recreational parkway "for public use and enjoyment" and to "conserve the scenery and the natural and historic objects and the wildlife [and] provide for the enjoyment of the same . . . by such means as will leave them unimpaired . . . for the enjoyment of future generations."[90]

Some Parkway supporters eloquently articulated these arguments. A Linville Falls, North Carolina, man reminded Weems and two congressmen in the midst of the facilities fight that the Parkway, "built by public funds, exists primarily for the benefit of the traveling public. It exists secondarily for the benefit of the communities through or near which it passes. In no sense does it exist for private benefit. Yet the inn-keepers seem to feel they have a vested right—a kind of contract with the government—to preserve a status which they feel to be favorable to themselves." Wrote longtime Parkway supporter R. L. Gwyn, "I am not one bit afraid of the National Park Service going into the hotel business, or any other business. [We] can be assured that whatever they do will be done right." Furthermore, Gwyn argued, it was "certainly to our interest that the Parkway may become something more than just a high speed road."[91]

Put on the defensive, however, the Parkway staff failed to make these arguments, and at a mid-1957 meeting with the North Carolina National Park, Parkway, and Forest Development Commission, Weems and the Park Service again capitulated to many of Morton and his allies' demands, agreeing to enlarge informational signs at Parkway intersections with major highways and to install bulletin boards with informational racks at all Parkway visitor centers. More importantly, the Park Service abandoned plans for expanded lodging facilities at Mt. Pisgah and the Bluff in North Carolina.[92]

Entrance Fees

The third issue that brought Morton to statewide prominence involved the Park Service's decision to resurrect an old proposal to impose entrance fees or tolls on the motor road. The Park Service could hardly have planned a better strategy to antagonize the regional tourism interests, whose support for the project was increasingly shaky. While some of the conflict may have been an inevitable part of protecting the Parkway from commercial encroachment, the array of issues also made resolving the Parkway route at Grandfather vastly more difficult.

The prospect of the Parkway as a (self-liquidating) toll road had bedeviled the project from the time it was first proposed in 1933 by Virginia Senator Harry F. Byrd. As negotiations regarding the Parkway proposal proceeded, however, the toll idea was dropped, and Ickes eventually accepted the project in late 1933 with the understanding that it would be completely federally funded beyond the states' land-buying costs. With federal funding waxing and waning through the 1930s, however, the toll idea remained on the table, and in 1942, with World War II under way and NPS starved for funds, Washington officials announced a plan to charge twenty-five cents per day to Parkway travelers as part of a nationwide policy of imposing fees on national parklands.[93]

The plan went nowhere, largely as a result of R. Getty Browning's direct intervention with Ickes. In letters and in a personal visit, Browning predicted that the policy would be "extremely unpopular" with North Carolinians and tourists. In addition to the considerable practical problems and inconvenience to drivers of collecting tolls on a road with so many entrance and exit points, Browning asserted, the Parkway operators had a moral obligation to keep promises made to local landowners. In often strained land-acquisition negotiations, he reminded the secretary, "we have contended that the Parkway was not to be a toll road, that it would be open to the rich and poor alike." Browning furthermore warned that "enemies of the Parkway . . . have heretofore taken the attitude that the National Government is planning to administer the Parkway in a high-handed, arbitrary fashion. [We] have tried to meet [this argument] by denying that any such policy would prevail, and cited personal experiences . . . supporting the belief that . . . the Park Service would encourage . . . the full use of the Parkway by every one." Though annoyed by Browning's all-out push to deluge his office with calls of opposition from North Carolina's congressional delegation, Ickes was at least convinced that imposing tolls might hinder acquisition of lands still needed to complete the Parkway. Overruling the NPS, he "indefinitely" postponed the toll plan. But he recounted in his diary that "I told Browning that he must have known that it was the intention from the beginning to charge tolls. The President would never have approved nor would I have recommended the road otherwise."[94]

Ickes's action did not lay the matter permanently to rest, however. In 1947 Parkway officials and the Interior Department were again planning to collect tolls on the Parkway beginning in 1948. But complaints from North Carolina Congressman Robert Doughton and the state's two senators as well as the slow progress of Parkway construction scotched that plan as well.[95]

In late 1954, however, a firestorm erupted when Governor Hodges learned that the NPS intended to begin collecting fees on the Parkway in the spring of 1955. Attempting to justify the decision, NPS staff cited the federal government's $40 million investment in the project and its $500,000 annual cost for maintenance. They also cited the federal policy of recouping some of such costs from a facility's users, noting that fees were already charged in several other national parks and along the Skyline Drive in Shenandoah National Park (where their imposition in 1939 had, according to a later account, left a "residue of bitterness").[96]

The 1955 plan met with a "loud and vehement volley of spoken and written protests," especially in North Carolina, which, unlike Virginia, had for years prided itself on its toll-free road system. In the six months before land-acquisition maps for Grandfather Mountain were posted in mid-1955, the strongest player in this volley was Hugh Morton. He quickly marshaled a comprehensive set of arguments — similar to those Browning had advanced in 1942 — against the fees: that they would represent "a moral, if not also contractual, breach of faith"; that the numerous Parkway entrances (opponents said six hundred, although the actual number was considerably smaller) would create a "cumbersome administrative problem" that would annoy travelers; that nothing guaranteed that the fees (once dumped into the general U.S. Treasury), would benefit the Parkway; and finally that the fees both would discriminate against local people who needed the road and would hurt the "No. 1 industry" of tourism. The "loss of good will by North Carolina and the National Park Service," Morton concluded, would outweigh the fees' benefits. The plan, he judged, was a "a blunder . . . in the making."[97]

Indeed it was. With characteristic energy and an astute multipronged public and political strategy, Morton over the next few months enlisted perhaps two hundred individuals, including the governor, several North Carolina senators and representatives, members of the State Board of Conservation and Development, longtime Parkway supporters (including Browning and former Highway Commission Chair Edwin B. Jeffress), local business associations, and the statewide news media in a concerted battle to defeat the fee proposal. In the end, their campaign again turned the tide, as the Interior Department "temporarily" delayed imposing the fees pending further investigation.[98]

Poring over the documentary record through the late 1950s, however, neither Morton's allies nor NPS staff uncovered evidence that a definitive agreement had been reached about the toll matter in the 1930s. Perhaps, given strongly differing feelings about it among early Parkway planners, the issue had intentionally been

Parkway fee-collection station, just north of the route 460 intersection north of Roanoke, 1955. The 1955 tolls proposal was the third of the Park Service's four pre-1960 attempts to impose entry fees on Parkway drivers. Photo by Sam Weems. Courtesy Blue Ridge Parkway.

left vague. Just as Ickes had claimed in 1942 that neither he nor Roosevelt would have approved the project had they not expected tolls eventually to be charged, North Carolinians Browning and Jeffress argued in the 1950s that neither they nor Governor J. C. B. Ehringhaus would have involved North Carolina in a project that promised to become a toll road. Browning and Jeffress, who had participated in all of the important meetings held at the Parkway's inception, believed that the toll idea had been abandoned for all time when Ickes had agreed to build the Parkway entirely with federal funds.[99]

Whether supported by previous agreement or not, commitment to the fee idea remained strong within the NPS, and the matter, like the concessions/facilities debate, thus festered into the late 1950s. Undaunted, the Park Service came forth in 1958 with yet another announcement that fee collection would be instituted on the Parkway. And once again, Morton and Hodges, bolstered by strong arguments put together by Browning, orchestrated North Carolina's by-now predictable opposition. Indeed, within three days after Hodges got wind of the latest fee plan, both Morton and Browning were in touch with him about strategy.[100]

Within a month, an avalanche of anti-fee articles crashed down on the proposal from newspapers in most of the state's major cities and many smaller ones. They argued that the "People's Parkway" had not been carved (like the western parks) from the public domain but had been assembled with state funds from private lands whose former owners had been promised a free road. "It would be a shame," one newspaper asserted, "to convert this masterpiece of nature into a commercial expressway." "What Price Parkway Beauty?," the *Skyland Post* in the mountain town of West Jefferson asked. That beauty was, the *Morganton News-Herald* chimed in, "being marred by the triple-dipped double-dealing and duplicity of federal agents [and the] power-hungry claws of a grasping bureaucracy." The Park Service wanted "to shake down guests of the hardtopped ribbon through wonderland. Tolls, the greedy caretaker wants!" If the decision were not reversed, the Morganton paper warned, the Park Service "will think that Custer's trouble at Little Big Horn was a pink tea by comparison."[101]

The media storm supplemented political maneuvers by Hodges, Morton, Browning, the State Board of Conservation and Development, the State Highway Commission, regional business associations, and the state's congressional delegation to carry the message of opposition to federal officials. Hodges's office quickly arranged for a North Carolina delegation that included the governor, North Carolina's senators and some members of Congress, Morton, Browning, Jeffress, and several others to plead their case directly to Secretary of the Interior Fred Seaton. There they stressed again the promises made to North Carolina landowners. From his experience handling many difficult land-acquisition negotiations, Browning told Seaton, "it is my firm belief that had we told these people that this was to be a toll road . . . some of the negotiations would have ended in bloodshed." Possibly at Browning's suggestion, the state's congressional representatives prepared to introduce legislation permanently prohibiting fees on the Parkway. That course of action was ultimately abandoned shortly after the meeting with the North Carolina opponents, when the secretary decisively killed the fee proposal. An Interior Department press release announced that Seaton's decision "finally disposes of the matter."[102]

A "SWITCHBLADE TO THE MONA LISA"?:
THE COMPETING ROUTES AT GRANDFATHER

In this environment of protracted suspicion and ill feeling between N PS and Parkway leaders on the one hand and Morton and the public supporters he had repeatedly organized and deployed on the other, the conflict over a revised Parkway route at Grandfather Mountain took place after 1955. The array of ill-considered policies the Park Service pursued in the 1940s and 1950s—the resistance to directional signs for local attractions, the announcement of ambitious plans for concessions and dogged adherence to the monopoly concessionaire model, and the repeated toll proposals—sewed discontent in North Carolina and set the stage for NPS troubles with Morton and his by-now loyal public. In addition to offering Morton a platform on which to build his statewide constituency, the conflicts allowed him to portray his battle with the Park Service over Grandfather lands as a public-spirited and popular campaign against widely disliked federal incursions. All the while, the growing numbers of visitors to Grandfather became a ready-made public constituency receptive to alarmist publicity about impending destruction of the mountain.[103]

These conflicts also took place during a period when the Park Service's role as an environmental steward had come under attack from emerging environmentalist constituencies and its long-standing alliance with conservationist groups was fracturing. Who then was likely the best conservator of a mountain that nearly everyone agreed should be protected? In this context of uncertainty, Morton paradoxically redeployed in service of private development of the mountain the preservationist discourse about Grandfather Mountain on which Kelsey's campaign for public purchase had relied.[104] At the same time, the Park Service's policy blunders impaired its ability to remind the public of its prior efforts to conserve Grandfather Mountain, to reiterate the NPS commitment to mitigating Parkway construction scars, and to present the real merits of the route it preferred there. Ineffectively opposed by a weakened Park Service, Morton shaped the public preservationist discourse to serve his private ends, which he portrayed as public ends.

The routing battle commenced with the state's abortive 1955 attempt to acquire the 779 acres and took thirteen years to resolve. In many respects, as Superintendent Weems later related, Morton "just outlasted the Park Service," aided by several North Carolina governors and a State Highway Commission unwilling to condemn the right-of-way lands the Park Service preferred. "Each time either the Park Service or the state threatened to condemn Morton's lands," Weems remembered, "he would go to the Governor and the Governor would just politely tell the United States Government that they weren't going to condemn Mr. Morton's land. So, in a nutshell, that was our problem." In any case, because the state was responsible for acquiring Parkway lands, the Park Service's hands were tied when Morton and the state presented a united front.[105]

In truth, the problem was more complex. It arose, as we have seen, out of years of bad feeling between Morton and the Park Service. The difficult situation was further compounded by the fact that as the conflict stretched into the 1960s, the Parkway's most knowledgeable, nimble, and skillful ally in state government, R. Getty Browning, who had been Morton's ally in the toll fight but his nemesis in nearly everything else, retired from the Highway Commission and lost the ear of state leaders. With Browning out of the way, Morton enlisted the support of the state bureaucracy—and a public constituency that grew as Grandfather's visitation increased—in a way no other private landowner in Parkway history had been able to do.

The conflict boiled down to a choice between a so-called high route, to which the Park Service committed itself in the late 1940s when it became clear that the effort to purchase all of Grandfather had failed, and two lower routes favored at various times by Morton: the 1939 Yonahlossee Road route and the middle or compromise route, which lay between the Yonahlossee and the high route. In the mid-1950s, Park Service and BPR engineers mapped and studied that middle route, but it subsequently faded from view for a few years. By the late 1950s and early 1960s, when Morton first took his case to the public, his favored low route seems to have been identical to the 1939 Yonahlossee Trail location—that is, an attempt to convince the Park Service to use the lands already acquired. All three routes remained under discussion, however, and after 1963 Morton shifted his support again to the middle route, which became the basis for the eventual solution, consummated in 1968.[106]

The question of alternative routes came into play after years of investigation by Park Service and BPR engineers in the 1940s revealed that the original (but always tentative) route along five miles of the torturous and curvy Yonahlossee Road (for which the state had bought 488 acres of land from the Linville Company in 1939) would not work well for the Parkway. As early as 1940, Stanley Abbott and his Parkway staff recognized the potential problems of the Yonahlossee, stemming from the cuts, fills, and tree cutting that would be needed to bring the 1890s-era road up to Parkway curvature and grade standards and from having to build another regular highway to carry the commercial traffic that depended on the Yonahlossee (U.S. 221). At the state's request, federal officials in 1940 flagged a new line "entirely clear of the present road" and lying higher up the mountain.[107]

The abandonment of the Yonahlossee route and the proposal of a new one could not—despite Morton's later statements to the contrary—have come as a surprise to anyone associated with the former Linville Company, as Morton was. Although land-acquisition documents drawn up in 1939 plainly connected the Yonahlossee acquisition with the construction of the Parkway, correspondence between state and Parkway officials and members of the MacRae family into the

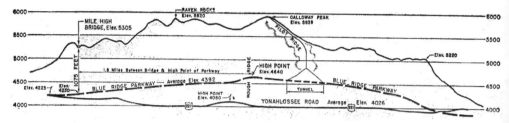

Southeast profile of Grandfather Mountain, proposed Blue Ridge Parkway high route location, showing its relation to crest of the mountain and U.S. highway 221 (former Yonahlossee Road). This diagram appeared in the *Skyland Post* and *Roanoke Times* in 1962. The final middle or compromise route lay between these two routes and did not include the Pilot Ridge tunnel.

1940s clearly stated that "no definite location of the Parkway in that area has yet been determined." Perhaps for this reason, no deed for the land turnover was filed at this time. Indeed, a 1945 map of lands proposed to be purchased under Harlan Kelsey's option—signed by Linville Company representatives Hugh Mac-Rae and Julian Morton—showed in dotted lines the "proposed Parkway" crossing Grandfather higher up the mountain on lands contiguous to but different from those bought from the Linville Company in 1939. Later reports from those closely involved in the 1939 purchase agreed that the Yonahlossee route had not been firmly set and that the purchase was made mainly at the instigation of the State Highway Commission's general counsel to help friends in the Linville Company in a difficult time, to forestall roadside development and timbering along the Yonahlossee side of Grandfather, and perhaps to bring the Yonahlossee right-of-way, which was at that point under lease to the state, firmly under state control (necessary whether or not the area was used for the Parkway). Thus, those involved in the 1939 arrangement for the Parkway right-of-way clearly knew that it was tentative.[108]

To some degree, however, the question of exactly where on Grandfather the Parkway would run had gotten lost in the discussions over federal acquisition of the entire mountain. If Kelsey's purchase plan had worked, all of the lands in question—for whatever route—would have been in federal hands. The issue of Parkway routing reemerged only after the failure of the Kelsey purchase. Official acquisition maps for the high route were sent to the state in 1948, and in 1949 Browning was instructed to post the acquisition maps for this land "at the earliest possible time." For reasons that remain unclear, the "earliest possible time" turned out to be nearly six years later.[109]

By this time, of course, Morton, who was not involved in the 1939 transaction, owned the mountain. In addition to maintaining that land required for the high route would exceed the limit of 125 acres per mile specified in North Carolina's 1930s laws, he portrayed the NPS commitment to that route as a "double cross" in which an "egotistical engineer" (probably Browning) and an "arrogant bureaucrat" (likely Wirth), unwilling to live up to previous agreements and disappointed in the failure of prior attempts to put Grandfather under public ownership, sought to steal the entire mountain.[110]

This argument was bolstered in Morton's long public campaign against the high route by the consistently repeated but no more accurate reports that that route would, in Morton's words, "go over the mountain, kill the development we have, and ruin much of the natural beauty of Grandfather." Morton cast himself as protecting a "sacred" Grandfather from the NPS's "expensive," "impractical," and "foolish" high route, which would, he insisted, make an "unsightly gash high up on Grandfather Mountain." "We just don't want it scarred up," he argued in 1962. The "Lord put it there," he continued, "and it would be like taking a switchblade to the Mona Lisa if you gash it up." He simultaneously maintained that the high route would approach within three hundred feet of his ubiquitously advertised Mile-High Swinging Bridge and "interfere with our attraction."[111] Morton seems to have perceived damage to the mountain and damage to his developed area as one and the same.

In truth, the facts about the high line were considerably less dramatic than Morton and his supporters indicated. Most importantly, the high route did not go over the top of Grandfather Mountain; it was so named only because it was higher than the other proposed routes. It also did not, as Morton and his partisans asserted, come "within a stone's throw" of the Swinging Bridge. Even the "great scar" Morton predicted the high route would leave was debatable: Park Service landscape architects and BPR engineers asserted that the high line, with a seventeen-hundred-foot tunnel that took the Parkway through rather than around Pilot Knob, "will be much less noticeable from the scar standpoint."[112]

The high route right-of-way (that is, the acquired land) at its highest vertical point lay somewhere between 4,850 and 4,920 feet, while the highest point on the proposed high roadway itself would have been at approximately 4,640 feet, both far below Grandfather's 5,964-foot peak. Furthermore, the highest roadway point on the high line was about 1.5 miles away laterally from Grandfather's highest peak and 1.8 miles laterally away from the Mile-High Swinging Bridge. Thus, although it was technically true in terms of elevation that the high line was only a few hundred feet lower than both of these major features, to characterize the high line as 300 feet from the bridge (as many accounts did and as a 1962

Morton speech to the Asheville Rotary Club implied) was at best disingenuous. The middle line, in contrast, reached its highest point at about 4,415 feet, while the high point on the low Yonahlossee Road lay between roughly 4,060 and 4,200 feet. Thus, in terms of the elevation of the roadway itself, the high line differed from the lowest line by 580 feet, while none of the three lines ascended near the top of the mountain.[113]

After several detailed investigations stretching from the 1940s through the early 1960s, NPS landscape architects, BPR engineers, and engineers in Browning's office agreed that the high route would best serve the Parkway. Rather than being "expensive," "impractical," and "foolish," as Morton claimed, they determined that it would be the cheapest, shortest, and easiest to build.[114] It would also, as Browning pointed out, permit continued use of the Yonahlossee for commercial and local traffic and would protect several small waterfalls and the timber belt saved along the Yonahlossee by the 1939 state purchase.[115]

Despite the experts' agreement, Morton was not swayed. After the State Highway Commission returned the high route lands to him in 1957, the situation languished in a stalemate through the late 1950s. Morton firmly refused the high line, Governor Hodges stalled while investigating the alternatives, the NPS redirected $2.5 million in funding from the Grandfather section to other areas where right-of-way was available, and Browning urged the Park Service to take stronger action to get its line approved.[116]

The conflict heated up considerably after new governor Terry Sanford took office in 1962. Of the three governors who came and went during the long struggle, Sanford was Morton's strongest ally. Sanford asked for further investigation and negotiation and worried that because of the statutory limit of 125 acres per mile, the state had no authority to take more than it already had. Meanwhile, in March 1962, Morton took his case to the public, and the ensuing deluge of favorable news coverage described Morton's fight to save a "Landmark in Peril."[117]

In a dramatic hearing at the end of May 1962, Morton and NPS director Conrad Wirth argued their cases before the State Highway Commission and, a few days later, in a joint appearance on Raleigh's WRAL-TV. In what may have been the conflict's turning point, Morton triumphed while Wirth squandered what was undoubtedly the Park Service's best chance to bring its case before the public. Editorializing on a Raleigh radio station, one observer summed up the Highway Commission hearing: "Hugh Morton mantrapped both the public interest and Conrad Wirth" by displaying "the smoothest, slickest, subtlest, suavist [sic] techniques in annihilation of a puny enemy I have ever seen in action." Morton,

'Touch Not A Hair On Yon Gray Head'

Cartoon in support of Hugh Morton's cause depicts him as an aggrieved and defiant mountaineer, *Charlotte Observer*, 27 March 1962. Reprinted with permission of the *Charlotte Observer*. © *Charlotte Observer*.

the commentator agreed, did precisely what was needed to defend his interests: he "touched every base, loaded the balances beautifully, blew every whistle, rang every bell."[118]

Wirth, by contrast, failed utterly to present the Park Service's most compelling arguments. "The public interest," the radio commentator noted, "did not directly make an appearance" during Wirth's numbingly dull and passionless page-by-page recital of the history of the conflict, a "pathetic effort" that "bored beyond belief." Worse, Wirth stated unequivocally that the Park Service would rather the Grandfather section remain uncompleted (thus leaving a gaping hole in the Parkway) than accept something other than the high route. This statement, perceived by many in North Carolina as a high-handed threat, tended to confirm, the commentator surmised, that Wirth was "as tyrannical, theivish [sic], socialistic, lying, and et cetera as he had been pictured." American citizens, the commentator concluded, were the losers. "The Government's defense against implications of all but sordid abuse of public powers can only be [countered] by a strong statement of the public case for the high road advocated by the government. As presented . . . there was no visible connection between the high road and the public interest" even though the "standards of engineering and beauty" that had produced the high route "were long ago adopted in the public interest." Even a sympathetic observer such as this commentator could not help but be crushed by the NPS director's poor performance.[119]

From this point forward, momentum was in Morton's favor. Legal questions surrounding the state's right to acquire high route lands in addition to the land bought in 1939 cleared up when the state attorney general ruled shortly after the hearing that the state had the authority to acquire the high route lands should the Highway Commission decide to do so. But Sanford soon declared the state unwilling to do so as long as Morton objected. After a yearlong investigation of all three routes by a Highway Commission subcommittee, the commission, Sanford, and Morton united in favor of the middle route, which the Park Service continued to resist. To settle for anything other than the high route, the NPS associate director declared, "would be like wearing a pair of old tennis shoes with a $65 suit." With all North Carolina constituencies arrayed against a steadfast Park Service, another stalemate ensued.[120]

Attempting to break the impasse with an end run around the Park Service one day before Sanford left office in early 1965, the Highway Commission and Morton signed legal documents exchanging some state-owned lands (from the 1939 acquisition) for some of Morton's lands along the compromise route, thus putting the state in possession of much of the land needed to build the middle route. The

Park Service—not invited to the discussions surrounding this transaction—still stood firm for the high route.[121]

After leaving office, Sanford revealed how completely he had internalized Morton's arguments by labeling the Park Service a "bureaucratic" organization that "insists on having its own way or it takes its baseball and breaks up the ball game." In North Carolina, Sanford said, "our people believe the best way to look at a mountain is not to bulldoze a highway across the top of it." At Grandfather, he alleged in the face of overwhelming evidence to the contrary, the "Park Service wants to go over the top."[122]

With Sanford out of office, the problem passed to his successor, Dan K. Moore. By the spring of 1966, Moore somehow convinced the Park Service to abandon the high route and build on the middle route. The arrival of new leadership at the Park Service (Wirth had retired in 1963) seems to have facilitated this solution; Browning's sudden death early in 1966 may also have helped. Small disagreements over particulars of the arrangement persisted, however, and not until 1968 did a celebratory luncheon at the visitor center atop Grandfather Mountain officially proclaim the end of the thirteen-year controversy. Morton's triumph was virtually complete.[123]

A "CASE IN THE PUBLIC INTEREST THAT HAS NOT BEEN MADE": THE OTHER SIDE OF THE STORY

How did Morton pull off this victory? Simply put, he overpowered a feckless Park Service by much more effectively getting his version of the controversy before the public and by defining the terms of the debate. As one observer put it, the high road "has a case in the public interest that has not been made. Charges now stand unrefuted which ought not to stand."[124] Using skills honed through managing publicity for Luther Hodges's successful 1956 gubernatorial campaign as well as his deft hand at marketing, Morton rallied the statewide media in support of his campaign. No fewer than forty articles in the state's newspapers broadcast his arguments during the thirteen-year struggle.[125]

Remembering the media campaign, Morton asserted nearly forty years later that the state's newspapers had sided with him because "they knew that I had never told them anything but the truth, and I think they knew these other people were daily telling them things that weren't completely truthful, and they knew that even if it was unfavorable to me, that I would tell them what was what."[126]

But, in reality, the 1960s media accounts overlooked crucial parts of the story. In addition to failing to point out either the "unnatural" state in which areas of

Grandfather Mountain had been left after timbering, the decidedly artificial nature of parts of the tourist attraction there, or Morton's private stake in the battle, the media accounts misrepresented both the history of Grandfather and the details of the Park Service's intentions there. Repeated so persistently and countered so ineffectively, Morton's portrayal of the conflict took on an air of objective truth that, after a time, he no longer had to continue asserting. Once inserted so strongly into public imagination, the details of the popular and resonant but inaccurate account of "Morton and His Mountain" were rarely questioned.[127]

Morton's media initiative might not have succeeded had it been countered by a vigorous response by the Park Service. But hobbled by the wounds inflicted during the tolls, facilities, and signs battles and appearing deaf to local concerns, Park Service officials found themselves frozen in Morton's headlights. Far from feeding untruths to the media, they were unable even to begin to get an alternative narrative about what was happening at Grandfather before the public until early 1962, seven years into the conflict, on the eve of Morton and Wirth's pivotal hearing before the State Highway Commission.

The Park Service's failure to make its case in public, however, does not mean that there was no effective case to be made. Indeed, high route supporters (both within NPS and in North Carolina) formulated a number of strong counterarguments in which they forcefully defended the route, highlighted the negative impacts of Morton's development of Grandfather, and questioned Morton's tactics. Though their voices were drowned out as the Morton-NPS conflict unfolded, they articulated a critical analysis of Morton's campaign and put forth an alternative narrative about what was afoot at Grandfather.

Internal correspondence from 1955 on reveals that Sam Weems, R. Getty Browning, and others inside both the Park Service and the North Carolina State Highway Commission recognized from the outset that Morton's public presentations of the story were misleading and that the record needed to be set straight. For example, when Morton issued a pamphlet titled *A Capsule of Facts Substantiating Opposition to a Possible Change in the Established Right of Way for the Blue Ridge Parkway at Grandfather Mountain*, Browning wrote a meticulous sixteen-page internal report rebutting the "facts" one by one. Casting his arguments confidently as those of "thoroughly unbiased engineers, who were motivated only by a determination to find a location which would be in keeping with the dignity of this great Parkway and which . . . would protect the interests of all the land owners involved to the greatest possible extent," Browning confronted Morton's assertions.[128]

Browning countered Morton's claim that travelers on the Yonahlossee route would view of number of "waterfalls in beautiful settings" by pointing out that most were "on very small drains or streams and, except during a heavy and pro-longed rainy season, could easily escape notice." He also challenged Morton's claim that the Linville Company had "provided" the Yonahlossee right-of-way, reminding readers that the state had paid for it to help the company during its fiscal crisis. Browning dismissed Morton's complaints about the "fantastically impractical" proposed high route tunnel, noting that "there is nothing fantastic or unusual about driving a tunnel" on a modern highway.[129]

This report and other correspondence also took on what would become Morton's central argument: that building along the high line would damage a mountain that Morton was committed to protecting. Supporters instead emphasized the damage Morton's building projects as well as the Linville Company's earlier activities had already wrought. In 1955, for example, Browning's senior locating engineer, George McKinley, noted that Morton "speaks of desecrating the beauty of Grandfather Mountain. I do not think this was given much consideration when the company sold the timber and pulpwood[,] for Grandfather was given a crew-cut and after some twenty years still looks rather bare and rocky." At Parkway headquarters that summer, staff scrambled to find photos to bolster their case: "Do you have any pictures," a staffer asked Weems, "of the Swinging Bridge and environs showing how that has messed up the mt.?" Early that fall, when BPR engineers and an NPS landscape architect gave state officials a requested report on the high route, they included photographs that showed "the scar resulting from [Morton's] so-called 'mile high' road and parking area." This scar, the report concluded, "is 500 or more feet higher in elevation than any scar that will be created" by the Parkway high line.[130]

Browning's 1957 report also challenged Morton's claim to want to protect the mountain. "From his own experience," Browning noted, Morton was "well-qualified to testify regarding the amount of rock and the scarcity of earth on that part of Grandfather Mountain where he laboriously blasted out a steep and winding road over the naked cliffs to his parking lot near the high bridge." Morton's toll road, Browning concluded, "forms a scar on the face of this lovely mountain that can never be erased." Citing with some pride the lengthy record of careful work done by engineers both to highlight scenic features and to minimize construction damage along the Parkway, Browning expressed confidence that the high route would be gentle on the mountain and that "neither the State engineers nor the engineers of the Park Service would undertake such a glaring, ruthless, irreparable job at this [or] at any point on the Parkway."[131]

For some reason, Browning's devastating report circulated internally but received no press attention until years later. Shortly after it was issued, however,

Aerial view of the Blue Ridge Parkway and Hugh Morton's road to the Swinging Bridge at Grandfather Mountain, 1976. Swinging Bridge, parking lot, and bridge access road are at top center; the Parkway intersection with U.S. 221 is at lower left; and the Parkway is the prominent road at lower middle. In the 1980s, the Linn Cove Viaduct was built just east (to the right) of where the Parkway ends here. Courtesy Blue Ridge Parkway.

Browning apparently lobbied influential citizens in the Blowing Rock area in favor of the high route, infuriating Morton. Browning, for his part, at that point seemed to want to avoid a public conflict because he judged the matter simply a "misunderstanding" based mainly on personal animosity between Morton and Weems that could with patience be worked out. Indeed, Browning reasoned, it could be argued that the high route would benefit Morton. Plans for the high line, Browning wrote to Hodges in 1958, included a large parking overlook from which "a clear and unobstructed view of Mr. Morton's high bridge" would in effect advertise the attraction. Furthermore, Browning thought it "quite feasible for [Morton] to build a branch of his toll road . . . to a point on Route 221 just west of the proposed Parkway crossing," easing tourist access from the Parkway. The only advantage to Morton of the lower line, Browning thought, was that it would allow him to retain ownership of a larger part of the top of the mountain.[132]

Realizing that the situation was politically delicate, however, Browning was reluctant to air publicly any of his counterarguments. Historian Herbert Evison, a retired Park Service chief of information who was gathering information for a history of the Parkway in the late 1950s, was intrigued by the Morton controversy, especially the abrupt Highway Commission decision to return the lands Browning's office had appropriated in 1955. Digging into the matter, however, Evison hit barriers at every turn and ultimately gave up in frustration. A note at the beginning of the transcript of his interview with Browning explained that whenever he had asked Browning about the land return, "he asked me to turn off the tape recorder."[133]

By early 1962, as Morton began to take his case more directly to the public, high route supporters awoke to the need to speak out. Acting Parkway Superintendent Howard B. Stricklin wrote to Browning for comment on newspaper clippings that presented a number of problematic elements in Morton's emerging narrative, which Stricklin listed one by one: the assertion that the Park Service planned to build the Parkway "over the top" of the mountain, "marring and defacing the whole mountain"; the statement that the route would come close enough to the swinging bridge to "ruin that enterprise"; the report that "the right of way 'given' by Morton would be better, cheaper and less destructive of scenic values"; and the notion that the Park Service was "holding out for the route 'over the top of the mountain' just to be stubborn, and to demonstrate their engineering skill in building a road in a bad place." Shortly thereafter, Weems wondered "whether a statement should be given the press to offset the exaggerations that have appeared in some North Carolina papers." But as Weems pondered, Morton moved, generating his 1962 media blitz. Indeed, Morton had spent at least four years contemplating the potential benefits of taking his story to the "man on the street," as he put it. Park Service supporters clearly were slow to get into the media game.[134]

Browning may have been constrained by his continued employment by the State Highway Commission, which by 1962 had ceased to cooperate with the Park Service. When he retired from his Parkway work with the commission in 1962, however, he became freer to speak. Convinced by then that the situation with Morton would never be negotiated without decisive state or federal action, he seems to have subsequently made some efforts to air his views more publicly while pressuring officials to stop stalling and take stronger action on behalf of the high route.

In 1962, for example, the *Raleigh News and Observer* reported that Browning's comprehensive 1957 internal report was belatedly "receiving attention by top State officials" and was "due some consideration." "I believe," Browning wrote to Wirth the same year, that Morton's "attitude is to prevent any development in that area which might in any way adversely affect his activities in connection with his high bridge and toll road." Given that "we had to compel some of the mountain people to abandon their homes completely and move to another local- ity and where we were obliged at time to cut their lands into awkward and isolated areas, I cannot understand why we should be so hesitant about dealing with the Grandfather Mountain situation." Morton, Browning observed, is "in a different class [because] he is a close personal friend of" former North Carolina gover- nor and current secretary of commerce Luther Hodges. Only a month before his death in 1966, Browning was quoted at length in two Raleigh newspapers assert- ing that the high route "fits the country better, it provides better scenery, it hurts the mountain the least and it benefits the property."[135]

Sam Beard, director of public affairs at Raleigh's conservative WRAL-TV and a Parkway supporter who had worked in the late 1950s as the public relations director for the State Highway Commission, also judged by 1962 that "the people of North Carolina are getting only one side of this story." But "I know very well," he wrote to Weems, "that there are two sides because I went into the records very thoroughly in 1958 in doing a special report for Governor Hodges." Indeed, Beard had originated the idea of having Morton and Wirth fight it out in the televised debate following their joint appearance before the Highway Commission in 1962. "I am not at all sure," Beard said, "that the newspaper climate in North Caro- lina is such that you would get a fair break especially since Hugh is selling his side strongly and since the [Sanford] administration is now backing him." Beard hoped, he wrote to Weems, that "the National Park Service side of this dispute can be aired properly." In the hours after their Highway Commission hearing, Wirth and Morton taped an episode of WRAL-TV's In My Opinion program. Unfortu- nately for Park Service supporters, the television appearance reinforced the pro- Morton newspaper reports. In Morton's recollections, he has described burying Wirth and converting scores of new supporters by bringing on fiddler and radio personality Arthur Smith to plead Grandfather's cause.[136]

In the wake of the 1962 hearing and the WRAL program, several state newspa- pers honed in on Wirth's stubborn assertion that he would rather see the Parkway left uncompleted than follow the "inferior" lower route. Editorials, articles, and a cartoon in the Greensboro Daily News characterized the Park Service as an obsti- nate bureaucracy holding the Parkway hostage. At this crucial moment when the Park Service had the chance to thrust its case into the public eye, however, Weems was taking an extended trip to Europe. It thus fell to Stricklin to write eloquent if ultimately ineffective letters to the editors of the Raleigh News and Observer, the

"If You Want To See Your Boy In One Piece, You'll Let Us Through!"

Cartoon depicting the Park Service holding the Parkway hostage by insisting on the high route, *Greensboro Daily News*, 2 June 1962. Reprinted with permission of the *Greensboro News and Record*.

Asheville Times, and the *Greensboro Daily News* requesting more balanced coverage of the conflict. By the time Weems returned, nearly two weeks after the hearing, the critical moment had passed.[137]

Following the hearing, Weems observed, "Much misinformation has been circulated about the proposed location around Grandfather Mountain." Perhaps, he suggested, "the National Park Service should have refuted this bit by bit." Instead, the service had withheld all its supporting materials and exhibits until Wirth could use them in his presentation to the Highway Commission. "Now that Mr. Wirth has stated the Park Service position," Weems wrote to an Asheville businessman, "we can elaborate on it for you." All in all, however, the Park Service's hesitant public relations effort in the spring of 1962 represented too little, too late.[138]

As late as 1965, after Morton orchestrated the unapproved land swap that gave the state the needed lands for the compromise route, Weems and the Park Service staff still did not make a forceful public case. "[It] is high time," Beard wrote to Weems, "for some statement of purpose from the National Park Service regarding Hugh's latest maneuver . . . and some definitive statement . . . regarding its view of the middle route. Is it possible that Washington is going to agree to Hugh's proposal? If not, . . . the Park Service [should] set the record straight."[139]

The Park Service, however, did not correct the record. Instead, several newspaper articles parroted Morton's press release announcing the middle route land swap. The *Greensboro News*, for example, trumpeted, "Mortons Give Property for Highway Route" (omitting mention of the land they had received from the state in exchange). This outraged one of the Parkway's staunchest media supporters, Stella Anderson of West Jefferson, North Carolina, who wrote to Weems lambasting the Greensboro report as "hogwash." Anderson, owner and editor of the *Skyland Post* and the *Alleghany News*, published several long articles between 1962 and 1966 that pointed out flaws in Morton's arguments. She detailed problems with both the Yonahlossee/221 and the middle routes and highlighted the case for the high line. A large graphic featured on the front page in July 1962 and again in a 1966 piece, for example, showed that the high route did not cross "over the top" of Grandfather and did not come as near the swinging bridge as Morton proclaimed. Anderson also pointed out, as most other media reports did not, that the high route disrupted only one landowner, and she reminded readers that elsewhere along the Parkway the state had not hesitated to relocate landowners whose homes lay in the Parkway's path.[140]

The most comprehensive critique of Morton and the clearest contemporary public statement of the politics of the controversy came, however, from national environmental writer Michael Frome. In a 1966 article for *American Forests*, Frome framed the Grandfather conflict as a choice of "beauty or the bulldozer." Frome alleged that former governor Sanford had been a captive of the tourist industry and that during his administration, sections of North Carolina had "deteriorated into unsightly tourist slums" while state highways had become "increasingly blighted with billboards" at the same time that adjoining states had passed laws to prevent billboard proliferation. With regard to the Parkway, Frome pointed out, Sanford and others had made a "gross misstatement" to say the Park Service wanted to go "over the top" of Grandfather Mountain. The source of this misinformation and of the associated "stream of printed material filled with invective against the Park Service" Frome identified as Morton, whom the writer characterized as "a personable and popular fellow [who was] active in many causes" but who was also "an alert political worker."[141]

Frome reported correctly that the "high route" remained well below Grandfather's crest. Furthermore, he noted, the route had been "selected by the state's own highway locating engineer, R. Getty Browning, a distinguished public servant." Browning told Frome that the high route was chosen in good faith, that it fit the topography better, offered superior scenery, promised less damage, and benefited Morton. Frome also pointed out—as virtually no one else in the media had, that "Morton has done some mountain gutting of his own" in building the road to the Swinging Bridge. "When Mr. Morton complains that the high route would 'kill Grandfather Mountain's principal charm,' he must surely be referring to the box office receipts," Frome concluded.[142]

Frome found the middle route problematic because it had been initially suggested and favored by Morton, who was "neither a highway engineer nor a landscape architect." Even if the route turned out to have some technical merit, Frome argued that the crucial question at hand was "whether a commercial tourist operator should be able to fix the location of a national park facility vis-à-vis his own property. [For] the National Park Service, serving the interest of all people, the prospect is devastating."[143]

Weems was thrilled with Frome's piece. "Thank goodness," he wrote as he forwarded a copy to Stella Anderson, "Mike Frome has come out with some stuff about the Parkway location around Grandfather Mountain which was written by him and not by Hugh Morton (for a change!)." Weems also called Frome's article to the attention of several in-state journalists but received only lukewarm responses. Predictably, some in the state media dismissed or ridiculed the piece. The publisher of the *Asheville Citizen-Times* said that Frome's article "really doesn't add a lot of new and constructive material to the discussion" and judged that it would only be "an irritant to a lot of the people involved in North Carolina." The

Winston-Salem Journal-Sentinel reported that Frome had "slipped the needle to North Carolina" but acknowledged that he might have been right to charge that "we as a people have been so determined to make this land green with tourist dollars that we are, in fact, despoiling it." The *Journal-Sentinel* brushed off Frome's charges about Morton, however, as "loaded with personal bias." Less charitable was the *Watauga Democrat*, which alleged that Frome had overlooked the Park Service's lax attempts to encourage Parkway tourists to patronize local businesses and lauded Morton for plowing his profits "right back into promoting [Grandfather Mountain] and adding . . . attractions around it, making the entire area more beautiful for the citizens of the USA to enjoy."[144]

The only North Carolina print journalist to risk laying bare the raw politics of the situation, West Jefferson's combative Anderson, repeated most of Frome's arguments in a long article also occasioned by the recent death of Getty Browning. Morton, Anderson pointed out, had "snowed the press with thousands of words insisting that the parkway is trying to ram its own plan down North Carolina's throat and mar the beauty of the mountain by gutting it." This argument was surprising, she continued, "coming from a man who has a commercial development on part of the mountain and who has done some gutting in order to build a road to the parking area at the foot of the mile-high swinging bridge." The compromise route, she continued, was "selected by Mr. Morton" and thus represented no compromise at all. Wasn't this, she asked, "a ram rod deal . . . attempting to ram a location down the throats of the parkway service?" Given the displacement of other landowners, she asked, "Is it justifiable that one man who operates a beautiful, but commercial tourist attraction, be able to fix the location of a link of the parkway to suit himself?"[145]

From the conflict's opening days in the mid-1950s until its resolution in the 1960s, then, a number of people understood how Morton's assertions of public-spirited concern for Grandfather's preservation masked a complicated mix of personal and private interests and how his victory emerged from the skillful deployment of a misleading story bolstered by political power and influence that most landowners affected by the Parkway had not been able to wield.

THE LINN COVE VIADUCT: A FINAL PARADOX

After the long struggle between Morton and the NPS finally subsided in 1968, construction on parts of the final section got under way immediately, and a 1969 article optimistically predicted that the segment would be finished by 1972 at a cost of $4 million. In fact, however, funding delays and construction challenges delayed closure of the "missing link" until 1987, nearly twenty years after the controversy with Morton ended. Given that the conflict with Morton ostensibly revolved around how to build the Parkway without damaging the mountain, it is perhaps a final paradox that a quandary about how to construct the Parkway without creating unacceptable scars and instability in the rocky Linn Cove area stalled progress long after the routing controversy was resolved.[146]

The construction problems in the Linn Cove boulder field, through which both the high and middle routes ran at the same location, had long been anticipated by NPS and federal highway staff. Huge rocks sat precariously piled among large old trees and scenic expanses of rhododendrons. After considerable study in the late 1960s and 1970s, the Parkway engineering and landscape team determined that neither a conventional roadbed with heavy infill nor a traditional bridge could be built without disfiguring or destabilizing the terrain beyond repair. Searching for an innovative solution that would maintain Parkway aesthetic and engineering standards, the Federal Highway Administration solicited proposals for bridge designs that would make use of the available spots for placing support piers while minimizing construction scars and disturbance to boulders, vegetation, and streams.[147]

The winning design came from the engineering firms of Barrett, Daffin, and Figg of Tallahassee, Florida, and Jean M. Muller–Europe Études of Paris, France (later combined to form the firm of Figg and Muller): a 1,243-foot S-shaped bridge now known as the Linn Cove Viaduct. Working under stringent controls that permitted cutting only trees situated directly below the bridge and that required specific approval for each tree cut, engineers devised a technique called progressive erection to build the bridge. Workers assembled the bridge out of 153 precast concrete sections (each one unique in its dimensions) by cantilevering out from the completed portion of the bridge to add each new segment, avoiding the need for construction access roads and minimizing tree cutting. Even the seven piers that supported the structure were built one by one, south to north, from the bridge top. Gently hugging the mountainside, the graceful, curving viaduct produced almost no construction scars, won numerous design awards, and provided a dramatic (and oft-photographed) highlight on an already spectacular parkway. The final cost, however, rose to an estimated $10 million.[148]

Despite the sensitivity to mitigating construction damage, the environmental concern that governed the building of the viaduct had more to do with maintaining longtime Parkway aesthetics of preserving scenery and minimizing scar than with a science-based environmental concern about the flora and fauna of Grandfather Mountain. Biologists, botanists, and environmental activists played no central role in the conception and planning of the viaduct, and the still-new National Environmental Policy Act (1969) had little influence on construction. Although the act required federal agencies to undertake scientific evaluation of the potential environmental impacts of federal development projects and to obtain public comment, the Park Service during the 1970s and 1980s accommodated itself only reluctantly—even "grudgingly," according to some critics—to the legislation's requirements. For the Grandfather Mountain section of the Parkway, planners wrote only a brief environmental impact assessment (modest by present-day standards) and solicited no public commentary. Indeed, one long-time Parkway staff member asserted that awareness of the significant numbers of rare and endangered plants and animals living on Grandfather emerged only after the viaduct and the associated N PS hiking trail there were under construction.[149]

Despite the after-the-fact emergence of the supporting ecological science, despite the fact that Hugh Morton was not involved in the bridge's conception or design, and despite the fact that the area traversed by the viaduct was included in both the high and middle routes, however, the viaduct—cloaked now in a mythology that attributes its building to a desire to protect fragile ecology—has provided a crucial retroactive justification for Morton's long resistance to the Park Service's high route. The passage of time has blurred and confused chronologies, so that most observers now read backward from a post-1970s notion of ecological protection and conclude that if an international team of engineers, an astoundingly difficult construction technique imported from Europe, and $10 million were needed to build a bridge less than a quarter of a mile long, Morton surely must have been right to persist so long in his crusade.[150]

DEVELOPER ENVIRONMENTALISM AND THE
BREAKDOWN OF PUBLIC-PRIVATE COOPERATION

Furthermore, every year that has passed has added credibility to this (mis)understanding of the Grandfather controversy and Morton's role in it because as the national environmental consciousness has evolved, so too has Hugh Morton's. In the 1980s and 1990s, long after the Parkway route question was resolved, Morton strengthened his credentials as a champion of the environment in the southern Appalachians. As chairman of Western North Carolina Tomorrow during the 1980s, he pushed the 1983 passage of North Carolina's Mountain Ridge Protection Act (the "ridge law"), which permitted counties to prevent construction of more of the kind of multistory structures that had already defaced Sugar Mountain. Not coincidentally, the ungainly Sugar Top condominium complex that spurred ridge law proponents into action stood glaringly in view across the valley from the Mile-High Swinging Bridge.[151]

Moreover, in the early 1990s, Morton legally protected parts of Grandfather Mountain from further development, primarily by donating conservation easements over lands that he continued to own or by facilitating purchase of lands by the Nature Conservancy. Since 1991, he has donated conservation easements of nearly 1,800 acres to the Conservancy, which has also purchased easements of 925 acres and bought another 900 acres outright. All in all, the Conservancy now helps to manage more than 4,000 acres of Grandfather Mountain. In this period, Grandfather Mountain, Inc., also expanded its efforts in ecological education, opening its Nature Museum and expanding its wildlife habitats. And in 1993, after Morton applied to the United Nations Educational, Scientific, and Cultural Organization at the suggestion of a member of the Parkway staff, Grandfather became a United Nations Biosphere Reserve.[152]

As chair of the North Carolina governor's Year of the Mountains Commission in 1996, Morton mobilized his photography skills to develop a widely shown slide presentation demonstrating the devastating effects of air pollution and acid rain on the mountains. Under his leadership, the commission also initiated a partnership with the Conservation Trust for North Carolina to acquire for the Blue Ridge Parkway critical viewshed lands threatened by development. As of 2004, this effort had led to the protection of well over twenty thousand acres of land adjacent to the Parkway. Morton also promoted (and in some ways genuinely demonstrated) himself as a friend of the Parkway through his efforts at land and view protection of many acres at Grandfather Mountain itself and through more mundane acts such as offering his staff's assistance in cleanup along the Parkway after a devastating 2003 ice storm.[153]

However admirable these activities, it is important to keep chronologies clear and to realize that most of these efforts took place long after the Grandfather routing controversy was settled. In addition, Morton's environmentalism has in many ways worked best when it was congruent with his longtime role as a tourism developer and promoter. The choice of the Nature Conservancy as a partner, the use of the conservation easement as a tool, and even the designation of the Biosphere Reserve were all compatible with the ongoing operation of Grandfather Mountain as a lucrative parklike tourist attraction. The Nature Conservancy, for its part, has built itself into a major protector of billions of dollars in environmental assets by becoming what the *Washington Post* has called "the leading proponent of a brand of environmentalism that promotes compromise between conservation and corporate America."[154]

From the standpoint of environmental protection, furthermore, conservation easements, through which owners retain title to their lands but permanently
prohibit certain kinds of development through restrictions placed on the deeds,
have met with mixed success. Such easements, which are donated to private, nonprofit land trusts such as the Nature Conservancy for certification, monitoring,
and management, also permit landowners to claim substantial federal income tax
deductions (and sometimes reduced estate taxes and local property taxes) based
on the reduction in the lands' value. The *Washington Post* in 2003 found wealthy
landowners and developers benefiting from the difficult-to-police easement system by tailoring easements to work in tandem with their development plans, by
donating easements covering otherwise "unusable acres," and often by giving up
very little in return for the large tax breaks. The Biosphere Reserve designation,
for its part, had the associated benefit of convincing Parkway staff to erect a long-
sought-after sign on the road directing travelers to Grandfather.[155]

More specifically, the most aggressive conservation efforts at Grandfather
came about after a very public battle in the late 1980s and early 1990s between
Morton and regional environmentalists who sought to stop his plans to sell nine
hundred acres (the so-called Wilmor tract that he owned jointly with an Oklahoma oil pipeline builder) on Grandfather's northwest side for tourism-related
development, including a ski resort. Several groups lobbied to preserve the tract
in a wild state and tried to raise funds to buy parts of it. Morton asserted that the
Wilmor tract was not really part of Grandfather Mountain proper, that "people
who you know are in good shape financially and have a good track record" could
be trusted to develop Wilmor in an environmentally sensitive way, and that, in any
event, "development is going to occur everywhere, and the best thing you can do
is try to make it good." He challenged critics to "name me a person who is more a
friend of Grandfather than I am." In the end, this conflict may have pushed Morton toward more active environmental protection efforts: in its wake he began his
official partnership with the Conservancy and subsequently facilitated either the
donation or the sale of more than two-thirds of the Wilmor property to the Nature
Conservancy while he and his partner developed a supermarket, restaurants, motels, and condominiums on the rest of the land.[156]

Statements made during the 1990 wrangle over the Wilmor tract revealed
how, in many respects, Morton's reputation and self-presentation as a "friend of
Grandfather" rides on the inaccurate but perdurable story of how he rescued the
mountain from the Park Service and its high Parkway route. A representative of
the Audubon Society noted that "if [Morton] had not saved that mountain, there
wouldn't be anything there for anyone to quarrel over," and the *Atlanta Journal and*

Constitution reported in a single breath that Morton won a "12-year [sic]" battle against National Park Service, "which was determined to run the Blue Ridge Parkway over the mountain," and led the fight for passage of North Carolina's ridge law.[157]

In an elegantly circular fashion, the epic tale of the earlier rescue thus undergirds Morton's present image as an environmentalist, while Morton's more recent conservation work, combined with the mythology surrounding the building of the Linn Cove Viaduct, gives credibility to the appealing story of how he saved the mountain. But reading this past through the rosy lenses of the present distorts a history that had much more to do with a fundamental conflict between public and private interests and with one man's ability to shape a public project to his personal benefit than it did to a lone, heroic conservationist's fight to fend off "arrogant bureaucrats" trying to steal Grandfather Mountain.[158]

That Morton has for all these years been able to push forward a private business development while simultaneously trading on emergent environmentalist discourse, that he so completely defined his interests as broad public interests at the expense of a public-serving agency whose goals he portrayed as self-serving, that he drove a wedge into the powerful public-private partnership that had brought the Parkway into being—all of these testify to his shrewdness and drive, to the complexity of his motivations, and to the powerful symbolism of Grandfather Mountain.

But Morton's success also issued from his brilliance in understanding some of the fundamental contradictions and fragile coalitions at the center of the Parkway project. Starting as a public project that came into being largely at the behest of private business boosters in collaboration with supportive state governments in a region whose economy was built partly on the tourism they hoped the Parkway would foster, yet funded by public monies and built by a federal public agency for the free use of all travelers, the Parkway project was from the beginning rent by internal tensions that have always been difficult to resolve. Should it primarily serve businesspeople such as Morton, Heriot Clarkson, and members of the Asheville Chamber of Commerce who owned and operated the state's "top scenic attractions"? How could it serve local and regional businesspeople who operated on a smaller scale? To what degree should the interests of regional business constituencies of whatever size or of individual landowners receive consideration in Parkway routing, design, and land use? What higher public interests could and should the project serve? When public interests and regional business interests or landowner concerns collide, how should conflicts be resolved?

Throughout the Parkway's development, the NPS shared responsibility with state agencies for managing and mediating these conflicts. In North Carolina, throughout the first thirty years of Parkway construction, the enthusiastic cooperation of state government, personified by R. Getty Browning, was critical to keeping business interests and the larger public good in balance and to resolving conflicts relatively quickly. In this period, Asheville succeeded in having the Parkway routed to its leaders' liking, along a route that, as Browning devised and promoted it, offered the public stunning mountaintop scenery and high elevation coolness. Clarkson forced a distractingly narrowed right-of-way through his Little Switzerland development, but the Park Service fended off his later attempts to commercialize the Parkway with advertising signs. The Eastern Band of Cherokees pushed a routing change that preserved their limited options for Cherokee-driven economic development yet gave the Parkway a good alignment on the ridges around the Qualla Boundary. None of these conflicts seriously threatened the business-state-federal (roads-parks-tourism) coalition that had brought the Parkway into being.

Yet this coalition ultimately was frail, and the balance between local and individual needs and the public interest was always hard to maintain, especially as responsibility for the Parkway shifted from the states to the N P S during the 1950s. In those years, the owners of the Peaks of Otter (who cooperated almost completely amicably with the Park Service) found themselves sidelined as the agency gave control of concessions to large-scale operators. Watching this process and other N P S efforts to impose its vision on the Parkway (through sign policies, facilities development, and tolls), Hugh Morton refused steadfastly to agree to anything other than what he wanted and managed to tip the balance at Grandfather almost completely in his favor, right down to the placement of directional signs on the Parkway that presently guide carloads of tourists to his attraction's front gates.

Morton's long campaign both exacerbated and benefited from the fracturing of the original coalition as the tourist business—feeling it had been "sold down the river"—turned against the Parkway and as the cooperative spirit of North Carolina's state bureaucracy ebbed away with Browning's waning influence. Intentionally or otherwise, Morton's strategy destabilized the industry-state-N P S/ federal alliance that had until the 1950s kept competing interests in check and produced the Parkway. While the Parkway and N P S could, with state support, rather quickly fend off or resolve challenges from businesses and landowners, its leadership could not prevail in the delicate land-acquisition process when the pillar of state cooperation crumbled, as it did under the weight of the Grandfather conflict.

Linn Cove Viaduct,
Grandfather Mountain, n.d.
Courtesy Historic American
Buildings Survey/Historic
American Engineering Record,
Library of Congress.

At Grandfather, more than anywhere else on the Parkway, the price of the early collaboration between Parkway supporters and business interests and the ultimate durability of state support for business (always percolating just below the surface of Parkway development) became clear. With the state's help, a powerful developer could indeed bring a federal project to a halt and shape it to his liking. The outcome at Grandfather revealed vividly the key lesson of the history of controversy over land, design, access, and use all along the road: that power politics, social pressures, and the resolution of cultural and class conflicts—every bit as much as vision, aesthetic sensibilities, landscape design, and engineering—created the landscape that became the Blue Ridge Parkway.

EPILOGUE

Over its entire history and along its entire 469-mile length, the Blue Ridge Parkway has been a study in the complicated and messy process of identifying and pursuing some version of a public good. For each of the episodes I have unpacked in this book, I could have explored several others in which public and private, individual and collective, environmental and social needs and wants were in tension and in which decisions had to be made that determined winners and losers and shaped the Parkway. In the midst of ever-shifting coalitions and alliances and competing agendas, it has not always been easy to see where a transcendent public interest lies and whether it is possible to distribute the costs of striving for it fairly and equitably in the face of challenges presented by constituencies with other interests at stake.

The process of balancing these issues and concerns has not ended and probably never will. Whatever the changes in historical context, the current array of challenges facing the Parkway and those who relate to it does not differ substantially from the challenges that faced North Carolina engineer R. Getty Browning, Parkway landscape architect Stanley Abbott, or any of the other founders, builders, managers, or regional and local private interests over the road's history. Far from living in times radically different from our own, countless others involved in the Parkway's development would instantly recognize many of the challenges the Parkway faces today.

Recent pressure from adjacent developers near Roanoke whose projects might compromise Parkway views? Not new to those who coped with Little Switzerland developer Heriot Clarkson and consented to the reduced right-of-way through Little Switzerland.

Ongoing problems with congestion and misuse of Parkway

access points in southern Virginia? Not new to Interior Secretary Harold Ickes, who in 1938 clamped down on new Parkway entrance points in response to their proliferation in this area.

Federal funding deficits? Not new to Superintendent Sam Weems and others who shepherded the Parkway through the slow-progress decade after World War II, when visitation spiked and funds were scarce.

Difficulties raising money from private sources for land protection and Parkway programs? Not new to the public-spirited Harlan Kelsey, who lamented the private sector's inability or unwillingness to step up to protect Grandfather Mountain in the 1940s.

Concessionaire problems and complaints? Not new to Hunter Miller and his colleagues in the Bedford-based Peaks of Otter, Inc.

Periodically reemerging proposals to raise funds for the Parkway by charging tolls? Not new to Weems, Browning, Ickes, or regional business leaders such as Hugh Morton, who argued over this matter repeatedly in the 1940s and 1950s.

Questions about what kind of historic scene to present along the Parkway and what to do with historic properties? Not new to the NPS history specialists who went looking for log cabins in the late 1930s or to Parkway historian F. A. "Andy" Ketterson, who tried to bring more accurate history telling to the Peaks of Otter in the 1970s.

Landowner and community discontent with the Parkway? Not new to North Carolina farmer S. A. Miller and other aggrieved Ashe County landowners or to Stanley Abbott, who inaugurated the *Blue Ridge Parkway News* to address a perceived public relations problems among Parkway neighbors in the 1930s.

Different degrees of commitment to Parkway viewshed protection and land acquisition in North Carolina and Virginia? Not new to Virginia Senator Harry F. Byrd, Virginia Highway Department Commissioner Henry G. Shirley, Browning, or Abbott, who made a range of decisions that, for good or ill, laid the foundation for the divergent situations in the two states today.

Challenges of relating the Parkway to the needs of regional business interests and tourism-promotion organizations whose agendas do not always mesh with Parkway plans? Not new to Weems, to the creators of the tourism-boosting Blue Ridge Parkway Association in the 1950s, or to Park Service director Conrad Wirth, who clashed with Morton.

Quandary over the degree to which a new visitor's center in Asheville should promote regional tourism and advertise nearby attractions? Not new to Asheville Chamber of Commerce manager Fred Weede or local developer George Stephens; *Asheville Citizen-Times* editor Charles Webb; President Franklin D. Roosevelt's confidant, Josephus Daniels; Heriot Clarkson; Weems; Browning; or Morton, all of whom recognized the Parkway's genesis among tourism promoters and struggled to achieve what each viewed as the optimal balance between the public's interests and the business community's needs.

Despite these clear antecedents for present-day Parkway policy and management problems, a persistent statement about the Parkway is that "it couldn't be built today." Underlying this belief may be a sense that things somehow were simpler in the undifferentiated deep past—that people were more giving, public-spirited, and unified, that they saw the Parkway as a relatively straightforward undertaking, that things just were not as controversial, and that the project brought people together in a time before they became jaded and cynical and the world became frustratingly complicated.

This view is dangerous, I fear, both for us and for the Parkway, because it turns the past into an unrepeatable and distant golden age while it robs us of power and choice in the present. Such statements are fundamentally ahistorical. Which past are we talking about? The New Deal and depression era? World War II or the Cold War periods? The Mission 66 age? The activist 1960s and 1970s, when social movements pushed the country to enact justice for its citizens and protections for its environment? The Parkway was pushed forward during all of these times, under an ever-changing set of historical circumstances.

Yet these specific contexts, like our own, did and do make a difference in the way issues and conflicts the project generated have been resolved. One episode from the 1970s will illustrate how the general question of building the Parkway, arising in a new historical moment, was answered in a way that produced an outcome very different from what resulted in the 1930s.

Beginning in the 1930s, people from Roosevelt on down had from time to time envisioned this Parkway as part of a much longer route running all the way up and down the eastern United States.[1] By the 1960s, the remnants of that plan had crystallized into a proposal to extend the Parkway south from North Carolina through the north Georgia mountains to Marietta, just north of Atlanta. Surveys went forward in the early 1960s, and congressional approval for the 190-mile extension came in 1967. Public hearings followed, and by 1970 it was clear that the project was encountering major opposition from both residents in the vicinity of Rabun County, Georgia, and from regional environmentalists.[2]

The conception of the Parkway itself had changed little from its 1930s form: plans still called for the states to acquire land not already in Forest Service hands according to the standard of 125 acres per mile long used in North Carolina, still envisioned a limited-access pleasure road, still called for private concessions operators to develop accommodations for travelers. Much of the Rabun County opposition, too, followed predictable lines: A Rabun Gap couple wrote to the Parkway superintendent, "We feel it is just a terrible thing to ruin the beauty of one side of this lovely mountain valley by taking out 14 or maybe 16 homes. . . . The parkway will not be of any advantage or profit to the people of this valley as you know it is only for the wealthy or rich people to enjoy except a few people that have motels or restaurants will reap some profit." Not surprisingly, developers too opposed the appropriation of lands.

Before long, a chorus of environmentalist complaints also arose, echoing the Wilderness Society's antiroads crusade that began in the 1930s but now strengthened by the emergence of a full-blown national environmental movement. A letter from a representative of Marietta's Wildlife Management Institute summarized the issues: "Our concern arises because the Parkway is but one facet of the proliferation of highways and highway proposals in the Appalachians of southern North Carolina and Georgia. . . . Even a road of the high quality of the Parkway substantially destroys the natural environment, reducing the human opportunity to enjoy a mountain forest experience shorn of the artificialities of humanity. With each highway, the quality of this experience is diminished. . . . We are amazed that the National Park Service, an agency ostensibly responsive to the protection of nature, is so involved in such a blatant tourist promotion."

The National Park Service, a press report indicated, "was stunned by the opposition coming from organizations which in the past have been supporters of park projects." During the 1930s, the article continued, "the parkway was viewed as a principal means of conserving spectacular mountain areas in western Virginia and North Carolina." But noting the changed context, the author observed that "modern conservationists balk at road building plans. They charged [that] the extension of the scenic highway to within a few minutes of Atlanta would 'guarantee a ribbon of pollution through unspoiled mountain areas.'" After an environmental-impact statement was drawn up in 1973, the project foundered and died.

The Georgia extension episode makes it clear that however persistent and recognizable the problems, in changed contexts, different outcomes are likely. Neither extending nor, for that matter, even maintaining the Blue Ridge Parkway in its present state are inevitable, immutable certainties. At present, we (and those who care for the Parkway on behalf of all of us) confront many challenges that are all too familiar to anyone with even a cursory understanding of the road's past. But instead of finding ourselves in the midst of a national economic depression at a time of rising public faith in the role of the federal government to provide for our common good, we live in an era where distrust of and hostility toward a strong and beneficent federal government have led to the erosion of our public agencies and of much of the public and social infrastructure built in the New Deal and Mission 66 periods.

On the Parkway, the consequences are evident: some overlooks are overgrown, "comfort stations" are increasingly uncomfortable, the roadway is patched, some campgrounds are ragged and ill equipped, rail fences sag, and historic sites are languishing. A 2003 study suggested that only a 40 percent budget increase would permit the Parkway to operate "at standard."[3] It is not inconceivable that the Parkway could be allowed simply to crumble.

History teaches us that the Parkway was created by human hands within all-too-human frameworks of divergent perspectives and interests, uncertainty about the wisdom of contending approaches, and the difficulty of predicting outcomes. Its present shape inscribes on the land the results of thousands of decisions small and large that balanced competing interests in a variety of ways. Its future lies in the decisions we all make as we are asked to figure out how to balance the competing needs that have been in tension in the project since its first day.

Taking more careful stock of what has changed (the broader sociopolitical context) and what has stayed the same (the broad array of competing constituencies and demands) helps us to seize the power each of us has to make decisions — individual and collective — that determine the shape of the Parkway and, more broadly, of the public good it has on the whole served so well for nearly seventy-five years. Like all of the people who influenced the Parkway's development during the twentieth century, we are presented with an array of difficult choices, and the results of our decisions will be written on the land. The ongoing creation of the Blue Ridge Parkway now lies in our hands.

NOTES

JWBP	Josiah William Bailey Papers, Duke University Library, Special Collections Department, Durham, North Carolina
LHH	Luther H. Hodges
LHP	Luther Hodges Papers, North Carolina State Archives, Raleigh
NPS	National Park Service
POF	President's Official Files, Franklin D. Roosevelt Presidential Library, Hyde Park, New York
PWA	Public Works Administration
RGB	R. Getty Browning
RGBP	R. Getty Browning Papers, Blue Ridge Parkway Archives, Asheville, North Carolina
RLD	Robert Lee Doughton
RLDP	Robert Lee Doughton Papers, Southern Historical Collection, University of North Carolina, Chapel Hill
RNO	*Raleigh News and Observer*
RPC	Tom Richardson, Bedford, Virginia, Private Collection (on loan to Blue Ridge Parkway Headquarters, Asheville, North Carolina)
SERG 75	Record Group 75, Cherokee Indian Agency Files, National Archives Southeast Region, East Point, Georgia
SHCRWD	State Highway Commission, Right of Way Department, Blue Ridge Parkway Records, North Carolina State Archives, Raleigh
SPW	Sam P. Weems
SWA	Stanley W. Abbott
TCV	Thomas C. Vint
TSP	Terry Sanford Papers, North Carolina State Archives, Raleigh

INTRODUCTION

1. According to longtime Parkway landscape architect Robert Hope, the Parkway is in fact 470 miles long, though the final milepost and official NPS pronouncements say 469. This discrepancy emerged because all the mileposts were laid out before completion of the final Parkway link at Grandfather Mountain, which turned out to be longer than anticipated. The "miles" around Grandfather are, therefore, slightly longer than one mile (Hope, interview).

2. All quotations are taken from the fall 2002 series "Parkway at a Crossroads," in the *Asheville Citizen-Times*. See <http://www.citizen-times.com/parkway/> (accessed 26 May 2003). Specific articles include Julie Ball, "Historic Scenic Roadway Plays Big Role in Region's Identity and Economy," ACT, 11 October 2002; Julie Ball, "Views Draw Visitors to Scenic Parkway," ACT, 17 October 2002.

3. BRP Foundation, "Family Visitor Collection"; "Our Thanksgiving Place: The Peaks of Otter."

4. Middleton, "Good Road of the Blue Ridge."

5. Myers, "Line of Grace." This account, along with most popular stories, focuses on the work of the Parkway's first resident landscape architect, Stanley W. Abbott. See also O'Connell and Myers, "Road to Match the Mountains"; Myers, "Variety and Interest"; Buxton and Beatty, *Blue Ridge Parkway*. See also Jolley, *Painting*; Davies, "Highway"; NPS, "Lying Lightly."

   A similar perspective dominates histories written within or for the NPS. See especially the account written by Abbott's son, Carlton Abbott et al., *Visual Character*; see also Quin and Marston, *Historic American Engineering Record*; Edward G. Speer, *Blue Ridge Parkway*; Ian J. W. Firth, "Historic Resource Study: Blue Ridge Parkway, Virginia and North Carolina [Draft]," August 1993 (revised November 2004), Blue Ridge Parkway Headquarters, Asheville, North Carolina.

6. A recent one is Graham, *Blue Ridge Parkway*.

7. Works following Jolley's approach include Catlin, *Naturalist's Blue Ridge Parkway*; Gentry, *Road That Rides the Fog*; Jolley, *Blue Ridge Parkway: First 50 Years*; Akers, *Mileposts and More*; *Northbound Visitor's Guide*; *Southbound Visitor's Guide*; Winokur, *Joy in the Mountains*; Bledsoe, *Blue Horizons*; Lord, *Blue Ridge Parkway Guide*; Skinner, *Bicycling the Blue Ridge*; Beney, *Land of the Sky*.

8. Jolley, *Blue Ridge Parkway*, 44, 51–56, 49, 90, 93–101, 115–19, 135–36.

9. "The Scenic Parkway" [editorial], *AC*, 4 February 1934, B6; "Scenic Parkway Seems Assured" [editorial], *AC*, 13 November 1933, 4; "Big News for Us" [editorial], *AC*, 17 November 1933, A4; "North Carolina and the Parkway" [editorial], *AC*, 28 June 1934, 4.

10. *Blue Ridge Parkway News* 1, no. 4 (February 1938). Page numbers are not available for this and many other newspaper clippings cited in the notes. Where available, page numbers are provided.

11. Julie Powers Rives, "Vanishing Vistas," *RNO*, 24 January 1993; Phil Alexander, "Popular Blue Ridge Parkway Marks Milestone of 60 Years," *ACT*, 21 August 1995; Todd Richissin, "Parkway Celebrates 60 Years," *RNO*, 11 September 1995; author's observations of presentation on history of BRP to campers at Crabtree Meadows Park by NPS Ranger Burgess, 3 August 1996; Buxton and Beatty, *Blue Ridge Parkway*, 99, 123–27.

12. S. A. Miller to Franklin D. Roosevelt, 7 January 1937, CCF7B, Box 2731.

13. HLI to U.S. Attorney General, 16 July 1938, CCF7B, Box 2719; Connie Johnson to RLD, July 1945, CCF7B, Box 2764; D. S. Bare to RLD, 16 August 1935, RLDP, Box 14.

14. Fred B. Bauer, "Cherokee Indian Explains Opposition to Scenic Road," *Charlotte Observer*, 15 January 1939.

15. Marie G. Dwight to RGB, 3 June 1935, Charles S. Dwight to ABC, 6 June 1935, Elizabeth Ogden to ABC, 3 October 1936, and other correspondence, all in CCF7B, Box 2714.

16. Granville Liles, "History of the Blue Ridge Parkway," n.d., BRPRG 5, Box 48; Whisnant, *Modernizing the Mountaineer*; Eller, *Miners, Millhands, and Mountaineers*; Pudup, Billings, and Waller, *Appalachia*; Lewis, *Transforming*.

17. Eminent domain is described nicely in "National Eminent Domain Power."

18. Brothers and Chen, *1995–96 Economic Impact*.

19. Jolley, *Blue Ridge Parkway*, 136.

20. SWA, "Blue Ridge Parkway: 500-Mile Super-Scenic Motorway."

CHAPTER 1

1. Powell, *Dictionary*, 1:382–83.

2. HC, Text of Speech, September 1919, HCP, Box 2. The "dallies" quotation is attributed to South Carolina Governor George McDuffie ("Giga Quotes").

3. Excellent discussions of these interrelated developments appear in Shaffer, *See America First*; Carr, *Wilderness by Design*.

4. Sellars, *Preserving Nature*, 51; McClelland, *Presenting Nature*, 109–11; Carr, *Wilderness by Design*, 1–50, 309.

5. McClelland, *Presenting Nature*, 11; Carr, *Wilderness by Design*, 1–9, 11, 17, 19, 29–34.

6. Carr, *Wilderness by Design*, 23, 24–25, 45–48, 82.

7. Ibid., 46; McClelland, *Presenting Nature*, 29–33.

8. Carr, *Wilderness by Design*, 48–53.

9. McClelland, *Presenting Nature*, 7, 40–45.

10. Ibid., 45–47.

11. Carr, *Wilderness by Design*, 53.

12. Shaffer, *See America First*, 137–61, offers a good discussion of the Good Roads movement and tourism.

13. Preston, Dirt Roads, 13, 37.
14. Ibid., 13–16, 19–25, 37–38; Cecil Kenneth Brown, State Highway System, 35–36.
15. Preston, Dirt Roads, 25–30, 40–41; Shaffer, See America First, 161. For a long discussion of early auto tourism (autocamping), see Belasco, Americans on the Road, 7–74.
16. Preston, Dirt Roads, 39–41; Shaffer, See America First, 138–40, 154–61.
17. McKown, "Roads and Reform," 40–100; Cecil Kenneth Brown, State Highway System, 53–123; Preston, Dirt Roads, 69–92.
18. George B. Tindall coined the term "business progressivism"; for a discussion of the idea in relationship to North Carolina's political climate in the 1920s and 1930s, see Badger, North Carolina, 7–8.
19. McKown, "Roads and Reform," 40–100; Cecil Kenneth Brown, State Highway System, 53–123, 171; CMW, North Carolina Roads, 1:29–44; Lefler and Newsome, North Carolina, 566; Preston, Dirt Roads, 154, 161.
20. Preston, Dirt Roads, 42–64, 64–66.
21. Blackwell P. Robinson, North Carolina Guide, 592; Blackmun, Western North Carolina, 215; Starnes, Creating the Land, 17–18; McKown, "Roads and Reform," 30–32, 34–39; Cecil Kenneth Brown, State Highway System, 33–36, 57–59; Preston, Dirt Roads, 21–25, 37–38.
22. McKown, "Roads and Reform," 33–39; Cecil Kenneth Brown, State Highway System, 57–59. This highway would have connected towns along the Blue Ridge from Virginia to Georgia, several of which (Blowing Rock, Little Switzerland, and Asheville) later lay along the Blue Ridge Parkway route.
23. Bowman, Highway Politics, 27–33; Heinemann, Harry Byrd, 33, 42; Heinemann, Depression and New Deal, 135.
24. Carr, Wilderness by Design, 55–63; McClelland, Presenting Nature, 73.
25. Clements, "Politics and the Park"; Ben Robert Martin, "Hetch Hetchy Controversy"; Hundley, "Urban Imperialism"; Carr, Wilderness by Design, 63–72.
26. Carr, Wilderness by Design, 74; McClelland, Presenting Nature, 73; Sellars, Preserving Nature, 31–46.
27. Sellars, Preserving Nature, 43, 45–46; Carr, Wilderness by Design, 78–80, 92–93.
28. Carr, Wilderness by Design, 1–10, 139–87, 146; Shaffer, See America First, 94.
29. Sutter, Driven Wild, 102–10. The publicity campaign preceded the official establishment of the National Park Service by about a year and itself formed part of Mather's effort to encourage the creation of a separate federal parks bureau. See also Carr, Wilderness by Design, 5–9, 77, 146–52; McClelland, Presenting Nature, 78, 104; Shaffer, See America First, 102–6, 117–19; Sellars, Preserving Nature, 41–43.
30. Shaffer, See America First, 26–39, 40–92, 93–160; Carr, Wilderness by Design, 1–10, 139–87; Sutter, Driven Wild, 100–111; Sellars, Preserving Nature, 47–53, 58–59.
31. Carr, Wilderness by Design, 1–10, 139–87; Sutter, Driven Wild, 100–111; Sellars, Preserving Nature, 47–53, 58–59, 60–65.
32. McClelland, Presenting Nature, 78, 104; Sutter, Driven Wild, 102–10; Shaffer, See America First, 102–6, 117–19; Carr, Wilderness by Design, 147, 151; Sellars, Preserving Nature, 59–60.
33. An Act to Establish a National Park Service, and for Other Purposes (39 Stat. 535, 1916), reprinted in Dilsaver, America's National Park System, 46; Carr, Wilderness by Design, 5–7.
34. Sutter, Driven Wild, 110; NPS, "Lying Lightly"; Sellars, Preserving Nature, 47–53, 61; McClelland, Presenting Nature, 108–9; Carr, Wilderness by Design, 7, 171–77.
35. NPS, "Lying Lightly"; Carr, Wilderness by Design, 180–87; Simmons, "Creation," 159.
36. Gibson and Jung, "Historical Census Statistics"; Pierce, Great Smokies, 52.
37. Preston, Dirt Roads, 109–32, 154–57; Carr, Wilderness by Design, 82–85.
38. Members of this group did not specify a particular location for the park they wanted, so their

efforts cannot be directly linked to agitation for a park in the Great Smoky Mountains. But they did list as possible areas the Great Smokies and parts of the Balsams and sent the Senate a map showing the general area desired for the park. See Carlos C. Campbell, *Birth*, 15; Smith, "Appalachian National Park Movement," 47–51, 53–54. Chase P. Ambler, a physician who had just moved from Ohio to Asheville, started the movement that culminated in the 1899 meeting. His petition drive for the park caught the attention of the Asheville Board of Trade, which convened the meeting.

39. Smith, "Appalachian National Park Movement," 46–47. Charles A. Webb, a prominent Asheville newspaperman who attended the 1899 gathering, reported years later that three hundred people had gathered. But minutes of the meeting itself (in Appalachian National Park Association Collection, North Carolina State Archives, Raleigh), give the more modest figure of forty-two attendees. See Smith, "Appalachian National Park Movement," 46; Charles A. Webb, *Fifty-eight Years*, 4, 11.

40. Margaret Lynn Brown, "Smoky Mountains Story," 122 (later published as Margaret Lynn Brown, *Wild East*); Smith, "Appalachian National Park Movement," 39, 52–53.

41. Ready, *Asheville*, 45; Smith, "Appalachian National Park Movement," 38, 52–53.

42. Frome, *Strangers*, 174–78; Smith, "Appalachian National Park Movement," 44–47; 52–65; Gatewood, "North Carolina's Role," 165–66; Margaret Lynn Brown, "Smoky Mountains Story," 122–23, 133–34; Eller, *Miners, Millhands, and Mountaineers*, 114–16.

43. Margaret Lynn Brown, *Wild East*, 49–77; Donald Edward Davis, *Where There Are Mountains*, 163–98; Eller, *Miners, Millhands, and Mountaineers*, 99–112; Lewis, *Transforming*; Clarkson, *Tumult*.

44. Eller, *Miners, Millhands, and Mountaineers*, 101; Margaret Lynn Brown, "Smoky Mountains Story," 82.

45. Margaret Lynn Brown, "Smoky Mountains Story," 99–115.

46. Ready, *Asheville*, 85–88; Tooman, "Evolving Economic Impact," 219–22; Margaret Lynn Brown, "Smoky Mountains Story," 125–32; Gatewood, "North Carolina's Role," 166.

47. Pierce, *Great Smokies*, 48–52.

48. Margaret Lynn Brown, "Smoky Mountains Story," 132–35; Gatewood, "North Carolina's Role," 167–71; Frome, *Strangers*, 181, 183; Simmons, "Creation," 5, 9–18; Pierce, *Great Smokies*, 52–53.

49. Heinemann, *Harry Byrd*, 87–89; Margaret Lynn Brown, "Smoky Mountains Story," 132–35; Gatewood, "North Carolina's Role," 167–71; Frome, *Strangers*, 181, 183; Simmons, "Creation," 5, 9–18.

50. Simmons, "Creation," 22–23, 159; Margaret Lynn Brown, "Smoky Mountains Story," 134; Frome, *Strangers*, 184–85, 203. Knoxville led the 1920s campaign for a national park in the Great Smoky Mountains area. Margaret Lynn Brown reports that park enthusiasts in the Asheville region had since the early part of the century favored instead a park in the Linville Gorge–Grandfather Mountain area of their state, further to the northeast. Only the National Park Committee's selection of the Great Smoky Mountains region for one of the eastern parks brought Asheville to work wholeheartedly with Knoxville. See "Smoky Mountains Story," 132–35; Frome, *Strangers*, 185, 189; Gatewood, "North Carolina's Role," 171–84.

51. H. C. E. Bryant, "Senator Bailey Heads Delegation Winning Fight at Road Conference," RNO, 5 April 1931; R. L. Gwyn to JCBE, 20 February 1933, JCBEP, Box 152.

52. Bryant, "Senator Bailey Heads Delegation." For map, see NPS in cooperation with Eastern National Park-to-Park Highway Association, Map of Eastern National Park-to-Park Highway, 1931, CCF7B, Box 2712.

53. R. L. Gwyn to E. B. Jeffress, 5 August 1932, JWBP, Box 310; R. L. Gwyn to JCBE, 20 February 1933, JCBEP, Box 152; Maurice H. Thatcher to E. B. Jeffress, 19 July 1933, RLDP, Box 10.

54. Maurice H. Thatcher to HLI, 21 October 1933, CCF7B, Box 2713.

55. See Major John A. Bechtel, "[Illegible] to Smoky Park: Tennessee Rapidly Going Forward with Plans for Western Entrance but N.C. Has No Major Proposals, Scenic Beauty, Short Mileage Routes Sought," *Carolina Motor News*, June 1932, A1; R. L. Gwyn to RLD, 4 August 1932, JWBP, Box 310; R. L. Gwyn to JCBE, 20 February 1933, JCBEP, Box 152.

56. R. L. Gwyn to E. B. Jeffress, 5 August 1932, R. L. Gwyn to RLD, 4 August 1932, both in JWBP, Box 310; R. L. Gwyn to JCBE, 20 February 1933, JCBEP, Box 152.

57. R. L. Gwyn to JCBE, 20 February 1933, JCBE to R. L. Gwyn, 27 February 1933, both in JCBEP, Box 152; Maurice Thatcher to E. B. Jeffress, 19 July 1933, RLDP, Box 10. Gwyn did not specifically mention the budget-cutting, but North Carolina's depression governors O. Max Gardner and J. C. B. Ehringhaus responded to the economic collapse with drastic cuts in state spending and a new sales tax, introduced in 1933. See Badger, *North Carolina and the New Deal*, 8–12; Abrams, *Conservative Constraints*, 17, 190–213.

58. Abrams, *Conservative Constraints*, 205, reports that the 1933 North Carolina General Assembly limited State Highway Commission spending on construction to $190,000 per year while appropriating $6.9 million for maintenance.

59. J. G. Stikeleather to JWB, 30 April 1931, JWBP, Box 310; "Ledge of Eastern America, Great Smoky Divide Centers Park Interest and Grandeur," *Carolina Motor News*, June 1932, A6; Bechtel, "[Illegible] to Smoky Park"; FLW to JWB, 29 January 1932, JWBP, Box 310; Charles A. Webb to JWB, 25 October 1932, JWBP, Box 310; W. H. Hipps to JCBE, 31 August 1933, JCBEP, Box 152; R. L. Gwyn to JCBE, 20 February 1933, JCBEP, Box 152.

60. Simmons, "Creation," 63–67, 75–80, 83, 90, 150–52.

61. Ibid., 25, 32–33, 56, 86, 112–19, 122–44, 156–59, 167–69, 171–75, 182–85, 194–96, 199–203. On the forcible removal from the park of local (and long-established) residents, see Charles L. Perdue and Martin-Perdue, "Appalachian Fables and Facts"; Charles L. Perdue and Martin-Perdue, "'To Build a Wall.'"

62. Simmons's telling of the story indicates that at the very least park and highway planners had only a dim understanding of mountain residents' needs or desires in the midst of the Great Depression. See Simmons, "Creation," 53–54, 75–78, 15–28, 138–44, 158, 166–67.

63. Whisnant, "Finding the Way," 152 n. 8; FLW, Biographical Sketch, 15 February 1952, Fred Weede Envelopes, *Asheville Citizen-Times* Library, Asheville, North Carolina.

64. FLW to JWB, 29 January 1932, JWBP, Box 310.

65. FLW, "Battle for the Blue Ridge Parkway," 1–6, North Carolina Collection, Sondley Research Room, Pack Memorial Library, Asheville, North Carolina. Weede pegged Asheville's involvement in the project to a July 1933 conversation in which J. Quince Gilkey of Marion, North Carolina, gave Weede a newspaper clipping describing a meeting the day before in Richmond, Virginia, where public works official and engineer Theodore Straus had suggested that the PWA construct a scenic highway connecting the Shenandoah and Great Smoky Mountains National Parks. Weede recalled that PWA officials had described Straus's proposal to Virginia political leaders at a September 1933 meeting of the League of Virginia Municipalities and that Virginia Governor John Garland Pollard had then appointed a committee headed by Senator Byrd to promote the project to the federal government and the other states involved. Unfortunately, I have been unable to document the events Weede described. Other sources refer to the Shenandoah–Great Smoky Mountains parkway project beginning only in late September and early October 1933, and Straus figures only tangentially in the later documents I have found on parkway planning. It does indeed appear to be true, in any case, that the specifics of the project were first discussed among Virginians.

66. See Title II of Public Law 67 [H.R. 5755], 73rd Congress, National Industrial Recovery Act,

which authorized the PWA, in HLI, *Back to Work*, 235–55; see also Carr, *Wilderness by Design*, 258, 264–65.

67. For information on Ickes's career as a reform-oriented Progressive, see Jeanne Nienaber Clarke, *Roosevelt's Warrior*, 4, 9, 13, 15–16, 19–23, 25–28, 33, 60, 67, 98; Leuchtenburg, *Franklin D. Roosevelt and the New Deal*, 70–71; T. H. Watkins, *Righteous Pilgrim*, 371–72; HLI, *Back to Work*, 39, 48, 51, 56.

68. Jeanne Nienaber Clarke, *Roosevelt's Warrior*, 65–70, 96, 157–58; Isakoff, *Public Works Administration*, 20; T. H. Watkins, *Righteous Pilgrim*, 369–70; HLI, *Back to Work*, 39–40, 60–62, 73, 78.

69. Jeanne Nienaber Clarke, *Roosevelt's Warrior*, 97–100; HLI, *Back to Work*, 81, 256; Leuchtenburg, *Franklin D. Roosevelt and the New Deal*, 133–34; T. H. Watkins, *Righteous Pilgrim*.

70. HLI, *Back to Work*, 64.

71. John Garland Pollard to JCBE, 5 October 1933, JCBEP, Box 152; FLW, "Battle for the Blue Ridge Parkway"; Harry F. Byrd to SPW, 7 December 1953, BRPRG 5, Box 54; R. L. Gwyn to M. H. Thatcher, 4 September 1933, RLDP, Box 7. Ickes gave a brief account of this day in his diary but did not mention any discussion of a parkway to the Great Smoky Mountains park. See HLI, Diaries, Microfilm Edition, 12 August 1933, HIP. The earliest mention of the Parkway in any document I have collected is "Byrd Outlines Park Road Plan," AC, 28 September 1933, 3. The first report I have seen linking the parkway proposal to FDR's visit to the Shenandoah park is "Construction of Scenic Highway Connecting National Parks Proposed," ACT, 1 October 1933, B1. See also J. Q. Gilkey to JWB, 5 October 1933, JWBP, Box 311.

72. Harry F. Byrd to JCBE, 7 October 1933, JCBEP, Box 152; R. L. Gwyn to RLD, 26 October 1933, RGBP, Box 2. One example of the many telegrams Ehringhaus received is G. Foard to JCBE, 7 October 1933, JCBEP, Box 152, which noted that Gwyn "originated this idea five years ago and has been the most active promoter."

73. "Minutes of Meeting in Office of Senator Harry F. Byrd of Virginia," 17 October 1933, BRPRG 5, Box 59.

74. Ibid. For further discussion of this meeting, see CLW to ABC and File, 18 October 1933, CCF7B, Box 2713; "Want Ridge Road from Washington to 'Smokies'" RNO, 18 October 1933. The initial proposal also suggested that the parkway run from Washington, D.C., to the Shenandoah park, where it would connect with the Skyline Drive and then continue south to the Great Smoky Mountains, but the Washington-Shenandoah section was quickly dropped. See George L. Radcliffe, Thomas H. MacDonald, E. B. Jeffress, O. F. Goetz, H. G. Shirley, R. Y. Stuart, and ABC to HLI, 17 October 1933, HIP, Box 248. The small committee included Radcliffe (PWA regional director), MacDonald (BPR chief), Jeffress (chair of the North Carolina State Highway and Public Works Commission), Goetz (head of Tennessee's highway department), Shirley (head of the Virginia Department of Highways), Stuart (head of the National Forest Service), and Cammerer (NPS director). See also Harry F. Byrd to JCBE, 7 October 1933, JCBEP, Box 152.

75. HLI to George L. Radcliffe, 19 October 1933, CCF7B, Box 2713. Ickes's opposition to having the federal government completely bankroll the project was well publicized. See, for example, Walter Brown, "Ickes Wants State Aid on Road Project," AC, 27 October 1933; Maurice H. Thatcher to HLI, 21 October 1933, CCF7B, Box 2713.

76. HLI to Maurice H. Thatcher, 30 October 1933, ABC to Harvey Broome, 25 October 1933, both in CCF7B, Box 2713.

77. RLD to R. L. Gwyn, 25 October 1933, RLDP, Box 7; RLD to R. L. Gwyn, 28 October 1933, RGBP, Box 2. Representative Robert Doughton, who was from the North Carolina mountains, worked especially hard in Washington on the Parkway's behalf. Doughton's brother, Rufus A. Doughton, was one of the original members of the State Highway Commission established by the

state's landmark 1921 highway legislation and served as the commission's chair from 1929 to 1931. See CMW, *North Carolina Roads*, 1:40–41, 45, 75. Doughton, who had served North Carolina's western Ninth District in Congress since 1910, was by the 1930s chair of the House Ways and Means Committee and the state's most powerful voice in Congress. Unlike many of North Carolina's other politicians, Doughton strongly supported the New Deal. See Abrams, *Conservative Constraints*, 216–17, 258–59.

78. RLD to J. Q. Gilkey, 31 October 1933, RGBP, Box 2; RLD to JCBE, 11 November 1933, JCBEP, Box 152; RLD to R. L. Gwyn, 11 November 1933, RLDP, Box 7; "Park Roadway Plan Will Go to Roosevelt," AC, 11 November 1933, A1; "Scenic Parkway Seems Assured" [editorial], AC, 13 November 1933, 4; ABC to AED, 14 November 1933, HLI to ABC, 18 November 1933, both in CCF7B, Box 2713. News of the approval was made public a few days prior to this communiqué. See, for example, Walter Brown, "Ickes Gives Approval to Plan for Building Park-to-Park Highway," AC, 17 November 1933, 1. On Ickes, see Jeanne Nienaber Clarke, *Roosevelt's Warrior*, 107–14, 160–61.

79. FLW to JWB, 29 January 1932, JWBP, Box 310.

80. Harry F. Byrd to JCBE, 7 October 1933, JCBEP, Box 152; Hugh MacRae to RLD, 12 October 1933, FLW to RLD, 24 October 1933, both in RLDP, Box 7; "Minutes of Meeting," 17 October 1933.

81. JWB to E. B. Jeffress, 9 October 1933, RGBP, Box 1; Abrams, *Conservative Constraints*, xiv–xv.

82. Heinemann, *Depression and New Deal*, 6, 15, 46, 28, 78, 129–32, 136–39, 172, 181.

83. "Minutes of Meeting," 17 October 1933. On MacDonald, see Seely, *Building the American Highway System*, 3, 56.

84. See, for example, RLD to JCBE, 25 October 1933, RLDP, Box 7; statement of Reynolds in "Minutes of Meeting," 17 October 1933; R. L. Gwyn to RLD, 26 October 1933, RGBP, Box 2.

85. Cutler, *Public Landscape*, 51; Gilmore D. Clarke, "Parkway Idea," 33–39; Nolen and Hubbard, *Parkways and Land Values*, 83; Phil Patton, *Open Road*, 69.

86. Gilmore D. Clarke, "Parkway Idea," 40–41; Cutler, *Public Landscape*, 52. Some of the so-called parkways built in New York under Moses's direction in the 1930s include the Henry Hudson Parkway, the Grand Central Parkway, the Cross Island Parkway and Gowanus Parkway, and the Interborough Parkway.

87. Cutler, *Public Landscape*, 53; Gilmore D. Clarke, "Parkway Idea," 42; Jakle, *The Tourist*, 139; Timothy Davis, "Mount Vernon Memorial Highway."

88. Radde, *Merritt Parkway*, 2–11, 23, 40, 44–47, 54, 61–75, 83–93, 115–16, 123.

89. See Thomas H. MacDonald and AED, "Parkways of the Future: Radio Address," Delivered 13 April 1935, Transcript Dated 14 April 1935, BRPRG 7, Box 51; Jakle, *The Tourist*, 139. The Colonial Parkway originated prior to the Blue Ridge but was completed in the 1950s under the tutelage of Stanley Abbott. See Bennett, "Colonial Parkway."

90. MacDonald and AED, "Parkways of the Future."

91. Jakle, *The Tourist*, 129; Phil Patton, *Open Road*, 71–75.

92. DOI, NPS, "Regulations and Procedure to Govern the Acquisition of Rights-of-Way for National Parkways," 8 February 1935, SHCRWD, Box 1.

93. See NPS, Natchez Trace Parkway Brochure, 1996; U.S. Congress, Senate, *Natchez Trace Parkway Survey*, 143–45; Dilsaver, *America's National Park System*, 111–13.

94. Alexander McKee to JCBE, 13 October 1933, John M. Geary to JCBE, 12 October 1933, both in JCBEP, Box 152.

95. See Gidcomb, "History and the Natchez Trace Parkway"; Crutchfield, *Natchez Trace*; NPS, Natchez Trace Parkway Brochure; U.S. Congress, Senate, *Natchez Trace Parkway Survey*, 2–4.

96. For visitation figures on both parkways and all other NPS sites, see NPS, Public Use Statistics Office, "Visitation Statistics"; DOI, NPS, Public Use Statistics Office, *National Park Service Statis-*

tical *Abstract*. In 1999, the Blue Ridge Parkway was (as it had been for decades) the most visited site in the National Park System, with 19,836,842 travelers, while Natchez Trace was in seventh place with 6,392,961.

97. Jurisdictional lines — not always clear, even to the participants — are perhaps most succinctly explained in G. A. Moskey to Clyde F. Smith, 6 July 1936, CCF7B, Box 2728, which says, "[The NPS] provides the landscape supervision, the State provides the surveys and the parkway land, and the Bureau of Public Roads provides the engineering supervision for this project." See also Granville Liles, "History of the Blue Ridge Parkway," BRPRG 5, Box 48; HLI to ABC, 18 November 1933, TCV to ABC, December 1933, both in CCF7B, Box 2713; HLI to Colonel Waite, 30 November 1933, HIP, Box 249; TCV to AED, 13 January 1936, CCF7B, Box 2731; Acting Chief Architect, DOI, NPS, Branch of Plans and Design, to Hillory Tolson, 28 June 1937, CCF7B, Box 2720; *Congressional Record*, 74th Cong., 2d sess., 20 June 1936, 80, part 10, 10582–89, 10610–15, 10894–96; Walter Brown, "Park Service Is Given Control of Blue Ridge Drive," ACT, 21 June 1936, A1. On hiring requirements for workers, see DOI, NPS, "Bid, Bid Bond, Special Provisions, and Supplemental Specifications, Project 2D4, Blue Ridge Parkway," and Proposal of Federation Construction Company, Inc., Myrtle Beach, South Carolina, 10 February 1938, both in CCF7B, Box 2756; Secretary of Agriculture, WPA Administrator, and Franklin D. Roosevelt, "Rules and Regulations for Carrying Out the Provisions of the Emergency Relief Appropriation Act of 1935," 8 July 1935, POF 129, Box 1. On early funding, see "President Signs Order for Funds to Build Parkway," AC, 26 September 1935, 1, which describes Doughton's crucial role in convincing Roosevelt to restore public works funding for the project after it had been diverted when the work had been too slow to get under way.

98. "Work on Scenic Parkway Link to Begin Very Soon," *Alleghany Times*, 12 September 1935; "Parkway Started Monday above Lowgap," *Mt. Airy News*, 19 September 1935; J. P. Dodge to CMW, 21 September 1935, RGBP, Box 1; "Parkway Bids to Be Opened Today," *Watauga Democrat*, 24 October 1935.

99. DOI, NPS, "Regulations and Procedure"; Jakle, *The Tourist*, 135–37; Phil Patton, *Open Road*, 66.

100. DOI, NPS, "Regulations and Procedure"; EHA, "History of the Blue Ridge Parkway," 8 February 1948, BRPRG 5, Box 48.

101. DOI, NPS, "Regulations and Procedure."

102. Sutter, *Driven Wild*, 10.

103. Ibid., 3–4, 232.

104. Sutter, *Driven Wild*, foreword, vii–viii, 3–5, 10, 15–18.

105. Ibid., 5–6.

106. Ibid., 20–23, 26–53.

107. HC, Text of Speech, September 1919, HCP, Box 2; Leopold, "River."

108. Marshall quoted in Sutter, *Driven Wild*, 233.

109. Sutter, *Driven Wild*, 51–53, 98; Harvey Broome to HLI, 14 October 1933, CCF7B, Box 2711. See also MacCannell, "Staged Authenticity," 589–95.

110. Broome, "Wilds, Parkways, and Dollars," 46.

111. Carr, *Wilderness by Design*.

CHAPTER 2

1. JD, Diaries, 13, 14, 15 June 1934, JDP, Box 7 (Microfilm Reel, Diaries 5–6); "Notables Are Welcomed to WNC Area," AC, 16 June 1934, A1. On the Ickeses' unhappy marriage, see T. H. Watkins, *Righteous Pilgrim*, 147–51, 168–71, 219–20, 237, 408–10; Jeanne Nienaber Clarke, *Roosevelt's Warrior*, 342–45.

2. JD, Diaries, 15 June 1934, JDP.

3. Ibid.; Junius G. Adams to R. A. Doughton, 16 June 1934, POF 6p, Box 14.

4. R. L. Gwyn to RLD, 18 November 1933, FLW to RLD, 24 October 1933, John M. Geary to RLD, 6 December 1933, all in RLDP, Box 7; JWB to E. B. Jeffress, 31 October 1933, JWBP, Box 311.

5. George L. Radcliffe, Thomas H. MacDonald, E. B. Jeffress, O. F. Goetz, H. G. Shirley, R. Y. Stuart, and ABC to HLI, 17 October 1933, HIP, Box 248; "Construction of Scenic Highway Connecting National Parks Proposed," ACT, 1 October 1933, B1; FLW to JWB, 12 October 1933, JWBP, Box 311; FLW to RLD, 24 October 1933, 13 December 1933, both in RLDP, Box 7; FLW to ABC, 7 December 1933, CCF7B, Box 2713.

6. J. Q. Gilkey to RLD, 28 October 1933, RLDP, Box 7.

7. HLI to ABC, 18 November 1933, CCF7B, Box 2713.

8. Gilkey worked for years as the southeastern regional sales manager for a "noted snuff manufacturer" based in New York. He had also owned a furniture manufacturing company and a lake resort and had served on the boards of several Marion banks and businesses. His letterhead indicates that in the early 1930s, he was heading a company called Gilkey Homespun Weavers, which was said to manufacture "Genuine Hand-Loomed Homespun and Novelty Rugs." See J. Q. Gilkey to RLD, 28 October 1933, RLDP, Box 7. Another letterhead he used in the 1930s listed him as one of the owners of "Lake Tahoma" ("In the Shadow of Mt. Mitchell"). See J. Q. Gilkey to RLD, 19 December 1933, RLDP, Box 7. See also "J. Quince Gilkey," in North Carolina Biography, 100–101.

9. North Carolina Committee on Federal Parkway, "Description of a Route through North Carolina Proposed as a Part of the Scenic Parkway to Connect the Shenandoah National Park with the Great Smoky Mountains National Park," 1934, CCF7B, Box 2711; Mary F. Henderson, Social Register. On Randolph, see London, North Carolina Manual, 1933. On Hutchins, see London, North Carolina Manual, 1935.

10. On the weakness of this committee, see Charles A. Webb to JD, 21 September 1934, JDP, Box 676, Great Smoky Mountains File; FLW, "Battle for the Blue Ridge Parkway," 1957, 12–13, North Carolina Collection, Sondley Research Room, Pack Memorial Library, Asheville, North Carolina.

11. On Weede, see Whisnant, "Finding the Way," 152 n. 8; FLW, Biographical Sketch, 15 February 1952, Fred Weede Envelopes, Asheville Citizen-Times Library, Asheville, North Carolina. On the Florida land boom, see Ballinger, Miami Millions; Frazer and Guthrie, Florida Land Boom. According to Ballinger, Miami Millions, 67, Weede left the Chamber in 1925 for the real estate firm of Lee and Brooks in hopes of personally profiting from the land speculation fever that gripped the city.

12. FLW, Biographical Sketch; Whisnant, "Finding the Way," 136–37, 152–53. Keenly conscious of his place in Asheville's history, Weede in 1957 wrote a lengthy account of the Parkway routing battle, attached to it some relevant correspondence, had the whole thing nicely bound, and presented it (apparently with some fanfare) to the Asheville Public Library. See FLW, "Battle for the Blue Ridge Parkway." While this is one of the few accounts of events written by someone directly involved, it must be used with caution. Weede's transparent desire to magnify his role in the process colored it significantly, causing him to overlook many developments in which he was perhaps only tangentially involved and leading him to minimize the roles of some other participants. In addition, Weede was forced out of the Chamber managership in 1940 and thus may have sought to defend himself by justifying his actions.

13. FLW to RLD, 13 December 1933, RLD to R. L. Gwyn, 15 December 1933, both in RLDP, Box 7; FLW to ABC, 7 December 1933, CCF7B, Box 2713.

14. The important part that the Miami Herald played (in conjunction with the Miami Chamber of Commerce) in encouraging Florida's earlier boom is discussed in Ballinger, Miami Millions,

5–7. For information on Webb, see Powell, *Dictionary*, vol. 6; "Charles A. Webb Rites Set Tuesday," *Asheville Times*, 12 December 1949, 1; Charles A. Webb, *Fifty-eight Years*.

15. Charles A. Webb, *Fifty-eight Years*, 17; Powell, *Dictionary*, vol. 6; "Charles A. Webb Rites Set Tuesday"; "Big News for Us" [editorial], *AC*, 17 November 1933, A2; "In Loving Memory of Charles A. Webb" [editorial], *Asheville Times*, 12 December 1949, 4. The *Times* editorial noted that Webb "considered the establishment of the Great Smoky Mountains National Park and the Blue Ridge Parkway essential to the fulfillment of the great destiny he envisioned for Western North Carolina."

16. Hanchett, "Sorting Out the New South City," 312–27 (later published as Hanchett, *Sorting Out the New South City*).

17. Hanchett, "Sorting Out the New South City," 367–69.

18. Ibid., 340–42, 366–67, 370.

19. Ibid., 369–80.

20. Ibid., 387–88 (gives date of Stephens's move to Asheville as 1922); Bailey, *Fashionable Asheville*, 217–18 (gives date of Stephens's move as 1919).

21. Reak, *Kanuga*, 9–16. By the 1920s, Kanuga Lake was faltering, and Stephens sold it to the Episcopal Church for a summer assembly. See also "George Stephens, Builder" [editorial], *Asheville Times*, 2 April 1946, 4.

22. RGB to George Stephens, 28 January 1942, RGBP, Box 2; FLW, "Battle for the Blue Ridge Parkway," 7–8. Stephens was friendly enough with Ehringhaus to address the governor as "My dear Blucher" in his letters (George Stephens to JCBE, 12 February 1934, JCBEP, Box 152).

23. E. B. Jeffress, "The Modern State of North Carolina, 1776–1955," 1955, E. B. Jeffress Papers, Folder 159, Southern Historical Collection, University of North Carolina, Chapel Hill; FLW, "Battle for the Blue Ridge Parkway," 27–28.

24. North Carolina State Highway and Public Works Commission, "Press Release upon Retirement of R. Getty Browning," 27 July 1956, BRPRG 5, Box 59; "Engineer Browning Dies at 82," *AC*, 31 January 1966, A1; [RGB?], "Blue Ridge Parkway," 7 October 1953, Robert C. Browning Private Collection, Raleigh, North Carolina.

25. These impressions come from the following sources: Jolley, *Painting*; author's observations of presentation on history of Blue Ridge Parkway to campers at Crabtree Meadows Park by NPS Ranger Burgess, 3 August 1996; author's conversations with Blue Ridge Parkway interpretive specialist Phil Noblitt, March 1996. Carr, *Wilderness by Design*; Sellars, *Preserving Nature* also discuss the dominance of landscape architects in the NPS. See also Ian J. W. Firth, "Historic Resource Study: Blue Ridge Parkway, Virginia and North Carolina [Draft]," August 1993 (revised November 2004), Blue Ridge Parkway Headquarters, Asheville, North Carolina; Carlton Abbott et al., *Visual Character*.

26. Resident Landscape Architect [SWA], "Report: Proposed Locations, Shenandoah–Great Smoky Mountains National Parkway, to Chief Landscape Architect, National Park Service," 8 June 1934, CCF7B, Box 2711. Browning devoted significantly more of his professional life to work on the Blue Ridge Parkway than did Abbott. Abbott was a member of the Parkway staff from 1933 to 1943 and again from 1946 to 1949, after which he moved on to other positions within the NPS. Browning was involved with Parkway land acquisition from 1933 until his retirement in 1962.

27. Herndon, "Pathfinder."

28. Browning republished his grandfather's memoirs in 1942. See Meshach Browning, *Forty-four Years*; CMW, *North Carolina Roads*, 1:90–91. On the development of civil engineering programs in the South, see Preston, *Dirt Roads*, 25–26.

29. CMW, *North Carolina Roads*, 1:90–91.

30. Herndon, "Pathfinder," 30–31; CMW, *North Carolina Roads*, 1:91.

31. Robert McKee, "Parkway Group Inspects N.C. Route," ACT, 25 March 1934, 1; TCV to E. B. Jeffress, 18 April 1934, George L. Radcliffe to RGB, 4 June 1934, both in SHCRWD, Box 1; "Parkway Group off to Visit Mt. Mitchell," *Asheville Times*, 22 May 1934, 1; RGB to George L. Radcliffe, 1 June 1934, CCF7B, Box 2711.

32. George L. Radcliffe to RGB, 4 June 1934, Theodore E. Straus to RGB, 11 June 1934, both in SHCRWD, Box 1.

33. E. B. Jeffress to RLD, 14 June 1934, SHCRWD, Box 1; JD, Diaries, 14 June 1934, JDP; ABC to JD, 19 June 1934, JDP, Box 676, Great Smoky Mountains File.

34. RGB to George Stephens, 28 January 1942, RGBP, Box 2; CLW to ABC and File, 18 October 1933, CCF7B, Box 2713; RGB to George L. Radcliffe, 1 June 1934, CCF7B, Box 2711.

35. FLW to RLD, 24 October 1933, R. L. Gwyn to RLD, 13 December 1933, J. Q. Gilkey to RLD, 19 December 1933, all in RLDP, Box 7; FLW to ABC, 7 December 1933, CCF7B, Box 2713; "Favor Scenic Grandeur for Park Highway," ACT, 17 December 1933, 1. The first routing proposals made by various groups in western North Carolina had small variations, but nearly all included these spots. In particular, the section between Blowing Rock and Asheville never generated much debate, while the route between Asheville and the park took a little more discussion to determine.

36. RGB to George L. Radcliffe, 1 June 1934, CCF7B, Box 2711; North Carolina Committee, "Description of a Route." Weede indicated that Browning (with help from Highway Commission member Frank Miller of Waynesville) developed the route west of Asheville. See FLW, "Battle for the Blue Ridge Parkway." Weede also reported that he wrote most of the state's official pamphlet, which was published under the name of the governor's Parkway committee, but Browning almost certainly assisted, since the two essentially ran North Carolina's campaign together and since language similar to that in the pamphlet appears in Browning's correspondence. The pamphlet segment entitled "The Rugged and Wild Balsams" bears a strong resemblance to Browning's note that much of the scenery between Asheville and Soco was "extremely wild and rugged" in RGB to Theodore Straus, 17 January 1934, CCF7B, Box 2711.

37. FLW, "Battle for the Blue Ridge Parkway," 10–12.

38. Ibid., 10–12. An alternative plan put together by the Hendersonville Chamber of Commerce suggested a more southerly route coming from Asheville to Hendersonville, Cashiers, Highlands, and the Nantahala Gorge. See Southern Appalachian Parkway Committee, "Proposed Southern Appalachian Highway," 1934, CCF7B, Box 2711; Francis J. Heazel to Theodore Straus, 20 January 1934, CCF7B, Box 2711. Asheville attorney Heazel's letter noted that several western North Carolina communities had started movements to get the Parkway in their regions, and he asked Straus not to be swayed by them. By his account, the route supported by the Asheville partisans and endorsed by the Highway Commission was supported by most western North Carolinians and should receive consideration by the federal committee because it had been chosen "independent of any local sentiment."

It would be useful to have details concerning the day-to-day interaction between the Weede group and R. Getty Browning, but relevant records no longer exist. In the foreword to his memoir, Weede recounted that "when I resigned as Manager of the Asheville Chamber of Commerce in 1940 . . . I left complete records, not only of my own administration, but also [of the] nearly half a century old civic organization," but they were destroyed by his successors. Weede reported that much of what he was writing was based on extensive Chamber of Commerce documents "now lost forever."

Contemporaneous documents basically bear out Weede's assertion that most of the lobbying for the Parkway in North Carolina was carried on by representatives of the Asheville Chamber of Commerce. It is clear in the record that the state Parkway committee, Governor Ehringhaus, and Asheville's elected city leaders were not involved in day-to-day planning for bringing the Parkway into North Carolina, as the state committee recommended. State elected officials in Washington (particularly Representative Doughton), however, played a somewhat larger role.

39. FLW, "Battle for the Blue Ridge Parkway," 8. The federal committee that chose the Parkway route considered three different possibilities—one that would have been just in Virginia and Tennessee, one that would have included portions of all three states, and the one North Carolina advocated, which included portions only of Virginia and North Carolina. See Resident Landscape Architect [SWA], "Report: Proposed Locations, Shenandoah–Great Smoky Mountains National Parkway"; PWA, "The Shenandoah–Smoky Mountain Parkway and Stabilization Project: Proceedings of the Meetings Held in Baltimore, February 5, 6, 7, 1934," 23–27, CCF18, Box 2. The three-state route would have divided the non-Virginia mileage approximately equally between Tennessee and North Carolina.

40. Tennessee State Parks, "Roan Mountain State Park"; Resident Landscape Architect [SWA], "Report: Proposed Locations, Shenandoah–Great Smoky Mountains National Parkway"; Map of Tennessee Route (known as the Maloney Route after the Knoxville engineer who laid it out), in Jolley, Blue Ridge Parkway, 62–63.

41. George Stephens to JCBE, 21 December 1933, JCBEP, Box 152; FLW to RLD, 13 December 1933, RLDP, Box 7. On the deluge of routing requests pouring into federal offices, see letters in CCF7B, Box 2711. See also TCV to W. T. Kennerly, 29 January 1934, CCF7B, Box 2713.

42. "This State to Submit Route for Park Road," AC, 3 February 1934, A1; Snow, Highway and the Landscape, v–vi.

43. Birnbaum and Crowder, Pioneers, 6. Abbott did not initially favor the location of the Parkway along the North Carolina–sponsored route (Resident Landscape Architect [SWA], "Report: Proposed Locations, Shenandoah–Great Smoky Mountains National Parkway").

44. PWA, "Shenandoah–Smoky Mountain Parkway and Stabilization Project," 5–37.

45. Ibid., 1–3, 54. North Carolina's strategy was finalized in last-minute meetings in Raleigh that included Weede, Stephens, and members of the State Highway Commission and the state Parkway committee ("Joint Meeting Will Be Held in Raleigh," AC, 31 January 1934, 5; "Push Plans for Scenic Parkway: Governor to Head Group before Federal Officials," RNO, 1 February 1934).

46. PWA, "Shenandoah–Smoky Mountain Parkway and Stabilization Project," 5–6. For Ickes's language, see HLI to ABC, 18 November 1933, CCF7B, Box 2713. The contents of this letter were read into the record at the beginning of each day of the hearings. Furthermore, according to the official booklet outlining North Carolina's routing proposal, the North Carolinians also drew on former Secretary of the Interior Hubert Work's instructions for selection of the southern Appalachian national parks in the 1920s. Work had noted that the areas chosen for those parks should include "scenery of a quality so unusual and impressive or natural features so extraordinary, as to possess National interest and importance as contra-distinguished from local interest" (North Carolina Committee, "Description of a Route").

47. Robert McKee, "North Carolina Group Scores at Parkway Hearing," AC, 7 February 1934, A1.

48. PWA, "Shenandoah–Smoky Mountain Parkway and Stabilization Project," 7–18.

49. McKee, "North Carolina Group Scores," A1.

50. PWA, "Shenandoah–Smoky Mountain Parkway and Stabilization Project," 27, 34, 36, 43.

51. Ibid., 23, 29, 38.

52. Ibid., 26, 35.

53. Ibid., 33–34.

54. Dona Brown, Inventing New England, 204–5.

55. PWA, "Shenandoah–Smoky Mountain Parkway and Stabilization Project," 50. The quotation is from Ehringhaus's statement concluding North Carolina's presentation.

56. Ibid., 51.

57. PWA, "Shenandoah–Smoky Mountain Parkway and Stabilization Project," 5–19.

58. Ibid., 11, 23–38. At the hearing and elsewhere, Tennessee's partisans generally advocated the three-state route and did not push a route that would have excluded North Carolina. Indeed, Maloney explicitly ruled out such a proposal, stating that it would be fundamentally unfair. For newspaper reports of the hearings, see McKee, "North Carolina Group Scores," A1; "Senator McKellar's Outburst" [editorial], AC, 8 February 1934, 4; Robert McKee, "Implications of M'Keller Stir Hearing," AC, 8 February 1934, A1.

59. McKee, "North Carolina Group Scores," A1; PWA, "Shenandoah–Smoky Mountain Parkway and Stabilization Project," 17.

60. George Stephens to JCBE, 2 February 1934, 24 September 1934, JCBEP, Box 152; Walter Brown, "North Carolina Park Road Body Is Well Pleased," AC, 8 February 1934, A1; FLW to JWB, 10 February 1934, JWBP, Box 311; C. A. Unchurch Jr., "Smoky Mountain Parkway Will Pierce Paradise of Majestic Splendor," RNO, 18 November 1934; FLW, "Battle for the Blue Ridge Parkway."

61. Ready, Asheville, 35–39; Tooman, "Evolving Economic Impact," 218–32; Starnes, "Creating the Land," 102–50. Earlier access to Asheville had been provided via stagecoach on the Buncombe Turnpike, which linked Asheville to Greenville, South Carolina, and opened in 1828. See Langley and Langley, Yesterday's Asheville, 23. On mid-nineteenth-century tourists, see Blethen, "Antebellum Visitors."

62. Ready, Asheville, 35–40. Christian Reid was a pen name for Frances Fisher Tiernan. On the role of the late-nineteenth-century local-color writers and others in promoting the idea of the Appalachian region as a land apart from the rest of America, see Shapiro, Appalachia. On the implications of the widespread adoption of these views of Appalachia in the region's economic, political, social, and cultural development, see Whisnant, Modernizing the Mountaineer; Whisnant, All That Is Native and Fine; Batteau, Invention; Dunn, Cades Cove; Waller, Feud; J. W. Williamson, Hillbillyland; Harkins, Hillbilly; Pudup, Billings, and Waller, Appalachia; Ready, Asheville, 35–39; Langley and Langley, Yesterday's Asheville, 32, 34.

63. Tooman, "Evolving Economic Impact," 219; Ready, Asheville, 73–81; Langley and Langley, Yesterday's Asheville, 76.

64. Ready, Asheville, 43–45; Langley and Langley, Yesterday's Asheville, 34; Smith-McDowell House Museum, "George Willis Pack." On Frank Coxe, see University of North Carolina at Asheville Library, "Asheville and the Coxe Family."

65. Ready, Asheville, 46–49; Langley and Langley, Yesterday's Asheville, 34; Whisnant, "Finding the Way," 136; Mead, Asheville, 44.

66. Langley and Langley, Yesterday's Asheville, 57–58, 73; Ready, Asheville, 49, 81.

67. Tooman, "Evolving Economic Impact," 219; Ready, Asheville, 85–88.

68. Tooman, "Evolving Economic Impact," 219; Ready, Asheville, 85–88; Langley and Langley, Yesterday's Asheville, 58; Whisnant, "Finding the Way."

69. Mead, Asheville, 93–98. On the Pisgah Inn, see materials in BRPRG 5, Box 58; Touring the Great Smoky Mountains National Park and the Southland (Asheville, N.C.: Southland Tourist, 1933); "Paved Roads Lead from Asheville to Scenic Points of Interest," ACT, 10 June 1934, G8; "Asheville and Environs."

70. Reak, Kanuga, 13; "Ridgecrest—History"; "Town of Montreat"; YMCA Blue Ridge Assembly; Eastern National Park-to-Park Highway Magazine, Good Will Tour Edition; Bright W. Padgitt, "Motorists Find Carolina Mountains Wonderland of Scenic Splendor," ACT, 13 June 1937; Dixon, Wildacres; Finger, Cherokee Americans, 32.

71. Ready, *Asheville*, 85–91; Van Noppen and Van Noppen, *Western North Carolina*, 386–88.

72. Ready, *Asheville*, 91–92; Langley and Langley, *Yesterday's Asheville*, 99.

73. Ready, *Asheville*, 92; C. R. Sumner, "Expect Huge Increase in Western North Carolina Tourist Business," *ACT*, 10 June 1934, F1.

74. See Badger, *North Carolina*, 7–12, 61–73. On sources of relief funds in Asheville, see Community Chests and Councils, Asheville Community Chest Survey Bureau, and Citizens' Committee of One Hundred, *Welfare Portrait*, 10.

75. PWA, "Shenandoah–Smoky Mountain Parkway and Stabilization Project," 54. Stephens noted that the name of the project had been changed after the hearings. "My idea," he wrote, "is that the word 'Stabilization' was added for the benefit of North Carolina, for the reason that they can build around it the arguments from an economic standpoint for the route we proposed" (George Stephens to JCBE, 12 February 1934, JCBEP, Box 152). AED to HLI, 10 February 1934, CCF7B, Box 2711, recommended the name change and indicated that Stephens was correct in his surmise.

76. Jolley, *Blue Ridge Parkway*, chapter 6.

77. Reuben B. Robertson to E. B. Jeffress, 9 March 1934, R. L. Gwyn to E. B. Jeffress, 12 March 1934, E. B. Jeffress to R. L. Gwyn, 13 March 1934, J. Q. Gilkey to E. B. Jeffress, 14 March 1934, all in SHCRWD, Box 1; Robert McKee, "Parkway Group Inspects N.C. Route," *ACT*, 25 March 1934, 1.

78. "Locating the Scenic Parkway" [editorial], *ACT*, 25 March 1934, B2.

79. Ibid.

80. "The Scenic Parkway" [editorial], *ACT*, 4 February 1934, B6. Stephens's arguments at the hearing (PWA, "Shenandoah–Smoky Mountain Parkway and Stabilization Project," 30–32) closely paralleled the editorial, indicating that perhaps the speech and the editorial were prepared together.

81. PWA, "Shenandoah–Smoky Mountain Parkway and Stabilization Project," 30–32; "The Scenic Parkway."

82. PWA, "Shenandoah–Smoky Mountain Parkway and Stabilization Project," 32.

83. Ibid. ; "Mrs. Franklin D. Roosevelt is Here for Visit," *AC*, 4 July 1934, A1.

84. On the mythicization of Appalachia as a handicraft-bound region and the commercialization of regional handicraft production in the 1930s, see Becker, *Selling Tradition*; PWA, "Shenandoah–Smoky Mountain Parkway and Stabilization Project," 31–32; "Mrs. Franklin D. Roosevelt Is Here," A1.

85. Whisnant, *All That Is Native and Fine*, 5–16, 43, 110–18, 161–63; Whisnant, *Modernizing the Mountaineer*, xv–xii, 8, 272; Eller, *Miners, Millhands, and Mountaineers*; Shapiro, *Appalachia*, ix–xix, 18, 30–31, 188–89; Waller, *Feud*; J. W. Williamson, *Southern Mountaineers in Silent Films*; J. W. Williamson, *Hillbillyland*.

    The literary examples mentioned here are just a few of the numerous articles and books on Appalachian people that spilled forth from publishers from the 1850s forward. See, for example, Fee, "Kentucky"; Clingman, "Western North Carolina"; Harney, "Strange Land and Peculiar People"; Rebecca Harding Davis, "Rose of Carolina"; Woolson, "Up in the Blue Ridge"; Murfree, "Romance of Sunrise Rock"; Jones, "In the Highlands of North Carolina"; Murfree, *Prophet of the Great Smoky Mountains*; Warner, *On Horseback*; Fox, *Cumberland Vendetta*; Fox, *Kentuckians*; Frost, "Our Contemporary Ancestors"; Frost, "Southern Mountaineer"; Semple, "Anglo-Saxons of the Kentucky Mountains"; Wright, "In the Highlands of North Carolina"; Wilson, *Southern Mountaineers*; Erskine, "Handicraftsmen"; Furman, *Sight to the Blind*; Bradley, "Hobnobbing"; Branson, *Our Carolina Highlanders*; James A. Robinson, "Artistic Weaving"; Olive Dame Campbell and Sharp, *English Folk Songs*; Kephart, *Our Southern Highlanders*; Koch, *Carolina Folk*

Plays; Borah, "Patriotic Pilgrimage"; Cabell Phillips, "New Scenic Ridge Road: Three States Combining with Government to Build Motor Way," *New York Times*, 11 February 1934, section 20, p. 8. Shapiro's *Appalachia* contains a comprehensive bibliography of such writings from 1850 to 1922.

86. CLW, *Parks, Politics, and the People*, 50–51.

87. Pudup, Billings, and Waller, *Appalachia*, documents the diversity of nineteenth-century southern mountain experiences and development.

88. Whisnant, *All That Is Native and Fine*, 5–16, 68, 78, 110–18, 161–63; Becker, *Selling Tradition*, 74–93; Eller, *Miners, Millhands, and Mountaineers*; Shapiro, *Appalachia*, ix–xix, 18, 30–31 188–89; Whisnant, *Modernizing the Mountaineer*, 3–17; *Mountain Life and Work* (1925–); Blackwell P. Robinson, *North Carolina Guide*, 599; University of North Carolina at Asheville, "Biltmore Industries Archive."

89. Whisnant, *All That Is Native and Fine*, 68–93, 151–53, 172–74, 264; Shapiro, *Appalachia*, 122–32.

90. Miles, *Spirit of the Mountains*; MacDonald, "Mountaineers in Mill Villages"; John C. Campbell, "From Mountain Cabin to Cotton Mill"; Dawley, "Our Southern Mountaineers"; Ross, *Machine Age*; Alva Taylor, "Sub-Marginal Standards of Living."

91. Grattan, "Trouble in the Hills," 290–91.

92. Ibid., 291–92.

93. Ibid., 292–94; "In Memoriam: C. Hartley Grattan."

94. PWA, "Shenandoah–Smoky Mountain Parkway and Stabilization Project," 32–33; "The Scenic Parkway," B6. For a discussion of the impacts of rising land values on local citizens, see Appalachian Land Ownership Task Force, *Who Owns Appalachia?*, 96–99.

95. HC to JD, 2 June 1934, JDP, Box 215.

96. "Rhododendron Festival" [advertisement], ACT, 10 June 1934; George L. Radcliffe, Thomas H. MacDonald, and ABC to HLI, 13 June 1934, POF 6p, Box 14.

97. Junius G. Adams to R. A. Doughton, 16 June 1934, POF 6p, Box 14.

98. "North Carolina and the Parkway" [editorial], AC, 28 June 1934, 4; "Asheville and the Parkway," AC, 22 June 1934, A4.

99. HLI to AED, 12 February 1934, CCF7B, Box 2711. This reaction may not have been surprising, for although Ickes was "one of the best friends" the NPS ever had and a vigorous advocate of expanding the national parks system (overseeing the acquisition of forty-seven new park areas plus more than fifty other sites gained through administrative reorganization), he was also less likely than his predecessors to emphasize the parks' value in promoting increased tourism. Instead, he favored parks more for their value in promoting wilderness conservation and had serious reservations about continued road building within them. A recent biographer notes that "Ickes told his audiences that he intended to keep roads and tourist facilities in and around the national parks to an absolute minimum, because 'crowds and parks are incompatible'" (Jeanne Nienaber Clarke, *Roosevelt's Warrior*, 108–14). See also Sutter, *Driven Wild*, 230–34, on Ickes's close alliance with Wilderness Society founder (and Skyline Drive opponent) Robert Marshall, whom Ickes sent to investigate the Parkway routes in August 1934. Finally, Ickes's reputation for incorruptibility, strict fairness, and scrupulous objectivity in designating PWA projects did not bode well for those seeking to use behind-the-scenes influence to override the results of a six-month professional investigation.

That the Asheville partisans understood Ickes's personality and views is indicated, for example, in Don S. Elias to JWB, 16 June 1934, CCF7B, Box 2713. Elias, the *Citizen's* vice president, wrote to Bailey reiterating the Asheville partisans' point that a parkway bypassing the city and leaving out the rest of the suggested North Carolina route would "be of very mediocre scenic value." Elias noted that "Mr. Ickes is not the man to play politics or be influenced to any great extent by them, and if the recommendations on this highway [from the Radcliffe Committee] are adverse to the arguments above I feel that the large national aspect and non-political viewpoint should be urged upon the Secretary of the Interior."

100. FLW, "Battle for the Blue Ridge Parkway," 40–45. Weede indicates that Daniels, though supportive of the Parkway, had to be cajoled into using his influence with Ickes and FDR, but Daniels's dairy entries from the time do not suggest such reluctance.

101. JD, Diaries, 16–18 June 1934, JDP.

102. FLW, "Battle for the Blue Ridge Parkway," 43–44; JD, Diaries, 25 June 1934, 18 June 1934, JDP; JD to HLI, 22 June 1934, HIP, Box 170; Walter Brown, "Hearing Will Be Held on W.N.C. Parkway Routes," AC, 22 June 1934, A1; "Parkway Case Will Be Laid before Ickes," AC, 23 June 1934, A1; "May Disclose New Parkway Route Today," AC, 24 June 1934, 1. See also "Strong Delegation on Parkway Trip Foreseen," ACT, 24 June 1934, 1; JWB to JCBE, 27 June 1934, JCBEP, Box 152; Walter Brown, "North Carolina Hearing on Parkway Postponed," AC, 27 June 1934, A1; JWB to Robert Lathan, 27 June 1934, JWBP, Box 312; JD, Diaries, 25–26 June 1934, JDP; RLD to Zebulon Weaver, 27 June 1934, RLDP, Box 10; HLI to RGB, 28 June 1934, HIP, Box 170.

103. JD to Franklin D. Roosevelt, 25 August 1934, POF 6p, Box 14; JD, Diaries, 26 June 1934, JDP. For Daniels's familiarity with the president, see, for example, JD to Franklin D. Roosevelt, 2 March 1934, CCF7B, Box 2713.

104. JD to HLI, 1 August 1934, JD to Franklin D. Roosevelt, 25 August 1934, HLI to Franklin D. Roosevelt, 1 September 1934, Franklin D. Roosevelt to HLI, 3 September 1934, all in POF 6p, Box 14.

105. JWB to Don S. Elias, 27 June 1934, JWB to JCBE, 27 June 1934, JWB to Robert Lathan, 27 June 1934, 12 July 1934, all in JWBP, Box 312; RLD to George Stephens, 3 July 1934, RLDP, Box 10. To Webb, Daniels wrote reassuringly that "I came away fully assured that the wrong about to be done to our entrance of the park would not be consummated" (JD to Charles A. Webb, 24 July 1934, JDP, Box 676, Great Smoky Mountains File). For a later account of the secrecy surrounding the Daniels initiative, see FLW, "Battle for the Blue Ridge Parkway," 40–45.

106. "North Carolina and the Parkway," 4. Another editorial emphasized that Tennessee had already benefited from considerable New Deal largesse in the form of the Tennessee Valley Authority and other appropriations and that North Carolina had not received aid proportionate to its federal tax contributions ("North Carolina: Red-Headed Stepchild," ACT, 19 August 1934, B2).

107. Charles A. Webb to JWB, 11 July 1934, JWBP, Box 312; Charles A. Webb to JD, 17 July 1934, JDP, Box 676, Great Smoky Mountains File; Charles A. Webb to E. B. Jeffress, 18 July 1934, SHCRWD, Box 1; "Reynolds Voices Plea for Parkway Interest," AC, 7 September 1934, A11.

108. JD to HLI, 1 August 1934, JD to Franklin D. Roosevelt, 25 August 1934, both in POF 6p, Box 14; JD to RGB, 22 August 1934, SHCRWD, Box 1; JD to RGB, 13 September 1934, JDP, Box 676, Great Smoky Mountains File.

109. JD to RGB, 22 August 1934, RGB to HLI, 15 August 1934, both in SHCRWD, Box 1; JD to HLI, 1 August 1934, JD to Franklin D. Roosevelt, 25 August 1934, both in POF 6p, Box 14; JD to HLI, 6 September 1934, JDP, Box 84, Harold Ickes Files; "Part of Parkway Route Announced," Baltimore Sun, 20 July 1934; Walter Brown, "Route for Parkway Is Designated as Far as Blowing Rock in N.C.," AC, 20 July 1934, 1.

110. Margaret Lynn Brown, Wild East, 83–87; Pierce, Great Smokies, 57.

111. George Stevens to JCBE, December 21, 1933, JCBEP, Box 152.

112. E. G. Frizzell to T. E. Straus, April 12, 1934, CCF7B, Box 2711; Margaret Lynn Brown, Wild East, 79, 88, 133, 174, 178; Sutter, Driven Wild, 3–18, 178, 187–90, 232–33, 241.

113. McDonald and Wheeler, Knoxville, 8, 14–26, 38, 41, 51, 54–55, 60–62; "Five Buildings under Way on Henley Street," Knoxville News-Sentinel, 13 August 1933, B8; Pierce, Great Smokies, 57–58; "Plane Factory Planned Here," Knoxville News-Sentinel, 18 August 1933, A1.

114. See Selznick, *TVA and the Grass Roots*; Whisnant, *Modernizing the Mountaineer*, 43–69.

115. "The Valley Gets Action," *Knoxville News-Sentinel*, 1 August 1933, A4; "TVA Leases 106 Offices in Knoxville," *Knoxville News-Sentinel*, 2 August 1933, A1; "50,000 Job Applications Filed with TVA Office," *Knoxville News-Sentinel*, 22 August 1933, A3; "TVA to Start Final Tests This Week on Site of Dam," *Knoxville News-Sentinel*, 28 August 1933, A1; "Dynamite Blasts open TVA Dam Work," *Knoxville News-Sentinel*, 31 August 1933, A1.

116. "TVA Sets Low Municipal Power Rates," *Knoxville News-Sentinel*, 14 September 1933, A1; "New Deal in Power," *Knoxville News-Sentinel*, 15 September 1933, A4.

117. "Knoxville to Vote on Public Power Issue on Nov. 25," *Knoxville News-Sentinel*, 1 October 1933, A1; "Begin Actual Construction at Norris Dam," *Knoxville News-Sentinel*, 9 November 1933, A1, 7; "City Power System Will Save Citizens $14,000,000 in 15 Years, Engineers Say," *Knoxville News-Sentinel*, 3 November 1933, A1; Steve Humphrey, "City Votes TVA Power Two to One," *Knoxville News-Sentinel*, 26 November 1933, 1; "First Money Is Given Road to Link Parks," *Knoxville News-Sentinel*, 8 December 1933, 10; "We Must Do Big Things in Return," *Knoxville News-Sentinel*, 8 December 1933, 4.

118. "TVA Offers $6,550,000 for TPS Plant," *Knoxville News-Sentinel*, 13 June 1934, 1, 3; "Mountain Road, $16 Million Job, to Start at Once," *Richmond Times-Dispatch*, 17 November 1933; Jolley, *Blue Ridge Parkway*, 44.

119. Resident Landscape Architect [SWA], "Report: Proposed Locations, Shenandoah–Great Smoky Mountains National Parkway"; TCV to NPS Director, 8 June 1934, CCF7B, Box 2711.

120. Resident Landscape Architect [SWA], "Report: Proposed Locations, Shenandoah–Great Smoky Mountains National Parkway."

121. RGB to George L. Radcliffe, 1 June 1934, CCF7B, Box 2711.

122. Ibid.

123. AED to RGB, 31 August 1934, CCF7B, Box 2714; AED to J. Ross Eakin, 31 August 1934, CCF7B, Box 2739; Walter Brown, "Ickes Decides against Going on Inspection," AC, 7 September 1934, A1; Sutter, *Driven Wild*, 231–34.

124. RGB to JD, 8 September 1934, JDP, Box 676, Great Smoky Mountains File; FLW to JWB, 8 September 1934, in FLW, "Battle for the Blue Ridge Parkway"; Charles A. Webb to JWB, 10 September 1934, JWBP, Box 312; George Stephens to JCBE, 11 September 1934, JCBEP, Box 152; "On to Washington!" [advertisement], AC, 16 September 1934, C10; "Expect 200 on Parkway Train from This State," ACT, 16 September 1934, A1; "Delegation off for Hearing on Parkway Today," AC, 18 September 1934, A1; Robert E. Williams, "Opposing Claims to Park Highway Put before Ickes," RNO, 19 September 1934; Robert McKee, "N.C. Presses Claims for Parkway at Hearing," AC, 19 September 1934, A1; Charles A. Webb to JD, 21 September 1934, JDP, Box 676, Great Smoky Mountains File.

125. "Delegation off for Hearing," A1; "State Parkway Case Outlined at Conference," AC, 18 September 1934, A1; Federal Emergency Administration on Public Works, "Hearing in Re: Route of Proposed Scenic Parkway Connecting Shenandoah and Great Smoky Mountains National Parks," CCF7B, Box 2712; Williams, "Opposing Claims."

126. Federal Emergency Administration on Public Works, "Hearing in Re: Route of Proposed Scenic Parkway."

127. Ibid.

128. Ibid.; McKee, "N.C. Presses Claims," A1; "Tennesseans Reveal Ickes's Committee Reported That Two-State Route Was Best," *Knoxville News-Sentinel*, 19 September 1934, 10.

129. David C. Chapman to HLI, 18 September 1934, JCBEP, Box 152; "Tennessee Loses Park-to-Park Road," *Knoxville News-Sentinel*, 12 November 1934, 1, 14.

130. David C. Chapman to HLI, 18 September 1934, JCBEP, Box 152.

131. Charles A. Webb to ABC, 20 September 1934, CCF7B, Box 2714. Ehringhaus apparently also favored a loop or fork proposal. See Albert L. Cox to JCBE, 19 September 1934, JCBE to Albert L. Cox, 21 September 1934, both in JCBEP, Box 152.

A flurry of correspondence in the aftermath of the hearing on the possibility of a forked Parkway indicates that most of the principal Asheville-based supporters, with the special encouragement of Bailey, were now pushing the fork solution. See George Stephens to JD, 20 September 1934, Charles A. Webb to JD, 21 September 1934, both in JDP, Box 676, Great Smoky Mountains File; Robert Lathan to JWB, 21 September 1934, 10 October 1934, JWB to Robert Lathan, 24 September 1934, JWB to Harry Slattery, 27 September 1934, all in JWBP, Box 312. See also FLW to Gilliland Stikeleather, 17 October 1934, POF 6p, Box 14.

For the Radcliffe Committee's discussion of a possible fork, see George L. Radcliffe, Thomas H. MacDonald, and ABC to HLI, 13 June 1934, POF 6p, Box 14. The report suggested that the new Parkway be thought of as "a unit in a National Parkway to serve the entire chain of Atlantic States" and that as such, the recommended route would allow for a forking at the Great Smoky Mountains National Park, with "one fork continuing on in Tennessee connecting with [the] Natchez Trail toward New Orleans, and the other branching toward Atlanta and Florida. The fork might also be placed in the vicinity of Grandfather Mountain utilizing much of the route proposed in North Carolina to the south of Asheville." According to the North Carolinians, if they had known of this portion of the Radcliffe Committee's recommendations, they would have argued for the forked parkway instead of asking for exclusive construction of their own route. See also Robert Lathan to HLI, 21 September 1934, CCF7B, Box 2714.

132. George Stephens to JD, 20 September 1934, Charles A. Webb to JD, 21 September 1934, both in JDP, Box 676, Great Smoky Mountains File; Robert Lathan to HLI, 21 September 1934, CCF7B, Box 2714.

133. RGB to JD, 22 September 1934, JDP, Box 676, Great Smoky Mountains File.

134. JCBE to HLI, 25 September 1934, JCBEP, Box 152. Ehringhaus almost certainly did not write the brief. Bailey reported that Browning was the author but that both Bailey and Stephens offered suggestions. See JWB to RGB, 21 September 1934, JWB to Robert Lathan, 24 September 1934, both in JWBP, Box 312; George Stephens to JCBE, 24 September 1934, JCBEP, Box 152.

135. HLI to JD, 2 October 1934, HLI to JD, 24 September 1934, both in JDP, Box 84, Harold Ickes Files. See also JD to Charles A. Webb, 25 September 1934, JD to George Stephens, 26 September 1934, both in JDP, Box 676, Great Smoky Mountains File. It is unclear how much Browning knew about Daniels's conversations with Ickes and Roosevelt in June 1934. He and Daniels certainly were the two men most intimately involved in making those contacts, and Browning followed up Daniels's visits with his own conferences with Ickes. Writing to Browning in September, Daniels mentioned few specifics, saying only that he was "confident when the final decision is made that the representations we made to Secretary Ickes will have full weight in his mind and that North Carolina will be treated fairly" (JD to RGB, 28 September 1934, JDP, Box 676, Great Smoky Mountains File). For Ickes's account of the September events, see HLI, Diaries, 20 September 1934, HIP.

136. Robert Lathan to HLI, 21 September 1934, CCF7B, Box 2714; Tooman, "Evolving Economic Impact," 296, 491.

137. Tooman, "Evolving Economic Impact." On development of the Land of the Sky image for Asheville, see Starnes, *Creating the Land*.

138. Tooman, "Evolving Economic Impact," 222–24, 231, 233, 252, 255, 259, 313, 494; Charles A. Webb, *Fifty-eight Years*, 13–15.

139. Ready, *Asheville*, 92; Charles A. Webb, *Fifty-eight Years*, 13–15; Tooman, "Evolving Economic Impact," 231, 255.

140. Tooman, "Evolving Economic Impact," 229, 252–55, 259, 295–96, 300, 313, 345.

141. Robert Lathan, typed manuscript regarding arguments for putting Parkway through Asheville, November 1934, POF 6p, Box 14.

142. Ickes's official announcement was carried in a letter to Governor Ehringhaus: HLI to JCBE, 10 November 1934, JCBEP, Box 152. A copy was released to the press on 12 November 1934 (DOI, "Memorandum for the Press," 12 November 1934, CCF7B, Box 2713).

143. HLI to JCBE, 10 November 1934, JCBEP, Box 152.

144. Charles A. Webb to JWB, November 15, 1934, JWBP, Box 312; "Tennessee Loses" [editorial], *Knoxville News-Sentinel*, 13 November 1934, 4; "McAlister Sees No Recourse from Ruling," *Knoxville News-Sentinel*, 12 November 1934, 14; Kenneth D. McKellar to Franklin D. Roosevelt, November 1934, POF 6p, Box 14; HLI, Diaries, 19 November 1934, HIP.

145. See, for example, "People Here Receive News with Delight," AC, 13 November 1934, A1. My findings here directly contradict the long-standing conventional wisdom that the Parkway was designed primarily as a relief project to aid out-of-work mountaineers.

146. Walter Brown, "Ickes' Decision Placing Route for Parkway in N.C. Hailed as Great Victory by Entire State," AC, 13 November 1934, A1. All quotations are from "People Here Receive News with Delight," A1.

147. "Shoulder to Shoulder and Eyes to the Front" [editorial], AC, 14 November 1934, A4; "The Parkway Decision" [editorial], AC, 13 November 1934, A4; "Editorial Comment on Routing of Scenic Parkway," AC, 15 November 1934.

148. "Surveys Will Be Started on Parkway Soon," AC, 13 November 1934, A1; "W.N.C. Leaders Highly Pleased over Decision," AC, 13 November 1934, A1; Jolley, *Blue Ridge Parkway*, 50–56.

149. Miles, *Spirit of the Mountains*, 191–200.

150. Becker, "Selling Tradition," 247, 250–324.

151. *Impact of Recreational Development*, 27, 35.

152. Tooman, "Evolving Economic Impact," abstract, 345, 488–89, 496.

153. Ibid., 231, 255, 494–95.

154. Weede explicitly thanked Browning and the rest of the staff at the North Carolina Highway Commission in his remarks quoted in the *Citizen* after the routing decision was announced ("People Here Receive News with Delight," A1). Stephens also acknowledged Browning's role in several letters and encouraged publicity for the engineer, who was hoping for a promotion (which he did not receive) to the Highway Commission's top staff position, chief engineer (George Stephens to Jonathan Daniels, 17 November 1934, George Erwin Cullet Stephens Papers, Folder 4, Southern Historical Collection, University of North Carolina, Chapel Hill). A long article on Browning's role also appeared in the Raleigh newspaper: C. A. Upchurch Jr., "Smoky Mountain Parkway Will Pierce Paradise of Majestic Splendor," RNO, 18 November 1934.

155. Ralph Howland, "Mr. Browning Moves Mountains; Once Even Changed Ickes' Mind," *Charlotte Observer*, 22 February 1953, D18.

156. RGB to HC, 3 July 1935, SHCRWD, Box 1.

CHAPTER 3

1. S. A. Miller to Franklin D. Roosevelt, 7 January 1937, CCF7B, Box 2731.

2. Jolley, *Painting*; SWA, interview, BRPLIB; NPS, "Lying Lightly."

3. EHA, interview, BRPLIB; Division of Resource Planning and Professional Services, BRP, "Blue Ridge Parkway Statement for Management," June 1988, BRPRG 5, Box 1.

4. U.S. Census Bureau, *Fifteenth Census*, table 3, 1:782–83; Foster, *Past Is Another Country*, 19, 145.

5. U.S. Census Bureau, *Census of Agriculture*, table 1, 448–56; U.S. Census Bureau, *Fifteenth Census*, table 20, vol. 3, part 2, 374–87; Foster, *Past Is Another Country*, 19, 25.

6. Virginia highway officials believed that state law required them to grant landowner access to the Parkway (C. K. Simmers to G. A. Moskey, 23 February 1938, CCF7B, Box 2731).

7. Ian J. W. Firth, "Historic Resource Study: Blue Ridge Parkway, Virginia and North Carolina [Draft]," August 1993 (revised November 2004), Blue Ridge Parkway Headquarters, Asheville, North Carolina; Lord, *Blue Ridge Parkway Guide.*

8. The analysis in the section that follows is based on the 1930 Census. On North Carolina, see U.S. Census Bureau, *Fifteenth Census,* table 13, vol. 3, part 2, 353–59, table 3, 1:782–83, table 14, vol. 3, part 2, 360–66, table 20, vol. 3, part 2, 374–87; U.S. Census Bureau, *Census of Agriculture,* table 1, 448–56. On Virginia, see U.S. Census Bureau, *Fifteenth Census,* table 3, vol. 1:1120–21, table 13, vol. 3, part 2, 1161–68, table 20, vol. 3, part 2, 1182–96; U.S. Census Bureau, *Census of Agriculture,* table 1, 448–56.

9. SWA, "Shenandoah–Great Smoky Mountains National Parkway," 26 June 1935, CCF7B, Box 2715; DOI Information Service, NPS, "Press Release on Blue Ridge Parkway," 28 April 1940, POF 200, Box 56.

10. DOI, "Memorandum for the Press," 15 April 1938, CCF18, Box 2; Sheila Gasperson, E-mail to Author, 18 August 2004. No county lost more than a small percentage of its lands to the project, however—less than 1.6 percent in the twelve Virginia counties as of the late 1970s (and less than 0.8 percent in eight counties). In North Carolina at the same time, the Parkway owned nearly 3 percent of all lands in two counties (Alleghany and Watauga) where large recreation areas were located but owned barely 1.3 percent in the remaining counties (NPS, BRP, "Land Acquisition Program Briefing Statement, Blue Ridge Parkway, Virginia–North Carolina," 6 March 1979, BRPRG 7, Box 54).

11. NPS, BRP, "Land Acquisition Program Briefing Statement"; Sheila Gasperson, E-mail to Author, 30 August 2004. For early summary figures, see SPW to NPS Region 1 Director, 18 September 1943, BRPRG 7, Box 5; Granville Liles, "History of the Blue Ridge Parkway," BRPRG 5, Box 48; NPS, BRP, "Blue Ridge Parkway Statistics," June 1975, BRPRG 7, Box 52; Division of Resource Planning and Professional Services, BRP, "Blue Ridge Parkway Statement for Management." Acreage figures and costs for the 1930s are discussed in SPW to NPS Region 1 Director, 18 September 1943, SWA to NPS Director, 4 November 1943, both in BRPRG 7, Box 5. The latter document gives acreage figures for "lands acquired by purchase" for every Parkway county in North Carolina, yielding a total of 20,386 acres, while the former letter breaks down land acquisition by the agency that obtained the lands. Cost figures for North Carolina are from RGB to Hillory A. Tolson, 25 February 1944, RGBP, Box 4; NPS, BRP, "Land Acquisition Program Briefing Statement."

12. SPW to NPS Region 1 Director, 19 September 1943, BRPRG 7, Box 5; SPW to NPS Director, 10 May 1940, CCF7B, Box 2733; EHA, "History of the Blue Ridge Parkway," 8 February 1948, BRPRG 5, Box 48; DOI, NPS, "Regulations and Procedure to Govern the Acquisition of Rights-of-Way for National Parkways," 8 February 1935, SHCRWD, Box 1.

13. Acting Chief Architect, DOI, NPS, Branch of Plans and Design, to Hillory Tolson, 28 June 1937, CCF7B, Box 2720.

14. NPS, "Great Smoky Mountains National Park Facts"; Frome, *Strangers,* 202; Margaret Lynn Brown, "Smoky Mountains Story," 140; Dunn, *Cades Cove,* 251; Division of Resource Planning and Professional Services, BRP, "Blue Ridge Parkway Statement for Management," 29; J. P. Dodge to Frank L. Dunlap, 9 January 1940, SHCRWD, Box 8. Several maps are also useful, all in BRPLF: NPS and North Carolina State Highway and Public Works Commission, "Map of Lands Acquired for the Blue Ridge Parkway: Ashe and Wilkes Counties from N.C. Route no. 18 to Horse Gap," 4 March 1940; DOI and North Carolina State Highway and Public Works Commission, "Map of Lands Acquired for the Blue Ridge Parkway: Alleghany and Wilkes Counties

from U.S. Route no. 21 to Air Bellows Gap," 15 June 1937; NPS and Virginia Department of Highways, "Map of Lands Acquired for the Blue Ridge Parkway: Floyd and Patrick Counties from Tuggle Gap to Rock Castle Gap," 15 January 1941. For construction, the Parkway was divided into forty-five units, each assigned a section number. Virginia section numbers began with 1, while North Carolina section numbers began with 2.

15. Early reports giving the two-hundred-foot figure include "U.S. to Approve Skyline Drive, Ickes Declares," *Richmond Times-Dispatch*, 11 November 1933; RLD to JCBE, 11 November 1933, JCBEP, Box 152; "The Park to Park Highway" [editorial], AC, 11 November 1933, 4; "Scenic Route Is Approved by Roosevelt," *Richmond Times-Dispatch*, 12 November 1933; "Scenic Parkway Seems Assured" [editorial], AC, 13 November 1933, 4; "Mountain Road, $16 Million Job, to Start at Once," *Richmond Times-Dispatch*, 17 November 1933; "Ickes' Approval of Great Scenic Road Claimed," *Washington Post*, 17 November 1933; "Ickes Approves Scenic Highway," RNO, 17 November 1933; "Favor Scenic Grandeur for Park Highway," ACT, 17 December 1933, 1; "This State to Submit Route for Park Road," AC, 3 February 1934, A1. The "Minutes of Meeting in Office of Senator Harry F. Byrd of Virginia," 17 October 1933, BRPRG 5, Box 59, however, report that the official proposal sent to Ickes asked for one thousand feet. See also HLI to ABC, 18 November 1933, CCF7B, Box 2713.

16. ABC to Harlean James, 9 December 1933, Frank A. Kittredge to ABC, 6 January 1934, CLW to Frank A. Kittredge, 19 January 1934, all in CCF7B, Box 2713; C. K. Simmers to AED, 7 July 1934, CCF7B, Box 2714.

17. HLI to AED, 17 July 1934, CCF7B, Box 2714; AED, TCV, H. J. Spelman, and C. K. Simmers, "Rights of Way and Scenic Easements on Parkway," 3 August 1934, CCF7B, Box 2711; Thomas H. MacDonald to E. B. Jeffress, 8 August 1934, SHCRWD, Box 1.

18. The one hundred acres in fee simple and fifty acres in scenic easements policy is set in DOI, NPS, "Regulations and Procedure." See also EHA, "History of the Blue Ridge Parkway." This policy is also discussed in DOI, NPS, "Requirements and Procedure to Govern the Acquisition of Land for National Parkways," 9 June 1941, BRPRG 7, Box 51; Granville Liles, "History of the Blue Ridge Parkway," BRPRG 5, Box 48. See also C. K. Simmers to NPS Director, 1 April 1935, BRPRG 7, Box 5; SPW to NPS Director, 10 May 1940, CCF7B, Box 2733.

19. Original stipulations given in HLI to ABC, 18 November 1933, CCF7B, Box 2713. As late as November 1934, the *Asheville Citizen* continued to report that the parkway's right-of-way would be two hundred feet wide (Walter Brown, "Ickes' Decision Placing Route for Parkway in N.C. Hailed as Great Victory by Entire State," AC, 13 November 1934, A1). The first public report I have seen that mentions land acquisition beyond the two-hundred-foot limit is C. A. Upchurch Jr., "Smoky Mountain Parkway Will Pierce Paradise of Majestic Splendor," RNO, 18 November 1934. This article stated that a right-of-way two hundred feet wide would be taken but that there would need to be five hundred to one thousand feet of "protected area" on either side of the highway to prevent unsightly development. The article did not, however, detail how this "protected area" was to be obtained. As late as March 1935, officials at the North Carolina Highway Commission were still confused about the amounts of right-of-way and easement they would be expected to acquire. Highway Commission Chair Capus M. Waynick reported this puzzlement to federal officials in CMW to H. J. Spelman, 4 March 1935, BPRRG 7, Box 5. Doughton reiterated several times the idea that landowners would donate their property (RLD to D. W. Adams, 9 December 1933, RLDP, Box 7; RLD to JCBE, 11 November 1933, JCBEP, Box 152).

20. SWA, "Annual Report of the Blue Ridge Parkway, Roanoke, Va., to the Director, National Park Service," 30 June 1938, CCF7B, Box 2717; EHA, "History of the Blue Ridge Parkway"; SPW, in-

terview, BRPLIB; RGB, interview, National Park Service, Harpers Ferry Center Library, Harpers Ferry, West Virginia.

21. Turner, *Paving Tobacco Road*, 1–45.

22. The state legislature affirmed this standard in 1937, amending the 1935 law that authorized the Highway Commission to proceed with land acquisition for the Parkway under its existing eminent domain procedures. The acquisition law for North Carolina is "North Carolina General Statutes, Chapter 136," § 19(g). See also C. K. Simmers to NPS Director, 1 April 1935, BRPRG 7, Box 5; SWA to AED, 19 April 1935, BRPRG 7, Box 7.

23. EHA, interview, BRPLIB; "Virginia's Sit-Down Strike" [editorial], *Roanoke World-News*, reprinted in *Richmond Times-Dispatch*, 23 June 1938; "Virginia Lags Behind" [editorial], *Roanoke World-News*, 16 April 1938; "The Parkway Deadlock" [editorial], *Roanoke World-News*, 16 February 1939.

24. Heinemann, *Harry Byrd*, 33, 42; Turner, *Paving Tobacco Road*, 12–13; Bowman, *Highway Politics*, 29–30.

25. Heinemann, *Harry Byrd*, 47, 104, 176; Bowman, *Highway Politics*, 33.

26. SWA, interview.

27. H. G. Shirley to H. J. Spelman, 18 October 1935, H. G. Shirley to HLI, 23 January 1935, H. G. Shirley to George C. Peery, 7 February 1935, George C. Peery to Louis Spilman, 5 May 1935, all in George C. Peery Papers, Box 41, Library of Virginia, Richmond; RGB, interview; H. G. Shirley to HLI, 26 September 1934, CCF7B, Box 2736; Virginia Department of Highways, 1942 *Supplement*; "Shirley Hopes to See Scenic Road Finished," *Richmond News-Leader*, 1 March 1935, 1; C. K. Simmers to NPS Director, 1 April 1935, BRPRG 7, Box 5.

28. SWA to AED, 19 April 1935, SWA to TCV, 17 December 1935, C. K. Simmers to AED, 20 November 1935, all in BRPRG 7, Box 7; George C. Peery to Louis Spilman, 5 May 1935, H. G. Shirley to H. J. Spelman, 18 October 1935, both in Peery Papers, Box 41.

29. In November 1935, another legal obstacle was removed with the Supreme Court's refusal in *Via v. Virginia* to overturn a state court ruling allowing the state to condemn and deed to the federal government lands for the Shenandoah National Park. See "State's Power Issue in Appeal," *Richmond News-Leader*, 19 November 1935; "Skyline Drive Snag Is Ended by Via Land Suit Dismissal," *Richmond Times-Dispatch*, 26 November 1935; H. E. van Gelder, "Virginia: Rights-of-Way: Report on Meeting on Scenic Easements in the Office of the State Highway Commission, Richmond," 28 December 1935, BRPRG 7, Box 7. See also SWA to TCV, 18 January 1937, BRPRG 7, Box 8; Virginia Department of Highways, 1942 *Supplement*; H. G. Shirley to AED, 28 October 1937, CCF7B, Box 2731.

30. SWA to TCV, 24 February 1936, 10 March 1936, BRPRG 7, Box 7; SWA to TCV, 18 January 1937, BRPRG 7, Box 8.

31. Abram P. Staples to AED, 27 December 1937, CCF7B, Box 2731; Virginia Department of Highways, 1942 *Supplement*; SWA to TCV, 18 January 1937, BRPRG 7, Box 8; SWA, interview; C. K. Simmers to NPS Director, 1 April 1935, BRPRG 7, Box 5; SPW to SWA, August 1936, CCF7B, Box 2746; SWA, "Annual Report of the Blue Ridge Parkway, Roanoke, Va., to the Director, National Park Service," 30 June 1940, BRPRG 7, Box 5; DOI, NPS, "Requirements and Procedure"; EHA, "History of the Blue Ridge Parkway"; Liles, "History of the Blue Ridge Parkway"; [SWA?], Bibliography of Correspondence, Virginia Right-of-Way, [March 1936?], BRPRG 7, Box 8.

32. HLI to James H. Price, 15 March 1938, CCF7B, Box 2732; EHA to TCV, 17 October 1939, BRPRG 7, Box 26.

33. In Virginia, the *Via* case stalled land acquisition. Confident that it was on firmer legal ground, North Carolina began in 1935 to acquire lands through eminent domain. See Charles Ross,

"Memorandum Regarding Legal Aspects of Deed from the State of North Carolina to the United States of America Covering Right-of-way of the Shenandoah–Great Smoky Mountains National Parkway," 25 July 1935, CMW, Ina L. Ferrell, and HLI, "Agreement," 5 August 1935, both in JCBEP, Box 160; HLI to CMW, 25 July 1935, BRPRG 7, Box 5.

34. Ross, "Memorandum Regarding Legal Aspects of Deed"; RGB, interview.

35. The legal details of this process are described in many documents, including Ross, "Memorandum Regarding Legal Aspects of Deed"; Nathan E. Margold to HLI, 10 August 1935, CCF7B, Box 2730; North Carolina State Highway and Public Works Commission, "General Statement Regarding the Acquisition of National Parkway Lands," 1937, BRPRG 5, Box 1; EHA, "History of the Blue Ridge Parkway."

36. EHA, "History of the Blue Ridge Parkway." A 1938 report noted that of the 639 parcels to be acquired along Virginia sections 1A and 1P–1W, only 94 had been condemned (DOI, NPS, "Land Acquisition Progress Report—Parkway Land," 1 February 1938, CCF7B, Box 2731).

37. H. E. van Gelder to SWA, 23 February 1937, BRPRG 7, Box 8.

38. ABC to Harlean James, 9 December 1933, CCF7B, Box 2713; SWA, "Appalachian National Parkway from Shenandoah National Park to Great Smoky Mountains National Park, Report on Recreation and Service Areas: Type and Scope of Development Proposed," 15 December 1934, CCF7B, Box 2711.

39. EHA, "History of the Blue Ridge Parkway"; William G. Lord, "History of the Blue Ridge Parkway," 1 December 1954, BRPRG 5, Box 49; Liles, "History of the Blue Ridge Parkway"; Quin and Marston, *Historic American Engineering Record*; Firth, "Historic Resource Study"; Thomas H. MacDonald and AED, "Parkways of the Future: Radio Address," Delivered 13 April 1935, Transcript dated 14 April 1935, BRPRG 7, Box 51.

40. ABC to Harlean James, 9 December 1933, CCF7B, Box 2713, discusses the president's role in suggesting the development of recreation areas; ABC to Frank A. Kittredge, 22 December 1933, CCF7B, Box 2713, mentions that Ickes and Roosevelt "insist that [the Parkway] should be bulged at certain points to provide recreational opportunities." See also SWA, "Appalachian National Parkway from Shenandoah National Park to Great Smoky Mountains National Park, Report on Recreation and Service Areas"; SWA to TCV, 15 April 1938, BRPRG 7, Box 57; SWA, "Progress Report: Development of Recreational Areas, Blue Ridge Parkway, for Mr. Vint," 24 April 1939, BRPRG 7, Box 50; Lord, "History of the Blue Ridge Parkway." The two parks under ' way by the end of the decade in North Carolina were Cumberland Knob and the Bluff (Doughton Park), and in 1937 Cumberland Knob became the first to open. See SWA to TCV, 15 April 1938, BRPRG 7, Box 57; HLI to Henry A. Wallace, 27 February 1935, CCF7B, Box 2736.

41. SWA, "Appalachian National Parkway from Shenandoah National Park to Great Smoky Mountains National Park, Report on Recreation and Service Areas." Abbott worried—with some foresight—that providing such facilities might provoke complaints of government interference with private enterprise in the region.

42. Figures from Quin and Marston, *Historic American Engineering Record*; Firth, "Historic Resource Study"; NPS, Blue Ridge Parkway Map, 2002.

43. Quin and Marston, *Historic American Engineering Record*.

44. Ibid.; "Brief Description of the Recreation Areas Adjacent to the Parkway, to Accompany the Master Plan Therof Drawn June 3, 1936," 3 June 1936, BRPRG 5, Box 9.

45. Quin and Marston, *Historic American Engineering Record*; "Brief Description of the Recreation Areas Adjacent to the Parkway"; SWA to NPS Director through TCV, 12 August 1938, CCF7B, Box 2735.

46. A Morganton attorney reported this confusion to the Highway Commission chair in H. J. Hatcher to CMW, 27 March 1937, SHCRWD, Box 2. See also RGB to H. J. Hatcher, 1 April 1937,

Ira T. Johnston to CMW, 6 March 1936, both in SHCRWD, Box 2; C. K. Simmers to AED, 29 February 1936, CCF7B, Box 2731; RGB to CMW, 24 February 1936, SHCRWD, Box 8.

47. G. A. Moskey, W. G. Carnes, and AED, "Memorandum of Information and Instructions for the Guidance of Land Representatives of the National Park Service Assigned to National Parkway Projects," 16 July 1936, BRPRG 7, Box 8.

48. SWA to TCV, 31 October 1936, BRPRG 7, Box 5; RGB to CMW, 8 December 1936, CMW to RGB, 7 March 1936, RGB to J. R. Cates, 10 March 1936, James P. Dodge to RGB, 10 August 1936, RGB to CMW, 8 December 1936, all in SHCRWD, Box 2; C. K. Simmers to AED, G. A. Moskey, and TCV, 21 January 1937, CCF7B, Box 2731; North Carolina State Highway and Public Works Commission, "General Statement"; AED to RGB, 9 January 1937, BRPRG 7, Box 6.

49. H. E. van Gelder to SWA, 23 February 1937, BRPRG 7, Box 8; Frazier E. Kelley to Franklin D. Roosevelt, 4 January 1937, CCF7B, Box 2731; Frazier E. Kelley records available at <http://awt. ancestry.com/cgi-bin/igm.cgi?ti=o&surname=kelley&given=frazier> (9 August 2005); Jean Haskell Speer and Russell, *Kelley School*, 6–12. For the Kelley acreage, see [Virginia Department of Highways?], "List of Property Owners, Sections 1P, 1Q, 1R, 1S, 1T, Blue Ridge Parkway," [1938?], BRPRG 7, Box 8.

50. On North Carolina, see U.S. Census Bureau, *Census of Agriculture*, table 1, 448–56; U.S. Census Bureau, *Fifteenth Census*, table 14, vol. 3, part 2, 360–66, table 20, vol. 3, part 2, 374–87. On Virginia, see U.S. Census Bureau, *Census of Agriculture*, table 1, 448–56; U.S. Census Bureau, *Fifteenth Census*, table 13, vol. 3, part 2, 1161–68, table 20, vol. 3, part 2, 1182–96.

51. Frazier E. Kelley to Franklin D. Roosevelt, 4 January 1937, CCF7B, Box 2731.

52. JCBE to JWB, 7 June 1935, JCBEP, Box 152.

53. J. P. Dodge to RGB, 10 June 1937, SHCRWD, Box 7; J. P. Dodge to Frank L. Dunlap, 9 January 1940, Ernest Gardner to RGB, 26 November 1943, both in SHCRWD, Box 8.

54. SPW to C. P. Grantham, 12 June 1935, SHCRWD, Box 1; RGB to J. R. Smith, 29 November 1938, SHCRWD, Box 3; "State Parkway Spending Now at $766,354 Figure," RNO, 15 November 1939. The record is not clear on whether the guidelines actually governed state acquisition policy, were simply recommendations, or applied only to federal-level recreation-area land acquisition. Without improvements figured in, the per-acre average was about thirty dollars. For North Carolina land values as assessed by the U.S. Census Bureau, see also U.S. Census Bureau, *Census of Agriculture*, table 1, 448–56; C. K. Simmers to G. A. Moskey, 31 August 1935, CCF7B, Box 2712.

55. "State Parkway Spending Now at $766,354 Figure." In April 1939, Browning reported an average thirty-five dollars per acre for about ten thousand acres then acquired (RGB to M. W. Torkelson, 12 April 1939, SHCRWD, Box 3). This figure was slightly higher than the average of about thirty-three dollars an acre reported in late 1938 ("Claims," RNO, 22 December 1938). See also "Cost of the Blue Ridge Parkway from Beginning to July 1, 1941," [1941?], SHCRWD, Box 4; SPW to NPS Region 1 Director, 18 September 1943, BRPRG 7, Box 5; RGB to Hillory A. Tolson, 25 February 1944, RGBP, Box 4. The state paid the Linville Company approximately fifty dollars an acre. See State Highway Commission, "Press Release," 1939, SHCRWD, Box 10; "$25,000 Is Paid for Road Rights," RNO, 26 May 1939.

56. NPS and Virginia Department of Highways, "Map of Lands Acquired for the Blue Ridge Parkway: Floyd and Patrick Counties"; C. K. Simmers to Mr. Sanders, 12 February 1940, CCF7B, Box 2763; SPW to NPS Region 1 Director, 18 September 1943, BRPRG 7, Box 5.

57. Ashe County, North Carolina, Superior Court Minutes, 1938, Microfilm reel C.006.30012, vol. L (1938–43), North Carolina State Archives, Raleigh; RGB to AED, 6 December 1935, SHCRWD, Box 8; Chester Davis, "Developers, Park Service Battle over Blue Ridge," *Winston-Salem Journal and Sentinel*, 25 January 1970.

58. J. P. Dodge to SWA, 18 January 1937, J. P. Dodge to RGB, 25 June 1938, both in SHCRWD, Box 8.

59. Ashe County, North Carolina, Superior Court Minutes, 1938, Microfilm reel C.006.30012, vol. L (1938–43); M. F. Miller, et al. v. North Carolina State Highway and Public Works Commission, Amended Petition in the Superior Court, Ashe County, North Carolina, 1938, FOCP; NPS and North Carolina State Highway and Public Works Commission, "Map of Lands Acquired for the Blue Ridge Parkway: Ashe and Wilkes Counties"; DOI, NPS, "Land Acquisition Progress Report — Parkway Land," 13 March 1938, CCF7B, Box 2732; W. A. Royal, "Press Release," 27 March 1937, CCF7B, Box 2731.

60. John R. Jones to Charles Ross, 6 July 1937, SHCRWD, Box 8. Some of the details of the land-acquisition process are outlined in weekly memos (titled "Status of Parkway Claims, Weekly Report") sent in by the Highway Commission's claims adjuster as he worked to settle with Parkway landowners. See, for example, J. Ray Cates to RGB, 18 January 1936, J. Ray Cates to RGB, 15 February 1936, 30 March 1936, James P. Dodge to RGB, 10 August 1936, all in SHCRWD, Box 2.

61. Charles Ross to John R. Jones, 12 July 1937, SHCRWD, Box 8.

62. G. A. Moskey to TCV, 10 August 1937, CCF7B, Box 2731. See also C. K. Simmers to AED, 31 March 1936, SWA to TCV, 6 August 1937, Hillory A. Tolson to Charles Ross, 28 August 1937, all in CCF7B, Box 2731; SWA to TCV, 31 October 1936, BRPRG 7, Box 5.

63. G. A. Moskey to TCV, 10 August 1937, CCF7B, Box 2731; J. P. Dodge to Charles Ross, 25 October 1937, 29 October 1937, SHCRWD, Box 2; "Buildings on the Blue Ridge Parkway Right-of-Way," 16 September 1936, SHCRWD, Box 2; SWA to RGB, 13 May 1938, BRPRG 7, Box 6.

64. Charles L. Perdue and Martin-Perdue, "Appalachian Fables and Facts," 90, traces this policy to an edict issued in 1934 by Cammerer, who insisted — as did Assistant Director G. A. Moskey in his 10 August 1937 letter cited in the preceding note — that the federal government would no longer accept title to any lands the states had obtained for national park areas as long as inhabitants remained on the lands. See also Dunn, Cades Cove, 241–54; Margaret Lynn Brown, "Smoky Mountains Story," 140–57; Powers with Hannah, Cataloochee; Simmons, "Creation"; Charles L. Perdue and Martin-Perdue, "Appalachian Fables and Facts," 84–104; Charles L. Perdue and Martin-Perdue, "'To Build a Wall.'" The Perdues note that about five hundred families were displaced from the Shenandoah National Park, while Margaret Lynn Brown writes that about fifty-six hundred people were removed from the Great Smoky Mountains National Park.

65. HLI to Clyde R. Hoey, 2 July 1938, CCF7B, Box 2732; C. K. Simmers to AED, G. A. Moskey, and TCV, 21 January 1937, CCF7B, Box 2731.

66. C. K. Simmers to AED, 31 March 1936, CCF7B, Box 2731.

67. SWA to NPS Director, 13 April 1939, CCF7B, Box 2733; AED, "Principles to Govern the Approval of Crossing of, or Access to, the Shenandoah–Great Smoky Mountains National Parkway in Virginia," 16 November 1935, BRPRG 7, Box 7; ABC, "Memorandum of Information and Instructions Governing the Preparation and Transmittal of Parkway Land Deeds," 23 August 1937, CCF7B, Box 2732; HLI, "Requirements and Procedure to Govern the Acquisition of Land for National Parkways," 9 November 1937; DOI, NPS, "Requirements and Procedure." See also C. K. Simmers to Chief Counsel, 1 September 1939, CCF7B, Box 2715.

68. M. F. Miller et al. v. North Carolina State Highway and Public Works Commission, Amended Petition in the Superior Court, Ashe County, North Carolina, 1938, FOCP.

69. AED to CMW, 8 January 1937, CCF7B, Box 2714; AED to H. G. Shirley, 13 February 1937, BRPRG 7, Box 8.

70. Superintendent, Blue Ridge Parkway, "Report on Private Crossings, Sections 1P, 1Q, 1R, 1S, 1T," 13 October 1937, BRPRG 7, Box 9; AED to H. G. Shirley, 26 October 1937, BRPRG 7, Box 8.

71. H. G. Shirley to AED, 28 October 1937, CCF7B, Box 2731.

72. EHA, "Memorandum for Files," [November 1937?], BRPRG 7, Box 6.

73. Ibid.

74. Jones and Ward [attorneys] to Charles Ross, 13 June 1936, SHCRWD, Box 9; Nelson MacRae to CMW, 25 June 1936, SHCRWD, Box 10; Linville Improvement Company, "Legal Protest to Capus M. Waynick," 26 June 1936, SHCRWD, Box 9; Linville Improvement Company, "Linville" [advertising pamphlet], [188?], North Carolina Collection, University of North Carolina, Chapel Hill; Covington, Linville.

75. HLI to Clyde R. Hoey, 2 July 1938, CCF7B, Box 2732; EHA, "Memorandum for Files"; C. K. Simmers to Chief Counsel, 1 September 1939, CCF7B, Box 2715. It seems that not everyone within the NPS favored a total ban on accesses, however, and BPR engineer H. J. Spelman discussed in 1939 the policy modifications that transpired subsequent to the secretary's pronouncement. A few days before Ickes wrote his letter, Stanley Abbott noted that the blanket "no access" policy being recommended by some within the NPS would be difficult to enforce and would make land-acquisition requirements much greater, but his opinion was apparently not adopted. See H. J. Spelman to AED, 19 April 1939, CCF7B, Box 2733; SWA, "Annual Report," 30 June 1938. Despite Ickes's statement, Spelman indicates that the policy remained under discussion for at least another year, especially because of state pressure for the NPS to allow some private accesses to facilitate the land-acquisition process. See a series of "special use" permits issued by the Interior Department in 1938 in CCF7B, Box 2746. See also Thomas H. MacDonald to AED, 19 May 1939, CCF7B, Box 2733. By 1940, however, the question apparently was mostly resolved within the NPS, with Demaray reporting that "the extension of right-of-way privileges for private accesses to nearby lands would violate parkway standards" and thus that "regulations of this Department have accordingly provided that private roads crossing the parkway at grade shall not be permitted" (AED to R. F. Camalier, 17 April 1940, CCF7B, Box 2715). By 1941, official Park Service guidelines stated flatly that "there shall be no private roads crossing the parkway road at grade" (DOI, NPS, "Requirements and Procedure"). The NPS also began by the late 1930s to tighten control over the proliferation of illegal Parkway accesses from private lands by prosecuting people using such unofficial roads as trespassers. See SPW to J. P. Dodge, 21 January 1939, CCF7B, Box 2732.

76. Walter H. Woodson to Frank L. Dunlap, 1 June 1939, Frank L. Dunlap to Walter H. Woodson, 2 June 1939, both in SHCRWD, Box 3.

77. SPW to NPS Director, 11 October 1940, CCF7B, Box 2747; SWA, "Superintendent's Monthly Narrative Report, February 1942," 10 March 1942, CCF7B, Box 2718.

78. SWA to NPS Director, 13 April 1939, CCF7B, Box 2733.

79. Ernest G. Whanger, "Superintendent's Monthly Narrative Report, March 1943," 12 April 1943, CCF7B, Box 2718; Ernest G. Whanger, "Superintendent's Monthly Narrative Report, August 1945," 11 September 1945, CCF7B, Box 2718.

80. AED to L. F. Caudill, 23 January 1936, CCF7B, Box 2731.

81. SPW to SWA, August 1936, CCF7B, Box 2746; National Park Service, "Press Release," 1 September 1936, CCF7B, Box 2728.

82. SWA, "Appalachian National Parkway from Shenandoah National Park to Great Smoky Mountains National Park, Report on Recreation and Service Areas."

83. Martha Armstrong to AED, 12 December 1937, Hillory A. Tolson to Martha Armstrong, 19 January 1938, both in CCF7B, Box 2746. Armstrong's is one of perhaps forty letters in this box making similar requests, all of which received form-letter responses.

84. G. C. Robbins to NPS Director, 14 December 1938, CCF7B, Box 2746; "Park Service Policies on Travel Housing Explained," Spruce Pine Tri-County News, 9 February 1939; S. J. Bruce to NPS,

12 August 1939, AED to G. C. Robbins, 30 December 1938, both in CCF7B, Box 2746; HLI, Diaries, 16 September 1939, HIP.

85. Charles Ross to G. A. Moskey, 24 June 1939, CCF7B, Box 2746.

86. Frank L. Dunlap to ABC, 6 June 1940, SHCRWD, Box 4; ABC to Frank L. Dunlap, 12 June 1940, CCF7B, Box 2747.

87. The difference of opinion between Abbott and Washington officials is reported in Charles L. Gable to NPS Director, 27 February 1940, CCF7B, Box 2747. But see also SWA to Files, 8 March 1940, SWA, "Special Analysis of Departmental Policy for Prospective Bidders for Operation of Tourist Facilities on the Blue Ridge Parkway in Virginia and North Carolina," 9 February 1940, SWA to Lyles Harriss, 27 March 1940, all in CCF7B, Box 2747.

88. Charles L. Gable to SWA, 16 May 1940, CCF7B, Box 2747. Abbott noted that at a meeting of NPS officials in Washington, sentiment strongly favored structuring the bid process to enable the "smaller business man" to win a concessionaire contract (SWA to Files, 8 March 1940, CCF7B, Box 2747). See also *Blue Ridge Parkway News* 3, no. 7 (May 1940); *Blue Ridge Parkway News* 3, no. 9 (August 1940).

89. Seven separate concessions units ultimately were planned for the length of the Parkway, with the possibility of a different concessionaire in charge of each section. See Hillory A. Tolson to Robert Landreth, 22 January 1941, CCF7B, Box 2747; SWA, "Annual Report of the Blue Ridge Parkway, Roanoke, Va., to the Director, National Park Service," 30 June 1941, CCF7B, Box 2718.

90. ABC to Frank L. Dunlap, 12 June 1940, CCF7B, Box 2747; *Blue Ridge Parkway News* 3, no. 7 (May 1940).

91. SPW to NPS Region 1 Director, 7 March 1946, BRPRG 5, Box 13; *Blue Ridge Parkway News* 3, no. 7 (May 1940).

92. SWA, "Annual Report," 30 June 1940; *Blue Ridge Parkway News* 3, no. 9 (August 1940); AED to HLI, 26 December 1941, Newton B. Drury to First Assistant Secretary of the Interior, 22 November 1940, Hillory A. Tolson to Robert Landreth, 22 January 1941, all in CCF7B, Box 2747; SWA, "Annual Report," 30 June 1941.

93. *Blue Ridge Parkway News* 5, no. 3 (April 1942); AED to HLI, 26 December 1941, CCF7B, Box 2747; NPS, "National Park Concessions, Inc.: Purposes, Reasons for Formation, History, Organization, and Functions," February 1957, BRPRG 3, Box 102. The Cumberland Knob shop lost money during its first year and closed in 1943 for the duration of World War II (SWA, "Annual Report of the Blue Ridge Parkway, Roanoke, Va., to the Director, National Park Service," 30 June 1943, CCF7B, Box 2718).

94. The decisions made in 1942 set the course for much of the future development of Parkway concessions. A 1988 NPS document indicated that the bureau had leased concessions at twelve sites to six different concessionaires but that the services were dominated by two firms, National Park Concessions and the Virginia Peaks of Otter Company, which together operated facilities at seven of the sites (Division of Resource Planning and Professional Services, BRP, "Blue Ridge Parkway Statement for Management").

95. JD to HLI, 26 December 1934, CCF7B, Box 2730; Bertha L. Cone to HLI, 12 March 1939, Bertha L. Cone to Franklin D. Roosevelt, 14 July 1939, both in CCF7B, Box 2733; Bertha L. Cone to RLD, 23 May 1937, RLD to Bertha L. Cone, 24 May 1937, both in RLDP, Box 17.

96. Harry Slattery to Bertha L. Cone, 23 April 1935, SHCRWD, Box 8; AED to HLI, 10 January 1935, CCF7B, Box 2730; Frank L. Dunlap to JD, 13 July 1938, JDP, Box 677, Great Smoky Mountains Files; Frank L. Dunlap to J. Gordon Hackett, 20 December 1938, Frank L. Dunlap to RLD, 24 January 1939, Frank L. Dunlap to Benjamin Cone, 20 July 1939, Bertha L. Cone to AED, 28 July 1939, Frank L. Dunlap to AED, 29 July 1939, Frank L. Dunlap to J. R. White, 7 August 1939, Bertha L. Cone to Frank L. Dunlap, 10 September 1939, ABC to Bertha L. Cone, 5 April 1939,

all in SHCRWD, Box 3; AED to Files, 25 May 1939, CCF7B, Box 2733; SWA, "Annual Report of the Blue Ridge Parkway, Roanoke, Va., to the Director, National Park Service," 30 June 1939, CCF7B, Box 2717. For a complete discussion of the Cones and their Blowing Rock estate, see Noblitt, *Mansion in the Mountains*.

97. Chester Davis, "Developers, Park Service Battle over Blue Ridge," *Winston-Salem Journal and Sentinel*, 25 January 1970; Ashe County, North Carolina, Superior Court Minutes, 1938, Microfilm reel C.006.30012, vol. L (1938–43); J. P. Dodge to B. T. Campbell, 14 June 1939, SHCRWD, Box 8.

98. Scott, *Weapons of the Weak*; M. F. Miller et al. v. *North Carolina State Highway and Public Works Commission*, Amended Petition in the Superior Court, Ashe County, North Carolina, 1938, FOCP; J. P. Dodge to RGB, 25 June 1938, SHCRWD, Box 8.

99. Hall et al., *Like a Family*, 293–94.

100. D. S. Bare to RLD, 16 August 1935, RLDP, Box 14.

101. RLD to D. S. Bare, 19 August 1935, RLDP, Box 14; RGB to CMW, 24 February 1936, J. P. Dodge to RGB, 30 August 1937, both in SHCRWD, Box 8.

102. RLD to D. S. Bare, 19 August 1935, RLDP, Box 14. Some landowners may have been induced to sell by NPS promises of jobs in building and development at the new recreation area. In SPW to Charles Miles, 8 February 1936, BRPRG 6, Box 2, the Parkway administrator in charge of the land acquisition for the Bluff personally authorized that such a guarantee be made. See also R. C. Jennings to Robert R. Reynolds, 10 August 1937, CCF7B, Box 2715; "The Bluff: List of Parcels," 1936, SPW to AED, 18 June 1937, Howard B. Shaw Jr. to SPW, 18 July 1938, Howard B. Shaw Jr. to Fielding Caudill, 18 July 1938, all in BRPRG 7, Box 13. The land-acquisition process for the Bluff (and other recreation areas where private lands were taken) had landowners initially sign options to sell their lands to the federal government, with the documents including information regarding the compensation they would accept. Federal surveyors then surveyed the lands, and the government decided whether to accept the valuation (various materials in BRPRG 6, Box 2).

103. SPW to R. Baldwin Myers, 2 May 1938, Eli Richardson to HLI, 27 July 1939, Carlisle W. Higgins to Charles E. Collett, 4 May 1939, SPW to Mr. Shaw, 10 May 1939, SPW to R. Baldwin Myers, 28 July 1938, all in BRPRG 7, Box 13; SWA to Director, 18 November 1942, CCF7B, Box 2716.

104. CLW to BRP Acting Superintendent, 20 May 1939, SPW to NPS Director, 15 June 1939, Amanda Osborne to HLI, 24 July 1939, CLW to SPW, 10 August 1939, all in BRPRG 7, Box 13.

105. Eli Richardson to HLI, 27 July 1939, SPW to G. A. Moskey, 22 June 1939, SPW to Eli Richardson, 17 August 1939, CLW to SPW, 10 August 1939, SPW to NPS Director, 26 August 1939, SPW to Amanda Osborne, 17 August 1939, all in BRPRG 7, Box 13.

106. Eli Richardson to SPW, 17 November 1939, 23 July 1940, SPW to Eli Richardson, 21 November 1939, Amanda Osborne to Eleanor Roosevelt, 22 June 1942, G. A. Moskey to Amanda Osborne, 1 July 1942, all in BRPRG 7, Box 13. Richardson apparently did not receive his money until July 1940, after Congress had passed an appropriations bill that gave the NPS the necessary funds (SPW to Eli Richardson, 17 October 1939, G. A. Moskey to BRP Acting Superintendent, 16 July 1940, both in BRPRG 7, Box 13).

107. SPW to NPS Director, 22 September 1939, CCF7B, Box 2721; SWA, "Superintendent's Monthly Narrative Report, February 1942"; SWA, "Superintendent's Monthly Narrative Report, May 1942," 11 June 1942, SWA, "Superintendent's Monthly Narrative Report, September 1942," 10 October 1942, SWA, "Superintendent's Monthly Narrative Report, November 1942," 9 December 1942, all in CCF7B, Box 2718. In most cases, the NPS seems not to have taken action against offenders but simply to have awaited state settlement of the claims for those parcels, which the agency hoped would take care of the problems. See C. K. Simmers to G. A. Moskey, 15 February 1938, CCF7B, Box 2719.

108. L. F. Caudill to HLI, 14 January 1936, Rufus A. Wagoner to SWA, 29 October 1937, both in CCF7B, Box 2731; C. K. Simmers to G. A. Moskey, 29 January 1938, HLI to U.S. Attorney General, 16 July 1938, both in CCF7B, Box 2719.

109. SWA to NPS Director, 6 April 1942, CCF7B, Box 2740.

110. EHA, "History of the Blue Ridge Parkway"; North Carolina State Highway and Public Works Commission, "General Statement"; SPW to SWA, August 1936, CCF7B, Box 2746; RGB to J. Q. Harris, 16 August 1935, AED to CMW, 6 December 1935, both in SHCRWD, Box 7; SWA to C. K. Simmers, 19 August 1935, CCF7B, Box 2719; SPW to Charles Ross, 22 July 1939, SHCRWD, Box 8; SWA to RGB, 22 April 1940, SHCRWD, Box 4; SWA to RGB, 15 April 1943, CCF7B, Box 2766.

111. SWA to TCV, 27 November 1935, SHCRWD, Box 7; Carlisle D. Higgins to Frank Chambers, 7 October 1936, CCF7B, Box 2719; SPW to SWA, August 1936, CCF7B, Box 2746.

112. C. A. Burns, "Destruction of Trees on the Blue Ridge Parkway, Near Glendale Springs, North Carolina," 7 August 1937, CCF7B, Box 2719.

113. J. R. Cates to RGB, 28 August 1936, SHCRWD, Box 8; William M. Austin to H. J. Spelman, 28 September 1936, Hillory A. Tolson to William M. Austin, 5 October 1936, R. A. Wagoner to C. K. Simmers, 12 October 1936, H. J. Spelman to AED, 13 November 1936, TCV to NPS Director, 4 August 1937, all in CCF7B, Box 2720; D. H. Rosier Jr. to NPS Director, 14 August 1937, Hillory A. Tolson to SWA, 26 August 1937, Donald E. Lee, Memorandum for File, 3 December 1936, all in CCF7B, Box 2719.

114. C. K. Simmers to AED and TCV, 21 January 1937, CCF7B, Box 2719; EHA to TCV, 18 February 1937, CCF7B, Box 2731.

115. RGB to AED, 14 March 1938, CCF7B, Box 2715.

116. *Blue Ridge Parkway News* 1, no. 2 (December 1937); SWA, "Annual Report," 30 June 1938; *Blue Ridge Parkway News* 2, no. 6 (July 1939); Isabelle F. Story to BRP Acting Superintendent, 22 April 1940, SWA to ABC, 17 November 1938, both in CCF7B, Box 2715; SWA to NPS Director, 28 March 1941, CCF7B, Box 2729; EHA, "History of the Blue Ridge Parkway"; SWA to NPS Director, 15 March 1940, CCF7B, Box 2728. Demaray specifically linked the commencement of publication of the *Blue Ridge Parkway News* to the rumors that the Parkway would be a road only for the wealthy (AED to RGB, 24 March 1938, CCF7B, Box 2715). By 1940, the paper was also being sent to chambers of commerce in Georgia and Florida, presumably to publicize the fact that many Parkway sections were ready for travelers (SWA to ABC, 14 March 1940, CCF7B, Box 2715).

117. *Blue Ridge Parkway News* 1, no. 4 (February 1938); *Blue Ridge Parkway News* 1, no. 6 (April 1938); *Blue Ridge Parkway News* 2, no. 3 (January 1939); *Blue Ridge Parkway News* 1, no. 3 (January 1938); *Blue Ridge Parkway News* 2, no. 3 (January 1939); *Blue Ridge Parkway News* 4, no. 3 (March 1941); *Blue Ridge Parkway News* 4, no. 4 (April 1941); SWA to TCV, 20 January 1938, CCF7B, Box 2728.

118. *Blue Ridge Parkway News* 3, no. 7 (May 1940).

119. SWA to Director, 18 November 1942, CCF7B, Box 2716.

120. Ibid.; SWA to J. P. Dodge, 29 April 1940, SHCRWD, Box 4; Thor Borreson, "Report on Mountain Culture and Handicraft, Blue Ridge Parkway," 7 October 1940, BRPRG 5, Box 61; Roy Edgar Appleman, "Report on Preservation of Mountain Culture, Marking of Historic Sites, and Promotion of Handicraft, Blue Ridge Parkway," 9 October 1940, BRPRG 5, Box 61.

121. AED to RGB, 24 March 1938, CCF7B, Box 2715; *Blue Ridge Parkway News* 3, no. 7 (May 1940).

122. "No Green Mountain Hot-Dogs," 9. Other factors also were involved in Vermont's decision, including many environmentalist arguments that were not as salient in North Carolina during this period.

CHAPTER 4

1. [HC?], "Thunder and Lightning over Little Switzerland," n.d. [November 1938], FOCP.
2. HC to Carol D. Taliaferro, 3 November 1938, FOCP.
3. Starnes, "Creating the Land," 198; Christopher Brenden Martin, "Selling the Southern Highlands."
4. Ledford, "Two Views from Grassy Mountain."
5. Powell, *Dictionary*, 1:382–83; Johnnie Virginia Anderson, "Heriot Clarkson"; various materials in HCP, Boxes 1, 4; CMW, *North Carolina Roads*, 1:39; McKown, "Roads and Reform," 96–100; Escott, *Many Excellent People*, 259–60; Tindall, "Business Progressivism."
6. Escott, *Many Excellent People*, 247–53.
7. Ibid., 252–59.
8. HC, "Important Events of My Life," n.d., HCP, Box 1; Typed Manuscript on HC's Life, n.d., HCP, Box 1; Carol D. Taliaferro, "Address Delivered on Occasion of the Presentation of the Portrait," 8 December 1939, HCP, Box 4; Powell, *Dictionary*, 1:382–83.
9. Taliaferro, "Address"; Typed Manuscript on HC's Life; Johnnie Virginia Anderson, "Heriot Clarkson," 37–49; Escott, *Many Excellent People*, 259–60.
10. A summary of this speech ("Race Fusion Is Unnatural," delivered 20 May 1900, HCP, Box 1) is virtually the only document in Clarkson's papers that details his racial views.
11. Johnnie Virginia Anderson, "Heriot Clarkson," 52–56; Powell, *Dictionary*, 1:382–83.
12. Johnnie Virginia Anderson, "Heriot Clarkson," 7, 21–24, 81–86.
13. CMW, *North Carolina Roads*, 1:39; McKown, "Roads and Reform," 96–100; Johnnie Virginia Anderson, "Heriot Clarkson," 68–75; Lefler and Newsome, *North Carolina*, 565–66.
14. Duls, *Story of Little Switzerland*; advertising copy for Little Switzerland, *Eastern National Park-to-Park Highway Magazine, Good Will Tour Edition*, 61; "Little Switzerland, North Carolina, Nature's Playground, the Beauty Spot of the Blue Ridge on the Scenic Highway State Route no. 19" [advertising pamphlet], 1 July 1931, North Carolina Collection, University of North Carolina, Chapel Hill.
15. Duls, *Story of Little Switzerland*, 3, 5–10.
16. Ibid., 11–23.
17. Ibid., 23–29, 178.
18. Ibid., 30; Switzerland Company, Taliaferro and Clarkson, Attorneys, "Memorandum Brief and Authorities to Mr. Taylor M. Landford, Internal Revenue Agent, Treasury Department, Internal Revenue Service, Raleigh, N.C.," 17 January 1944, FOCP.
19. Duls, *Story of Little Switzerland*, 33–34; HC to RGB, 21 March 1936, FOCP.
20. Duls, *Story of Little Switzerland*, 33–39; Cecil Kenneth Brown, *State Highway System*, 167–68; Frank L. Dunlap to FOC, 27 August 1937, FOCP.
21. Ledford, "Two Views from Grassy Mountain," 7–8; HC to Athan Hollifield, 11 May 1937, FOCP; *Switzerland Company v. North Carolina State Highway and Public Works Commission*, 216 N.C. 450 (1939), Mitchell North Carolina Appeal Record, 35.
22. *Eastern National Park-to-Park Highway Magazine, Good Will Tour Edition*, 61; Committee of Mass Meeting, *What Citizens Think*; Duls, *Story of Little Switzerland*, 2–38.
23. Constance Jolley Duncan, "Little Switzerland Colony Founded 27 Years Ago by Justice Clarkson," *ACT*, 5 July 1936; Duls, *Story of Little Switzerland*, 244–46.
24. Duls, *Story of Little Switzerland*, 14–19, 23–25; Switzerland Company Financial Records, 1936, 1941, FOCP; Duncan, "Little Switzerland Colony."
25. Duls, *Story of Little Switzerland*, 90–94.
26. Ibid., 81–90, 104.

27. Ruth Moore, "Little Switzerland Is One of Most Popular Resorts in Blue Ridge," *ACT*, 25 July 1937.

28. Ibid.; Hoyt M'Afee, "Much Pride Shown in Little Switzerland by Justice Clarkson," *AC*, 19 June 1938; Hoyt McAfee, "Justice Clarkson — An Intimate View of Jurist at Summer Home," *Charlotte Observer*, 26 September 1937; Hoyt McAfee, "Little Switzerland, Scenic Beauty Spot of Blue Ridge," *Charlotte Observer*, 15 August 1937; Ashton Chapman, "Many Charlotteans Enjoy Little Switzerland Homes," *Charlotte Observer*, 15 June 1941.

29. McAfee, "Little Switzerland."

30. Nelson MacRae to JCBE, 7 October 1933, JCBEP, Box 152; HC to JD, 2 June 1934, JDP, Box 215; "Strong Delegation on Parkway Trip Foreseen," *ACT*, 24 June 1934, 1; HC to Wilson Warlick, 11 April 1939, FOCP; JD to HC, 28 June 1934, HCP, Box 4; HC to HLI, 2 July 1934, CCF7B, Box 2714; North Carolina Committee on Federal Parkway, "Description of a Route through North Carolina Proposed as a Part of the Scenic Parkway to Connect the Shenandoah National Park with the Great Smoky Mountains National Park," 1934, CCF7B, Box 2711; FOC to RGB, 18 August 1937, HC to J. P. Dodge, 11 May 1937, 22 May 1937, all in FOCP.

31. HC to RGB, 29 June 1935, SHCRWD, Box 1; HC to J. P. Dodge, 11 May 1937, 22 May 1937, FOCP; Moore, "Little Switzerland"; McAfee, "Little Switzerland"; Duncan, "Little Switzerland Colony."

32. HC to RGB, 21 March 1936, FOCP; Duncan, "Little Switzerland Colony"; McAfee, "Little Switzerland"; Switzerland Company Financial Records, 1937, 1944, FOCP; Committee of Mass Meeting, *What Citizens Think*; HC to Carol D. Taliaferro, 12 December 1938, FOCP.

33. Articles advertising Little Switzerland appeared frequently throughout the 1930s in both the Asheville and Charlotte newspapers. See M'Afee, "Much Pride Shown."

34. James R. Hollowell to RGB, 10 May 1936, RGB to J. R. Hollowell, 13 May 1936, both in SHCRWD, Box 11; RGB to William M. Austin, 2 June 1936, SHCRWD, Box 2; CMW to ABC, 3 November 1936, CCF7B, Box 2714; HC to RGB, 29 June 1935, SHCRWD, Box 1; Parkway correspondence, 1936–37, FOCP.

35. SWA to Lynn Harriss (cc to RGB), 18 November 1936, J. P. Dodge to Lynn Harriss, 3 December 1936, both in SHCRWD, Box 11. See also J. P. Dodge to FOC, 2 September 1937, FOCP.

36. HC to J. P. Dodge, 22 May 1937, 4 June 1937, Switzerland Company and James H. Walker, Brief for the North Carolina Highway Commission, 30 April 1962, J. P. Dodge to FOC, 2 September 1937, all in FOCP. See also FOC to J. P. Dodge, 7 August 1937, HCP, Box 4. The taking was to include about seventy-five acres in fee and another twelve in scenic easements ("Under the Dome," *RNO*, 8 July 1938).

37. The per-acre average paid by North Carolina crept upward through the late 1930s but generally remained between thirty and forty dollars during this period ("Claims," *RNO*, 22 December 1938; RGB to FOC, 20 August 1937, Frank L. Dunlap to FOC, 27 August 1937, both in FOCP). Both the Cherokee and Linville negotiations ended with per-acre payments of fifty dollars or less.

38. FOC to RGB, 22 September 1937, FOCP; "Resort Asks State to Pay $50,000 for Right-of-Way," *RNO*, 6 July 1938; "Clarkson Gives Claim of Resort," *RNO*, 8 July 1938; "Under the Dome," 8 July 1938; Editorial, *RNO*, 8 July 1938; Switzerland Company and Walker, Brief.

39. See summary of events in Switzerland Company case in FOC to Jonathan Daniels, 18 November 1939, FOCP. The specifics of the appraisers' decision are outlined in HC to Carol D. Taliaferro, 12 December 1938, FOCP. See also Guy T. Carswell to J. A. McMillan, 28 December 1938, FOCP; "State to Resist Clarkson Claims" *RNO*, 17 December 1938; Frank L. Dunlap to J. Gordon Hackett, 20 December 1938, HC to E. L. McKee, 11 April 1939, both in SHCRWD, Box 3; "Little Switzerland Land Company Suit for Damages from Highway Commission in Court," *Spruce Pine*

Tri-County News, 6 April 1939. My discussion of arguments and legal maneuvers in the case is informed by the official transcripts and records of the case (*Switzerland Company v. North Carolina State Highway and Public Works Commission*, 216 N.C. 450 [1939], contained in the *Mitchell North Carolina Appeal Record*) and the decision (*North Carolina Reports*, vol. 216).

40. Clarkson frequently employed the "Chinese wall" image: see, for example, "Clarkson Gives Claim"; FOC to Jonathan Daniels, 18 November 1939, FOCP (later printed as a letter to the editor, RNO, 28 November 1939); HC to Ida C. Jones, 1 November 1937, FOCP; Switzerland Company and Walker, Brief. See also numerous letters in HCP, Box 4; FOC, "Little Switzerland Again" [letter to the editor], RNO, 18 September 1938.

41. "Resort Asks State to Pay $50,000."

42. Ibid.; "Clarkson Gives Claim"; "Under the Dome," 8 July 1938; Editorial, RNO, 8 July 1938; Frank L. Dunlap to FOC, 27 August 1937, 1 September 1937, FOC to RGB, 1 September 1937, all in FOCP; Report of Highway Commission Response in the Switzerland Company's Lawsuit in "Asserts Parkway to Help Property," RNO, 14 July 1938.

43. J. P. Dodge to FOC, 2 September 1937, 14 May 1938, FOCP; Switzerland Company and Walker, Brief. See also J. P. Dodge to RGB, 6 June 1938, Charles Ross to AED, 10 February 1939, both in SHCRWD, Box 11; "Resort Asks State to Pay $50,000"; "Asserts Parkway to Help Property"; SWA to NPS Director, 1 June 1939, CCF7B, Box 2733; SPW and SWA, "Special Report on the Switzerland Company Land Holdings," 24 February 1941, CCF7B, Box 2737; FOC to Jonathan Daniels, 18 November 1939, FOCP; Charles Ross to Donald E. Lee, 21 July 1941, CCF7B, Box 2768; EHA to J. P. Dodge, 26 January 1939, SHCRWD, Box 11; "Cooperative Agreement" between the North Carolina State Highway and Public Works Commission and the Interior Department "Relating to the Relocation, Abandonment, and Maintenance of Public Roads on Parkway Lands, Section 2-L," 30 August 1938, included on p. 271 of the trial record.

44. "Award of $25,000 to Little Switzerland Company Is Upheld," *Asheville Times*, 8 November 1939; "Evenly Divided Court Upholds $25,000 Award," RNO, 9 November 1939; Switzerland Company and Walker, Brief; Switzerland Company Financial Records, 1939, FOCP.

45. See HC to Allen Austin, 4 January 1939, FOC to HC, 16 December 1939, Taliaferro and Clarkson, "Switzerland Company in Account with Taliaferro & Clarkson," 16 December 1939, FOC to HC, 21 December 1939, all in FOCP; HC to Julia L. Clarkson, 24 January 1940, HC to John D. Curtis, 10 February 1940, HC to A. E. Clarkson, 23 February 1940, all in HCP, Box 4.

46. See HC to FOC, 18 April 1939, 8 January 1940, both in FOCP; HC to Annie Clarkson, 12 March 1940, HC to James P. Burke, 18 January 1940, HC to Thomas S. Clarkson, 14 May 1940, all in HCP, Box 4; Duls, *Story of Little Switzerland*, 195; "Little Switzerland Is Dignified Resort," *Spruce Pine Tri-County News*, 12 June 1941, 12; Chronology of Parkway Construction, n.d., BRPRG 5, Box 49.

47. Duls, *Story of Little Switzerland*, 193–215, 216–21; Ashton Chapman, "Little Switzerland Area Boasts Many Top Tourist Attractions," ACT, 27 July 1958.

48. HC to E. L. McKee, 3 January 1938, HCP, Box 4; HC to FOC, 4 January 1938, 22 January 1938, 14 May 1938, 12 May 1938, 16 December 1939, Switzerland Company, Contract with Attorneys, December 1939, all in FOCP; Taliaferro and Clarkson, "Switzerland Company in Account."

49. See FOC, "Little Switzerland Again"; FOC to E. B. Jeffress, 26 December 1938, FOCP; "Resort Asks State to Pay $50,000"; "Under the Dome," 10 September 1938.

50. "Clarkson Gives Claim"; "Under the Dome," 8 July 1938; Editorial, RNO, 8 July 1938; "Asserts Parkway to Help Property."

51. See HC to FOC, 20 July 1938, FOC to JCBE, 28 July 1938, both in FOCP; "Clarksons Reply in Parkway Case," RNO, 3 August 1938.

52. HC to FOC, 20 July 1938, FOCP; FOC to J. P. Dodge, 7 August 1937, HCP, Box 4.

53. Report of Meeting, 1 August 1938, HCP, Box 4; Committee of Mass Meeting, *What Citizens Think*; Duls, *Story of Little Switzerland*, 108–10; "List of Plaintiff's Witnesses in the Superior Court, March–April Term 1939," "Mitchell County: List of Plaintiff's Witnesses before the Commissioners," 1939, both in FOCP.

54. HC to FOC, 3 August 1938, 10 August 1938, 3 September 1938, 4 September 1938, FOCP; Committee of Mass Meeting, *What Citizens Think*. For information on the pamphlet's production, see Wade Lucas, "The Political Pinwheel," RNO, 6 September 1938.

55. Lucas, "Political Pinwheel"; "Trial by Pamphlet," RNO, 10 September 1938.

56. "Issue of 'Ethics' Raised in Case," RNO, 10 September 1938; "Trial by Pamphlet"; "Under the Dome," 10 September 1938; FOC to Editor, RNO, 14 September 1938, FOCP, printed as FOC, "Little Switzerland Again"; "A Plea for Simple Truth and Justice," RNO, 2 October 1938; HC to Walter C. Watt, 3 October 1938, FOCP. See also HC to FOC, 17 September 1938, 18 September 1938, 28 September 1938, W. Ray Deal to Frank Daniels, September 19, 1938, all in FOCP.

57. See HC to Carol D. Taliaferro, 3 November 1938, FOC to Jonathan Daniels, 3 January 1939, FOC to John A. Park, 17 January 1939, HC to Allen Austin, 4 January 1939, all in FOCP. Another battle with the *News and Observer* over publication of a long Francis Clarkson letter to the editor took place in late 1939. See FOC to Jonathan Daniels, 18 November 1939, 24 November 1939, FOC to HC, 24 November 1939, FOC to Frank Smethurst, 25 November 1939, all in FOCP; Switzerland Company, "Little Switzerland and the State," RNO, 28 November 1939.

58. HC to FOC, 3 May 1938, 28 September 1938, HC to Clyde R. Hoey, 23 May 1939, all in FOCP; HC to FOC, 15 February 1940, HCP, Box 4. For further public and private examples of Clarkson's overblown rhetoric, see "Clarkson Gives Claim"; Committee of Mass Meeting, *What Citizens Think*; Lucas, "Political Pinwheel"; "Issue of 'Ethics' Raised in Case"; FOC to JCBE, 29 October 1938, HC to Clyde R. Hoey, 23 May 1939, both in FOCP; HC to Thomas S. Clarkson, 14 May 1940, HCP, Box 4.

59. This language is taken from the Switzerland Company's legal documents filed in the initial complaint and is quoted in "Clarkson Gives Claim."

60. R. F. Crouse to FOC, 17 August 1938, FOC to R. F. Crouse, 15 August 1938, both in FOCP.

61. FOC to E. B. Jeffress, 26 December 1938, HC to FOC, 14 May 1938, FOC to Jonathan Daniels, 3 January 1939, FOC to John A. Park, 17 January 1939, HC to RGB, 12 January 1939, all in FOCP.

62. HC to Wilson Warlick, 11 April 1939, HC to FOC, 10 April 1939, both in FOCP; "A Statement by Hon. Heriot Clarkson," *Spruce Pine Tri-County News*, 13 April 1939.

63. The protracted affair is described in North Carolina Historical Commission, "Matters Presented to Mr. Samuel P. Weems, Asst. Supt. Blue Ridge Parkway," 10 August 1940, SPW to NPS Director and G. A. Moskey, 13 September 1940, FOC to E. M. Dale, 14 October 1940, SPW to NPS Director, 17 October 1940, AED to Harry McMullan, 22 October 1940, all in CCF7B, Box 2733; FOC to SPW, 4 November 1940, FOC to AED, 4 November 1940, K. C. McCarter to FOC, 25 November 1940, FOC to Newton B. Drury, 16 December 1940, SPW to Ranger Liles, 2 April 1941, C. K. Simmers to Chief Counsel, NPS, 30 April 1941, SWA to AED, 21 August 1940, AED to FOC, 29 January 1941, AED to Acting Superintendent, Blue Ridge Parkway, 21 April 1941, all in CCF7B, Box 2737; SPW and SWA, Special Report; HC to SPW, 7 October 1940, SPW to HC, 12 October 1940, FOC to AED, 4 November 1940, 13 February 1941, Newton B. Drury to FOC, 3 December 1940, 8 January 1941, AED to HLI, 1 March 1941, all in CCF7B, Box 2768.

64. CMW to ABC, 3 November 1936, CCF7B, Box 2714.

65. Pierce, "Boosters, Bureaucrats, Politicians and Philanthropists," 223–34 (later published as Pierce, *Great Smokies*); Rothman, *Devil's Bargains*; Sellars, *Preserving Nature*, 280–90.

CHAPTER 5

1. See Prucha, *Great Father*, 338; Graham D. Taylor, *New Deal and American Indian Tribalism*, 93–94.

2. U.S. Congress, House, Committee on Public Lands, *Establishing the Blue Ridge Parkway*; Finger, *Cherokee Americans*, 7, 54–55, 75–78. The estimate of 5 percent (three thousand of the tribe's sixty thousand total acres) comes from Fred Bauer's testimony in U.S. Congress, House, Committee on Public Lands, *Establishing the Blue Ridge Parkway*, 72. See also Theda Perdue, *The Cherokee*, 96–99; Theda Perdue, *Native Carolinians*, 36–44; Hill, "Cherokee Patterns," 428–46, 463 (later published as *Weaving New Worlds*); EBCCM.

3. Finger, *Cherokee Americans*, 32, 67–74, 84.

4. Finger, *Eastern Band*; Theda Perdue, *Native Carolinians*, 36–44; Finger, *Cherokee Americans*, xi, 9.

5. Finger, *Cherokee Americans*, 9–10.

6. Prucha, *Great Father*, 326, 338–39; Graham D. Taylor, *New Deal and American Indian Tribalism*, 93–94; Philp, *John Collier's Crusade*; Kelley, *Assault on Assimilation*.

7. Prucha, *Great Father*, 272–77; Philp, *John Collier's Crusade*, 24; Dorman, *Revolt of the Provinces*, 63.

8. Dorman, *Revolt of the Provinces*, 60, 61–62, 63, 64, 66–72; Prucha, *Great Father*, 317; Graham D. Taylor, *New Deal and American Indian Tribalism*, introduction; Philp, *John Collier's Crusade*, 161.

9. Prucha, *Great Father*, 317, 277; Graham D. Taylor, *New Deal and American Indian Tribalism*, introduction; Philp, *John Collier's Crusade*, 161; Dorman, *Revolt of the Provinces*, 67–69, 71–74.

10. Prucha, *Great Father*, 320, 305 (on land allotment), 323–24, 326, 327–28, 339; Graham D. Taylor, *New Deal and American Indian Tribalism*, 27–29, 31–32; Philp, *John Collier's Crusade*, 159–60. See also T. H. Watkins, *Righteous Pilgrim*, 543; Finger, *Cherokee Americans*, 79–81, 82–83.

11. Philp, *John Collier's Crusade*, 4; Collier, *From Every Zenith*, 31. Most of this discussion is drawn from Collier, *From Every Zenith*, 27–33, 49–56.

12. Finger, *Cherokee Americans*, 80, 84–85. In their initial votes, 181 tribes (with a population of 129,750) voted to accept the IRA, while 77 tribes (86,365 Indians) repudiated it (Prucha, *Great Father*, 324–35). See also Charles J. Weeks, "Eastern Cherokee and the New Deal"; Hauptman, "American Indian Federation." The slogan was that of Joseph W. Latimer, quoted in Hauptman, "American Indian Federation," 387.

13. Charles J. Weeks, "Eastern Cherokee and the New Deal"; Finger, *Cherokee Americans*, 84–91. The Bauers' views on the Eastern Cherokees' relationship to the federal government are most completely spelled out in Fred Bauer, *Land*.

14. EBCCM, 7 January 1935; U.S. Congress, Senate, Subcommittee of the Committee on Indian Affairs, *Survey of Conditions*, 20596, 20616, 20633; U.S. Congress, House, Committee on Public Lands, *Establishing the Blue Ridge Parkway*, 55, 61; Catherine A. Bauer to CMW, 20 October 1935, SHCRWD, Box 15; *North Carolina Atlas and Gazetteer*. See map of North Carolina in *Rand McNally Road Atlas*, 1936, 62–63, and descriptions of poor road conditions on the reservation in the 1930s in Hill, "Cherokee Patterns," 453, 457–58. There is some confusion about exactly what action the council took at its January meeting. Council minutes seem to indicate that it "granted" the right-of-way. Catherine Bauer reported, however (Bauer to CMW, 20 October 1935, SHCRWD, Box 15), that the council simply granted state and federal officials the right to survey for a right-of-way for the Parkway on the reservation, a much more cautious move. At any rate, the January council was clearly much more amenable to the possibility of the Parkway coming to the reservation than later councils would be.

15. Finger, *Cherokee Americans*, 78–79; EBCCM, 7 January 1935; U.S. Congress, Senate, Subcommittee of the Committee on Indian Affairs, *Survey of Conditions*, 20596, 20616, 20619, 20633; U.S. Congress, House, Committee on Public Lands, *Establishing the Blue Ridge Parkway*, 55, 61; Catherine A. Bauer to CMW, 20 October 1935, SHCRWD, Box 15; E. B. Jeffress to Theodore E. Straus, 1 June 1934, CCF7B, Box 2711.

16. Catherine Bauer reported that at the time the council approved the two-hundred-foot right-of-way and agreed to allow surveying, "NO MENTION of restrictions was made. . . . NO MENTION was then made of the amount of easements, of a utility road, of underpasses, not even of recompense for damage" (Catherine A. Bauer to CMW, 20 October 1935, SHCRWD, Box 15; John Collier to ABC, 21 February 1935, CCF7B, Box 2734).

17. John Collier to ABC, 21 February 1935, AED to TCV, 23 February 1935, both in CCF7B, Box 2734. On the petition, see U.S. Congress, Senate, Subcommittee of the Committee on Indian Affairs, *Survey of Conditions*, 20596–97.

    I have been unable to locate a copy of this petition to review directly. The information here comes from hearings before a Senate committee critical of the Indian New Deal. The transcript of these hearings notes that many of the signatures "are indecipherable," and I have no way of knowing to what degree this petition reflected the views of which Cherokees. See also Catherine A. Bauer to CMW, 20 October 1935, SHCRWD, Box 15; U.S. Congress, Senate, Subcommittee of the Committee on Indian Affairs, *Survey of Conditions*, 20596–20600, 20614–17. Bauer's letter is referred to in U.S. Congress, Senate, Subcommittee of the Committee on Indian Affairs, *Survey of Conditions*, 20599. Catherine Bauer apparently did not receive a response from Eleanor Roosevelt.

18. Prucha, *Great Father*, 335; John Collier to ABC, 4 March 1935, AED to John Collier, 18 April 1935, both in CCF7B, Box 2734.

19. John Collier to Harold W. Foght, 30 April 1935, CCF7B, Box 2734.

20. Catherine A. Bauer to CMW, 20 October 1935, SHCRWD, Box 15; HLI, "Message to the Cherokee Tribe," 20 May 1935, CCF7B, Box 2734. All evidence indicates that Ickes, who had long been interested in Indian issues, strongly supported Collier's new Indian Bureau policies. See Prucha, *Great Father*, 316–17; T. H. Watkins, *Righteous Pilgrim*, 535.

21. Harold W. Foght and Jarrett Blythe to HLI, 24 June 1935, CCF7B, Box 2734.

22. U.S. Congress, House, Committee on Public Lands, *Establishing the Blue Ridge Parkway*, 66; Finger, *Cherokee Americans*, 75–76; Harold W. Foght and Jarrett Blythe to HLI, 24 June 1935, CCF7B, Box 2734; Catherine A. Bauer to CMW, 20 October 1935, SHCRWD, Box 15.

23. Finger, *Cherokee Americans*, 85; Fred Bauer, *Land*, introductory page; Jane Hall, "Hall Marks," RNO, 8 July 1962; "3 Groups Plan Grave Marker for 19th-Century Architect," RNO, 14 January 1986; Prioli, "Indian 'Princess' and the Architect," 296, 300; CMW, "Half Indian Is Chief of Tribe of Cherokees," RNO, 1 December 1935.

24. Adams, *Education for Extinction*, 48–59, 307–33; Coleman, *American Indian Children at School*; U.S. Congress, Senate, Subcommittee of the Committee on Indian Affairs, *Survey of Conditions*, 20628; Finger, *Cherokee Americans*, 85. In the introduction to *Land*, Fred Bauer notes that he taught and coached at the Phoenix Indian School in Arizona (founded 1891) and the Mt. Pleasant Indian School in Michigan (founded 1893).

25. CMW, "Half Indian Is Chief"; Finger, *Cherokee Americans*, 85, 89; Catherine Bauer to JWB, 22 January 1937, JWBP, Box 314.

26. Finger, *Cherokee Americans*, 82, 85–87.

27. Harold W. Foght to John Collier, 15 March 1937, SERG 75, Series 6, Box 10; Finger, *Cherokee Americans*, 88–89; Catherine A. Bauer to CMW, 20 Oct. 1935, SHCRWD, Box 15; U.S. Congress, Senate, Subcommittee of the Committee on Indian Affairs, *Survey of Conditions*, 20644–46.

28. Harold W. Foght to John Collier, 15 March 1937, SERG 75, Series 6, Box 10; Finger, *Cherokee Americans*, 80–81, 88; U.S. Congress, Senate, Subcommittee of the Committee on Indian Affairs, *Survey of Conditions*, 20644–47; Fred Bauer, *Land*, 39–40.

29. Harold W. Foght to John Collier, 15 March 1937, SERG 75, Series 6, Box 10.

30. EBCCM, 7 October 1935; Finger, *Cherokee Americans*, 85–91. Controversy arose at the October

1935 tribal council meeting about whether to seat Bauer as vice chief. Tribal regulations required the vice chief to be at least 50 percent Cherokee, and council members and witnesses differed as to whether Bauer met this requirement (he did not). It was finally agreed, however, that it would be legal to install him as vice chief, and, after a vote (ten to two in favor) on the issue, he was sworn in.

31. Finger, *Cherokee Americans*, 93; John Parris, "Retiring Cherokee Chief Jarrett Blythe Honored," *AC*, 4 October 1967; "Death Claims Noted Cherokee Leader, 90," *Cherokee One Feather*, 20 May 1977; Adams, *Education for Extinction*, 44–48, 326–28. On Blythe's work with the Indian Service, see U.S. Congress, Senate, Subcommittee of the Committee on Indian Affairs, *Survey of Conditions*, 20629; for an example of public testimony in which neither Bauer nor Blythe acknowledged their relationship, see U.S. Congress, House, Committee on Public Lands, *Establishing the Blue Ridge Parkway*.

32. Catherine A. Bauer to CMW, 20 October 1935, SHCRWD, Box 15.

33. Harold W. Foght and Jarrett Blythe to HLI, 24 June 1935, CCF7B, Box 2734; Fred Bauer, *Land*, 41.

34. Catherine A. Bauer to CMW, 20 October 1935, SHCRWD, Box 15; U.S. Congress, Senate, Subcommittee of the Committee on Indian Affairs, *Survey of Conditions*, 20618–19. Testimony in these hearings gives the date of the *Citizen* article as 22 June 1935 and says that the article was derived from a press release sent from the BIA agency at Cherokee. The testimony quotes the article as saying that "the Appalachian Scenic Parkway will run through the Cherokee Reservation for a distance of 11 miles after a majestic swing through Soco Gap from the Balsam Range. . . . Both Dr. Harold W. Foght, superintendent of the reservation, and Jarrett Blythe, present chief, are greatly interested in the new deal that is coming to the Eastern Band of Cherokees." See also Jack Jackson, Henry Bradley, and Meroney French to HLI, 25 June 1935, CCF7B, Box 2734.

35. Catherine A. Bauer to CMW, 20 October 1935, SHCRWD, Box 15.

36. Waffling is evident in ABC to Harold W. Foght, 3 July 1935, CCF7B, Box 2734 (announcing abandonment of Soco Valley route); M. H. McIntyre to Charles A. Webb, 22 July 1935, POF 129, Box 1 (expressing the Executive Office's sense that "we are in doubt as to what can be done" in the Cherokee section); ABC to Charles A. Webb, 23 August 1935, CCF7B, Box 2714 (reiterating the uncertainty about what the Park Service would do in light of the rejection); AED to Thomas H. MacDonald and TCV, 26 September 1935, CCF7B, Box 2730 (announcing Ickes's decision to continue to pursue the Soco route and negotiations with the Cherokees). The Weaver quotation is repeated in Catherine A. Bauer to CMW, 20 October 1935, SHCRWD, Box 15.

37. AED to Thomas H. MacDonald and TCV, 26 September 1935, CCF7B, Box 2730; Catherine A. Bauer to CMW, 20 October 1935, RGB to CMW, 29 October 1935, both in SHCRWD, Box 15; CMW to HLI, 20 November 1935, John Collier to HLI, December 1935, both in CCF7B, Box 2734.

38. Fred Bauer, *Land*, 41; Harold W. Foght and Jarrett Blythe to HLI, 24 June 1935, CCF7B, Box 2734; EBCCM, 13 December 1935.

39. Walter Brown, "One-Fourth of Parkway Work Now Allotted," *AC*, 17 December 1935, 1; "Ickes Says Cherokees Should Favor Parkway," *AC*, 18 December 1935, 1; RGB to HLI, 18 December 1935, AED to HLI, 24 December 1935, both in CCF7B, Box 2734.

40. Fred B. Bauer to HLI, 27 December 1935, CCF7B, Box 2734; Harold W. Foght to RGB, 30 December 1935, RGB to Harold Foght, 4 January 1936, both in SHCRWD, Box 15.

41. Harold W. Foght to HLI, 23 January 1936, Cherokee Indians to HLI, 14 January 1936, both in CCF7B, Box 2734.

42. Cherokee Indians to HLI, 14 January 1936, Harold W. Foght to John Collier, 30 January 1936,

both in CCF7B, Box 2734. Foght's letter was also signed and approved by Blythe. It further noted that the Bauer-McCoy group was circulating other petitions against the IRA, the chief, and the agent, many of which "have been signed . . . by children and others on promise of being placed on the ration list for the old and needy."

43. See John Collier to HLI, 5 March 1936, HLI to AED, 9 March 1936, J. R. Eakin to Director, National Park Service, 9 March 1936, J. R. Eakin, "Report on Proposed Exchange of Lands between Great Smoky Mountains National Park and Quallah Indian Reservation," 19 March 1936, all in CCF7B, Box 2734; Walter Brown, "Submits Plan for Cherokee Parkway Link," ACT, 17 May 1936, A1; "Should Solve the Problem" [editorial], AC, 18 May 1936, 4. The most careful and thorough discussion in the press of the proposed swap is "Foght Predicts Land Swap Will Please Indians," AC, 20 May 1936, 1, which detailed the terms of the swap as a transfer of 1,547 acres of land in the Ravensford area of the Great Smoky Mountains National Park for 1,202 acres of the reservation near Smokemont. The article makes clear that the exchange would not have involved a direct swap for the Parkway lands but would have constituted part of a package deal. See also U.S. Congress, House, Committee on Public Lands, Report no. 3003.

44. EBCCM, 15 March 1937. This package was originally presented to the band at the December 1936 meeting but was tabled until the March meeting (EBCCM, 10 December 1936).

45. Harold W. Foght to William Zimmerman Jr., 17 March 1937, SERG 75, Series 6, Box 10.

46. Frank L. Dunlap to JD, 7 June 1937, George Stephens to Frank L. Dunlap, 1 July 1937, both in SHCRWD, Box 2.

47. Catherine A. Bauer to CMW, 20 October 1935, SHCRWD, Box 15; U.S. Congress, House, Committee on Public Lands, Establishing the Blue Ridge Parkway, 47.

48. Dunn, Cades Cove, 241–54; Powers with Hannah, Cataloochee; Woody, "Cataloochee Homecoming." The original boundary line for the Great Smoky Mountains National Park was drawn by then Park Service associate director Arno B. Cammerer. The "Cammerer Line," embracing a much larger area than was ultimately included in the park, encompassed some Cherokee lands not included in the final park boundaries. By the time the Parkway negotiations got under way, Cammerer, long an advocate of the aggressive use of powers of eminent domain, was director of the Park Service, a fact that likely disconcerted the Cherokees contemplating the Parkway. See Margaret Lynn Brown, "Smoky Mountains Story," 142–50. Margaret Lynn Brown, Wild East, is the fullest available study of the removal of more than fifty-six hundred people from the area taken into the park.

49. Fred Bauer, Land, 39; Fred B. Bauer, "Cherokee Indian Explains Opposition to Scenic Road," Charlotte Observer, 15 January 1939.

50. Fred B. Bauer, "Cherokee Indian Explains Opposition."

51. In these as in so many other cases, MacCannell's employment (in his "Staged Authenticity," 590, 597) of Goffman's typology of front and back regions and of the ubiquitous tourist desire to have "authentic experiences" by gaining admission to normally forbidden back regions is useful.

52. "Park Development Plans Revealed," ACT, 16 October 1932, A1.

53. North Carolina Committee on Federal Parkway, "Description of a Route through North Carolina Proposed as a Part of the Scenic Parkway to Connect the Shenandoah National Park with the Great Smoky Mountains National Park," 1934, CCF7B, Box 2711.

54. HLI, "Message to the Cherokee Tribe"; Hoyt McAfee, "Scenic Grandeur along Crest Way," Charlotte Observer, 10 July 1938. See also "Progress of the Parkway" [editorial], AC, 14 December 1935, 4; Roy, "Rambling around the Roof"; Sass, "Land of the Cherokee."

55. U.S. Congress, House, Committee on Public Lands, Establishing the Blue Ridge Parkway, 74. A basis certainly existed for seeing such an agenda: Foght had previously written that the imple-

mentation of his plans for craft cooperatives under the IRA awaited only the routing of the Parkway. See Harold W. Foght and Jarrett Blythe to HLI, 24 June 1935, CCF7B, Box 2734. See also Fred Bauer, *Land*, 38–39, which discusses the committees Foght had formed in 1934 to plan tribal cooperatives and revitalize Cherokee traditions.

56. Catherine Bauer originally reported the results of this council survey (which apparently covered 1934) in Catherine A. Bauer to CMW, 20 October 1935, SHCRWD, Box 15. Fred Bauer reiterated the arguments, also referencing an independent study conducted in 1937 by journalist Eleanor Patterson, in his testimony before the House Committee on Public Lands (U.S. Congress, House, Committee on Public Lands, *Establishing the Blue Ridge Parkway*, 74–76).

57. Becker, *Selling Tradition*, 126–30; Hall et al., *Like a Family*, 298–99.

58. U.S. Congress, Senate, Subcommittee of the Committee on Indian Affairs, *Survey of Conditions*, 20707; Catherine Bauer, "Problems."

59. Catherine Bauer, "Problems." On post–World War II tourism development in the Great Smoky Mountains area, see Tooman, "Evolving Economic Impact," 223, 242–43; Finger, *Cherokee Americans*, 104, 138.

60. Fred Bauer, *Land*, 7. Finger, *Cherokee Americans*, 177, notes that U.S. courts ultimately ruled against Bauer's interpretation of Eastern Cherokee history.

61. Lowell Kirk, "The Cherokee Legend of 'Tsali,'" *Tellico Plains Mountain Press*, July 2005, <http://www.telliquah.com/Tsali2.htm> (11 August 2005); Mooney, *Myths*; Fred Bauer, *Land*, 9–33; Finger, *Cherokee Americans*, 44.

62. JD to Mr. West, 3 July 1937, CCF7B, Box 2734; U.S. Congress, House, Committee on Public Lands, *House Report no. 3003*; U.S. Congress, House, Committee on Public Lands, *House Report no. 937*; U.S. Congress, House, Committee on Public Lands, *Establishing the Blue Ridge Parkway*, 36–37; "Indians to Vote on Park Route," RNO, 25 August 1937; EBCCM, 13 March 1937; HLI to JD, 8 October 1937, SHCRWD, Box 2; Finger, *Cherokee Americans*, 92–93; Fred Bauer, *Land*, 42.

63. RGB to JD, 9 July 1938, SHCRWD, Box 3; HLI to JD, 8 October 1937, SHCRWD, Box 2.

64. RGB to JD, 20 October 1937, JD to RGB, 13 October 1937, FLW to RGB, 8 December 1937, RGB to HLI, 20 December 1937, all in SHCRWD, Box 2; AED to Files, 9 March 1938, CCF7B, Box 2734.

65. EBCCM, 31 May 1938; RGB to JD, 9 July 1938, RGB to William Zimmerman Jr., 20 July 1938, SHCRWD, Box 3; U.S. Congress, House, Committee on Public Lands, *Establishing the Blue Ridge Parkway*, 5–7, 48–49. See also Finger, *Cherokee Americans*, 94.

66. EBCCM, 1 June 1938; C. M. Blair to Commissioner of Indian Affairs, 2 June 1938, SERG 75, Series 6, Box 10. According to Blair, some council members (possibly encouraged by Bauer) still appeared to fear that agreeing to the terms of the agreement would allow the state to turn over the Soco Valley right-of-way to the NPS for the Parkway. See also Fred Bauer, *Land*, 43; Finger, *Cherokee Americans*, 93.

67. RGB to JD, 3 August 1938, 9 July 1938, RGB to FLW, 2 August 1938, all in SHCRWD, Box 3; Hillory A. Tolson to ABC, 9 July 1938, CCF7B, Box 2732; Frank L. Dunlap to JD, 13 July 1938, JDP, Box 677.

68. RGB to JD, 3 August 1938, RGB to Clyde Blair, 2 August 1938, both in SHCRWD, Box 3. See also Fred Bauer, *Land*, 43; [RGB], "Memorandum for File," 9 August 1938, SHCRWD, Box 15; Frank M. Dunlap to JD, 18 August 1938, SHCRWD, Box 3. In *Land of the North Carolina Cherokees*, 43, Bauer writes that the *Asheville Citizen* reported that the council had approved the compromise. The *News and Observer* certainly did so. See Robert E. Williams, "Parkway Route Given Approval," RNO, 2 September 1938; Resolution Presented to Cherokee Council [copy], 5 August 1938, Fred Bauer to HLI, 3 September 1938, Fred B. Bauer to Clyde R. Hoey, 6 September 1938, all in SHCRWD, Box 3.

69. George Stephens to Curtis B. Johnson, 19 August 1938, Curtis B. Johnson to George Stephens, 23 August 1938, both in Stephens Papers.

70. HLI, Diaries, 1933–51, Microfilm Edition, 25 November 1938, HIP; JD to RGB, 20 July 1938, RGB to JD, 20 September 1938, RGB to FLW, 7 January 1939, all in SHCRWD, Box 3; AED to Oscar L. Chapman, 8 September 1938, Nathan R. Margold to HLI, 4 October 1938, both in CCF7B, Box 2734. Several scholars have substantiated the AIF's ties to fascist organizations: see Prucha, *Great Father*, 333–35; Hauptman, "American Indian Federation," 396–99; Philp, *John Collier's Crusade*, 202.

71. William Zimmerman Jr. to C. M. Blair, 29 October 1938 (referring to a 14 August article carried by the *Raleigh News and Observer*), C. M. Blair to William Zimmerman Jr., 8 November 1938, 30 January 1939, all in SERG 75, Series 6, Box 23; Fred B. Bauer, "Cherokee Indian Explains Opposition to Scenic Road," *Charlotte Observer*, 15 January 1939; Frank Dunlap to Jarrett Blythe, 20 February 1939, Jarrett Blythe to Frank Dunlap, 16 February 1939, both in SHCRWD, Box 3.

72. U.S. Congress, House, Committee on Public Lands, *Establishing the Blue Ridge Parkway*, 1–3; Finger, *Cherokee Americans*, 94. See also Harold D. Smith to Stephen Early, 7 June 1940, POF 5708, Box 18.

73. Charles E. Ray Jr. to RGB, 1 June 1939, SHCRWD, Box 3.

74. EBCCM, 9 December 1938; Finger, *Cherokee Americans*, 94; U.S. Congress, House, Committee on Public Lands, *Establishing the Blue Ridge Parkway*, 45–50.

75. U.S. Congress, House, Committee on Public Lands, *Establishing the Blue Ridge Parkway*, 51–61, 66–79.

76. Ibid., 53, 66–67, 78–79.

77. Ibid., 66, 68, 74–75.

78. Ibid., 70–71, 75.

79. Charles E. Ray Jr. to Frank L. Dunlap, 13 April 1940, SHCRWD, Box 4; EBCCM, 2 October 1939; Frank L. Dunlap to C. M. Blair, 15 September 1939, C. M. Blair to Frank Dunlap, 14 September 1939, both in SHCRWD, Box 3; Finger, *Cherokee Americans*, 94–96. Some evidence, recounted in later testimony before the Senate Indian Affairs Committee by AIF lobbyist Alice Lee Jemison, indicates that the BIA used (unspecified) underhanded methods to ensure Bauer's defeat (U.S. Congress, Senate, Subcommittee of the Committee on Indian Affairs, *Survey of Conditions*, 20858).

80. Frank L. Dunlap to C. M. Blair, 15 September 1939, SHCRWD, Box 3; *U.S. Statutes at Large*, 299–301; Frank L. Dunlap to Zebulon Weaver, 26 March 1940, SHCRWD, Box 4; Frank L. Dunlap to HLI, 10 January 1941, CCF7B, Box 2734; EBCCM, 6 February 1940; Fred Bauer, *Land*, 44; map of North Carolina in *Rand McNally Road Atlas*, 1944, 66–67; Finger, *Cherokee Americans*, 97. See also materials on Parkway dedication ceremonies in BRPRG 1, Series 23, Box 12. After his defeat in the 1939 election, Bauer's influence ebbed, although he continued to speak out in tribal politics up into the 1950s. He subsequently left the reservation for nearby Brevard, North Carolina, where shortly before his death in 1971 he published his antigovernment account of Eastern Cherokee history, *Land of the North Carolina Cherokees*. See "N.C. Cherokee, Ex-Chief Dies," RNO, 1 June 1971. After her husband's death, Catherine Bauer moved back to the Qualla Boundary, where she was murdered near the Parkway in January 1979. See "Woman's Death Being Probed," *Asheville Times*, 2 January 1979; "Widow, 74, Found Dead in Cherokee," AC, 3 January 1979. No further reference to Bauer's murder appeared in the *Asheville Citizen* in the week following the discovery of her body, and I do not know if the crime was ever solved.

81. Finger reports that by the late 1970s, "several court decisions had systematically repudiated the contentions of the late Fred Bauer and generations of state officials by holding that the Eastern Band is indeed a tribe, that it occupies a reservation that, whatever its origins, is similar to

other Indian reservations, and that federal authority is preeminent and virtually identical to that exercised over other federally recognized tribes" (*Cherokee Americans*, 177).

82. Parris, "Retiring Cherokee Chief Jarrett Blythe Honored"; "Death Claims Noted Cherokee Leader, 90." *Unto These Hills* was originally sponsored by the Cherokee Historical Association, a white-dominated nonprofit group set up in 1947 by the business-oriented Western North Carolina Associated Communities. The Cherokee Historical Association also developed the Oconaluftee Village and the Museum of the Cherokee Indian. See Finger, *Cherokee Americans*, 112–17, 137–38; Fred Bauer, *Land*, 54–55, 58, 184–85; Hill, "Cherokee Patterns," 505–9; Finger, "Saga of Tsali."

83. Fred Bauer, *Land*, 58; Finger, *Cherokee Americans*, 184; Hill, "Cherokee Patterns," 505–9, 588–90.

84. Finger, *Eastern Band*, 16, 18, 29, 42, 44, 105–6, 110, 120–21, 125, 144, 147, 155, 172–75. The tribe's history remains a subject of contention. See, for example, discussion of the Eastern Cherokees' exhibit at the National Museum of the American Indian in Bob Thompson, "Where Myth Meets Reality," *Washington Post*, 14 September 2004, <http://www.washingtonpost.com/wp-dyn/articles/A19201-2004Sep13.html> (28 August 2005). Debate also goes on about tourism as a development base. In 1995, Tooman held that the predominance of tourism in Swain County, where much of the Cherokee reservation is located, combined with the lack of other industrial development, had produced higher-than-average levels of unemployment and had failed significantly to raise the overall standard of living. See Tooman, "Evolving Economic Impact," 297, 310, 315, 342, 344–46, 490, 496. Tooman's analysis preceded the opening of Harrah's Cherokee Casino in 1997; for a discussion of the casino, see Oakley, "Indian Gaming." Although the casino's revenues have cured unemployment and helped provide important public facilities and services, its social, political, and cultural implications have been the subject of great internal debate reminiscent of the Parkway battles sixty years earlier.

85. Prucha, *Great Father*, 339. See also T. H. Watkins, *Righteous Pilgrim*, 540–41; Graham D. Taylor, *New Deal and American Tribalism*, 93–94, 101–2, 112; Philp, *John Collier's Crusade*, 186, 211–13, 244; Hauptman, "American Indian Federation," 401–2.

86. See *Indigenous Peoples*, xii, 43–67, 93–101, for an overview of major land-related issues facing indigenous peoples; Burger, *Report from the Frontier*, 1–4, 195–203, which discusses the ways in which the BIA facilitated mining on the Navajo and Hopi reservations and talks about the enmeshment of tribal councils in this process; Lawson, *Dammed Indians*, xix–xxxi, which covers the most damaging public works project ever brought to Indian lands in the United States.

87. See Foster's account of the late-1960s and early 1970s resistance to the Appalachian Power Company's plans to build a hydroelectric dam on the New River in Ashe County, North Carolina, in *Past Is Another Country*. Fisher, *Fighting Back*, reports on community resistance to a range of social, environmental, and other threats since the 1960s. Bartlett, *Troubled Waters*, discusses community-based opposition to Champion International paper company's continued pollution of the Pigeon River in western North Carolina and east Tennessee in the 1980s and 1990s.

CHAPTER 6

1. Viemeister, *Peaks of Otter*, 211; E. L. Johnson, "Memoir of Life at the Peaks of Otter," 21 December 1960, BRPRG 5, Box 52; Peaks of Otter, Inc., "Peaks of Otter, Inc.: An Unusual Opportunity for a Safe and Sound Investment," 1931, CCF7B, Box 2736.

2. E. L. Johnson, "Memoir of Life"; F. A. Ketterson Jr. to Liles et al., 11 October 1972, reproduced in Jean Haskell Speer, Russell, and Worsham, *Johnson Farm*, appendixes, vol. 6.

3. Alanen and Melnick, "Introduction," 8; Howett, "Integrity as a Value," 205.

4. Ketterson, interview. On the layering of cultural landscapes, see Alanen and Melnick, "Introduction," 3–6.

5. Granville Liles, "History of the Blue Ridge Parkway," BRPRG 5, Box 48.

6. Lowenthal, "Pioneer Museums"; Loewen, *Lies across America*; Howett, "Integrity as a Value," 205; Shackel, *Myth*; MacCannell, "Staged Authenticity," 590.

7. Alanen, "Considering the Ordinary," 127–38; Howett, "Integrity as a Value," 205–7.

8. Viemeister, *Peaks of Otter*, 15; SWA, "Appalachian National Parkway from Shenandoah National Park to Great Smoky Mountains National Park, Report on Recreation and Service Areas: Type and Scope of Development Proposed," 15 December 1934, CCF7B, Box 2711; "Brief Description of the Recreation Areas Adjacent to the Parkway, to Accompany the Master Plan Therof Drawn June 3, 1936," 3 June 1936, BRPRG 5, Box 9.

9. Viemeister, *Peaks of Otter*, 15–47. Present-day Route 43 through the Peaks follows closely the path of the Liberty-Buchanan Turnpike. For conflicting information regarding the date of the turnpike's construction, see Robert F. Hunter, "Turnpike Movement," 279–80; Sarvis, "Turnpike Tourism"; Jean Haskell Speer, Russell, and Worsham, *Johnson Farm*, 10–11.

10. Sarvis, "Turnpike Tourism," 17–19; Robert F. Hunter, "Turnpike Construction"; Robert F. Hunter, "Turnpike Movement"; Viemeister, *Peaks of Otter*, 72–90, 97; Jean Haskell Speer, Russell, and Worsham, *Johnson Farm*, 10–20; Crayon, "Virginia Illustrated"; Daniel, *Bedford County*.

11. Jean Haskell Speer, Russell, and Worsham, *Johnson Farm*, 29–33.

12. Ibid., 17–18, 33–38; Rosemary Johnson et al., "Johnson Farm"; Viemeister, *Peaks of Otter*, 112–30.

13. Viemeister, *Peaks of Otter*, 123–33, 136–37.

14. Jean Haskell Speer, Russell, and Worsham, *Johnson Farm*, 17–18, 33–38; Rosemary Johnson et al., "Johnson Farm"; Viemeister, *Peaks of Otter*, 112–30.

15. Viemeister, *Peaks of Otter*, 131–51; Jean Haskell Speer, Russell, and Worsham, *Johnson Farm*, 20.

16. Jean Haskell Speer, Russell, and Worsham, *Johnson Farm*, 17–18, 33–38.

17. Viemeister, *Peaks of Otter*, 150–51.

18. Ibid., 152.

19. Ibid., 151–67; Dodson, *General Assembly of Virginia*.

20. T. W. Richardson to A. Willis Robertson, 17 February 1917, A. Willis Robertson to T. W. Richardson, 19 February 1917, both in RPC.

21. T. W. Richardson to Charles W. Rosenberg, 11 August 1916, RPC; "Proposed Plan for Development of the Peaks of Otter and Mons Hotel," [1927], RPC; Jean Haskell Speer, Russell, and Worsham, *Johnson Farm*, 20–23; Myriam P. Moore to Tom Givens, 13 March 1969, in Jean Haskell Speer, Russell, and Worsham, *Johnson Farm*, appendixes, vol. 3; David T. Catlin, "Notes Made at the Offices of the *Bedford Bulletin-Democrat*, Nov. 9, 1979," in Jean Haskell Speer, Russell, and Worsham, *Johnson Farm*, appendixes, vol. 3; Viemeister, *Peaks of Otter*, 154–59, 166–73.

22. "Hotel Mons and Peaks of Otter" [brochure], [1930s], BRPRG 5, Box 52; "Hotel Mons and the Peaks of Otter, Bedford, Virginia. Mrs. Fredonia Z. Putnam, Manager" [brochure], [1930?], BRPRG 5, Box 54; Myriam P. Moore to Tom Givens, 13 March 1969, Moore, interview, both in Jean Haskell Speer, Russell, and Worsham, *Johnson Farm*, appendixes, vol. 3.

23. Myriam P. Moore to Tom Givens, 13 March 1969, in Jean Haskell Speer, Russell, and Worsham, *Johnson Farm*, appendixes, vol. 3; "Hotel Mons and Peaks of Otter"; "Hotel Mons and the Peaks of Otter, Bedford, Virginia. Mrs. Fredonia Z. Putnam, Manager"; "Proposed Plan for Development of the Peaks of Otter and Mons Hotel"; Jean Haskell Speer, Russell, and Worsham, *Johnson Farm*, 21; Moore, interview, in Jean Haskell Speer, Russell, and Worsham, *Johnson Farm*, appendixes, vol. 3. The rates charged by the hotel are roughly equivalent to about sixty dollars per night in 2000 (Nash et al., *American People* 2:822–23; U.S. Census Bureau, "DP-3, Profile of Selected Economic Characteristics: 2000").

24. Myriam Putnam Moore to Ranger Clifton, 2 December 1956, Myriam P. Moore to Tom Givens,

[372] NOTES TO PAGES 217–24

13 March 1969, both in Jean Haskell Speer, Russell, and Worsham, *Johnson Farm*, appendixes, vol. 3; "Hotel Mons and Peaks of Otter."

25. Jean Haskell Speer, Russell, and Worsham, *Johnson Farm*, 35–38.

26. Ibid., 35–38, 50–62. Most details in the Speer study are taken from a large interview project conducted in the 1970s by Rosemary Johnson et al., "Johnson Farm."

27. Jean Haskell Speer, Russell, and Worsham, *Johnson Farm*, 35–38, 50–62; Rosemary Johnson et al., "Johnson Farm."

28. Jean Haskell Speer, Russell, and Worsham, *Johnson Farm*, 35–38, 50–62; Rosemary Johnson et al., "Johnson Farm."

29. Viemeister, *Peaks of Otter*, 97, 162–68; Peaks of Otter, Inc., "Peaks of Otter, Inc."; T. W. Richardson to E. T. Brown, 6 June 1928, RPC; "Hotel Mons and the Peaks of Otter, Bedford, Virginia. Mrs. Fredonia Z. Putnam, Manager"; "Hotel Mons and Peaks of Otter"; T. W. Richardson to Messrs. Pollard and Bagby, 15 October 1927, 19 October 1927, RPC.

30. T. W. Richardson to Charles W. Rosenberg, 11 August 1916, RPC; "Hotel Mons and the Peaks of Otter, Bedford, Virginia. Mrs. Fredonia Z. Putnam, Manager"; Myriam P. Moore to Tom Givens, 13 March 1969, in Jean Haskell Speer, Russell, and Worsham, *Johnson Farm*, appendixes, vol. 3; Hunter Miller to AED, 11 May 1936, CCF7B, Box 2736; *Touring the Great Smoky Mountains National Park and the Southland*, (Asheville, N.C.: Southland Tourist, 1933). Assuming a family income in the 1920s of $2,000 per year and an annual family income in 2000 of $42,000, the admission charge equates to approximately $10.50 per person to ascend Sharp Top. The actual cost in 2002 was $4.50 per adult.

31. Moore, interview, in Jean Haskell Speer, Russell, and Worsham, *Johnson Farm*, appendixes, vol. 3; "Proposed Plan for Development of the Peaks of Otter and Mons Hotel"; "Income from Admissions, Etc., Peaks of Otter," [1927?], RPC.

32. "The Peaks of Otter," [1929?], RPC; "The Tourist Gold Mine: Millions of Dollars Brought into Virginia by Visitors to Her Scenic Wonders," *Bedford Bulletin*, [1931?], RPC.

33. With regard to the Bryant family at the Johnson Farm, a similar idea is put forth in Jean Haskell Speer, Russell, and Worsham, *Johnson Farm*, 57.

34. "Hotel Mons and Peaks of Otter"; Lee H. Williamson, "Appraisal, Peaks of Otter, Inc. Lands," 5 September 1935, CCF7B, Box 2736; T. W. Richardson to E. T. Brown, 6 June 1928, RPC; Myriam P. Moore to Tom Givens, 13 March 1969, in Jean Haskell Speer, Russell, and Worsham, *Johnson Farm*, appendixes, vol. 3; T. W. Richardson to E. Hilton Jackson, 28 June 1930, RPC.

35. T. W. Richardson to E. T. Brown, 6 June 1928, T. W. Richardson to E. Hilton Jackson, 28 June 1930, T. W. Richardson to William E. Carson, 31 January 1931, all in RPC.

36. T. W. Richardson to E. Hilton Jackson, 28 June 1930, RPC; "The Peaks of Otter," [1930?]; T. W. Richardson to Colonel Holden, 5 December 1927, RPC.

37. Many letters in the Peaks of Otter Corporation correspondence from 1927 to 1932 make clear that both the corporation and many Bedford citizens aggressively lobbied the Highway Commission. See "Proposed Plan for Development of the Peaks of Otter and Mons Hotel"; T. W. Richardson to E. Hilton Jackson, 28 June 1930, "The Peaks of Otter," [1930?], T. W. Richardson to Colonel Holden, 5 December 1927, T. W. Richardson to Messrs. Pollard and Bagby, 15 October 1927, 19 October 1927, T. W. Richardson to E. T. Brown, 6 June 1928, T. W. Richardson to William E. Carson, 31 January 1931, all in RPC; Hunter Miller to SWA, 17 December 1934, CCF7B, Box 2736. The Richardson correspondence gives the date of the road's incorporation into the state system as 1931, but reading about the history of Virginia road building leads me to conclude that this action must have been part of the Secondary Roads Act of 1932, when Virginia took all public roads that had been under local control into the state system. See Bowman, *Highway Politics*, 31.

38. Peaks of Otter, Inc., "Peaks of Otter, Inc."; T. W. Richardson to E. T. Brown, 6 June 1928, T. W. Richardson to Colonel Holden, 5 December 1927, T. W. Richardson to E. Hilton Jackson, 28 June 1930, T. W. Richardson to J. W. Hurt, 15 December 1930, T. W. Richardson to William E. Carson, 31 January 1931, T. W. Richardson to T. C. Northcott, 2 May 1931, T. W. Richardson to Morton G. Thalheimer, 20 June 1931, Hunter Miller to F. H. Winter and Company, 2 May 1932, all in RPC.

39. John J. Palmer, "Memorandum for Files—Chief Park Naturalist," 20 October 1967, in Jean Haskell Speer, Russell, and Worsham, *Johnson Farm*, appendixes, vol. 6. See also Jean Haskell Speer, Russell, and Worsham, *Johnson Farm*, 35–38, 50–62; Rosemary Johnson et al., "Johnson Farm"; Viemeister, *Peaks of Otter*, 180.

40. "$7,500,000 Plan for Scenic Road Headed by Byrd," *Richmond Times-Dispatch*, 23 September 1933.

41. John Garland Pollard to Secretary of the Commonwealth, 6 October 1933, Hunter Miller to John Garland Pollard, 11 December 1933, both in John Garland Pollard Papers, Box 19, Library of Virginia, Richmond. See also Mrs. F. P. Petty, Minutes of Meeting, 17 October 1933, CCF7B, Box 2711; PWA, "The Shenandoah–Smoky Mountain Parkway and Stabilization Project: Proceedings of the Meetings Held in Baltimore, February 5, 6, 7, 1934," CCF18, Box 2; Hunter Miller to SWA, 17 December 1934, CCF7B, Box 2736.

42. Viemeister, *Peaks of Otter*, 184.

43. Hunter Miller to ABC, 13 April 1934, William E. Carson to ABC, 7 May 1934, John Garland Pollard to ABC, 7 May 1934, A. Willis Robertson to ABC, 7 May 1934, E. Lee Trinkle to ABC, 7 May 1934, all in CCF7B, Box 2736. This collection contains eleven more such letters of support for this project. See also SWA, "Appalachian National Parkway from Shenandoah National Park to Great Smoky Mountains National Park, Report on Recreation and Service Areas."

44. Lee H. Williamson, "Appraisal"; Hunter Miller to ABC, 19 January 1935, J. W. Rader and C. K. Simmers, "Appraisal Report—Peaks of Otter Project," 27 December 1935, National Forest Service, "Summary of Lands Recommended for Purchase," 1936, all in CCF7B, Box 2736.

45. Hunter Miller to SWA, 3 January 1935, Hunter Miller to TCV, 2 February 1935, J. Callaway Brown to C. A. Woodrum, 27 December 1934, all in CCF7B, Box 2736.

46. AED to HLI, 4 March 1936, HLI to AED, 10 March 1936, Hunter Miller to TCV, 2 February 1935, Hunter Miller to HLI, 17 March 1936, Peaks of Otter, Inc., "Option to Sell Real Estate to the United States Government," 28 July 1936, SWA to ABC, 3 December 1938, all in CCF7B, Box 2736. The "Financial Statement, Peaks of Otter, Inc., Dec. 31, 1936," RPC, indicates two dollars cash in the bank and assets consisting mostly of the Peaks property, balanced against liabilities consisting mostly of stock issued. On the CCC, see Viemeister, *Peaks of Otter*, 182–87. The Forest Service bought the lands through an executive order authorizing the use of emergency funds for the purchase. See Franklin D. Roosevelt, Executive Order, "Purchase of Forest Lands for Emergency Conservation Work," June 1936, CCF7B, Box 2736; Deed for Purchase of Peaks of Otter Property, 16 April 1937, BRPRG 7, Box 17.

47. H. A. Wallace to James H. Price, 6 November 1939, Hunter Miller to ABC, 5 December 1939, both in BRPRG 7, Box 17. See also DOI, NPS, Branch of Plans and Design, "Master Plan, Blue Ridge Parkway, Second Edition, 1941," with maps, 8 May 1941, Record Group 79 (National Park Service), Blue Ridge Parkway Master Plans, Folders 1–4, Cartographic Research Room, National Archives II, College Park, Maryland. This Parkway master plan explains that lands were obtained through the Resettlement Administration submarginal lands acquisition program at Pine Spur, Rocky Knob, and Smart View (Virginia) and at the Bluff (Doughton Park) and Cumberland Knob (North Carolina). Later correspondence indicates that debt pressure on the company leaders (who had taken responsibility for the loans the company had taken out)

was a major reason for their coming to agreement with the NPS. See W. Richardson to John Tucker Percy, 24 February 1957, RPC.

48. This long process is discussed in massive correspondence (1937–42) in the National Archives II and the Blue Ridge Parkway Archives. See Hunter Miller to SWA, 25 October 1938, G. A. Moskey to NPS Director, 1 July 1939, Hunter Miller to NPS Director, 4 October 1939, all in CCF7B, Box 2736. See also AED to Carter Glass, 4 March 1941, CCF7B, Box 2735; Hunter Miller to ABC, 5 December 1939, BRPRG 7, Box 17; Hunter Miller to ABC, 29 May 1940, Hunter Miller to AED, 22 June 1940, 27 September 1940, Hunter Miller to SWA, 2 November 1940, SWA to J. Callaway Brown, 1 March 1941, Hunter Miller to Ira T. Yarnall, 4 February 1942, AED to HLI, 5 March 1942, all in BRPRG 7, Box 18; DOI, NPS, Branch of Plans and Design, "Master Plan, Blue Ridge Parkway, Second Edition"; Jean Haskell Speer, Russell, and Worsham, *Johnson Farm*, 65–67; *Blue Ridge Parkway News* 5, no. 2 (February–March 1942).

49. "List of Land Tracts Composing Peaks of Otter Park," 20 March 1950, BRPRG 7, Box 18; Viemeister, *Peaks of Otter*, 197–98; Jean Haskell Speer, Russell, and Worsham, *Johnson Farm*, 69–70; Robert A. Hope and D. H. Robinson, "Historic Structures Report, Part I, Johnson Farm Group, Class CC, Blue Ridge Parkway," 30 January 1964, in Jean Haskell Speer, Russell, and Worsham, *Johnson Farm*, appendixes, vol. 6.

50. SPW, "Superintendent's Monthly Narrative Report, November 1945," 11 December 1945, NPS, "Blue Ridge Parkway Annual Report, Fiscal Year 1948," 1948, both in CCF7B, Box 2718; J. Carlisle Crouch, "Superintendent's Monthly Narrative Report, April 1947," 13 May 1947, [SPW], "Superintendent's Monthly Narrative Report, July 1948," 10 August 1948, both in CCF7B, Box 2719; J. Carlisle Crouch, "Annual Report of the Blue Ridge Parkway to the Director, National Park Service, 1948 Fiscal Year," 12 July 1948, "Annual Report of the Blue Ridge Parkway to the Director, National Park Service, 1958," both in Box F217.B6U55, Blue Ridge Parkway Archives; Hunter Miller to W. L. Lyle, 14 March 1939, Webster Richardson to Hunter Miller, 22 April 1941, "Bus Service to Peaks Started," 31 July 1948, all in RPC.

51. Hunter Miller to Stockholders of the Peaks of Otter, Inc., 10 January 1950, RPC.

52. The decline is summarized in Webster Richardson to CLW, 13 March 1958, RPC. See also Hunter Miller to Stockholders of the Peaks of Otter, Inc., 10 January 1950, 27 April 1950, 1 March 1952, Hunter Miller to Webster Richardson, 3 January 1952, Hunter Miller to Elbert Cox, 18 January 1952, Webster Richardson to Hunter Miller, 17 July 1953, Webster Richardson to Directors, Peaks of Otter, Inc., 24 March 1955, "Annual Report of Peaks of Otter, Inc., Blue Ridge Parkway, to the United States Department of the Interior, National Park Service for the Year Ended December 31, 1953," 3 December 1953, all in RPC.

53. Howard B. Stricklin to NPS Director, 8 April 1957, BRPRG 5, Box 43; Edward G. Speer, *Blue Ridge Parkway*, 46–47; Quin and Marston, *Historic American Engineering Record*, 190. See also Hunter Miller to Mary Lee R. Harvey, 14 November 1951, Hunter Miller to Stockholders, Peaks of Otter, Inc., 1 March 1952, Hunter Miller to Webster Richardson, 27 January 1953, 28 February 1959, Webster Richardson to Richard H. Poff, 21 January 1957, all in RPC.

54. Hunter Miller to Webster Richardson, 3 January 1952, Hunter Miller to Elbert Cox, 18 January 1952, Hunter Miller to Stockholders, Peaks of Otter, Inc., 1 March 1952, Hunter Miller to Mary Lee Harvey, 24 June 1953, Webster Richardson to Hunter Miller, 17 July 1953, Webster Richardson to Directors, Peaks of Otter, Inc., 24 March 1955, Webster Richardson to Richard H. Poff, 21 January 1957, Webster Richardson to John Tucker Percy, 24 February 1957, Webster Richardson to CLW, [1957?], 13 March 1958, all in RPC.

55. The new policy was announced in November 1956. See Webster Richardson to Wendell B. Barnes, 18 February 1957, Mary Lee R. Harvey to Harry F. Byrd, 2 October 1956, Webster Richardson to Richard H. Poff, 21 January 1957, John T. Perry to Webster Richardson, 21 January

1957, Webster Richardson to John Tucker Percy, 24 February 1957, 19 April 1957, Webster Richardson to CLW, 16 September 1957, [1957?], 13 March 1958, all in RPC.

56. Webster Richardson to Wendell B. Barnes, 18 February 1957, Webster Richardson to Hunter Miller, 17 July 1953, Webster Richardson to Directors, Peaks of Otter, Inc., 24 March 1955, Mary Lee R. Harvey to Harry F. Byrd, 2 October 1956, Webster Richardson to Richard H. Poff, 21 January 1957, Vice President, Peaks of Otter, Inc., to CLW, 26 April 1957, Webster Richardson to CLW, 16 September 1957, 13 March 1958, Application for Concession Contract, December 9, 1957, all in RPC.

57. SPW to Mary Lee R. Harvey, 24 September 1958, William T. Stevens to Mary Lee R. Harvey, 12 November 1958, William T. Stevens to SPW, 20 December 1961, Bryce Wagoner to SPW, 8 January 1962, all in BRPRG 3, Box 65; Webster Richardson to Wendell B. Barnes, 18 February 1957, Webster Richardson to CLW, 16 September 1957, 13 March 1958, all in RPC. See also Quin and Marston, Historic American Engineering Record, 199.

58. Hunter Miller to Webster Richardson, 28 February 1959, RPC.

59. Executive Vice President, Virginia Peaks of Otter Company, to Stuart Udall, 6 April 1965, BRPRG 3, Box 17; Acting Superintendent, BRP, to NPS Region 1 Director, 5 March 1962, BRPRG 3, Box 65.

60. Granville Liles, "History of the Blue Ridge Parkway," BRPRG 5, Box 48.

61. Sellars, Preserving Nature, 136–37; Tyler, Historic Preservation, 57–58; Unrau and Williss, Administrative History; Hosmer, Preservation Comes of Age, 1:529–76, 866–950; Mackintosh, Interpretation, chapter 2.

62. Matzko, Reconstructing Fort Union, 2; Greenspan, Creating Colonial Williamsburg; Handler and Gable, New History; Mackintosh, Interpretation, chapter 2.

63. DOI, "Memorandum for the Press," 24 February 1939, POF 200, Box 56.

64. Roy Edgar Appleman, "Report on Preservation of Mountain Culture, Marking of Historic Sites, and Promotion of Handicraft, Blue Ridge Parkway," 9 October 1940, BRPRG 5, Box 61.

65. NPS, "Planning the Complete Landscape Development: The Problem and the Program," 1939, BRPRG 7, Box 51; Ronald F. Lee to NPS Region 1 Director, 19 August 1940, Roy E. Appleman to J. P. Dodge, 5 September 1940, both in CCF7B, Box 2733. The bias toward pioneer life was not unique to the Parkway or to the Appalachian region. Lowenthal, "Pioneer Museums," 119, notes that by the 1960s, both subjects had become very popular among tourists nationally.

66. Appleman, "Report on Preservation"; Thor Borreson, "Report on Mountain Culture and Handicraft, Blue Ridge Parkway," 7 October 1940, BRPRG 5, Box 61; Ned J. Burns, Comment on the Appleman-Borreson Report on "Preservation of Mountain Culture, Marking of Historic Sites, and Promotion of Handicrafts, Blue Ridge Parkway, October 10, 1940," 30 October 1940, CCF7B, Box 2717; Roy Edgar Appleman, "Recommendations (for Blue Ridge Parkway)," 9 October 1940, BRPRG 5, Box 61; SWA, "Superintendent's Monthly Narrative Report, January 1941," 6 February 1941, SWA, "Annual Report of the Blue Ridge Parkway, Roanoke, Va., to the Director, National Park Service," 30 June 1941, both in CCF7B, Box 2718.

67. Thor Borreson, "Inspection Report, Blue Ridge Parkway, Old Log Cabins and Other Old Structures along the Parkway," 24 September 1941, SWA to NPS Region 1 Director, 10 October 1941, both in BRPRG 5, Box 61; SWA, "Superintendent's Monthly Narrative Report, April 1942," 12 May 1942, CCF7B, Box 2718.

68. Borreson, "Report on Mountain Culture"; Appleman, "Report on Preservation." See also SWA to NPS Region 1 Director, 15 October 1940, CCF7B, Box 2717, which noted that the NPS might have to find craftspersons trained "at a handicraft school" to staff Parkway displays. Park Service personnel were naively wandering into a long-trafficked bog (later thoroughly ex-

plored by Whisnant, *All That Is Native and Fine*; Becker, *Selling Tradition*) of which they had little knowledge.

69. SWA to NPS Region 1 Director, 13 September 1941, CCF7B, Box 2737; SWA, "Annual Report," 30 June 1941; SWA, "Superintendent's Monthly Narrative Report, May 1942," 11 June 1942, CCF7B, Box 2718. See also SWA to NPS Director, 10 November 1942, BRPRG 5, Box 70; SWA, "Draft of the Interpretive Statement of the Blue Ridge Parkway," December 1942, BRPRG 5, Box 13. A full interpretive statement was incorporated into the 1943 Parkway master plan. See SWA, "Annual Report of the Blue Ridge Parkway, Roanoke, Va., to the Director, National Park Service," 30 June 1943, CCF7B, Box 2718.

70. *Blue Ridge Parkway News* 5, no. 3 (April–July 1942); SWA, "Draft of the Interpretive Statement." In 1950, Abbott discussed his commitment to the preservation of vernacular structures in SWA, "Historic Preservation."

71. O. B. Taylor to Regional Director, 9 June 1945, BRPRG 5, Box 33.

72. EHA, "History of the Blue Ridge Parkway," 8 February 1948, BRPRG 5, Box 48. See also J. Carlisle Crouch, "Annual Report of the Blue Ridge Parkway to the Director, National Park Service, 1953," "Annual Report of the Blue Ridge Parkway to the Director, National Park Service, 1956," both in Box F217.B6U55, Blue Ridge Parkway Archives; "Research and Interpretation" (Section of Blue Ridge Parkway Master Plan), October 1950, BRPRG 5, Box 13; Hope and Robinson, "Historic Structures Report, Part I"; EHA, interview, BRPLIB; SWA, "Annual Report of the Blue Ridge Parkway, Roanoke, Va., to the Director, National Park Service," 30 June 1940, CCF7B, Box 2717; D. W. Levandowsky, "Monthly Narrative Report to Acting Superintendent of Blue Ridge Parkway," 31 October 1940, April 1942, BRPRG 7, Box 50. See also O. B. Taylor to Regional Director, 9 June 1945, BRPRG 5, Box 33; Liles, "History of the Blue Ridge Parkway"; Westmacott, "Historic Agriculture."

73. Jean Haskell Speer, Russell, and Worsham, *Johnson Farm*, 11.

74. Hope and Robinson, "Historic Structures Report, Part I."

75. Palmer, "Memorandum for Files"; Bruce Gregory et al., "Transcript of Recording of Meeting at Johnson Farm Group to Discuss Restoration of the Main House," 2 November 1966, in Jean Haskell Speer, Russell, and Worsham, *Johnson Farm*, appendixes, vol. 6.

76. Gregory et al., "Transcript of Recording."

77. Ibid.

78. Palmer, "Memorandum for Files."

79. Mackintosh, *National Historic Preservation Act*, v–viii, 1–17, 20–21; Richard M. Nixon, Executive Order 11593, in Dilsaver, *America's National Park System*, 377–79; NPS, Denver Service Center, "Other Laws."

80. As Mackintosh, an NPS historian, noted, the sense of crisis was not new. Interpretation in the Park Service, he said, "has always been in crisis, it seems" (*Interpretation*, chapter 5). Criticism of the interpretive program—frequently starved for funds and personnel—continued into the 1980s.

81. Ketterson, interview; F. A. Ketterson Jr. to Granville Liles et al., 11 October 1972, in Jean Haskell Speer, Russell, and Worsham, *Johnson Farm*, appendixes, vol. 6.

82. F. A. Ketterson Jr. to Granville Liles et al., 11 October 1972, in Jean Haskell Speer, Russell, and Worsham, *Johnson Farm*, appendixes, vol. 6.

83. Ibid.

84. "Interpretive Prospectus, Johnson Farm, Peaks of Otter, Blue Ridge Parkway," 26 March 1973, in Jean Haskell Speer, Russell, and Worsham, *Johnson Farm*, appendixes, vol. 6.

85. Ibid.; Mackintosh, *Interpretation*; Leon and Piatt, "Living-History Museums," 65–72; Mel Lee, E-mail to Author, 23 December 2004, January 3, 2005. The *Foxfire* journal (1967) and book se-

ries (twelve volumes, continuing into the 1980s) were issued by Eliot Wigginton's Foxfire secondary schools pedagogical project, based in Rabun Gap, Georgia. See Wigginton, *Sometimes a Shining Moment*.

86. Karen Lee, "Seasonal Evaluation, 1974," Melvin Lee, "Seasonal Evaluation, 1974," both in Jean Haskell Speer, Russell, and Worsham, *Johnson Farm*, appendixes, vol. 6; Mel Lee, E-mail to Author, 23 December 2004.

87. Mel Lee, E-mail to Author, 23 December 2004, January 27, 2005; Karen Lee, "Seasonal Evaluation, 1974"; Melvin Lee, "Seasonal Evaluation, 1974."

The dulcimer had been in evidence (if sparsely) in the region for many decades and had remained in limited use in certain areas (especially eastern Kentucky) well into the twentieth century. Its revival and popularity at midcentury were traceable mainly to the influence of the 1960s counterculture, the folk revival, and several prominent outmigrant musicians such as eastern Kentucky's Jean Ritchie (Ritchie, *Jean Ritchie's Dulcimer People*). Both the instrument itself and its associated (mostly ballad) repertoire lodged easily in the popular imagination primarily because they appeared neatly congruent with cherished images of romantic Appalachia. For more detailed discussion, see Whisnant, *All That Is Native and Fine*, 47–56, 93–100, 187–91.

88. Mel Lee, E-mail to Author, 27 January 2005.

89. Jean Haskell Speer, Russell, and Worsham, *Johnson Farm*, 76–80, 93; Rosemary Johnson et al., "Johnson Farm," 1:3–5, 9–10; Mel Lee, E-mail to Author, 23 December 2004, 27 January 2005; Karen Lee, "Seasonal Evaluation, 1974"; Melvin Lee, "Seasonal Evaluation, 1974."

90. Mel Lee, E-mail to Author, 27 January 2005.

91. Mel Lee, E-mail to Author, 3 January 2005; Jean Haskell Speer, Russell, and Worsham, *Johnson Farm*, 76–80, 86, 93; Rosemary Johnson et al., "Johnson Farm."

92. Jean Haskell Speer, Russell, and Worsham, *Johnson Farm*, 91–96.

93. Scholarship on Appalachia has continued to mushroom in the 1990s and 2000s. A few examples include Margaret Lynn Brown, *Wild East*; Stephen Wallace Taylor, *New South's New Frontier*; Pudup, Billings, and Waller, *Appalachia*; J. W. Williamson, *Hillbillyland*; Becker, *Selling Tradition*; Harkins, *Hillbilly*; Lewis, *Transforming*; Howell, *Culture, Environment, and Conservation*; Jean Haskell Speer, Russell, and Worsham, *Johnson Farm*.

94. "Research and Interpretation" (Section of Blue Ridge Parkway Master Plan), October 1950, BRPRG 5, Box 13.

95. For a broader examination of such exhibits, see Noblitt, "Blue Ridge Parkway," 394–98. In *Cades Cove*, a study of a community taken into the Great Smoky Mountains National Park, Dunn argues that mountain people, like the rest of mainstream America, were involved with local, state, national politics; participated in the market economy; and used state laws and the court system to organize their lives and settle their differences. Inscoe, *Mountain Masters*, 8–10, traces the connectedness of western North Carolina communities into the nineteenth century, when affluent mountain residents participated in far-flung trade and tourism networks. The unexceptional character of life in the region in the nineteenth century is the central argument of Pudup, Billings, and Waller, *Appalachia*.

96. For a trenchant analysis of the guild, see Becker, *Selling Tradition*, 73–92. See also Noblitt, "Blue Ridge Parkway," 400–404; for a complete discussion of the history of the Cone estate, see Noblitt, *Mansion in the Mountains*, 143–59.

97. SWA, "Annual Report," 30 June 1943; Noblitt, *Mansion in the Mountains*, 148–59.

98. Leon and Piatt, "Living-History Museums," 72.

99. Middleton, "Good Road of the Blue Ridge."

100. Glassberg, *Sense of History*, 6–7, 209; Sheridan Morley quoted in Lowenthal, *Past Is a Foreign Country*, 4; see also 8.

101. SWA, interview, BRPLIB.

102. Lowenthal, *Past Is a Foreign Country*, 28–29, 49; Greenspan, *Creating Colonial Williamsburg*, 170–73; Leon and Piatt, "Living-History Museums," 74–77.

103. See Loewen, *Lies across America*, 21, 36; Kammen, *Mystic Chords*, 538–39.

104. Kammen, *Mystic Chords*, 7, 538–39, 626–28; Loewen, *Lies across America*, 41.

105. Rosenzweig and Thelen, *Presence of the Past*, 20–21, 32, 179–97; Mel Lee, E-mail to Author, 27 January 2005.

106. Rosenzweig and Thelen, *Presence of the Past*, 20–21, 32, 195.

107. An excellent recent example of a highly self-reflexive film about the Appalachian region is Barret's *Stranger with a Camera*.

108. Kaye, "Making of American Memory," 257; Rosenzweig and Thelen, *Presence of the Past*, 188–89.

CHAPTER 7

1. C. D. Hogue Jr. to RGB, 7 June 1955, SHCRWD, Box 9; Charles Ross, "Memorandum Regarding Legal Aspects of Deed from the State of North Carolina to the United States of America Covering Right of Way of the Shenandoah–Great Smoky Mountains National Parkway," 25 July 1935, JCBEP, Box 160.

2. HM to LHH, 8 September 1955, TSP, Box 81. For this chronology, see [HM?], "Events Relating Directly and Indirectly to the Construction of the Blue Ridge Parkway at Grandfather Mountain, North Carolina, 1889–1962," [March 1962?], SHCRWD, Box 9. See also HM to William Medford, n.d., enclosed with William Medford to RGB, 11 March 1957, SHCRWD, Box 9; "Chronological History: Blue Ridge Parkway around Grandfather Mountain," [1964], BRPLF; "Battle of Grandfather Mountain," *Concord Tribune*, 25 March 1962; HM to J. Fleming Snipes, 30 October 1956, Sam Beard to LHH, 29 April 1959, both in TSP, Box 81; HM, interview. As Morton told this story in 2004, the appearance of the machinery preceded the taking of the lands (and thus constituted trespassing on his lands), but his account is not supported by the historical documents (including the 1962 chronology, which he almost certainly wrote), which place the encounter in late June 1955, after the posting of the courthouse maps.

3. "Weather Doesn't Stop Thousands from Enjoying Festivities of Dedication '87," *Blowing Rock (N.C.) Blowing Rocket*, 18 September 1987, B1–4.

4. [SPW?] to Southeast Region Director, 2 September 1965, BRPLF.

5. Morton laid out much of the narrative on which the popular account is based in a 1988 book chapter he titled "Blue Ridge Parkway: 52 Years Later: Truth about 'Missing Link.'" As recently as 2002–3, numerous respected statewide media outlets including the *Carolina Alumni Review*, the University of North Carolina public television station (UNC-TV), the *Charlotte Observer*, the *Raleigh News and Observer*, and the *Asheville Citizen-Times* have interviewed Morton and told versions of the compelling tale. Charlotte's Levine Museum of the New South published the story in the profile of Morton included in Covington and Ellis, *North Carolina Century*.

6. David E. Brown, "Long View"; Gross, "Hugh Morton's Mountain"; HM in "Hearing, Blue Ridge Parkway Grandfather Mountain Vicinity," 31 May 1962, transcript in BRPLF; UNC-TV, "Biographical Conversations with Hugh Morton"; Jack Betts, "Through a Lens: Hugh Morton Used Images to Influence Public Opinion," *Charlotte Observer*, 12 October 2003, available at <http://www.charlotte.com/mld/observer/news/columnists/jack_betts/6994687.htm> (12 October 2003); Mary E. Miller, "North Carolina through Hugh Morton's Lens," RNO, 28 September 2003, D1; Hensley, "Blue Ridge Parkway"; "Grandfather Mountain's Hugh Morton Sets Standards for Conservation That Are World-Class," ACT, 28 August 2003; Marvin Eury, "You've Heard of 'Battle of Kings Mountain, but Have You Heard of . . . 'Battle of Grandfather Moun-

tain,'" *Concord Tribune*, 25 March 1962; Grandfather Mountain, Inc., "Blue Ridge Parkway." Almost all the elements were included in Ralph Grizzle, "Hugh Morton," in Covington and Ellis, *North Carolina Century*, 499–502.

7. "Fight for a Mountain" [editorial], *Reidsville Review*, 28 March 1962.

8. The Blue Ridge Parkway drew approximately 2 million visitors in 1950 and 5.5 million by 1960. Its closest competitor was the Great Smoky Mountains National Park (1.5 million/4.5 million). The most popular western parks (Yosemite, Grand Canyon, Yellowstone) lagged far behind, with 665,000–1.1 million in 1950 and 1.2–1.4 million ten years later. See NPS, Public Use Statistics Office, "Visitation Statistics." By 2004, Parkway visitation had risen to 18 million.

9. In a 1962 hearing before the State Highway Commission, Morton mentioned the NPS's recent construction of a modernist observation tower at Clingman's Dome in the Great Smoky Mountains National Park, a structure that had been the target of considerable conservationist criticism. Conservationist language as it developed from its late-nineteenth-century beginnings up through the 1950s represented a conglomeration of many different emphases—aesthetics, health, ecology, conservationist use, wilderness. The modern U.S. environmental movement was spurred by Rachel Carson's 1962 book, *Silent Spring*, and by 1970's inaugural Earth Day. The most concrete constraint on Parkway construction imposed by rising environmentalism was the early 1970s defeat by a coalition of environmentalists and property owners of the effort to extend the Parkway into northern Georgia. "Hearing, Blue Ridge Parkway Grandfather Mountain Vicinity"; Kline, *First Along the River*, 51–84; Hays, *History of Environmental Politics*, 22–35; Sellars, *Preserving Nature*, 185–86; Rothman, *Greening of a Nation?*; Roy Parker Jr., "Group Fighting Parkway, TVA Plan," RNO, 30 November 1970; "Petition Protesting the Route of the Extension of the Blue Ridge Parkway through the Persimmon Community of Rabun County, Ga.," 8 November 1970, BRPRG 5, Series 12, Box 15; Noel Yancey, "Mountain Owner, Engineer Still Debate Parkway Route," [RNO?], December 1965; Noel Yancey, "Grandfather Mountain Road: Park Service, Morton Still Debate Routing," *Raleigh Times*, 8 December 1965.

10. Walter Brown, "Park Service Is Given Control of Blue Ridge Drive," ACT, 21 June 1936, A1; HLI to AED, 23 January 1936, CCF7B, Box 2714; *Congressional Record*, 74th Cong., 2nd sess., 20 June 1936, 80, part 10, 10582–89, 10610–15, 10894–896; Public Law 848, 74th Cong., 1st sess., 30 June 1936; SWA, "Annual Report of the Blue Ridge Parkway, to the Director, NPS," 30 June 1942, CCF7B, Box 2717; NPS, DOI, *Blue Ridge Parkway, 1941* [pamphlet], CCF7B, Box 2715; "Beautiful Parkway Nears Completion," *Spruce Pine Tri-County News*, 12 June 1941, 9; SWA, "Annual Report of the Blue Ridge Parkway, Roanoke, Va., to the Director, National Park Service," 30 June 1941, SWA, "Annual Report of the Blue Ridge Parkway, Roanoke, Va., to the Director, National Park Service," 30 June 1943, both in CCF7B, Box 2718; DOI, NPS, "Statement of Funds Available and the Expenditures Incurred against Appropriations and Allocations for the Blue Ridge and Natchez Trace Parkways as of March 31, 1941," 13 May 1941, SHCRWD, Box 4.

11. SWA, "Annual Report," 30 June 1943; NPS Division of Recreation Resource Surveys, "Economic Effects of the Blue Ridge Parkway," January 1962, BRPRG 1, Series 28, Box 24; NPS Press Release, 23 July 1956, TSP, Box 81; NPS, Public Use Statistics Office, "Visitation Statistics."

12. Sellars, *Preserving Nature*, 181 (quotation supposedly from Wirth); SPW to RGB, 19 July 1954, Harriet Browning Davant Private Collection, Blowing Rock, North Carolina.

13. RGB to Sam Smith, 13 April 1943, SHCRWD, Box 4; SPW, "Superintendent's Monthly Narrative Report, July 1946," 12 August 1946, SWA, "Superintendent's Monthly Narrative Report, September 1946," 9 October 1946, NPS, "Blue Ridge Parkway Annual Report, Fiscal Year 1948," 1948, all in CCF7B, Box 2718. Major construction was halted in the fall of 1942; only a small crew of government maintenance workers remained on the job. Amid some uncertainty about

whether the project would continue after the war, Parkway builders remained optimistic that public works funds to employ returning soldiers would allow construction to be resumed. Thus, land acquisition was planned to proceed in both states during the war. See *Blue Ridge Parkway News* 6, no. 1 (December 1942–April 1943); "Chronology of Parkway Construction: Virginia and North Carolina," n.d., tables 1, 2, Blue Ridge Parkway Headquarters.

14. On Mission 66, see CLW, *Parks, Politics, and the People,* 237; see also 162; NPS, "Mission 66 for Blue Ridge Parkway," n.d., LHP, Box 217; Sellars, *Preserving Nature,* 173–91, 281.

15. NPS, "Mission 66"; NPS Press Release, 23 July 1956, TSP, Box 81; SPW to NPS Region 1 Director, 17 December 1956, BRPRG 3, Series 17, Box 101; HM, "Report on Plan for Government-Sponsored Hotels and Eating Places on the Blue Ridge Parkway," 7 January 1957, LHP, Box 271; CLW, *Parks, Politics, and the People,* 271–72; "Chronology of Parkway Construction," tables 1, 2.

16. Eivind T. Scoyen to LHH, 3 August 1956, TSP, Box 81; North Carolina State Highway and Public Works Commission, "Press Release upon Retirement of R. Getty Browning," 27 July 1956, BRPRG 5, Series 44, Box 59; "Man Who Put Blue Ridge Parkway in N.C. Retiring," *Charlotte Observer,* 3 August 1956, C20; E. T. Scoyen to RGB, 30 August 1956, Davant Private Collection.

17. HM to LHH, 14 August 1958, HM to S. Herbert Evison, 21 September 1959, both in TSP, Box 81; HM, "Open Forum: Morton Gives His Objections to High Route of Parkway," *West Jefferson Skyland Post,* 28 April 1966.

18. Nelson MacRae and Frank L. Dunlap, "Legal Agreement Filed in Avery & Caldwell Counties, N.C. in Re Land Acquisition, Blue Ridge Parkway, Project SPP-18, Section 2-H," 24 May 1939, J. P. Dodge to Charles Ross, 26 August 1938, 30 November 1938, Charles E. Ross to Mr. Smith, 24 May 1939, all in SHCRWD, Box 10.

19. AED to Files, 25 May 1939, CCF7B, Box 2733, indicates that the state was pushing the NPS to designate the right-of-way on Parkway section 2-H at Grandfather at a point after the Linville Company had been paid. MacRae was certainly aware that final word on the route at Grandfather had not come. See Charles Ross to Nelson MacRae, 11 August 1941, SHCRWD, Box 10; "North Carolina General Statutes," chap. 136, sec. 19; Morton's annotations on map, "Property of the Linville Company, Linville, North Carolina," April 1943 [revised April 1962], BRPLF.

20. Morton maintains that the legal argument was critical to his ultimate victory, but the documents indicate that it was only one of an array of arguments and probably not the most important. HM, interview; RGB to EHA, 31 July 1957, RGB to CLW, 27 May 1958, both in SHCRWD, Box 9; SPW to William F. Babcock, 28 March 1962, BRPLF; "On Grandfather Mountain: Ruling Gives SHC Right to Acquire High Route," *Asheville Times,* 29 June 1962.

21. HM to LHH, 14 August 1958, TSP, Box 81. The concept of "wilderness" has been under intense discussion in American environmental historiography over the last decade. Important has been the recognition, central to William Cronon's work, that "wilderness" is a culturally constructed category, not an identifiable, absolute state of nature on which everyone can agree. See the essays in Cronon, *Uncommon Ground,* including his piece, "The Trouble with Wilderness," 69–90; Hays, *History of Environmental Politics,* 22–51, 94–108.

22. "An Artist's Wife," "North Carolina Mountains"; Dugger, *Balsam Groves*; North Carolina Audubon Society, <www.ncaudubon.org/IBAs/Mtn/grandfather_mountain.htm>.

23. Tyson, *Blood Done Sign My Name,* 272–23; State Library of North Carolina, "Alex Manly."

24. Tyson, *Blood Done Sign My Name,* 272–73; State Library of North Carolina, "Alex Manly"; Powell, *Dictionary,* 4:191–92. See also Ralph Grizzle's profile, "Hugh MacRae," in Covington and Ellis, *North Carolina Century,* 24–26.

25. Linville Improvement Company, Linville Advertising Pamphlet, [188?], North Carolina Collection, University of North Carolina, Chapel Hill; Donald Edward Davis, *Where There Are Mountains,* 164–98; Covington, *Linville,* 7; Dugger, *War Trails,* 147.

26. Donald Edward Davis, *Where There Are Mountains*, 165–66; Silver, *Mount Mitchell*, 138–39; Lewis, *Transforming*.

27. Covington, *Linville*, 3–7; Silver, *Mount Mitchell*, 140, 175–80; Linville Improvement Company, Linville Advertising Pamphlet.

28. Van Noppen and Van Noppen, *Western North Carolina*, 185, 265, 351–52; Dugger, *War Trails*; Nelson MacRae to CMW, 25 June 1936, State Highway Commission, "Press Release," 1939, both in SHCRWD, Box 10; Powell, *Dictionary*, 4:191–92; Dugger, *Balsam Groves*, 232; Vining, *Eseeola Inn and Annex*; Covington, *Linville*, 8–17, 61–64, 78.

29. Van Noppen and Van Noppen, *Western North Carolina*, 185, 265, 351–52; Dugger, *War Trails*; Nelson MacRae to CMW, 25 June 1936, State Highway Commission, "Press Release," 1939, both in SHCRWD, Box 10; Powell, *Dictionary*, 4:191–92; Dugger, *Balsam Groves*, 232; Vining, *Eseeola Inn and Annex*; Covington, *Linville*, 8–17, 61–64, 78.

30. Covington, *Linville*, 1–62; Van Noppen and Van Noppen, *Western North Carolina*, 265–66; Silver, *Mount Mitchell*, 144.

31. Covington, *Linville*, 1–78. The fact that the Yonahlossee became the major commercial route through the area complicated plans to use the road for the Parkway and increased the importance of the question of access rights in this section. See Frank L. Dunlap to RLD, 24 January 1939, SHCRWD, Box 3.

32. Dugger, *War Trails*, 147; J. P. Dodge to L. M. Harriss, 19 July 1939, SHCRWD, Box 10; SPW to NPS Region 1 Director, 7 March 1946, BRPRG 5, Series 10, Box 13; Covington, *Linville*, 75; Covington, *Linville*, 77, 95–96; Alabama Business Hall of Fame, "William McWane."

33. Covington, *Linville*, viii–ix, 5–95; Grizzle, "Hugh MacRae," 25; Linville Improvement Company, Linville Advertising Pamphlet; Long, "Historical Sketch."

34. Linville Improvement Company, Linville Advertising Pamphlet; Hugh MacRae to Oscar W. Underwood, 20 January 1916, CCF7B, Box 2738; Covington, *Linville*, 43; Donald Edward Davis, *Where There Are Mountains*, 171–74; Pierce, *Great Smokies*, 67; Shankland, *Steve Mather*, 172; Frome, *Strangers*, 179.

35. Pierce, *Great Smokies*, 52–53, 66–86; Frome, *Strangers*, 182–85.

36. Grizzle, "Hugh Morton," 500; HM, interview.

37. Covington, *Linville*, 78–79, 81–85.

38. J. P. Dodge to Charles Ross, 10 December 1938, Reuben B. Robertson to CMW, 29 October 1935, RGB to CMW, 6 November 1935, Nelson MacRae to CMW, 25 June 1936, all in SHCRWD, Box 10; AED to H. J. Spelman, 28 February 1936, CCF7B, Box 2731; Tager, *Grandfather Mountain*, 85–109; "Preservation Plan for Big Grandfather Mountain Area Urged," *Asheville Times*, 13 July 1933; L. A. Sharpe, "Report of Inspector L. A. Sharpe on Grandfather Mountain National Park," 23 June 1935, CCF7B, Box 2738. Carlos C. Campbell, *Birth*, 30 n. 4, indicates that most of the virgin timber from Grandfather's slopes had, in fact, been cut by 1924. See also Nancy Alexander, "Old Friend of 'Grandfather,' Joe Hartley, Recalls the Land That Was," *Asheville Times*, 20 August 1959.

39. Silver, *Mount Mitchell*, 146–54; Mrs. J. L. Nelson to RLD, 31 August 1933, R. L. Gwyn to M. H. Thatcher, 4 September 1933, Bessie Beall Reid to RLD, 13 September 1933, Mrs. A. M. Yates to RLD, 30 September 1933, Mrs. A. G. Jones to RLD, 2 October 1933, Mrs. R. Z. Linney to RLD, 28 October 1933, RLD to Mrs. R. Z. Linney, 30 October 1933, all in RLDP, Box 7. See also R. L. Gwyn to RLD, 26 August 1935, RLDP, Box 14; AED to H. J. Spelman, 28 February 1936, CCF7B, Box 2731. The women's clubs may have been spurred to action by Gwyn, who was writing to Senator Josiah Bailey, President Roosevelt, and other government officials about threats to Grandfather from logging by Champion Paper and Fibre ("Preservation Plan"; R. L. Gwyn to JWB, [193?], CCF7B, Box 2730).

40. RGB to CMW, 7 April 1936, Nelson MacRae to CMW, 25 June 1936, both in SHCRWD, Box 10; SWA to TCV, 1 May 1936, BRPRG 7, Series 33, Box 47; CMW to AED, 4 May 1936, SHCRWD, Box 2; H. J. Spelman to CMW, 21 May 1936, quoted in "Chronological History."

41. SWA, "Appalachian National Parkway from Shenandoah National Park to Great Smoky Mountains National Park, Report on Recreation and Service Areas, Type and Scope of Development Proposed," 15 December 1934, CCF7B, Box 2711; Donald Edward Davis, *Where There Are Mountains*, 165–71; Silver, *Mount Mitchell*, 134–62.

42. The second maps were posted in Avery County in December 1938. See [HM?], "Events Relating Directly and Indirectly to the Construction of the Blue Ridge Parkway." The degree of federal approval for this course of action is unclear. Most of the correspondence cited in "Chronological History" makes clear that federal officials had serious reservations about using the Yonahlossee route and that the BPR and the NPS continued studying the route for section 2-H well into the 1940s. But, perhaps because the North Carolina State Highway Commission was being pressed to settle with the Linville Company, the NPS did give the go-ahead in 1939 for acquisition on the basis of the Yonahlossee route. See, for example, AED to Frank L. Dunlap, 18 May 1939, in "Chronological History": "This letter will confirm your understanding that the existing plans designate the right-of-way for Section 2-H, and acquisition by the State is requested on the basis of these plans." The agreement reached is MacRae and Dunlap, "Legal Agreement." This agreement was filed in 1939, but the quitclaim deed for the transfer of these lands was not filed until 1957, apparently as a result of "unavoidable delays" that prevented the Highway Commission from "finish[ing] the surveys . . . and furnish[ing] the Linville Company with the necessary description to be placed in the deed" (RGB to W. F. Babcock, 1 July 1958, SHCRWD, Box 9). See also Quitclaim Deed, Avery and Caldwell Counties, North Carolina, 28 December 1957, SHCRWD, Box 9; and [State Highway Commission?], "Press Release," 1939, SHCRWD, Box 10.

43. AED to Frank L. Dunlap, 30 April 1940, SHCRWD, Box 4; J. P. Dodge to Charles Ross, 30 November 1938, J. P. Dodge to Charles Ross, 10 December 1938, both in SHCRWD, Box 10; "$25,000 Is Paid for Road Rights: 500 Acres Bought from Linville Company for Blue Ridge Parkway Stretch," RNO, 26 May 1939; State Highway Commission, "Press Release," 1939, SHCRWD, Box 10. Continued access to the Yonahlossee Road/U.S. 221 was central to Highway Commission negotiations with the MacRaes. That access, Linville Company officials knew, was critical for continued exploitation of the timber, building stone, and shrubbery higher up the mountain and for any contemplated real estate development. In short, the company worried that without access to the Yonahlossee (or to another commercial highway that might be built through the area), it could not carry on with the activities that concerned Parkway planners. In that event, company officials claimed, the market value of five thousand acres of their lands would plummet and the company "would sustain great damage" (Nelson MacRae to CMW, 25 June 1936, SHCRWD, Box 10; Linville Improvement Company, Legal Protest to CMW, 26 June 1936, SHCRWD, Box 9). Champion Paper and Fibre officials, for their part, worried about continued access to the fifteen hundred acres of spruce timber the company had purchased at Grandfather and was removing over expensive plank roads connected to the Yonahlossee. Jones and Ward (attorneys) to Charles Ross, 13 June 1936, SHCRWD, Box 9; "Parkway Link Needs Completing . . . But Not on Route That Would Mar Grandeur of Grandfather Mountain" (editorial), *Elkin Tribune*, 19 March 1962; "Morton and His Mountain," *Newton (N.C.) Observer and News-Enterprise*, reprinted in *Watauga Democrat*, 16 March 1962; Eury, "You've Heard of 'Battle of Kings Mountain.'"

44. J. P. Dodge to L. M. Harriss, 19 July 1939, SHCRWD, Box 10; AED to Files, 25 May 1939, CCF7B, Box 2733; MacRae and Dunlap, "Legal Agreement"; J. P. Dodge to Charles Ross, 26 August

1938, 30 November 1938, 10 December 1938, CMW to Nelson MacRae, 24 July 1936, Nelson MacRae to J. P. Dodge, 13 December 1938, Nelson MacRae to Major and Mrs. J. P. Dodge, 12 September 1938, all in SHCRWD, Box 10.

45. Nelson MacRae to Major and Mrs. J. P. Dodge, 12 September 1938, SHCRWD, Box 10; SPW, interview, BRPLIB.

46. J. P. Dodge to L. M. Harriss, 19 July 1939, Lynn M. Harriss to J. P. Dodge, 3 August 1939, both in SHCRWD, Box 10. See also Covington, *Linville*, viii–ix, 5–62, 72–73, 80–95; SWA to NPS Director, 18 February 1942, BRPRG 7, Box 16; Hugh MacRae to HPK, 24 February 1942, CCF7B, Box 2766; Tager, *Grandfather Mountain*, 85–89.

47. MacRae and Dunlap, "Legal Agreement."

48. SWA to NPS Director, 2 May 1939, CCF7B, Box 2766. In fact, as early as 1935, Browning suggested trying to interest Ickes in authorizing federal purchase of between five thousand and six thousand acres on the mountain. See RGB to CMW, 6 November 1935, SHCRWD, Box 10; SWA to TCV, 20 May 1939, BRPRG 7, Box 16; AED to Frank L. Dunlap, 27 May 1939, quoted in "Chronological History"; ABC to HPK, 9 March 1940, CCF7B, Box 2733; Frank L. Dunlap to AED, 9 June 1939, SHCRWD, Box 3.

49. Frome, *Strangers*, 181; Linville Improvement Company, Linville Advertising Pamphlet; Covington, *Linville*, 5–6.

50. ABC to HPK, 17 April 1940, CCF7B, Box 2733. Indeed, as Drury noted two years later, the original 1936 plans for the Parkway had included a recreation area at Grandfather, but since then "the Service has more or less 'given up' mainly because the high price asked the Forest Service for the 2,000 acres above the 5,000-foot contour level was beyond consideration" (Newton B. Drury to HPK, 16 February 1942, CCF7B, Box 2766). On NPS willingness to accept donation of Grandfather as part of the Parkway (not as a freestanding national park), see Newton B. Drury to HPK, 28 December 1943, CCF7B, Box 2738. See also DOI, NPS, Branch of Plans and Design, "Master Plan, Blue Ridge Parkway, Second Edition, 1941," 8 May 1941, Record Group 79 (National Park Service), Blue Ridge Parkway Master Plans, Folders 1–4, Cartographic Research Room, National Archives II, College Park, Maryland.

51. Newton B. Drury to HPK, 12 March 1942, R. Bruce Etheridge to Newton B. Drury, 17 April 1942, both in CCF7B, Box 2766; Newton B. Drury to R. Bruce Etheridge, 7 May 1942, BRPRG 7, Box 16; Hugh MacRae to HPK, 27 July 1942, HPK to Newton B. Drury, 2 December 1947, both in CCF7B, Box 2738; HPK to ABC, 8 April 1940, CCF7B, Box 2733; HPK to Horace M. Albright, 13 April 1943, CCF7B, Box 2716.

52. Hugh MacRae to HPK, 25 February 1942, CCF7B, Box 2766; SPW to NPS Director, 2 March 1945, J. W. Morton to HPK, 3 December 1943, Newton B. Drury to HPK, 13 December 1943, HPK to Horace M. Albright, 11 March 1944, HPK to Newton B. Drury, 7 March 1944, all in CCF7B, Box 2738. The reference to the "return" of the fauna suggests, of course, that they had departed.

53. Hugh MacRae to HPK, 25 February 1942, HPK to Hugh MacRae, 2 March 1942, both in CCF7B, Box 2766. See also Silver, *Mount Mitchell*, 135; Kline, *First Along the River*, 51–69.

54. AED to NPS Director, 5 February 1945, HPK to Horace M. Albright, 11 March 1944, J. W. Morton to HPK, 22 March 1944, all in CCF7B, Box 2738.

55. J. W. Morton to HPK, 22 January 1945, SPW to NPS Director, 2 March 1945, both in CCF7B, Box 2738. On the sale in 1944 of sixteen hundred acres of the Linville community itself (including the inn and golf course) to the newly organized Linville Resorts, Inc., controlled by the families of several cottage owners, see Covington, *Linville*, 96–109. See also Long, "Historical Sketch." Other correspondence gives a larger figure for the acreage sold: see AED to NPS Director, 5

February 1945, CCF7B, Box 2738. According to Weems, the Forest Service was buying similar lands for $2.50 to $5.00 per acre (SPW, interview, BRPLIB).

56. AED to NPS Director, 5 February 1945, SPW to NPS Region 1 Director, 22 March 1946, both in CCF7B, Box 2738; SPW, "Superintendent's Monthly Narrative Report, December 1945," 14 January 1946, CCF7B, Box 2718; HPK, "Shall Grandfather Mountain Be Saved?"; HPK to Horace M. Albright, 13 April 1943, CCF7B, Box 2716; SPW, "Superintendent's Monthly Narrative Report, July 1946."

57. HPK to Newton B. Drury, 7 March 1944, CCF7B, Box 2738; HPK, "Grandfather Mountain: Shall It Be Saved?"; HPK, "Shall Grandfather Mountain Be Saved?"; Ervin, "Shall Grandfather Mountain Be Saved?"; Burke Davis, "Grandfather Mountain May Yet Be Saved from Woodman's Axe," *Charlotte News*, 23 November 1946, 10-A; "Make Grandfather a Park" [editorial], *Winston-Salem Journal*, 3 April 1945; HPK, "Grandfather Mountain: 'Gem of the Southern Appalachians,'" ACT, 14 July 1946, B1.

58. HPK to ABC, 8 April 1940, CCF7B, Box 2733; Covington, *Linville*, 102; HPK to Newton B. Drury, 12 April 1945, CCF7B, Box 2738.

59. Hugh MacRae to HPK, 27 July 1942, HPK to HM, 20 November 1947, SPW to NPS Region 1 Director, 22 March 1946, CLW to AED, 8 December 1947, HPK to SPW, 15 September 1948, HPK to Newton B. Drury, 2 December 1947, SPW to HPK, 27 April 1948, 2 September 1948, all in CCF7B, Box 2738. See also SWA, "Superintendent's Monthly Narrative Report, September 1946"; SPW, "Superintendent's Monthly Narrative Report, January 1947," 12 February 1947, CCF7B, Box 2719.

60. HPK to SPW, 29 April 1948, CCF7B, Box 2738.

61. HPK to Horace M. Albright, 22 April 1947, HPK to SPW, 29 April 1948, 15 September 1948, all in CCF7B, Box 2738.

62. HM, interview; HPK to SPW, 29 April 1948, HM to HPK, 7 October 1946, both in CCF7B.

63. HPK, "Grandfather Mountain: Shall It Be Saved?"; HPK quoted in Jay Jenkins, "Grandfather Mountain Provokes $165,000 Argument across State," RNO, 9 March 1947; HM to HPK, 26 November 1946, 13 December 1946, both in CCF7B, Box 2738.

64. "Minutes of Meeting of the North Carolina Park, Parkway and Forest Development Commission, Linville, N.C., August 23, 1948: Statements of Mr. Morton and Mr. Weems," 23 August 1948, BRPRG 3, Box 101; W. Ralph Winkler, E. C. Guy, and Raymond W. Sutton to Charles E. Ray, 10 April 1948, CCF7B, Box 2738; Margaret Lynn Brown, *Wild East*, 49–77.

65. SPW to HPK, 2 September 1948, CCF7B, Box 2738; SPW, "Superintendent's Monthly Narrative Report, April 1948," 10 May 1948, CCF7B, Box 2719.

66. HM to HPK, 26 November 1946, 13 December 1946, 28 November 1947, all in CCF7B, Box 2738.

67. "Hugh MacRae Dead at 86," RNO, 22 October 1951; Deed, State of North Carolina, County of New Hanover, 23 December 1952, SHCRWD, Box 9; [HM?], "Events Relating Directly and Indirectly to the Construction of the Blue Ridge Parkway."

68. SPW to NPS Region 1 Director, 6 August 1949, BRPRG 3, Box 101; *Grandfather Mountain*; Govert, "Godfather of Grandfather"; Grandfather Mountain, Inc., "Grandfather Mountain"; HM to LHH, 14 August 1958, TSP, Box 81; Don Bedwell, "Hugh Morton: The Man and His Mountain," *Charlotte Observer*, 21 September 1980; Johnny Corey, "Promoter Helps Self, N.C.," RNO, 5 August 1956; HM to RGB, 31 October 1952, 20 September 1952, both in SHCRWD, Box 9.

69. Ad campaign described in Corey, "Promoter Helps Self, N.C."; Highland Games discussed in Grandfather Mountain, Inc., "Grandfather Mountain"; HM to LHH, 14 August 1958, TSP, Box 81.

70. [HM?], "Events Relating Directly and Indirectly to the Construction of the Blue Ridge Parkway"; "New Visitor Center Built atop Grandfather Mountain," ACT, 15 October 1961. Other development at the site after the Parkway battle was resolved included the creation of a wild animal habitat in the 1970s and a nature museum in 1991. See Elizabeth Hunter, "Up on Grandfather Mountain"; UNC-TV, "Biographical Conversations with Hugh Morton"; Bedwell, "Hugh Morton."

71. "Morton, Jenkins Named to Conservation Board," ACT, 27 June 1951; Sharpe, "Photo by Morton"; UNC-TV, "Biographical Conversations with Hugh Morton"; SPW to NPS Region 1 Director, 6 August 1949, BRPRG 3, Box 101; Govert, "Godfather of Grandfather."

72. HM to Bill Sharpe, 7 November 1946, CCF7B, Box 2738; HM, "Review and Appraisal of the NPS Statement to the North Carolina Board of Conservation and Development on January 7, 1957," 21 January 1957, BRPRG 3, Box 102.

73. HM to HPK, 13 December 1946, CCF7B, Box 2738; SPW, "Superintendent's Monthly Narrative Report, February 1947," 14 March 1947, CCF7B, Box 2719; SPW to RLD, 11 February 1949, BRPRG 3, Box 101; HM to SPW, 13 May 1958, SHCRWD, Box 9.

74. SPW, "Superintendent's Monthly Narrative Report, October 1945," 13 November 1945, CCF7B, Box 2718; Van Noppen and Van Noppen, Western North Carolina, 371–412; Chambers, Drinking the Waters; Starnes, Creating the Land; Massengill, Western North Carolina; Greenberg and Kahn, Asheville History; Compton, Early Tourism. These works include pictures of numerous hotels and inns dating from the nineteenth century, including Asheville's Eagle Hotel (ca. 1814), Swannanoa Hotel (1880), Kenilworth Inn (1891), Battery Park Hotel (1886), and Grove Park Inn (1913); Catawba County's White Sulphur Springs (1859); Madison County's Warm Springs Hotel (before 1850); Waynesville's Haywood White Sulphur Springs Hotel (1879); Hot Springs's Mountain Park Hotel (1850s); the Mt. Mitchell Hotel (1882); Blowing Rock's Mayview Manor (1921); Waynesville's Eagle's Nest Hotel (1900); Burnsville's Nu-Wray Inn (1833); Little Switzerland's Switzerland Inn (1910); and many other small motor courts of more recent vintage. See also SPW to NPS Region 1 Director, 7 March 1946, BRPRG 5, Box 13.

75. Paul R. Franke to Supervisor of Concessions, NPS, 31 December 1946, CCF7B, Box 2736; SPW to RLD, 11 February 1949, BRPRG 3, Box 101; "Charge and Retort" [editorial], Roanoke Times, 3 September 1948; "Minutes of Meeting of the North Carolina Park, Parkway, and Forest Development Commission"; NPS, BRP, "Visitor Accommodations on the Blue Ridge Parkway," 8 September 1949, BRPRG 3, Box 101.

76. Starnes, "Creating the Land," 177–87. As early as 1946, the North Carolina Travel Council and the Roanoke American Automobile Association had worked with Abbott to develop information highlighting private accommodations near the Parkway (SWA, "Superintendent's Monthly Narrative Report, September 1946").

77. Dilsaver, America's National Park System, 53, 80, 269–70, 298–301.

78. Barringer, Selling Yellowstone, 109–67; Carr, "Modernism," 39–46; Dilsaver, America's National Park System, 269–70, 298–301.

79. NPS, "National Park Concessions, Inc.: Purposes, Reasons for Formation, History, Organization, and Functions," February 1957, BRPRG 3, Box 102.

80. AED to Monroe M. Redden, 21 February 1950, BRPRG 3, Box 101; NPS, "National Park Concessions, Inc."; Webster Richardson to Hunter Miller, 17 July 1953, RPC.

81. NPS, "Blue Ridge Parkway Annual Report, Fiscal Year 1948"; NPS, BRP, "Visitor Accommodations." The Bluff's facilities had been in the plans since the 1930s. See SPW to HPK, 2 September 1948, CCF7B, Box 2738; "Minutes of Meeting of the North Carolina Park, Parkway, and Forest Development Commission"; HM, "Talk before the Asheville Board of Realtors," 3 August 1949, Charles E. Ray to Newton B. Drury, 11 February 1949, North Carolina National

Park, Parkway, and Forest Development Commission, "Resolution, Adopted at a Meeting of the Commission in Raleigh, N.C.," 3 February 1949, all in BRPRG 3, Box 101; J. Carlisle Crouch, "Superintendent's Monthly Narrative Report, August 1948," 15 September 1948, CCF7B, Box 2719.

82. "Charge and Retort"; "Minutes of Meeting of the North Carolina Park, Parkway, and Forest Development Commission"; NPS, BRP, "Visitor Accommodations."

83. SPW to NPS Director, 8 September 1949, BRPRG 3, Box 101; NPS, BRP, "Visitor Accommodations."

84. Charles E. Ray to Commissioners, 25 January 1950, SPW to NPS Region 1 Director, 17 December 1956, both in BRPRG 3, Box 101.

85. SPW to Charles Ray, 27 August 1948, SPW to NPS Region 1 Director, 6 August 1949, both in BRPRG 3, Box 101; "No Vast Room for Argument" [editorial], AC, 26 August 1948.

86. Blowing Rock Chamber of Commerce and Boone Chamber of Commerce, "We Are Not Going to Sit Still"; John W. Caffey to LHH, 4 February 1957, LHP, Box 217; Mrs. Sam J. Huskins to Monroe M. Redden, 6 February 1950, Frances L. Oakley to SPW, 22 June 1950, both in BRPRG 3, Box 101. Mission 66 plans for the Parkway are discussed in NPS, "Mission 66." See also Bunny Harris and Walt Damtoft, "Row over Parkway Concessions Mounts," Charlotte Observer, 24 February 1957.

87. Asheville leaders, Morton reported, "have feelings just as strong as my own about the attempts of the Government to skim the cream of the Parkway tourist business." See HM to LHH, 1 December 1956, 2 January 1957, LHP, Box 217; HM, "Report on Plan"; HM, "Review and Appraisal."

88. Martin Morgan to William M. Tuck, 5 March 1957, BRPRG 3, Box 103; Superintendent, BRP, "Annual Report of the Blue Ridge Parkway to the NPS Director, 1957," Box Ref. F217.B6U55, Blue Ridge Parkway Archives; NPS, "General Information Concerning the Granting of Concessions in the Areas Administered by the National Park Service," February 1957, BRPRG 3, Box 102; SPW to NPS Region 1 Director, 17 December 1956, BRPRG 3, Box 101.

89. Harris and Damtoft, "Row over Parkway Concessions Mounts"; "Parkway Plan Critics Tell N.C. Congressmen How They Look at It," Galax Gazette, 4 February 1957.

90. An Act to Establish a National Park Service, and for Other Purposes (National Park Service Organic Act), Title 16, U.S. Code, § 1, approved 25 August 1916 (39 Stat. 535).

91. M. A. Wright to George Shuford, 1 March 1957, BRPRG 3, Box 103; R. L. Gwyn to William B. Medford, 3 April 1957, LHP, Box 217.

92. William Medford, Press Release, 28 August 1957, William Medford to John W. Caffey, 27 January 1958, both in LHP, Box 300; "Park Service Yields on Parkway Facilities," AC, 30 August 1957.

93. "Byrd Outlines Park Road Plan," AC, 28 September 1933; Walter Brown, "Ickes Gives Approval to Plan for Building Park-to-Park Highway," AC, 17 November 1933, 1; Blue Ridge Parkway News 5, no. 2 (February–March 1942).

94. RGB to HLI, 28 April 1942, JDP, Box 677; RGB to Mr. Prince, 16 April 1942, E. K. Burlew to RGB, 8 May 1942, both in RGBP, Box 2; HLI, Diaries, 2 May 1942, HIP.

95. SWA, "Superintendent's Monthly Narrative Report, March 1947," 10 April 1947, CCF7B, Box 2719; CLW to LHH, 23 December 1954, A. H. Graham to Roy Morse, 8 March 1955, both in LHP, Box 24.

96. CLW to LHH, 23 December 1954, NPS, "Pertinent Information Concerning the Charging of Vehicle Fees on the Blue Ridge Parkway," [1955?], both in LHP, Box 24; Simmons, "Creation."

97. Superintendent, BRP, "Annual Report of the Blue Ridge Parkway to the NPS Director, NPS, 1955," Box Ref. F217.B6U55, Blue Ridge Parkway Archives; HM to [LHH], "Research into the

Blue Ridge Parkway Toll Situation," [1955?], HM to Don Shoemaker, 18 February 1955, HM to Sam J. Ervin, 12 January 1955, all in LHP, Box 24. NPS, BRP, "Land Acquisition Program Briefing Statement, Blue Ridge Parkway, Virginia–North Carolina," 6 March 1979, BRPRG 7, Box 54, indicates that in 1979, there were 162 public road crossings and accesses and 130 private road accesses and crossings (of which 104 were in Virginia). See also NPS, "Pertinent Information."

98. See LHH to George Shuford, 11 January 1955, HM to Sam J. Ervin Jr., 12 January 1955, 7 February 1955, North Carolina Board of Conservation and Development, "Resolution Unanimously Adopted . . . in Opposition to the Proposal to Levy Tolls on the Blue Ridge Parkway," 24 January 1955, Blue Ridge Parkway Association, "Resolution Unanimously Adopted . . . in Opposition to the Proposal to Levy Tolls on the Blue Ridge Parkway," 27 January 1955, John D. Norton to LHH, 13 February 1955, E. B. Jeffress to A. H. Graham, 1 March 1955, Orme Lewis to LHH, 19 April 1955, all in LHP, Box 24.

99. See HM to [LHH], "Research into the Blue Ridge Parkway Toll Situation"; [NPS?], "Analysis of the Record Presented by the State of North Carolina," 19 April 1955, E. B. Jeffress to A. H. Graham, 1 March 1955, HM to LHH, 17 February 1955, HM to Don Shoemaker, 18 February 1955, A. H. Graham to Roy W. Morse, 8 March 1955, all in LHP, Box 24; RGB to W. F. Babcock, 11 March 1958, CLW to LHH, 25 February 1958, W. M. Johnson to LHH, 27 March 1955, all in LHP, Box 300. See also HLI, Diaries, 2 May 1942, HIP.

100. CLW to LHH, 25 February 1958, HM to LHH, 27 February 1958, both in LHP, Box 300.

101. Editorial, *Hickory (N.C.) Record*, 28 February 1958; "There Should Be No Tolls on Parkway" [editorial], AC, 28 February 1958; Editorial, *Charlotte Observer*, 1 March 1958; "Keep Toll Collectors off the Parkway" [editorial], *Charlotte News*, 1 March 1958; "Parkway Toll Battle" [editorial], *Greensboro Record*, 1 March 1958; "U.S. Government Wrong: Parkway Toll Plans Real Shock to N.C." [editorial], *Asheville Times*, 1 March 1958; "Levying a Toll Charge on Blue Ridge Parkway" [editorial], *Durham Herald*, 2 March 1958; "Parkway Fee Fuss" [editorial], *Winston-Salem Journal-Sentinel*, 2 March 1958; "The People's Parkway" [editorial], *Greensboro Daily News*, 2 March 1958; "Bureaucrats Are Persistent" [editorial], *Henderson Daily Dispatch*, 3 March 1958; "A Long-Standing Peeve of Ours" [editorial], *Forest City Courier*, 3 March 1958; "Not Commercial Enterprise" [editorial], *Lexington Dispatch*, 3 March 1958; "Congressman Hugh Alexander Strongly Opposes Tolls on Blue Ridge Parkway" [editorial], *Lenoir News-Topic*, 5 March 1958; "Toll Temerity" [editorial], *Salisbury Evening Post*, 5 March 1958; "Parkway Tolls Again" [editorial], *Watauga Democrat*, 6 March 1958; "What Price Parkway Beauty?" [editorial], *West Jefferson Skyland Post*, 6 March 1958; "Ammunition for Toll Road Fight" [editorial], *Greensboro Daily News*, 7 March 1958; "Great White Father and His Forked Tongue" [editorial], *Morganton (N.C.) News-Herald*, 7 March 1958; "The Case against Parkway Fees" [editorial], AC, 15 March 1958.

102. E. L. Rankin Jr., Memorandum, 12 March 1958, Charles Raper Jonas to HM, 28 March 1958, RGB to W. F. Babcock, 11 March 1958, all in LHP, Box 300; RGB, "Statement of Mr. R. Getty Browning, Federal Parkway Engineer, Regarding the Proposed Imposition of Tolls on the Blue Ridge Parkway, Prepared for Meeting between Governor Hodges and Secretary Seaton at Washington, D.C.," 19 March 1958, Davant Private Collection; DOI Information Service, Press Release, "Secretary Seaton Cancels Proposed Fees for Blue Ridge Parkway," 26 March 1958, FOCP.

The Seaton decision may not have been as final as people thought. A Parkway business plan commissioned in 2003 again raised the possibility that "entrance fees" might be a way to supplement still insufficient Parkway funds. However, federal policy now permits 80 percent of the funds to be kept by the collecting park. See NPS, *Blue Ridge Parkway Business Plan* (Asheville, N.C.: BRP, 2003); Julie Ball, "Parkway Seeks Ways to Increase Budget," ACT, 21 October 2003.

Predictably, the *Asheville Citizen-Times* immediately condemned the idea: "Yes, Parkway Needs More Funds, but Let's Quickly Eliminate Entry Fee Idea" [editorial], *ACT*, 22 October 2003; Phil Noblitt, Management Assistant, BRP, Conversation with Author, 1 July 2005.

103. See, for example, J. P. Brady, "Grandfather Is a Symbol," *Franklin Press*, 29 March 1962; Joseph G. McClung to John F. Kennedy, 2 March 1962, Catawba Valley Camera Club, Petition to CLW, 16 April 1962, both in BRPLF; Betina Cox to Terry Sanford, 9 April 1962, Gurney Franklin to Terry Sanford, 9 April 1962, Ellen Townsend to Terry Sanford, 9 April 1962, Elmore Wise to Terry Sanford, 9 April 1962, all in TSP, Box 199.

104. Julian Scheer, "He Fights Again to Save Mountain," *Charlotte News*, 17 March 1962; Rothman, *Greening of a Nation?*, 50–62.

105. SPW quoted in Charlie Peek, "Adversaries Found That Morton Was a Man to Match His Mountain," *Winston-Salem Journal*, 6 September 1987; SPW, interview, BRPLIB; RGB to CLW, 31 January 1962, Davant Private Collection.

106. Distinctions among the three routes are somewhat clarified in RGB to LHH, 7 November 1958, SHCRWD, Box 9. Morton seems to have proposed and favored the middle or compromise route in 1955. See H. J. Spelman to W. H. Rogers Jr., 14 September 1955, SHCRWD, Box 9; E. L. Rankin Jr. to LHH, 19 October 1955, TSP, Box 81; HM, *A Capsule of Facts Substantiating Opposition to a Possible Change in the Established Right of Way for the Blue Ridge Parkway at Grandfather Mountain*, [1957?], BRPLF; "Hearing, Blue Ridge Parkway Grandfather Mountain Vicinity." See also "Comparison of Alternate Locations of Section 2H . . . ," 9 April 1964, BRPLF; Clifton L. Benson et al., Blue Ridge Parkway Committee, North Carolina State Highway Commission, "Report of Blue Ridge Parkway Committee," 2 May 1963, TSP, Box 413. On the final route being the middle route, see "Route Picked for Parkway Link in N.C.," *Winston-Salem Journal-Sentinel*, 21 May 1966.

107. EHA and SWA, Memorandum, 20 December 1940, BRPLF; RGB, Report, "Blue Ridge Parkway, Section 2-H," [1957?], BRPLF.

108. HM to LHH, 8 September 1955, TSP, Box 81; MacRae and Dunlap, "Legal Agreement"; "$25,000 Is Paid for Road Rights"; Charles Ross to Nelson MacRae, 11 August 1941, SHCRWD, Box 10. Morton wrote in 1955, "My family believes that we have made a real contribution to the State by the cooperation which we extended to you in being among the first to convey the needed right of way for the Blue Ridge Parkway, and that the agreement reached in 1939 covers all land needed by the Parkway through our holdings. At no time have we made any statement that would cause anyone to think otherwise" (HM to A. H. Graham, 22 March 1955, SHCRWD, Box 9). A 1955 article quoted Morton as saying that he always thought the Parkway officials would go ahead with the earlier plans to use the Yonahlossee route. See Marjorie Hunter, "Parkway Link Fought," *Winston-Salem Journal*, 6 July 1955. Browning noted in a 1965 interview that the upper route had been approved by the state and the Park Service and BPR for years before Morton complained. "It wasn't a matter of sneaking up on any of the property owners. Hugh had every opportunity to complain then if he didn't like it" (Yancey, "Grandfather Mountain Road").

The Yonahlossee lands were not deeded to the state until 1957, in the midst of the Park Service's battle with Morton. See Quitclaim Deed, Avery and Caldwell Counties, North Carolina, 28 December 1957, SHCRWD, Box 9; DOI, NPS Branch of Engineering, "Grandfather Mountain Area Acquisition Map, Section 2-H, Blue Ridge Parkway," 1945, North Carolina Collection, University of North Carolina, Chapel Hill.

R. Getty Browning wrote in the 1950s that "this purchase was made before it was definitely decided whether or not the Parkway could be adapted to the . . . Yonahlossee Trail; but since there was some uncertainty about the final location of the Parkway, the Highway Commission, upon recommendation of Charles Ross, who, at that time was Chief Counsel for the Commission, reluctantly granted the urgent request of the Linville Company to buy this section of right of way because it was so badly in need of money" (RGB, Report, "Blue Ridge Parkway, Section 2-H"). In a 1960 interview, Weems recounted essentially the same story (SPW, interview, BRPLIB).

109. "Chronological History."

110. HM to LHH, 8 September 1955, TSP, Box 81; "Quit Trying to Steal Mountain, Says Owner," *Winston-Salem Journal*, 8 March 1962; HM, Press Release, 4 January 1965, BRPLF; HM to *Greensboro Daily News* [letter to the editor], 18 June 1962, BRPLF; Granville Liles, "History of the Blue Ridge Parkway," BRPRG 5, Box 48; "Hearing, Blue Ridge Parkway Grandfather Mountain Vicinity"; "North Carolina General Statutes, Chapter 136," § 19.

111. Marjorie Hunter, "Parkway Link Fought"; Scheer, "He Fights Again to Save Mountain"; HM to LHH, 14 August 1958, 3 December 1958, 8 September 1955, HM to S. Herbert Evison, 29 September 1959, all in TSP, Box 81; Yancey, "Grandfather Mountain Road"; William Medford to RGB, 11 March 1957, SHCRWD, Box 9; "Hearing, Blue Ridge Parkway Grandfather Mountain Vicinity."

112. "Parkway Link Needs Completing"; Jay Jenkins, "High Route Promises 'Great Scar' — Morton," *Charlotte Observer*, 1 June 1962; "Chronological History."

113. H. J. Spelman to W. H. Rogers Jr., 14 September 1955, SHCRWD, Box 9; HM and SPW, Remarks by Hugh Morton in Color Slide Presentation to the Asheville Rotary Club [with Interpolated Responses by Weems], 26 April 1962, BRPLF; "Blue Ridge Parkway Location around Grandfather Mountain," 3 April 1962, BRPLF; CLW, "Statement of Mr. Conrad L. Wirth, Director, National Park Service on the Grandfather Mountain Section of the Blue Ridge Parkway in North Carolina," 31 May 1962, BRPLF; "Chronological History"; "Comparison of Alternate Locations," BRPLF. For the assertion that the road would come within three hundred feet of the attractions, see, for example, "Grandfather Mountain Subject of Controversy" [editorial], *North Wilkesboro (N.C.) Journal-Patriot*, 19 April 1962; HM and SPW, Remarks; HM, "Old Grandfather: A Man Defends His Mountain" (excerpts from a talk to the Asheville Rotary Club in April 1962), *Greensboro Daily News*, 27 May 1962; HM, "Open Forum." See also "Like Horatius at the Bridge" [editorial], *Burke County (N.C.) News-Herald*, 1 October 1963.

114. A Bureau of Public Roads study of the routes in 1955 revealed that the high route, with its seventeen-hundred-foot tunnel through Pilot Knob, would be approximately 6 miles long. Construction costs — the cheapest for any of the three routes — were estimated to be $1,930,000. The low (middle) line went around instead of through Pilot Knob, was just over 7 miles long, and would cost only slightly more than the high route. The (lowest) Yonahlossee route was about 6.5 miles and would cost the most to build ($2,174,600). See BRP, "Blue Ridge Parkway Project 2H1: Preliminary Estimate 'High Line,'" 25 August 1955, H. J. Spelman to W. H. Rogers Jr., 14 September 1955, both in SHCRWD, Box 9; RGB, Report, "Blue Ridge Parkway, Section 2-H." In a 2004 interview, Morton claimed that the high route included two tunnels (Pilot Ridge and Rough Ridge), but I can find no documentary evidence that more than one (Pilot Ridge) was ever contemplated. After the routing controversy was mostly resolved in 1966–68, however, correspondence between Morton and state highway officials discussed a projected Rough Ridge tunnel to which Morton had apparently acquiesced, but it was never built. See G. A. Wilkins (signed by Elmer R. Haile Jr.) to W. F. Babcock, 23 December 1966, Unsigned Letter, [December 1967], HM to J. G. Gibbs, 13 April 1967, J. G. Gibbs to HM, 11 April 1967, all in SHCRWD, Box 9; HM, interview; "Comparison of Alternate Locations."

115. See "Chronological History"; H. J. Spelman to W. H. Rogers Jr., 14 September 1955, SHCRWD,

Box 9; RGB, Report, "Blue Ridge Parkway, Section 2-H"; "Comparison of Alternate Locations." Although Morton later asserted that the BPR did not care which route was used, bureau representatives consistently concurred with the Park Service that the high line was superior. See A. Clark Stratton to Dan K. Moore, 29 September 1965, DKMP, Box 143.

116. SPW to NPS Southeast Region Director, 2 September 1965, BRPLF; RGB to CLW, 31 January 1962, Davant Private Collection; RGB to LHH, 7 November 1958, RGB to CLW, 27 May 1958, both in SHCRWD, Box 9.

117. Terry Sanford to CLW, 5 April 1962, BRPLF; Scheer, "He Fights Again to Save Mountain."

118. Wade Marr Jr. to Stewart Udall, 1 June 1962, with attached transcript of "Capital Comment: An Editorial Report on Yesterday's Highway Commission Hearing," delivered on WKIX radio, BRPLF.

119. "Hearing, Blue Ridge Parkway Grandfather Mountain Vicinity"; Wade Marr Jr. to Stewart Udall, 1 June 1962, with attached transcript of "Capital Comment: An Editorial Report on Yesterday's Highway Commission Hearing," delivered on WKIX radio, BRPLF; Sanders, "If You Want to See Your Boy in One Piece, You'll Let Us Through" [cartoon], *Greensboro Daily News*, 2 June 1962; "Grandfather Confrontation" [editorial], *Greensboro Daily News*, 2 June 1962.

120. "On Grandfather Mountain"; "Parkway Route Left to SHC," AC, 29 June 1962; Terry Sanford to C. E. Evans, 18 July 1962, TSP, Box 199; Clifton L. Benson et al., Blue Ridge Parkway Committee, North Carolina State Highway Commission, "Report of Blue Ridge Parkway Committee"; "Route by Mountain Approved," *Durham Sun*, 2 May 1963; David Cooper, "Park Bureau Spurns Parkway Compromise," RNO, 5 September 1963; Terry Sanford to Stewart Udall, 7 October 1963, BRPLF; Cliff Sessions, "Owner of Mountain Refuses to Let U.S. Build Parkway," United Press International, 10 April 1964, DKMP, Box 143.

121. W. F. Babcock to J. G. Gibbs, 4 December 1964, J. G. Gibbs to Harrison Lewis, 14 December 1964, Meeting Minutes, North Carolina State Highway Commission, 22 December 1964, Deed, Avery, Caldwell, and Watauga Counties, 5 January 1965, all in SHCRWD, Box 9; Terry Sanford to Stewart L. Udall, 30 December 1964, HM, Press Release, 4 January 1965, Stewart Udall to Dan K. Moore, 15 October 1965, all in BRPLF. See also "Across Grandfather: Compromise Route for Parkway Backed," AC, 23 December 1964; "Mortons Give Property for Highway Route," *Greensboro Daily News*, 28 January 1965.

122. Sanford, "New Era Ahead for Your State."

123. Stewart Udall to Dan K. Moore, 15 October 1965, BRPLF; A. Clark Stratton to Dan K. Moore, 29 September 1965, Dan K. Moore, Press Release, 20 May 1966, both in DKMP, Box 143; "Route Picked for Parkway Link in N.C."; Dan K. Moore, Press Release, 19 October 1968, DKMP, Box 373.2.

124. Wade Marr Jr. to Stewart Udall, 1 June 1962, BRPLF.

125. See, for example, Bedwell, "Hugh Morton"; *Winston-Salem Journal*, March 1962; Editorial, *Hickory Daily Record*, 12 March 1962.

126. HM, interview.

127. "Morton and His Mountain."

128. HM, *Capsule of Facts*; RGB, Report, "Blue Ridge Parkway, Section 2-H"; HM, interview.

129. HM, *Capsule of Facts*; RGB, Report, "Blue Ridge Parkway, Section 2-H"; HM, interview.

130. George A. McKinley to RGB, 27 June 1955, H. J. Spelman to W. H. Rogers Jr., 14 September 1955, both in SHCRWD, Box 9. See also EHA to SPW, 19 August 1955, BRPLF.

131. RGB, Report, "Blue Ridge Parkway, Section 2-H."

132. HM to LHH, 3 December 1958, 8 December 1958, TSP, Box 81; RGB to CLW, 27 May 1958, RGB to LHH, 7 November 1958, both in SHCRWD, Box 9.

133. RGB, interview.

134. Howard B. Stricklin to RGB, 19 March 1962, SPW to William F. Babcock, 28 March 1962, both in BRPLF; HM to LHH, 14 August 1958, TSP, Box 81.

135. HM, *Capsule of Facts*; RGB, Report, "Blue Ridge Parkway, Section 2-H"; "Two Sides" [editorial], RNO, 18 May 1962; "Road Engineers Disagree with Hugh Morton," RNO, 17 May 1962; RGB to CLW, 31 January 1962, Davant Private Collection; Yancey, "Mountain Owner, Engineer Still Debate Parkway Route"; Yancey, "Grandfather Mountain Road"; T. K. Pease to Superintendent, [2 July 1962], BRPLF; RGB to Terry Sanford, 2 July 1962, Terry Sanford to Cliff Benson, 24 September 1962, both in TSP, Box 199; W. F. Babcock to J. G. Gibbs, 5 November 1964, SHCRWD, Box 9; J. M. Eden to Superintendent, 4 February 1965, BRPLF.

136. Sam Beard to SPW, 18 April 1962, [SPW] to Dudley, [28 January 1963?], EHA to Chief, EODC, 13 June 1962, all in BRPLF; Sam Beard to LHH, 29 April 1959, TSP, Box 81; "Sam Beard Picked to Head Highway Public Relations," RNO, 12 July 1957; Peek, "Adversaries Found"; HM, interview. I have been unable to corroborate the report of Smith's appearance from contemporary sources: WRAL-TV maintains that there are no video archives of this program.

137. Jenkins, "High Route Promises 'Great Scar'"; "Park Service Director Holds out for Carolina's 'High Route' on the Parkway," *Roanoke Times*, 1 June 1962; "Wirth-Morton Battle Flames Anew" [editorial], *Asheville Times*, 1 June 1962; Noel Yancey, "Wirth Holds out the Prospect of Uncompleted Parkway Link," AC, 1 June 1962; "Grandfather Confrontation"; "Idea of an Uncompleted Parkway Is Unacceptable" [editorial], *Asheville Times*, 2 June 1962; "Time for Decision" [editorial], RNO, 2 June 1962; Sanders, "If You Want to See Your Boy in One Piece, You'll Let Us Through"; Howard B. Stricklin to Jonathan Daniels, 8 June 1962, Howard B. Stricklin to Robert Bunnelle, 8 June 1962, Howard B. Stricklin to H. W. Kendall, 8 June 1962, all in BRPLF; Howard B. Stricklin, "A Grandfatherly Rebuttal," *Greensboro Daily News*, 12 June 1962.

138. SPW to George Coggins, 22 June 1962, BRPLF.

139. Sam Beard to SPW, 27 January 1965, BRPLF.

140. "Mortons Give Property for Highway Route"; "Hugh Morton Explains Grandfather Settlement," *Hickory Daily Record*, 28 January 1965; HM, "Morton Thinks Parkway Route Argument Laid to Rest," *Watauga Democrat*, 4 February 1965; [SPW] to Dudley, [28 January 1963?], Stella W. Anderson to Superintendent, [27 January 1965?], both in BRPLF; "Will 'Mission 66' Be Missed with Link of Blue Ridge Parkway around Grandfather Mountain Still Unfinished?," *West Jefferson Skyland Post*, 12 July 1962; "Another Season Finds the Missing Link of Blue Ridge Parkway around Grandfather Mountain Still Unfinished," *West Jefferson Skyland Post*, 31 March 1966. On Stella Anderson, see Lefler, *History*, 608; *Heritage of Ashe County*, 113–14; HM, interview; Stella W. Anderson to SPW, 30 March 1966, BRPLF.

141. Frome, "Beauty or the Bulldozer?"; University of Idaho Manuscripts Collection, "Brief Biography."

142. Frome, "Beauty or the Bulldozer?"

143. Ibid.

144. SPW to Stella Anderson, 5 March 1966, Robert Bunnelle to SPW, 8 March 1966, both in BRPLF; Chester Davis, "Has N.C. Spoiled Its Beauty?," *Winston-Salem Journal-Sentinel*, 10 March 1966; Herman W. Wilcox, "Calls Attention to Frome Article on Parkway Link," *Watauga Democrat*, 10 March 1966.

145. "Another Season Finds the Missing Link of Blue Ridge Parkway Around Grandfather Mountain Still Unfinished," *West Jefferson Skyland Post*, 31 March 1966. For a rather comprehensive report on the long-running Morton-NPS controversy written decades after the events, see Peek, "Adversaries Found."

146. John Parris, "Grandfather Mountain Land Donated for Parkway Link," AC, 19 June 1969; Liles, "Grandfather and the Blue Ridge Parkway."

147. For clarifying that both the high and middle routes included the Linn Cove section, I am indebted to Bob Hope, former Parkway resident landscape architect. See also Gary W. Johnson, E-mail to author, 13 February 2004; Schreffler, "Bridge Closes Blue Ridge Gap"; Ed Spears, "Parkway Viaduct May Be Finished Sooner Than Planned Five Years," AC, 9 November 1978; Muller and Barker, "Design and Construction"; Hope, interview. Hope credits FHWA engineer Rex Cocroft with the idea of using precast segmental construction to bridge the area; Cocroft and his staff then sought outside consultation on how to do so.

148. The construction of the viaduct is detailed in Muller and Barker, "Design and Construction"; "DSC Seeks Blue Ridge 'Missing Link'"; Schreffler, "Bridge Closes Blue Ridge Gap"; Spears, "Parkway Viaduct May Be Finished." See also Quin and Marston, Historic American Engineering Record, 124–27.

149. This legislation and its effect on the NPS is discussed (and the full text is included) in Dilsaver, America's National Park System, 271, 364–69. See also Sellars, Preserving Nature, 234, 240–42, 279–80; Gary W. Johnson, interview; Hope, interview. A substantial number of rare and endangered plants and animals live on Grandfather Mountain; for one list, see the Grandfather Mountain Web site at <http://www.grandfather.com/conservation/endangered.htm>.

150. Edward G. Speer, Blue Ridge Parkway, 49.

151. North Carolina General Statutes, §§ 113A-205–214; School of Journalism and Mass Communication, University of North Carolina at Chapel Hill, "North Carolina Public Relations Hall of Fame."

152. The Grandfather Mountain reserve was part of a five-unit consortium under the umbrella of the Southern Appalachian Biosphere Reserve. See Grandfather Mountain, Inc. "Grandfather Mountain"; Grandfather Mountain, Inc., "Fast Facts." See also Nature Conservancy, "Grandfather Mountain." On the U.S. Man and the Biosphere Program, see "U.S. List of Biosphere Reserves"; Grandfather Mountain, Inc., "Grandfather Mountain: A Biosphere Reserve"; Grandfather Mountain, Inc., "Wildlife Habitats."

153. Sheila Gasperson, "Blue Ridge Parkway Land Acquisition Ranking System," [2004?], Obtained from Phil Noblitt, Blue Ridge Parkway Headquarters, Asheville, North Carolina; "Conservation Trust for North Carolina"; HM, Report to the Governor; HM, interview.

154. David B. Ottaway and Joe Stephens, "Nonprofit Land Bank Amasses Billions," Washington Post, 4 May 2003.

155. Joe Stephens and David B. Ottaway, "Developers Find Payoff in Preservation," Washington Post, 21 December 2003; HM, interview.

156. Bruce Henderson, "Blue Ridge Rivals Say They Aren't Making Mountain of Molehill," Atlanta Journal-Constitution, 20 May 1990; "Grandfather Mountain Source of Development Fears," AC, 2 April 1990; UNC-TV, "Biographical Conversations with Hugh Morton." This conflict is also discussed in Tager, Grandfather Mountain, 89–109. Acreage figures are from Grandfather Mountain, Inc., "Fast Facts."

157. Bruce Henderson, "Blue Ridge Rivals."

158. HM, Press Release, 4 January 1965, BRPLF; HM, "Morton Thinks Parkway Route Argument Laid to Rest"; "Hugh Morton Explains Grandfather Settlement."

EPILOGUE

1. "This Project Appeals" [editorial], AC, 24 October 1933; TCV to NPS Director, 2 November 1934, CCF7B, Box 2740; Walter Brown, "Parkway May Be Built to New England," AC, 12 July 1935, A1.

2. The story of the proposed Georgia extension that follows is assembled from the following sources: DOI, "North Carolina–Georgia Extension of the Blue Ridge Parkway: A Report to the Congress of the United States," 12 June 1963, DKMP, Box 51; Dan K. Moore, Press Release, 19 October 1968, DKMP, Box 373.2; Quin and Marston, *Historic American Engineering Record*, 101–5; John Parris, "Parkway Extension Plans Unveiled," AC, 18 November 1970; Roy Parker Jr., "Group Fighting Parkway, TVA Plan," RNO, 30 November 1970. See also "Petition Protesting the Route of the Extension of the Blue Ridge Parkway through the Persimmon Community of Rabun County, Georgia," 8 November 1970, Mr. and Mrs. James Keener to Superintendent, Blue Ridge Parkway, 22 October 1970, Leonard E. Foote to Granville Liles, 30 November 1970, Granville B. Liles to Director, Southeast Region, NPS, 8 December 1970, all in BRPRG 5, Box 15.

3. NPS, *Blue Ridge Parkway Business Plan* (Asheville, N.C.: BRP, 2003).

BIBLIOGRAPHY

ARCHIVAL COLLECTIONS

Asheville, North Carolina

    Asheville Citizen-Times Library

        Charles Webb Envelopes

        Fred Weede Envelopes

    Blue Ridge Parkway Archives

        Blue Ridge Parkway Record Groups 1, 3, 5, 6, 7, 9, 11, 63

        R. Getty Browning Papers

        Superintendent's Annual Reports

    Blue Ridge Parkway Headquarters

        Engineering and Technical Services Map Files

        Lands Files

        Photograph Collection

        Tom Richardson, Bedford, Virginia, Private Collection (on loan)

    Blue Ridge Parkway Library, District Ranger Office

        Stanley W. Abbott, interview by S. Herbert Evison, 1958.

        Edward H. Abbuehl, interview by S. Herbert Evison, 9 April 1971.

        Sam P. Weems, interview by S. Herbert Evison, 26 July 1960, 16 July 1971.

    Pack Memorial Library

        Grandfather Mountain Clipping File and Other Materials

        Sondley Research Room

            North Carolina Collection

    University of North Carolina at Asheville, D. Hiden Ramsey Library, Special Collections

        Heritage of Western North Carolina Collection

        Photographic Collections

Blacksburg, Virginia

    Virginia Tech Digital Library and Archives

Blowing Rock, North Carolina

    Harriet Browning Davant Private Collection

Chapel Hill, North Carolina

    University of North Carolina

        North Carolina Collection

            Clipping Files and Other Materials

        Southern Historical Collection

            Francis O. Clarkson Papers, 1983 Addition

            Heriot Clarkson Papers

            Robert Lee Doughton Papers

            E. B. Jeffress Papers

            George Erwin Cullet Stephens Papers

College Park, Maryland

    National Archives II

        Record Group 30 (Bureau of Public Roads)

Record Group 79 (National Park Service), Central Classified Files, 1933–49, Entry 7B, "National Parkways–Blue Ridge," Boxes 2711–75

Record Group 79 (National Park Service), Central Classified Files, 1933–49, Entry 18, "Records of Arno B. Cammerer, 1920–1940," Box 2

Cartographic Research Room

Record Group 79 (National Park Service), Blue Ridge Parkway Master Plans, Folders 1–4

Still Picture Research Room

Record Group 30 (Bureau of Public Roads), Boxes 103, 104, 110, 111

Record Group 79-G (NPS Prints, Charles W. Porter Collection), Box 1

Record Group 79SM (Stephen Mather Collection), Boxes 1, 7

Durham, North Carolina

Duke University Library, Special Collections Department

Josiah William Bailey Papers

East Point, Georgia

National Archives Southeast Region

Record Group 75, Cherokee Indian Agency Files

Elmsford, New York

Westchester County Archives

Grandfather Mountain, North Carolina

Hugh Morton Private Collection

Harpers Ferry, West Virginia

National Park Service, Harpers Ferry Center Library

R. Getty Browning, interview by S. Herbert Evison, 9 December 1958.

Hyde Park, New York

Franklin D. Roosevelt Presidential Library

President's Official Files 6p, 27, 129, 200, 237, 1606, 2383, 5708

President's Personal Files 2812, 3860, 611

President's Speech Files 1299, 880, 914

Memphis, Tennessee

Memphis Public Library and Information Center

Senator Kenneth McKellar Papers

Raleigh, North Carolina

Robert C. Browning Private Collection

North Carolina State Archives

Appalachian National Park Association Collection

Ashe County, North Carolina, Superior Court Minutes, 1938–43

Blue Ridge Parkway Photographic Collection, 1931–59

Eastern Band of Cherokee Indians, Cherokee Indian Council Minutes, 1931–62. Microfilm copy of English minutes.

J. C. B. Ehringhaus Papers

Luther Hodges Papers

Dan K. Moore Papers

Terry Sanford Papers

State Highway Commission, Right of Way Department, Blue Ridge Parkway Records

Richmond, Virginia

Library of Virginia

George C. Peery Papers

John Garland Pollard Papers

Washington, D.C.
    Library of Congress, Manuscripts Division
        Josephus Daniels Papers
        Harold Ickes Papers

GOVERNMENT DOCUMENTS

Biennial Report of the Attorney General of the State of North Carolina. Vol. 36 (1960–62). Raleigh, N.C.:
    Department of Justice, 1886–1970.

Mather, Stephen. *Report of the Director of the National Park Service to the Secretary of the Interior for the Fiscal*
    Year Ended June 30, 1920, and the Travel Season 1920. Washington, D.C.: Government Printing
    Office, 1920.

Mooney, James. *Myths of the Cherokee.* Nineteenth Annual Report of the Bureau of American
    Ethnology, part 1. Washington, D.C.: Government Printing Office, 1900.

National Park Service Organic Act of 1916. 16 U.S.C. §§1–18f., 39 Stat. 585.

Public Law 593, *An Act to Authorize the Secretary of the Interior to Convey to the State of North Carolina for*
    Use in Connection with the Blue Ridge Parkway Certain Land within the Cherokee Indian Reservation in the
    State of North Carolina, U.S. Statutes at Large, 54, part 1, chapter 318 (1941).

Quin, Richard, and Christopher Marston. *Historic American Engineering Record: Blue Ridge Parkway,*
    HAER no. NC-42. Historic American Buildings Survey/Historic American Engineering Record
    (HABS/HAER) Division, National Park Service, 1997.

"Record and Case on Appeal of the Plaintiff: In the Supreme Court of North Carolina, Fall Term,
    1939: *Switzerland Company v. North Carolina State Highway and Public Works Commission* (from
    Mitchell), before Warlick, Judge, March Term, 1939, Mitchell Superior Court—Defendant
    Appealed (Case Is 216 N.C. 450)." In *North Carolina Appeal Record* (216 N.C. 450). Vol. 216.
    Raleigh, N.C.: Commercial, 1939.

Speer, Edward G. *The Blue Ridge Parkway: An Administrative History* [Draft]. Written under Cooperative
    Agreement no. 1443CA514098007 (Jean Haskell, Principal Investigator). U.S. Department of
    the Interior, National Park Service, 2000.

Speer, Jean Haskell, and Frances H. Russell. *The Kelley School (Pate/Ware Store).* Historic Resource
    Study/Historic Structure Report. 2 vols. U.S. Department of the Interior, National Park Service,
    Blue Ridge Parkway, 1989.

Speer, Jean Haskell, Frances H. Russell, and Gibson Worsham. *The Johnson Farm at Peaks of Otter,*
    Blue Ridge Parkway, Milepost 86. Historic Resources Study and Historic Structures Report. U.S.
    Department of the Interior, National Park Service, Blue Ridge Parkway, 1990.

Switzerland Company v. North Carolina State Highway and Public Works Commission. In Mitchell North
    Carolina Appeal Record, vol. 216 (fall term 1939). Raleigh, N.C.: Commercial, 1939.

Switzerland Company v. North Carolina State Highway and Public Works Commission. In North Carolina
    Reports, vol. 216, *Cases Argued and Determined in the Supreme Court of North Carolina,* spring term
    1939, fall term 1939, edited by John M. Strong. Raleigh, N.C.: Bynum, 1940.

U.S. Census Bureau. *Fifteenth Census of the United States, 1930: Population.* 3 vols. Washington, D.C.:
    Government Printing Office, 1931–33.

———. *U.S. Census of Agriculture, 1935,* vol. 1, *Reports for States with Statistics for Counties and a*
    Summary for the United States, pt. 2, *Southern States.* Washington, D.C.: Government Printing
    Office, 1931–33.

U.S. Congress. House of Representatives. *Congressional Record.* vol. 80, pt. 10, 74th Cong., 2nd sess.,
    1936.

U.S. Congress. House of Representatives. Committee on Public Lands. *Report no. 3003 to Accompany*
    H.R. 12789. 74th Cong., 2nd sess., 1936.

————. *Report no. 937 to Accompany H.R. 5472*. 75th Cong., 1st sess., 1937.

————. *Establishing the Blue Ridge Parkway in North Carolina: Hearings before the House Committee on Public Lands*. 76th Cong., 1st sess., 1939.

U.S. Congress. Senate. *Natchez Trace Parkway Survey*. 76th Cong., 3rd sess., 26 February 1940.

U.S. Congress. Senate. Subcommittee of the Committee on Indian Affairs. *Survey of Conditions of the Indians in the United States: Hearings before a Subcommittee of the Committee on Indian Affairs*. 76th Cong., part 37, 1937–39.

U.S. Department of the Interior, National Park Service, Public Use Statistics Office. *National Park Service Statistical Abstract 1999*. Denver: National Park Service Public Use Statistics Office, 1999.

U.S. Statutes at Large. Washington, D.C.: Government Printing Office, 1941.

Unrau, Harlan D., and G. Frank Williss. *Administrative History: Expansion of the National Park Service in the 1930s*. <http://www.cr.nps.gov/history/online_books/unrau-williss/adhi.htm>. 8 December 2002.

Westmacott, Richard. *Long-Term Landscape Change and Management of Historical Agricultural Landscapes in Southern Appalachian Parks: Summary Report*. Washington, D.C.: U.S. Department of the Interior, National Park Service, Southeast Region, [1994?].

INTERVIEWS

Browning, Robert C. Interview by author. 17 May 2000.

Davant, Harriet Browning. Interview by author. 15 May 2000.

Frome, Michael. Telephone interview by author. 21 May 2005.

Hope, Robert. Telephone interview by author. 9 June 2004.

Johnson, Gary W. Telephone interview by author. 22 June 2004.

Ketterson, F. A., Jr. Interview by Jim Williams. 5 August 1991. <http://www.nps.gov/hstr/OHP/ketterson_f/ketterson_interview.htm>.

Moore, Myriam Putnam. Interview by David Catlin. 25 July 1979. In possession of author.

Morton, Hugh. Interview by author. 18 May 2004.

BOOKS, ARTICLES, AND THESES

"1900-Mile Park-to-Park Highway." *Manufacturers Record* 49, no. 22 (1931): 43.

Abbott, Carlton, William Douglas Mettler, Mollianne George, Roberta A. Young, Nancy L. S. Abbott, Tina A. McCurry, and Ashley Powell. *Visual Character of the Blue Ridge Parkway*. Williamsburg, Va.: Carlton Abbott and Partners and National Park Service, [1997?].

Abbott, Stanley W. "The Blue Ridge Parkway: 500-Mile Super-Scenic Motorway: A New Element in Recreational Planning within Day's Drive of 60,000,000 People." In *The Eastern National Park-to-Park Annual and The Blue Ridge Parkway Guide*, 10–12. Asheville, N.C.: Park-to-Park, 1941.

————. "The Blue Ridge Parkway: A New Element in Recreational Planning." *Regional Review* 3, no. 1 (July 1939): 3–6.

————. "Historic Preservation: Perpetuation of Scenes Where History Becomes Real." *Landscape Architecture* 40, no. 4 (1950): 153–57.

————. "Parks and Parkways: A Creative Field Even When the Task Is to Avoid Creation." *Landscape Architecture* 44, no. 1 (1953): 22–24.

Abrams, Douglas Carl. *Conservative Constraints: North Carolina and the New Deal*. Jackson: University Press of Mississippi, 1992.

Adams, David Wallace. *Education for Extinction: American Indians and the Boarding School Experience, 1875–1928*. Lawrence: University Press of Kansas, 1995.

"Advertising Virginia: Tourism in the Old Dominion in the Twenties and the Great Depression." *Virginia Cavalcade* 44, no. 1 (1994): 28–39.

Aguar, Charles E. "Mackaye, Benton." In *Pioneers of American Landscape Design*, edited by Charles A. Birnbaum and Robin Carson, 233–36. New York: McGraw-Hill, 2000.

Akers, Rhonda, ed. *Mileposts and More: The Blue Ridge Parkway*. Radford, Va.: Radford University, 1985.

Alanen, Arnold R. "Considering the Ordinary: Vernacular Landscapes in Small Towns and Rural Areas." In *Preserving Cultural Landscapes in America*, edited by Arnold R. Alanen and Robert Z. Melnick, 112–42. Baltimore: Johns Hopkins University Press, 2000.

Alanen, Arnold R., and Robert Z. Melnick. "Introduction: Why Cultural Landscape Preservation?" In *Preserving Cultural Landscapes in America*, edited by Arnold R. Alanen and Robert Z. Melnick, 1–21. Baltimore: Johns Hopkins University Press, 2000.

Alleghany County Historical Committee. *History of Alleghany County, 1859 through 1976, Sparta, North Carolina*. Winston-Salem, N.C.: Hunter, 1976.

Alleghany Historical-Genealogical Society. *Alleghany County Heritage, 1983*. Winston-Salem, N.C.: Hunter, 1983.

Anderson, Johnnie Virginia. "Heriot Clarkson: A Social Engineer of North Carolina." Master's thesis, Wake Forest University, 1972.

Anderson, Larry. *Benton MacKaye: Conservationist, Planner, and Creator of the Appalachian Trail*. Baltimore: Johns Hopkins University Press, 2002.

Anderson, Michael Francis. "Polishing the Jewel: An Administrative History of Grand Canyon National Park." Ph.D. diss., Northern Arizona University, 1999.

Annese, Domenico. "Clarke, Gilmore David." In *Pioneers of American Landscape Design*, edited by Charles A. Birnbaum and Robin Karson, 56–60. New York: McGraw-Hill, 2000.

Appalachian Land Ownership Task Force. *Who Owns Appalachia?: Landownership and Its Impact*. Lexington: University Press of Kentucky, 1983.

"An Artist's Wife." "The North Carolina Mountains." *Appleton's Journal* (1870). <http//www.ls.net/ffinewriver/nc/appl1870.htm>. 17 January 2005.

"Asheville and Environs." *Eastern National Park-to-Park Highway Magazine* (1935): 8–12.

Badger, Anthony J. *North Carolina and the New Deal*. Raleigh: North Carolina Department of Cultural Resources, Division of Archives and History, 1981.

Bailey, David Coleman. *Fashionable Asheville*. Vol. 1, *The Fascinating Social History of a Famous Mountain Town, 1880–1930*. Charleston, S.C.: BookSurge, 2004.

Ballinger, Kenneth. *Miami Millions: The Dance of the Dollars in the Great Florida Land Boom of 1925*. Miami, Fla.: Franklin, 1936.

Barringer, Mark Daniel. *Selling Yellowstone: Capitalism and the Construction of Nature*. Lawrence: University Press of Kansas: 2002.

Bartlett, Richard A. *Troubled Waters: Champion International and the Pigeon River Controversy*. Knoxville: University of Tennessee Press, 1995.

Batteau, Allen W. *The Invention of Appalachia*. Tucson: University of Arizona Press, 1990.

Bauer, Catherine. "Problems of the Indians." *The State: A Weekly Survey of North Carolina* 14, no. 18 (1946): 3–21.

Bauer, Fred B. *Land of the North Carolina Cherokees*. Brevard, N.C.: Buchanan, 1970.

Bawden, Timothy Todd. "Reinventing the Frontier: Tourism, Nature, and Environmental Change in Northern Wisconsin, 1880–1930." Ph.D. diss., University of Wisconsin at Madison, 2002.

Becker, Jane S. *Selling Tradition: Appalachia and the Construction of an American Folk, 1930–1940*. Chapel Hill: University of North Carolina Press, 1998.

Belasco, Warren James. *Americans on the Road: From Autocamp to Motel, 1910–1945*. Cambridge: MIT Press, 1979.

Beney, Peter. *Land of the Sky: Wonders of the Blue Ridge and Great Smoky Mountains.* Atlanta: Longstreet, 1990.

Biles, Roger. *A New Deal for the American People.* De Kalb, Ill.: Northern Illinois University Press, 1991.

———. *The South and the New Deal.* Lexington: University Press of Kentucky, 1994.

Birnbaum, Charles A., and Lisa E. Crowder, eds. *Pioneers of American Landscape Design: An Annotated Bibliography.* Washington, D.C.: U.S. Department of the Interior, National Park Service, 1993.

Blackford, Mansel G. *Fragile Paradise: The Impact of Tourism on Maui, 1959–2000.* Lawrence: University Press of Kansas, 2001.

Blackmun, Ora. *Western North Carolina: Its Mountains and Its People to 1880.* Boone, N.C.: Appalachian Consortium, 1977.

Bledsoe, Jerry. *Blue Horizons: Faces and Places from a Bicycle Journey along the Blue Ridge Parkway.* Asheboro, N.C.: Down Home, 1993.

Blight, David W. "Historians and 'Memory.'" *Common-Place* 2, no. 3 (April 2002). <http//www.historycooperative.org/journals/cp/vol-02/no-03/author/index.shtml>. 1 January 2005.

Blowing Rock Historical Society. *Post Cards of Historic Blowing Rock.* Boone, N.C.: Parkway, 2002.

Borah, Leo A. "A Patriotic Pilgrimage to Eastern National Parks: History and Beauty Live along Paved Roads, Once Indian Trails, through Virginia, North Carolina, Tennessee, Kentucky, and West Virginia." *National Geographic* 65, no. 6 (1934): 663–97.

Bowman, Gary M. *Highway Politics in Virginia.* Fairfax, Va.: George Mason University Press, 1993.

Bradley, William Aspenwall. "Hobnobbing with Hillbillies." *Harper's Magazine* 132 (1915): 91–103.

Branson, E. C. *Our Carolina Highlanders.* Chapel Hill: University of North Carolina Extension Bureau, 1916.

Broom, Leonard. "The Acculturation of the Eastern Cherokee." Ph.D. diss., Duke University, 1937.

Broome, Harvey. "The Wilds, Parkways, and Dollars [letter to the editor]." *Nation* 139, no. 3601 (1934): 46.

Brothers, Gene, and Rachel J. C. Chen. *1995–96 Economic Impact of Travel to the Blue Ridge Parkway North Carolina and Virginia.* Raleigh: Office of Parks, Tourism Research, North Carolina State University, [1996].

Brown, Cecil Kenneth. *The State Highway System of North Carolina: Its Evolution and Present Status.* Chapel Hill: University of North Carolina Press, 1931.

Brown, David E. "The Grandfather of Parkway Preservation." *Carolina Alumni Review,* September–October 1998, 49.

———. "The Long View from the Top." *Carolina Alumni Review,* September–October 2003, 36–44.

Brown, Dona. *Inventing New England: Regional Tourism in the Nineteenth Century.* Washington, D.C.: Smithsonian Institution Press, 1995.

Brown, Margaret Lynn. "Captains of Tourism: Selling a National Park in the Great Smoky Mountains." *Journal of the Appalachian Studies Association* 4 (1992): 42–49.

———. "Smoky Mountains Story: Human Values and Environmental Transformation in a Southern Bioregion, 1900–1950." Ph.D. diss., University of Kentucky, 1995.

———. *The Wild East: A Biography of the Great Smoky Mountains.* Gainesville: University Press of Florida, 2000.

Brownell, Blaine A. Review of *Sorting Out the New South City: Race, Class, and Urban Development in Charlotte, 1875–1975,* by Thomas W. Hanchett. *American Historical Review* 104, no. 3 (1999): 918–19.

Browning, Meshach. *Forty-four Years of the Life of a Hunter: Being Reminiscences of Meshach Browning, a Maryland Hunter, Roughly Written Down by Himself; Revised and Illustrated by E. Stabler.* Introduction by R. Getty Browning. Winston-Salem, N.C.: Winston, 1942.

Brundage, W. Fitzhugh, ed. *Where These Memories Grow: History, Memory, and Southern Identity*. Chapel Hill: University of North Carolina Press, 2000.

Burger, Julian. *Report from the Frontier: The State of the World's Indigenous Peoples*. London: Zed, 1987.

Buxton, Barry M., and Steven M. Beatty, eds. *Blue Ridge Parkway: Agent of Transition*. Proceedings of the Blue Ridge Parkway Golden Anniversary Conference. Boone, N.C.: Appalachian Consortium, 1986.

Cammerer, Arno B. "National Government Services through Recreation in Our National Parks." *Recreation* 28 (1935): 465–67.

Campbell, Carlos C. *Birth of a National Park in the Great Smoky Mountains*. Knoxville: University of Tennessee Press, 1960.

Campbell, John C. "From Mountain Cabin to Cotton Mill." *Child Labor Bulletin* 2, no. 1 (1913): 74–84.

———. *The Southern Highlander and His Homeland*. 1921; reprint, Lexington: University Press of Kentucky, 1969.

Campbell, Olive Dame, and Cecil J. Sharp. *English Folk Songs from the Southern Appalachians: Comprising 122 Songs and Ballads and 323 Tunes*. New York: Putnam's, 1917.

Caro, Robert A. *The Power Broker: Robert Moses and the Fall of New York*. New York: Vintage, 1975.

Carr, Ethan. *Wilderness by Design: Landscape Architecture and the National Park Service*. Lincoln: University of Nebraska Press, 1998.

Catlin, David T. *A Naturalist's Blue Ridge Parkway*. Knoxville: University of Tennessee Press, 1984.

Chafe, William H. *Civilities and Civil Rights: Greensboro, North Carolina, and the Black Struggle for Freedom*. Oxford: Oxford University Press, 1980.

Chambers, Thomas A. *Drinking the Waters: Creating an American Leisure Class at Nineteenth-Century Mineral Springs*. Washington, D.C.: Smithsonian Institution Press, 2002.

Clark, Elmer T. *Junaluska Jubilee: A Short History of the Lake Junaluska Assembly, Inc., on the Occasion of Its Fiftieth Anniversary*. New York: World Outlook, 1963.

Clarke, Gilmore D. "The Parkway Idea." In *The Highway and the Landscape*, edited by W. Brewster Snow, 33–55. New Brunswick, N.J.: Rutgers University Press, 1959.

Clarke, Jeanne Nienaber. *Roosevelt's Warrior: Harold L. Ickes and the New Deal*. Baltimore: Johns Hopkins University Press, 1996.

Clarkson, Roy B. *Tumult on the Mountains: Lumbering in West Virginia, 1770–1920*. Parsons, W.Va.: McClain, 1964.

Clements, Kendrick A. "Politics and the Park: San Francisco's Fight for Hetch Hetchy, 1908–1913." *Pacific Historical Review* 48 (1979): 185–215.

Clingman, T. L. "Western North Carolina." *Appleton's Journal* 5 (1871): 587.

Coleman, Michael C. *American Indian Children at School, 1850–1930*. Jackson: University Press of Mississippi, 1993.

Collier, John. *From Every Zenith: A Memoir and Some Essays on Life and Thought*. Denver: Sage, 1963.

Community Chests and Councils, Asheville Community Chest Survey Bureau, and Citizens' Committee of One Hundred. *Welfare Portrait of Asheville, North Carolina: A Community Welfare Study of the Year 1938*. N.p.: n.p., 1940.

Compton, Stephen C. *Early Tourism in Western North Carolina*. Charleston, S.C.: Arcadia, 2004.

Covington, Howard E., Jr. *Linville: A Mountain Home for 100 Years*. Linville, N.C.: Linville Resorts, 1992.

Covington, Howard E., Jr., and Marion A. Ellis, eds. *The North Carolina Century: Tar Heels Who Made a Difference, 1900–2000*. Charlotte, N.C.: Levine Museum of the New South, 2002.

Crayon, Porte [David Hunter Strother]. "Virginia Illustrated: Adventures of Porte Crayon and His Cousins." *Harper's New Monthly Magazine* 55 (December 1854): 1–26; 57 (February 1855): 289–310; 63 (August 1855): 289–311; 75 (September 1856): 303–24.

Cronon, William, ed. *Uncommon Ground: Rethinking the Human Place in Nature*. New York: Norton, 1995.

Crum, Mason. *The Story of Lake Junaluska*. Greensboro, N.C.: Piedmont, 1950.

Crutchfield, James A. *The Natchez Trace: A Pictorial History*. Nashville, Tenn.: Rutledge Hill, 1985.

Cutler, Phoebe. *The Public Landscape of the New Deal*. New Haven: Yale University Press, 1985.

Dabney, Virginius. *Virginia: The New Dominion: A History from 1607 to the Present*. Charlottesville: University Press of Virginia, 1971.

Daniel, W. Harrison. *Bedford County, Virginia, 1840–1860: The History of an Upper Piedmont County in the Late Antebellum Era*. Bedford, Va.: Virginia Baptist Historical Society, 1985.

Davies, Jay. "Highway in the Sky." *Wildlife in North Carolina* 52, no. 9 (1988): 8–14.

Davis, Donald Edward. *Where There Are Mountains: An Environmental History of the Southern Appalachians*. Athens: University of Georgia Press, 2000.

Davis, Rebecca Harding. "The Rose of Carolina." *Scribner's Monthly* 8 (1874): 723–36.

Davis, Timothy. "Mount Vernon Memorial Highway and the Evolution of the American Parkway." Ph.D. diss, University of Texas at Austin, 1997.

Dawley, Thomas R. "Our Southern Mountaineers: Removal the Remedy for the Evils That Isolation and Poverty Have Brought." *World's Work* 19 (1910): 12704–14.

Dilsaver, Lary M., ed. *America's National Park System: The Critical Documents*. Lanham, Md.: Rowman and Littlefield, 1994.

Dixon, Thomas. *Wildacres in the Land of the Sky*. Little Switzerland, N.C.: Wildacres Development Company/Mt. Mitchell Association of Arts and Sciences, 1926.

Dodson, E. Griffith. *General Assembly of Virginia, 1919–1939: Register and Index*. Richmond, Va.: State Publication, 1939.

Dorman, Robert L. *Revolt of the Provinces: The Regionalist Movement in America, 1920–1945*. Chapel Hill: University of North Carolina Press, 1993.

Dugger, Shepherd M. *The Balsam Groves of the Grandfather Mountain*. 1907; reprint, Banner Elk, N.C.: Puddingstone, 1974.

———. *The War Trails of the Blue Ridge*. 1932; reprint, Banner Elk, N.C.: Puddingstone, 1974.

Duls, Louisa DeSaussure. *The Story of Little Switzerland*. Richmond, Va.: Whittet and Shepperson, 1982.

Dunn, Durwood. *Cades Cove: The Life and Death of a Southern Appalachian Community, 1818–1937*. Knoxville: University of Tennessee Press, 1988.

"DSC Seeks Blue Ridge 'Missing Link.'" *Courier: The National Park Service Newsletter* 2, no. 11 (1979): 13.

The Eastern National Park-to-Park Highway Guide. Asheville, N.C.: Park-to-Park, 1939.

The Eastern National Park-to-Park Highway Magazine, Good Will Tour Edition. Asheville, N.C.: Park-to-Park, 1935.

Eiler, Lyntha Scott, Terry Eiler, and Carl Fleischhauer, eds. *Blue Ridge Harvest: A Region's Folklife in Photographs*. Washington, D.C.: Library of Congress, 1981.

Eller, Ronald D. *Miners, Millhands, and Mountaineers: Industrialization of the Appalachian South, 1880–1930*. Knoxville: University of Tennessee Press, 1982.

Erbe, Carl. "The Last Frontier." *Eastern National Park-to-Park Highway Magazine*, 1935, 3.

Erskine, Ralph. "The Handicraftsmen of the Blue Ridge: A Simple, Homeloving Folk Who Have Lived Their Own Lives, Heedless of the March of Events." *Craftsman* 13 (1907): 158–67.

Escott, Paul D. *Many Excellent People: Power and Privilege in North Carolina, 1850–1900*. Chapel Hill: University of North Carolina Press, 1985.

Famighetti, Robert, ed. *The World Almanac and Book of Facts, 1995*. Mahwah, N.J.: Funk and Wagnalls, 1994.

Fee, John G. "Kentucky." *American Missionary* 10 (1855): 13–14.

Ferrell, Henry C. Jr. Review of *The Blue Ridge Parkway*, by Harley E. Jolley. *American Historical Review* 75, no. 4 (1970): 1202–3.

Finger, John R. *Cherokee Americans: The Eastern Band of Cherokees in the Twentieth Century.* Lincoln: University of Nebraska Press, 1991.

———. *The Eastern Band of Cherokees, 1819–1900.* Knoxville: University of Tennessee Press, 1984.

———. "The Saga of Tsali: Legend versus Reality." *North Carolina Historical Review* 56, no. 1 (January 1979): 1–18.

Fisher, Stephen L., ed. *Fighting Back in Appalachia: Traditions of Resistance and Change.* Philadelphia: Temple University Press, 1993.

Fixico, Donald L. *The Invasion of Indian Country in the Twentieth Century: American Capitalism and Tribal Resources.* Niwot: University Press of Colorado, 1998.

Flippen, J. Brooks. *Nixon and the Environment.* Albuquerque: University of New Mexico Press, 2000.

Foppes, Ellen K., and Robert M. Utley. "Present at the Creation: Robert M. Utley Recalls the Beginnings of the National Historic Preservation Program." *Public Historian* 24, no. 2 (2002): 61–81.

Foster, Stephen William. *The Past Is Another Country: Representation, Historical Consciousness, and Resistance in the Blue Ridge.* Berkeley: University of California Press, 1988.

Fox, John, Jr. *A Cumberland Vendetta and Other Stories.* New York: Harper and Brothers, 1895.

———. *The Kentuckians.* New York: Harper, 1897.

Francaviglia, Richard. "Selling Heritage Landscapes." In *Preserving Cultural Landscapes in America,* edited by Arnold R. Alanen and Robert Z. Melnick, 44–69. Baltimore: Johns Hopkins University Press, 2000.

Frazer, William, and John J. Guthrie Jr. *The Florida Land Boom: Speculation, Money, and the Banks.* Westport, Conn.: Quorum, 1995.

Frazier, Kevan D. "Outsiders in the Land of the Sky: City Planning and the Transformation of Asheville, North Carolina, 1921–1929." *Journal of Appalachian Studies* 4 (Fall 1998): 299–316.

Frome, Michael. "Beauty or the Bulldozer?" *American Forests,* February 1966, 6–9, 40–41.

———. *Strangers in High Places: The Story of the Great Smoky Mountains.* Expanded ed. Knoxville: University of Tennessee Press, 1980.

Frost, William Goodell. "Our Contemporary Ancestors in the Southern Mountains." *Atlantic Monthly* 83 (March 1899): 311–19.

———. "The Southern Mountaineer: Our Kindred of the Boone and Lincoln Type." *American Review of Reviews* 21 (1900): 303–11.

Furman, Lucy. *Sight to the Blind: A Story.* New York: Macmillan, 1914.

Garrett, Robert B. "Browning Knob." *Glades Star* 4, no. 7 (1970): 134–38.

Gatewood, Willard Badgette, Jr. "North Carolina's Role in the Establishment of the Great Smoky Mountains National Park." *North Carolina Historical Review* 37, no. 2 (1960): 165–84.

Gentry, Diane Koos. *Road That Rides the Fog: A Golden Anniversary Look at the Blue Ridge Parkway.* Lakewood, Calif.: American Association of Retired Persons, 1985.

Gidcomb, Barry Doyle. "History and the Natchez Trace Parkway." Ph.D. diss., Illinois State University, 2000.

Glassberg, David. *Sense of History: The Place of the Past in American Life.* Amherst: University of Massachusetts Press, 2001.

Govert, Gary. "The Godfather of Grandfather." *Carolina Lifestyle,* July 1982, 42–51.

Graham, J. Scott. *Blue Ridge Parkway: America's Favorite Journey.* Johnson City, Tenn.: Graham, 2003.

Grattan, C. Hartley. "Trouble in the Hills." *Scribner's* 98, no. 5 (1935): 290–94.

Green, Elna C., ed. *The New Deal and Beyond: Social Welfare in the South since 1930*. Athens: University of Georgia Press, 2003.

Greenberg, Sue, and Jan Kahn. *Asheville: A Postcard History*. 2 vols. Dover, N.H.: Arcadia, 1997.

Greenspan, Anders. *Creating Colonial Williamsburg*. Washington, D.C.: Smithsonian Institution Press, 2002.

Hall, Jacquelyn Dowd, James Leloudis, Robert Korstad, Mary Murphy, Lu Ann Jones, and Christopher B. Daly. *Like a Family: The Making of a Southern Cotton Mill World*. New York: Norton, 1987.

Hanchett, Thomas W. "Sorting Out the New South City: Charlotte and Its Neighborhoods." Ph.D. diss., University of North Carolina at Chapel Hill, 1993.

———. *Sorting Out the New South City: Race, Class, and Urban Development in Charlotte, 1875–1975*. Chapel Hill: University of North Carolina Press, 1998.

Handler, Richard, and Eric Gable. *The New History in an Old Museum*. Durham, N.C.: Duke University Press, 1997.

Harmon, Rick. *Crater Lake National Park: A History*. Corvallis: Oregon State University Press, 2000.

Harkins, Anthony. *Hillbilly: A Cultural History of an American Icon*. New York: Oxford University Press, 2004.

Harney, Will Wallace. "A Strange Land and Peculiar People." *Lippincott's Magazine* 12 (1873): 429–38.

Hauptman, Laurence M. "The American Indian Federation and the Indian New Deal: A Reinterpretation." *Pacific Historical Review* 52 (1983): 378–402.

Hays, Samuel P. *A History of Environmental Politics since 1945*. Pittsburgh: University of Pittsburgh Press, 2000.

Heaney, Thomas Michael. "The Call of the Open Road: Automobile Travel and Vacations in American Popular Culture, 1935–1960." Ph.D. diss., University of California at Irvine, 2000.

Heinemann, Ronald L. *Depression and New Deal in Virginia: The Enduring Dominion*. Charlottesville: University Press of Virginia, 1983.

———. *Harry Byrd of Virginia*. Charlottesville: University Press of Virginia, 1996.

Henderson, Mary F., ed. *The Social Register of North Carolina*. N.p., 1936.

Hensley, Bill F. "Blue Ridge Parkway: Why It Took 52 Years to Complete 'America's Most Scenic Drive.'" *North Carolina Magazine*. 2003. <http://www.nccbi.org/NCMagazine/2003/mag-10-03tht.htm>. 16 November 2003.

The Heritage of Ashe County North Carolina. Vol. 1. Winston-Salem, N.C.: Ashe County Heritage Book Committee, [1984].

Herndon, Booton. "The Pathfinder of the Moonshine Mountains." *Saturday Evening Post*, March 29, 1952, 30–31, 190–94.

Hill, Sarah Hitch. "Cherokee Patterns: Interweaving Women and Baskets in History." Ph.D. diss., Emory University, 1991.

———. *Weaving New Worlds: Southeastern Cherokee Women and Their Basketry*. Chapel Hill: University of North Carolina Press, 1997.

Hosmer, Charles B., Jr. *Preservation Comes of Age: From Williamsburg to the National Trust, 1926–1949*. Charlottesville: University Press of Virginia, 1981.

Howell, Benita J., ed. *Culture, Environment, and Conservation in the Appalachian South*. Urbana: University of Illinois Press, 2002.

———, ed. *Cultural Heritage Conservation in the American South*. Athens: University of Georgia Press, 1990.

Howett, Catherine. "Integrity as a Value in Cultural Landscape Preservation." In *Preserving Cultural Landscapes in America*, edited by Arnold R. Alanen and Robert Z. Melnick, 186–207. Baltimore: Johns Hopkins University Press, 2000.

Hubbard, Henry Vincent, and Theodora Kimball. *An Introduction to the Study of Landscape Design*. New York: Macmillan, 1927.

Hufford, Mary, ed. *Conserving Culture: A New Discourse on Heritage*. Urbana: University of Illinois Press, 1994.

Hundley, Norris, Jr. "Urban Imperialism: A Tale of Two Cities." In *The Great Thirst: Californians and Water, 1770s–1990s*. Berkeley: University of California Press, 1992.

Hunter, Elizabeth. "Up on Grandfather Mountain." *Blue Ridge Country*, January–February 1996, 40–44.

Hunter, Robert F. "Turnpike Construction in Antebellum Virginia." *Technology and Culture* 4, no. 2 (1963): 177–200.

———. "The Turnpike Movement in Virginia, 1816–1860." *Virginia Magazine of History and Biography* 69, no. 3 (1961): 278–89.

Ickes, Harold L. *Back to Work: The Story of the PWA*. New York: Macmillan, 1935.

———. *The Secret Diary of Harold L. Ickes*. 3 vols. New York: Simon and Schuster, 1954.

The Impact of Recreational Development in the North Carolina Mountains. Durham: North Carolina Public Interest Research Group, 1975.

Indigenous Peoples: A Global Quest for Justice. London: Zed, 1987.

Inscoe, John C. *Mountain Masters, Slavery, and the Sectional Crisis in Western North Carolina*. Knoxville: University of Tennessee Press, 1989.

Isakoff, Jack F. *The Public Works Administration*. Urbana: University of Illinois Press, 1938.

Jackson, John Brinckerhoff. *Discovering the Vernacular Landscape*. New Haven: Yale University Press, 1984.

Jakle, John A. "Landscapes Redesigned for the Automobile." In *The Making of the American Landscape*, edited by Michael P. Conzen, 293–210. Boston: Unwin Hyman, 1990.

———. *The Tourist: Travel in Twentieth-Century North America*. Lincoln: University of Nebraska Press, 1985.

Johnson, Rosemary, Karen Lee, Mel Lee, and Julie Savage. *The Johnson Farm "Back in 'At Day 'N Time": A Social and Historical Study of the Johnson Farm and Its Inhabitants, 1852–1941*. 6 vols. Asheville: Blue Ridge Parkway, 1975.

Jolley, Harley E. *The Blue Ridge Parkway*. Knoxville: University of Tennessee Press, 1969.

———. *Blue Ridge Parkway: The First 50 Years*. Boone, N.C.: Appalachian Consortium, 1985.

———. *Painting with a Comet's Tail: The Touch of the Landscape Architect on the Blue Ridge Parkway*. Boone, N.C.: Appalachian Consortium, 1987.

Jones, Louise Coffin. "In the Highlands of North Carolina." *Lippincott's Magazine* 32 (1883): 378–86.

Judd, Richard W., and Christopher S. Beach. *Natural States: The Environmental Imagination in Maine, Oregon, and the Nation*. Washington, D.C.: Resources for the Future, 2003.

Julin, Suzanne Barta. "Public Enterprise: Politics, Policy, and Tourism Development in the Black Hills through 1941." Ph.D. diss., Washington State University, 2001.

Kammen, Michael. *Mystic Chords of Memory: The Transformation of Tradition in American Culture*. New York: Vintage, 1993.

Kaye, Harvey J. "The Making of American Memory." *American Quarterly* 46, no. 2 (1994): 251–59.

Kelley, Lawrence C. *The Assault on Assimilation: John Collier and the Origins of Indian Policy Reform*. Albuquerque: University of New Mexico Press, 1983.

Kelsey, Harlan P. "Grandfather Mountain: Shall It Be Saved?" *Planning and Civic Comment*, April 1944, 3–5.

———. "Shall Grandfather Mountain Be Saved?" *National Parks Magazine*, April–June 1944, 1–3.

Kephart, Horace. *Our Southern Highlanders*. New York: Macmillan, 1921.

Ketterson, F. A., Jr. "Interpretation in the National Park System." *Cultural Resource Management* 13, no. 3 (1990). <http://crm.cr.nps.gov/archive/13-3/13-3-all.pdf>. 9 March 2003.

Kline, Benjamin. *First Along the River: A Brief History of the U.S. Environmental Movement.* 2nd ed. Lanham, Md.: Acada, 2000.

Koch, Frederick H., ed. *Carolina Folk Plays.* New York: Holt, 1922.

Langley, Joan, and Wright Langley. *Yesterday's Asheville.* Miami, Fla.: Seemann, 1975.

Lawson, Michael L. *Dammed Indians: The Pick-Sloan Plan and the Missouri River Sioux, 1944–1980.* Norman: University of Oklahoma Press, 1994.

Lefler, Hugh T. *History of North Carolina.* Vol. 4, *Family and Personal History.* New York: Lewis Historical, 1956.

Lefler, Hugh T., and Albert Ray Newsome. *North Carolina: The History of a Southern State.* Rev. ed. Chapel Hill: University of North Carolina Press, 1963.

Leon, Warren, and Margaret Piatt. "Living-History Museums." In *History Museums in the United States: A Critical Assessment,* edited by Warren Leon and Roy Rosensweig, 64–97. Urbana: University of Illinois Press, 1989.

Leopold, Aldo. "The River of the Mother of God." In *The River of the Mother of God and Other Essays,* edited by Susan Flader and J. Baird Callicott, 123–27. Madison: University of Wisconsin Press, 1991.

Leuchtenburg, William E. *The FDR Years: On Roosevelt and His Legacy.* New York: Columbia University Press, 1995.

———. *Franklin D. Roosevelt and the New Deal, 1932–1940.* New York: Harper and Row, 1963.

Lewis, Ronald L. *Transforming the Appalachian Countryside: Railroads, Deforestation, and Social Change in West Virginia, 1880–1920.* Chapel Hill: University of North Carolina Press, 1998.

Liles, Granville. "Grandfather and the Blue Ridge Parkway." *The State: Down Home in North Carolina* 55, no. 3 (1987): 18–20, 24.

Lingo, Karen, and Morris Glenn. "The Blue Ridge Parkway Winds through Ages." *Southern Living* 14, no. 5 (1979): 98–105.

Loewen, James W. *Lies across America: What Our Historic Sites Get Wrong.* New York: New Press, 1999.

London, H. M., ed. *North Carolina Manual, 1933.* Raleigh: North Carolina Historical Commission, Legislative Reference Library, 1933.

———, ed. *North Carolina Manual, 1935.* Raleigh: North Carolina Historical Commission, Legislative Reference Library, 1935.

Lord, William George. *Blue Ridge Parkway Guide.* Rev. ed. Birmingham, Ala.: Menasha Ridge, 1992.

Lowenthal, David. *The Past Is a Foreign Country.* Cambridge: Cambridge University Press, 1985.

———. "Pioneer Museums." In *History Museums in the United States: A Critical Assessment,* edited by Warren Leon and Roy Rosensweig, 115–27. Urbana: University of Illinois Press, 1989.

———. *Possessed by the Past: The Heritage Crusade and the Spoils of History.* New York: Free Press, 1996.

Lutts, Ralph H. "Like Manna from God: The American Chestnut Trade in Southwestern Virginia." *Environmental History* 9, no. 3 (July 2004). <http//www.historycooperative.org/journals/eh/9.3/lutts.html>. 1 January 2005.

MacCannell, Dean. "Staged Authenticity: Arrangements of Social Space in Tourist Settings." *American Journal of Sociology* 79 (November 1973): 589–603.

———. *The Tourist: A New Theory of the Leisure Class.* New York: Schocken, 1976.

MacDonald, Lois. "Mountaineers in Mill Villages." *Mountain Life and Work* 4 (1929): 3–7.

MacKaye, Benton. "Flankline vs. Skyline." *Appalachia* 20, no. 4 (July 1934): 104–8.

Mackintosh, Barry. *Interpretation in the National Park Service: A Historical Perspective.* Washington, D.C.: National Park Service, 1986. <http://www.cr.nps.gov/history/online_books/mackintosh2/index.htm>. 27 December 2004.

————. *The National Historic Preservation Act and the National Park Service: A History*. Washington, D.C.: History Division, National Park Service, 1986.

Martin, Ben Robert. "The Hetch Hetchy Controversy: The Value of Nature in a Technological Society." Ph.D. diss., Brandeis University, 1982.

Martin, Christopher Brenden. "Selling the Southern Highlands: Tourism and Community Development in the Mountain South." Ph.D. diss., University of Tennessee at Knoxville, 1997.

Mason, Kathy Sue. "Before the Park Service: Standards and Management in the United States National Parks, 1872–1916." Ph.D. diss., Miami University, 1999.

Mason, Robert J. *Contested Lands: Conflict and Compromise in New Jersey's Pine Barrens*. Philadelphia: Temple University Press, 1992.

Massengill, Stephen E. *Western North Carolina: A Visual Journey through Stereo Views and Photographs*. Charleston, S.C.: Arcadia, 1999.

Mathews, Rich. *The Era of the Grand Hotels and Boarding Houses*. Asheville: Preservation Society of Asheville and Buncombe County, 2005. <http://www.psabc.org/Resource-800/edochotels.pdf>. 26 September 2005.

Matzko, John. *Reconstructing Fort Union*. Lincoln: University of Nebraska Press, 2001.

McClelland, Linda Flint. *Building the National Parks: Historic Landscape Design and Construction*. Baltimore: Johns Hopkins University Press, 1998.

————. *Presenting Nature: The Historic Landscape Design of the National Park Service, 1916 to 1942*. Washington, D.C.: Government Printing Office, 1993.

McDonald, Michael J., and John Muldowny. *TVA and the Dispossessed: The Resettlement of Population in the Norris Dam Area*. Knoxville: University of Tennessee Press, 1982.

McDonald, Michael J., and William Bruce Wheeler. *Knoxville: Continuity and Change in an Appalachian City*. Knoxville: University of Tennessee Press, 1983.

McKown, Harry Wilson, Jr. "Roads and Reform: The Good Roads Movement in North Carolina, 1885–1921." Master's thesis, University of North Carolina, 1972.

McMenamin, Brigid. "Golden Arch." *Forbes*, 16 November 1998, 131.

McNeil, W. K., ed. *Appalachian Images in Folk and Popular Culture*. Knoxville: University of Tennessee Press, 1995.

Mead, Martha Norburn. *Asheville . . . In Land of the Sky*. Richmond, Va.: Dietz, 1942.

Middleton, Harry. "The Good Road of the Blue Ridge." *Southern Living*, September 1985, 72–79.

Miles, Emma Bell. *The Spirit of the Mountains*. 1905. Facsimile ed., with a foreword by Roger D. Abrahams and introduction by David E. Whisnant. Knoxville: University of Tennessee Press, 1975.

Mitchell, Anne V. "Culture, History, and Development on the Qualla Boundary: The Eastern Cherokees and the Blue Ridge Parkway, 1935–40." *Appalachian Journal* 24 (Winter 1997): 144–91.

————. "Parkway Politics: Class, Culture, and Tourism in the Blue Ridge" Ph.D. diss., University of North Carolina at Chapel Hill, 1997.

Morton, Hugh. "Blue Ridge Parkway: 52 Years Later: Truth about 'Missing Link.'" In *Making a Difference in North Carolina*, by Hugh Morton and Edward L. Rankin Jr., 134–43. Raleigh, N.C.: Lightworks, 1988.

————. *Report to the Governor: Mountain Legacies: Actions and Recommendations for the Future*. [Raleigh?]: Year of the Mountains Commission, 1996.

Morton, Jack. "My Grandfather and His Camera." *Metro Magazine* 4, no. 11 (December 2003). <www.metronc.com/issues/issue12_03/Morton/morton.html>. 12 January 2004.

Muller, Jean M., and James M. Barker. "Design and Construction of Linn Cove Viaduct." *PCI Journal* 30, no. 5 (1985): 2–17.

Murfree, Mary Noailles [Charles Egbert Craddock, pseud.]. *The Prophet of the Great Smoky Mountains.* Boston: Houghton, Mifflin, 1885.

———. "The Romance of Sunrise Rock." *Atlantic Monthly* 46 (December 1880): 775–86.

Myers, Mary E. "The Line of Grace: Principles of Road Aesthetics in the Design of the Blue Ridge Parkway." *Landscape Journal* 23 (February 2004): 121–40

———. "Variety and Interest: What Makes the Blue Ridge Parkway Beautiful?" *Landscape Architecture* 92, no. 3 (2002): 71–73, 93–95.

Nash, Gary B., Allen F. Davis, Allan M. Winkler, Peter J. Frederick, John R. Howe, and Julie Roy Jeffrey. *The American People: Creating a Nation and a Society.* 4th ed., New York: Longman, 1998.

National Parks and Conservation Association. "Paved Crossings May Fragment Scenic Parkway." *National Parks* 72, no. 6 (November–December 1998): 19.

"No Green Mountain Hot-Dogs: Vermonters, through Town Meetings, Make Sure Barkers Will Not Cry in Their Unspoiled Wilderness by Vetoing Federal Parkway." *Literary Digest,* 14 March 1936, 9.

Noblitt, Phil. "The Blue Ridge Parkway and the Myths of the Pioneer." *Appalachian Journal* 21 (1994): 394–409.

———. *A Mansion in the Mountains: The Story of Moses and Bertha Cone and Their Blowing Rock Manor.* Boone, N.C.: Parkway, 1996.

Nolen, John, and Henry V. Hubbard. *Parkways and Land Values.* Cambridge: Harvard University Press, 1937.

North Carolina Atlas and Gazetteer. Freeport, Me.: DeLorme Mapping, 1993.

North Carolina Biography. Vol. 6 of *History of North Carolina.* Chicago: Lewis, 1919.

North Carolina Roadways: A Magazine for Employees of the State Highway Commission 5, no. 9 (1956): 11.

Oakley, Christopher Arris. "Indian Gaming and the Eastern Band of Cherokee Indians." *North Carolina Historical Review* 78, no. 2 (April 2001): 133–55.

O'Connell, Kim A., and Mary Myers. "Grandfather Mountain and Beyond." *Landscape Architecture* 92, no. 3 (2002): 74–75.

———. "A Road to Match the Mountains." *Landscape Architecture* 92, no. 3 (2002): 68–70.

Olson, Ted. "In the Public Interest? The Social and Cultural Impact of the Blue Ridge Parkway, a Depression-Era Appalachian 'Public Works' Project." In *The New Deal and Beyond: Social Welfare in the South since 1930,* edited by Elna C. Green, 100–115. Athens: University of Georgia Press, 2003.

Patton, James W., ed. *Messages, Addresses, and Public Papers of Luther Hartwell Hodges, Governor of North Carolina, 1954–61.* Raleigh: Council of State, State of North Carolina, 1962.

Patton, Phil. *Open Road: A Celebration of the American Highway.* New York: Simon and Schuster, 1986.

"The Peaks of Otter: Grandstand of the Blue Ridge." *Virginia Cavalcade,* Autumn 1951, 23–28.

Perdue, Charles L., Jr., and Nancy J. Martin-Perdue. "Appalachian Fables and Facts: A Case Study of the Shenandoah National Park Removals." *Appalachian Journal* 7 (1979–80): 84–104.

———. "'To Build a Wall around These Mountains': The Displaced People of Shenandoah." *Magazine of Albemarle County History* 49 (1991): 49–71.

Perdue, Theda. *The Cherokee.* New York: Chelsea House, 1989.

———. *Native Carolinians: The Indians of North Carolina.* Raleigh: Division of Archives and History, North Carolina Department of Cultural Resources, 1985.

Philippon, Daniel J. "The Bridge of Words: Encounters with Virginia's Natural Bridge." *Southern Cultures* 6, no. 3 (2000): 36–46.

Philp, Kenneth R. *John Collier's Crusade for Indian Reform, 1920–1954.* Tucson: University of Arizona Press, 1977.

A Pictorial History of Haywood County. Asheville, N.C.: Asheville Citizen-Times, 1994.

Pierce, Daniel Smith. "Boosters, Bureaucrats, Politicians, and Philanthropists: Coalition Building in the Establishment of the Great Smoky Mountains National Park." Ph.D. diss., University of Tennessee, 1995.

———. *The Great Smokies: From Natural Habitat to National Park.* Knoxville: University of Tennessee Press, 2000.

Pleasants, Julian M. *Buncombe Bob: The Life and Times of Robert Rice Reynolds.* Chapel Hill: University of North Carolina Press, 2000.

Powell, William S., ed. *Dictionary of North Carolina Biography.* 6 vols. Chapel Hill: University of North Carolina Press, 1979–96.

Powers, Elizabeth, with Mark Hannah. *Cataloochee: Lost Settlement of the Smokies.* Charleston, S.C.: Powers-Hannah, 1982.

Preston, Howard Lawrence. *Dirt Roads to Dixie: Accessibility and Modernization in the South, 1885–1935.* Knoxville: University of Tennessee Press, 1991.

Prichard, James A. *Preserving Yellowstone's Natural Conditions: Science and the Perception of Nature.* Lincoln: University of Nebraska Press, 1999.

Prioli, Andrew Carmine. "The Indian 'Princess' and the Architect: Origin of a North Carolina Legend." *North Carolina Historical Review* 60 (1983): 283–303.

Prucha, Francis Paul. *The Great Father: The United States Government and the American Indians.* Lincoln: University of Nebraska Press, 1986.

Pudup, Mary Beth, Dwight B. Billings, and Altina L. Waller, eds. *Appalachia in the Making: The Mountain South in the Nineteenth Century.* Chapel Hill: University of North Carolina Press, 1995.

Radde, Bruce. *The Merritt Parkway.* New Haven: Yale University Press, 1993.

Raitz, Karl B., and Richard Ulack. *Appalachia: A Regional Geography.* Boulder, Colo.: Westview, 1984.

Rand McNally Road Atlas of the U.S., Canada, and Mexico. Chicago: Rand McNally, 1936.

Rand McNally Road Atlas of the U.S., Canada, and Mexico. Chicago: Rand McNally, 1944.

Ready, Milton. *Asheville: Land of the Sky.* Northridge, Calif.: Windsor, 1986.

———. "Enduring Vision: Early Planners Helped Make Asheville Great." *Mountain Express,* November 2000. <http://www.mountainx.com/opinion/2000/1115ready.php>. 4 August 2005.

Reak, Jack. *Kanuga: Story of a Gathering Place.* Hendersonville, N.C.: Kanuga Conferences, 1993.

Ritchie, Jean. *Jean Ritchie's Dulcimer People.* New York: Oak, 1975.

Robinson, Blackwell P., ed. *The North Carolina Guide.* Chapel Hill: University of North Carolina Press, 1955.

Robinson, James A. "Artistic Weaving in the Mountains of North Carolina." *Art World* 2 (1917): 484–85.

Robinson, Nancy, and Ian Firth. "Abbott, Stanley William." In *Pioneers of American Landscape Design,* edited by Charles A. Birnbaum and Robin Karson, 1–3. New York: McGraw-Hill, 2000.

Rose, Mark H. *Interstate: Express Highway Politics, 1939–1989.* Knoxville: University of Tennessee Press, 1990.

Rosenzweig, Roy, and David Thelen. *The Presence of the Past: Popular Uses of History in American Life.* New York: Columbia University Press, 1998.

Ross, Malcolm. *Machine Age in the Hills.* New York: Macmillan, 1933.

Rothman, Hal K. *Devil's Bargains: Tourism in the Twentieth-Century American West.* Lawrence: University Press of Kansas, 1998.

———. *The Greening of a Nation?: Environmentalism in the United States since 1945.* Fort Worth, Tex.: Harcourt Brace College, 1998.

Roy, Leonard C. "Rambling around the Roof of Eastern America." *National Geographic* 70, no. 2 (1936): 242–66.

Russell, Mattie U. "Devil in the Smokies: The White Man's Nature and the Indian's Fate." *South Atlantic Quarterly* 73 (Winter 1974): 53–69.

Sanford, Terry. "New Era Ahead for Your State." *Nation's Business*, July 1965, 57–64.

Sarvis, Will. "A Difficult Legacy: Creation of the Ozark National Scenic Riverways." *Public Historian* 24, no. 1 (2002): 31–52.

———. "Turnpike Tourism in Western Virginia, 1830–1860." *Virginia Cavalcade* 48, no. 1 (1999): 15–23.

Sass, Herbert Ravenel. "Land of the Cherokee." *Collier's*, 29 February 1937.

Schreffler, Robert E. "Bridge Closes Blue Ridge Gap." *Courier: The National Park Service Newsletter* 2, no. 1 (1978): 1.

Schwarzkopf, S. Kent. *A History of Mt. Mitchell and the Black Mountains: Exploration, Development, and Preservation*. Raleigh: Division of Archives and History, North Carolina Department of Cultural Resources, 1985.

Scott, James C. *Weapons of the Weak: Everyday Forms of Peasant Resistance*. New Haven: Yale University Press, 1985.

Sears, John F. *Sacred Places: American Tourist Attractions in the Nineteenth Century*. New York: Oxford University Press, 1989.

Seely, Bruce E. *Building the American Highway System: Engineers as Policy Makers*. Philadelphia: Temple University Press, 1987.

Sellars, Richard West. *Preserving Nature in the National Parks: A History*. New Haven: Yale University Press, 1997.

Selznick, Philip. *TVA and the Grass Roots: A Study in the Sociology of Formal Organization*. Berkeley: University of California Press, 1949.

Semple, Ellen Churchill. "The Anglo-Saxons of the Kentucky Mountains: A Study in Anthropogeography." *Geographical Journal* 17 (1901): 588–623.

Shackel, Paul A. *Myth, Memory, and the Making of the American Landscape*. Gainesville: University Press of Florida, 2001.

Shaffer, Marguerite S. *See America First: Tourism and National Identity, 1880–1940*. Washington, D.C.: Smithsonian Institution Press, 2001.

Shankland, Robert. *Steve Mather of the National Parks*. New York: Knopf, 1951.

Shapiro, Henry D. *Appalachia on Our Mind: The Southern Mountains and Mountaineers in the American Consciousness, 1870–1920*. Chapel Hill: University of North Carolina Press, 1978.

Sharpe, Bill. *A New Geography of North Carolina*. Raleigh, N.C.: Sharpe, 1954.

———. "'Photo by Morton.'" *The State* 18 (2 December 1950): 4–5.

Silver, Timothy. *Mount Mitchell and the Black Mountains: An Environmental History of the Highest Peaks in Eastern America*. Chapel Hill: University of North Carolina Press, 2003.

Simmons, Dennis Elwood. "The Creation of Shenandoah National Park and the Skyline Drive, 1924–1936." Ph.D. diss., University of Virginia, 1978.

Skinner, Elizabeth. *Bicycling the Blue Ridge: A Guide to the Skyline Drive and the Blue Ridge Parkway*. Birmingham, Ala.: Menasha Ridge, 1990.

Smith, Charles Dennis. "The Appalachian National Park Movement, 1885–1901." *North Carolina Historical Review* 37, no. 1 (1960): 38–65.

Snow, W. Brewster, ed. *The Highway and the Landscape*. New Brunswick, N.J.: Rutgers University Press, 1959.

Speer, Jean Haskell. "The Hegemony of Landscape in Appalachian Culture." *Journal of the Appalachian Studies Association* 4 (1992): 24–33.

———. "'Hillbilly Sold Here': Appalachian Folk Culture and Parkway Tourism." *Parkways Conference Proceedings*. n.d.: 212–20.

Starnes, Richard D., "Creating the Land of the Sky: Tourism and Society in Western North Carolina." Ph.D. diss., Auburn University, 1999.

———. *Creating the Land of the Sky: Tourism and Society in Western North Carolina.* Tuscaloosa: University of Alabama Press, 2005.

———, ed. *Southern Journeys: Tourism, History, and Culture in the Modern South.* Tuscaloosa: University of Alabama Press, 2003.

Stine, Jeffrey K. *Mixing the Waters: Environment, Politics, and the Building of the Tennessee-Tombigbee Waterway.* Akron, Ohio: University of Akron Press, 1993.

Sutter, Paul. *Driven Wild: How the Fight against Automobiles Launched the Modern Wilderness Movement.* Seattle: University of Washington Press, 2002.

———. "Reflections: What Can U.S. Environmental Historians Learn from Non-U.S. Environmental Historiography?" *Environmental History* 8, no. 1 (January 2003). <http://www.historycooperative.org/journals/eh/8.1/sutter.html>. 2 January 2005.

———. Review of *Yellowstone: The Creation and Selling of an American Landscape, 1870–1903*, by Chris J. Magoc. *Journal of American History* 88, no. 2 (2001): 677–78.

Tager, Miles. *Grandfather Mountain: A Profile.* Boone, N.C.: Parkway, 1999.

Taylor, Alva. "Sub-Marginal Standards of Living in the Southern Mountains." *Mountain Life and Work* 14 (1938): 12–14.

Taylor, Graham D. *The New Deal and American Indian Tribalism: The Administration of the Indian Reorganization Act, 1934–45.* Lincoln: University of Nebraska Press, 1980.

Taylor, Stephen Wallace. *The New South's New Frontier: A Social History of Economic Development in Southwestern North Carolina.* Gainesville: University Press of Florida, 2001.

Teer, Nello, Robert D. Teer, Robert D. Teer Jr., and Anna Daugird. *Courage Ever: An American Success Story — Nello L. Teer Sr. and His Company.* Durham, N.C.: Teer Associates, 2001.

Thomas, Jerry Bruce. *An Appalachian New Deal: West Virginia in the Great Depression.* Lexington: University Press of Kentucky, 1998.

Tindall, George B. "Business Progressivism: Southern Politics in the Twenties." *South Atlantic Quarterly* 62 (1963): 92–106.

Tooman, L. Alex. "The Evolving Economic Impact of Tourism on the Greater Smoky Mountain Region of East Tennessee and Western North Carolina." Ph.D. diss., University of Tennessee at Knoxville, 1995.

Topping, John D. "Millions to Be Reaped from Tourist Travel When New Parkway Is Completed." *Eastern National Park-to-Park Highway Magazine*, 1935, 69.

Turner, Walter R. *Paving Tobacco Road: A Century of Progress by the North Carolina Department of Transportation.* Raleigh: Office of Archives and History, North Carolina Department of Cultural Resources, 2003.

Tyler, Norman. *Historic Preservation: An Introduction to Its History, Principles, and Practice.* New York: Norton, 2000.

Tyson, Timothy B. *Blood Done Sign My Name: A True Story.* New York: Crown, 2004.

Unrau, Harlan D., and G. Frank Williss. *Administrative History: Expansion of the National Park Service.* Denver, Colo.: National Park Service, 1983. <http://www.cr.nps.gov/history/online_books/unrau-williss/adhi.htm>. 13 August 2005.

Van Noppen, Ina W., and John J. Van Noppen. *Western North Carolina since the Civil War.* Boone, N.C.: Appalachian Consortium, 1973.

Viemeister, Peter. *The Peaks of Otter: Life and Times.* Bedford, Va.: Hamilton's, 1992.

Vining, James P. *Eseeola Inn and Annex.* Linville, N.C.: n.p., n.d.

Virginia Department of Highways. *1942 Supplement to Laws of Virginia Relating to the State Highway Commission.* Richmond, Va.: Division of Purchase and Printing, 1942.

Walbert, David. *Garden Spot: Lancaster County, the Old Order Amish, and the Selling of Rural America*. New York: Oxford University Press, 2002.

Waller, Altina L. *Feud: Hatfields, McCoys, and Social Change in Appalachia, 1860–1900*. Chapel Hill: University of North Carolina Press, 1988.

Warner, Charles Dudley. *On Horseback: A Tour through Virginia, North Carolina, and Tennessee*. Boston: Houghton, Mifflin, 1888.

Watkins, Charles Alan. "Merchandising the Mountaineer: Photography, the Great Depression, and Cabins in the Laurel." *Appalachian Journal* 12, no. 3 (1985): 215–38.

Watkins, T. H. *Righteous Pilgrim: The Life and Times of Harold L. Ickes, 1874–1952*. New York: Holt, 1990.

Waynick, Capus. *North Carolina Roads and Their Builders*. Raleigh, N.C.: Superior Stone, 1952.

Weals, Vic. *Last Train to Elkmont: A Look Back at Life on the Little River in the Great Smoky Mountains*. Knoxville, Tenn.: Olden, 1993.

Webb, Charles A. *Fifty-eight Years in Asheville*. Asheville, N.C.: Asheville Citizen-Times, 1948.

Webb, Melody. "Cultural Landscapes in the National Park Service." *Public Historian* 9, no. 2 (1987): 77–90.

Weeks, Charles J. "The Eastern Cherokee and the New Deal." *North Carolina Historical Review* 53 (1976): 311–19.

Weeks, Jim. *Gettysburg: Memory, Market, and an American Shrine*. Princeton: Princeton University Press, 2003.

Whisnant, David E. *All That Is Native and Fine: The Politics of Culture in an American Region*. Chapel Hill: University of North Carolina Press, 1983.

———. "Finding the Way between the Old and the New: The Mountain Dance and Folk Festival and Bascom Lamar Lunsford's Work as a Citizen." *Appalachian Journal* 7, no. 1–2 (1979): 135–54.

———. *Modernizing the Mountaineer: People, Power, and Planning in Appalachia*. 1980; rev. ed., Knoxville: University of Tennessee Press, 1994.

Whitaker, Stephen Paul. "A New Wave of Colonization: The Economics of the Tourism and Travel Industry in Appalachian Kentucky." *Journal of Appalachian Studies* 6 (Spring–Fall 2000): 35–48.

White, Graham, and John Maze. *Harold Ickes of the New Deal: His Private Life and Public Career*. Cambridge: Harvard University Press, 1985.

Wigginton, Eliot. *Sometimes a Shining Moment: The Foxfire Experience*. Garden City, N.Y.: Anchor Press/Doubleday, 1985.

Williams, Michael Ann. *Great Smoky Mountains Folklife*. Jackson: University Press of Mississippi, 1995.

Williamson, J. W. *Hillbillyland: What the Movies Did to the Mountains and What the Mountains Did to the Movies*. Chapel Hill: University of North Carolina Press, 1995.

———. *Southern Mountaineers in Silent Films: Plot Synopses of Movies about Moonshining, Feuding, and Other Mountain Topics, 1904–1929*. Jefferson, N.C.: McFarland, 1994.

Wilson, Samuel Tyndale. *The Southern Mountaineers*. New York: Literature Department, Presbyterian Home Missions, 1906.

Winokur, Lou. *Joy in the Mountains*. Boca Raton, Fla.: Winokur, 1977.

Wirth, Conrad L. *Parks, Politics, and the People*. Norman: University of Oklahoma Press, 1980.

Woody, Robert H. "Cataloochee Homecoming." *South Atlantic Quarterly* 49 (January 1950): 8–17.

Woolson, Constance Fenimore. "Up in the Blue Ridge." *Appleton's Journal* 5 (1878): 104–25.

Wright, Frances M. "In the Highlands of North Carolina." *Southern Workman* 31 (1902): 206–10.

Wrobel, David M., and Patrick T. Long, eds. *Seeing and Being Seen: Tourism in the American West*. Lawrence: University Press of Kansas, 2001.

UNPUBLISHED MATERIALS

Blethen, H. Tyler. "Antebellum Visitors to Appalachian North Carolina." Paper presented at the
 Appalachian Studies Association meeting, 1996.
Carr, Ethan. "Modernism in the Wilderness: National Parks, MISSION 66, and the Post-War
 American Landscape" [draft proposal]. 27 October 2004.
Ledford, Katherine. "Two Views from Grassy Mountain: Founding and Development of Little
 Switzerland, North Carolina." [1994?].
Westmacott, Richard. "Historic Agriculture of the Blue Ridge: Real and Idealized Landscapes."
 1994.

NEWSPAPERS

Alleghany (N.C.) Times
Asheville (N.C.) Citizen
Asheville (N.C.) Citizen-Times
Asheville (N.C.) Times
Baltimore Sun
Bedford (Va.) Bulletin
Blue Ridge Parkway News
Carolina Motor News
Charlotte (N.C.) News
Charlotte (N.C.) Observer
Cherokee One Feather
Concord (N.C.) Tribune
Durham (N.C.) Sun
Elkin (N.C.) Tribune
Forest City (N.C.) Courier
Franklin (N.C.) Press
Galax (Va.) Gazette
Greensboro (N.C.) Daily News
Greensboro (N.C.) Record
Henderson (N.C.) Daily Dispatch
Hickory (N.C.) Daily Record
Johnson City (Tenn.) Staff-News
Knoxville (Tenn.) Journal
Knoxville (Tenn.) News-Sentinel
Lenoir (N.C.) News-Topic
Lexington (N.C.) Dispatch
Mt. Airy (N.C.) News
New York Times
Raleigh (N.C.) News and Observer
Raleigh (N.C.) Times
Reidsville (N.C.) Review
Richmond (Va.) News-Leader
Richmond (Va.) Times-Dispatch
Roanoke (Va.) Times
Roanoke (Va.) World-News
Salisbury (N.C.) Evening Post
Spruce Pine (N.C.) Tri-County News

Washington Post
Watauga (N.C.) Democrat
West Jefferson (N.C.) Skyland Post
Wilmington (N.C.) Morning Star
Wilmington (N.C.) News
Winston-Salem (N.C.) Journal
Winston-Salem (N.C.) Journal and Sentinel

OTHER MATERIALS

Advertisement for Asheville, N.C. *Eastern National Park-to-Park Highway Magazine*, 1935, 6–7.

Barret, Elizabeth. *Stranger with a Camera* [video]. Whitesburg, Ky.: Appalachian Film Workshop, 2000.

Committee of Mass Meeting of Little Switzerland Community. *What Citizens Think about Attorney Chas. Ross' Attack on the Switzerland Co. and Its Stockholders* [pamphlet]. 1938.

Grandfather Mountain [brochure]. Linville, N.C.: Grandfather Mountain, 194?.

Northbound Visitor's Guide to the Blue Ridge Parkway: An Interpretive Guide from Cherokee to Blowing Rock [audiocassette]. Woodruff, S.C.: Rogers Associates, 1987.

Southbound Visitor's Guide to the Blue Ridge Parkway: An Interpretive Guide from Blowing Rock to Cherokee [audiocassette]. Woodruff, S.C.: Rogers Associates, 1988.

U.S. Department of the Interior, National Park Service. *The Natchez Trace Parkway, 1996* [brochure]. Denver, Colo.: National Park Service Public Use Statistics Office, 1999.

We Are Not Going to Sit Still while the Tourist Business Is Sold down the River! [flyer]. Boone and Blowing Rock, N.C.: Blowing Rock and Boone Chambers of Commerce, 1958.

WEB PAGES

Alabama Business Hall of Fame. "William McWane, Inducted 1989." <http://www.cba.ua.edu/alumni/halloffame/89WM.html>. 3 January 2004.

Bennett, Michael G. "The Colonial Parkway (National Park Service)." <http://www.nps.gov/colo/Colonial_Parkway/ColPkway.htm>. 21 August 2005.

Blue Ridge Parkway Foundation. "Family Visitor Collection." <http://www.brpfoundation.org/archives/exhibit1/vexmain1.htm>. 3 March 2005.

———. "Family Visitor Collection." <http://www.brpfoundation.org/archives/exhibit1/e10112a.htm>. 3 March 2005.

"Conservation Trust for North Carolina." <http://www.ctnc.org/main.asp?template=about_ctnc&level1=blue_ridge_parkway>. 23 June 2004.

"The Eseeola Lodge at Linville Golf Club." <http://www.eseeola.com/lodge-history.asp>. 4 June 2005.

Gibson, Campbell, and Kay Jung. "Historical Census Statistics on Population Totals by Race, 1790 to 1990, and by Hispanic Origin, 1970 to 1990, for the United States, Regions, Divisions, and States. Working Paper Series 56, Division, U.S. Census Bureau." September 2002. <http://www.census.gov/population/www/documentation/twps0056.html>. 15 December 2004.

"Giga Quotes." <http://www.giga-usa.com/gigaweb1/quotes2/qutopdoubtx001.htm>. 10 December 2004.

Grandfather Mountain, Inc. "The Blue Ridge Parkway." <http://www.grandfather.com/conservation/parkway.htm>. 23 June 2004.

———. "Fast Facts." <http://www.grandfather.com/media/facts.htm#conservancy>. 10 July 2005.

———. "Grandfather Mountain." <http://www.grandfather.com/index.htm>. 4 January 2004.

———. "Grandfather Mountain: A Biosphere Reserve." <http://grandfather.com/conservation/biosphere.htm>. 10 July 2005.

———. Wildlife Habitats. <http://grandfather.com/habitats/habitats.htm>. 10 July 2005.

Gross, Andrea. "Hugh Morton's Mountain." <http://www.americanprofile.com/issues/20000910/20000910se_307.asp>. 16 October 2003.

"In Memoriam: C. Hartley Grattan." <http://www.utexas.edu/faculty/council/2000-2001/memorials/AMR/Grattan/grattan.html>. 25 May 2005.

Long, W. Ray. "Historical Sketch of Eseeola Lodge and the Linville Community." <http://www.eseeola.com/history.html>. 22 December 2003.

Middleton Family. "Photograph of Middleton Family at Peaks of Otter Lodge Parking Lot, 1976." <http://www.brpfoundation.org/archives/exhibit1/e101112a.htm>. 3 March 2005.

"Mountain Ridge Protection Act of 1983 (Ridge Law)." <http://www.cals.ncsu.edu/wq/LandPreservationNotebook/statutes/nc/mountainridgeprotection.htm>. 23 June 2004.

"National Eminent Domain Power." <http://caselaw.lp.findlaw.com/data/constitution/amendment05/14.html>. 15 March 2005.

National Park Service. "Lying Lightly on the Land: Building America's National Park Roads and Parkways." <http://www.cr.nps.gov/habshaer/lll>. 9 December 2004.

———. "Great Smoky Mountains National Park Facts." <http://www.nps.gov/grsm/pphtml/facts.html>. 25 May 2005.

National Park Service, Denver Service Center. "Other Laws Affecting the National Park Service: Cultural Resources." http://workflow.den.nps.gov/staging/11_Laws/laws_cultural.htm>. 27 December 2004.

National Park Service, Public Use Statistics Office. "Visitation Statistics." <http://www2.nature.nps.gov/stats/visitbody.htm>. 23 May 2005.

Nature Conservancy. "Grandfather Mountain." <http://nature.org/wherewework/northamerica/states/northcarolina/preserves/art5604.html>. 24 June 2004.

"North Carolina General Statutes, Chapter 136." <http://www.ncleg.net/statutes/generalstatutes/html/bychapter/chapter_136.html>. 1 August 2004.

"Our Thanksgiving Place: The Peaks of Otter." <http://www.brpfoundation.org/MiddletonStory.php>. 3 March 2005.

"Ridgecrest—History." <http://www.lifeway.com/reservations/history.htm>. 13 August 2005.

School of Journalism and Mass Communication, University of North Carolina at Chapel Hill. "North Carolina Public Relations Hall of Fame." <http://www.jomc.unc.edu/specialprograms/famepublicrelations.html#Morton>. 23 June 2004.

Smith-McDowell House Museum. "George Willis Pack and the Development of Pack Square." <http://www.wnchistory.org/museum/pack.htm>. 4 August 2005.

State Library of North Carolina. "Alex Manly—Wilmington Race Riots." <http://statelibrary.dcr.state.nc.us/nc/bio/afro/riot.htm>. 5 September 2005.

Tennessee State Parks. "Roan Mountain State Park." <http://www.state.tn.us/environment/parks/parks/RoanMtn/>. 17 December 2004.

"Town of Montreat, N.C.—A Brief History." <http://www.townofmontreat.org/history.htm>. 13 August 2005.

U.S. Census Bureau. "DP-3, Profile of Selected Economic Characteristics: 2000." <http://factfinder.census/gov>. 23 November 2002.

U.S. Man and the Biosphere Program. "U.S. List of Biosphere Reserves." <http://www.mabnet.org/brprogram/usbrl.html>. 23 June 2004.

University of Idaho Manuscripts Collection. "A Brief Biography of Michael Frome." <http://www.lib.uidaho.edu/special-collections/Manuscripts/mg174.htm>. 18 April 2004.

University of North Carolina at Asheville. "Biltmore Industries Archive." <http://toto.lib.unca.edu/findingaids/mss/biltmore_industries/Default.htm>. 13 August 2005.

University of North Carolina at Asheville Library. "Asheville and the Coxe Family." <http://toto.lib.unca.edu/findingaids/mss/speculation_lands/biographies/coxe_family.htm>. 4 August 2005.

UNC-TV. "Biographical Conversations with Hugh Morton." <http://www.unctv.org/biocon/hmorton/index.html> and <http://www.unctv.org/biocon/hmorton/timeline00.html>. 22 October 2003.

YMCA Blue Ridge Assembly. <http://www.blueridgeassembly.org/centennial.html>. 13 August 2005.

INDEX

Abbott, Stanley W., 218; Appalachian stereotypes and, 243, 244–45, 256, 257–58; *Blue
Ridge Parkway News* and, 151–52, 327; commercial traffic on Parkway and, 136–37;
Grandfather Mountain land acquisition
and, 277–78, 280–81, 283–84, 303; land
acquisition for Parkway and, 127, 132; landowner access to Parkway and, 357 (n. 75);
landscape architecture, Parkway and, 60,
66–67, 94, 96, 116, 132, 278, 326, 341
(n. 26); Little Switzerland and, 169; NPS
interpretive program and, 240, 243, 244,
266–67, 377 (n. 70); Peaks of Otter and,
232–33, 238, 240, 377 (n. 70); recreation
areas for Parkway and, 125–26, 354 (n. 41);
right-of-way for Parkway in Virginia and,
121, 123; Tennessee vs. North Carolina
route and, 65–66, 94–95, 96, 343 (n. 43);
timber cutting on Parkway land and, 124,
149; tourist concessions on Parkway and,
116, 139, 140–41, 142, 354 (n. 41), 358
(nn. 87, 88)
Abbott Lake (Va.), 218, 236
Abbuehl, E. B., 96
Acadia National Park (Maine), 26
Access to Parkway. *See* Landowner access to
Parkway
Adams, Junius G., 87
African Americans: disfranchisement of, late
nineteenth century, 159–60, 270; Fusion
government, late nineteenth century and,
158–59; in Linville, early twentieth century
and, 275; Little Switzerland and, 164, 166
Agricultural Adjustment Administration, 82
Agriculture, 82, 114–15; Cherokees and, 185,
189, 190–91, 205; Peaks of Otter and, 219,
221, 225–26
Albright, Horace M., 241, 281, 282, 283, 284,
292
Alleghany County, N.C., 110, 115, 118, 145, 148
Alligator Back (N.C.), xix

American Automobile Association, 49, 69
American Enka Corporation, 56, 101
American Forestry Association, 48
American Forests, 316
American Indian Defense Association, 186
American Indian Federation (AIF), 188, 207,
209, 370 (nn. 70, 79)
American Indian Movement (AIM), 213
American parkway movement. *See* Parkway
movement
Anderson, Stella, 316, 317, 318
Appalachian Mountain Club, 281
Appalachian people: cultural and historical
understanding of, 252–55, 378 (nn. 93,
95); music of, 250, 252, 378 (n. 87); NPS
interpretive program and, 250–54; opposi-
tion to Parkway and, 152, 153–55; Parkway,
and possibility of relief work, 103–4;
removal from Great Smoky Mountains
National Park, 132, 199; routing of Parkway
and, 112–16; stereotyping and, 83–84, 86,
152–53, 200–201, 212, 218, 240, 241–45,
249, 251–58, 261, 292, 345 (n. 84); tourism,
Parkway and, 82–86, 104–5, 143–50, 291
Appalachian National Forest Reserve Association, 27
Appalachian National Park Association
(ANPA), 26–27, 335 (n. 39)
Appalachian Realty Company, 58
Appalachian Trail, 48
Apple Orchard Mountain (Va.), 113
Ashe County, N.C.: environmental protection
in, after Parkway, 371 (n. 87); land acquisition for Parkway and, 108–12, 118; land
acquisition payment and, 130, 145, 149;
landowner access to Parkway and, 133;
opposition to Parkway and, 145–46, 149–
50, 154, 327; tourism in, lack of, 110
Asheville, N.C.: Battery Park Hotel and, 73,
74; Cherokee opposition to Parkway route
and, 198; completion of Parkway and, 113,

Champion Paper and Fibre Company, 27, 81, 102; Grandfather Mountain, lumber industry and, 276–77, 382 (n. 39); landowner access to Parkway and, 135

Chapman, David C., 28, 91

Charlotte, N.C., urban development in, 57–58

Charlotte Observer, 57, 166, 178, 201, 207, 296–97, 307

Charlottesville, Va., 238

Chase, Richard, 252

Cherokee, N.C., 1, 194, 210, 213; routing of Parkway and, 63, 65, 113, 190, 202

Cherokee Elementary School, 194

Cherokee Fair, 76, 185

Cherokee Indian Agency, 194

Cherokees, Eastern Band, 60; agriculture and, 185, 189, 190–91, 205; arts and crafts and, 200–202, 368–69 (n. 55), 369 (n. 56); BIA and culture of, 185, 199–201, 203–4, 208–9, 210; BIA and NPS and fear of cultural exploitation of, 199–201, 208–9, 210; BIA and opposition to Parkway and, 190, 195, 196, 198, 199, 205, 208–9; BIA and tourism of, 202, 211–13; Blue Ridge Parkway beginnings and, 63; as corporation, 185–86; ethnic identity, 184; Great Depression and, 184–85; Great Smoky Mountains National Park and, 184, 197, 198, 199, 208, 368 (nn. 43, 48); history of independence, 185–86, 203–4, 210, 370–71 (n. 81); identity, after Parkway resistance, 211–13; Indian New Deal and, 188; land acquisition payment and, 170, 205, 208, 209, 279, 362 (n. 37); land-exchange strategy for, 197–98, 204, 208, 368 (n. 43); landowner access to Parkway and, 196; legislation to resolve Parkway route through reservation of, 207–10; lumber industry and, 184–85; Mooney, James, and, 203; opposition to Parkway and, 1, 5, 10, 145, 154–55, 182, 183–213, 240, 324, 366 (n. 17); right-of-way for Parkway and, 188–91, 196–97, 365 (n. 14), 366 (n. 16); state highway development and, 5, 188–89, 200, 205, 209, 369 (n. 66); tourism and, 76, 185, 371 (n. 84); tourism, Parkway and, 185, 189, 196, 201–2, 205, 210, 371 (n. 82); Tsali, 203, 210

—Eastern Band Tribal Council: alternative route possibility and, 204–10, 369 (n. 66), 369 (n. 68), 370 (n. 79); arts and crafts and, 201; Bauer, Fred, and, 193, 209, 366–67 (n. 30), 370 (n. 79); Great Depression and, 185; legal standing, 185–86; opposition to Parkway and, 193, 194, 196–98, 365 (n. 14); Soco Valley route and, 188–91, 194, 204–5

Chestnut Ridge (N.C.), 161

Chimney Rock (N.C.), 75, 227, 229

Civilian Conservation Corps (CCC), 32, 34, 36, 40; Blue Ridge Parkway beginnings and, 45; Blue Ridge Parkway construction and, 266; Sharp Top mountain road and, 233

Civil Works Administration, 34

Clansman, The (Dixon), 76

Clarke, Gilmore D., 66, 70, 71

Clarkson, Francis O., 55, 162, 167, 170; campaign against Parkway, 176–80, 181, 364 (n. 57)

Clarkson, Heriot, 239; early life and career of, 158–61; land acquisition payment and, 169–70, 171–72; landowner access to Parkway and, 170–71, 181–82, 363 (n. 40); Little Switzerland, establishment of, 13, 76, 161–62; Little Switzerland development and, 164–67; opposition to Parkway and, 144, 156–57, 158, 173–82, 183, 328; right-of-way for Parkway and, 169, 324; road building and, 18–19, 49, 160–61, 162–63; routing of Parkway and, 55; support for Parkway and, 13–14, 87, 167, 168–69; tourism, commercial and, 5, 10, 13, 144, 154; White Supremacy and, 159–60, 164, 166. *See also* Little Switzerland; Switzerland Company

Cleary, George, 147–48

Clinch River Valley (Tenn.), 93

Cocke, Norman A., 274, 285

Cold Springs Mountain (Tenn.), 65

Collier, John, 186–88, 203; Cherokee opposition to Parkway and, 189–90, 193, 196, 197, 204, 212

Colonial Parkway, Va., 42

Colonial Williamsburg, Va., 29, 241, 247, 251, 257, 258

Compensation, for land acquisition, 124, 128–31, 147, 355 (n. 54); Ashe County and, 130,

268–69, 381 (n. 19); routing conflict and, 301–9, 390 (n. 114), 390–91 (n. 115); routing conflict, media coverage and, 306–8, 309–10, 317–18; tourism, commercial vs. NPS and, 5, 11, 144, 154, 158, 234, 239, 261–62, 296; tourism, commercial vs. NPS, entrance fees and, 297–301; tourism, commercial vs. NPS, signs and, 291, 297, 324; tourist developments on, after Parkway completion, 322, 323; tourist developments on, before Parkway completion, 270–80, 286–89, 303, 386 (n. 70); Wilmor land tract and, 322. *See also* Linville Improvement Company; Morton, Hugh M.

Grandfather Mountain Park Association, 284

Grandmother Mountain (N.C.), 283

Grassy Mountain (N.C.), 161

Grattan, C. Hartley, 85–86

Great Depression: in Asheville, 53, 78–79, 101, 102; Cherokees and, 184–85; highway construction and, 3–4, 32–39, 45, 121; Indian Emergency Conservation Work Program and, 194; in Knoxville, Tenn., 92; Little Switzerland and, 168; Peaks of Otter and, 227–29, 230–31

Great Smoky Mountains Conservation Association, 28

Great Smoky Mountains National Park (N.C. and Tenn.): Blue Ridge Parkway beginnings and, 33–34, 35–36, 48; Blue Ridge Parkway ending at, 2, 33, 36, 48, 54, 63, 67, 91, 98, 113, 231; Cherokees, Eastern Band and, 184, 197, 198, 199, 208, 368 (nn. 43, 48); environmental movement and, 380 (n. 9); formation of, 26–29, 53, 56, 88, 91, 184, 334–35 (n. 38), 335 (n. 50); Grandfather Mountain and, 275–76; land acquisition for, 117; lumber industry and, 278; resident removal from, 132, 199, 356 (n. 64), 368 (n. 48); routing of Parkway and, 65, 69, 91, 98, 103, 194; tourism and, 30; tourism, Parkway and, 79, 92, 213

Green, Ottis, 104

Greensboro Daily News, 314–16

Greenspan, Anders, 258

Grossman, Charles, 246–47

Grove, Edwin Wiley, 73

Grove Arcade (Asheville, N.C.), 74

Grove Park Inn (Asheville, N.C.), 73, 75, 81, 104; Parkway dinner and, 1934, 52–53, 61, 87

Gwyn, R. L., 297; Blue Ridge Parkway beginnings and, 30, 36, 39, 53, 55; Grandfather Mountain and, 277, 382 (n. 39)

Hanchett, Thomas, 57

Harkening Hill (Peaks of Otter, Va.), 218, 219, 221

Hartford, Tenn., 65

Hendersonville, N.C., 58, 342–43 (n. 38)

Hendersonville Times-News, 104

Highway construction: Blue Ridge Parkway, post-World War II and, 267, 380–81 (n. 13); Blue Ridge Parkway beginnings and, 45–46, 266–67; Blue Ridge Parkway completion and, 113, 264–68, 312, 318–20, 332 (n. 1); Blue Ridge Parkway design and construction, 4, 44–47, 123, 266–68; Blue Ridge Parkway through Peaks of Otter and, 234; Good Roads movement and, 17–21, 24; Great Depression and, 3–4, 32–39, 45, 121, 336 (n. 57); National Park Service and, 24–26, 29; North Carolina, 1920s-30s and, 17, 28, 29–32, 39, 75, 120, 121, 162–63; North Carolina, early twentieth century and, 17–21; parkway movement and, 40–44, 338 (n. 86); Peaks of Otter and, 222–23, 229–30, 231, 373 (n. 37); public vs. scenic, 5, 15–16, 39–40, 45–46, 95, 106–7; taxes and, 19; in Virginia, 21, 121; Wilmington-Charlotte-Asheville Road project, 13; World War II stoppage on Parkway, 234, 235, 267, 380–81 (n. 13). *See also* State highway development

Historical exhibits on Parkway: Brinegar cabin as, 244, 257–58; constraints and contradictions in, 255–62; Johnson Farm development as, 215, 218, 245–55; log cabins as, 242–43, 244; Mabry Mill, 2, 6, 242–43, 244, 246, 255–56, 257–58; NPS interpretive program and, 10–11, 200, 215, 216, 217–18, 240, 243, 244, 248, 249–55, 259, 266–67, 327, 377 (nn. 70, 80); Peaks of Otter and, 10–11, 217–18, 245–55; pioneer bias and, 242, 244–45, 255, 256, 376 (n. 65)

Historic Sites Act (1935), 241

161–62; campaign against Parkway and, 160–61, 176–82; Citizens' Committee of, 163; Clarkson, development of, and, 63, 76, 164–67; development after Parkway settlement, 172–73; exclusivity of, 158, 164, 166; Geneva Hall at, 177; Great Depression and, 168; Kilmichael Tower at, 165, 167, 168, 172; labor and, 164–65; land acquisition for Parkway and, 157, 169–70, 171, 178; land acquisition payment and, 169–70, 279; local citizens of, 164–65; opposition to Parkway and, 156–82; state road development and, 162–63, 177; support for Parkway and, 63, 87; tourism, commercial vs. NPS and, 5, 10, 144, 145, 153, 154, 157, 169, 172, 181, 182, 234, 239, 324; tourism, early and, 158, 161–62, 242

Loewen, James W., 258

Long Island State Park Commission, 40

Love, Spencer, 274

Lowenthal, David, 257

Low Gap, N.C., 45

Lumber industry, 187–88, 256; in 1920s, 27–28; Champion Paper and Fibre Company and, 27, 81, 102, 135, 276–77, 382 (n. 39); Cherokees and, 184–85; and defiance of land acquisition, 124, 149–50, 151; environmental protection and, 1920s and, 27–28; environmental protection, Grandfather Mountain and, 276–77, 281–83, 382 (nn. 38, 39); at Grandfather Mountain, 276–79, 287, 311, 382 (nn. 38, 39); Great Smoky Mountains National Park and, 278; Linville Improvement Company and, 135, 271–74, 276–77, 280, 281–83, 286, 382 (n. 38)

Lumina pavilion (Wrightsville Beach, N.C.), 270

Luray Cave (Va.), 228

Lyle, Walter L., 222, 234, 238

Lynchburg-Bedford-Roanoke road, 222

Mabry, Ed, 2, 243, 244

Mabry Mill (Va.), 2, 6, 242–43, 244, 246, 255–56, 257–58

MacDonald, Thomas H., 37, 39, 55

Machine Age in the Hills (Ross), 85

MacKaye, Benton, 48, 92

MacRae, Agnes. *See* Morton, Agnes

MacRae, Hugh, 38, 270–71, 275, 276, 280, 281, 282–83, 284, 285, 304

MacRae, Nelson, 269, 273, 279, 280, 281, 282, 381 (n. 19)

Maloney, Frank, 71, 344 (n. 58)

Mammoth Cave National Park (Ky.), 29, 142

Marion, N.C., 163

Marshall, Robert, 48, 49–50, 97

Mather, Stephen, 22–24, 28, 275, 281, 292

Matthews Cabin, 244

McAlister, Hill, 103

McCoy, Pearson, 193, 197

McKellar, Kenneth, 37, 70–71, 103

McKinley, George, 311

McKinney, Alphonzo "Fons," 164–65, 177

McWane, William, 274

McWane Cast Iron and Pipe Company, 274

Meadowbrook State Parkway (N.Y.), 40

Merritt Parkway (Conn.), 41–42

Miami tourism development, and Parkway, 55, 56, 75

Mile-High Swinging Bridge, on Grandfather Mountain, 287–88, 305, 311, 312, 316, 318, 321

Mileposts, 2, 113, 332 (n. 1)

Miles, Emma Bell, 85, 104–5

Miller, Hunter, 222, 230, 231, 232–33, 234, 236–38, 239, 327

Miller, S. A., 5, 108, 109, 110, 112, 118, 127, 128, 153, 327

Mining, 135, 270–71

Mission 66 program, 45, 238, 245; completion of Parkway and, 266–68; funding increase for NPS and, 267–68, 296

Mons hotel. *See* Hotel Mons

Montreat religious assembly (N.C.), 76

Mooney, James, 203

Moore, Dan K., 309

Moore, Myriam Putnam, 224

Morganton News-Herald, 301

Morrison, Cameron, 19, 161

Morton, Agnes, 276

Morton, Hugh M.: and conflict with NPS over entrance fees, 297–301, 327; conservationist arguments and, 265–66, 286, 302, 320–24, 380 (n. 9); early life of, 276; Grandfather Mountain, agreements and, 1930s, 268–69; Grandfather Mountain, environmental concerns after conflict and, 320–24; Grandfather Mountain, routing conflict and, 301–9, 311–18, 389–90 (n. 108), 390 (n. 114), 390–91 (n. 115); Grandfather Mountain, routing conflict, media coverage and, 306–8, 309–10, 313, 314, 316, 392 (n. 136); Grandfather Mountain land acquisition and, 263–66, 269–70, 285–86, 379 (n. 2), 381 (n. 20); Grandfather Mountain tourist developments and, 287–89, 322, 323, 386 (n. 70); growing fame and public service of, 289–90; Linn Cove Viaduct and, 320; Linville and, 273, 276, 286; and Linville Improvement Company leadership, post-World War II, 285–86, 287, 290; tourism, commercial vs. NPS and, 5, 11, 144, 154, 158, 239, 261–62, 291, 293–96, 328, 387 (n. 87)

Morton, Julian, 276, 282, 283, 284, 304

Moses, Robert, 40

Moses Cone Memorial Park (N.C.), 145

Mountain Dance and Folk Festival, 75, 79

Mountain Ridge Protection Act (N.C., 1983), 320

Mt. Mitchell (N.C.), 61, 63, 68, 75, 113, 135, 227

Mt. Pisgah (N.C.), 61, 63, 75, 113, 297

Mount Vernon Memorial Highway (Md.), 41

"Museum of the Managed American Countryside," 245

Myers, A. G., 274

Myers Park suburb (Charlotte, N.C.), 57–58

Mystic Chords of Memory (Kammen), 259

Natchez Trace Association, 44

Natchez Trace Parkway, 42, 43, 44, 338–39 (n. 96)

National Environmental Policy Act (1969), 320

National Forest Service. *See* U.S. Forest Service

National Geographic, 83

National Historic Preservation Act (1966), 247

National Industrial Recovery Act (1933), 34

National Park Concessions (NPC), 238, 293–94, 297

National Park Service (NPS): Appalachian stereotypes and, 83–84, 152–53, 200–201, 212, 240, 241–45, 249, 251–55, 261, 292; Blue Ridge Parkway beginnings and, 37,

38, 39, 49; and Blue Ridge Parkway design and construction, 44–46, 60, 123, 182; *Blue Ridge Parkway News* and, 4, 151–53, 154, 157, 327, 360 (n. 116); boosting of Parkway by, 4, 11; Cherokee culture and, 182, 199–201; Cherokee opposition to Parkway and, 189–90, 196, 203–4; Cherokee route and, 204–7; Cherokees, tourism and, 201–2, 212; concessions and, 138–43, 189, 234, 235–39, 292–95, 297, 327–28, 358 (nn. 87, 88, 94); Cone property and, 144–45, 154, 256; crafts and, 83–84, 242, 243, 256, 376–77 (n. 68); current developments, Parkway and, 330; distortion of history and, 214–18, 235, 241–43, 245–49, 255–56; early twentieth century projects and, 13–14; eastern park formation and, 26–29, 334–35 (n. 38); entrance fees on Parkway and, 297–301, 327, 388–89 (n. 102); formation of, 22–23, 59, 334 (n. 29); funding drop, post-World War II and, 267; Georgia extension of Parkway and, 328–29; Grandfather Mountain, commercial tourism vs., 5, 11, 144, 154, 158, 234, 239, 261–62, 296; Grandfather Mountain, entrance fees and, 297–301; Grandfather Mountain, lumber industry and, 277–78; Grandfather Mountain, Parkway, North Carolina folklore and, 264–66; Grandfather Mountain, routing conflict and, 301–9, 310–18, 320–21, 390 (n. 114), 390–91 (n. 115); Grandfather Mountain, routing conflict, media coverage and, 306–8, 310, 313–16, 317–18, 392 (n. 136); Grandfather Mountain signs and, 291, 297, 324; Grandfather Mountain land acquisition and, 263–66, 268–70, 280–81, 381 (n. 19), 383 (n. 42); Grandfather Mountain as recreation area and, 281–84, 285, 384 (n. 48); Grove Park Inn dinner and, 1934, 52–53, 61, 87; and historical sites of Parkway, current constraints with, 255–62; interpretive program and, 10–11, 200, 215, 216, 217–18, 240, 243, 244, 248, 249–55, 259, 266–67, 327, 377 (nn. 70, 80); land acquisition for Parkway and, 116–17, 124, 127, 131–32, 144–50, 150–51, 351 (n. 11); land acquisition payments and, 129, 146–49, 359 (n. 106); landowner access to Parkway and, 132–38, 151, 357 (n. 75); landscape architecture, Parkway and, 10–11, 60, 66–67, 94, 96, 116, 132, 247, 278, 326, 332 (n. 5), 341 (n. 26); and landscaping ideals, early twentieth century, 16, 51; and landscaping ideals, for Parkway, 182, 216; Linn Cove Viaduct construction and, 265, 318–20, 323, 393 (n. 147); Little Switzerland and, 5, 10, 144, 145, 153, 154, 157, 169, 172, 181, 182, 234, 239, 324; logging in defiance of land acquisition and, 124, 149–50, 151; Mission 66 program and, 45, 238, 245, 266–68, 296; Museum Division of, 243; National Register of Historic Places and, 247; Native American stereotypes and, 200–201; and Peaks of Otter, acquisition of, 125, 232–34, 374–75 (n. 47); Peaks of Otter, Johnson Farm acquisition and, 234; Peaks of Otter, Johnson Farm development and, 245–55; Peaks of Otter development and, 214–18, 235–39, 241, 258–61; Peaks of Otter interpretive program and, 10–11, 200, 215, 216, 217–18, 245–55; pioneer bias and, 255, 256; Public Works Administration (PWA) and, 34; recreation areas and, 124–26, 238, 281–84, 285, 355 (n. 54), 384 (n. 48); resident removal from parks and, 32–33, 132, 199, 356 (n. 64), 368 (n. 48); resident removal from Parkway and, 314; road building in the East and, 29–33; road building in the West and, 24–26, 43; routing of Parkway and, 52–53, 66–71, 96, 343 (n. 43), 346–47 (n. 99); tourism, Asheville commercial vs., 294, 296, 387 (n. 87); tourism, commercial vs., 5, 10, 11, 144, 145, 153–55, 158, 181, 182, 234, 239, 261–62, 289–301, 323–24, 387 (n. 87); tourism, early promotions and, 22–24; vandalism on Parkway and, 148–50, 359 (n. 107); visitor accommodation and, 141–42, 291–97. See also Land acquisition, for Parkway

National Parks Portfolio (NPS), 23
National Parks Touring Association, 24
National Park-to-Park Highway, 24–25, 29
National Recovery Administration, 82
National Register of Historic Places, 247
Native Americans: American Indian Defense Association and, 186; American Indian

Federation (AIF) and, 188, 207, 209, 370 (nn. 70, 79); American Indian Movement (AIM) and, 213; assimilation vs. traditionalism and, 192–93; crafts and, 187; federal government seizing lands of, 213, 371 (n. 86); Indian New Deal and, 188, 192, 193, 199, 208, 211–12, 366 (n. 17); Indian schools and, 192, 194, 366 (n. 24); New Deal and, 183, 186–88, 195, 197, 366 (n. 17); Pueblo Indians and, 186. See also Cherokees, Eastern Band

Natural Bridge (Va.), 223, 227, 228–29, 230
Natural Style in Landscape Gardening, The (Waugh), 16
Nature Conservancy, 321, 322
New Deal: Blue Ridge Parkway and, 336 (n. 65); Blue Ridge Parkway beginnings and, 45–46, 48–49, 54, 339 (n. 97); Blue Ridge Parkway funding and, 4, 9, 33–39, 42; Blue Ridge Parkway vs. other parkways and, 43–44; Indian New Deal, 188, 192, 193, 199, 208, 211–12, 366 (n. 17); Native Americans and, 183, 186–88, 195, 197, 366 (n. 17); parkway construction and, 42–44; Penderlea resettlement community and, 270; Skyline Drive construction and, 32–33; Tennessee Valley Authority (TVA) and, 92–94, 347 (n. 106)
New York Zoological Society, 40
Niagara Falls, 15
Niles, John Jacob, 252
Nolen, John, 57–58
Nolichucky River Gorge (N.C. and Tenn.), 65
Norfolk and Western Railroad, 221
Norris Dam (Tenn.), 93
North Carolina Board of Conservation and Development, 289, 299, 301
North Carolina Committee on the Federal Parkway, 55
North Carolina Conservation and Development Commission, 37, 284
North Carolina Department of Conservation and Development, 281–82, 296
North Carolina Geological Survey, 20
North Carolina Good Roads Association, 19
North Carolina Park, Parkway, and Forest Development Commission, 286–87, 294, 296, 297

172, 180; landowner access to Parkway and, 170–71; right-of-way for Parkway and, 169, 171–72; state road development and, 163; tourism, commercial vs. NPS and, 183

Switzerland Inn (Little Switzerland, N.C.), 161, 162, 165

Taylor, Alva, 85

Teer, Nello, 45

Tennessee: forked Parkway suggestion and, 98–99, 349 (n. 131); North Carolina vs., for Parkway route, 52–54, 64–71, 78, 87, 89, 91–94, 97–99, 103, 157, 343 (n. 39), 344 (n. 58), 347 (n. 106)

Tennessee State Highway Commission, 71

Tennessee Valley Authority (TVA), 92–94, 96, 98, 347 (n. 106)

Thatcher, Maurice H., 29, 37

Thelen, David, 259

"Thunder and Lightning over Little Switzerland," 156–57

Timber industry. See Lumber industry

Tolls, 297–301, 327, 387–88 (n. 97), 388–89 (n. 102); Sharp Top mountain and, 233; Skyline Drive and, 32–33

Tompkins Knob (N.C.), 61

Tooman, Alex, 101, 105, 106

Topography, of Parkway, 113–14

Tourism: Asheville, history of, 19–20, 72–79, 344 (n. 61); automobiles and, 17–24, 30, 32, 33; at Blowing Rock, 63, 256; Cherokees, Eastern Band and, 76, 185, 371 (n. 84); development, nineteenth century New England and, 70; economic limitations of, 105–6; Great Smoky Mountains National Park and, 30; highway construction in North Carolina, 1930s and, 75, 120; historical sites and, 29, 257, 258–61; Linville, before Parkway and, 242, 271–74; Little Switzerland, before Parkway and, 158, 161–62, 242; lumber industry and, 27–28; National Parks and, 22–24; National Parks in East and, 26–29, 30; Peaks of Otter, before Parkway and, 214, 216, 218–31; in Virginia, 29

Tourism, Parkway, 1–3, 5–6, 9–11; Appalachian people and, 82–86, 104–5, 143–50, 291; Ashe County, lack of, 110; Asheville, vs.

NPS and, 294, 296, 387 (n. 87); Asheville and, 9, 38, 39, 43–44, 47, 54–56, 59, 63–64, 79, 97, 106, 143–44, 323, 342–43 (n. 38); Asheville, "little farms" and, 81–87, 98, 138; automobiles and, 13–14, 34, 48, 49–51; at Blowing Rock, 140; Cherokees and, 185, 189, 196, 201–2, 205, 210, 371 (n. 82); Cherokees, BIA and, 202, 211–13; commercial benefits and, 138–43, 357 (n. 83); commercial vs. NPS conflicts and, 289–301; conflicts and, 47; conflict with NPS, entrance fees and, 297–301; farmers and, 110; Grandfather Mountain and, 5, 11, 144, 154, 158, 234, 239, 261–62, 296; Grandfather Mountain, entrance fees and, 297–301; Grandfather Mountain, after Parkway completion and, 322, 323; Grandfather Mountain, before Parkway completion and, 270–80, 286–89, 303, 386 (n. 70); Grandfather Mountain, signs and, 291, 297, 324; Great Smoky Mountains National Park and, 79, 92, 213; historical sites of Parkway, current constraints with, 255–62; Little Switzerland and, 144, 145, 153, 154, 157, 169, 172, 181, 182, 234, 239, 324; manufacturing vs., 115; Miami tourism development and, 55, 56, 75; success of, 265, 380 (n. 8); in Tennessee, 92; in Virginia, 128, 139, 141; visitation numbers and, 44, 267, 338–39 (n. 96), 380 (n. 8); visitor accommodations and, 291–97, 386 (nn. 74, 76); wilderness definitions and, 269–70, 381 (n. 21)

Trail of Tears, 185, 203

Trail Ridge Road, Rocky Mountain National Park (Colo.), 26

Tsali, 203, 210

Tyson, Timothy, 270

Unicoi, Tenn., 65

United Nations Educational, Scientific, and Cultural Organization, 321

U.S. Congress, Cherokee opposition to Parkway and, 204

U.S. Daughters of the War of 1812, 44

U.S. Department of the Interior, 34, 96–97, 99, 108, 149–50, 183, 190, 293; Cherokee opposition to Parkway and, 194–96, 200,

204, 207–8; entrance fees on Parkway and, 299, 301, 388–89 (n. 102); Grandfather Mountain and, 275

U.S. Forest Service: Georgia extension of Parkway and, 328; Grandfather Mountain and, 275, 277, 284; land acquisition for Parkway and, 116, 118; Peaks of Otter and, 222, 223, 230, 231, 233, 374 (n. 46); recreation areas for Parkway and, 125

University of North Carolina, 158

Unto These Hills (outdoor Cherokee drama), 210, 371 (n. 82)

Urban planning: Asheville and, 58; Myers Park suburb and, 57–58

Vandalism, in opposition to Parkway, 148–50, 359 (n. 107)

Vanderbilt, George Washington, 73

Vanderbilt University, 85

Vermont, Parkway proposal and, 154, 155, 360 (n. 122)

Vint, Thomas C., 66, 94

Virginia: Blue Ridge Parkway beginnings and, 33, 39; counties affected by Parkway, 114–15, 351 (n. 10); land acquisition for Parkway and, 112, 118, 122–24, 127–28, 351 (nn. 6, 10), 351–52 (n. 14), 353–54 (n. 33), 354 (n. 36); land acquisition payments and, 129–30; landowner access to Parkway and, 133–35, 137, 138; National Parks and, 28; Peaks of Otter and, 214–62; recreation areas for Parkway and, 126; right-of-way for Parkway and, 119–23, 127–28, 353 (n. 29); road building and, 21; routing of Parkway and, 54, 67, 231; Skyline Drive construction and, 32; tourism, historic towns and, 29; tourism, Parkway, "little farms" and, 128; tourist concessions on Parkway in, 139, 141

Virginia Conservation and Development Commission, 32, 232

Virginia Peaks of Otter Company, 238, 358 (n. 94). *See also* Peaks of Otter Corporation

Virginia State Highway Commission, 121–22, 134, 138, 327; Peaks of Otter and, 230, 373 (n. 37)

Wantagh State Parkway (N.Y.), 40

Warm Springs, N.C., 19, 21

Washington, D.C.: forked Parkway suggestion and, 99–100, 349 (n. 131); Radcliffe Committee and, 54–55, 66–71, 80–81, 87–91, 98; routing of Parkway and, 60, 61, 66–71, 87–91, 103, 342–43 (n. 38), 343 (n. 39), 344 (n. 58); tourist concessions on Parkway and, 140–41, 358 (nn. 87, 88)

Watauga Democrat, 318

Waterrock Knob (N.C.), 1, 6

Waugh, Frank, 16

Wawona Road, Yosemite National Park (Calif.), 26

Waynesboro, Va., 113

Waynesville, N.C., 1

Weaver, Zebulon, 88, 195–96, 208, 209

Webb, Charles A., 30, 56, 79, 101, 102, 327, 341 (n. 15); Tennessee vs. North Carolina route and, 80, 90, 99, 103

Weede, Fred L., 33, 38, 53, 58–59, 75, 79, 151, 327, 336 (n. 65); Tennessee vs. North Carolina route and, 67, 71, 80, 88, 97, 343 (n. 45), 350 (n. 154); tourism, Parkway and, 55–56, 63–64, 101, 340 (nn. 11, 12), 342 (n. 36), 342–43 (n. 38)

Weems, Sam, 147, 300, 327, 328; completion of Parkway and, 267; Grandfather Mountain, routing conflict and, 310, 311, 313, 316, 317; Grandfather Mountain land acquisition and, 264, 280, 283–84, 287, 302; landowner access to Parkway and, 136; Peaks of Otter and, 238; right-of-way for Parkway and, 119–20; tourism, commercial vs. NPS and, 294–97; tourist concessions on Parkway and, 138–39; visitor accommodations and, 291, 292

Westchester County Parkway Commission, 66

Western North Carolina Associated Communities, 292

Western North Carolina Railroad, 72

Western North Carolina Tomorrow, 320

Western North Carolina Tourist Association, 292

West Jefferson, N.C., 301, 316, 318

What Citizens Think about Attorney Chas. Ross' Attack on the Switzerland Co. and its Stockholders, 178

Wheeler-Howard Act. *See* Indian Reorganization Act (IRA) (1934)